# Praise for *Core PHP Programming*

"Bought your book *Core PHP Programming* at a Barnes and Noble here in Tucson. Normally I absolutely hate books in terms of learning, preferring instead to sort of just mess around with something with online docs until I know it, but your book is exceptional. I was telling my girlfriend about it; it's concise and thorough without being annoyingly wordy, and it is a spiffing reference for PHP, which I'm sort of teaching myself from the ground up.

The simple act of buying your book affirms all of the essential aspects of capitalism—I got more out of it than what I paid for it, and I assume you are reaping windfalls that made all the work worth it. You should be proud. I have a whole stack of books that I abandoned because they were organized badly.

I have recommended it unhesitatingly to hacker-minded (in the good sense) friends. I have MySQL running here now, and I shall actively seek out your book on that subject in coming months when I have time.

Best wishes to you, and hope for your continued success."

**—Chris Hizny**

"I am a Web designer/developer in NYC. I just want to let you know that I just purchased your book, *Core PHP Programming*, 2nd Edition, and I think it is wonderful!!! Very easy to read—and retain—so far . . . I just want to thank you ahead of time because all the other PHP books I've purchased and read got me nowhere!"

**—Neal Levine**
*http://www.ilaonline.com*

"I recently purchased your *Core PHP Programming* book, and I just wanted to let you know that it is one of the best programming books I've ever read. Thank you for taking the time to do the book right."

**—Jordan**

"I gotta tell you, I enjoyed the book, *Core PHP Programming*. It has helped me a lot. I even went so far as to sell my first edition and bought the second."

**—Kreg Steppe**

"I'm enjoying *Core PHP Programming*, 2nd Edition, enormously. I'm about 50 pages in and it is a real page-turner; unlike many technical books, this one can actually be read word for word due to your fine writing style."

**—Stuart**

"Just wanted to say how much I have enjoyed your book, very well done, I am learning a lot from it, Congratulations on an excellent book! It has opened a whole new world to me, I have written Perl, ASP, Delphi, VB apps before—but it is PHP that I am most excited about. It must have been a huge project to complete."

**—R.A. McCormack,** P.Eng.
Professor of Multimedia, Confederation College
CASE.org's "Outstanding Canadian College Professor of the Year"

"I corresponded with you about 6 to 9 months ago regarding your *Core PHP Programming* book (first version) and recently purchased your second version. I enjoyed the update for PHP 4.0. Your first version book was falling apart on me!"

**—TDavid**
*http://www.tdscripts.com/contact.html*

"I'm a French PHP programmer, and I would like to thank you for the book *Core PHP Programming*. I'm 17 years old and with your book (I read completely the book ;–)), I programmed a Web site *http://www.tutorials-fr.com/*, a tutorials directory and the internal Web site of my secondary school. Thanks very much for all :–)) "

**—GML**

"I was first introduced to your expertise through the FreeTrade project, which we actively use for one of our sites. I also reference your *Core PHP Programming* almost daily, which has brought me a long way."

**—Bob Bennett**

"First of all, I want to say that your book *Core PHP Programming* is a Great book with clear examples. This is the book that learned me PHP a couple of years ago. Now I'm much more experienced and created a PHP 4 template class recently, called TemplatePower. You're probably very busy, but if you find a little time, could you take a look at it? I would be very pleased. You can read more about it at *http://templatepower.codocad.com/.*"

**—Ron**
The Netherlands

"I'm a French PHP Webmaster, and I've began in PHP with your book. I'm not a developer but a graphist, and I wanted to learn a programmation language . . . . It's done with your help!!!

Thanks a lot for all, and excuse my English that is tooooooooooo bad!!!! I've made a link from my site to yours, and I would like to know if you are agree. Please send me a mail if you don't want to be in my site, or if you have any question, suggestion, or else . . . .

Thanks for all, I really don't know how to say in English that I'm very happy to have learn PHP with your help!!  : )) "

**—Vincent Pontier**

"You write very clearly and succinctly, which is a rare gift among programmers. My copy is looking fairly tired now—time for a second edition? A bit more on the built-in session manager would be good, also some examples of using the PHP extensions, e.g., ming, would be useful. I have adopted your dynamic selection boxes to use as a function, and wondered whether you would be interested in putting it on your code exchange site?"

**—Dr. Tom Hughes**
MD, MSc, MBA, MRCP, FRCS

"My name is Marcus Andersson, and I'm a 22-year-old student from Sweden. I bought your book *Core PHP Programming*, 2nd Edition, and I find it really good. It didn't take me long to notice that PHP is really great for building dynamic Web sites. Thank you for a great book!"

**—Marcus**

"I bought your *Core PHP Programming*, 2nd Edition, a couple of weeks ago, and I must say it's a great book. Well done! It's nice to see you've set up an errata section on your site, wish more authors would be more forthcoming."

**—Murray**
"A Web 4 U Designs"
*www.aweb4u.co.nz*

"Your book has, in large part, helped me to implement a complex (at least by typical non-corporate standards), databased Web site in PHP . . . something I would never have accomplished without it. Thanks and take care."

**—Eric Geddes**
Fringe Group Inc.

"Nice book, easy read (I'm reading it front to back). Based on the usability of this book, I am looking forward to picking up a copy of your MySQL book for my library."

**—Nolan**

# core
# PHP
# PROGRAMMING

# PRENTICE HALL PTR
# CORE SERIES

*\*Sun Microsystems Press titles*

*c o r e*

# PHP PROGRAMMING

## LEON ATKINSON

PRENTICE
HALL
PTR

PRENTICE HALL
Professional Technical Reference
Upper Saddle River, NJ 07458
www.phptr.com

**Library of Congress Cataloging-in-Publication Data**

A CIP catalog record for this book can be obtained from the Library of Congress.

*Editorial/Production Supervision*: Faye Gemmellaro
*Composition*: Vanessa Moore
*Cover Design Director*: Jerry Votta
*Art Director*: Gail Cocker-Bogusz
*Interior Design*: Meg Van Arsdale
*Manufacturing Manager*: Alexis R. Heydt-Long
*Manufacturing Buyer*: Maura Zaldivar
*Editor-in-Chief* : Mark Taub
*Editorial Assistant*: Noreen Regina
*Developmental Editor*: Russ Hall
*Marketing Manager*: Curt Johnson

© 2004 Pearson Education, Inc.
Publishing as Prentice Hall Professional Technical Reference
Upper Saddle River, New Jersey 07458

**Prentice Hall PTR offers excellent discounts on this book when ordered in quantity for bulk purchases or special sales. For more information, please contact: U.S. Corporate and Government Sales, 1-800-382-3419, corpsales@pearsontechgroup.com. For sales outside of the U.S., please contact: International Sales, 1-317-581-3793, international@pearsontechgroup.com.**

Printed in the United States of America

First Printing
Text printed on recycled paper
ISBN 0-13-046346-9

Pearson Education Ltd.
Pearson Education Australia Pty., Limited
Pearson Education Singapore, Pte. Ltd.
Pearson Education North Asia Ltd.
Pearson Education Canada, Ltd.
Pearson Educación de Mexico, S.A. de C.V.
Pearson Education—Japan
Pearson Education Malaysia, Pte. Ltd.

# About Prentice Hall Professional Technical Reference

With origins reaching back to the industry's first computer science publishing program in the 1960s, and formally launched as its own imprint in 1986, Prentice Hall Professional Technical Reference (PH PTR) has developed into the leading provider of technical books in the world today. Our editors now publish over 200 books annually, authored by leaders in the fields of computing, engineering, and business.

Our roots are firmly planted in the soil that gave rise to the technical revolution. Our bookshelf contains many of the industry's computing and engineering classics: Kernighan and Ritchie's *C Programming Language*, Nemeth's *UNIX System Adminstration Handbook*, Horstmann's *Core Java*, and Johnson's *High-Speed Digital Design*.

PH PTR acknowledges its auspicious beginnings while it looks to the future for inspiration. We continue to evolve and break new ground in publishing by providing today's professionals with tomorrow's solutions.

# Contents

## 29    DESIGN PATTERNS    1002

# Foreword

When I wrote the Foreword for Leon's second edition, PHP 4 had just started making it big, taking over the market share from PHP 3. The new version made great promises, and looking back it met all of its promises and more. We can see that at present PHP 4 has no doubt not only replaced almost all PHP 3 installations, but has conquered the Web application development market with its millions of installations and use in enterprise companies.

Today, we are again facing exciting times. PHP 5 is about to be released, promising major improvements to the growing PHP community. As with previous versions, the major improvements are at the language level. Zeev and I redesigned the object model—at last dumping the problematic model, which originated from our work in PHP 3. Some of the other changes we made include:

- Treating objects as handles and not native types, allowing for other new features and fixing some odd behavior.
- Allowing for private, public, and protected access restrictions on members and methods.
- Introducing exception handling a la C++'s try/catch.
- Providing interfaces similar to the ones found in Java giving.
- And lots more…

PHP 5 is also expected to feature improvements and additions in other areas, including better all-around XML support, improved streams support, and more.

In the 3rd edition of *Core PHP Programming*, Leon has invited my partner Zeev Suraski to cover the PHP 5 language changes. No doubt that Leon's experience in writing PHP books and Zeev's superior knowledge of PHP 5 and its internals have led to a must-buy book for PHP developers.

I hope you enjoy this book and that it accompanies you during the adoption phase of PHP 5.

*Andi Gutmans*
*Herzelyia, Israel*

# Preface

My first inkling that I might like to write a book about PHP was borne out of the frustration I felt with the original PHP manual. It was a single, large HTML file with all the functions in alphabetical order. It was also on a Web server thousands of miles away from me in Canada, so it was slow to show up in my browser, even across a T1 connection. It wasn't long before it was saved on my desktop. After struggling for several months, it started to dawn on me that I could probably organize the information into a more usable format. Around that time the next version of PHP began to take shape, and with it a new manual was developed. It was organized around PHP's source code, but was less complete than the old PHP manual. I contributed descriptions for some of the missing functions, but I still had the idea to write my own manual. In the spring of 1998 Prentice Hall gave me the opportunity to do so. It is an honor for my book to be among Prentice Hall classics such as *The C Programming Language* by Brian Kernighan and Dennis Ritchie.

This book assumes a certain familiarity with the Internet, the Web, and HTML programming, but it starts with the most basic ideas of programming. It will introduce you to concepts common to all programming languages and how they work in PHP. You can expect this book to teach you how to create rich, dynamic Web sites. You can also expect it to remain on your desk as a reference for how PHP works, or even as a recipe book for solving common design problems.

This book is not for dummies, nor is it for complete idiots. That you are considering PHP is a great indication of your intelligence, and I'd hate to insult it. Some of the ideas in this book are hard to understand. If you don't quite get them the first time, I encourage you to reread and experiment with the examples.

If you are uncomfortable writing HTML files, you may wish to develop this skill first. Marty Hall's *Core Web Programming* provides an excellent introduction. Beyond HTML, numerous other topics I touch on fall out of scope. Whenever I can, I suggest books and Web sites that provide more information. There are even some aspects of PHP that range too far from the focus on writing PHP scripts. An example is writing extensions for PHP in C. This involves a healthy knowledge of C programming that I cannot provide here. Related to this is compiling and installing PHP. I attempt to describe the process of installing PHP, which can involve compiling the source code, but I can't attempt to pursue all the different combinations of operating system, Web server, and extensions. If you are comfortable running `make` files, you will find the information that comes with the PHP source code more than adequate.

Along with the explanation text I've provided real-world examples. Nothing is more frustrating than trying to adapt some contrived academic problem to the Web site you must have working by the end of the week. Some of the examples are based on code from live Web sites I have worked on since discovering PHP in 1997. Others are distilled from the continual discussion being conducted on the PHP mailing lists.

This book is organized into four main sections: an introduction to programming; a reference for all the functions in PHP; a survey of common programming problems; and finally a guide for applying this knowledge to Web site development. The first section deals with the issues involved with any programming language: what a PHP script looks like; how to control execution; how to deal with data. The second section organizes the functions by what they do and gives examples of their use. PHP offers many functions, so this section is larger than the rest. The third section deals with solving common programming problems such as sorting and generating graphics. The last section offers advice about how to create a whole Web site with PHP.

I've chosen a few conventions for highlighting certain information, and I'm sure you will find them obvious, but for the sake of clarity I'll spell them out. Whenever I use a keyword such as the name of a script or a function, I place it in a monospace font. For example, I may speak about the `print` function. Another convention I've used is to place email addresses and Web addresses inside angle brackets. Examples are the email address by which you can contact me, `<corephp@leonatkinson.com>`, and my Web site, `<http://www.leonatkinson.com/>`.

It can be difficult to describe a subject that changes rapidly. PHP 5 underwent a methodical design process and implementation, which made it easier to write about ahead of finalization. Yet, there are bound to be changes between the time of writing and when you're reading the text. Most changes PHP acquires take the form of new functions or slight changes to existing functions. Sometimes, though, entirely new features appear or provisional features disappear. Just before going to press, the namespace keyword described in Chapter 6 was removed. A spirited debate on the PHP mailing lists included passionate supporters of keeping and removing namespaces. In the end, the arguments for removal won, with the decision to continue to seek a feasible solution to the problem of namespaces.

Please visit my Web site, `<http://www.leonatkinson.com/>`, for updates about the book. Aside from news, you'll find the inevitable list of errata and a link for downloading all the listings.

# Acknowledgments

Thank you for picking up this book. I love sharing PHP. It's offered the platform for many interesting projects over that past six years. I'm delighted to have introduced PHP to so many people. If you're one of the many people who took the time to write with questions, comments, and corrections, know that I really appreciate it. The feedback from the very beginning has always been overwhelmingly positive.

Without my family, I would never have finished the first edition of this book. They put up with long hours I spent writing instead of being with them. I'm grateful for their patience over the years. Your dedication and pride in me inspires me.

My wife, Vicky, deserves particular thanks for reading through the entire text from start to finish. I also benefited from unique perspective of Bob Dibetta, my long-time friend.

I'm happy to have Zeev helping out with the book this time around. His understanding of the new object model was invaluable. The PHP community is fortunate to have such a passionate and wise advocate. Thanks also to Andi for writing another great Foreword.

No PHP book is complete without thanks going out to the PHP developers. It all started with Rasmus Lerdorf, but the project continues to benefit from contributions from many people. I encourage you to visit the PHP mailing lists and contribute to the PHP project. It's refreshing to find the important members of the development team are genuine individuals, willing to interact on a personal level.

Working with Prentice Hall has been a pleasure. I've enjoyed the wisdom and guidance of Mark Taub. Faye Gemmellaro kept the production process going under a tight deadline.

*Leon Atkinson*
*August 2003*

I would like to thank Andi Gutmans, without whom the PHP project wouldn't have materialized, and there would be no topic to write this book about; Ophir Prusak, for getting me acquainted with php/fi 2 and making the birth of PHP possible; and my colleagues at Zend Technologies, for giving me a lot of ideas and insights.

I'd like to express my gratitude to Leon Atkinson and Mark Taub for giving me the opportunity to get involved in writing this book. I would like to thank my family that encouraged me to continue with the PHP project throughout the years. And finally, I would like to thank my girlfriend for putting up with the weekends I had to spend writing.

*Zeev Suraski*
*August 2003*

# core
# PHP
# PROGRAMMING

# PROGRAMMING
# WITH PHP

# Part

The first part of this book is a thorough discussion of PHP as a programming language. You will be introduced to common concepts of computer science and how they are implemented in PHP. No prior programming experience beyond the use of simple mark-up languages is necessary. That is, you must be familiar with HTML. These chapters focus on building a foundation of understanding rather than on how to solve specific problems. If you have experience programming in a similar language, such as C or Perl, you may choose to read Chapter 1 and skim the rest, saving it as a reference. In most situations, PHP treats syntax much as these two languages do.

Chapter 1 is an introduction to PHP—how it began and what it looks like. It may be sufficient for experienced programmers, since it moves quickly through PHP's key features. If you are less experienced, I encourage you to treat this chapter as a first look. Don't worry too much about exactly how the examples work. I explain the concepts in depth in later chapters.

Chapter 2 introduces the concepts of variables, operators, and expressions. These are the building blocks of a PHP script. Essentially, a computer stores and manipulates data. Variables let you name values; operators and expressions let you manipulate them.

Chapter 3 examines the ways PHP allows you to control program execution. This includes conditional branches and loops.

Chapter 4 deals with functions, how they are called and how to define them. Functions are packages of code that you can call upon repeatedly.

Chapter 5 is about arrays—collections of values that are identified by either numbers or names. Arrays are a very powerful way to store information and retrieve it efficiently.

Chapter 6 is about classes, presenting an object-oriented approach to grouping functions and data. Although not strictly an object-oriented language, PHP supports many features found in OO languages such as Java.

Chapter 7 deals with how PHP sends and receives data. Files, network connections, and other means of communication are covered.

# An Introduction to PHP

# Chapter 1

This chapter introduces you to PHP. You learn how it came about, what it looks like, and why it is the best server-side technology. It also exposes the most important features of the language.

PHP began as a simple macro replacement tool. Like a nice pair of shoes, it got you where you needed to go, but you could go only so far. On the hyperspeed development track of the Internet, PHP has become the equivalent of a 1960s muscle car. It's cheap, it's fast, and there's plenty of room under the hood for you and your virtual wrench.

This chapter lets you poke around the PHP engine, get your hands a little dirty, and take it for a spin. There are lots of small examples you can try immediately. Like all the examples in this book, you can easily adapt them to provide real solutions. Don't be intimidated if you don't fully understand the PHP code at first. Later chapters deal with all the issues in detail.

This chapter talks about some things that you already know, such as what a computer is, just to make sure we're all on the same page. You may be a wizard with HTML but not fully appreciate the alien way computers are put together. Or you may find you learned all these things in a high school computer class. If you get bored with the basics, skip to Chapter 2.

# 1.1 The Origins of PHP

Wonderful things come from singular inspiration. PHP began life as a simple way to track visitors to Rasmus Lerdorf's resume. It also could embed SQL queries in Web pages. But as often happens on the Web, admirers quickly asked for their own copies. As a proponent of the Internet's ethic of sharing, and as a generally agreeable person, Rasmus unleashed upon an unsuspecting Web his Personal Home Page Tools version 1.0.

"Unleashed upon himself" may be more accurate. PHP became very popular. A consequence was a flood of suggestions. PHP 1.0 filtered input, replacing simple commands for HTML. As its popularity grew, people wondered if it couldn't do more. Loops, conditionals, rich data structures—all the conveniences of modern structured programming seemed like a next logical step. Rasmus studied language parsers, read about YACC and GNU Bison, and created PHP 2, otherwise known as PHP/FI.

PHP/FI allowed developers to embed structured code inside HTML tags. PHP scripts could parse data submitted by HTML forms, communicate with databases, and make complex calculations on the fly. And it was very fast because the freely available source code compiled into the Apache Web server. A PHP script executed as part of the Web server process and required no forking, often a criticism of Common Gateway Interface (CGI) scripts.

PHP was a legitimate development solution and began to be used for commercial Web sites. In 1996, Clear Ink created the SuperCuts site (*www.supercuts.com*) and used PHP to create a custom experience for the Web surfer. The PHP Web site tracks the popularity of PHP by measuring how many different Web sites use the PHP module. When writing the second edition of this text, it seemed really exciting that PHP had grown from 100,000 sites to 350,000 sites during 1999. The most recent data show more than 10 million domains using PHP!

In 1997, a pair of Israeli students named Andi Gutmans and Zeev Suraski attempted to use it for building an online shopping cart, considered cutting-edge enough to be a university project. Shortly after they started, they stumbled upon various bugs in PHP that made them look under the hood at the source code. To their surprise, they noticed that PHP's implementation broke most of the principles of language design, which made it prone to unexpected behavior and bugs. Always looking for good excuses not to study for exams, they started creating a new implementation. In part, the task was a test of their programming abilities, in part a recreation. A few months later, they had rewritten PHP from scratch, making it a *real*, consistent, and robust language for the first time. Having spent so much time on the project, they asked the course teacher, Dr. Michael Rodeh, for academic credit in an attempt to avoid unnecessary exams. Being the manager of the IBM Research Lab in Haifa and well aware of the overwhelming number of different languages to choose from, he agreed—with the stipulation that they cooperate with the existing developers of PHP/FI instead of starting their own language.

When Andi and Zeev emailed Rasmus with the news about their rewrite, they wondered if he would accept this new work, as it essentially meant discarding his implementation. Rasmus did accept it, and a new body was formed—the PHP Core Team, known today as the PHP Group. Along with Andi, Rasmus, and Zeev, three other developers—Stig Bakken, Shane Caraveo, and Jim Winstead—were accepted to the Core Team. A community of developers started growing around PHP.

After seven months of development, alpha and beta testing, PHP version 3.0 was officially released on June 6, 1998, and started bending the curve of PHP's growth to unprecedented angles. PHP's functionality was growing on a daily basis, and PHP applications were popping up everywhere. Following the release, Open Source projects written in PHP flourished. Projects like Phorum tackled long-time Internet tasks such as hosting online discussion. The PHPLib project provided a framework for handling user sessions that inspired new code in PHP. FreeTrade, a project I led, offered a toolkit for building e-commerce sites.

Writing about PHP increased as well. More than 20 articles appeared on high-traffic sites such as *webmonkey.com* and *techweb.com*. Sites dedicated to supporting PHP developers were launched. The first two books about PHP were published in May 1999. Egon Schmid, Christian Cartus, and Richard Blume wrote a book in German called *PHP: Dynamische Webauftritte professionell realisieren*. Prentice Hall published the first edition of my book, *Core PHP Programming*. Since then, countless books about PHP fill bookstore shelves.

Given this background, there were no reasons not to be happy with the way PHP was back then. Perhaps the internal knowledge of what was going on under the hood and the feeling familiar to every developer—"I could have done it much better"— were the reasons that Andi and Zeev were some of the very few people who felt unhappy with PHP 3. As if out of habit, they withdrew from the PHP community and attempted to design a new approach towards executing PHP scripts.

A few months later, on January 4, 1999, Zeev and Andi announced a new framework that promised to increase dramatically the performance of PHP scripts. They dubbed the new framework the Zend Engine. Early tests showed script execution times dropping by a factor of 100. In addition, new features for compiling scripts into binary, debugging, optimization, and profiling were planned. This announcement officially ended the PHP 3.1 project, which was supposed to bring better Windows support to PHP 3 but failed to gain momentum, and officially started the planning of PHP 4.

Work on the Zend Engine and PHP 4 continued in parallel with bug fixes and enhancements to PHP 3. During 1999, eight incremental versions were released, and on December 29, 1999, PHP version 3.0.13 was announced. A PHP beta based on the Zend Engine became publicly available in July 19, 1999, and was followed by an intense development period of various components, some of which were brand new, such as built-in session handling, output buffering, and a Web server abstraction layer. The release of PHP 4 on May 22, 2000, marked another important milestone on PHP's journey to becoming the most popular Web development platform on earth. The number of people working on various levels of PHP has grown immensely, and new projects, most notably PEAR, gained momentum and started pushing PHP to new heights of popularity.

The PHP community drives the development of new features. Many programmers find inspiration in object-oriented programming. PHP 3 introduced objects as syntactic sugar. That is, while the syntax used for objects was different, the underlying implementation varied little from arrays. It attracted many object-oriented advocates, but the limited implementation left them desiring more. PHP 5 addresses these needs with a strong, rebuilt object system.

PHP is not a shrink-wrapped product made by faceless drones or wizards in an ivory tower. PHP started as a simple tool brought into the bazaar described by Eric Raymond in his essay *The Cathedral and the Bazaar*. Once it appeared, anyone could make improvements, and many did. Their aim seems to be to achieve solutions of direct, personal interest. If a client comes along who requires a project to use a database not supported by PHP, you simply write an extension. Then you give it to the PHP project. Soon, other people are fixing your bugs.

Yet, the vast majority of PHP users never write an extension. They happily find everything they need in the contributed works of others. Those who've contributed thousands of lines of code to PHP perhaps never consider themselves heroes. They don't trumpet their accomplishments. But because each part of PHP came from a real person, I would like to point them out. When appropriate, I'll note who added a particular extension.

You can find an up-to-date list of credits on the PHP site `<http://www.php.net/credits.php>`.

# 1.2  PHP Is Better Than Its Alternatives

In previous years, skeptics may have asked, Why should I learn PHP? Today, PHP's popularity is enough to generate interest in learning it. PHP is a standard feature offered by most Web hosting companies. However, it is interesting to understand why so many people choose PHP over alternatives.

Perl adapted well to being a CGI solution. Microsoft provides its Active Server Pages with Internet Information Server. Middleware, like Macromedia's Cold Fusion, is yet another solution. ServerWatch.com lists hundreds of Web technologies, some costing tens of thousands of dollars. Why should you choose PHP over any of these alternatives?

The short answer is that PHP is better. It is faster to code and faster to execute. The same PHP code runs unaltered on different Web servers and different operating systems. Additionally, functionality that is standard with PHP is an add-on in other environments. A more detailed argument follows.

PHP is free. Anyone may visit the PHP Web site `<http://www.php.net/>` and download the complete source code, licensed under a BSD-style license `<http://www.php.net/license/>`. Binaries are also available for Windows. The result is easy entry into the experience. There is very little risk in trying PHP, and its license allows the code to be used to develop works with no royalties. This is unlike products such as Allaire's Cold Fusion, which costs thousands of dollars for the software to interpret and serve scripts. Even commercial giants like Netscape and IBM now recognize the advantages of making source code available.

PHP runs on UNIX, Windows, and Macintosh OS X. PHP is designed to integrate with the Apache Web server. Apache, another free technology, is the most popular Web server on the Internet and comes with source code for UNIX and Windows. PHP works with other Web servers, including Microsoft's Internet Information Server. Scripts may be moved between server platforms without alteration. PHP supports ISAPI to allow for the performance benefits of tight coupling with Microsoft Web servers.

PHP is modifiable. PHP is designed to allow for future extension of functionality. PHP is coded in C and provides a well-defined application programming interface (API). Capable programmers may add new functionality easily. The rich set of functions available in PHP is evidence that they often do. Even if you aren't interested in changing the source code, it's comforting to know you can inspect it. Doing so may give you greater confidence in PHP's robustness.

PHP was written for Web page creation. Perl, C, and Java are very good general languages and are certainly capable of driving Web applications. The unfortunate sacrifice these alternatives make is the ease of communication with the Web experience. PHP applications may be rapidly and easily developed because the code is encapsulated in the Web pages themselves.

Support for PHP is free and readily available. Queries to the PHP mailing lists are often answered within minutes. A custom bug-tracking system on the PHP site shows each problem along with its resolution. Numerous sites, such as *phpbuilder.com* and *zend.com,* offer original content to PHP developers.

PHP is popular. Internet service providers find PHP to be an attractive way to allow their customers to code Web applications without the risks exposed by CGIs. Developers worldwide offer PHP programming. Sites coded in PHP will have the option of moving from one host to another as well as a choice of developers to add functionality.

Programming skills developed in other structured languages can be applied to PHP. PHP takes inspiration from both Perl and C. Experienced Perl and C programmers learn PHP very quickly. Likewise, programmers who learn PHP as a first language may apply their knowledge toward not only Perl and C, but other C-like languages such as Java.

# 1.3  Interfaces to External Systems

Originally, PHP was famous for interfacing with many different database systems, but it also has support for other external systems. Support comes in the form of modules called extensions. They either compile directly into PHP or are loaded dynamically. New extensions are added to the PHP project regularly. The extensions expose groups of functions for using these external systems. As mentioned, some of these are databases. PHP offers functions for talking natively with most popular database systems, and it provides access to ODBC drivers. Other extensions give you the ability to send messages using a particular network protocol, such as LDAP or IMAP. These functions are described in detail in Part II. Because PHP developers are enthusiastic and industrious, you will undoubtedly find more extensions have been added since I wrote this.

Pspell is a system for checking spelling. An extension provides support for numbers of arbitrary precision. There is an extension for dealing with various calendar systems. An extension provides support for DBM-style databases. You can use the SNMP, IMAP, and LDAP protocols. The Interbase and Informix databases are supported natively, as are mSQL, MySQL, MS SQL, Sybase, Oracle, and PostgreSQL. You can also parse XML or create WDDX packets. You can even extract meta information about your digital pictures using the EXIF extension. At the time of writing, automated coffee making is not yet supported.

# 1.4  How PHP Works with the Web Server

The normal process a Web server goes through to deliver a page to a browser is as follows. It all begins when a browser makes a request for a Web page. Based on the URL, the browser resolves the address of the Web server, identifies the page it would like, and gives any other information the Web server may need. Some of this information is about the browser itself, like its name (Mozilla), its version (4.08), or the operating system (Linux). Other information given the Web server could include text the user typed into form fields.

If the request is for an HTML file, the Web server will simply find the file, tell the browser to expect some HTML text, and then send the contents of the file. The browser gets the contents and begins rendering the page based on the HTML code. If you have been programming HTML for any length of time, this will be clear to you.

Hopefully, you have also had some experience with CGI scripts. When a Web server gets a request for a CGI, it can't just send the contents of the file. It must execute the script first. The script will generate some HTML code, which then gets sent to the browser. As far as the browser is concerned, it's just getting HTML.

When a PHP page is requested, it is processed exactly like a CGI, at least to the extent that the script is not simply sent to the browser. It is first passed through the PHP engine, which gives the Web server HTML text.

# 1.5  Hardware and Software Requirements

One great advantage of Open Source software is that it provides the opportunity for adaptation to new environments. This is true of PHP. Although originally intended as a module for the Apache Web server, PHP has since abstracted its Web server interface. The new abstraction layer allowed an ISAPI module to be written, which allows it to work equally well with Microsoft's Internet Information Server. With regard to hardware requirements, I have personally witnessed PHP running on 100-MHz Pentium machines running Slackware Linux and Windows NT respectively. Performance was fine for use as a personal development environment. That the engines for PHP 3 and 4 were developed on Intel 486 CPUs must have helped. A site expected to receive thousands of requests a day would need faster hardware, of course. Although more resources are needed when comparing a PHP-powered site to a flat HTML site, the requirements are not dramatically different. Despite my example, you are not limited to Intel hardware. PHP works equally well on PowerPC, Sparc, and other 32-bit or better CPUs.

When choosing an operating system, you have the general choice between Windows and a UNIX-like OS. PHP will run on older Windows operating systems, although these operating systems aren't suited for high-traffic Web servers. It will also run on Windows 2000 and Windows XP. For UNIX operating systems, PHP works well with Linux and Solaris as well as others. If you have chosen a PPC-based system, such as a Macintosh, you may choose LinuxPPC, a version of Linux. Chad Cunningham contributed patches for compiling PHP in Apple's OS X. There's even support of IBM's OS/2 and Novell Netware.

PHP still works best with the Apache Web server. But it now works very well with IIS. It also compiles as a module for the fhttpd Web server. You can make PHP work with almost any Web server using the CGI version, but I don't recommend this setup for production Web sites.

## Installation on Apache for UNIX

If you are using Linux, you can easily find an RPM for Apache and PHP, but this installation may not include every PHP feature you want. I recommend this route as a very quick start. You can always pursue compiling Apache and PHP from scratch later. PHP will compile on most versions of UNIX-like operating systems, including

Solaris and Linux. If you have ever compiled software you've found on the Net, you will have little trouble with this installation. If you don't have experience extracting files from a tar archive and executing `make` files, you may wish to rely on your system administrator or someone else more experienced. You will need to have root privileges to completely install PHP.

The first step is to download the tar files and unpack them. Download the newest versions from the PHP site `<http://www.php.net/downloads.php>` and the Apache site `<http://httpd.apache.org/>`. At the time of writing, Apache 2 is considered stable. Support for `mod_php` in Apache is not complete. The following instructions assume Apache 1.3 and Apache 2 may require a few changes.

After unpacking the tar file, the first step is to configure Apache. This is done by running the configure script inside the Apache directory. Listing 1.1 shows a minimal configuration.

| Listing 1.1 | *Configuring Apache* |
|---|---|

```
./configure \
--server-uid=nobody \
--enable-module=so
```

The script will examine your system and prepare a `make` file for Apache. This builds Apache for using shared libraries, one of which will be PHP. You should follow the configuration step with `make install`, which will compile Apache and install the binaries in the default location. You may wish to test Apache by starting it with the `/usr/local/apache/bin/apachectl` script.

Next, configure and compile PHP. Listing 1.2 shows a command for configuring PHP with a few extensions, executed within the PHP source code directory. Follow this with a `make install`. In most cases, PHP can find the libraries it needs for extensions. In Listing 1.2, I'm specifically using the MySQL libraries I have in `/usr/libs` rather than the MySQL libraries included in the PHP distribution.

Appendix E lists the compile-time configuration directives. You can also get information by running `./configure --help`. Running `make` will create the PHP library, and `make install` places the PHP module in Apache's directory of modules. It also installs the latest PEAR classes, a collection of standard PHP code.

| Listing 1.2 | *Configuring PHP* |
| --- | --- |

```
./configure \
--with-apxs=/usr/local/apache/bin/apxs \
--with-zlib \
--with-bz2 \
--with-openssl \
--with-gd \
--enable-exif \
--with-jpeg-dir=/usr \
--with-freetype-dir \
--with-t1lib \
--enable-gd-native-ttf \
--with-mysql=/usr
```

To supply additional configuration options, PHP uses a file called `php.ini`. This file should reside in `/usr/local/lib`, so copy it from the PHP source directory (Listing 1.3):

| Listing 1.3 | *Copying `php.ini`* |
| --- | --- |

```
cp php.ini-dist /usr/local/lib/php.ini
```

You may not need to edit this file. It controls certain aspects of PHP, including support for historic behavior. Chapter 15 discusses configuration directives you may use in `php.ini`. Many of them are in the default file. Some you must add.

The last step is to make sure Apache recognizes PHP scripts. Somewhere in Apache's configuration file, `httpd.conf`, you need an `AddType` directive that matches scripts ending in `.php` with `application/x-httpd-php`. You also need to load the PHP module. If the lines in Listing 1.4 do not appear in `httpd.conf`, add them.

| Listing 1.4 | *Activating PHP for Apache* |
| --- | --- |

```
LoadModule php5_module libexec/libphp5.so
AddType application/x-httpd-php .php
AddModule mod_php5.c
```

This causes all files with the extension `.php` to be executed as PHP scripts. You may also wish to insert `index.php` as a default document. When the Apache server is started, it will process PHP scripts. The documentation for Apache has hints for starting Apache automatically. If you have been running Apache previously, you will need to restart it, not just use a `kill -HUP` command.

## Installation on Apache for Windows

Compiling PHP for Windows is not an ordinary task. Windows users typically use binaries available on the PHP Web site. The same is true for Apache. Both packages include automated installers, which makes installation easy. Installing Apache this way is fine. I prefer to install PHP manually, using the archive, because it allows for better flexibility.

Unzip the PHP archive into a directory. I use `C:\PHP`, but you can really put it anywhere. Next, copy the file `php.ini-dist` into your system root directory, which is probably `C:\Windows`. Rename it `php.ini`. When PHP is invoked, it looks first for `php.ini` in this directory. Although you don't need to, you may wish to edit it to change configuration parameters, including automatically loading extensions. Comments in the file explain the purpose of each configuration directive. Chapter 15 discusses them in detail.

The next step is to make sure the required DLL files are in your path. One way is to copy required files to your system directory, such as `C:\Windows\system32`. Alternatively, you can click on the `system` icon in the control panel and add your PHP directory to the system path. Your Web server must be able to find `php4ts.dll`, which is in the root of the PHP installation directory.

Next, configure Apache to load the PHP module. Edit `httpd.conf` and add the lines in Listing 1.5. These lines load the module and associate the `.php` extension with PHP script. The final step is restarting Apache.

| **Listing 1.5** | *Activating PHP for Apache on Windows* |
| --- | --- |

```
LoadModule php5_module c:/php/sapi/php5apache.dll
AddType application/x-httpd-php .php
AddModule mod_php5.c
```

## Editing Scripts

PHP scripts are just text files, and you can edit and create them just as you would HTML files. Certainly, you can telnet into your Web server and start creating files with vi. Or you can create files with Notepad and use FTP to upload them one by one. But these aren't ideal experiences. One handy feature of newer editors is built-in FTP. These editors can open files on a remote Web server as if they were on a local drive. A single click saves them back to the remote Web server. Another feature you may enjoy is syntax highlighting. This causes PHP keywords to be colored in order to help you read the code faster.

Everyone has a favorite editor for PHP scripts. I use UltraEdit `<http://www.ultraedit.com/>`. I know many Windows users prefer Macromedia's Dreamweaver `<http://www.macromedia.com/software/dreamweaver/>` or HomeSite `<http://www.macromedia.com/software/homesite/>` to edit PHP scripts. The Macintosh users I know prefer BBedit `<http://www.barebones.com/products/bbedit/bbedit.html>`.

On a UNIX operating system, you may prefer emacs or vi, of course. You might also consider nEdit `<http://nedit.org/>`. A module for PHP is available in the contrib directory. The topic of which editor is best appears frequently on the PHP mailing list. Reading the archives can be amusing and informative `<http://www.progressive-comp.com/Lists/?l=php3-general>`.

Although I continue to use a text editor for building PHP applications, many people prefer an integrated development environment, otherwise known as an IDE. There are several IDEs designed specifically for PHP. PHPEdit `<http://www.phpedit.net/>` is one example. The Zend Studio `<http://www.zend.com/store/products/zend-studio.php>` is another very popular choice.

## Algorithms

Whenever we interact with a computer, we are instructing it to perform some action. When you drag an icon into the wastebasket on your desktop, you are asking the computer to remove the file from your hard disk. When you write an HTML file, you are instructing the computer in the proper way to display some information. There are usually many incremental steps to any process the computer performs. It may first clear the screen with the color you specified in the body tag. Then it may begin writing some text in a particular color and typeface. As you use a computer, you may not be entirely aware of each tiny step it takes, but you are giving it a list of ordered instructions that you expect it to follow.

Instructions for baking a cake are called a recipe. Instructions for making a movie are called a screenplay. Instructions for a computer are called a program. Each of these is written in its own language, a concrete realization of an abstract set of instructions. Borrowing from mathematics, computer science calls the abstract instructions an algorithm.

You may at this moment have in mind an algorithm that you'd like to implement. Perhaps you wish to display information in a Web browser that changes frequently.

Imagine something simple, such as displaying today's date. You could edit a plain HTML file once a day. You could even write out a set of instructions to help remind you of each step. But you cannot perform the task with HTML alone. There's no tag that stands for the current date.

PHP is a language that allows you to express algorithms for creating HTML files. With PHP, you can write instructions for displaying the current date inside an HTML document. You write your instructions in a file called a script. The language of the script is PHP, a language that both you and the computer can understand.

# 1.6  What a PHP Script Looks Like

PHP exists as a tag inside an HTML file. Like all HTML tags, it begins with a less than symbol, or opening angle bracket (<), and ends with a greater than symbol, or closing angle bracket (>). To distinguish it from other tags, the PHP tag has a question mark (?) following the opening angle bracket and preceding the closing angle bracket. All text outside the PHP tag is simply passed through to the browser. Text inside the tag is expected to be PHP code and is parsed.

To accommodate XML and some picky editors such as Microsoft's Front Page, PHP offers three other ways to mark code. Putting php after the opening question mark makes PHP code friendly to XML parsers. Alternatively, you may use a script tag as if you were writing JavaScript. Finally, you can use tags that appear like ASP, using <% to start blocks of code. Appendix D explains how these alternatives work. In my own coding, I frequently use the simple <? and ?> method because I can be sure I can configure PHP to accept them. For code you share with others, it's best to use <?php for the opening tag, as I have in the examples.

Listing 1.6 shows an ordinary HTML page with one remarkable difference: the PHP code between the <?php and the ?>. When this page is passed through the PHP module, it will replace the PHP code with today's date. It might read something like Friday May 1, 1999 (see Figure 1.1).

| Listing 1.6 | *Printing today's date* |
|---|---|

```
<html>
<head>
<title>Listing 1-6</title>
</head>
<body>
Today's date: <?php print(Date("l F d, Y")); ?>
</body>
</html>
```

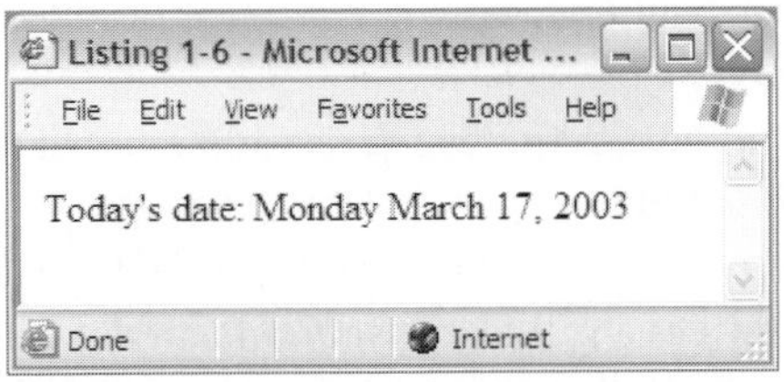

**Figure 1.1**   Output from Listing 1.6.

Whitespace—that is, spaces, tabs, and carriage returns—is ignored by PHP. Used judiciously, it can enhance the readability of your code. Listing 1.7 is functionally the same as the previous example, though you may notice more easily that it contains PHP code.

---

**Listing 1.7**   *Reformatting for readability*

```
<html>
<head>
<title>Listing 1-7</title>
</head>
<body>
Today's date:
<?php
    /*
    ** print today's date
    */
    print(Date("l f d, y"));
?>
</body>
</html>
```

---

You may also notice the line of code in Listing 1.7 that begins with a slash followed by an asterisk. This is a comment. Everything between /* and */ is equivalent to whitespace. It is ignored. Comments can be used to document how your code works. Even if you maintain your own code, you will find comments necessary for all but simple scripts.

In addition to the opening and closing comment statements, PHP provides two ways to build a single-line comment. Double slashes or a pound sign will cause everything after them to the end of the line to be ignored by the parser.

After skipping over the whitespace and the comment in Listing 1.7, the PHP parser encounters the first word: print. This is one of PHP's functions. A function collects code into a unit you may invoke with its name. The print function sends text to the browser. The contents of the parentheses will be evaluated, and if it produces output, `print` will pass it along to the browser.

Where does the line end? Unlike BASIC and JavaScript, which use a line break to denote the end of a line, PHP uses a semicolon. On this issue PHP takes inspiration from C.

The contents of the line between `print` and `;` is a call to a function named `date`. The text between the opening and closing parentheses is the parameter passed to `date`. The parameter tells `date` in what form you want the date to appear. In this case we've used the codes for the weekday name, the full month name, the day of the month, and the four-digit year. The current date is formatted and passed back to the `print` function.

The string of characters beginning and ending with double quotes is called a string constant or string literal. PHP knows that when quotes surround characters, you intend them to be treated as text. Without the quotes, PHP will assume you are naming a function or some other part of the language itself. In other words, the first quote is telling PHP to keep hands off until it finds another quote.

Notice that `print` is typed completely in lowercase letters, yet `date` has a leading uppercase letter. I did this to illustrate that PHP takes a lenient attitude toward the names of its built-in functions. `Print`, `PRINT`, and `PrInT` are all valid calls to the same function. However, for the sake of readability, it is customary to write PHP's built-in functions using lowercase letters only.

## 1.7  Saving Data for Later

Often it is necessary to save information for later use. PHP, like most programming languages, offers the concept of variables. Variables give a name to the information you want to save and manipulate. Listing 1.8 expands on our example by using variables (see Figure 1.2).

The first block of PHP code puts values into some variables. The four variables are `YourName`, `Today`, `CostOfLunch`, and `DaysBuyingLunch`. PHP knows they are variables because they are preceded by a dollar sign (`$`). The first time you use a variable in a PHP script, some memory is set aside to store the information you wish to save. You don't need to tell PHP what kind of information you expect to be saved in the variable; PHP can figure this out on its own.

The script first puts a character string into the variable `YourName`. As I noted earlier, PHP knows it's textual data because I put quotes around it. Likewise, I put today's date into a variable named `Today`. In this case PHP knows to put text into the variable because the `date` function returns text. This type of data is referred to as a string, which is shorthand for character string. A character is a single letter, number, or any other mark you make by typing a single key on your keyboard.

Notice that there is an equal sign (=) separating the variable and the value you put into it. This is the assignment operator. Everything to its right is put into a variable named to its left.

| Listing 1.8 | *Assigning values to variables* |

```php
<?php
    $YourName = "Leon";
    $Today = date("l F d, Y");
    $CostOfLunch = 3.50;
    $DaysBuyingLunch = 4;
?>
<html>
<head>
<title>Listing 1-8</title>
</head>
<body>
Today's Date:
<?php
    /*
    ** print today's date
    */
    print("<h3>$Today</h3>\n");

    /*
    ** print message about lunch cost
    */
    print("$YourName, you will be out ");
    print($CostOfLunch * $DaysBuyingLunch);
    print(" dollars this week.<br>\n");
?>
</body>
</html>
```

**Figure 1.2**    Output from Listing 1.8.

The third and fourth assignments are putting numerical data into variables. The value 3.5 is a floating-point, or fractional, number. PHP calls this type a double, showing some of its C heritage. The value 4 in the next assignment is an integer, or whole number.

After printing some HTML code, another PHP code block is opened. First the script prints today's date as a level-three header. Notice that the script passes some new types of information to the `print` function. You can give string literals or string variables to `print`, and they will be sent to the browser.

When it comes to variables, PHP is not so lenient with case. `Today` and `today` are two different variables. Since PHP doesn't require you to declare variables before you use them, you can accidentally type `today` when you mean `Today` and no error will be generated by default. If variables are unexpectedly empty, check your case. You can also catch these sorts of errors by configuring PHP to warn you of uninitialized variables. See Chapter 15's description of error reporting.

The script next prints `Leon, you will be out 14 dollars this week`. The line that prints the total has to calculate it with multiplication, using the * operator.

# 1.8  Receiving User Input

Manipulating variables that you set within your script is somewhat interesting, but hardly anything to rave about. Scripts become much more useful when they use input from the user. When you call PHP from an HTML form, the form fields are turned into variables. Listing 1.9 is a form that calls Listing 1.10, a further modification of our example script.

| Listing 1.9 | *HTML form for lunch information* |
|---|---|

```
<html>
<head>
<title>Listing 1-9</title>
</head>
<body>
<form action="1-10.php" method="post">
Your name:
<input type="text" name="YourName"><br>
```

---

| Listing 1.9 | *HTML form for lunch information (cont.)* |
|---|---|

```
Cost of a lunch:
<input type="text" name="CostOfLunch"><br>
Days buying lunch:
<input type="text" name="DaysBuyingLunch"><br>
<input type="submit" value="Compute">
</form>
</body>
</html>
```

---

Listing 1.9 is a standard HTML form. If you have dealt at all with CGIs, it will look familiar. There are three form fields that match up with the variables from our previous example. Instead of simply putting data into the variables, we will provide a form and use the information the user types. When the user presses the submit button, the script named in the ACTION attribute will receive the three form fields, and PHP will convert them into variables (see Figure 1.3).

---

| Listing 1.10 | *Computing the cost of lunch from a form* |
|---|---|

```php
<?php
    $Today = date("l F d, Y");
?>
<html>
<head>
<title>Listing 1-10</title>
</head>
<body>
Today's date:
<?php
    /*
    ** print today's date
    */
    print("<h3>$Today</h3>\n");

    /*
    ** print message about lunch cost
    */
    print($_REQUEST['YourName'] . ", you will be out ");
    print($_REQUEST['CostOfLunch'] *
        $_REQUEST['DaysBuyingLunch']);
    print(" dollars this week.<br>\n");
?>
</body>
</html>
```

---

**Figure 1.3**   Output from Listing 1.10.

Notice that in the first segment of the PHP script, I have eliminated the lines setting the variables, except for today's date. See how instead of using $CostOfLunch, I used $_REQUEST['CostOfLunch']? PHP collects all the variables sent by forms and cookies into a collection called _REQUEST. The technical name for this type of data is array, the subject of Chapter 5.

Try experimenting with the scripts by entering nonsense in the form fields. One thing you should notice is that if you put words where the script expects numbers, PHP seems to just assign them values of zero. The variables are set with a text string, and when the script tries to treat it as a number, PHP does its best to convert the information. Entering 10 Little Indians for the cost of lunch will be interpreted as 10.

# 1.9  Choosing Between Alternatives

PHP allows you to test conditions and execute certain code based on the result of the test. The simplest form of this is the if statement. Listing 1.11 shows how you can customize the content of a page based on the value of a variable (see Figure 1.4).

The Today variable is set with the name of today's weekday. The if statement evaluates the expression inside the parentheses as either true or false. The == operator compares the left side to the right side. If Today contains the word Friday, the block of code surrounded by curly braces ({ and }) is executed. In all other cases the block of code associated with the else statement is executed.

| Listing 1.11 | *Conditional daily message* |
|---|---|

```
<html>
<head>
<title>Listing 1-11</title>
</head>
<body>
<h1>
<?php
    /*
    ** Get today's day of the week
    */
    $Today = date("l");

    if($Today == "Friday")
    {
        print("Thank goodness it's Friday!");
    }
    else
    {
        print("Today is $Today.");
    }
?>
</h1>
</body>
</html>
```

**Figure 1.4**   Output from Listing 1.11.

# 1.10  Repeating Code

The last type of functionality in this brief introduction is looping. Looping allows you to repeat the execution of code. Listing 1.12 is an example of a `for` loop. The `for` statement expects three parameters separated by semicolons. The first parameter is executed once before the loop begins. It usually initializes a variable. The second parameter makes a test. This is usually a test against the variable named in the first parameter. The third parameter is executed every time the end of the loop is reached (see Figure 1.5).

**Listing 1.12** *Today's daily affirmation*

```
<html>
<head>
<title>Listing 1-12</title>
</head>
<body>
<h1>Today's Daily Affirmation</h1>
Repeat three times:<br>
<?php
    for($count = 1; $count <= 3; $count++)
    {
        print("<b>$count</b> I'm good enough, ");
        print("I'm smart enough, ");
        print("and, doggone it, people like me!<br>\n");
    }
?>
</h1>
</body>
</html>
```

**Figure 1.5**   Output from Listing 1.12.

The `for` loop in Listing 1.12 will execute three times. The initialization code sets the variable `count` to be one. Then the testing code compares the value of `count` to three. Since one is less than or equal to three, the code inside the loop executes. Notice that the script prints the value of `count`. When you run this script, you will find that `count` will progress from one to three. The reason is that the third part of the `for` statement is adding one to `count` each time through the loop. The `++` operator increments the variable immediately to its left.

The first time through the loop, `count` is one, not two. This is because the increment of `count` doesn't occur until we reach the closing curly brace. After the third time through the loop, `count` will be incremented to four, but at that point four will not be less than or equal to three, so the loop will end. Execution continues at the command following the loop code block.

# VARIABLES, OPERATORS, AND EXPRESSIONS

**Topics in This Chapter**

- A Top-Down View
- Data Types
- Variables
- Constants
- Operators
- Building Expressions

# Chapter 2

This chapter discusses fundamental building blocks of PHP scripts: variables, operators, expressions, and statements. A statement is a piece of code that instructs PHP to do something. For instance, a statement may compute a value and store it in memory, it may print something, or it may save something to the disk. There are many different types of statements in PHP. Function calls, variable assignments, loops, and `if` conditions are all statements.

Although the description of identifiers, expressions, and statements may seem simplistic, they are important building blocks that allow you to understand how scripts execute. The technique of breaking a sentence into its parts helps the student of a human language gain an appreciation for the important rules of communication. The same idea applies to programming languages.

## 2.1 A Top-Down View

Every PHP script is a collection of one or more statements. Each statement instructs PHP to perform a subtask, which is part of the greater algorithm. The statement appears as a collection of names, numbers, and special symbols. At the end is either a semicolon or a block of statements inside curly braces. For clarity, you may add any number of line breaks and spaces within the statement. Any block of PHP code that does work and ends in a semicolon is a statement. Listing 2.1 shows several simple statements.

| Listing 2.1 | *Simple statements* |
| --- | --- |

```php
<?php
    //an expression statement
    2 + 3;

    //another expression statement
    print("PHP!");

    //a control statement
    if(3 > 2)
    {
        //an assignment statement
        $a = 3;
    }
?>
```

The first statement is the addition of two numbers. It produces no output. The second prints a string to the browser. The third decides whether to execute a block of code based on an expression. Consider the 2 + 3 expression in the first line of the script. PHP understands that the + operator uses the 2 and the 3, and the entire expression evaluates to the quantity 5.

PHP includes many types of statements. Some are simple, stand by themselves, and compare well with functions. The print statement is a good example. Other statements fall naturally into groups, such as the if statement, which changes the flow of execution. The simplest statements contain only an expression.

An expression is any piece of code that represents a value. For example, 2 + 3 is an expression representing 5, "Zeev" is an expression representing four letters, and strlen("Leon") is an expression that represents 4 by way of a function call. The semicolon that ends a statement is not part of the expression.

Generally, PHP evaluates expressions from left to right and from inside parentheses outward. With each pass, PHP replaces the expression with its value until the entire expression becomes a single value. The latter part of this chapter discusses the complex rules PHP uses for evaluating expressions.

PHP can use literal values, such as numbers or blocks of text in expressions. It can also use identifiers that give names to the abstract parts of PHP: variables, functions, and classes. Some of them are created by PHP in the form of built-in functions or environment variables.

Operators join values. Most operators look for a value on their left and a value on their right. The operator defines a specific method for combining the values. For example, the + operator performs addition.

The simplest expression statements do nothing. The first statement in Listing 2.1 performs arithmetic but does not communicate the value of the expression. That is, the value isn't saved and it isn't displayed. It disappears as soon as the script creates it.

# 2.2  Data Types

PHP has eight different types of values, or data types. The first five are basic: integers, floating-point numbers, strings, booleans, and null. Two others are composed of the basic types, otherwise known as composite types. These include arrays, discussed in Chapter 5, and objects, discussed in Chapter 6. Additionally, the resource type denotes a non-native type, such as an open file or a database connection.

## Integers

Integers are whole numbers. The range of integers in PHP is equivalent to the range of the so-called long data type of the C language. Typically, this means they range from –2,147,483,648 to +2,147,483,647 on a 32-bit architecture, but may vary depending on your platform.

PHP allows you to write integers in three ways: decimal, octal, and hexadecimal. Decimal digits are the ordinary, base-10 numbers we use in day-to-day life. You write decimal values as a sequence of digits, without leading zeros. The sequence may begin with a plus (+) or minus (-) sign to show whether the number is negative or positive. You may not include commas in integers.

Octal, or base-8 numbers, consist of a sequence of digits from 0 to 7, prefixed by a leading zero. Octal numbers are useful in some contexts, such as file permissions. You may have experienced setting the permissions on a UNIX file with an octal number like 0744.

Hexadecimal, or base-16 values, begin with 0x, followed by a sequence of digits (0 to 9) or letters ranging from A to F. The case of the letters does not matter.

## Floating-Point Numbers

Floating-point numbers represent numeric values with decimal digits, which are equivalent to the range of the double data type of the C language. Floating-point numbers are also called real numbers or doubles. The range and accuracy of real numbers varies from one platform to another. Usually, this range is significantly greater than the range of integers. You can write a floating-point number in the ordinary way: a sequence of digits, a decimal point, and a sequence of digits. You may also write floating-point numbers in scientific notation, otherwise known as exponential notation. This form allows for the letter E followed by a power of 10.

For example, you can write 3.2 billion as `3.2E9`. The E may be uppercase or lower-case. The power of 10 must be an integer, of course.

Unlike integers, floating-point values have limited accuracy. Each floating-point number uses a block of memory, part of which holds the values of the digits and part of which holds the power of 10 applied to those digits. At times, a floating-point value may appear to gain or lose a very small amount of value due to the quirks of the floating-point number format. A detailed discussion is beyond the scope of this text. However, knowing they perform this way, you should take care not to use them in situations where you need exact precision.

You can perform arithmetic of arbitrarily large precision with PHP's BC library, discussed in Chapter 13.

## Strings

Web applications usually move text around more often than they make complex mathematical calculations. Strings represent a sequence of characters of limited length and can contain any kind of data, including binary data. You can write a string value by surrounding it by single-quotes (`'`) or double-quotes (`"`). Whichever you choose, the opening quote character must match the closing quote character.

PHP interprets characters inside single quotes as-is: Each character between quotes becomes one character in the string. If you need to include a single quote in the string, you may place a backslash (`\`) immediately before it. PHP understands the `\'` sequence stands for a single character and does not treat the single quote as the end of the string literal. Likewise, you may use two backslashes to represent a single backslash in the string value. Generally, these are called escape sequences.

Strings in double quotes may contain variables and additional escape sequences. PHP replaces references to variables with their values. Table 2.1 contains escape sequences recognized by PHP.

**Table 2.1**    Escape Sequences

| Code | Description |
| --- | --- |
| `\"` | Double quotes |
| `\\` | Backslash character |
| `\n` | New line |
| `\r` | Carriage return |
| `\t` | Horizontal tab |
| `\x00 - \xFF` | Hex characters |

Borrowing from UNIX shells, PHP also allows what are sometimes called HERE docs. A special operator allows you to specify your own string of characters that stands for the end of the string. This is helpful when you have large blocks of text that span multiple lines and contain quotes. Backslash codes and variables are recognized inside the text block, just as they are with strings surrounded by double quotes. To mark an area of text, begin by using the <<< operator. Follow it by the identifier you'll use to end the string. When that identifier is found alone on a line, PHP will consider it equivalent to a closing quote character. You can use numbers, letters, and underscores for the identifier, but it must begin with a letter or an underscore. It's customary to use HERE or EOD (end of data). See Listing 2.2 for an example.

| Listing 2.2 | *HERE docs* |
|---|---|

```php
<?php
    print <<< HERE
This text can contain both double quotes
and single quotes. It's "simple."

Note that the line break following the
first HERE and the one before the last
HERE are not included in the string. And
PHP is smart enough to recognize that the
line above was not the real end of the string.

You can also embed variables and backslash
codes in this string.

        The only downside is that any tabs or
        spaces you use to index the text will
        pass through, too.
HERE;

?>
```

# Booleans

The boolean type, named after mathematician George Boole, contains only two values—true and false. The control statements discussed in Chapter 3 use boolean values to decide whether to execute blocks of code, and the comparison operators discussed later in this chapter resolve to boolean values.

You can write boolean values with the TRUE and FALSE constants. You can also allow PHP to convert a string, integer, or floating-point value to boolean. Table 2.2 describes how PHP converts values of other types to booleans.

**Table 2.2**   Converting Other Types to Booleans

| Data Type | Value | Boolean Value |
|---|---|---|
| Integer or Floating-Point | 0 | FALSE |
| | Any other value | TRUE |
| String | "" (empty string) "0" | FALSE |
| | Any other value | TRUE |
| Array | Array with no elements | FALSE |
| | Array with one or more elements | TRUE |
| Object | Any instantiated object | TRUE |
| Null | NULL | FALSE |

## Null

Null is a special type that stands for the lack of value. It is typically used to initialize and reset variables or to check whether or not a variable is initialized. You can use the NULL constant to unset a variable.

## Resources

Resources are a data type that allows PHP scripts to hold handles to external data structures. Resources are different from the elementary types, since they don't contain native PHP values but rather point to non-native elements such as open files or database connections. If you attempt to use a resource like a string, it returns something sensible, such as Resource id #1.

# 2.3  Variables

Although you've seen variables in the previous pages, you may wonder what they are exactly. Variables in PHP give you access to memory storage in a part of a computer called RAM, or random access memory. RAM is a volatile medium for storing information. That is, it all disappears when you shut off the machine. The computer sees this memory as a long array of memory cells that reside in sequential addresses. In PHP, however, you cannot actually get to memory at this level.

You must use a variable. When you assign a value to a variable with `$result = 2 + 5`, or retrieve the value of a variable with `print($result)`, PHP takes care of matching the variable name you specified with the right piece of memory in RAM.

Every use of a variable in PHP begins with `$`, followed by letters, numbers, or underscores. After the `$`, the first character must be either a letter or an underscore. Table 2.3 shows examples of some valid and invalid variable names.

Using dollar signs in variable names has a long tradition in programming languages. BASIC, a popular language created in the 1960s, uses them, and so does PERL. Other languages, such as C and Java, do not. The dollar sign helps you distinguish a variable from a function, a keyword, or any other part of PHP. You may wish to consider `$` part of the variable name, or you may choose to think of it as an operator that references memory with a given name. When speaking about variables, it's more common to say "user equals three" rather than "dollar-sign-user equals three." In written language, which lacks nuance, it's common to see `$` included, but it's not necessary. In both cases, you will be understood, and it's mostly a matter of personal and community preference.

**Table 2.3**   Examples of Variable Names

| Name | Validity | Comment |
| --- | --- | --- |
| `i` | Valid | Single-letter variables are good for temporary purposes, such as loop counters. |
| `1` | Invalid | The first character following the dollar sign may not be a number. |
| `_1` | Valid | Traditionally, variables that begin with an underscore have special meaning to the local namespace. |
| `firstName` | Valid | Variables that look like words help make your scripts easier to understand. |
| `7Lucky` | Invalid | The first character following the dollar sign may not be a number. Use `Lucky7` instead. |
| `~password` | Invalid | ~ is not an alpha character and may not be used in variable names. |
| `Last!Visit` | Invalid | ! is not an alpha character and may not be used in variable names. Use `LastVisit` or `last_visit` instead. |
| `Compute-Mean` | Invalid | – is not an alpha character and may not be used in variable names. Use `Compute_Mean` instead. |

The equal sign (`=`) is used to set the value of a variable. This is called the assignment operator. On the left side of the assignment operator is a variable that will receive a value. On the right side is an expression, which could be a simple string constant or a complex combination of operators, variables, and constants. The simplest form of assignment is from a constant expression. This could be a number or a string surrounded by quotes. Table 2.4 lists some examples.

**Table 2.4** Examples of Variables Assignments

| String Constants | Integer Constants | Double Constants |
|---|---|---|
| `$myString = "leon";` | `$myInteger = 1;` | `$myDouble = 123.456;` |
| `$myString = "\n";` | `$myInteger = -256;` | `$myDouble = -98.76e5;` |

Most compiled languages, such as C or C++, require you to declare every variable along with the type of value that it will contain, and they require every code piece to state in advance what kind of values it is designed to work with. Most interpreted languages, such as PHP, allow variables to store any type of value and allow code units to work with any type of value. PHP doesn't even require you to explicitly declare a variable before you use it. Instead, the first time you assign a variable with some value, it is created. This simplifies development and helps you produce and maintain working programs more quickly. It also can lead to bugs when you use a variable before initializing it.

Variables in PHP don't have designated types. Instead, the type of the variable is considered to be the type of the value that it contains. The type of value that variables contain may be changed at any time. For example, assigning an integer to a variable that previously held a string converts the variable to an integer. This is in contrast to C, where each variable has a designated type. Assigning a value to a variable of a different type will make C attempt to convert the value so that it fits the variable.

You may use a variable in any context that expects an expression. You can use variables to create complex expressions and assign their results to other variables. Listing 2.3 uses a variable in an expression to set the value of a second variable.

**Listing 2.3** *Using a variable in a computation*

```php
<?php
    //create variable
    $result = 2 + 5;

    //create another variable
    $doubleResult = $result * 2.001;

    //print the second variable
    print($doubleResult);
?>
```

As mentioned earlier, double-quoted strings and HERE docs may contain embedded variables. You may write a variable inside a string surrounded by double quotes, and its value appears in its place. This even works with arrays and objects. Listing 2.4 is an example of this technique. Notice that the name variable appears within a print statement between double quotes.

| Listing 2.4 | *Embedded variables* |
|---|---|

```php
<?php
    $name = "Zeev";

    //Greet Zeev
    print("Hello, $name!\n");

    //Greet Zeev again
    print <<< EOD
Hello again, $name!
How is it going?
EOD;
?>
```

# Freeing Memory

PHP applications, like any kind of computer applications, consume memory. PHP uses some memory for internal purposes. Some memory stores the data that you work with in your application, mostly in variables. Typically, PHP applications consume small amounts of memory, so you don't have to worry about conserving memory. During the course of execution, PHP does its best to determine which memory pieces are no longer in use and frees them automatically for reuse by other parts of the script. At the end of each request, PHP frees any memory used by this specific request.

Larger applications that make use of many variables may consume larger chunks of memory, and conserving memory may become an issue. In this context, PHP needs help identifying variables you no longer need. To accomplish this, you have two methods: set the variable to NULL or use the unset function.

If you set a variable to NULL, the variable itself remains, but it does not point to any memory. PHP uses a small amount of memory itself to maintain the variable, but the memory consumed isn't enough to be a concern. This approach carries the side effect that if your script reads from the variable later, PHP cannot warn you about using an undefined variable.

The unset function completely removes a variable from memory. This saves the overhead PHP needs for any variable, and any read of the variable generates a notice.

After using either method, you can test whether a variable contains a value with the isset and empty functions. If you need to know if a variable points to NULL, you can use is_null. Chapter 11 discusses these functions.

# References

By default, assigning the value of a variable to another variable creates a copy of the data. Listing 2.5 illustrates this behavior. The value of b remains intact even after a is modified. In most cases, this would be the desired behavior. If you wish two variables to share storage, use the reference operator (&).

| Listing 2.5 | *Assigning variables with variables* |
|---|---|

```php
<?php
    //create variable
    $a = "Apple";

    //assign $a to $b
    $b = $a;

    //change $a
    $a = "Ball";

    //prints Apple
    print($b);
?>
```

Listing 2.6 demonstrates the & operator. In this example, a and b share the same block of memory. Assigning a value with either variable changes the value they share. You can think of b as an alias to a, except that existence of b does not depend on a. Internally, PHP understands there are two references to that block of memory. Of course, you can create many references to a single value if you wish. There are two ways to break a reference: unset the variable or set it to reference another value.

---

**Listing 2.6** *Assigning by reference*

```php
<?php
    //create variable
    $a = "Apple";

    //create references
    $b = &$a;

    //change value of both $a and $b
    $a = "Ball";

    //remove $a
    unset($a);

    //prints Ball
    print($b);
?>
```

---

# String Offsets

If a variable contains a string, you may refer to each character using curly braces. PHP numbers each character starting with zero. To refer to the seventh character in the s variable, type `$s{6}`. You may also set a single character with this notation with an expression like `$s{6} = 'x'`. PHP uses only the first character of the value on the right-hand side to replace the specified character. If the variable on the left-hand side is not a string, it remains unchanged. Listing 2.7 demonstrates the use of curly brackets to reference single characters.

---

**Listing 2.7** *Referencing a single character*

```php
<?php
    //replace space with underscore
    $s = "a string";
    $s{1} = "_";
    print($s);
?>
```

---

Historically, PHP used square brackets to refer to string offsets. However, due to an ambiguity with the access notation for arrays, this syntax is now deprecated.

# 2.4 Constants

Constants are similar to variables, but they may be set only once. Some of them are created automatically by PHP; others you will create with the `define` function discussed in Chapter 11. You do not use the dollar-sign operator to get the value of a constant, and you may never use a constant on the left side of an assignment operator.

Although it is not necessary, it is customary to name constants exclusively with capital letters. This helps make them stand out in your script, as in Listing 2.8. PHP creates many constants upon startup, as described in Chapter 8.

| Listing 2.8 | *Using a constant* |
|---|---|

```php
<?php
    define("STANDARD_GREETING", "Hello, World!");
    print(STANDARD_GREETING);
?>
```

# 2.5 Operators

As stated earlier, an operator is a symbol that tells PHP to perform a mathematical or logical operation on one or more operands. An expression such as `$result = 2 + 5` contains three operators. The `$` operator lets PHP know you're using a variable named `result`. The = operator assigns the value on the right to the variable on the left. The + operator adds the values on each side of it.

Most operators work on two operands and are called binary operators. Others operate on only one operand and are referred to as unary operators. PHP also has one operator that works with three operands, known as the ternary operator. With some exceptions, most operators fall into five categories: arithmetic, logical, bitwise, assignment, and control.

Most operators expect their operands to be of a certain type. For example, the arithmetic operators generally expect their arguments to be numeric. What happens if you feed them a string? Fortunately, PHP in general and its operators in particular were designed not to make a big fuss about mismatched data types.

If you give an operator a type that differs from the one it expects, PHP does its best to convert the type meaningfully. When converting from strings to numbers, PHP ignores leading spaces and trailing characters. For example, PHP converts both

"4.5test" and "4.5" to 4.5. If PHP is unable to find any numeric meaning to the string, it evaluates to zero. If PHP expects an integer, it drops any digits after the decimal point.

Using floating-point numbers where PHP expects an integer results in truncation of the fraction. You can use the round function discussed in Chapter 13 to round a floating-point number to the nearest integer.

Empty strings and zero become FALSE where PHP expects a boolean. A string containing a single zero character becomes FALSE. All other strings and all other numeric values become TRUE. Arrays, discussed in Chapter 4, become TRUE unless they contain no elements. Allowing PHP to convert an array to a boolean is unusual. NULL values are always FALSE. Resources and objects are always TRUE.

Because PHP converts all other types to booleans with no complaints, you must be careful. Some functions return FALSE on failure and return a number or string when successful. If you simply test the return value and the function returns an empty string or zero, it is indistinguishable from failure. The === and !=== operators discussed later in this chapter allow you to avoid this ambiguity.

When converting other types to strings, PHP returns a sensible representation. Integers become strings of digits. Floating-point numbers become strings of digits with a decimal point. PHP returns extremely large and extremely small numbers in exponential notation. Composite types become strings naming the type. Treating composite types as strings is useful only for debugging purposes. Table 2.5 summarizes conversion between types.

**Table 2.5**   Type Conversion Rules

| Given Type | Expected Type | Conversion Performed |
|---|---|---|
| String | Integer or Floating-Point | Ignore leading spaces and use digits. Truncate digits after the decimal point if expecting an integer. |
| String | Boolean | The empty string and the string containing a single zero character are FALSE. Any other strings are TRUE. |
| Integer or Floating-Point | Boolean | Zero values are FALSE. All other values are TRUE. |
| Integer or Floating-Point | String | PHP creates a string representation of the number. |
| Floating-Point | Integer | Any digits after the decimal sign are truncated. |
| Boolean | String | TRUE becomes "1". FALSE becomes an empty string. |
| Boolean | Integer or Floating-Point | TRUE becomes 1. FALSE becomes 0. |

**Table 2.5**    Type Conversion Rules *(cont.)*

| Given Type | Expected Type | Conversion Performed |
|---|---|---|
| Array | Integer or Floating-Point | An integer stating the number of elements in the array—most of the time. Do not rely on this functionality. |
| Array | Boolean | Arrays with one or more elements are converted to TRUE. Empty arrays are converted to FALSE. This conversion is rarely used. |
| Array | String | The string literal "Array". |

# Arithmetic Operators

Addition, subtraction, multiplication, and division are familiar concepts. They may be applied to any numeric value, including integers and floating-point numbers. When used with other types of values, such as a string, PHP first converts them to numeric value and then performs the operation. The result type of an arithmetic expression can be either an integer or a floating-point number. PHP determines the result type based on whether a decimal point is necessary to describe the result or not. This is unlike strict-typed languages such as C that determine the result based only on the operand types. Table 2.6 displays the arithmetic operators. Listing 2.9 demonstrates their use.

**Table 2.6**    Arithmetic Operators

| Operator | Operation It Performs | Example |
|---|---|---|
| + | Addition<br>Explicit positive sign | 12 + 43<br>+13 |
| − | Subtraction<br>Negation | 100 − 50<br>−3 |
| * | Multiplication | 3 * 4 |
| / | Division | 5 / 2 |
| % | Modulo division | 5 % 2 |
| ++ | Post-increment<br>Pre-increment | $a++<br>++$a |
| -- | Post-decrement<br>Pre-decrement | $a--<br>--$a |

Modulo division returns the integer remainder of a division and is therefore defined only for integers. When used with other types of values, it first converts them to integer values and then performs the operation. The result of modulo division is always an integer.

The + operator has a different meaning when applied to arrays. See Chapter 5 for a discussion of using + with arrays.

---

**Listing 2.9**  *Using arithmetic operators*

```php
<?php
    //prints 6 (not 8!)
    print(2 + 2 * 2);
    print("<br>\n");

    //prints 2.5
    print(5 / 2);
    print("<br>\n");

    //prints 1
    print(5 % 2);
    print("<br>\n");

    //prints 35
    print(" 7 little Indians" * 5);
    print("<br>\n");
?>
```

---

The increment and decrement operators are shorthand for adding or subtracting 1 from a variable. They cannot be used with anything other than a variable, so something like 5++ is illegal. These operators work for integers and floating-point numbers. The increment operators also work with strings: PHP increments the last character in the string to the next character in the character set. Decrement operators do not work with strings, but they do not produce an error.

As you can see in Table 2.6, there are two different notations for each operator. In many situations, where these operators are used simply to increment or decrement a variable, the two different notations result in much the same behavior. However, if you use the increment expression as an argument for a function or for another operator, the difference in notation affects the value of the expression.

The value of an increment expression is always the value of the variable. The location of the increment operator only determines whether the expression evaluates to the value of the variable before or after the increment. When placing the operator to the right, PHP uses the value of the variable and then increments it. This is called post-increment. When placing the operator to the left, PHP increments the variable and then uses the new value. This is called pre-increment. Listing 2.10 demonstrates this concept.

**Listing 2.10**   *Comparing pre-increment to post-increment*

```php
<?php
    $VisitorsToday = 1;

    //prints 1
    print($VisitorsToday++);

    //VisitorsToday is now 2
    print("<br>\n");

    //prints 3
    print(++$VisitorsToday);
    print("<br>\n");

    //prints 4.14
    $pi = 3.14;
    $pi++;
    print($pi);
    print("<br>\n");

    //prints PHQ
    $php = "PHP";
    $php++;
    print($php);
    print("<br>\n");

    //prints PHP
    $php = "PHP";
    $php--;
    print($php);
    print("<br>\n");
?>
```

# Assignment Operators

There really is only one assignment operator, but PHP offers a handful of shortcut operators for combining assignment with another operator, often referenced as assign-op. Table 2.7 lists all the assignment operators.

**Table 2.7** Assignment Operators

| Operator | Operation Performed | Example |
|---|---|---|
| = | Assign right side to left side | $a = 13 |
| += | Add right side to left side | $a += 2 |
| -= | Subtract right side from left side | $a -= 3 |
| *= | Multiply left side by right side | $a *= 5 |
| /= | Divide left side by right side | $a /= 4 |
| %= | Set left side to left side modulo right side | $a %= 2 |
| &= | Set left side to bitwise-AND of left side and right side | $a &= $b |
| \|= | Set left side to bitwise-OR of left side and right side | $a \|= $b |
| ^= | Set left side to bitwise-XOR of left side and right side | $a ^= $b |
| .= | Set left side to concatenation of left side and right side | $a .= "more text" |

All the assignment operators put a value into a variable. Specifically, they put a value on the right side into a variable on the left side. You may not reverse the order. The operators that combine another operator with an assignment operator operate on both the right and left sides and then put the result in the variable on the left. Listing 2.11 demonstrates equivalent statements.

**Listing 2.11** *Using assignment operators*

```php
<?php
    //Add 5 to Count
    $Count = 0;
    $Count = $Count + 5;

    //Add 5 to Count
    $Count = 0;
    $Count += 5;

    //prints 13
    print($a = $b = 13);
    print("<br>\n");

    //prints 7
    $Count = 2;
    print($Count += 5);
    print("<br>\n");
?>
```

Assignment expressions resolve to the value being assigned. This allows you to use an assignment expression where you would otherwise place a variable alone. It also allows you to chain assignments. For example, `print($a = $b = 13)` prints 13 and assigns 13 to both a and b. The operators that combine another operator with an assignment operator resolve to the final value assigned, not to the right-hand value.

## Logical and Relational Operators

Relational operators compare values and return either TRUE or FALSE. Logical operators perform logical operations on TRUE and FALSE. Values used with a logical operator are converted into booleans prior to being evaluated. For numerical values, zero will be interpreted as FALSE, and other values will be TRUE. Empty strings are considered to be FALSE, and any nonempty string is TRUE. Table 2.8 lists the logical and relational operators.

**Table 2.8**   Logical and Relational Operators

| Operator | Operation Performed | Example |
| --- | --- | --- |
| < | Is less than | $a < 14 |
| > | Is greater than | $a > $b |
| <= | Is less than or equal to | $a <= 3 |
| >= | Is greater than or equal to | 6 >= $a |
| == | Is equal to (equality) | $a == 13 |
| === | Is identical | $a === NULL |
| != | Is not equal to | $a != 7 |
| !== | Is not identical | $a !== FALSE |
| AND | Logical and | $a AND $b |
| && | Logical and | $a && $b |
| OR | Or | $a OR $b |
| \|\| | Or | $a \|\| $b |
| XOR | Exclusive or | $a XOR $b |
| ! | Not | ! $a |

These operators allow you to determine the relationship between two operands. When both operands are strings, the comparison is done lexicographically. If at least one of the operands is not a string, then the comparison is done arithmetically. Non-numeric values are converted to numbers on the fly according to the conversion rules before the comparison takes place.

Notice that the equality operator is very similar to the assignment operator. That's reasonable. One performs the action of making both sides equal; the right-side value is copied to the variable on the left side. The other asks the question, Are both sides equal? The danger is that it's difficult to notice when the two are confused. PHP will allow you to put an assignment inside the parentheses of an `if` statement. If you have an `if` statement that always seems to evaluate one way, check to make sure you haven't typed = when you meant ==. If you're testing the value of a variable and a constant, put the constant on the left. If you accidentally use an assignment operator, PHP generates an error.

If you are unfamiliar with logical operations, refer to Table 2.9. The first two columns enumerate all the possible combined values of `p` and `q`, which stand for relational expressions. The other four columns show the results of performing a logical operation on `p` and `q`.

**Table 2.9**   Truth Table for Logical Operators

| p | q | p AND q | p OR q | p XOR q | !p |
|-------|-------|---------|--------|---------|-------|
| FALSE | FALSE | FALSE | FALSE | FALSE | TRUE |
| FALSE | TRUE | FALSE | TRUE | TRUE | TRUE |
| TRUE | FALSE | FALSE | TRUE | TRUE | FALSE |
| TRUE | TRUE | TRUE | TRUE | FALSE | FALSE |

You might have noticed two versions of the logical operators in Table 2.8. For instance, there is both `&&` and `AND`. Operationally, they are the same, but they differ in precedence—a topic discussed at the end of this chapter. Aside from precedence, you are free to use them interchangeably.

PHP evaluates an expression only to the point of determining its ultimate value. With most binary operators, this requires taking both of the operands into account. For instance, you can't really tell what the sum of 4 + 6 is without taking both 4 and 6 into account. There are two operators that are an exception to this rule—the logical-AND and logical-OR operators.

Listing 2.12 demonstrates short-circuit logical expressions.

| Listing 2.12 | *Short-circuit logical expressions* |
| --- | --- |

```php
<?php
    $numerator = 5;
    $divisor = 0;
    if(($divisor == 0) OR (($num / $divisor) > 1))
    {
        print("The result is greater than 1");
    }
?>
```

The `if` statement first checks whether the divisor is zero. Dividing a number by 0 generates a warning. Mathematically, it evaluates to infinity. If PHP determines the divisor is zero, it doesn't evaluate the rest of the logical-OR expression. It already knows the entire expression is TRUE. This avoids the generation of an error message. Likewise, a logical-AND expression is FALSE if the expression on the left is FALSE.

The `===` and `!==` operators compare both value and type. For example, the integer 0 and the floating-point number 0.00 are equal, and the expression 0 == 0.00 evaluates to TRUE. They are of two different types, so 0 === 0.00 evaluates to FALSE. This can be most useful when a function returns an integer or string when successful and FALSE or NULL on error. If the function returns zero or an empty string, it appears to return FALSE. The `===` operator allows you to distinguish between other types that become FALSE when converted to booleans and values defined explicitly as booleans.

## Bitwise Operators

If you're not familiar with the notion of bits, this paragraph provides some background information. If you are, you can safely skip to the next paragraph. Bits are the smallest memory unit in computers. They are able to contain a single binary digit, or in other words, either 1 or 0. Internally, computers work on binary representations of data. A binary representation of a number is the value of the number in base-2. For example, when you ask the computer to add 3 and 5, it actually converts these numbers to binary, 0011 and 0101 respectively. It then performs the requested operation, in this case addition, and arrives at the result, 1000. Only then, the binary result is converted back to the decimal base, and we get the result—15.

Bitwise operators are similar to logical operators, except they perform on the binary representation of their arguments. In case both arguments are strings, the operation is performed between parallel character offsets, and the result is stored in the same offset in the result string. In all other cases, the arguments are converted to integer representation, and the operation is then performed.

When using logical operators, 1 and 10 are both considered TRUE. A logical-AND of 1 and 10 results in TRUE. However, if we look at these numbers from a binary perspective, a decimal 1 is 0001 in binary and a decimal 10 is 1010 in binary. A bitwise-AND of 1 and 10 results in 0. This is because each bit of the two numbers is compared by a bitwise-AND. Table 2.10 lists PHP's bitwise operators.

**Table 2.10** Bitwise Operators

| Operator | Operation Performed | Example |
|----------|---------------------|---------|
| & | And | $a & $b |
| \| | Or | $a \| 1001 |
| ^ | Exclusive or | $a ^ $b |
| ~ | One's complement or NOT | ~$a |
| >> | Shift all bits to the right | $a >> 3 |
| << | Shift all bits to the left | $a << 2 |

See Figure 2.1 for an example of a bitwise operation, which shows that (12 & 10) == 8. Matching bits are operated on. In the rightmost position 0 and 0 are operated on with a bitwise-AND. The result is 0, so a 0 is put in this position of the result.

```
    1   1   0   0  | (12)

&   1   0   1   0  | (10)
_____
    1   0   0   0  | (8)
```

**Figure 2.1** Bitwise-AND of 12 and 10.

Bitwise operators are very useful in C, from which PHP takes inspiration, but you rarely will need to use them in a PHP script. You will find some functions in the reference chapters (8 through 20) that use bitfields.

## Casting Operators

The automatic conversion of values depending on the context allows you to ignore exact types most of the time. However, in certain situations you may wish to explicitly state what kind of value you need. The operation of changing a value of a certain type to an equivalent value of a different type is called casting. Table 2.11 contains PHP's casting operators.

PHP provides several casting operators. The notation for casting operators is simply the type to which you wish to cast enclosed in parentheses. The expression that you wish to cast appears to the right of the casting operator.

**Table 2.11**    Casting Operators

| Operator | Operation Performed | Example |
|---|---|---|
| (int)<br>(integer) | Integer cast | (integer)$i |
| (float)<br>(double)<br>(real) | Floating-point cast | (float)$f |
| (string) | String cast | (string)$s |
| (bool)<br>(boolean) | Boolean cast | (boolean)($a - 3) |
| (array) | Array cast | (array)$c |
| (object) | Object cast | (object)$a |

Note that casting a variable does not change the variable itself. Instead, it creates an expression whose value is of the required type. If you wish to change the type of a value that is stored inside a variable, you can use the settype function, described in Chapter 11.

Explicitly converting the type of an expression may be necessary in situations where PHP interfaces with less forgiving environments. For example, PHP can cope with extra characters following a number in a string converted to an integer. SQL, the language used by most relational databases, cannot.

## Miscellaneous Operators

There are operators that don't fit into any of the previous categories: the concatenation operator, the variable marker, the reference operator, and others. Table 2.12 lists them.

**Table 2.12**    Miscellaneous Operators

| Operator | Operation Performed | Example |
|---|---|---|
| . | Concatenate | $a . $b |
| $ | Indirect reference | $$a |
| @ | Silence (suppress error messages) | @($a/$b) |

**Table 2.12**   Miscellaneous Operators *(cont.)*

| Operator | Operation Performed | Example |
|---|---|---|
| ? : | Ternary conditional expression | `($a == 3) ? "yes" : "no"` |
| {} | Variable embedded in a string | `{$a}` |
| ` ` | Execute a string in the command shell | `` `ls -1` `` |
| => | Assign array element index | `array(1=>'January')` |
| -> | Reference an object | `$c->method()` |
| :: | Reference a class | `myClass::method()` |
| instanceof | Tests if an object is an instance of a certain class | `$c instanceof myClass` |

The concatenation operator is similar to the addition operator except that it joins two strings. Nonstring operands are converted automatically according to the conversion rules. I find this operator indispensable. When issuing a `print`, it is convenient to concatenate several strings. I also use the concatenation operator to build database queries. Listing 2.13 is an example of doing this.

**Listing 2.13**   *The concatenation operator*

```php
<?php
    $Query = "SELECT LastName, FirstName " .
        "FROM Clients " .
        "WHERE Disposition = 'Pleasant' " .
        "ORDER BY LastName ";

    print($Query);
?>
```

When variables were discussed earlier, it was shown that a dollar sign always precedes the name of a variable. This is true whether the variable is global, local, or a function argument. The operator can be taken to mean "use the value stored in the named variable." This can be useful if you want to create a piece of code where you don't know the name of the variable you would like to reference at the time of development. The dollar-sign operator may also operate on the result of another dollar-sign operator or the result of a complex expression inside curly braces. Note that indirect reference is not supported inside quoted strings or HERE docs unless you use curly braces.

Curly braces (`{` and `}`) group variables as parentheses do for arithmetic. This eliminates the ambiguity that can arise when referencing variables. They allow you to specify elements of multidimensional arrays inside strings. But even when not strictly necessary, it's a good idea to use curly braces. Listing 2.14 demonstrates indirect reference and the use of curly braces. It's clear that the script uses a variable to name another variable here.

---

**Listing 2.14**  *Using indirect reference*

```php
<?php
    //set variables
    $var_name = "myValue";
    $myValue = 123.456;

    $array_name = "myArray";
    $myArray = array(1, 2, 3);

    //prints "123.456"
    print($$var_name . "<br>\n");

    //prints "$myValue", perhaps not what you expect
    //$var_name expands to "myValue", but indirect
    //reference doesn't work inside quoted strings,
    //and the extra dollar sign is printed as-is
    print("$$var_name<br>\n");

    //prints "123.456"
    //Uses special notation to embed complex variables
    //inside strings
    print("{$$var_name}<br>\n");

    //prints "3"
    print(${$array_name}[2] . "<br>\n");
?>
```

---

The `@` operator suppresses any error messages when it precedes an expression. Normally, when a built-in function encounters an error, PHP sends text directly to the browser. Sometimes this is just warning text. If you want to suppress any error or warning messages, place `@` directly before the name of the function. You may also place `@` before an expression if you anticipate an error condition, such as division by zero. Error messages may also be suppressed for all functions in a script with the `error_reporting` directive. See Listing 2.15.

| Listing 2.15 | *The silence operator* |
|---|---|

```php
<?php
    $a = 7;
    $b = 0;

    //suppress division-by-zero warning
    @ $c = $a / $b;
?>
```

The ? operator is equivalent to an `if` statement. It is called a ternary operator because it takes three parameters: an expression that is evaluated to be TRUE or FALSE, an expression that is evaluated if the first is TRUE, and an expression that is evaluated if the first is FALSE. A complete discussion of the ? operator appears in Chapter 3.

The -> operator is used strictly to reference either methods or properties of objects, which are discussed in Chapter 6. The left-hand side of the operator is the name of an instantiated class; the right-hand side is the name of a function or variable inside the class. The :: operator allows you to refer to a member of a class. This allows you to call methods in classes without instantiating objects. The right side of the :: operator should be the name of a class known to the current scope. The left side may be the name of a method or constant. The `instanceof` operator tests whether an object on the left is a member of the class on the right.

The -> and :: operators may be chained. Both $a->$b->c() and ClassA::ClassB::methodC() are valid expressions.

PHP supplies three special names for use on the left side of the :: operator: self, parent, and main. The self namespace refers to the local namespace. You may not use it outside of a class definition. The parent namespace refers to the class the current class extends. The main namespace refers to the global scope.

The => operator is used in declaring arrays, discussed in Chapter 5. When creating an array with the `array` statement, you may specify the index for an element with the => operator. The left-hand side of the operator is the index, and the right-hand side is the value. This operator is also used by the `foreach` statement in much the same way.

You may use backticks (`) to execute a command in the shell. The backtick character is on the extreme left of most keyboards. The expression evaluates to the output of the command. This is the same functionality implemented by the shell_exec function described in Chapter 9. Listing 2.16 shows a simple example of the backtick operator.

| Listing 2.16 | *The backtick operator* |
|---|---|

```
<?
    //print directory contents
    print(nl2br(`ls -la`));
?>
```

# 2.6  Building Expressions

When computing the value of an expression made out of several operators, PHP evaluates operators according to their precedence value, as shown in Table 2.13. Operators with lower precedence values evaluate first. Consider the evaluation of 2 + 2 * 2. Since the multiplication operator * has precedence over the addition operator +, evaluation begins with the computation of 2 * 2. PHP then adds 2 to 4 and returns the result of 6.

Precedence alone, however, is not enough. Consider the expression 12 / 2 * 3. Both operators appearing in this expression, division and multiplication, have the same precedence. However, the result of this expression will vary depending on which operation we perform first. That is, (12 / 2) * 3 is not equal to 12 / (2 * 3).

Since we expect PHP to adhere to the rules of arithmetic we're all used to from grade school, it is crucial that ambiguities between operators in the same precedence level are properly resolved. We expect the expression to be 18 because we learned to execute operators of equal precedence from left to right. In computer science, we call this associativity. Operators may be right associative, left associative, or nonassociative.

Ordinary multiplication is left-associative. PHP evaluates the expression from left to right. Assignments are right-associative. PHP computes the value on the right of the operator before assigning it to the variable on the left. An expression with a nonassociative operator cannot be used as an operand for another expression that uses a nonassociative operator. Composing such an expression will result in a parse error unless you use parentheses to isolate the nonassociative expression.

Because precedence and associativity are difficult to remember, use the following two rules when building expressions. Multiplication and division come before addition and subtraction. Put parentheses around everything else. It may seem humorous, but these rules will save you hours of debugging.

Table 2.13 describes the precedence and associativity of PHP's operators.

**Table 2.13**   PHP's Operators

| Precedence | Operator | Operation It Performs | Associativity |
|---|---|---|---|
| 1 | !<br>~<br>++<br>--<br>@<br>(int)<br>(float)<br>(string)<br>(bool)<br>(array)<br>(object) | logical not<br>bitwise not<br>increment<br>decrement<br>silence operator<br>integer cast<br>floating-point cast<br>string cast<br>boolean cast<br>array cast<br>object cast | Right |
| 2 | *<br>/<br>% | multiply<br>divide<br>modulo | Left |
| 3 | +<br>-<br>. | add<br>subtract<br>concatenate | Left |
| 4 | <<<br>>> | bitwise shift left<br>bitwise shift right | Left |
| 5 | <<br><=<br>><br>>= | is smaller<br>is smaller or equal<br>is greater<br>is greater or equal | Nonassociative |
| 6 | ==<br>!=<br>===<br>!== | is equal<br>is not equal<br>is identical<br>is not identical | Nonassociative |
| 7 | && | logical and | Left |
| 8 | \|\| | logical or | Left |
| 9 | ? : | question mark operator | Left |

**Table 2.13** PHP's Operators *(cont.)*

| Precedence | Operator | Operation It Performs | Associativity |
|---|---|---|---|
| 10 | = | assign | Right |
|  | =& | assign by reference |  |
|  | += | assign add |  |
|  | –= | assign subtract |  |
|  | *= | assign multiply |  |
|  | /= | assign divide |  |
|  | %= | assign modulo |  |
|  | ^= | assign bitwise xor |  |
|  | &= | assign bitwise and |  |
|  | \|= | assign bitwise or |  |
|  | .= | assign concatenate |  |
| 11 | AND | logical and | Left |
| 12 | XOR | logical xor | Left |
| 13 | OR | logical or | Left |

# CONTROL STATEMENTS

**Topics in This Chapter**

- The `if` Statement
- The `?` Operator
- The `switch` Statement
- Loops
- `exit, die,` and `return`
- Exceptions
- Declare

# Chapter 3

Control statements allow you to execute blocks of code depending on conditions. They allow you to repeat a block of code, which leads to simpler, more efficient scripts. This chapter introduces the decision-making statements `if` and `switch`. It also discusses loops using `for` and `while`.

## 3.1 The `if` Statement

Figure 3.1 lays out the form of an `if` statement.

```
if(expression1)
{
    This block gets executed if expression1 is true.
}
elseif(expression2)
{
    This block gets executed if expression1
    is false and expression 2 is true.
}
else
{
    This block gets executed if both expression1
    and expression2 are false.
}
```

**Figure 3.1**   The form of an `if` statement.

The `if` statement executes a statement if the expression inside the parentheses evaluates to true; otherwise, the code is skipped. It may be a single statement followed by a semicolon. Usually it's a compound statement surrounded by curly braces. An `else` statement may appear immediately after the statement and have a statement of its own. It too may be either single or compound. It is executed only when the previous expression is false. In between an `if` statement and an `else` statement you may put as many `elseif` statements as you like. Each `elseif` expression is evaluated in turn, and control skips past those that are false. If an `elseif` statement evaluates to true, then the rest of the code in the greater `if` statement is skipped. That is, PHP accepts only one match. Listing 3.1 demonstrates an `if-elseif-else` statement.

| Listing 3.1 | An `if-elseif-else` statement |
| --- | --- |

```php
<?php
    $name = "Leon";
    if($name == "")
    {
        print("You have no name.");
    }
    elseif(($name == "leon") OR ($name == "Leon"))
    {
        print("Hello, Leon!");
    }
    else
    {
        print("Your name is '$name'.");
    }
?>
```

Of course, you are not obligated to have an `elseif` or an `else`. Sometimes you might want to build a very simple `if` statement, as in Listing 3.2.

| Listing 3.2 | A simple `if` statement |
| --- | --- |

```php
<?php
    if(date("D") == "Mon")
    {
        print("Remember to put the trash out.");
    }
?>
```

You can use if to build a series of checks that covers all possible cases. Just start by checking for the first condition with an if; then check for each following condition with an elseif. If you put an else at the end, you will have accounted for all possible cases. Listing 3.3 uses this method to print the day of the week in German. The script gets today's name and then compares it to the days Monday through Saturday. If none match, it is assumed to be Sunday.

**Listing 3.3**   *Covering all cases with* `if-elseif-else`

```php
<?php
    /*
    ** Get today's weekday name
    */
    $englishDay = date("l");

    /*
    ** Find the today's German name
    */
    if($englishDay == "Monday")
    {
        $deutschDay = "Montag";
    }
    elseif($englishDay == "Tuesday")
    {
        $deutschDay = "Dienstag";
    }
    elseif($englishDay == "Wednesday")
    {
        $deutschDay = "Mittwoch";
    }
    elseif($englishDay == "Thursday")
    {
        $deutschDay = "Donnerstag";
    }
    elseif($englishDay == "Friday")
    {
        $deutschDay = "Freitag";
    }
    elseif($englishDay == "Saturday")
    {
        $deutschDay = "Samstag";
    }
    else
    {
        // It must be Sunday
        $deutschDay = "Sonntag";
    }
```

| Listing 3.3 | *Covering all cases with `if-elseif-else` (cont.)* |
|---|---|

```
    /*
    ** Print today's English and German names
    */
    print("<h2>German Lesson: Day of the Week</h2>\n" .
        "<p>\n" .
        "In English: <b>$englishDay</b>.<br>\n" .
        "In German:  <b>$deutschDay</b>\n" .
        "</p>\n");
?>
```

# 3.2 The ? Operator

PHP offers an abbreviated version of the `if` statement, which borrows syntax from C. It uses the question mark as a ternary operator. Figure 3.2 outlines the format.

```
conditional expression ? true expression : false expression;
```

**Figure 3.2**   The ? operator.

The conditional expression is evaluated to be either true or false. If true, the expression between the question mark and the colon is executed. Otherwise, the expression after the colon is executed. The following code fragment

```
($clientQueue > 0) ? serveClients() : cleanUp();
```

does the same thing as

```
if($clientQueue > 0)
        serveClients();
else
        cleanUp();
```

The similarity is deceiving. Although the abbreviated form seems to be equivalent to using `if-else`, at a deeper level it is not. As I said, ? is an operator, not a statement. This means that the expression as a whole is evaluated. The value of the matched expression takes the place of the ? expression. In other words, something like

```
print(true ? "it's true" : "it's false");
```

is a valid statement. Since the conditional expression is true, the line is equivalent to

```
print("it's true");
```

which is something you can't do with an `if` statement.

The `?` operator can be confusing to read and is never necessary. It wouldn't be bad if you never used it. However, it allows you to write very compact code.

## 3.3  The `switch` Statement

An alternative to `if-elseif-else` structures is the `switch` statement, which works on the assumption that you compare a single expression to a set of possible values. Figure 3.3 demonstrates the structure of a `switch` statement.

```
switch(root-expression)
{
    case case-expression:
    default:
}
```

**Figure 3.3**   The `switch` statement.

The root expression inside a switch statement is evaluated and then compared to each expression following a `case` statement. At the end of the list of cases you can put a `default` statement that works exactly like an `else` statement; it matches if no other case matches.

Notice that cases don't have curly braces after them. This reveals an important difference between `if` and `switch`. When an `if` block matches and is executed, control skips to the end of the entire `if` statement. In Listing 3.3, if today is Tuesday, `deutsch_Day` is set to `Deinstag`, and control jumps down to after the curly brace closing the `else` block.

A `case` statement serves as a starting point for execution. The root expression is compared to each case expression until one matches. Each line of code after that is executed. If another `case` statement is reached, it is ignored. Sometimes this is useful, but most often a `break` statement is used to escape from the `switch` statement.

Take a look at Listing 3.4. I've recoded Listing 3.3 using a `switch` statement. The best argument for using `switch` is that it can be much easier to understand. Since PHP allows you to compare strings, the `switch` statement is much more useful than in other languages. If you have experience with BASIC, you might wonder if PHP's `switch` statement allows cases to contain ranges. It doesn't. It's probably best to code this situation with an `if-elseif-else` statement.

---

| **Listing 3.4** | *Covering all cases with* `switch` |
|---|---|

```php
<?php
    /*
    ** Get today's weekday name
    */
    $englishDay = date("l");

    /*
    ** Find the today's German name
    */
    switch($englishDay)
    {
        case "Monday":
            $deutschDay = "Montag";
            break;
        case "Tuesday":
            $deutschDay = "Dienstag";
            break;
        case "Wednesday":
            $deutschDay = "Mittwoch";
            break;
        case "Thursday":
            $deutschDay = "Donnerstag";
            break;
        case "Friday":
            $deutschDay = "Freitag";
            break;
        case "Saturday":
            $deutschDay = "Samstag";
            break;
        default:
            // It must be Sunday
            $deutschDay = "Sonntag";
    }

    /*
    ** Print today's English and German names
    */
    print("<h2>German Lesson: Day of the Week</h2>\n" .
        "<p>\n" .
        "In English: <b>$englishDay</b>.<br>\n" .
        "In German:  <b>$deutschDay</b>\n" .
        "</p>\n");
?>
```

# 3.4 Loops

Loops allow you to repeat lines of code based on some condition. You might want to read lines from a file until the end is reached. You might want to print a section of HTML code exactly ten times. You may even wish to attempt to connect to a database three times before giving up. You may want to read data from a file until there's no more data to read. You can do all of these things with loops.

Each execution of the code inside a loop is an iteration. Loops iterate on the code until a stop condition is met. PHP supports four types of loops that vary from each other in what they iterate on, the actions taken before the loop begins, and whether the stop condition is checked at the beginning of each iteration or at its end.

## The `while` Statement

The simplest of loops is the `while` statement. When first reached, the expression is evaluated. If false, the code block is skipped. If true, the block is executed and then control returns to the top where, again, the expression is evaluated. Figure 3.4 shows the structure of a `while` statement.

```
while(expression)
{
    Zero or more statements
}
```

**Figure 3.4** The `while` statement.

A `while` loop is useful when you aren't sure exactly how many times you will need to iterate through the code—for example, when reading lines from a file or fetching rows from a database query. For the sake of a simple demonstration, let's examine some code that prints the days of the week between now and Friday.

The `while` loop in Listing 3.5 tests that the date stored in `currentDate` is not a Friday. If it is, then the loop will be finished, and execution will continue after the closing curly brace. But if the current date is not a Friday, then a list item with the name of the day is printed, and `currentDate` is advanced 24 hours. At that point, the end of the code block is reached, so control jumps back to the beginning of the loop.

Again the current date is tested for being a Friday. Eventually, `currentDate` will be a Friday and the loop will end. But what if I had done something silly, such as comparing the current date to `"Workday"`? There is no weekday with that name, so the expression will always be true. That is, `date("l", $currentDate) != "Workday"` must always be true. The result is a loop that goes on forever. I might as well write it as `while(TRUE)` and make it very clear.

**Listing 3.5**    *Using while to print day names*

```php
<?php
    //get the current date in number of seconds
    $currentDate = time();

    //print some text explaining the output
    print("Days left before Friday:\n");
    print("<ol>\n");

    while(date("l", $currentDate) != "Friday")
    {
        //print day name
        print("<li>" . date("l", $currentDate) . "</li>\n");

        //add 24 hours to currentDate
        $currentDate += (60 * 60 * 24);
    }

    print("</ol>\n");
?>
```

When a loop continues with no end, it's called an infinite loop. If you find your page loading forever and ever, you may have accidentally written an infinite loop. Fortunately, PHP stops all scripts by default after they use 30 seconds of CPU time. You can change the timeout with the set_time_limit function. At times, you may intentionally create an infinite loop but stop execution somewhere in the middle of the code block. This is accomplished with the break statement.

# The break Statement

When a break statement is encountered, execution jumps outside the innermost loop or switch statement. You've seen that this is essential to the usefulness of switch statements. It also has some application for loops. There are cases when you need to leave a loop block somewhere in the middle. Listing 3.6 shows this in action.

**Listing 3.6**    *Leaving a loop using break*

```php
<?php
    while(TRUE)
    {
        print("This line is printed.");
        break;
        print("This line will never be printed.");
    }
?>
```

The break statement may also break out of multiple levels if you place an integer after it. Listing 3.7 demonstrates breaking out two levels.

**Listing 3.7** *Breaking multiple levels*

```php
<?php
    while(TRUE)
    {
        while(TRUE)
        {
            print("This line is printed.");
            break 2;
        }
        print("This line will never be printed.");
    }
?>
```

# The `continue` Statement

The continue statement is similar to the break statement except that instead of stopping the loop entirely, only the current execution of the loop is stopped. Control is returned to the closing curly brace and the loop continues. Inside for loops, described below, increments will occur just as if control had reached the end of the loop otherwise.

As you might imagine, this statement is used to skip parts of a loop when a condition is met. Listing 3.8 demonstrates this idea. Random numbers are generated inside a loop until ten numbers, each greater than the previous, are produced. Most of the time the body of the loop is skipped due to the if statement that triggers a continue statement.

As with the break statement, you may follow the continue statement with an integer. Control passes up the levels to the top of the specified loop.

**Listing 3.8** *The `continue` statement*

```php
<?php
    /*
    ** get ten random numbers,
    ** each greater than the next
    */
    //init variables
    $count = 0;
    $max = 0;
```

---

| Listing 3.8 | *The* `continue` *statement (cont.)* |
| --- | --- |

```php
    //get ten random numbers
    while($count < 10)
    {
        $value = rand(1,100);

        //try again if $value is too small
        if($value < $max)
        {
            continue;
        }

        $count++;
        $max = $value;

        print("$value <br>\n");
    }
?>
```

---

## The `do...while` Statement

You can delay the decision to continue executing a loop until the end by using a
do...while statement. Listing 3.9 retools Listing 3.5. You won't notice a difference
unless you run the script on a Friday. On Fridays the original will print nothing in its
list of days. The new version will put Friday in the list because the body of the loop is
executed before currentDate is tested. By switching to a do...while loop, the loop
now lists the days until next Friday.

---

| Listing 3.9 | *Using do...while to print day names* |
| --- | --- |

```php
<?php
    /*
    ** get the current date in number of seconds
    */
    $currentDate = time();

    //print some text explaining the output
    print("Days left before next Friday:\n");
    print("<ol>\n");
```

**Listing 3.9** *Using do...while to print day names (cont.)*

```
do
{
    /*
    ** print day name
    */
    print("<li>" . date("l", $currentDate) . "</li>\n");

    /*
    ** add 24 hours to currentDate
    */
    $currentDate += (60 * 60 * 24);
}
while(date("l", $currentDate) != "Friday");

print("</ol>\n");
?>
```

## The `for` Statement

Strictly speaking, the `for` loop is unnecessary. Any `for` loop can be implemented as easily as a `while` loop. What `for` offers is not new functionality, but a better structure for building the most common loops. Many loops involve incrementing a counter variable every time through the loop, iterating until some maximum is reached.

Imagine that you wanted to step through the numbers 1 through 10. Using `while`, you would first set a variable to be 1. Then you would make a `while` loop that tests if your counter is less than or equal to 10. Inside the code block you would increment your counter, making sure you do this as the last statement in the block.

The problem is that it is very easy to forget to put the increment in. The result is an infinite loop. The `for` loop puts all this functionality in one place. Inside the `for` statement you give it three things: an initialization expression, a boolean continue expression, and an increment expression. Figure 3.5 defines a `for` loop.

```
for(initialization; continue; increment)
{
    Zero or more statements
}
```

**Figure 3.5** The `for` statement.

When first encountered, the initialization expression is executed. This traditionally takes the form of assigning a variable to be 0 or 1. Then, as with a `while` statement, the boolean expression is evaluated. If FALSE, control jumps to just after the code block. Otherwise, the code block is executed. Before the expression is evaluated again, the increment expression is executed. This puts all the information needed for running the loop in one place and forces you to think about all the steps. Listing 3.10 is a very simple `for` loop but is typical in form.

| Listing 3.10 | *A typical `for` loop* |
|---|---|

```php
<?php
    for($counter = 1; $counter <= 10; $counter++)
    {
        print("counter is $counter<br>\n");
    }
?>
```

Most `for` loops look like Listing 3.10. They use a counter that increments by one each time through the loop. However, the `for` statement is not particular about what you put in the three slots. You can use more complex expressions if you wish. The initialization slot allows a comma-separated list of assignments. This can be used to assign values to two or more variables. You may also leave a slot blank. Listing 3.11 converts the code in Listing 3.5 into a `for` loop. I've added line breaks to the `for` statement to keep the code from wrapping. It also makes it easier to see the three parts. Although the `for` statement is longer and looks more complicated, it really is no different from the simple example in Listing 3.9. A variable, in this case currentDate, is set to some initial value. That value is used to test for an end condition, and the value is incremented by the number of seconds in a day instead of by just one.

| Listing 3.11 | *Using `for` to print day names* |
|---|---|

```php
<?php
    /*
    ** print some text explaining the output
    */
    print("Days left before Friday:\n");
    print("<ol>\n");
```

**Listing 3.11** *Using `for` to print day names (cont.)*

```
for($currentDate = date("U");
    date("l", $currentDate) != "Friday";
    $currentDate += (60 * 60 * 24))
{
    /*
    ** print day name
    */
    print("<li>" . date("l", $currentDate) . "</li>\n");
}

print("</ol>\n");
?>
```

# The `foreach` Statement

PHP's `foreach` statement provides a formalized method for iterating over arrays, discussed in Chapter 5. An array is a collection of values referenced by keys. The `foreach` statement retrieves values from an array, one at a time. Like other looping structures, the `foreach` statement may have a simple or compound statement that's executed each time through the loop. Figure 3.6 shows the structure of a `foreach` statement.

```
foreach(array as key=>value)
{
    Zero or more statements

}
```

**Figure 3.6** The `foreach` statement.

The `foreach` statement expects an array, the keyword `as`, and a definition of the variables to receive each element. If a single value follows `as`, such as `foreach($array as $value)`, then with each turn of the loop, the variable named `value` will be set with the value of the next array element. You may capture the index of the array element if you form the `foreach` statement like `foreach($array as $key=>$value)`. Keep this statement in mind, and we will revisit it in Chapter 5.

# 3.5 `exit`, `die`, and `return`

Like `break`, the `exit` statement offers a way to escape from execution, but the `exit` statement stops all execution. Not even text outside of PHP tags is sent to the browser. This is useful when an error occurs and it would be more harmful to continue executing code than to just abort. This is often the case when preparing database queries. If the SQL statement cannot be parsed, it makes no sense to try to execute it.

The `die` statement is similar to `exit` except that it may be followed by an expression that will be sent to the browser just before aborting the script. Using the fact that subexpressions are evaluated according to precedence and associativity, and given the short-circuit nature of the logical operators, the idiom in Listing 3.12 is allowed. Notice the parentheses around the string to be printed when the `open` fails. They are required.

| Listing 3.12 | *Idiom for using the `die` statement* |
| --- | --- |

```
$fp = fopen("somefile.txt", "r") OR die("Unable to open file");
```

The precedence of the `OR` operator in Listing 3.12 has particular importance. That is, it has lower precedence than the assignment operator does. This allows PHP to assign the return value of `fopen` to `fp` and then evaluate the `OR` expression. The `||` operator, functionally identical to `OR`, has higher precedence than the assignment operator does. Using it in this situation would cause PHP to resolve the `||` expression first, ending the script.

Chapter 4 discusses the traditional use of the `return` statement, but there is an unusual use of `return` offered by PHP when a script uses the `include` statement, described in Chapter 7. If called outside of a function, the `return` statement stops execution of the current script and returns control to the script that made a call to `include`. That is, when a script uses the `include` function, the included script may return prematurely. If you use `return` in a script that was not invoked by `include`, the script will simply terminate as if `exit` were used.

I admit this is a strange concept, and it probably deserves to have its own name instead of sharing one with the statement for returning `from` functions. On the other hand, in certain special cases, it allows for tidy code.

# 3.6 Exceptions

When errors occur, PHP sends text to the browser. Some errors halt execution. For the error conditions that don't halt execution, you may trap them with a function you register with `set_error_handler`. See Chapter 15 for a discussion of this function. You can even generate your own errors with `trigger_error`, discussed in Chapter 9.

Alternatively, you may use exceptions. Figure 3.7 shows the form. Exceptions are object-oriented error conditions. They occur within the context of a `try` statement. To initiate an exception, you make a `throw` statement. Control then passes to a `catch` block, which receives a copy of the thrown exception. Add a `catch` block for each type of exception you wish to catch, or simply use PHP's built-in `Exception` class. The built-in `Exception` class includes two methods: `getFile`, which returns the path to file that generated the exception, and `getLine`, which returns the line number in that file.

If you've worked with an object-oriented programming language, such as Java, the concept of exceptions is familiar. If you prefer a procedural style of programming, they may not appeal to you. Listing 3.13 demonstrates the use of exceptions. Chapter 6 discusses objects in depth. If you don't feel comfortable with objects yet, make a note to return to this chapter after you've read Chapter 6.

```
try
{
    Zero or more statements
    throw Exception
    Zero or more statements
}
catch(class $variable)
{
    Zero or more statements
{
```

**Figure 3.7** The `try` statement.

---

**Listing 3.13** *Using a `try` statement*

```php
<?php
    //derive math exception from base class
    class mathException extends Exception
    {
        public $type;
```

| Listing 3.13 | *Using a try statement (cont.)* |
| --- | --- |

```php
        public function __construct($type)
        {
            //get filename and line number
            parent::Exception();
            $this->type = $type;
        }
    }

    //try a division
    $numerator = 1;
    $denominator = 0;
    try
    {
        //throw exception on divide by zero
        if($denominator == 0)
        {
            throw new mathException("Division by zero");
        }

        print($numerator/$denominator);
    }
    catch(mathException $e)
    {
        //we caught a math exception
        print("Caught Math Exception ($e->type) in " .
            "$e->file on line $e->line<br>\n");
    }
    catch(Exception $e)
    {
        //we caught some other type of exception
        print("Caught Exception in " .
            $e->file() . " on line " .
            $e->line() . "<br>\n");
    }
?>
```

# 3.7  Declare

The declare statement marks a block of code for execution under a set of conditions. Figure 3.8 shows the form of a declare statement.

```
declare(directive)
{
    Zero or more statements
}
```

**Figure 3.8**   The declare statement.

At the time of writing, PHP accepts only one directive: ticks. The ticks directive paired with the register_tick_function cause PHP to pause execution of a script periodically to execute a function. Each tick represents a lowest-level event determined by the parser. This functionality is not meant for general programming, and PHP does not guarantee any matching between the number of ticks and the number of statements inside the declare block. Listing 3.14 shows an example of a registered tick function.

**Listing 3.14**   *Using a declare Statement*

```php
<?php
    //define a tick function
    function logTick($part)
        {
        static $n = 0;
        print("Tick $n $part " . microtime() . "<br>\n");
        $n++;
    }

    print("Start " . microtime() . "<br>\n");

    //register the tick function
    register_tick_function("logTick", "doing square roots");

    //run code inside declare block
    declare(ticks=1)
    {
        1;1;1;
    }

    //unregister the tick function
    unregister_tick_function("logTick");

    print("Done " . microtime() . "<br>\n");
?>
```

It's possible the `declare` statement may receive additional directives in the future. As the `ticks` directive has little use beyond curiosity, you may feel comfortable ignoring declare statements.

# FUNCTIONS

**Topics in This Chapter**

- Declaring a Function
- The `return` Statement
- Scope
- Static Variables
- Arguments
- Recursion
- Dynamic Function Calls

# Chapter 4

You probably have noticed the use of several functions in the preceding chapters. `Date` and `print` are built-in functions that are always available for you. PHP also allows you to declare your own functions.

Functions expand the idea of repeating a block of code. They allow you to execute a block of code arbitrarily throughout your script. You declare a block of code as a function, and then you are able to call the function anywhere. When calling a function, you pass any number of arguments, and the function returns a value.

## 4.1 Declaring a Function

When you declare a function, you start with the `function` statement. Next comes a name for your function. Inside the parentheses is a list of arguments separated by commas. You may choose to have no arguments. Figure 4.1 shows you the form of a function declaration.

In other languages, including older versions of PHP, you must declare a function above any call to it. This is not true of PHP 4. You may put a function declaration after calls made to it. When you call a function, you write its name followed by parentheses, even if there are no arguments to pass.

```
function function_name(arguments)
{
    code block
}
```

**Figure 4.1**    Declaring a function.

Functions allow you to put together a block of code that you will repeat several times throughout your script. Your motivation may be to avoid typing identical code in two or more places, or it could be to make your code easier to understand. Consider Listing 4.1. It declares a function called `printBold` that prints any text with bold tags around it.

---

| Listing 4.1 | *A simple function* |
|---|---|

```php
<?php
    function printBold($text)
    {
        print("<b>$text</b>");
    }

    print("This Line is not Bold<br>\n");
    printBold("This Line is Bold");
    print("<br>\n");
    print("This Line is not Bold<br>\n");
?>
```

---

# 4.2 The `return` Statement

At some point a function will be finished, ready to return control to its caller. This happens, for example, when execution reaches the end of the function's block of code. Execution then picks up directly after the point where the function was called. Another way to stop execution of the function is to use the `return` statement.

You may have multiple `return` statements in your function, though you have to consider how this reduces the readability of your code. Multiple `return` statements can be a barrier to understanding the flow of execution. Ideally, functions should have one way in and one way out. In practice there are cases when multiple `return` statements are acceptable.

If you follow `return` with an expression, the value of the expression will be passed back. Listing 4.2 demonstrates this idea by taking a string and returning it wrapped in bold tags.

**Listing 4.2**    *A simple function using `return`*

```php
<?php
    function makeBold($text)
    {
        $text = "<b>$text</b>";
        return($text);
    }

    print("This Line is not Bold<br>\n");
    print(makeBold("This Line is Bold") . "<br>\n");
    print("This Line is not Bold<br>\n");
?>
```

For most data types, return values are passed by value. Objects, discussed in Chapter 6, pass by reference. You can force a function to return a reference by placing a `&` immediately before the name. In PHP 4, objects were passed by value, which hindered some techniques involving functions returning objects. Listing 4.3 demonstrates a function returning a reference to an array. Each call to the function creates a new array, fills it with 10 numbers, and returns its reference.

The `getRandArray` function creates a new array with each call. Ordinarily, PHP discards variables inside functions when the function returns control to the calling process. In this case, the function returns a reference to the array. The function scope dissolves, and PHP decrements the count of references to the array. However, `myNewArray` now references the array and the array persists.

**Listing 4.3**    *Function returning a reference*

```php
<?php
    function &getRandArray()
    {
        $a = array();

        for($i=0; $i<10; $i++)
        {
            $a[] = rand(1,100);
        }

        return($a);
    }

    $myNewArray = &getRandArray();
?>
```

# 4.3 Scope

In order to avoid clashes between variables in different functions, PHP includes the notion of scope. Each line of code belongs to a certain scope. Code that appears inside a function is considered to belong to the function's scope. Code that appears outside of any function is considered to belong to the global scope. The scope is the property that determines which memory table is used for storing variables and in turn which variables are accessible.

Variables declared inside a function scope are local variables. Local variables are the private property of a function and may never be seen or manipulated outside the scope of the function. Variables used outside the scope of any function are global variables. Unlike some other languages, global variables in PHP are not immediately available outside the global scope.

The code in Listing 4.4 assigns local variable name to Zeev inside assignName, but this does not change the contents of name in the global scope. The local name variable does not persist in any way once the function returns. There are two ways a function may access variables in the global scope: the global statement and the GLOBALS array.

| Listing 4.4 | *Experimenting with scope* |
|---|---|

```php
<?php
    function assignName()
    {
        $name = "Zeev";
    }

    $name = "Leon";

    assignName();

    //prints Leon
    print($name);
?>
```

The global statement brings a variable into a function's namespace. Thereafter the variable may be used as if it were outside the function. Any changes to the variable will persist after execution of the function ceases. In the same way, it is possible to refer to global variables through the array GLOBALS. The array is indexed by variable names, so if you create a variable named userName, you can manipulate it inside a function by writing $GLOBALS["userName"].

Listing 4.5 sets up a function, printCity, that prints out the name of a city. It will be used to show the contents of the variables named capital. Variables is plural because there are actually three variables in the script named capital. One is global and the other two are local to the California and Utah functions.

| Listing 4.5 | *Using the global scope* |
| --- | --- |

```
<?
    $capital = "Washington DC";

    function Nation()
    {
        global $capital;
        printCity($capital);
    }

    function printCity($NameOfCity)
    {
        print("The city is $NameOfCity.<br>\n");
    }

    function California()
    {
        $capital = "Sacramento";
        printCity($capital);
    }

    function Utah()
    {
        $capital = "Salt Lake City";
        printCity($capital);
    }


    Nation();
    California();
    Utah();
    Nation();
?>
```

When you run this script, you will find that the cities are printed in the order Washington DC, Sacramento, Salt Lake City, and Washington DC. Notice that even though we have given capital a new value inside California and Utah, it is not the same variable we set to Washington DC. The variables inside California and Utah are local, and the one containing Washington DC is global.

# 4.4 Static Variables

It is important to remember that when you create a variable inside a function, it exists only while that function is executing. Once execution finishes and control is passed back to the calling process, all the variable space for that function is cleaned up. Sometimes this is not desirable; sometimes you want the function to remember the values of the variables between calls. You could implement this by using global variables, but a more elegant solution is to use the `static` statement.

At the beginning of a function, before any other commands, you may declare a static variable. The variable will then retain any value it holds even after leaving the function. You might wonder why you would ever need to do this. Suppose you'd like to build a table where the rows alternate in background color. Listing 4.6 does just this.

| Listing 4.6 | *Demonstration of static variables* |
|---|---|

```
<?
    function useColor()
    {
        //remember the last color we used
        static $ColorValue = "#00FF00";

        //choose the next color
        if($ColorValue == "#00FF00")
        {
            $ColorValue = "#CCFFCC";
        }
        else
        {
            $ColorValue = "#00FF00";
        }

        return($ColorValue);
    }

    print("<table width=\"300\">\n");
    for($count=0; $count < 10; $count++)
    {
        //get color for this row
        $RowColor = useColor();

        /*
        ** print out HTML for row
        ** set background color
        */
```

| Listing 4.6 | *Demonstration of static variables (cont.)* |

```
        print("<tr>" .
            "<td style=\"background: $RowColor\">" .
            "Row number $count" .
            "</td>" .
            "</tr>\n");
    }
    print("</table>\n");
?>
```

Chapter 6 discusses static class members, which are different from static variables in functions.

# 4.5 Arguments

When declaring a function, you may declare arguments inside the parentheses, each separated by a comma. The arguments must be preceded by a dollar sign. They become variables inside the function. When the function is called, it expects values to be passed that will fill the arguments in the order declared.

Arguments, by default, copy the passed value into the local variable, otherwise known as pass-by-value. If the function argument is preceded by the & operator, the variable instead becomes an alias for the passed variable. This is commonly referred to as a variable reference. Changes made to referenced variables change the original. Chapter 2 contains a discussion of variable references.

To demonstrate this idea, imagine we wanted a function that stripped commas from numbers. That way, if we got something like 10,000 from an input field, we would know it was ten thousand, not ten. We could build the function by passing a string and returning it with the commas removed. But in this case we want to just pass the variable and have it be changed. Listing 4.7 demonstrates this functionality.

It is also possible to make an argument optional. Many built-in functions provide this functionality. The date function is one you should be familiar with by now. You can pass one or two arguments to date. The first argument is the format of the return value. The second argument is the timestamp, a date expressed in seconds since January 1, 1970. If the second argument is omitted, the current time is used.

| Listing 4.7 | *Passing arguments by reference* |
|---|---|

```php
<?php
    function stripCommas(&$text)
    {
        $text = str_replace(",", "", $text);
    }

    $myNumber = "10,000";

    stripCommas($myNumber);
    print($myNumber);
?>
```

You do this in your own functions by providing a default value using the = operator immediately after the argument. The right side of = is a literal value that the variable will be assigned. See Listing 4.8. Since arguments are matched up left to right, you must provide a default value for every argument after the first with a default value.

| Listing 4.8 | *Arguments with default values* |
|---|---|

```php
<?php
    function printColor($text,
        $color="black", &$count=NULL)
    {
        //print the text with style
        print("<span style=\"color: $color\">" .
            "$text</span>");

        //if given a count, increment it
        if(isset($count))
        {
            $count++;
        }
    }

    //call with one argument
    printColor("This is black text");
    print("<br>\n");

    //override default color
    printColor("This is blue text", "blue");
    print("<br>\n");
```

---

**Listing 4.8** *Arguments with default values (cont.)*

```
    //pass in count reference
    $c = 0;
    printColor("This is red text", "red", $c);
    print("<br>\n");
    printColor("This is green text", "green", $c);
    print("<br>\n");
    print("Count: $c<br>");
?>
```

---

You can give a default value to an optional argument. Use the same syntax for any other optional argument. If you call the function without this argument, changing its value will have no effect outside the function. However, if you set the default to NULL, you can test if it appears in the call and use it only if it does appear. You may set any argument to be unset by default by making it equal to NULL.

Other than named arguments, you may also access arguments by their position using three functions: `func_get_arg`, `func_get_args`, `func_num_args`. These functions are described in Chapter 8. You may either fetch one argument at a time using `func_get_arg` or fetch them all as an array using `func_get_args`. To find out how many arguments were passed, use `func_num_args`. There is an implication lurking here. Calling a function with a number of arguments different from the prototype is not an error unless you write your function that way.

You might wonder why you'd ever want to pull arguments out using the functions mentioned above instead of naming them in the declaration. It's possible that you do not know how many arguments you will be given. Consider a function that creates a list, given any number of items. You could first place those items in an array, then pass the array to the function, which in turn would pull the items out of the array. Alternatively, you could write a function that accepted a variable number of arguments, as in Listing 4.9.

---

**Listing 4.9** *Function with variable number of arguments*

```
<?php
    function makeList()
    {
        print("<ol>\n");
```

| Listing 4.9 | *Function with variable number of arguments (cont.)* |

```
    for($i=0; $i < func_num_args(); $i++)
    {
        print("<li>" . func_get_arg($i) . "</li>\n");
    }

    print("</ol>\n");
}

makeList("Linux", "Apache", "MySQL", "PHP");
?>
```

# 4.6 Recursion

Your functions may make calls to other functions, and they may also make calls to themselves. The process of a function calling itself is recursion. This circular definition usually leads to elegant algorithms. The problem is broken down into a small task that's repeated many times.

Recursive definitions are common in mathematics. Consider this definition of an integer: the sum or difference between one and any other integer, with one being an integer. Is three an integer? Yes, because one plus one must be an integer, which is two, and the sum of one and two must also be an integer.

Recursion is a difficult concept to understand. Some people use it because you can express an algorithm in fewer lines. Equivalent iterative algorithms usually must maintain this state on their own rather than relying on PHP to keep track of variables in the function for each call. Consider that 10 calls to a function requires PHP to keep 10 copies of all the variables the function uses. In many cases it's more efficient to manage the values yourself.

Take a look at Listing 4.10. The function checkInteger takes a number as input. We know that the difference between an integer and one is an integer. So, if the function gets a number bigger than one, it simply checks the number minus one. If we start out with a number less than zero, we multiply it by negative one and check it. Eventually, unless we are passed zero, we will reach one or a number between zero and one, which is an integer.

**Listing 4.10** *Using recursion*

```php
<?php
    function checkInteger($Number)
    {
        if($Number > 1)
        {
            // integer minus one is still an integer
            return(checkInteger($Number-1));
        }
        elseif($Number < 0)
        {
            //numbers are symmetrical, so
            //check positive version
            return(checkInteger((-1)*$Number-1));
        }
        else
        {
            if(($Number > 0) AND ($Number < 1))
            {
                return("no");
            }
            else
            {
                //zero and one are
                //integers by definition
                return("yes");
            }
        }
    }

    print("Is 0 an integer? " .
        checkInteger(0) . "<br>\n");
    print("Is 7 an integer? " .
        checkInteger(7) . "<br>\n");
    print("And 3.5? " . checkInteger(3.5) . "<br>\n");
    print("What about -5? " . checkInteger(-5) . "<br>\n");
    print("And -9.2? " . checkInteger(-9.2) . "<br>\n");
?>
```

# 4.7 Dynamic Function Calls

You might find yourself in the position of not knowing which function should be called when you are writing a script. You want to decide based on data you have during execution. One way to accomplish this is to set a variable with the name of a function and then use the variable as if it were a function.

If you follow a variable with parentheses, the value of the variable will be treated as the name of a function. Listing 4.11 demonstrates this. Keep in mind that you can't refer to built-in functions in this way. Setting myFunction to be print will cause an error.

---

**Listing 4.11** *Calling a function dynamically*

```php
<?php
    function write($text)
    {
        print($text);
    }

    function writeBold($text)
    {
        print("<b>$text</b>");
    }

    $myFunction = "write";
    $myFunction("Hello!");
    print("<br>\n");

    $myFunction = "writeBold";
    $myFunction("Goodbye!");
    print("<br>\n");
?>
```

---

If you do not know exactly how a function should operate until runtime, you may create an anonymous function with the create_function function. See Chapter 11 for a description of this function.

# Arrays

**Topics in This Chapter**

- Single-Dimensional Arrays
- Indexing Arrays
- Initializing Arrays
- Multidimensional Arrays
- Casting Arrays
- The + Operator
- Referencing Arrays Inside Strings

# Chapter 5

Arrays collect values into lists. You refer to an element in an array using an index, which is often an integer but can also be a string. The value of the element can be text, a number, or even another array. When you build arrays of arrays, you get multi-dimensional arrays. Arrays are used extensively by PHP's built-in functions, and coding would be nearly impossible without them. There are many functions designed simply for manipulating arrays. They are discussed in detail in Chapter 11.

## 5.1 Single-Dimensional Arrays

To refer to an element of an array, you use square brackets. Inside the brackets you put the index of the element, as in Listing 5.1. This construct may be treated exactly like a variable. You may assign a value or pass its value to a function. You do not have to declare anything about the array before you use it. Like variables, any element of an array will be created on the fly. If you refer to an array element that does not exist, it will evaluate to be zero or an empty string depending on the context.

| Listing 5.1 | *Referencing array elements* |
| --- | --- |

```php
<?php
    $Cities[0] = "San Francisco";
    $Cities[1] = "Los Angeles";
    $Cities[2] = "New York";
    $Cities[3] = "Martinez";

    print("I live in $Cities[3].<br>\n");
?>
```

Single-dimensional arrays are lists of values under a common name. But you might wonder, Why bother? You could just as easily create variables like $Cities1, $Cities2, $Cities3 and not worry about square brackets. One reason is that it's easy to loop through all values of an array. If you know that all the elements of an array have been added using consecutive numbers, you can use a for loop to get each element. PHP makes it easy to create arrays that work this way; if you leave out an index when assigning an array element, PHP will start at zero and use consecutive integers thereafter. If you run the code in Listing 5.2, you will discover that the four cities have indexes of 0, 1, 2, and 3.

| Listing 5.2 | *Adding to an array* |
| --- | --- |

```php
<?php
    $Cities[] = "San Francisco";
    $Cities[] = "Los Angeles";
    $Cities[] = "New York";
    $Cities[] = "Martinez";

    // count number of elements
    $indexLimit = count($Cities);

    // print out every element
    for($index=0; $index < $indexLimit; $index++)
    {
        print("City $index is $Cities[$index]. <br>\n");
    }
?>
```

# 5.2 Indexing Arrays

So far we've only seen arrays indexed by integers, but it is also permissible to use strings. Sometimes these are called associative arrays, or hashes. They are helpful in situations where you are collecting different types of information into one array. You could build into your code a system where element zero is a name, element one is a location, and element two is an occupation. Listing 5.3 is a more elegant way to accomplish this.

| Listing 5.3 | *Indexing arrays with strings* |
|---|---|

```php
<?php
    // fill in some information
    $UserInfo["Name"] = "Leon Atkinson";
    $UserInfo["Location"] = "Martinez, California";
    $UserInfo["Occupation"] = "Programmer";

    //loop over values
    foreach($UserInfo as $key=>$value)
    {
        print("$key is $value.<br>\n");
    }
?>
```

Since we aren't indexing the array with integers, we can't just pull out each value starting at zero. If you've turned ahead briefly to skim the array functions in Chapter 11, you may have noticed functions like reset, next, and current. These functions offer one way to step through an array, and they are the best way if you need to do more than simply step through the array in order. You can also use the each function. However, PHP 4 added a new statement called foreach specifically for stepping through an array. The foreach statement is discussed in Chapter 3. It is like a for loop but designed to pull elements from an array. You may wish to turn back and review it.

# 5.3 Initializing Arrays

In the situations where you want to fill an array with several values before you use it, it can become cumbersome to write an assignment for each element. PHP offers the array function to help in this matter. It takes a list of values and returns an array. Listing 5.4 uses array to build an array of the months of the year.

Each value is just as it would be if it were on the right side of the assignment operator. Commas separate the values. By default, as with using empty brackets, elements are numbered starting with zero. You can override this by using the => operator. In Listing 5.4 I have set January to have the index 1. Each subsequent element is indexed by the next integer.

---

**Listing 5.4**   *Initializing an array*

```php
<?php
    $monthName = array(1=>"January", "February", "March",
        "April", "May", "June", "July", "August",
        "September", "October", "November", "December");

    print("Month 5 is $monthName[5]<br>\n");
?>
```

---

You aren't limited to setting the index for the first element, of course. You can assign the index for every element. And you aren't limited to assigning integers as indexes. Listing 5.5 builds an array for translating various ways to write a month into a single form.

---

**Listing 5.5**   *Using an array to translate values*

```php
<?php
    $monthName = array(
        1=>"January", "February", "March",
        "April", "May", "June",
        "July", "August", "September",
        "October", "November", "December",

        "Jan"=>"January", "Feb"=>"February",
        "Mar"=>"March", "Apr"=>"April",
        "May"=>"May", "Jun"=>"June",
        "Jul"=>"July", "Aug"=>"August",
        "Sep"=>"September", "Oct"=>"October",
        "Nov"=>"November", "Dec"=>"December",

        "January"=>"January", "February"=>"February",
        "March"=>"March", "April"=>"April",
        "May"=>"May", "June"=>"June",
        "July"=>"July", "August"=>"August",
```

---

| Listing 5.5 | *Using an array to translate values (cont.)* |

```
        "September"=>"September", "October"=>"October",
        "November"=>"November", "December"=>"December"
        );

    print("Month 5 is " . $monthName[5] . "<br>\n");
    print("Month Aug is " . $monthName["Aug"] . "<br>\n");
    print("Month June is " .
        $monthName["June"] . "<br>\n");
?>
```

---

# 5.4 Multidimensional Arrays

An array element can be any type of data. You've seen numbers and strings, but you can even put an array inside an array. An array of arrays is also called a multidimensional array. Imagine a 10-by-10 grid. You've got 100 different squares, each of which can have its own value. One way to represent this in code is with a two-dimensional array: a 10-element array of 10-number arrays, 10 rows of 10 columns.

To reference a single element, you first use square brackets to pick the first dimension (row), then use a second pair of brackets to pick the second dimension (column). Row 3, column 7, would be written as `$someArray[3][7]`.

Listing 5.6 initializes a multidimensional array using the `array` function. This shows that multidimensional arrays are just arrays of arrays. You may create arrays with any number of dimensions.

---

| Listing 5.6 | *Creating and referencing a multidimensional array* |

```
<?php
    $Cities = array(
        "California"=>array(
            "Martinez",
            "San Francisco",
            "Los Angeles"
            ),
        "New York"=>array(
            "New York",
            "Buffalo"
            )
        );

    print($Cities["California"][1]);
?>
```

# 5.5  Casting Arrays

You can cast an array as another data type to get results of various usefulness. When you cast an array as an integer, double, or boolean, you will get a value of 1. When you cast an array as a string, you will get the word Array. This is useful as an indicator of when you have mistakenly used an array as a string. An array will be promoted to a string containing Array if you use it in a context that demands a string, such as in a print statement. You can't use an array in a context that expects a number, such as with the addition operator. This will cause an error. Listing 5.7 explores casting an array as other data types.

| Listing 5.7 | *Casting arrays as other data types* |
|---|---|

```php
<?php
    $userInfo = array(
        "Name"=>"Leon Atkinson",
        "Location"=>"Martinez, California",
        "Occupation"=>"Programmer",
        "PHP Version"=>5.0);

    //Whether a boolean, integer or double,
    //PHP converts the array to 1
    $asBool = (boolean)$userInfo;
    print("Boolean: $asBool<br>\n");

    $asInt = (integer)$userInfo;
    print("Integer: $asInt<br>\n");

    $asDouble = (double)$userInfo;
    print("Double: $asDouble<br>\n");

    //When converting to a string, PHP
    //returns the string "Array"
    $asString = (string)$userInfo;
    print("String: $asString<br>\n");

    //When converting the array to an object,
    //PHP tries to convert all elements to properties.
    //Elements with spaces in their keys are not lost,
    //but are inaccessible.
    $asObject = (object)$userInfo;
    print("Object: $asObject->Location<br>\n");
    print("$asObject->PHP Version<br>\n"); //doesn't work!
```

---

| Listing 5.7 | *Casting arrays as other data types (cont.)* |

```
    //uncommented, the following is a parse error
    //print($userInfo + 1);

    //PHP knows how to promote an array to a string, though
    //not with useful results.
    print("Promoted to string:" . $userInfo . "<br>\n");

    //PHP won't promote an array to an object
    print($userInfo->Name . "<br>\n");
?>
```

---

The most useful cast of an array you can perform is to an object. The elements of the array become properties of the object. However, elements indexed by values that are illegal as property names remain inaccessible. These values are not lost, and if you recast the variable as an array, they become available again. Objects are discussed in Chapter 6.

# 5.6  The + Operator

The + operator has a special meaning for arrays. It merges the elements from the array on the right into the array on the left. The keys of the arrays are important. If a key exists in the array on the left, it remains unchanged. Only elements from the array on the right with different keys merge into the array on the left. Listing 5.8 demonstrates this functionality.

---

| Listing 5.8 | *Using the + with arrays* |

```
<?php
    //define a couple of arrays
    $a = array(
        0=>"Apple",
        2=>"Ball");
    $b = array(
        1=>"Cat",
        2=>"Dog");

    foreach(($a + $b) as $key=>$value)
    {
        print("$key: $value<br>\n");
    }
?>
```

---

Figure 5.1 shows that Listing 5.8 prints an array with three elements. The element indexed by 2 uses the value from a, not b.

Chapter 11 discusses the `array_merge` function, which performs a different merge of arrays.

```
0: Apple
2: Ball
1: Cat
```

**Figure 5.1**    Output from Listing 5.8.

# 5.7  Referencing Arrays Inside Strings

As you know from Chapter 2, you may place a variable inside a string using double quotes. The variable's value will replace it. A single-dimensional array indexed by integers will be interpreted correctly inside double quotes, but other uses of arrays are problematic. To force the use of multidimensional arrays, use curly braces. These suspend the normal parsing that occurs within a double-quoted string. Of course, you may always concatenate strings. Listing 5.9 explores some different ways to use arrays inside strings.

**Listing 5.9** | *Referencing arrays in strings*

```php
<?php
    $monthInfo = array(
        1=>array("January", 31),
        array("February", 28),
        array("March", 31),
        array("April", 31),
        array("May", 31),
        array("June", 31),
        array("July", 31),
        array("August", 31),
        array("September", 30),
        array("October", 31),
        array("November", 30),
        array("December", 31));
```

**Listing 5.9**   *Referencing arrays in strings (cont.)*

```
$userInfo = array(
    "Name"=>"Leon Atkinson",
    "Location"=>"Martinez, California",
    "Occupation"=>"Programmer");

//This does not parse as expected. It prints
//Array[0] because [0] isn't considered part of
//the expression.
print("$monthInfo[1][0] <br>\n");

//Here the curly braces alert the parser to
//consider the entire array expression,
//including the second dimension.
print("{$monthInfo[1][0]} has {$monthInfo[1][1]} days<br>\n");

//Here we've avoided the confusion by keeping
//the array values outside of the strings, perhaps
//at the expense of some readability.
print($monthInfo[1][0] . " has " . $monthInfo[1][1]
    . " days <br>\n");

//This line would cause a parse error if uncommented
//print("Name is $userInfo["Name"]<br>\n");

//Once again, curly braces are used to clear up
//confusion for the parser.
print("Name is {$userInfo["Name"]}<br>\n");
?>
```

# CLASSES AND OBJECTS

**Topics in This Chapter**

- Object-Oriented Programming
- The PHP 5 Object Model
- Defining a Class
- Constructors and Destructors
- Cloning
- Accessing Properties and Methods
- Static Class Members
- Access Types
- Binding
- Abstract Methods and Abstract Classes
- User-Level Overloading
- Class Autoloading
- Object Serialization
- Namespaces
- The Evolution of the Zend Engine

# Chapter 6

This chapter discusses object-oriented programming and PHP's implementation of objects. If you're a PHP veteran, you will find many new features in this chapter. If you're relatively new to PHP, you may feel overwhelmed, in which case you way wish to set this chapter aside and return to it later. The functionality discussed here is useful but not necessary to most programming tasks.

## 6.1 Object-Oriented Programming

Object-oriented programming was devised as a solution to problems associated with large software projects where many programmers work on a single system. When source code grows to be tens of thousands of lines of code or more, each change can cause unexpected side effects. This happens when modules form secret alliances, as nations did in pre-WWI Europe. Imagine a module for handling logins that allows a credit card processing module to share its database connection. Surely it was done with the best intentions, probably to save the overhead of acquiring another connection. Some time later, the login module severs the agreement by changing the variable name. The credit card processing code breaks; then the module that handles invoices breaks. Soon, totally unrelated modules are dragged into the fray.

So, I'm being a bit dramatic. Most programmers pick up an appreciation for coupling and encapsulation. Coupling is the measure of how dependent two modules are. Less coupling is better. We'd like to take modules from existing projects and reuse them in new projects. We'd like to make wholesale changes to the internals of modules without worrying about how they affect other modules. The solution is to follow the principle of encapsulation. Modules are treated as independent states, and exchanges between modules are done through narrow, structured interfaces. Modules do not spy on each other by reaching into each other's variables. They ask politely through functions.

Encapsulation is a principle you can apply in any programming language—if you have discipline. In PHP and many procedural languages it's easy to be tempted to be lazy. Nothing prevents you from building a web of conceit between your modules. Object-oriented programming is a way of making it nearly impossible to violate encapsulation.

In object-oriented programming, modules are organized into objects. These objects have methods and properties. From an abstract perspective, methods are things an object does, and properties are the characteristics of the object. From a programming perspective, methods are functions and properties are variables. In an ideal object-oriented system, each part is an object. The system consists of objects exchanging objects with other objects using methods.

A class defines the attributes of objects. If you were baking a batch of cookie objects, the class would be the cookie cutter. The properties and methods of the class are called members. People may qualify the expression by saying *data* members or *method* members.

Each language takes a different approach to objects. PHP borrows from C++ and offers a data type that may contain functions and variables under a single identifier. When PHP was first conceived, and even when version 3 was created, PHP wasn't intended to be capable of powering projects of 100,000 lines or more of code. As PHP and the Zend Engine evolved, it became possible to write larger projects, but no matter the size of your project, building your scripts with classes will certainly aid you in writing code that can be reused. This is a good idea, especially if you wish to share your code.

The idea of objects is one of those mind-blowing concepts in computer science. It's hard to grasp at first, but I can attest that once you get it, it becomes quite natural to think in its terms. Nevertheless, you can ignore objects if you wish and return to this chapter later. Some built-in functions return objects. You can find alternatives that don't, or you can cast the objects as arrays, as described at the end of this chapter.

# 6.2 The PHP 5 Object Model

PHP 5 has a single-inheritance, access-restricted, and overloadable object model. Inheritance, discussed in detail later in this chapter, involves a parent-child relationship between classes. Other languages allow for multiple parents; PHP allows for one parent per child. Additionally, PHP supports restricting access to properties and methods. You may declare members private, disallowing access from outside the class. Finally, PHP allows a child class to overload the members of its parent class.

The object model in PHP 5 treats objects differently from any other kind of value that is available in PHP and implements implicit, pass-by-reference behavior. That is, PHP does not require you to explicitly pass or return objects by reference. The reasoning for moving to a handle-based object model is closely detailed at the end of this chapter. It's the most important new feature of PHP 5.

In addition to providing a more intuitive object model, the handle-based system has several additional advantages: improved performance, reduced memory consumption, and increased flexibility.

In previous versions of PHP, scripts copied objects by default. Unless this functionality specifically broke your design, it was easy to let PHP move big chunks of memory. PHP now moves only a handle, which requires less time. This increases performance of a given script because it avoids unnecessary copies. The performance benefit increases in step with the complexity of the object hierarchy. Fewer copies means using less memory too. This may increase performance of the system as a whole, since more memory remains available for all processes.

The Zend Engine 2 allows for more flexibility. One happy consequence of the new design is allowance for destructors, class methods that execute immediately before destroying an object. This also benefits memory use, as PHP knows exactly when no references to an object remain, allowing it to make the memory available for other uses.

# 6.3 Defining a Class

When you declare a class, you are really making a template for the creation of objects. You list all the variables the object should have and all the functions it will need. These are called properties and methods respectively. Figure 6.1 displays the form of a class declaration. Note that inside the curly braces you can declare only variables or functions. Listing 6.1 shows the definition of a class with three properties and two methods.

```
class Name extends Another Class
{
    Access Variable Declaration

    Access Function Declaration
}
```

**Figure 6.1**  Defining a class.

**Listing 6.1**  *Using a class*

```php
<?php
    //define class for tracking users
    class User
    {
        //properties
        public $name;
        private $password, $lastLogin;

        //methods
        public function __construct($name, $password)
        {
            $this->name = $name;
            $this->password = $password;
            $this->lastLogin = time();
            $this->accesses++;
        }

        // get the date of the last login
        function getLastLogin()
        {
            return(date("M d Y", $this->lastLogin));
        }
    }

    //create an instance
    $user = new User("Leon", "sdf123");

    //get the last login date
    print($user->getLastLogin() ."<br>\n");

    //print the user's name
    print("$user->name<br>\n");
?>
```

When you declare a property, you don't specify a data type. It is a variable like any other, and it may contain an integer, a string, or even another object. Depending on the situation, it might be a good idea to add a comment near the declaration of the property that states its intended use and data type.

When you declare a method, you do so just as you would declare a function outside a class definition. Both methods and properties exist within their own scope, or namespace. That means you can safely create methods that have the same name as functions declared outside of class definitions without conflicts. For example, a class can define a method named date. You cannot name a method after a PHP keyword, such as for or while.

Class methods may include what PHP calls *type hints*. A type hint is the name of another class that precedes an argument to the method. If your script calls the method and passes a variable that is not an instance of the named class, PHP generates a fatal error. You may not give type hints for other types, such as integer, string, or boolean. At the time of writing, there was some debate over whether type hints should include the array type.

Type hints are a shortcut for testing argument type with functions or the instanceof operator. You may always fall back on this method. Checking the type yourself allows you to force an argument to be an integer, for example. Listing 6.2 demonstrates the use of type hints to ensure the Assembler class makes Widget instances only.

| Listing 6.2 | *Type hints* |
|---|---|

```php
<?php
    //Widget class needs a helper class
    class Widget
    {
        public $name='none';
        public $created=FALSE;
    }

    //Assembler makes widgets only
    class Assembler
    {
        public function make(Widget $w)
        {
            print("Making $w->name<br>\n");
            $w->created=TRUE;
        }
    }
```

**Listing 6.2**    *Type hints (cont.)*

```
    //Create a widget
    $thing = new Widget;
    $thing->name = 'Gadget';

    //Assemble the widget
    Assembler::make($thing);
?>
```

Aside from the variables passed as arguments, methods contain a special variable called `this`. It stands for the particular instance of the class. You must use `this` to refer to properties and other methods of the object. Some object-oriented languages assume an unqualified variable refers to a local property, but in PHP any variables referred to within a method are simply variables local to that scope. Note the use of the `this` variable in the constructor for the `user` class in Listing 6.1.

PHP looks for an access type before property and method declarations. These are `public`, `private`, and `protected`. Additionally, you can mark a member with the `static` keyword. You can also declare constants within classes with the `const` directive. A discussion of the various access types appears later in the chapter.

You may list properties of the same access type on a single line, using commas to separate them. In Listing 6.1, the `User` class contains two private properties, defined with `private $password, $lastLogin`.

## 6.4  Constructors and Destructors

If you choose to declare a function within a class named `__construct`, the function will be considered a constructor and will be executed immediately upon creating an object from that class. To be clear, the first two characters are underscores. Like any other function, the constructor may have parameters and even default values. You can set up classes that allow you to create an object and set all its properties in one statement. You may also define a method named `__destruct`. PHP calls this method when it destroys the object. It's called a destructor.

One powerful aspect of classes is inheritance, the idea that a class can extend the functionality of another class. The new class will contain all the methods and properties of the class it extends, plus any others it lists within its body. You may also override methods and properties from the extended class. As shown in Figure 6.1, you extend a class using the `extends` keyword.

One issue you might wonder about is whether and how constructors are inherited. While they are inherited along with all other methods, they cease to have the property of being called when an object is created from the class. If you require this functionality, you must write it explicitly by calling the parent class's constructor within the child class's constructor. Recall the `::` operator from Chapter 2. It allows you to refer to namespaces. The special `parent` namespace refers to the immediate ancestor. You can call the parent constructor with `parent::__construct`.

Some object-oriented languages name constructors after the class. Previous versions of PHP used this method, and for the time being, it's still supported. That is, if you call you class `Animal` and you place a method inside named `Animal`, PHP uses it as the constructor. If the class has both `__construct` and a method named after the class, PHP uses `__construct`. This allows classes written for previous versions to continue to work as expected. Any new scripts should use `__construct`.

PHP's new convention for naming the constructor offers the ability to reference constructors with a unified name regardless of the name of their containing class. It allows you to change your class hierarchies without having to change the actual code in the class itself.

You may give constructors an access type like other methods in PHP. The access type will affect the ability of instantiating the object from certain scopes. This allows for implementation of certain design patterns, such as the Singleton pattern.

Destructors, as their name implies, are the opposite of constructors. PHP calls them each time it frees an object from memory. By default, PHP simply frees the memory of the properties in the object and destroys any resources that the object referenced. Destructors allow you to execute arbitrary code to properly clean up after your object.

Destructors are called as soon as PHP determines that your script no longer references the object. Inside a function namespace, that happens as soon as the function returns. For global variables, this typically happens when the script terminates. If you wish to explicitly destroy an object, you can assign any other value to every variable pointing to the object. Assigning `NULL` to a variable or calling unset is customary.

The class in Listing 6.3 counts the number of objects that were instantiated from it. The class counter is incremented in the constructor and decremented in the constructor.

Once you have defined a class, you use the `new` statement to create an instance of the class, an object. If the definition of the class is the blueprint, the instance is the widget rolling off the assembly line. The `new` statement expects the name of a class and returns a new instance of that class. If a constructor with parameters has been declared, you may also follow the class name with parameters inside parentheses. Look for the lines in Listing 6.3 that use the `new` statement.

**Listing 6.3** *Constructors and destructors*

```php
<?php
    class Counter
    {
        private static $count = 0;

        function __construct()
        {
            self::$count++;
        }

        function __destruct()
        {
            self::$count--;
        }

        function getCount()
        {
            return self::$count;
        }
    }

    //create one instance
    $c = new Counter();

    //print 1
    print($c->getCount() . "<br>\n");

    //create a second instance
    $c2 = new Counter();

    //print 2
    print($c->getCount() . "<br>\n");

    //destroy one instance
    $c2 = NULL;

    //print 1
    print($c->getCount() . "<br>\n");
?>
```

When you create an instance, memory is set aside for all the properties. Each instance has its own set of properties. However, the methods are shared by all instances of that class.

# 6.5 Cloning

The object model in PHP 5 treats objects in a unique way by implementing an implicit by-reference paradigm. In some situations, you may wish to create a replica of an object so that changes to the replica are not reflected in the original object. For that purpose, PHP defines a special method, named __clone. As with __construct and __destruct, use two underscores for the first two characters of the method name.

Every object has a default implementation for __clone. The default implementation creates a new object containing the same values and resources as the original object. If you wish to override this default implementation, you may declare your own version of __clone in your class.

The clone method accepts no arguments, but it includes both this and a second object pointer named that, which corresponds to the object being replicated. If you choose to implement __clone yourself, you have to take care of copying any information that you want your object to contain, from that to this. PHP will not perform any implicit value copying if you create your own implementation of __clone.

Listing 6.4 illustrates a simple way of automating objects with serial numbers.

---

**Listing 6.4** | *The __clone method*

```php
<?php
    class ObjectTracker
    {
        private static $nextSerial = 0;
        private $id;
        private $name;

        function __construct($name)
        {
            $this->name = $name;
            $this->id = ++self::$nextSerial;
        }

        function __clone()
        {
            $this->name = "Clone of $that->name";
            $this->id = ++self::$nextSerial;
        }
```

| Listing 6.4 | *The __clone method (cont.)* |

```
    function getId()
    {
        return($this->id);
    }

    function getName()
    {
        return($this->name);
    }
}

$ot = new ObjectTracker("Zeev's Object");
$ot2 = $ot->__clone();

//1 Zeev's Object
print($ot->getId() . " " . $ot->getName() . "<br>");

//2 Clone of Zeev's Object
print($ot2->getId() . " " . $ot2->getName() . "<br>");
?>
```

# 6.6  Accessing Properties and Methods

The properties of an instance are variables, just like any other PHP variable. To refer to them, however, you must use the -> operator. You do not use a dollar sign in front of the property name. For an example, refer to line in Listing 6.1 that prints the name property of the user object.

Use of -> can be chained. If an object's property contains an object itself, you can use two -> operators to get to a property on the inner object. You may even place these expressions within double-quoted strings. See Listing 6.5 for an example of an object that contains an array of objects.

Accessing methods is similar to accessing properties. The -> operator is used to point to the instance's method. This is shown in Listing 6.1 in the call to getLastLogin. Methods behave exactly as functions defined outside classes.

If a class extends another, the properties and methods of all ancestor classes are available in the child class despite not being declared explicitly. As mentioned previously, inheritance is very powerful. If you wish to access an inherited property, you may simply refer to it as you would any other local property. Alternatively, you may specify a specific namespace using the :: operator.

---

**Listing 6.5** | *Objects containing other objects*

```php
<?php
    class Room
    {
        public $name;

        function __construct($name="unnamed")
        {
            $this->name = $name;
        }
    }

    class House
    {
        //array of rooms
        public $room;
    }

    //create empty house
    $home = new house;

    //add some rooms
    $home->room[] = new Room("bedroom");
    $home->room[] = new Room("kitchen");
    $home->room[] = new Room("bathroom");

    //show the first room of the house
    print($home->room[0]->name);
?>
```

---

PHP recognizes two special namespaces within objects. The `parent` namespace refers to the immediate ancestor class. The `self` namespace refers to the current class. Listing 6.6 demonstrates the use of the `parent` namespace to call parent constructors recursively. It also uses `self` to call another method from within a constructor.

---

**Listing 6.6** | *The `parent` and `self` namespaces*

```php
<?php
    class Animal
    {
        public $blood;
        public $name;
```

| Listing 6.6 | *The `parent` and `self` namespaces (cont.)* |

```php
        public function __construct($blood, $name=NULL)
        {
            $this->blood = $blood;
            if($name)
            {
                $this->name = $name;
            }
        }
    }

    class Mammal extends Animal
    {
        public $furColor;
        public $legs;

        function __construct($furColor, $legs, $name=NULL)
        {
            parent::__construct("warm", $name);
            $this->furColor = $furColor;
            $this->legs = $legs;
        }
    }

    class Dog extends Mammal
    {
        function __construct($furColor, $name)
        {
            parent::__construct($furColor, 4, $name);

            self::bark();
        }

        function bark()
        {
            print("$this->name says 'woof!'");
        }
    }

    $d = new Dog("Black and Tan", "Angus");
?>
```

Chapter 4 introduced the idea of dynamic function calls, where a variable stands for the name of a function. The same technique applies for object members. For example, if you need to determine the name of a property at runtime, you can write an expression like `$this->$dynamicProperty`. Similarly, you can write an expression like `$obj->$method(1.23)` to call a method you choose with the `method` variable.

You can also use the return value of a function with the `->` operator, which was not allowed in previous versions of PHP. For example, you can write an expression like `$obj->getObject()->callMethod()`. This avoids using an intermediate variable. It also aids the implementation of some design patterns, such as the Factory pattern.

# 6.7 Static Class Members

Static class members are different from regular class members: They don't relate to an object instance of the class, but to the class itself. They are used to implement functionality and data that the class should encapsulate but that does not belong to any particular object. As with regular class members, there are static methods and static properties.

Static properties contain data that should be encapsulated in a class but that should be shared among all class instances. Practically, static class properties are very similar to global variables, except that they belong to a certain class and can be access-restricted.

We already used a static property in Listing 6.3: `Counter::$count` is a static property. It belongs to the `Counter` class, not to any particular instance of the `Counter` class. You cannot refer to it with `this`, but you may use `self` or any other valid namespace expression. In Listing 6.3, the `getCount` method returns `self::$count`. Instead, it could have used `Counter::$count`.

Static methods implement functionality that should be encapsulated in a class but that does not relate to any particular object. In very much the same way that static properties are similar to global variables, static methods are similar to global functions. Static methods enjoy full access to the properties of the class to which they belong as well as to object instances of that class, regardless of access restrictions.

In Listing 6.3, `getCount` is an ordinary method, called with the `->` operator. PHP creates the `this` variable, although the body of the method makes no use of it. However, much like `count` itself, `getCount` does not belong to any particular object. In certain situations, we may even wish to call it without even having an object instance available. Static methods fit these situations well. PHP does not create `this` inside static methods, even when you call them from an object.

Listing 6.7 modifies Listing 6.3 to make `getCount` a static method. The `static` keyword does not prevent calling `getCount` from an instance with the `->` operator, but PHP does not create `this` inside the method. You can attempt to call any method statically with the proper syntax. If the method uses `this`, PHP generates an error.

You can write a method to behave different depending on whether it's called statically or not by testing if `this` is set. Of course, if you use the `static` keyword, the method will always be static regardless of how it's called.

Your classes may also define constant properties. Instead of using `public static`, you use the `const` keyword. You may only refer to constant properties statically. They are properties of the class, not of objects that instantiate the class.

**Listing 6.7** *Static members*

```php
<?php
    class Counter
    {
        private static $count = 0;
        const VERSION = 2.0;

        function __construct()
        {
            self::$count++;
        }

        function __destruct()
        {
            self::$count--;
        }

        static function getCount()
        {
            return self::$count;
        }
    };

    //create one instance
    $c = new Counter();

    //print 1
    print(Counter::getCount() . "<br>\n");

    //print the version of the class
    print("Version used: " . Counter::VERSION . "<br>\n");
?>
```

# 6.8 Access Types

Access types allow developers to restrict access to members of their classes. They are new to PHP 5, but are a well-known feature of many object-oriented languages. Access types provide a fundamental building block of reliable object-oriented applications and are a crucial requirement for reusable object-oriented infrastructure libraries.

Like C++ and Java, PHP features three kinds of access types: `public`, `private`, and `protected`. A class member may be one of these. If you do not specify an access type, the member is public. You may give an access type to a static member, in which case the access type should precede the `static` keyword.

Public members can be accessed with no restrictions. Any code outside of the class may read and write public properties. You may call a public method from any part of your script. In previous versions of PHP all methods and properties were public, which invoked the thought that objects were little more than fancy arrays.

Private members are visible to members of the same class only. You cannot change or even read the value of a private property outside of a method in the class. Likewise, only other methods in the class may call a private method. Even child classes have no access to private members.

It's important to keep in mind that any member of a class, not just a particular instance, may access private members. Consider Listing 6.8. The `equals` method compares two widgets. The `==` operator compares the properties of two objects of the same class, but in this example each instance gets a unique ID. The `equals` method compares name and price only. Note how `equals` accesses the private properties of another instance of `Widget`. Java and C allow the same behavior.

---

**Listing 6.8**  *Private members*

```php
<?php
    class Widget
    {
        private $name;
        private $price;
        private $id;

        public function __construct($name, $price)
        {
            $this->name = $name;
            $this->price = floatval($price);
            $this->id = uniqid();
        }
```

| Listing 6.8 | *Private members (cont.)* |

```
        //checks if two widgets are the same
        public function equals($widget)
        {
            return(($this->name == $widget->name)AND
                ($this->price == $widget->price));
        }
    }

    $w1 = new Widget('Cog', 5.00);
    $w2 = new Widget('Cog', 5.00);
    $w3 = new Widget('Gear', 7.00);

    //TRUE
    if($w1->equals($w2))
    {
        print("w1 and w2 are the same<br>\n");
    }

    //FALSE
    if($w1->equals($w3))
    {
        print("w1 and w3 are the same<br>\n");
    }

    //FALSE, == includes id in comparison
    if($w1 == $w2)
    {
        print("w1 and w2 are the same<br>\n");
    }
?>
```

If you don't have a lot of experience with object-oriented programming, you may wonder about the purpose of private members. Recall the ideas of encapsulation and coupling discussed at the beginning of the chapter. Private members help encapsulate data within an object. They remain hidden inside and untouched by outside code. They also encourage loose coupling. If code from outside of the data structure cannot access properties directly, it cannot implement a hidden dependency.

Of course, most private properties still represent information to be shared with code outside of the object. The solution is a pair of public methods for getting and setting them. The constructor typically accepts initial values for properties too. This forces interaction with members through a narrow, well-defined interface. It also offers the opportunity to alter values as they pass through the method. Note how the constructor in Listing 6.8 forces the price to be a floating-point number.

Protected members can be accessed by methods of their containing class and any derived class. Public properties allow circumvention of the spirit of encapsulation because they allow subclasses to depend on writing to a particular property directly. Protected methods, however, pose less of a threat. You may think of protected members as being for experts only. A subclass that uses a protected method should know its ancestors well.

In Listing 6.9 the code from Listing 6.8 evolves to include a subclass of Widget named Thing. Note how Widget now includes a protected method called getName. Calling this method from an instance of Widget is not allowed: $w1->getName() generates an error. The getName method inside the subclass Thing, however, may call this protected method. This example is too simple to warrant making Widget::getName protected, of course. In practice, use protected methods for routines that rely on an understanding of the internal structure of an object and provide functionality useful outside of the class.

**Listing 6.9**   *Protected members*

```php
<?php
    class Widget
    {
        private $name;
        private $price;
        private $id;

        public function __construct($name, $price)
        {
            $this->name = $name;
            $this->price = floatval($price);
            $this->id = uniqid();
        }

        //checks if two widgets are the same
        public function equals($widget)
        {
            return(($this->name == $widget->name)AND
                ($this->price == $widget->price));
        }

        protected function getName()
        {
            return($this->name);
        }
    }
```

| Listing 6.9 | *Protected members (cont.)* |
|---|---|

```php
class Thing extends Widget
{
    private $color;

    public function setColor($color)
    {
        $this->color = $color;
    }

    public function getColor()
    {
        return($this->color);
    }

    public function getName()
    {
        return(parent::getName());
    }
}

$w1 = new Widget('Cog', 5.00);
$w2 = new Thing('Cog', 5.00);
$w2->setColor('Yellow');

//TRUE (still!)
if($w1->equals($w2))
{
    print("w1 and w2 are the same<br>\n");
}

//print Cog
print($w2->getName());
?>
```

A child class may change the access type assigned to member by overriding it; however, there are some restrictions. If you override a public class member, it must remain public in the derived class. If you override a protected class member, it may remain protected or become public. Private members remain visible within their local class only. Declaring a member with a name matching a private member of a parent class simply creates a distinct member in the containing class. Technically, therefore, you can't override private members. You may assign any access type you wish.

The `final` keyword offers another way to restrict access to a member method. Derived classes cannot override methods marked final in any of their ancestors. The `final` keyword does not apply to properties.

## 6.9 Binding

Other than restricting access, access types also determine which method will be called or which property will be accessed in subclasses that override methods or properties. Linking between function calls and their corresponding function, and between member accesses and the memory location of variables, is called binding.

There are two main types of binding in computer languages—static binding and dynamic binding. Static binding matches references to data structures and the data structures themselves. Static binding occurs during compilation and consequently cannot make use of any runtime information. It matches function calls to function bodies, and it matches variables to their block of memory. Since PHP is a dynamic language, it doesn't use static binding. However, there are portions of PHP that emulate static binding.

Dynamic binding matches access requests made at runtime, using information available only during runtime. In the context of object-oriented code, dynamic binding means determining which method to call or which property to access based on the class of `this`, not based on the scope in which the access is made.

Public and protected members behave similarly to the way methods behaved in previous versions of PHP and are bound using dynamic binding. This means that if a method accesses a class member that was overridden in a child class, and our `this` is an instance of the child class, the child's member will be accessed.

Consider Listing 6.10. This code prints "Hey! I am Son." because when PHP reaches `getSalutation`, `this` is an instance of `Son`, which overrides salutation. If `salutation` were public, PHP would produce identical results. Overridden methods operate similarly. The call to `identify` binds to the method in `Son`.

Dynamic binding occurs even if the access type in derived classes is weakened from protected to public. Per the rules of access type usage, it is impossible to increase the access restrictions on class members. Changing the access type from public to protected is not possible.

| Listing 6.10 | *Dynamic binding* |
|---|---|

```php
<?php
    class Father
    {
        protected $salutation = "Hello there!";

        public function getSalutation()
        {
            print("$this->salutation\n");
            $this->identify();
        }

        protected function identify()
        {
            print("I am Father.<br>\n");
        }
    };

    class Son extends Father
    {
        protected $salutation = "Hey!";

        protected function identify()
        {
            print("I am Son.<br>\n");
        }
    };

    $obj = new Son();
    $obj->getSalutation();
?>
```

Private members exist only to their containing class. Unlike public and protected members, PHP emulates static binding for private class members. Consider Listing 6.11. It displays "Hello there! I am Father.", despite the Child class overriding the value of salutation. The script must bind this->salutation to the immediate class, Father. Similar rules apply to the private method, identify.

**Listing 6.11**  *Binding and private members*

```php
<?php
    class Father
    {
        private $salutation = "Hello there!";

        public function getSalutation()
        {
            print("$this->salutation\n");
            $this->identify();
        }

        private function identify()
        {
            print("I am Father.<br>\n");
        }
    }

    class Son extends Father
    {
        private $salutation = "Hey!";

        private function identify()
        {
            print("I am Son.<br>\n");
        }
    }

    $obj = new Son();
    $obj->getSalutation();
?>
```

The advantage of dynamic binding is that it allows derived classes to alter the behavior of their parents while still taking advantage of their parents' interfaces and functionality. See Listing 6.12. Thanks to dynamic binding, the version of isAuthorized that is called inside deleteUser is determined based on the type of our object. If this is an ordinary user, PHP calls User::isAuthorized, which returns FALSE. If this is an instance of AuthorizedUser, PHP calls AuthorizedUser::isAuthorized, which allows deleteUser to work as expected.

**Listing 6.12**    *The advantages of dynamic binding*

```php
<?php
    class User
    {
        protected function isAuthorized()
        {
            return(FALSE);
        }

        public function getName()
        {
            return($this->name);
        }

        public function deleteUser($username)
        {
            if(!$this->isAuthorized())
            {
                print("You are not authorized.<br>\n");
                return(FALSE);
            }

            //delete the user
            print("User deleted.<br>\n");
        }
    }

    class AuthorizedUser extends User
    {
        protected function isAuthorized()
        {
            return(TRUE);
        }
    }

    $user = new User;
    $admin = new AuthorizedUser;

    //not authorized
    $user->deleteUser("Zeev");

    //authorized
    $admin->deleteUser("Zeev");
?>
```

Why do private class members emulate static binding? In order to answer that question, you must recall the reasons for having private members in the first place. That is, when does it make sense to use them instead of protected members?

Use private members only when you don't want to let deriving classes change or specialize the parent class's behavior. Such cases are fewer than you might expect. Generally, a good object hierarchy should allow most of the functionality to be specialized, improved, or altered by deriving classes: It is one of the foundations of object-oriented programming. Certain cases demand private methods or variables, such as when you're certain you don't want to allow deriving classes to alter a particular aspect of the class.

# 6.10  Abstract Methods and Abstract Classes

Object-oriented programs are built around class hierarchies. In a single inheritance language such as PHP, class hierarchies are trees. A root class has one or more classes that descend from it, with one or more classes derived from each of them. Of course, there may be multiple root classes, which implement different families of classes. In a well-designed hierarchy, each root class will expose a useful interface, which can be used by application code. If our application code is designed to work with a root class, chances are it will also be able to work with any specialized derivative of that class.

Abstract methods are methods that behave like placeholders for regular methods in derived classes and—unlike regular class methods—do not contain any code. The existence of one or more abstract method in a class turns the class into an abstract class. You may not instantiate abstract classes. You must extend them and instantiate the child class. You can also think of an abstract class as a template for derived classes.

If you override all of the abstract methods in it, the child class becomes an ordinary class that matches the expectations defined by the abstract class. If you define a subset of methods, the child class remains abstract. If a class contains any abstract methods, you must declare the class itself abstract by adding the `abstract` keyword before the `class` keyword.

The syntax for declaring abstract methods differs from that of declaring regular methods. In place of the function body, surrounded by curly braces, abstract methods simply have a semicolon.

In Listing 6.13, we define class `Shape` to contain the `getArea` method. However, since it is not possible to determine the area of `shape` without knowing its type, we declare the `getArea` method to be abstract. You cannot instantiate a `Shape` object, but you can extend it or use it in an `instanceof` expression, as shown in Listing 6.13.

If you create a class with abstract methods only, you define an interface. To clarify this situation, PHP includes the `interface` and `implements` keywords. You may use `interface` in place of `abstract class` and `implements` in place of `extends` to show that your class defines or uses an interface. For example, you might write `class myClass implements myInterface`. Use of either idiom is left to personal preference.

**Listing 6.13** *Abstract classes*

```php
<?php
    //abstract root class
    abstract class Shape
    {
        abstract function getArea();
    }

    //abstract child class
    abstract class Polygon extends Shape
    {
        abstract function getNumberOfSides();
    }

    //concrete class
    class Triangle extends Polygon
    {
        public $base;
        public $height;

        public function getArea()
        {
            return(($this->base * $this->height)/2);
        }

        public function getNumberOfSides()
        {
            return(3);
        }
    }

    //concrete class
    class Rectangle extends Polygon
    {
        public $width;
        public $height;
```

**Listing 6.13**   *Abstract classes (cont.)*

```
    public function getArea()
    {
        return($this->width * $this->height);
    }

    public function getNumberOfSides()
    {
        return(4);
    }
}

//concrete class
class Circle extends Shape
{
    public $radius;

    public function getArea()
    {
        return(pi() * $this->radius * $this->radius);
    }
}

//concrete root class
class Color
{
    public $name;
}

$myCollection = array();

//make a rectangle
$r = new Rectangle;
$r->width = 5;
$r->height = 7;
$myCollection[] = $r;
unset($r);

//make a triangle
$t = new Triangle;
$t->base = 4;
$t->height = 5;
$myCollection[] = $t;
unset($t);
```

| Listing 6.13 | *Abstract classes (cont.)* |
| --- | --- |

```php
//make a circle
$c = new Circle;
$c->radius = 3;
$myCollection[] = $c;
unset($c);

//make a color
$c = new Color;
$c->name = "blue";
$myCollection[] = $c;
unset($c);

foreach($myCollection as $s)
{
    if($s instanceof Shape)
    {
        print("Area: " . $s->getArea() .
            "<br>\n");
    }

    if($s instanceof Polygon)
    {
        print("Sides: " .
            $s->getNumberOfSides() .
            "<br>\n");
    }

    if($s instanceof Color)
    {
        print("Color: $s->name<br>\n");
    }

    print("<br>\n");
}

?>
```

# 6.11  User-Level Overloading

PHP 4 introduced the ability for module developers to overload the object-oriented syntax and create mappings into external object models, such as Java or COM. PHP 5 brings the power of object-oriented overloading syntax to PHP developers, allowing them to create custom behaviors for accessing properties and invoking methods.

User-level overloading is done by defining one or more of the following special methods: __get, __set, and __call. PHP calls these methods when the Zend Engine attempts to access a member and does not find it in the current scope.

In Listing 6.14 __get and __set relay all property accesses to the properties array. If necessary, you can implement any kind of filtering you wish. For example, the script could disallow setting of properties that begin with a certain prefix or that contain specific types of values.

The __call method illustrates how you can capture calls to undefined methods. The callback receives the method name as well as an array with the list of arguments that the method received. PHP passes the return value of __call on as the return value of the original call to the undefined method.

**Listing 6.14**    *User-level overloading*

```php
<?php
    class Overloader
    {
        private $properties = array();

        function __get($property_name)
        {
            if(isset($this->properties[$property_name]))
            {
                return($this->properties[$property_name]);
            }
            else
            {
                return(NULL);
            }
        }

        function __set($property_name, $value)
        {
            $this->properties[$property_name] = $value;
        }

        function __call($function_name, $args)
        {
            print("Invoking $function_name()<br>\n");
            print("Arguments: ");
            print_r($args);

            return(TRUE);
        }
    }
```

| Listing 6.14 | *User-level overloading (cont.)* |
|---|---|

```
    $o = new Overloader();

    //invoke __set()
    $o->dynaProp = "Dynamic Content";

    //invoke __get()
    print($o->dynaProp . "<br>\n");

    //invoke __call()
    $o->dynaMethod("Leon", "Zeev");
?>
```

# 6.12  Class Autoloading

When you attempt to use a class you haven't defined, PHP generates a fatal error, of course. The obvious solution to this situation involves adding a class definition, probably by issuing an `include` statement. After all, you should know which classes a script uses. However, PHP offers class autoloading, which may save programming time. When you attempt to use a class PHP does not recognize, it looks for a global function named `__autoload`. If it exists, PHP calls it with a single parameter, the name of the class. Inside the function, you may take the necessary steps to create the class.

Listing 6.15 demonstrates the use of `__autoload`. It uses a simple scheme that assumes files in the current directory match each class. When the script attempts to instantiate `User`, PHP executes `__autoload`. The script assumes `class_User.php` contains the class definition. Despite the letter case used to invoke a class, PHP returns the name in lowercase.

| Listing 6.15 | *Class autoloading* |
|---|---|

```
<?php
    //define autoload function
    function __autoload($class)
    {
        include("class_" . ucfirst($class) . ".php");
    }

    //use a class that must be autoloaded
    $u = new User;
    $u->name = "Leon";
    $u->printName();
?>
```

# 6.13 Object Serialization

The `serialize` function, discussed in Chapter 15, converts variables, including objects, into strings. You can store the serialized variable in a file or send it across the network. Afterwards, `unserialize` can convert the string back into the appropriate value. As long as you define a class prior to unserializing an object of that class, PHP can successfully restore the object's properties and methods. In some situations you may need to prepare an object prior to serialization and likewise perform some procedure immediately after unserialization. For these purposes, PHP looks for the `__sleep` and `__wakeup` methods.

When serializing an object, PHP calls the `__sleep` method if it exists. After unserializing an object, PHP calls the `__wakeup` method. Neither method accepts arguments. The `__sleep` method must return an array of properties to include in the serialization. PHP discards other property values. Without a `__sleep` method, PHP preserves all properties.

Listing 6.16 demonstrates serialization of an object with `__sleep` and `__wakeup` methods. The `id` property is a temporary value not meant to remain with a stored object. The `__sleep` method ensures PHP does not include it in the serialized object. When unserializing a `User` object, the `__wakeup` method creates a new value for `id`. This example may be contrived for the sake of being self-contained. In practice, you may find objects that contain resources, such as image or stream handles, require these methods.

---

**Listing 6.16** *Object serialization*

```php
<?php

    class User
    {
        public $name;
        public $id;

        function __construct()
        {
            //give user a unique ID
            $this->id = uniqid();
        }
```

| Listing 6.16 | *Object serialization (cont.)* |
|---|---|

```
        function __sleep()
        {
            //do not serialize this->id
            return(array("name"));
        }

        function __wakeup()
        {
            //give user a unique ID
            $this->id = uniqid();
        }
    }

    //create object
    $u = new User;
    $u->name = "Leon";

    //serialize it
    $s = serialize($u);

    //unserialize it
    $u2 = unserialize($s);

    //$u and $u2 have different IDs
    print_r($u);
    print_r($u2);
?>
```

# 6.14 Namespaces

Naming variables, functions, and classes is difficult. Aside from the artistic process of finding a name that communicates purpose, you must worry whether the name is used anywhere else. Within the context of a short script, this second problem is elementary. When you consider reusing your code, any future project must avoid using your names. Generally, reusable code finds itself inside functions or classes, which takes care of many variable name conflicts. But functions and classes may find themselves in conflict with duplicate names. You can try to avoid this situation by adding prefixes to the names of all classes you create, or you can use a namespace statement.

The namespace statement gives a name to a block of code. From outside the block, scripts must refer to the parts inside with the name of the namespace using the :: operator. This is the same way you refer to static members of classes. Inside the namespace the code does not specify the namespace; it's the default. This method offers an advantage over simply prefixing names. Your code may become more compact and more readable.

You may wonder whether you can create a hierarchy of namespaces. You cannot. However, PHP allows you to include a colon in the name of a namespace. You may recall that variables, functions, and classes may not include a colon in their names. Namespaces allow colons as long as they are not the first character, the last character, or next to another colon. Colons in namespace names do not imply any meaning to PHP, but if you use them to divide the names of your namespaces into logical partitions, they may suggest parent-child relationships to anyone who reads your code.

You may not include anything other than function, class, or constant definitions inside a namespace statement. This may prevent you from using them to retrofit older function libraries if they used global variables. Namespaces fit best with the object-oriented paradigm. Constants within namespaces follow the same syntax used for class constants. You may not create constants with the `define` function inside a namespace block.

Listing 6.17 demonstrates the use of a namespace to hold a simple class.

---

**Listing 6.17** *Using a namespace*

```php
<?php
    namespace core_php:utility
    {
        class textEngine
        {
            public function uppercase($text)
            {
                return(strtoupper($text));
            }
        }

        //make non-OO interface
        function uppercase($text)
        {
            $e = new textEngine;
            return($e->uppercase($text));
        }

    }
```

---

**Listing 6.17**  *Using a namespace (cont.)*

```
//test class in namespace
$e = new core_php:utility::textEngine;
print($e->uppercase("from object") . "<br>");

//test function in namespace
print(core_php:utility::uppercase("from function") . "<br>");

//bring class into global namespace
import class textEngine from core_php:utility;
$e2 = new textEngine;
?>
```

---

The `import` statement brings part of a namespace into the global namespace. To import a single member of the namespace, specify the type with `constant`, `function`, or `class` followed by the name of the member. If you wish to import all members of a particular type, you may use * in place of the name. If you wish to import all members of all types, use * by itself. Following the members, specify the namespace preceded by the `from` keyword. All together, you might write something like `import * from myNamespace` or `import class textEngine from core_php:utility`, as shown in Listing 6.17.

# 6.15  The Evolution of the Zend Engine

For the rest of this chapter, Zeev discusses the object model introduced in Zend Engine 2, especially with regard to how it differs from earlier object models in PHP.

When we implemented PHP 3, PHP/FI's replacement, back in the summer of 1997, we had no plans for object-oriented capabilities. It got pretty far without having any notion of classes or objects. It was to be a purely structured language. However, class support was added to the PHP 3 alpha source tree on the night of August 27. Adding a feature to the language at that time required little discussion because few people had discovered PHP. Starting August 1997, PHP made the first step toward becoming an object-oriented–friendly language.

Indeed, it was just the first step. Since relatively little thought contributed to the design, object support wasn't very powerful or impressive. Objects were nothing beyond a cool way of accessing arrays. Instead of having to use `$foo["bar"]`, you could use the nicer looking `$foo->bar`. The object-oriented approach's main advantage was simply the ability to store functionality in the form of member functions, or methods. Listing 6.18 demonstrates a typical block of code from that era. However, this isn't significantly different from Listing 6.19.

**Listing 6.18**   *PHP 3 object-oriented programming*

```php
<?php
    class Example
    {
        var $value = "some value";
        function PrintValue()
        {
            print $this->value;
        }
    }
    $obj = new Example();
    $obj->PrintValue();
?>
```

**Listing 6.19**   *PHP 3 structural programming*

```php
<?php
    function PrintValue($arr)
    {
        print $arr["value"];
    }

    function CreateExample()
    {
        $arr["value"] = "some value";
        $arr["PrintValue"] = "PrintValue";

        return $arr;
    }

    $arr = CreateExample();

    //Use PHP's indirect reference
    $arr["PrintValue"]($arr);
?>
```

We did save a couple of lines of code in the class version, and we did have to explicitly pass arr to our function (the this equivalent), but considering PHP 3 didn't offer programmers any other serious differences between these two options, one could still consider the object model as syntactic sugar for accessing arrays.

People who wanted to use PHP for object-oriented development, especially those using design patterns, quickly found themselves against a brick wall. Luckily, there weren't too many of those people during the PHP 3 era.

PHP 4 improved the situation. The new version introduced the notion of references, which allowed multiple symbols in PHP's symbol space to actually refer to the same place in memory. This means that you could have two or more names for the same variable, as shown in Listing 6.20.

| Listing 6.20 | *PHP 4 references* |
|---|---|

```php
<?php
    $a = 5;

    //$b points to the same place in memory as $a
    $b = &$a;

    //we're changing $b, since $a is pointing to
    //the same place - it changes too
    $b = 7;

    //prints 7
    print $a;
?>
```

Since building networks of objects that point to each other is a fundamental building block of almost all object-oriented design patterns, this new addition to PHP's arsenal was quite significant. However, things were far from being idyllic. While references allowed for building of more powerful object-oriented applications, the fact that PHP treated objects like any other data type brought much agony to those brave enough to try it. As any object-oriented PHP 4 programmer will tell you, such applications suffered from the WTMA (Way Too Many Ampersands) syndrome. To see how annoying things could get if you were trying to build real-world object-oriented applications, consider Listing 6.21.

| Listing 6.21 | *Problems with objects in PHP 4* |
| --- | --- |

```
1    class MyFoo {
2        function MyFoo()
3        {
4            $this->me = &$this;
5            $this->value = 5;
6        }
7
8        function setValue($val)
9        {
10           $this->value = $val;
11       }
12
13       function getValue()
14       {
15           return $this->value;
16       }
17
18       function getValueFromMe()
19       {
20           return $this->me->value;
21       }
22   }
23
24       function CreateObject($class_type)
25       {
26           switch ($class_type) {
27               case "foo":
28                   $obj = new MyFoo();
29                   break;
30               case "bar":
31                   $obj = new MyBar();
32                   break;
33           }
34           return $obj;
35       }
36
37       $global_obj = CreateObject ("foo");
38       $global_obj->setValue(7);
39
40       print "Value is " . $global_obj->getValue() . "\n";
41       print "Value is " . $global_obj->getValueFromMe() . "\n";
```

Let's go through it step by step. We have a class, MyFoo. In the constructor, we keep a reference to ourselves in this->me, and we also set this->value to 5.

We also have three other member functions: one that sets the value of `this->value`, another one that returns the value of `this->value`, and another one that returns the value of `this->value->me`. But wait a minute—aren't `$this` and `$this->me` the same thing? Won't `MyFoo::getValue()` and `MyFoo::getValueFromMe()` always return the same thing?

Let's see. First off, we call `CreateObject("foo")`, which returns an object of type `MyFoo`. Then, we call `MyFoo::setValue(7)`. Finally, we call `MyFoo::getValue()` and `MyFoo::getValueFromMe()`, expecting to get the same result—7.

Of course, if we were to receive 7 in both cases, this would have been one of the most pointless examples in the history of books, so I'm sure you guessed it by now—if there's one result that we will definitely not get, it's two 7s.

But what result will we get, and more importantly, why?

The result we will get is 7 and 5 respectively. As to why—there are actually three good reasons.

First, let's consider the constructor. While we're inside the constructor, we're establishing a reference between `this` and `this->me`. In other words, `this` and `this->me` are virtually the same thing. But the key element in the sentence was *while we're inside the constructor*. As soon as the constructor terminates, PHP has the job of assigning the newly created object (the result of `new MyFoo`, line 28) into `obj`. Since objects are not special and are treated like any other data type in PHP, assigning X to Y means making Y *a copy* of X. In other words, `obj` becomes *a copy* of `new MyFoo`, that is, a copy of the `this` object that we had inside the constructor. What about `obj->me`? Since it is a reference, it stays intact during the copy process and goes on pointing to the same object as it did before—`this` that we had inside the constructor. Voila—`obj` and `obj->me` are no longer the same thing: Changing one will not affect the other.

That was reason number one—and we promised three. Fortunately, you will find the other reasons very similar to the first one. Let's say that miraculously we managed to overcome the problem in the instantiation of the object (line 28). Still, as soon as we assign the return value of `CreateObject` into `global_object`, we would bump into the same problem—`global_object` would become a replica of the return value, and again, `global_object` and `global_object->me` wouldn't have been the same (reason number two).

But, as a matter of fact, we wouldn't have gone that far, even—we would have broken the reference as soon as we returned from `CreateObject` as `return $obj` (line 34, reason number three).

So, how can we fix all this? There are two options. Option one is to add ampersands all over the place, as I have in Listing 6.22 (lines 24, 28, 31, and 37). Option two, if you're lucky enough to be using PHP 5, is to thank your good fortune and forget about all this, as PHP 5 takes care of it for you. Still, if it interests you to understand *how* PHP 5 is taking care of this, read on.

---

**Listing 6.22** *WTMA syndrome in PHP 4*

---

```
1   class MyFoo {
2       function MyFoo()
3       {
4           $this->me = &$this;
5           $this->value = 2;
6       }
7
8       function setValue($val)
9       {
10          $this->value = $val;
11      }
12
13      function getValue()
14      {
15          return $this->value;
16      }
17
18      function getValueFromMe()
19      {
20          return $this->me->value;
21      }
22   };
23
24      function &CreateObject($class_type)
25      {
26          switch ($class_type) {
27              case "foo":
28                  $obj =& new MyFoo();
29                  break;
30              case "bar":
31                  $obj =& new MyBar();
32                  break;
33          }
34          return $obj;
35      }
36
37      $global_obj =& CreateObject ("foo");
38      $global_obj->setValue(7);
39
40      print "Value is " . $global_obj->getValue() . "\n";
41      print "Value is " . $global_obj->getValueFromMe() . "\n";
```

PHP 5 is the first version of PHP to treat objects as different beings, separate from all other types of values. From an end user's perspective, this manifests itself in a very clear way—objects in PHP 5 are always passed by reference, even in situations where other types of values (such as integers, strings, or arrays) are passed by value. Most notably, there is no need to use ampersands at any point in order to pass your objects by reference—they do that out of the box.

If you read the example, the motivation for making objects behave that way should be obvious. Object-oriented programming makes extensive use of object networks and complex relationships between objects, which requires using references. The transparent replication employed by previous versions of PHP, while making good sense when dealing with strings or arrays, is counterintuitive when we're dealing with objects. Therefore, moving objects by reference by default and creating copies only if explicitly requested makes more sense than the other way around.

How is it done?

Before PHP 5, all value types in PHP were stored in a special structure called zval (Zend VALue). These values could store simple values, such as numbers or strings, and complicated values, such as arrays or objects. When sent to or returned from functions, these values were duplicated, creating another structure with identical contents in another place in memory.

With PHP 5, values are still stored in the same way inside zval structures, except for objects. Objects are located elsewhere, in a place called *Object Store,* and are each given identification numbers called *handles*. A zval, instead of storing an object itself, stores a handle of the object. When replicating a zval that holds an object, such as when we're passing an object as a function argument, we no longer copy any data. We simply retain the same object handle and notify the object store that this particular object is now pointed to by another zval. Because the object itself sits in the Object Store, any changes we make to it will be reflected in all of the zval structures that hold its handle. This additional level of indirection makes PHP objects behave as if they're always passed by reference, in a transparent and efficient manner.

We can now go back to our example in Listing 6.21, get rid of all of the ampersands, and everything would still work fine. As a special bonus, there's no need even to use an ampersand when we're keeping a reference to ourselves inside the constructor on line 4.

# I/O and
# Disk Access

**Topics in This Chapter**

- HTTP Connections
- Writing to the Browser
- Output Buffering
- Environment Variables
- Getting Input from Forms
- Passing Arrays in Forms
- Cookies
- File Uploads
- Reading and Writing to Files
- Sessions
- The `include` and `require` Functions
- Don't Trust User Input

# Chapter 7

Ultimately, in order to be useful, a script must communicate with the outside world. We've seen PHP scripts that send text to the browser and get some information from functions like date. In this chapter we examine all the ways a PHP script can exchange data without using special interfaces. This includes reading from local disk drives, connecting to remote machines on the Internet, and receiving form input.

PHP is similar to other programming environments—with one notable exception: User input generally comes from HTML forms. The fields in forms are turned into variables. You can't stop your script in the middle and ask the user a question. This situation provides unique challenges. Each time a script runs, it is devoid of context. It is not aware of what has gone on before unless you make it so.

## 7.1 HTTP Connections

It will be helpful to review how data travels between a browser and a Web server. I will review it simply for purposes of illustration, but you may wish to refer to detailed descriptions, such as those found on the W3C Web site <http://www.w3.org/Protocols/>.

When you type a URL into the location box on your browser, the first task of the browser is to break it up into important parts, the first of which is the protocol, HTTP. Next is the name of the Web server to which the browser makes a connection. The browser must identify the document it wants from the Web server, and it does so using the HTTP protocol. Before completing the request, the browser may provide lines of extra information called headers. These headers let the server know the brand of the browser, the type of documents the browser can accept, and perhaps even the URL of a referring page.

The Web server places these headers into environment variables to conform with the Common Gateway Interface (CGI). When a PHP script begins, PHP converts the environment variables into PHP variables. One of the most useful headers describes the brand and version of the Web browser. This header is sent by the browser as `User-agent`. The Web server creates an environment variable called `HTTP_USER_AGENT` that holds the value of the header. PHP adds an element to the `_SERVER` array with this same name. You can refer to it with `$_SERVER['HTTP_USER_AGENT']`. If you are using Apache, you also have the option of using the `getallheaders` function. It returns an array of all headers exchanged between the browser and the server.

As a PHP script begins to execute, the HTTP exchange is in the stage where some headers have been sent to the browser, but no content has. This is a window of opportunity to send additional headers. You can send headers that cause the browser to ask for authentication, headers that request that the browser cache a page, or headers that redirect the browser to another URL. These are just some of the many HTTP headers you can send using the `header` function. Some common tasks are described in the last section of this book.

PHP places outgoing headers in a list. At the first place where PHP must send content, it dumps all the headers in the list. Once any content is sent, the opportunity to send headers is lost. Content includes any text outside of PHP tags, even if it's just a linefeed. If you try to send a header after content is sent, PHP generates an error message. You can use the `headers_sent` function to test whether it's safe to add more headers to the stack or whether it's too late. Cookies, described below, use headers and therefore are limited in the same way.

As a script runs and sends content, the Web server buffers the output. There is a bit of overhead to every network action, so a small amount of memory temporarily stores the information to be sent out in batches. The Web server owns this buffer. PHP does not have control of it. However, you may request that the buffer be flushed—immediately sent to the browser—by using the `flush` function. This is most useful in long scripts. Both browsers and people have limits to how long they wait for a response, so you can let them know you're making progress by flushing the output.

Two events can make a script halt unexpectedly: when the script runs too long and when the user clicks the stop button. By default, PHP limits scripts to a number of seconds specified in `php.ini`. This is usually 30 seconds, but you can change it. Look for the `max_execution_time` directive. But 30 seconds is a good setting. In case you write a script that could run forever, you want PHP to stop it. Otherwise, a few errant scripts could slow your server to a crawl. For the same reason, you usually want to allow users to be able to abort a page request.

There are times when you do want a script to run to completion, and you can instruct PHP to ignore time limits and user aborts. The `set_time_limit` function resets PHP's timer. See Chapter 15 for a complete description and example. I've written some scripts that run on their own once a night, perhaps doing a lot of work. These scripts I allow to run for an hour or more. Likewise, `ignore_user_abort` tells PHP to continue even after the user clicks the stop button.

Instead of just letting a script run, you may wish it to halt but deal with the reason it halted with special code. To do this, you must first tell PHP to execute a special function whenever a script ends. This is done with `register_shutdown_function`. This function will execute regardless of why a script ended. It even executes when the script ends normally. You can test for the reason with two functions: `connection_aborted` and `connection_timeout`. Chapter 9 discusses these functions.

# 7.2 Writing to the Browser

Three functions in PHP will send text to the browser: `echo`, `print`, and `printf`. Each does the same thing: They take values and print them to the browser. The `printf` function allows you to specify the format of the output rather than sending values as-is. I've used `print` so far in my examples, mostly out of personal preference. I don't usually need the formatting that `printf` provides. Many older PHP examples you will find on the Web use `echo` because it existed in PHP/FI. All three functions are discussed in Chapter 8.

It is important to remember everything you write is in the context of a Web browser. Unless you take measures to make it otherwise, your output will be treated as HTML text. If you send text that is HTML code, it will be decoded by the browser into its intended form. I've been sending `<br>` via `print` throughout the book so far, but Listing 7.1 is a more dramatic example of this concept.

| Listing 7.1 | *Sending HTML with* `print` |

```php
<?php
    print("You're using " .
        $_SERVER['HTTP_USER_AGENT'] .
        " to see this page.<br>\n");
?>
```

Of course, PHP sends anything outside its tags directly to the browser. This is undoubtedly the fastest and least flexible way to send content. You might wonder at this point when it's appropriate to use `print` and when you should place text outside PHP tags. There are issues of efficiency and readability to worry about, but put them aside for now. The final section of the book deals with this issue at length.

## 7.3  Output Buffering

As stated, the Web server buffers content sent to the browser, and you can request that the buffer be flushed. PHP also includes a mechanism for buffering output you can control completely. Among the output buffering functions described in Chapter 8 are `ob_start`, `ob_end_flush`, and `ob_end_clean`.

When you call the `ob_start` function, PHP places anything you send to the browser into a buffer. This includes text outside of PHP tags. The Web server does not receive this content until you call the `ob_end_flush` function. There are several powerful applications of these functions. One is to avoid the problem associated with sending headers. Because PHP sends all headers at once, before any content, you have to take care when using the `header` function. This results in a script design in which early parts of a script are declared a "no output" zone, which can be annoying. If you use output buffering, you can safely add headers to the stack where you wish and delay sending content until the last line of your script.

Another application of these functions is in building HTML tables. Imagine creating a table filled with data from a database. You first print the opening tags for the table. You execute a query and loop over the results being returned. If everything executes without error, you print a closing table tag. If an error occurs within the loop, you may have to abort, and the code that closes the table is never reached. This is bad because of the behavior of Netscape Navigator: It won't display information inside an unclosed table. The solution is to turn on output buffering before assembling the table. If assembly completes successfully, you can flush the buffer. Otherwise, you can use `ob_end_clean`, which throws away anything in the buffer.

## 7.4  Environment Variables

PHP also makes environment variables available. These are the variables that are created when you start a new shell. Some are the standard variables like `PATH`. Others are variables defined by the CGI. Examples are `REMOTE_ADDR` and `HTTP_USER_AGENT`. PHP adds them all to the `_SERVER` array for your convenience.

Similar to environment variables are the variables that PHP itself creates for you. The first is GLOBALS, which is an associative array of every variable available to the script. Exploring this array will reveal all the environment variables as well as a few other variables. Similar to GLOBALS are _GET, _POST, _COOKIE, _SERVER, and _REQUEST. As their names suggest, they are associative arrays of the variables created by the three methods the browser may use to send information to the server. The _REQUEST array merges _GET, _POST, and _COOKIE into one array.

The combination of Web server and operating system will define the set of environment variables. You can always write a script to dump the GLOBALS array to see which are available to you. Alternatively, you can simply view the output of the phpinfo function.

# 7.5  Getting Input from Forms

Sending text to the browser is easy to understand. Getting input from forms is a little tricky. HTML offers several ways to get information from the user via forms. There are text fields, text areas, selection lists, and radio buttons, among others. Each of these becomes a string of text offered to the Web server when the user clicks the submit button.

When someone clicks the submit button in a form, PHP turns each form field into an element of the _REQUEST array. PHP creates them as if you had written the PHP code yourself. This means that if you put two form variables on a page with the same name, the second one may overwrite the value of the first. This allows you to send arrays in form fields, as discussed later in this chapter.

All form fields from the GET method also go into _GET, and all form fields from the POST method go into _POST. In the case where a GET variable and a POST variable share the same name, PHP uses the variables_order directive to determine which to apply first. By default, PHP fills the _REQUEST array with GET variables, then POST variables, and finally cookies. For example, if a cookie and a POST variable share the same name, the cookie value overwrites the value in _REQUEST.

Listing 7.2 is an example of using variables created from form fields. The script expects a variable named color. The first time this page is viewed, color is empty, so the script sets it to be six Fs, the RGB code for pure white. On subsequent calls to the page, the value of the text box contains the background color of the page. Notice that the script also prepopulates the input fields with color. This way, each time you submit the form, it remembers what you entered. As an aside, you should also take note of the technique used here, in which a page calls itself.

| Listing 7.2 | *Getting form input* |
|---|---|

```php
<?php
    print("<html>\n");
    print("<head>\n");
    print("<title>Figure 7-2</title>\n");
    print("</head>\n");

    // if here for the first time
    // use white for bgcolor
    if(!isset($_REQUEST['color']))
    {
        $_REQUEST['color'] = "FFFFFF";
    }

    // open body with background color
    print("<body bgcolor=\"#{$_REQUEST['color']}\">\n");

    // start form, action is this page itself
    print("<form " .
        "action=\"{$_SERVER['PHP_SELF']}\" " .
        "method=\"post\">\n");

    // ask for a color
    print("<b>HTML color:</b> " .
        "<input type=\"text\" name=\"color\" " .
        "value=\"{$_REQUEST['color']}\">\n");

    // show submit button
    print("<input type=\"submit\" value=\"Try It\">\n");

    print("</form>\n");
    print("</body>\n");
    print("</html>\n");
?>
```

# 7.6  Passing Arrays in Forms

Though it may not be apparent, it is possible to pass arrays from a form. To understand how, you must recall how form fields are turned into PHP variables. Each field is read in order by PHP and turned into an assignment statement. An URL such as `http://www.example.com/script.php?name=leon` executes an assignment like `$name = "leon"`. By default, PHP places these assignments into a set of associative arrays.

PHP treats the name of the form field as the left side of an assignment statement. This means that if other special characters appear as part of the name of the field, PHP interprets them accordingly. You can include square brackets to force the variable to be an array. An empty pair of square brackets will add a value to an array using consecutive integers. So, if you name multiple fields in a form with the same name that ends in a pair of empty brackets, an array will be constructed for you when the form is submitted. Listing 7.3 illustrates this method.

**Listing 7.3** *Passing an array via a form*

```php
<?php
    print("<html>\n");
    print("<head>\n");
    print("<title>Listing 7-3</title>\n");
    print("</head>\n");

    print("<body>\n");

    if(isset($_REQUEST['part']))
    {
        print("<h3>Last Burger</h3>\n");
        print("<ul>\n");

        foreach($_REQUEST['part'] as $part)
        {
            print("<li>$part</li>\n");
        }

        print("</ul>\n");
    }

    $option = array("mustard", "ketchup",
        "pickles", "onions", "lettuce", "tomato");

    print("<h3>Create a Burger</h3>\n");
    print("<form action=\"{$_SERVER['PHP_SELF']}\">\n");

    foreach($option as $o)
    {
        print("<input type=\"checkbox\" " .
            "name=\"part[]\" value=\"$o\">" .
            "$o<br>\n");
    }
```

| Listing 7.3 | *Passing an array via a form (cont.)* |

```
    print("<input type=\"submit\">\n");
    print("</form>\n");

    print("</body>\n");
    print("</html>\n");
?>
```

# 7.7 Cookies

Cookies are small strings of data created by a Web server but stored on the client. In addition to having names and values, cookies have an expiration time. Some are set to last for only a matter of minutes. Others persist for months. This allows sites to recognize you without requiring a password when you return. To learn more about cookies, you may wish to visit Netscape's site `<http://developer.netscape.com/docs/manuals/communicator/jsguide4/cookies.htm>`.

Using cookies with PHP is almost as easy as using form fields. Any cookies passed from the browser to the server are converted automatically into entries in _COOKIE and _REQUEST.

If you wish to send a cookie, you use the `setcookie` function, described in Chapter 8. The Web server sends a cookie to the browser as a header. Just like other headers, you must set cookies before sending any content. When you do set a cookie, the browser may refuse to accept it. Many people turn off cookies, so you cannot count on the cookie being present the next time a user requests a page. However, cookies have become so common that it's not unusual for sites to require cookies for certain functionality—it's a design decision.

Setting a cookie does not create a value in _COOKIE—not immediately. When setting a cookie, you are asking the browser to store information that it will return when it next requests a page. Subsequent page requests will cause the cookie to be created as a variable for your use. If you write a script that requires the cookie variable always be set, set it immediately after sending the cookie.

Cookies are a sensitive topic, although they are less so than in the past. Some people view them as intrusive. You are asking someone to store information on their computer, although each cookie is limited in size. My advice with cookies is to keep them minimal. In most cases it is practical to use a single cookie for your entire site. If you can identify that user with a unique ID, you can use that ID to look up information you know about them, such as preferences. Keep in mind that each page load causes the browser to send the cookie. Imagine an extreme case in which you have created ten 1K cookies. That's 10K of data the browser must send with each page request.

# 7.8  File Uploads

A file upload is a special case of getting form input. Half of the task is putting together the correct HTML. File uploads are specified in RFC 1867. They are supported by Netscape Navigator 2 and above as well as by Internet Explorer 4 and above. Placing an input tag inside an HTML form with the type attribute set to `file` causes a text box and a button for browsing the local filesystem to appear on the Web page. Browsers that do not support uploads will likely render this as a text box, so it's best to present uploading forms only to capable browsers. The forms must use the `post` method to allow for uploads, and they must also contain the `enctype` attribute with a value of `multipart/form-data`. A hidden form variable, `MAX_FILE_SIZE`, must precede the file input tag. Its value is the maximum file size in bytes to be accepted.

When the form is submitted, PHP detects the file upload and places it in a temporary directory on the server, such as `/var/tmp`. PHP creates an entry in the `_FILES` array. As with other form fields, PHP uses the name of the form field for the key of the entry in `_FILES`. The entry is an array itself with the elements shown in Table 7.1. For example, you can find the name of an uploaded file from a field named portrait with `$_FILE['portrait']['name']`.

**Table 7.1**   File Upload Array Elements

| Element | Description |
| --- | --- |
| error | An error code matching a constant from Table 7.2. |
| name | The name of the file on the remote client. |
| size | The size of the file in bytes. |
| type | The MIME type of the uploaded file. |
| tmp_name | The path in the local filesystem to the uploaded file. |

**Table 7.2**   File Upload Error Codes

| Error Code | Description |
| --- | --- |
| UPLOAD_ERR_FORM_SIZE | The file exceeds `MAX_FILE_SIZE`. |
| UPLOAD_ERR_INI_SIZE | The file exceeds the `upload_max_filesize` directive. |

**Table 7.2** File Upload Error Codes *(cont.)*

| Error Code | Description |
| --- | --- |
| UPLOAD_ERR_NO_FILE | The browser didn't send a file. |
| UPLOAD_ERR_OK | The upload completed successfully. |
| UPLOAD_ERR_PARTIAL | The browser did not complete the upload. |

If you plan to use the file later, move the new file into a permanent spot. If you do not, PHP will delete the file when it finishes executing the current page request. Listing 7.4 accepts uploads and immediately deletes them.

**Listing 7.4** *File upload*

```
<html>
<head>
<title>Listing 7.4</title>
</head>
<body>
<?php
    //check for file upload
    if(isset($_FILES['upload_test']))
    {
        if($_FILES['upload_test']['error'] != UPLOAD_ERR_OK)
        {
            print("Upload unsuccessful!<br>\n");
        }
        else
        {
                //delete the file
            unlink($_FILES['upload_test']['tmp_name']);

            //show information about the file
            print("Local File: " .
                $_FILES['upload_test']['tmp_name'] .
                "<br>\n");
            print("Name: " .
                $_FILES['upload_test']['name'] .
                "<br>\n");
            print("Size: " .
                $_FILES['upload_test']['size'] .
                "<br>\n");
```

| Listing 7.4 | *File upload (cont.)* |
|---|---|

```php
            print("Type: " .
                $_FILES['upload_test']['type'] .
                "<br>\n");
            print("<hr>\n");
        }
    }
?>

<form enctype="multipart/form-data"
    action="<?= $_SERVER['PHP_SELF'] ?>" method="post">
<input type="hidden" name="MAX_FILE_SIZE" value="1024000">
<input name="upload_test" type="file">
<input type="submit" value="test upload">
</form>
</body>
</html>
```

File uploads are limited in size by a directive in php.ini, upload_max_filesize. It defaults to two megabytes. If a file exceeds this limit, your script will execute as if no file were uploaded. A warning will be generated as well.

# 7.9  Reading and Writing to Files

Communication with files follows the pattern of opening a stream to a file, reading from or writing to it, and then closing the stream. When you open a stream, you get a resource that refers to the open stream. Each time you want to read from or write to the file, you use this stream identifier. Internally, PHP uses this integer to refer to all the necessary information for communicating with the file.

To open a file on the local file system, you use the fopen function. It takes a name of a file and a string that defines the mode of communication. This may be r for read-only or w for write-only, among other modes. It is also possible to specify an Internet address by starting the filename with http:// or ftp:// and following it with a full path including a host name. The file functions are fully defined in Chapter 9.

Two other commonly used functions create file streams. You may open a pipe with the popen function, or you may open a socket connection with the fsockopen function. If you have much experience with UNIX, you will recognize pipes as temporary streams of data between executing programs. A common Perl method for sending mail is to open a pipe to sendmail, the program for sending mail across the Internet. Because PHP has so many built-in functions, it is rarely necessary to open pipes, but it's nice to know it's an option.

You can open a file stream that communicates through TCP/IP with `fsockopen`. This function takes a hostname and a port and attempts to establish a connection. It is described in Chapter 10 along with the rest of the network-related functions.

Once you have opened a file stream, you can read or write to it using commands like `fgets` and `fputs`. Listing 7.5 demonstrates their use. Notice how the script uses a `while` loop to get each line from the example file. It tests for the end of the file with the `feof` function. When you are finished with a file, end of file or not, you call the `fclose` function. PHP will clean up the temporary memory it sets aside for tracking an open file.

---

**Listing 7.5**   *Writing to and reading from file*

```php
<?php
    // open file for writing
    $filename = "/tmp/data.txt";
    if(!($myFile = fopen($filename, "w")))
    {
        print("Error: ");
        print("'$filename' could not be created\n");
        exit;
    }

    //write some lines to the file
    fputs($myFile, "Save this line for later\n");
    fputs($myFile, "Save this line too\n");

    //close the file
    fclose($myFile);

    // open file for reading
    if(!($myFile = fopen($filename, "r")))
    {
        print("Error:");
        print("'$filename' could not be read\n");
        exit;
    }

    while(!feof($myFile))
    {
        //read a line from the file
        $myLine = fgets($myFile, 255);

        print("$myLine<br>\n");
    }

    //close the file
    fclose($myFile);
?>
```

Keep in mind that PHP scripts execute as a specific user. Frequently, this is the "nobody" user. This user probably won't have permission to create files in your Web directories. Take care with allowing your scripts to write in any directory able to be served to remote users. In the simple case where you are saving something like guest book information, you will be allowing anyone to view the entire file. A more serious case occurs when those data files are executed by PHP, which allows remote users to write PHP that could harm your system or steal data. The solution is to place these files outside the Web document tree.

# 7.10  Sessions

If you build a Web application, it's likely you will have information to associate with each user. You may wish to remember the user's name from page to page. You may be collecting information on successive forms. You could attempt to pass the growing body of information from page to page inside hidden form fields, but this is impractical. An elegant solution is to use the idea of a session. Each visitor is assigned a unique identifier with which you reference stored information, perhaps in a file or in a database.

In the past, PHP developers were required to create their own code for handling sessions, but Sascha Schumann and Andrei Zmievski added new functions for session handling to PHP 4. The original system involved registering global variables with the session handler. The preferred method uses the _SESSION array. PHP saves this array in files on the server. When the user requests another page, PHP restores the array.

The session identifier is a long series of numbers and letters sent to the user as a cookie. It is possible that the user will reject the cookie, so PHP creates a constant that allows you to send the session identifier in a URL. The constant is SID and contains a full GET method declaration suitable for attaching to the end of a URL.

Consider Listing 7.6, a simple script that tracks a user's name and the number of times the user has visited the page. To activate sessions, call the session_start function. This sends the cookie to the browser, and therefore it must be called before sending any content. In previous versions of PHP, you had to call session_register for each global variable to be stored in the session. Since PHP 4.1, the _SESSION array provides a better interface to session data.

Listing 7.6 uses two session variables, Name and Count. The former tracks the user's name, and the latter counts the number of times the user views the page. Once placed in _SESSION, these values remain in the session until the session expires or you explicitly unset them. Before starting the HTML document, the example script sets Name with input from a form submission if present, and then it increments the page counter.

| Listing 7.6 | *Using sessions* |

```php
<?php
    //start session
    session_start();

    //Set variable based on form input
    if(isset($_REQUEST['inputName']))
    {
        $_SESSION['Name'] = $_REQUEST['inputName'];
    }

    //Increment counter with each page load
    if(isset($_SESSION['Count']))
    {
        $_SESSION['Count']++;
    }
    else
    {
        //start with count of 1
        $_SESSION['Count'] = 1;
    }

?>
<html>
<head>
<title>Listing 7-6</title>
</head>
<body>
<?php
    //print diagnostic info
    print("<b>Diagnostic Information</b><br>\n");
    print("Session Name: " . session_name() . "<br>\n");
    print("Session ID: " . session_id() . "<br>\n");
    print("Session Module Name: " . session_module_name() .
        "<br>\n");
    print("Session Save Path: " . session_save_path() . "<br>\n");
    print("Encoded Session:" . session_encode() . "<br>\n");

    print("<hr>\n");

    if(isset($_SESSION['Name']))
    {
        print("Hello, {$_SESSION['Name']}!<br>\n");
    }

    print("You have viewed this page " .
        $_SESSION['Count'] . " times!<br>\n");
```

| Listing 7.6 | *Using sessions (cont.)* |
| --- | --- |

```
    //show form for getting name
    print("<form " .
        "action=\"{$_SERVER['PHP_SELF']}\" " .
        "method=\"post\">" .
        "<input type=\"text\" name=\"inputName\" " .
            "value=\"\"><br>\n" .
        "<input type=\"submit\" value=\"change name\"><br>\n" .
        "</form>");

    //use a link to reload this page
    print("<a href=\"{$_SERVER['PHP_SELF']}\">reload</a><br>\n");
?>
</body>
</html>
```

The first bit of content the page provides is diagnostic information about the session. The session name is set inside php.ini along with several other session parameters. It is used to name the cookie holding the session identifier. The identifier itself is a long string of letters and numbers, randomly generated. By default, PHP stores sessions in /tmp using a built-in handler called files. This directory isn't standard on Windows, and if it is not present, sessions will not work correctly.

You have the option of creating your own handler in PHP code using the session_set_save_handler function. Chapter 8 contains an example of a session save handler. PHP encodes session data using serialization, a method for compacting variables into a form suitable for storing as text strings. If you examine the files saved in /tmp, you will find they match the strings returned by session_encode.

As stated earlier, PHP sends session identifiers with cookies, but a browser may refuse them. PHP can detect when a browser does not accept cookies, and in this situation it modifies all forms and links to include the session identifier. It only modifies relative URLs to prevent sending session identifiers to another site. As a backup, you can use the SID constant. It will contain a string consisting of the session name, an equal sign, and the session identifier. This is suitable for placing in a URL. If the browser returns a session cookie to the script, the SID constant will be empty.

# 7.11 The `include` and `require` Functions

The `include` and `require` functions take the path to a file. The file is parsed as if it were a standalone PHP script. This is similar to the `include` directive in C and the `require` directive in Perl. There is a subtle difference between the two functions. When the `require` function is processed, it is replaced with the file it points to. The `include` function acts more like a function call.

The difference is most dramatic inside a loop. Imagine having three files you wanted to execute one after the other. You could put an `include` inside a `for` loop, and if the files were named something like `include1.php`, `include2.php`, and `include3.php`, you would have no problem. You could just build the name based on a counter variable.

If you used `require`, however, you would execute the first file three times. That's because on the first time through the loop, the call to `require` would be replaced with the contents of the file. As I said, the difference is subtle but can be very dramatic.

Listing 7.7 and Listing 7.8 show one possible use of the `include` function. Here we revisit an example from the chapter on arrays. I've taken the definition of the array from the main file and put it into its own file. All the code that matches ways to refer to months with a preferred output form is not necessarily interesting to the main script. It is enough to know that we've included the translation array. This makes the script in Listing 7.8 easier to understand.

| Listing 7.7 | *Included file* |
| --- | --- |

```php
<?php
    /*
    ** Build array for referencing months
    */
    $monthName = array(
        1=>"January", "February", "March",
        "April", "May", "June",
        "July", "August", "September",
        "October", "November", "December",

        "Jan"=>"January", "Feb"=>"February",
        "Mar"=>"March", "Apr"=>"April",
        "May"=>"May", "Jun"=>"June",
        "Jul"=>"July", "Aug"=>"August",
        "Sep"=>"September", "Oct"=>"October",
        "Nov"=>"November", "Dec"=>"December",
```

| Listing 7.7 | *Included file (cont.)* |

```
        "January"=>"January",  "February"=>"February",
        "March"=>"March",  "April"=>"April",
        "May"=>"May",  "June"=>"June",
        "July"=>"July",  "August"=>"August",
        "September"=>"September",  "October"=>"October",
        "November"=>"November",  "December"=>"December"
    );
?>
```

| Listing 7.8 | *Including a file* |

```
<?php
    /*
    ** Get monthName array
    */
    include("7-7.php");

    print("Month 5 is " . $monthName[5] . "<br>\n");
    print("Month Aug is " . $monthName["Aug"] . "<br>\n");
    print("Month June is " . $monthName["June"] . "<br>\n");
?>
```

This strategy of modularization will enhance the readability of your code. It gives the reader a high-level view. If more detail is needed, it takes a few clicks to open the included file. But more than enhancing readability, coding in this way tends to help you write reusable code. Today you may use the translation array for a catalog request form, but in a week you may need it for displaying data from a legacy database. Instead of duplicating the array definition, you can simply include it.

Chapter 27 discusses modularization with `include` in depth.

# 7.12 Don't Trust User Input

The examples in this chapter take a naïve approach to user input. They expect users to send information to the scripts only though the HTML forms. They also assume users won't submit data outside expected values. Some values may be harmless. Giving a word where the script expects a number will simply result in zero. Some values may disturb the user interface. For example, a long string without any spaces may stretch an HTML page to a width that exceeds the viewable area. Randal Schwartz coined the purple dinosaur technique that involves submitting an HTML image tag where an application expects plain text. Some values may actually be harmful, such as shell commands smuggled into text fields.

Malicious users are not limited to using the HTML interface to your forms. They can submit their own values to the Web server directly. They can edit the value in the location box or modify your forms. They can even write program to submit the data they wish to send. You must account for these situations if you wish to protect your server.

One precaution you can take involves massaging user input to fit size and type. If your script expects a numeric ID, use a casting operator. If the script expects text that shouldn't exceed a certain length, use the `substr` function discussed in Chapter 12.

Be aware of the special meaning of any text provided by users. Angle brackets surround HTML tags. If you pass user input out of the browser unchanged, it may contain HTML that changes the way your application behaves. User input can even include JavaScript or links to other sites. This technique is generally called cross-site scripting. If you don't expect HTML in user input, pass it through `htmlentities` before printing it. Likewise, some characters have special meaning to command shells. Never pass unchanged user input to a call to `system`, `exec`, or similar functions. The `escapeshellcmd` function does a good job of adding backslashes to special characters.

# FUNCTIONAL REFERENCE

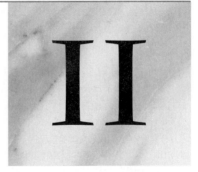

Part **II**

The chapters in this section of the book, Chapters 8 through 14, are a functional reference. They describe how each PHP function works: what arguments are expected, what value is returned, and how they ought to be used. The functions are grouped generally by what they do.

Chapter 8 is concerned with communication with the browser. In addition to printing text, this chapter covers pregenerated variables and HTTP headers.

Chapter 9 discusses interaction with the operating system, including the local filesystem. There are functions for running other programs, functions for reading and writing files, and a collection of functions to help you debug your scripts.

Chapter 10 describes networking functions. There are functions for generalized network I/O and specialized groups of functions for FTP, HTTP and SNMP transfers.

Chapter 11 is all about data structures. There are functions for handling arrays, objects, and your own functions.

Chapter 12 is concerned with transforming strings. This includes cutting strings into pieces, making hash keys, and executing regular expressions.

Chapter 13 is concerned with mathematics. Aside from the standard mathematical functions you expect, PHP offers some unique features for handling arbitrarily large or small numbers.

Chapter 14 describes time and date functions, including support of alternative calendars.

Chapter 15 discusses configuration of PHP. It lists configuration directives and the functions used to manipulate them.

Chapter 16 is a chapter on graphics functions. The GD library allows you to create and manipulate images on the fly.

Chapter 17 describes the most popular database extensions. This includes MySQL and PostgreSQL.

Chapter 18 is concerned with object layers: COM, CORBA, and Java.

Chapter 19 contains miscellaneous functions, most of which interface with specialized libraries, such as functions for communicating with IMAP and mnoGo-Search servers.

Chapter 20 discusses XML functions.

Throughout this section I've used a standard format for showing how a function works. Each description begins with a prototype for the function. This tells you what type of data the function returns and what type of data is expected to be passed. When a function returns nothing, it isn't preceded with a datatype. Likewise, if a function takes no arguments, the parentheses following the function's name are empty.

Following the prototype is a description of the function. If arguments are optional, it's noted. If an argument needs to be passed by reference, it is noted here. If the function is related to another function, it is referred to here as well.

For most functions, after the description, an example appears. It gives you an idea of how the function might work a real script. In many cases I've come up with pieces of code that could be dropped into your own script unaltered. Occasionally, I'll point you to another example in the same section where I've grouped several functions in one clear example. Most of the database functions, for example, make little sense outside the context of a complete script.

# BROWSER I/O

**Topics in This Chapter**

- Pregenerated Variables
- Pregenerated Constants
- Sending Text to the Browser
- Output Buffering
- Session Handling
- HTTP Headers

# Chapter 8

If you are experienced in traditional application development, you may be challenged by the unique characteristics of a stateless operating environment. Your script can't sit in a loop and get input from the user until the quit button is clicked. Although there are ways to force the preservation of state—that is, a collection of variables for each user—I encourage you to work within PHP's world. You may come to find what at first were limitations are refreshing opportunities.

## 8.1 Pregenerated Variables

Before executing a script, PHP creates a set of variables available in a superglobal namespace. They are available inside functions and classes without any extra declaration.

### _COOKIE

The `_COOKIE` variable is an array of cookies sent from the browser to the server. The keys in the array are names of cookies.

### _ENV

The `_ENV` variable is an array of environment variables that existed when the script began. The keys in the array are the names of the environment variables.

## _FILES

The _FILES array (Table 8.1) contains information about uploaded files. The keys to the array are the names of the form variables. Each value is an array of information about each file. See Chapter 7 for a discussion of file uploads.

**Table 8.1**    Elements of _FILES Array

| Element | Description |
| --- | --- |
| error | The error message, if any, associated with the uploaded file. |
| name | The name of the uploaded file as supplied by the uploading browser. |
| size | The size in bytes of the uploaded file. |
| tmp_name | The path in the local file system to the uploaded file. |
| type | The MIME type of the uploaded file, provided by the browser. |

### _GET

The _GET array contains values for all fields passed using the GET method. Keys in this array are the names of the variables passed in the request.

### GLOBALS

The GLOBALS array contains every variable in the global scope.

### php_errormsg

This variable holds a string describing the last error if track_errors is turned on. It's overwritten with each error.

### _POST

The _POST array contains values for all fields passed using the POST method. Keys in this array are the names of the variables passed in the request.

### _REQUEST

The _REQUEST array combines the contents of _GET, _POST, _COOKIES, and _FILES. In the case of variables with identical names, PHP overwrites entries according to the variables_order directive in php.ini.

## _SERVER

The _SERVER array contains information describing the server and its environment. The following list of elements may appear in the _SERVER array, depending on the Web server or if the script is run from a shell.

### argc
If run from the command line, PHP will place an integer in this variable representing the number of arguments passed.

### argv
If run from the command line, PHP will set this variable with an array. Each element of the array represents one argument passed. When running within a Web server, PHP places the query string in this variable.

### DOCUMENT_ROOT
This value contains the path to document root. A typical value for Apache is `/usr/local/apache/htdocs`.

### GATEWAY_INTERFACE
This value describes the version of the Common Gateway Interface (CGI) used by the Web server.

### HTTP_ACCEPT
This value mirrors the Accept header sent by the Web server. It is a comma-delimited list of MIME types.

### HTTP_ACCEPT_CHARSET
This value mirrors the Accept-Charset header sent by the Web server.

### HTTP_ACCEPT_ENCODING
This value mirrors the Accept-Encoding header sent by the Web server.

### HTTP_ACCEPT_LANGUAGE
This value mirrors the Accept-Language header sent by the Web server.

### HTTP_CONNECTION
This value mirrors the Connection header sent by the Web server.

### HTTP_HOST
This value mirrors the Host header sent by the Web server.

**HTTP_REFERER**

This value mirrors the Referer header sent by the browser.

**HTTP_USER_AGENT**

This value mirrors the User-Agent header sent by the browser.

**PATH_TRANSLATED**

This value is the path to the requested PHP script.

**PHP_AUTH_PW**

This value is the password sent by the browser.

**PHP_AUTH_TYPE**

This value describes the authentication type.

**PHP_AUTH_USER**

This value is the user name sent by the browser.

**PHP_SELF**

This value is the path to the requested script relative to the document root.

**QUERY_STRING**

This value is the complete query string.

**REMOTE_ADDR**

This value is the IP address of the browser.

**REMOTE_PORT**

This value is the port on the browser's machine used for receiving data from the server.

**REQUEST_METHOD**

This value describes the method used in the request by the browser. It may contain GET, HEAD, POST, or PUT.

**REQUEST_URI**

This value is the Universal Resource Identifier (URI) requested by the browser. Of the information that appears in a browser's location box, it excludes only the transport protocol and server name.

**SCRIPT_FILENAME**
This value is the path in the server's local filesystem to the requested script.

**SCRIPT_NAME**
This value is the external path to the requested script.

**SERVER_ADMIN**
This value is the email address of the Web server's administrator.

**SERVER_NAME**
This value is the domain name of the server.

**SERVER_PORT**
This value is the port on which the server listens for requests.

**SERVER_PROTOCOL**
This value contains a description of the version of HTTP used by the server.

**SERVER_SIGNATURE**
This value is a description of the server.

**SERVER_SOFTWARE**
This value describes the Web server software.

**_SESSION**
The `_SESSION` array contains variables placed in PHP's built-in sessions.

# 8.2 Pregenerated Constants

**DEFAULT_INCLUDE_PATH**
This constant contains the paths used by `include`, `include_once`, `require`, and `require_once`.

**__CLASS__**
This constant returns the name of the class in which the executing code is. It is an empty string when used outside a class.

**E_ALL**
This constant represents error messages of all levels.

### E_COMPILE_ERROR

This constant represents an error encountered when the Zend Engine attempts to compile the page.

### E_COMPILE_WARNING

This constant represents a problem encountered by the Zend Engine that doesn't halt compilation.

### E_CORE_ERROR

This constant represents an error generated by PHP's core.

### E_CORE_WARNING

This constant represents a warning generated by PHP's core.

### E_ERROR

This constant represents an error encountered by a PHP function that halts execution.

### E_NOTICE

This constant represents a possible error condition reported by a function.

### E_PARSE

This constant represents an error generated by PHP's parser.

### E_USER_ERROR

This constant represents an error generated by `trigger_error`.

### E_USER_NOTICE

This constant represents a notice generated by `trigger_error`.

### E_USER_WARNING

This constant represents a warning generated by `trigger_error`.

### E_WARNING

This constant represents a warning generated by a PHP function. Warnings don't halt script execution.

### __FILE__

This constant holds the full path to the executing script.

## __FUNCTION__

This constant holds the name of the function in which it is viewed.

## __LINE__

This constant holds the line number in the executing script.

## PEAR_EXTENSION_DIR

This constant holds the path where loadable extensions are kept according to PEAR. By default, PEAR sets this to `PHP_EXTENSION_DIR`, but it may be overridden.

## PEAR_INSTALL_DIR

This constant holds the path to the PEAR library, which is usually `/usr/local/lib/php`.

## PHP_BINDIR

This constant holds the path to the PHP command-line executable.

## PHP_CONFIG_FILE_PATH

This constant holds the path to the configuration file, `php.ini`.

## PHP_DATADIR

This constant holds a path to a directory for read-only architecture independent data files used by PHP. A typical value for this constant is `/usr/local/share`. At the time of writing, PHP's core doesn't use this constant.

## PHP_EXTENSION_DIR

This constant holds the default path to loadable extensions.

## PHP_LIBDIR

This constant holds the path to PHP's library of code. In addition to PEAR, there are several other general-purpose functions and classes for your use.

## PHP_LOCALSTATEDIR

This constant holds a path to data files that PHP may need to modify while running. It's usually set to `/usr/local/var`.

## PHP_OS

This constant holds a string describing the operating system. It's no more descriptive than "Linux."

### PHP_OUTPUT_HANDLER_CONT

This constant is used as a flag for the status value returned by `ob_get_status`. If this bit is set, output buffering has begun and the buffer has been flushed.

### PHP_OUTPUT_HANDLER_END

This constant is used as a flag for the status value returned by `ob_get_status`. If this bit is set, output buffering has ended.

### PHP_OUTPUT_HANDLER_START

This constant is used as a flag for the status value returned by `ob_get_status`. If this bit is set, output buffering has begun.

### PHP_SYSCONFDIR

This constant holds the path to files that pertain to the configuration of the server.

### PHP_VERSION

This constant holds a string representing the version of PHP. This is the same value returned by `php_version`. It's common to treat this value as a double in order to enforce a certain version of PHP in a script. See Listing 8.1.

| Listing 8.1 | *Example of testing PHP's version* |
| --- | --- |

```php
<?php
    if(PHP_VERSION < 5.0)
    {
        print('This script requires PHP 5 or better.');
        exit();
    }
?>
```

# 8.3 Sending Text to the Browser

Any text outside PHP tags is automatically sent to the browser. This is as you would expect. Chapter 26 deals with the decision to send text via a PHP function. PHP offers three functions that simply send text to the browser: `echo`, `print`, and `printf`.

### echo string first, string second, ..., string last

The `echo` function (Listing 8.2) sends any number of parameters, separated by commas, to the browser. Each will be converted to a string and printed with no space between them. Unlike most other PHP functions, the `echo` function does not require parentheses. In fact, echo is more of a statement than a function.

| Listing 8.2 | *echo* |
|---|---|

```php
<?php
    echo "First string", 2, 3.4, "last string";
?>
```

### flush()

As text is sent to the browser via functions like `print` and `echo`, it may be stored in a memory buffer and written out only when the buffer fills. The `flush` function (Listing 8.3) attempts to force the buffer to be dumped to the browser immediately. Since the Web server ultimately controls communication with the browser, the flush may not be effective.

PHP provides another layer of output buffering, as described later in this chapter.

| Listing 8.3 | *flush* |
|---|---|

```php
<?php
    //simulate long calculation
    //flush output buffer with each step
    for($n=0; $n<5; $n++)
    {
        print("Calculating...<br>\n");
        flush();
        sleep(3);
    }
    print("Finished!<br>\n");
?>
```

### print(string output)

The output argument of `print` (Listing 8.4) is sent to the browser. Like `echo`, print does not require parentheses.

**Listing 8.4** *print*

```php
<?php
    print("hello world!<br>\n");
?>
```

### printf(string format, …)

The `printf` function (Listing 8.5) converts and outputs arguments to the browser based on a format string. The format string contains codes, listed in Table 8.2, for different data types. These codes begin with a percentage sign, %, and end with a letter that determines the type of data. The codes match up with a list of values that follow the format string in the argument list. Any text outside these codes will be sent unchanged to the browser.

**Listing 8.5** *printf*

```php
<?php
    printf("%-10s %5d %05.5f <br>\n", "a string", 10, 3.14);
?>
```

**Table 8.2**   `printf` Type Specifiers

| Type Specifier | Description |
| --- | --- |
| d | Integer, decimal notation. |
| o | Integer, octal notation. |
| x, X | Integer, hexadecimal notation. x will use lowercase letters; X will use uppercase letters. |
| b | Integer, binary notation. |
| c | Character specified by integer ASCII code. See Appendix B for a complete list of ASCII codes. |
| s | String. |
| f | Double. |
| e | Double, using scientific notation such as 1.2e3. |
| % | Print a percentage sign. This does not require a matching argument. |

You also have the option of placing characters between the % and the type specifier that control how the data is formatted. Immediately following the % you may place any number of flags. These flags control padding and alignment. They are listed in Table 8.3.

**Table 8.3**   `printf` Flags

| Flag | Description |
| --- | --- |
| - | Align text to the left. |
| space | Pad output with spaces. This is the default padding character. |
| 0 | Pad output with zeros. |
| ' plus any character | Pad output with the character. |

After any flags, you may specify a minimum field length. The converted output will be printed in a field at least this wide, longer if necessary. If the output is shorter than the minimum width, it will be padded with a character, a space by default. The padding will normally be placed to the left but, if the - flag is present, padding will be to the right.

Next, you may specify a precision. It must start with a period to separate it from the minimum field length. For strings, the precision is taken to mean a maximum field length. For doubles, the precision is the number of digits that appear after the decimal point. Precision has no meaning for integers.

### vprintf(string format, array values)
The `vprintf` function operates similarly to `printf`, except that values for format codes are passed in an array.

## 8.4  Output Buffering

The output buffering commands add a layer of buffering controlled by PHP in addition to whatever buffering the Web server uses. Some performance penalty may be incurred by adding another layer of buffering, but you may decide the greater control you have is worth the price.

When `ob_start` is called, all output by functions such as `print` and `echo` is held back in a buffer, a large area of memory. The contents of the buffer may be sent to the browser using `ob_end_flush`, or it may be thrown away using `ob_end_clean`. As you recall from Chapter 7, headers cannot be sent after the first content is sent. Therefore, these functions allow you to avoid errors created by sending headers after content.

### ob_clean()

This function erases the contents of the output buffer but does not end output buffering. Following content will accumulate in the buffer.

### ob_end_clean()

The `ob_end_clean` function halts output buffering and eliminates the contents of the buffer. Nothing is sent to the browser.

### ob_end_flush()

The `ob_end_flush` function halts output buffering and sends the contents of the buffer to the browser.

### ob_flush()

The `ob_flush` function sends the contents of the buffer to the browser and erases the buffer.

### string ob_get_clean()

The `ob_get_clean` function returns the contents of the buffer and then empties the buffer. This is exactly what you'd get if you called `ob_getcontents` and then `ob_clean`.

### string ob_get_flush()

The `ob_get_flush` function returns the contents of the buffer, sends the buffer out the browser, and then empties the buffer. This is exactly what you'd get if you called `ob_getcontents` and then `ob_flush`.

### string ob_get_contents()

The `ob_get_contents` function returns the contents of the output buffer.

### integer ob_get_length()

This function returns the number of bytes in the output buffer.

### integer ob_get_level()

The `ob_get_level` function returns the level of output buffer nesting. Each call to `ob_start` begins a new output buffer nested in the outer output buffer. Outside any call to `ob_start`, this function returns 1.

### array ob_get_status(boolean full)

The `ob_get_status` function returns an array describing the current output buffering status. By default, it returns an associative array with the following elements: `level`, `type`, `status`, `name`, `del`. If the `full` argument is set to TRUE, the return value is an array indexed by nesting level. At the time of writing, this function was still in an experimental stage.

### ob_gzhandler(string buffer, integer mode)

The `ob_gzhandler` function returns the given buffer after compressing it with the gzip algorithm. It's meant to be used as a handler for `ob_start`.

### ob_iconv_handler(string buffer, integer mode)

The `ob_iconv_handler` function converts text from internal to external character encoding. It's meant to be used as a handler for `ob_start`. This handler becomes available with the `iconv` extension.

You can set the character set used by this handler with `iconv_set_encoding`. You can get the current character set with `iconv_get_encoding`. You can encode individual strings with `iconv`.

### ob_implicit_flush(boolean on)

This `ob_implicit_flush` function causes PHP to flush the buffer after every instruction that creates output.

### array ob_list_handlers()

The `ob_list_handlers` function returns an array of handlers available.

### ob_start(string callback)

The `ob_start` function (Listing 8.6) begins output buffering. All text sent by `print` and similar functions is saved in a buffer. It will not be sent to the browser until `ob_end_flush` is called. The buffer will also be flushed when the script ends.

The optional `callback` argument allows you pass all output through your own function. The function should accept a string and return a string.

**Listing 8.6**    *ob_start*

```php
<?php
    //begin output buffering
    ob_start();
?>
<html>
<head>
<title>ob_start</title>
</head>
<body>
<?php
    print("At this point ");
    print(strlen(ob_get_contents()));
    print(" characters are in the buffer.<br>\n");
?>
</body>
</html>
<?php
    //add a test header
    header("X-note: COREPHP");

    //dump the contents
    ob_end_flush();
?>
```

# 8.5  Session Handling

The functions in this section work with the session-handling capabilities of PHP. This functionality takes some inspiration from session handling in other technologies, such as Microsoft ASP and PHPLIB. The original vision was one of global variables registered as part of a session that persist with each page load. PHP has moved away from global variables created by the core, and I find it prudent to present these functions in that spirit. I recommend the use of _SESSION rather than turning on register_globals. This leads you toward compact, simple code. Chapter 7 discusses the purpose and use of sessions.

Sessions are managed by passing a cookie with a unique value between the server and the browser. This cookie indexes an entry in a systemwide session cache. All values in _SESSION are written into the cache when a script completes. PHP restores the contents of _SESSION on the next request. You may start a session manually with session_start, or you can configure PHP to automatically start sessions with the session.auto_start directive in php.ini.

Listing 8.7 creates a session and initializes it with three variables. The script increments a counter with each request, which proves that PHP is keeping the counter value in the session and updating after the script finishes.

| Listing 8.7 | *Session variables* |
| --- | --- |

```php
<?php
    //start session
    session_start();

    //initialize a set of session variables
    if(!isset($_SESSION['a']))
    {
        print("Initializing Session<br>");

        $_SESSION['a'] = 'Session Var A';
        $_SESSION['b'] = 123.45;
        $_SESSION['c'] = 0;
    }

    //update session with access count
    $_SESSION['c']++;

    print("Access count: " . $_SESSION['c'] . "<br>");

    print("Session Dump: " . session_encode() . "<br>");
?>
```

As sessions use cookies, keep in mind that cookies are matched to specific domains. You may find that sessions created for www1.yourdomain.com are lost when a browser moves to www2.yourdomain.com. You can cope with this in many cases by editing php.ini or using session_set_cookie_params.

### boolean output_add_rewrite_var(string name, string value)

The output_add_rewrite_var function adds a variable and its value to the registry of variables added to all URLs. The session handler uses this functionality to add the session identifier to anchor tags you send to the browser.

### boolean output_reset_rewrite_vars()

The output_reset_rewrite_vars function erases the registry of variables added to all URLs.

### integer session_cache_expire(integer minutes)

The `session_cache_expire` function returns the number of minutes a session is allowed to remain idle before it expires and the system removes it. Optionally, you may provide a new expiration value. By default, sessions expire after 180 minutes.

### string session_cache_limiter(string limiter)

The `session_cache_limiter` function returns the method for limiting caching of generated pages by browsers. The optional argument allows you to change the limiter. By default, the session system uses the `nocache` setting, which prevents most browsers from keeping a page in the cache.

PHP's sessions handling assumes that pages requiring session identifiers will contain data that immediately expires. It's a reasonable assumption, but it's not always true. This function allows you to override the setting in `php.ini`. Table 8.4 shows the four choices for limiters and the HTTP headers they produce. November 19, 1981, is simply a date in the past that forces browsers to keep a page out the cache; 10800 is the number of seconds in 180 minutes and may vary depending on the value set with `session_cache_expire`. The expiration time given by the `public` limiter is the current time.

**Table 8.4**  Session Cache Limiters

| Limiter | HTTP Headers Sent |
| --- | --- |
| nocache | Expires: Thu, 19 Nov 1981 08:52:00 GMT<br>Cache-Control: no-store, no-cache,<br>must-revalidate, post-check=0, pre-check=0<br>Pragma: no-cache |
| private | Expires: Thu, 19 Nov 1981 08:52:00 GMT<br>Cache-Control: private, max-age=10800,<br>pre-check=10800 |
| private_no_expire | Cache-Control: private, max-age=10800,<br>pre-check=10800 |
| public | Expires: Mon, 23 Jun 2003 19:32:00 GMT<br>Cache-Control: public, max-age=10800 |

Refer to the HTTP/1.1 specification <http://www.w3.org/Protocols/rfc2068/rfc2068> to better understand the headers in Table 8.4.

### boolean session_decode(string code)

Use `session_decode` to read encoded session data and set the values of global variables in the session. This happens automatically when you start a session with `session_start`.

### boolean session_destroy()

The `session_destroy` function eliminates all the data stored in the session. It does not destroy any global variables associated with the session, however.

### string session_encode()

The `session_encode` function returns a string that contains encoded information about the current session.

### array session_get_cookie_params()

The `session_get_cookie_params` function returns an array describing the session's cookie. The returned array contains the following keys: domain, lifetime, path, secure.

### string session_id(string id)

Use `session_id` to get the value of the session identifier. If you wish to change the session identifier, supply the optional `id` argument. If you do, take care to do so before calling `session_start`. The default session handler accepts only letters and numbers in session identifiers.

### boolean session_is_registered(string name)

The `session_is_registered` function returns TRUE if the specified variable is registered with the session. Note that this function expects the name of the variable, not the variable itself. Instead of using this function, check for an entry in `_SESSION`.

### string session_module_name(string name)

The `session_module_name` function returns the name of the module that handles session duties. This is the same value set by the `session.save_handler` directive inside `php.ini`. You can change the module name if you supply the optional `name` argument. The default module is named `files`. If you compile PHP using the `--with-mm` configuration, you can set the session module to `mm`. This module uses shared memory for storing sessions.

If you wish to implement your own handler in PHP, see the `session_set_save_handler` function.

### string session_name(string name)

The `session_name` function returns the current name for the session variable. The session may be renamed with the optional `name` argument. This name is used as the name of the cookie that contains the session identifier. It's also used for the back-up `GET` variable. If you wish to override the name of the session defined in `php.ini`, you must do so prior to registering any variables or starting the session.

### session_readonly()

This function reads in the session data without locking it against writing from other processes.

### boolean session_regenerate_id()

The `session_regenerate_id` function makes a new session identifier for the current session.

### boolean session_register(...)

The `session_register` function accepts any number of arguments, each of which may be a string or an array. Each argument names a global variable that will be attached to the session. Arrays passed as arguments will be traversed for elements. You can even pass multidimensional arrays. Each registered variable that is set when the script ends will be serialized and written into the session information. When the user returns with a later request, the variables will be restored.

Note that this function expects the name of the variable as a string, not the variable itself. Because this function works on global variables, it isn't as interesting as it once was. You are encouraged to set values in `_SESSION` directly.

### string session_save_path(string path)

The `session_save_path` function returns the path in the file system used to save serialized session information. This is `/tmp` by default. The optional `path` argument will change the path. Keep in mind that the permissions for this directory must include read/write access for the Web server.

### session_set_cookie_params(integer lifetime, string path, string domain, bool secure)

The `session_set_cookie_params` function sets the four parameters used for session cookies. You are required to supply the lifetime only.

**session_set_save_handler(string open, string close, string read, string write, string destroy, string garbage)**

The `session_set_save_handler` function allows you to implement an alternative method for handling sessions. Each argument is the name of a function for handling a certain aspect of the session-handling process. See Table 8.5. You can implement these as standalone functions or as class methods. If you choose the latter, as I have in Listing 8.8, you must pass the method names as two-element arrays. The first element should reference an object or class. The second element names the method. If you wish to use static methods, pass the name of the class. If you wish to use an object, pass the reference to the object as the first element, as I have done below.

**Table 8.5**  Functions for Use with `session_set_save_handler`

| Function | Arguments | Description |
| --- | --- | --- |
| open | string path, string name | Begins the session. |
| close | none | Ends the session. |
| read | string id | Returns the encoded session data. |
| write | string id, data | Writes encoded session data. |
| destroy | none | Removes session from data store. |
| garbage | integer lifetime | Cleans up stale sessions. |

**Listing 8.8**  *Session save handler*

```php
<?php
    class mySession
    {
        //prefix with which to mark session files
        var $mark;

        //path for storing session files
        var $path;

        //name of session cookie
        var $name;


        function mySession($mark='mySession_')
        {
            $this->mark = $mark;
        }
```

**Listing 8.8**   *Session save handler (cont.)*

```php
function getFilePath($id)
{
    return($this->path . '/' . $this->mark . $id);
}

function open($path, $name)
{
    $this->path = $path;
    $this->name = $name;

    return(TRUE);
}

function close()
{
    return(TRUE);
}

function read($id)
{
    if($fp = @fopen(getFilePath($id), "r"))
    {
        return(fread($fp,
                filesize($this->getFilePath($id))));
    }
    else
    {
        return("");
    }
}

function write($id, $data)
{
    if($fp = @fopen($this->getFilePath($id), "w"))
    {
        return(fwrite($fp, $data));
    }
    else
    {
        return(FALSE);
    }
}

function destroy($id)
{
    return(@unlink($this->getFilePath($id)));
}
```

**Listing 8.8**   *Session save handler (cont.)*

```php
    function garbage($lifetime)
    {
        $d = dir($this->path);

        while($f = $d->read())
        {
            //file begins with mark and it's too old
            if((strpos($f, $this->mark) == 0) AND
                (time() > (fileatime($f) + $lifetime)))
            {
                unlink("$this->path/$f");
            }

        }
        $d->close();
        return(TRUE);
    }
}

$s = new mySession();

session_set_save_handler(
    array($s, 'open'),
    array($s, 'close'),
    array($s, 'read'),
    array($s, 'write'),
    array($s, 'destroy'),
    array($s, 'garbage')
    );

//start session
session_start();

//initialize a set of session variables
if(!isset($_SESSION['a']))
{
    print("Initializing Session<br>");

    $_SESSION['a'] = 'Session Var A';
    $_SESSION['b'] = 123.45;
    $_SESSION['c'] = 0;
}

//update session with access count
$_SESSION['c']++;

print("Access count: " . $_SESSION['c'] . "<br>");

print("Session Dump: " . session_encode() . "<br>");
?>
```

### boolean session_start()

Use session_start to activate a session. If no session exists, one will be created. Since this involves sending a cookie, you must call session_start before sending any text to the browser. You can avoid using this function by configuring PHP to automatically start sessions with each request. This is done with the session.auto_start directive in php.ini. Once you start a session, the contents of the _SESSION array are preserved for the session user.

### boolean session_unregister(string name)

Use session_unregister to remove a global variable from the session. It will not be saved with the session when the script ends. Instead of using this function, remove the appropriate entry from the _SESSION array.

### session_unset()

The session_unset function clears all session variables from _SESSION.

### session_write_close()

This function immediately writes the session to save handler. Ordinarily, PHP will write session variables when output to the browser finishes, making this function unnecessary. If you have simultaneous connections using the same session, as you would with an HTML frameset, you may improve throughput by closing sessions manually. Otherwise, each request will block until the locks on the session are released. This has the visual affect of loading each frame, one at a time.

## 8.6  HTTP Headers

HTTP headers are special commands sent between the browser and Web server before the browser receives any content. Some of the headers let the server know which file the browser wants. Others may instruct the browser about the type of file it will soon send. To learn more about headers, refer to the HTTP specification, originally described in RFC 1945 and currently described in RFC 2616. It and other documents may be found at the W3C site, which has a section devoted to the HTTP protocol <http://www.w3.org/Protocols/>. For an overview of how headers work with PHP, turn back to Chapter 7.

## boolean header(string http_header, boolean replace, integer response)

The `header` function (Listing 8.9) sends an HTTP header to the browser. Unless you use the output buffering described earlier in this chapter, `header` must be called before any output is sent to the browser. You may wish to turn back to the description of HTTP connections in Chapter 7. Many different kinds of headers may be sent. Perhaps the most common is a location header, which redirects the browser to another URI.

Each time you call `header`, the HTTP is added to a list that's dumped to the browser when the first output is sent to the browser. The headers are sent in the same order you created them. Setting a header a second time will replace the previous value unless you set the optional second argument to FALSE, in which case PHP will send both headers.

The optional third argument sets the HTTP response code returned by the server.

PHP treats two header cases specially. The first is when you send the response header. This is the first line returned by a Web server. PHP detects this by looking for HTTP/ at the beginning of the string you pass to `header`. PHP will always send this header first.

The other special case concerns the `Location` header. PHP will change the response code to 302 to match `Location` headers unless you set the response header manually to a value that begins with 3.

Headers are also used to send cookies, but PHP's `setcookie` function is better suited for this purpose.

One common trick the `header` function provides is sending a user to another page, as demonstrated in the example below. Another is to force the browser to either download the file or display it in an OLE container. This is done by setting the `Content-type` header, which PHP defaults to `text/html`. Sending a value of `application/octet-stream` will cause most browsers to prompt the user for where to save the file. You can also use other MIME types to get the browser to run a helper application. For example, if you use `application/vnd.ms-excel`, a Windows machine with Microsoft Excel installed will launch Excel in an OLE container inside the browser window. In this case you don't need to send an actual Excel file. A simple tab-delimited file will be interpreted correctly.

| Listing 8.9 | *header* |
|---|---|

```php
<?php
    // redirect request to another address
    header("Location: http://www.leonatkinson.com/");
?>
```

### boolean setcookie(string name, string value, integer expire, string path, string domain, integer secure)

Use `setcookie` (Listing 8.10) to set a cookie to the browser. Cookies are sent as headers during an HTTP connection. Since cookie headers are more complex than other headers, it is nice to have a function specifically for sending cookies. Keep in mind that all headers must be sent prior to any content. Also, calling `setcookie` does not create a PHP variable until the cookie is set back by the browser on the next page load.

If `setcookie` is called with only the name argument, the cookie will be deleted from the browser's cookie database. Otherwise, a cookie will be created on the client browser with the name and value given.

The optional `expire` argument sets a time when the cookie will automatically be deleted by the browser. This takes the form of seconds since January 1, 1970. PHP converts this into Greenwich Mean Time and the proper form for the Set-Cookie header. If the expire argument is omitted, the browser will delete the cookie when the session ends. Usually, this means when the browser application is shut down.

The `path` and `domain` arguments are used by the browser to determine whether to send the cookie. The hostname of the Web server is compared to the domain. If it is left empty, the complete hostname of the server setting the cookie is used. The path is matched against the beginning of the path on the server to the document. The cookie specification requires that domains contain two periods. This is to prevent scripts that get sent to every top-level domain (`.com`, `.edu`, `.net`). It also prevents a domain value of `leonatkinson.com`. Just remember to add a leading dot.

The `secure` argument is used to tell the browser to send the cookie only over secure connections that use Secure Socket Layers. Use a value of 1 to denote a secure cookie.

Like other headers, those created by the `setcookie` function are pushed onto a stack, which causes them to be sent in reverse order. If you set the same cookie more than once, the first call to `setcookie` will be executed last. Most likely, this isn't what you intend. Keep track of the value you intend to set as the value of the cookie, and call `setcookie` once.

Netscape, which developed cookies, offers more information about them in a document titled "Persistent Client State: HTTP Cookies." Its URL is `<http://developer.netscape.com/docs/manuals/communicator/jsguide4/cookies.htm>`.

How do you know if a browser accepts your cookie? The only way is to send one and test that it is returned on the next page request.

**Listing 8.10**  *setcookie*

```php
<?php
    /*
    ** mark this site as being visited
    ** for the next 24 hours
    */
    setcookie("HasVisitedLast24Hours", "Yes", time()+86400);
?>
```

# OPERATING SYSTEM

## Topics in This Chapter

- Files
- Compressed File Functions
- Direct I/O
- Debugging
- POSIX
- Shell Commands
- Process Control

# Chapter 9

This chapter describes functions that interact with the operating system and the underlying hardware. Most of these functions deal with files. Others interact with command shells, allowing you to execute programs. Additionally, this chapter discusses debugging functions that return reflexive information about PHP.

## 9.1 Files

These functions manipulate or return information about files. Many of them are wrappers for the commands you execute in a UNIX or Windows command shell. When the functions in this section call for a filename or a directory, you may name a file in the same directory as the script itself. You may also use a full or relative path. The . and .. directories are valid in both UNIX and Windows. You may also specify drive letters on a Windows machine. Backslashes can delimit directories and filenames when running under Windows, but forward slashes are interpreted correctly, so stick with them.

### boolean chdir(string directory)

When a PHP script begins to execute, its default path is the path to the script itself. That is, if the fully qualified path to the script were /users/leon/ public_html/somescript.php, then all relative paths would work off /users/leon/public_html/. You may change this default path with the chdir function (Listing 9.1). It returns TRUE if the change was made, FALSE if the script was unable to change directories.

---

**Listing 9.1** *chdir*

```php
<?php
    if(chdir("/tmp"))
    {
        print("current directory is /tmp");
    }
    else
    {
        print("unable to change to /tmp");
    }
?>
```

---

### boolean chgrp(string filename, string group)

The chgrp function (Listing 9.2) invokes the UNIX idea of changing the group to which a file belongs. If successful, TRUE is returned. If the group cannot be changed, FALSE is returned. Under Windows this function always returns TRUE and leaves the file unchanged. Two similar functions are chmod and chown. If you want to find the group to which a file is currently assigned, use the filegroup function. You may wish to refer to the UNIX man page for the shell command of the same name.

---

**Listing 9.2** *chgrp*

```php
<?php
    if(chgrp("log.txt", "editors"))
    {
        print("log.txt changed to editors group");
    }
    else
    {
        print("log.txt not changed to editors group");
    }
?>
```

---

## boolean chmod(string filename, integer mode)

The chmod function (Listing 9.3) sets the UNIX permissions for the given file based on the mode supplied. The mode is interpreted like the UNIX shell command except that it is not converted to octal. Unless prefixed with a 0, chmode is treated as a decimal number.

Under UNIX, three octal numbers specify access privileges for owner, group, and others respectively. The modes may be added in order to combine privileges. For example, to make a file readable and executable, use mode 5. Refer to Table 9.1. You also may wish to refer to the man page for chmod on your UNIX system.

**Table 9.1**   File Modes

| Mode | Description |
|------|-------------|
| 0 | No access |
| 1 | Execute |
| 2 | Write |
| 4 | Read |

Under Windows, chmod has limited use. The modes described in Table 9.2 are defined by Microsoft. They may be combined with the bitwise-OR (|) but in practice only write permission has any meaning. All files in Windows are readable, and the file extension determines whether the file will execute.

**Table 9.2**   Windows File Modes

| Mode | Description |
|------|-------------|
| 0000400 | Read permission, owner |
| 0000200 | Write permission, owner |
| 0000100 | Execute/search permission, owner |

This function is part of a group of three functions that change similar information about files. The other two are chgrp and chown. The fileperms function will tell you the file's current modes.

| Listing 9.3 | *chmod* |
|---|---|

```php
<?php
    /*
    ** allow everyone to read and write to file
    ** when running PHP under UNIX
    */
    if(chmod("data.txt", 0666))
    {
        print("mode change successful");
    }
    else
    {
        print("mode change unsuccessful");
    }
?>
```

### boolean chown(string filename, string user)

The owner of the named file is changed by the chown function (Listing 9.4). If successful, TRUE is returned. Otherwise, the function returns FALSE. Under Windows, this function does nothing and always returns TRUE. This function is similar to chgrp and chmod. If you need to know the current owner of a file, use the fileowner function.

| Listing 9.4 | *chown* |
|---|---|

```php
<?php
    /*
    ** change owner to leon
    */
    if(chown("data.txt", "leon"))
    {
        print("owner changed");
    }
    else
    {
        print("couldn't change owner");
    }
?>
```

### boolean chroot(string path)

The `chroot` function changes the root directory to the given path. This disallows all access to any directories above the root. This change will remain with the server process until it ends, which means it may not be useful when PHP runs as an Apache module. This function is not available on Windows.

### closedir(integer directory_handle)

The `closedir` function (Listing 9.5) closes a directory after it has been opened with the `opendir` function. PHP will close a directory connection for you when the script ends, so use of this function is not strictly necessary.

| Listing 9.5 | *closedir* |
| --- | --- |

```php
<?php
    // print the current directory in unordered list
    print("<ul>\n");

    // open directory
    $myDirectory = opendir(".");

    // get each entry
    while(FALSE !== ($entryName = readdir($myDirectory)))
    {
            print("<li>$entryName</li>\n");
    }

    // close directory
    closedir($myDirectory);

    print("</ul>\n");
?>
```

### boolean copy(string source, string destination)

The `copy` function (Listing 9.6) copies a file specified by the `source` argument into the file specified by the `destination` argument. This results in two separate and identical files. You may wish to create a link to the file instead, in which case you should use `link` or `symlink`. If you wish to move a file to another directory, consider `rename`.

This function supports URLs for both arguments.

**Listing 9.6** *copy*

```php
<?php
    if(copy("data.txt", "/tmp/data.txt"))
    {
        print("data.txt copied to /tmp");
    }
    else
    {
        print("data.txt could not be copied");
    }
?>
```

### float disk_free_space(string path)

The `disk_free_space` function (Listing 9.7) returns the number of free bytes for the given path.

**Listing 9.7** *disk_free_space*

```php
<?php
    $total = disk_total_space("/");
    $free = disk_free_space("/");
    $ratio = sprintf("%.2f", $free/$total*100.00);

    print("Disk Usage: $ratio% free ($free/$total)");
?>
```

### float disk_total_space(string path)

This function returns the number of bytes of disk space in the given path.

### object dir(string directory)

The `dir` function (Listing 9.8) creates a directory object to be used as an alternative to the group of functions that includes `opendir` and `closedir`. The returned object has two properties: `handle` and `path`. The `handle` property can be used with other directory functions, such as `readdir`, as if it were created with `opendir`. The `path` property is the string used to create the directory object. The object has three methods: `read`, `rewind`, and `close`. These behave exactly like `readdir`, `rewinddir`, and `closedir`.

| Listing 9.8 | *dir* |
|---|---|

```php
<?php
    // print the current directory in unordered list
    print("<ul>\n");

    // open directory
    $myDirectory = dir(".");

    // get each entry
    while(FALSE !== ($entryName = $myDirectory->read()))
    {
        print("<li>$entryName</li>\n");
    }

    // close directory
    $myDirectory->close();

    print("</ul>\n");
?>
```

### boolean fclose(resource file)

The `fclose` function (Listing 9.9) closes an open file. When a file is opened, you are given an integer that represents a file handle. This file handle is used to close the file when you are finished using it. The functions used to open files are `fopen` and `fsockopen`. To close a pipe, use `pclose`.

| Listing 9.9 | *fclose* |
|---|---|

```php
<?php
    // open file for reading
    $myFile = fopen("data.txt", "r");

    // make sure the open was successful
    if(!($myFile))
    {
        print("file could not be opened");
        exit;
    }

    while(!feof($myFile))
    {
```

**Listing 9.9** *fclose (cont.)*

```
        // read a line from the file
        $myLine = fgets($myFile, 255);
        print("$myLine <br>\n");
    }

    // close the file
    fclose($myFile);
?>
```

### boolean feof(resource file)

As you read from a file, PHP keeps a pointer to the last place in the file you read. The feof function returns TRUE if you are at the end of the file. It is most often used in the conditional part of a while loop where a file is being read from start to finish. See Listing 9.9 for an example of use. If you need to know the exact position you are reading from, use the ftell function.

### boolean fflush(resource file)

The fflush function flushes any buffers associated with the given file handle, as returned by fopen, fsockopen, or popen. If you wish to flush buffers used for data sent to the browser, turn back to Chapter 8 and read about flush and ob_flush.

### string fgetc(resource file)

The fgetc function (Listing 9.10) returns a single character from a file. It expects a file handle as returned by fopen, fsockopen, or popen. Some other functions for reading from a file are fgetcsv, fgets, fgetss, fread, and gzgetc.

**Listing 9.10** *fgetc*

```php
<?php
    // open file and print each character
    if($myFile = fopen("data.txt", "r"))
    {
        while(!feof($myFile))
        {
            $myCharacter = fgetc($myFile);
            print($myCharacter);
        }

        fclose($myFile);
    }
?>
```

### array fgetcsv(resource file, integer length, string separator)

The `fgetcsv` function (Listing 9.11) is used for reading comma-separated data from a file. It requires a valid file handle as returned by `fopen`, `fsockopen`, or `popen`. It also requires a maximum line length. The optional `separator` argument specifies the character to separate fields. If left out, a comma is used. Fields may be surrounded by double quotes, which allow embedding of commas and linebreaks in fields. The return value is an array containing one field per element, starting with element zero.

**Listing 9.11**   *fgetcsv*

```
<?
    // open file
    if($myFile = fopen("data.csv", "r"))
    {
        print("<table border=\"1\">\n");

        while(!feof($myFile))
        {
            print("<tr>\n");

            $myField = fgetcsv($myFile, 1024);

            $fieldCount = count($myField);
            for($n=0; $n<$fieldCount; $n++)
            {
                print("\t<td>");
                print($myField[$n]);
                print("</td>\n");
            }

            print("</tr>\n");
        }

        fclose($myFile);

        print("</table>\n");
    }
?>
```

### string fgets(resource file, integer length)

The `fgets` function (Listing 9.12) returns a string that it reads from a file specified by the file handle, which must have been created with `fopen`, `fsockopen`, or `popen`. It will attempt to read as many characters as specified by the `length` argument less one. If you leave out the `length` argument, PHP defaults it to

1024. A linebreak character is treated as a stopping point, as is the end of the file. Linebreaks are included in the returned string. Keep in mind that different operating systems use different linebreaks. Some other functions for reading from a file are `fgetc`, `fgetcsv`, `fgetss`, `fread`, and `gzgets`.

---

**Listing 9.12**   *fgets*

```php
<?php
    // open file and print each line
    if($myFile = fopen("data.txt", "r"))
    {
        while(!feof($myFile))
        {
            $myLine = fgets($myFile, 255);
            print($myLine);
        }
        fclose($myFile);
    }
?>
```

---

### string fgetss(resource file, integer length, string ignore)

The `fgetss` function (Listing 9.13) is in all respects identical to `fgets` except that it attempts to strip any HTML or PHP code before returning a string. The optional `ignore` argument specifies tags that are allowed to pass through unchanged. Note that if you wish to ignore a tag, you need only specify the opening form. Some other functions for reading from a file are `fgetc`, `fgetcsv`, `fgetss`, `fread`, and `gzgets`. If you wish to preserve HTML but prevent it from being interpreted, you can use the `htmlentities` function.

---

**Listing 9.13**   *fgetss*

```php
<?php
    // open file and print each line,
    //stripping HTML except for anchor tags
    if($myFile = fopen("index.html", "r"))
    {
        while(!feof($myFile))
        {
            $myLine = fgetss($myFile, 1024, "<a>");
            print($myLine);
        }
        fclose($myFile);
    }
?>
```

### array file(string filename, boolean use_include_path)

The `file` function returns an entire file as an array. Each line of the file is a separate element of the array, starting at zero. Linebreaks are included in each array element. The optional `use_include_path` argument causes PHP to search for the file in your default include path.

Prior to the introduction of `file_get_contents`, many PHP scripts used the `implode` function to combine all lines into one string, as in Listing 9.14.

The `file` function is not binary-safe. That is, it is not appropriate for working with binary files that may contain NUL characters.

If you are planning on sending a file directly to browser, use `readfile` instead.

**Listing 9.14** *file*

```php
<?php
    // open file
    $myFile = file("data.txt");

    //fold array elements into one string
    $myFile = implode("", $myFile);

    //print entire file
    print($myFile);
?>
```

### boolean file_exists(string filename)

The `file_exists` function returns TRUE if the specified file exists and FALSE if it does not. This function is a nice way to avoid errors with the other file functions. Listing 9.15 tests that a file exists before trying to send it to the browser.

Unlike many other file system functions, this function does not accept URLs. You may attempt to check for the existence of a file by using `fopen` and suppressing error messages with the @ operator. Beware that a Web server will usually return a 404 error document for a missing file, which makes the file appear to be available. You may need a more sophisticated solution that looks at the response code from the Web server in this situation.

| Listing 9.15 | *file_exists* |
|---|---|

```php
<?php
    $filename = "data.txt";

    //if the file exists, print it
    if(file_exists($filename))
    {
        readfile($filename);
    }
    else
    {
        print("'$filename' does not exist");
    }
?>
```

### string file_get_contents(string filename, boolean use_include_path)

This `file_get_contents` function returns the entire contents of the named files as a string. This function is binary-safe, which makes it appropriate for loading image files. The optional `use_include_path` argument causes PHP to search for the file in the default include path. This function will read files specified by URLs. If you are planning on sending a file directly to browser, use `readfile` instead.

### boolean file_~~set~~put_contents(string filename, string contents)

The `file_set_contents` function creates the named file with the given contents. If the file exists, PHP replaces it.

### integer fileatime(string filename)

The `fileatime` function (Listing 9.16) returns the last access time for a file in standard timestamp format, the number of seconds since January 1, 1970. FALSE is returned if there is an error. A file is considered accessed if it is created, written, or read. Unlike some other file-related functions, `fileatime` operates identically on Windows and UNIX. Two other functions for getting timestamps associated with files are `filectime` and `filemtime`.

**Listing 9.16** *fileatime, filectime, filemtime*

```php
<?php
    $filename = 'data.txt';
    $LastAccess = fileatime($filename);
    $LastChange = filectime($filename);
    $LastMod = filemtime($filename);

    print("Last access was " .
        date("l F d, Y", $LastAccess) .
        "<br>\n");

    print("Last change was " .
        date("l F d, Y", $LastChange) .
        "<br>\n");

    print("Last modification was " .
        date("l F d, Y", $LastMod) .
        "<br>\n");
?>
```

### integer filectime(string filename)

When running on UNIX, the `filectime` function returns the last time a file was changed in standard timestamp format, the number of seconds since January 1, 1970. A file is considered changed if it is created or written to or its permissions have been changed. When running on Windows, `filectime` returns the time the file was created. If an error occurs, FALSE is returned. Two other functions for getting timestamps associated with files are `fileatime` and `filemtime`.

### integer filegroup(string filename)

The `filegroup` function (Listing 9.17) returns the group identifier for the given file, or FALSE when there is an error. This function always returns FALSE under Windows. Other functions that return information about a file are `fileinode`, `fileowner`, and `fileperms`. To change a file's group, use `chgrp`.

| Listing 9.17 | *filegroup, fileinode, fileowner, fileperms, filesize, filetype* |
|---|---|

```php
<?php
    $filename = 'data.txt';

    $groupID = filegroup($filename);
    $groupInfo = posix_getgrgid($groupID);

    $inode = fileinode($filename);

    $userID = fileowner($filename);
    $userInfo = posix_getpwuid($userID);

    print("Filename: $filename<br>\n");
    print("Group: $groupID [{$groupInfo['name']}]<br>\n");
    print("Owner: $userID [{$userInfo['name']}]<br>\n");
    printf("Permissions: %o<br>\n", (fileperms($filename)
        & 0777));
    print("Size: " . filesize($filename) . "<br>\n");
    print("Type: " . filetype($filename) . "<br>\n");
?>
```

### integer fileinode(string filename)

The `fileinode` function returns the inode of the given file, or FALSE on error. This function always returns FALSE under Windows. Similar functions are `filegroup`, `fileowner`, and `fileperms`.

### integer filemtime(string filename)

The `filemtime` function returns the last time a file was modified in standard timestamp format, the number of seconds since January 1, 1970. FALSE is returned if there is an error. A file is considered modified when it is created or its contents change. Operation of this function is identical under any operating system. There are two other functions related to timestamps on files: `fileatime` and `filectime`.

### integer fileowner(string filename)

The `fileowner` function returns the user identifier of the owner, or FALSE if there is an error. This function always returns FALSE under Windows. If you need to change the owner of a file, use the `chown` function. Similar functions for getting information about a file are `filegroup`, `fileinode`, and `fileperms`.

### integer fileperms(string filename)

The `fileperms` function returns the permission number for the given file, or `FALSE` when there is an error. If you are using UNIX, you may wish to refer to the man page for the stat system function. You may be surprised to find that printing this number in octal, as is customary, produces six digits. The first three give you information about the file that doesn't actually refer to read/write/execute permissions. You may wish to filter that information out, as I have in Listing 9.17, by performing a logical AND operation. If you need to change the mode of a file, use the `chmod` function.

### integer filesize(string filename)

The `filesize` function returns the size of the given file in bytes.

### string filetype(string filename)

The `filetype` function returns the type of the given file as a descriptive string. Possible values are `block`, `char`, `dir`, `fifo`, `file`, `link`, and `unknown`. This function is an interface to C's stat function, whose man page may be helpful in understanding the different file types.

### boolean flock(resource file, integer mode)

Use the `flock` function (Listing 9.18) to temporarily restrict access to a file. PHP uses its own system for locking, which works across multiple platforms. However, all processes must be using the same locking system, so the file will be locked for PHP scripts but likely not locked for other processes.

The `file` argument must be an integer returned by `fopen`. The `mode` argument determines whether you obtain a lock that allows others to read the file (`LOCK_SH`), you obtain a lock that doesn't allow others to read the file (`LOCK_EX`), or you release a lock (`LOCK_UN`). Add `LOCK_NB` to `LOCK_SH` or `LOCK_EX` to turn off blocking

When obtaining a lock, the process may block. That is, if the file is already locked, it will wait until it gets the lock to continue execution. If you prefer, you may turn off blocking using modes 5 and 6. Table 9.3 lists the modes.

---

**Listing 9.18**   *flock*

```php
<?php
    $fp = fopen("/tmp/log.txt", "a");

    //get lock
    flock($fp, (LOCK_EX + LOCK_NB));
```

**Listing 9.18** *flock (cont.)*

```
//add a line to the log
fputs($fp, date("h:i A l F dS, Y\n"));

//release lock
flock($fp, LOCK_UN);

fclose($fp);

//dump log
print("<pre>");
readfile("/tmp/log.txt");
print("</pre>\n");
?>
```

**Table 9.3** flock Modes

| Mode | Value | Operations Allowed |
|------|-------|-------------------|
| LOCK_SH | 1 | Allow reads. |
| LOCK_EX | 2 | Disallow reads. |
| LOCK_UN | 3 | Release lock. |
| LOCK_SH + LOCK_NB | 4 | Allow reads, do not block. |
| LOCK_EX + LOCK_NB | 5 | Disallow reads, do not block. |

### resource fopen(string filename, string mode, boolean use_include_path, resource context)

The fopen function (Listing 9.19) opens a file for reading or writing. The function expects the name of a file and a mode. It returns an integer, which is called a file handle. Internally, PHP uses this integer to reference a block of information about the open file. The file handle is used by other file-related functions, such as fputs and fgets.

Setting use_include_path to TRUE will cause PHP to search for the named file in the default include path. Its use is optional.

You may optionally provide a stream context as the fourth argument. This allows you to configure some aspects of the open stream and monitor I/O. See stream_context_create.

Ordinarily, the `filename` argument is a path to a file. It can be fully qualified or relative to the path of the script. If the filename begins with `http://` or `ftp://`, the file will be opened using HTTP or FTP protocol over the Internet.

The `mode` argument determines whether the file is to be read from, written to, or added to. Modes with a plus sign (+) are update modes that allow both reading and writing. If the letter `b` appears as the last part of the mode, the file is assumed to be a binary file, which means no special meaning will be given to end-of-line characters. Table 9.4 lists all the modes.

**Table 9.4** File Read/Write Modes

| Mode | Operations Allowed |
| --- | --- |
| r[b] | reading only [binary] |
| w[b] | writing only, create if necessary, discard previous contents if any [binary] |
| a[b] | append to file, create if necessary, start writing at end of file [binary] |
| r+[b] | reading and writing [binary] |
| w+[b] | reading and writing, create if necessary, discard previous contents if any [binary] |
| a+[b] | reading and writing, create if necessary, start writing at end of file [binary] |

While it is an error to open a file for writing when an HTTP URL is specified, this is not the case with FTP. You may upload an FTP file by using write mode. However, this functionality is limited. You can create remote files, but you may not overwrite existing files. With either HTTP or FTP connections, you may only read from start to finish from a file. You may not use `fseek` or similar functions.

Sometimes files on HTTP and FTP servers are protected by usernames and passwords. You can specify a username and a password exactly as popular Web browsers allow you to do. After the network protocol and before the server name, you may insert a username, a colon, a password, and an at-symbol (@).

Three other ways to open a file are the `fsockopen`, `gzopen`, and `popen` functions.

**Listing 9.19** *fopen*

```php
<?php
    print("<h1>HTTP</h1>\n");

    //open a file using http protocol
    //Use username and password
    if(!($myFile =
            fopen("http://leon:password@www.php.net/", "r")))
    {
        print("file could not be opened");
        exit;
    }

    while(!feof($myFile))
    {
        // read a line from the file
        $myLine = fgetss($myFile, 255);
        print("$myLine <br>\n");
    }

    // close the file
    fclose($myFile);
    print("<hr>\n");


    print("<h1>FTP</h1>\n");

    // open a file using ftp protocol
    if(!($myFile = fopen("ftp://php.he.net/welcome.msg", "r")))
    {
        print("file could not be opened");
        exit;
    }

    while(!feof($myFile))
    {
        // read a line from the file
        $myLine = fgetss($myFile, 255);
        print("$myLine <br>\n");
    }

    // close the file
    fclose($myFile);

    print("<hr>\n");
```

| Listing 9.19 | *fopen (cont.)* |
| --- | --- |

```
    print("<h1>Local</h1>\n");

    // open a local file
    if(!($myFile = fopen("data.txt", "r")))
    {
        print("file could not be opened");
        exit;
    }

    while(!feof($myFile))
    {
        // read a line from the file
        $myLine = fgetss($myFile, 255);
        print("$myLine <br>\n");
    }

    // close the file
    fclose($myFile);
?>
```

### boolean fpassthru(resource file)

The fpassthru function (Listing 9.20) prints the contents of the file to the browser. Data from the current file position to the end are sent, so you can read a few lines and output the rest. The file is closed after being sent. If an error occurs, fpassthru returns FALSE. The gzpassthru function offers the same functionality for compressed files. The readfile function will save you the bother of opening the file first.

| Listing 9.20 | *fpassthru* |
| --- | --- |

```
<?php
    /*
    ** Get a Web page, change the title tag
    */

    // open a file using http protocol
    if(!($myFile = fopen("http://www.php.net/", "r")))
    {
        print("file could not be opened");
        exit;
    }
```

| Listing 9.20 | *fpassthru (cont.)* |
|---|---|

```
$KeepSearching = TRUE;

while(!feof($myFile) AND $KeepSearching)
{
    // read a line from the file
    $myLine = fgets($myFile, 1024);

    //watch for body tag
    if(eregi("<body", $myLine))
    {
        //no chance to find a title tag
        //after a body tag
        $KeepSearching = FALSE;
    }

    //try adding some text after the title tag
    $myLine = eregi_replace("<title>",
        "<title>(fpassthru example)", $myLine);

    //send line to browser
    print("$myLine");
}

// send the rest of file to browser
fpassthru($myFile);
?>
```

### fprintf(resource file, string format, ...)

The fprintf function operates like printf except that it sends output to a file. See the description of printf in Chapter 8.

### integer fputs(resource file, string output)

The fputs function is an alias for fwrite.

### string fread(resource file, integer length)

The fread function (Listing 9.21) is a binary-safe version of the fgets function. That means it does not pay attention to end-of-line characters. It will always return the number of bytes specified by the length argument unless it reaches the end of the file. This function is necessary if you wish to read from binary files, such as jpeg image files.

**Listing 9.21** *fread*

```php
<?php
    /*
    ** Check that a file is a GIF89
    */

    $filename = "php.gif";

    $fp = fopen($filename, "r");

    //get first 128 bytes
    $data = fread($fp, 128);

    //close file
    fclose($fp);

    //check for GIF89
    if(substr($data, 0, 5) == "GIF89")
    {
        print("$filename is a GIF89 file.\n");
    }
    else
    {
        print("$filename isn't a GIF89 file.\n");
    }
?>
```

### array fscanf(resource file, string format, ...)

The `fscanf` function (Listing 9.22) reads a line from an open file and attempts to break it into variables according to the `format` argument. If only two arguments are given, `fscanf` returns an array. Otherwise, it attempts to place the values in the supplied list of variable references.

The `format` argument is a series of literal characters and codes compared to the input string. Literal characters must match the input string. The codes specify various data types, which `fscanf` converts from text into native data types. Whitespace in the format stands for any amount of whitespace in the input. For example, a single space in the format can match several tab characters in the input.

Each format code begins with the `%` character and ends with a character specifying the type. Table 9.5 shows codes available. Between the `%` and code, you may specify a width as an integer. The input must match this width exactly.

Additionally, you may place an asterisk (*) between the leading % and the width. This causes the field to be scanned and discarded.

PHP also includes `sscanf` for evaluating strings, described in Chapter 12.

**Table 9.5**   Format Codes for `fscanf`

| Code | Description |
|------|-------------|
| % | A literal % character. |
| d | An optionally signed decimal integer. |
| I | An optionally signed integer, recognized as hex if it starts with 0x or 0X, recognized as octal if it starts with k. |
| o | An octal integer. |
| u | An unsigned integer. |
| x | An unsigned hexadecimal integer. |
| f | A double-precision floating-point number. |
| s | A sequence of non-whitespace characters. |
| c | Any number of non-whitespace characters specified by a width flag or by 1 if no width is given. |
| [ ] | A regular expression. |
| n | The number of characters read so far. |

**Listing 9.22**   *fscanf*

```php
<?php
    $fp = fopen('data.txt', 'r');

    while(!feof($fp))
    {
        $a = fscanf($fp,
                    "%*4d %*i %o %u %x %f %s %3c %[a-zA-Z] %n");
        print_r($a);
        print("<br>");
    }

    fclose($fp);
?>
```

### integer fseek(resource file, integer offset, integer from)

To change PHP's internal file pointer, use `fseek` (Listing 9.23). It expects a valid file handle as created by `fopen`. It also expects an offset, the number of bytes past the beginning of the file. If an error occurs, `fseek` returns negative one (–1); otherwise it returns zero (0). Take note that this is different from most other PHP functions.

The optional third argument changes how PHP interprets the `offset` argument. By default, or if specified as `SEEK_SET`, `fseek` starts from the beginning of the file. You can start from the end of the file with `SEEK_END`, but don't forget to use a negative offset in that case. You can use `SEEK_CUR` to offset from the current position, in which case negative and positive values are valid.

Seeking past the end of the file is not an error; however, using `fseek` on a file opened by `fopen` if it was used with `http://` or `ftp://` is forbidden.

If you need to know where the file pointer points, use the `ftell` function.

---

**Listing 9.23** *fseek*

```php
<?php
    // open a file
    if($myFile = fopen("data.txt", "r"))
    {
        // jump 32 bytes into the file
        fseek($myFile, 32);

        // dump the rest of the file
        fpassthru($myFile);
    }
    else
    {
        print("file could not be opened");
    }
?>
```

---

### array fstat(resource file)

The `fstat` function gets information from C's `stat` function about an open file and returns it in an associative array. The elements of the array are `atime`, `blksize`, `blocks`, `ctime`, `dev`, `gid`, `ino`, `mode`, `mtime`, `nlink`, `rdev`, `size`, and `uid`. This function returns the same information returned by `stat` and `lstat`.

### integer ftell(resource file)

Given a valid file handle, `ftell` returns the offset of PHP's internal file pointer. If you wish to move the file pointer, use the `fseek` function.

### boolean ftruncate(resource file, integer size)

The `ftrunctate` function truncates a file to a specified size, expressed in number of bytes. It does not change the current file position, even if the truncation would place the position past the end of the file. You may need to use `fseek` to restore the file pointer to a valid position.

### integer fwrite(resource file, string data, integer length)

The `fwrite` function (Listing 9.24) writes a string to a file. The `file` argument must be an integer returned by `fopen`, `fsockopen`, or `popen`. The `length` argument is optional and sets the maximum number of bytes to write. If present, it causes the magic quotes functionality to be suspended. This means backslashes inserted into the string by PHP to escape quotes will not be stripped before writing.

**Listing 9.24**    *fwrite*

```php
<?php
    // open file for writing
    $myFile = fopen("data.txt","w");

    // make sure the open was successful
    if(!($myFile))
    {
        print("file could not be opened");
        exit;
    }

    for($index=0; $index<10; $index++)
    {
        // write a line to the file
        fwrite($myFile, "line $index\n");
    }

    // close the file
    fclose($myFile);
?>
```

## array get_meta_tags(string filename, boolean use_include_path)

The `get_meta_tags` function (Listing 9.25) opens a file and scans for HTML meta tags. The function assumes it is a well-formed HTML file that uses native linebreaks. An array indexed by the `name` attribute of the `meta` tag is returned. If the name contains any characters illegal in identifiers, they will be replaced with underscores.

The optional `use_include_path` will cause `get_meta_tags` to look for the file in the include path instead of the current directory. The include path is set in `php.ini` and normally is used by the `include` function.

Like many of the file functions, `get_meta_tags` allows specifying a URL instead of a path on the local filesystem.

---

**Listing 9.25** *get_meta_tags*

```
<html>
<head>
<title>get_meta_tags</title>
<meta name="description" content="Demonstration of
get_meta_tags.">
<meta name="keywords" content="PHP, Core PHP, Leon Atkinson">
<meta name="Name with Space" content="See how the name changes">
</head>
<body>
<?php
    $tag = get_meta_tags($_SERVER["PATH_TRANSLATED"]);

    //dump all elements of returned array
    print("<pre>");
    print_r($tag);
    print("</pre>\n");

?>
</body>
</html>
```

---

## array glob(string pattern, integer flags)

The `glob` function applies a pattern to the current working directory and returns an array of matching files. The pattern may contain typical shell wildcards, such as * and ?. The flags passed in the optional second argument control certain aspects of the pattern matching. At the time of writing, their exact implementation was unfinished.

### include(string filename)

The `include` function causes the PHP parser to open the given file and execute it. The file is treated as a normal PHP script. That is, text is sent directly to the browser unless PHP tags are used. You may use a variable to specify the file, and if the call to include is inside a loop, it will be reevaluated each time.

You may also specify files by URL by starting them with `http://` or `ftp://`. PHP will fetch the file via the stated protocol and execute it as if it were in the local filesystem.

Compare this function to `require`.

### include_once(string filename)

The `include_once` function is identical to `include` except that it will process a file only once. Any attempt to include the file a second time will result in silent failure.

### boolean is_dir(string filename)

The `is_dir` function (Listing 9.26) returns TRUE if the given filename is a directory; otherwise it returns FALSE. Similar functions are `is_file` and `is_link`.

| | |
|---|---|
| **Listing 9.26** | *is_dir, is_executable, is_file, is_link, is_readable, is_uploaded_file, is_writeable* |

```php
<?php
    $filename = "data.txt";

    print("$filename is...<br>\n");

    if(is_dir($filename))
    {
        print("...a directory.");
    }
    else
    {
        print("...not a directory.");
    }
    print("<br>\n");
```

| Listing 9.26 | *is_dir, is_executable, is_file,*<br>*is_link, is_readable, is_uploaded_file,*<br>*is_writeable (cont.)* |
|---|---|

```php
if(is_executable($filename))
{
    print("...executable.");
}
else
{
    print("...not executable.");
}
print("<br>\n");

if(is_file($filename))
{
    print("...a file.");
}
else
{
    print("...not a file.");
}
print("<br>\n");

if(is_link($filename))
{
    print("...a link.");
}
else
{
    print("...not a link.");
}
print("<br>\n");

if(is_readable($filename))
{
    print("...readable.");
}
else
{
    print("...not readable.");
}
print("<br>\n");
```

| Listing 9.26 | *is_dir, is_executable, is_file,*<br>*is_link, is_readable, is_uploaded_file,*<br>*is_writeable (cont.)* |
|---|---|

```
if(is_uploaded_file($filename))
{
    print("...an upload.");
}
else
{
    print("...not an upload.");
}
print("<br>\n");


if(is_writeable($filename))
{
    print("...writeable.");
}
else
{
    print("...not writeable.");
}
print("<br>\n");
?>
```

### boolean is_executable(string filename)

The is_executable function returns TRUE if a file exists and is executable; otherwise it returns FALSE. On UNIX this is determined by the file's permissions. On Windows this is determined by the file extension. Two related functions are is_readable and is_writeable.

### boolean is_file(string filename)

The is_file function returns TRUE if the given filename is neither a directory nor a symbolic link; otherwise it returns FALSE. Similar functions are is_dir and is_link.

### boolean is_link(string filename)

The is_link function returns TRUE if the given filename is a symbolic link; otherwise it returns FALSE. Similar functions are is_dir and is_file.

### boolean is_readable(string filename)

The `is_readable` function returns TRUE if a file exists and is readable; otherwise it returns FALSE. On UNIX this is determined by the file's permissions. On Windows, TRUE is always returned if the file exists. This function is similar to `is_executable` and `is_writeable`.

### boolean is_uploaded_file(string filename)

The `is_uploaded_file` function returns TRUE if a file was uploaded in an HTML form during the current request. Its purpose is to ensure that the file you expect to treat as an upload was indeed uploaded.

### boolean is_writeable(string filename)

The `is_writeable` function returns TRUE if a file exists and is writeable; otherwise it returns FALSE. Similar functions are `is_executable` and `is_readable`.

### boolean link(string source, string destination)

The `link` function creates a hard link. A hard link may not point to a directory, may not point outside its own filesystem, and is indistinguishable from the file to which it links. See the man page for `link` or `ln` for a full description. The `link` function expects a source file and a destination file. On Windows this function does nothing and returns nothing. You can create a symbolic link with the `symlink` function.

### integer linkinfo(string filename)

The `linkinfo` function calls the C function `lstat` for the given filename and returns the `st_dev` field `lstat` generates. This may be used to verify the existence of a link. It returns FALSE on error. You can read more about `lstat` on the man page or in the help file for Microsoft Visual C++.

### array lstat(string filename)

The `lstat` function (Listing 9.27) executes C's `stat` function and returns an array. The array contains 13 elements, numbered starting with zero. If the filename argument points to a symbolic link, the array will reflect the link, not the file to which the link points. The `stat` function always returns information about the file when called on a symbolic link. Table 9.6 lists the contents of the array, which contains two copies of the data. One copy is referenced by integer, the other by name.

**Table 9.6** Array Elements Returned by the `lstat` and `stat` Functions

| Integer | Name | Description |
| --- | --- | --- |
| 0 | dev | This is a number identifying the device of the `filesystem`. On Windows this number denotes the drive letter the file is on, with the A drive being zero. |
| 1 | ino | A unique identifier for the file, always zero on Windows. This is the same value you get from the `fileinode` function. |
| 2 | mode | This is the same value you will get from `fileperms`, the read/write/execute permissions. |
| 3 | nlink | Number of links to file. On Windows this will always be 1 if the file is not on an NTFS partition. |
| 4 | uid | User ID of the owner, always zero on Windows. This is the same value you will get from the `fileowner` function. |
| 5 | gid | Group ID, always zero on Windows. This is the same value you will get from the `filegroup` function. |
| 6 | rdev | This is the type of the device. On Windows it repeats the device number. |
| 7 | size | Size of the file in bytes, which is the same as reported by `filesize`. |
| 8 | atime | Last time the file was accessed, as defined in the description of `fileatime`. |
| 9 | mtime | Last time the file was modified, as defined in the description of `filemtime`. |
| 10 | ctime | Last time the file was changed, as defined in the description of `filectime`. On Windows this is the time the file was created. |
| 11 | blksize | Suggested block size for I/O to file, –1 under Windows. |
| 12 | blocks | Number of blocks used by file, –1 under Windows. |

**Listing 9.27**  *lstat*

```php
<?php
    $statInfo = lstat("data.txt");

    if(eregi("windows", PHP_OS))
    {
        // print useful information for Windows
        printf("Drive: %c <br>\n", ($statInfo[0]+65));
        printf("Mode: %o <br>\n", $statInfo[2]);
        print("Links: $statInfo[3] <br>\n");
        print("Size: $statInfo[7] bytes<br>\n");
        printf("Last Accessed: %s <br>\n",
            date("F d, Y", $statInfo[8]));
        printf("Last Modified: %s <br>\n",
            date("F d, Y", $statInfo[9]));
        printf("Created: %s <br>\n",
            date("F d, Y", $statInfo[10]));
    }
    else
    {
        // print UNIX version
        print("Device: $statInfo[0] <br>\n");
        print("INode: $statInfo[1] <br>\n");
        printf("Mode: %o <br>\n", $statInfo[2]);
        print("Links: $statInfo[3] <br>\n");
        print("UID: $statInfo[4] <br>\n");
        print("GID: $statInfo[5] <br>\n");
        print("Device Type: $statInfo[6] <br>\n");
        print("Size: $statInfo[7] bytes<br>\n");
        printf("Last Accessed: %s <br>\n",
            date("F d, Y", $statInfo[8]));
        printf("Last Modified: %s <br>\n",
            date("F d, Y", $statInfo[9]));
        printf("Last Changed: %s <br>\n",
            date("F d, Y", $statInfo[10]));
        print("Block Size: $statInfo[11] <br>\n");
        print("Blocks: $statInfo[12] <br>\n");
    }
?>
```

### string md5_file(string filename)

The md5_file function returns the MD5 hash for the given file. MD5 hashes are 128-bit numbers, usually expressed as text strings, that uniquely identify files.

### boolean mkdir(string directory, integer mode)

The mkdir function (Listing 9.28) creates a new directory with the supplied name. Permissions will be set based on the mode argument, which follows the same rules as chmod. On Windows the mode argument is ignored. You can use the rmdir function to remove a directory.

---

**Listing 9.28** *mkdir*

```php
<?php
    if(mkdir("myDir", 0777))
    {
        print("directory created");
    }
    else
    {
        print("directory cannot be created");
    }
?>
```

---

### boolean move_uploaded_file(string filename, string destination)

The move_uploaded_file function combines the functionality of is_uploaded_file and rename. If the named file is an uploaded file, it will be renamed to the destination name. If the file is not an upload or if the rename fails, the function returns FALSE.

### array parse_ini_file(string filename, boolean process_sections)

The parse_ini_file function parses a text file that conforms to the common format used by configuration files, particularly those postfixed with .ini. Named settings are followed by values separated by an equal sign (=). Values that contain special characters should be surrounded by quotation marks ("). Semicolons (;) begin comments, which are ignored by the parser.

You may break the configuration settings into sections by surrounding section names with square brackets. Listing 9.29 shows a sample configuration file. Listing 9.30 demonstrates parsing the contents of Listing 9.29. Figure 9.1 shows the results. If you leave process_sections out, the sections will be ignored. If you set it to TRUE, the returned array will be two-dimensional, dividing settings into subarrays named by section.

---

**Listing 9.29** *Example configuration file*

```
; Sample Configuration file: test.ini
; Use Semicolons to begin comments.

[User Interface]
text         =    "#333333"
highlight    =    "#FF3333"

[Database]
username     =    php
password     =    secret
dbname       =    ft3
```

---

**Listing 9.30** *parse_ini_file*

```php
<?php
    print_r(parse_ini_file('test.ini'));
    print("\n");
    print_r(parse_ini_file('test.ini', TRUE));
?>
```

---

```
Array
(
    [text] => #333333
    [highlight] => #FF3333
    [username] => php
    [password] => secret
    [dbname] => ft3
)

Array
(
    [User Interface] => Array
        (
            [text] => #333333
            [highlight] => #FF3333
        )

    [Database] => Array
        (
            [username] => php
            [password] => secret
            [dbname] => ft3
        )

)
```

**Figure 9.1**  Output from `parse_ini_file`.

### integer opendir(string directory)

The opendir function (Listing 9.31) requires a directory name and returns a directory handle. This handle may be used by readdir, rewinddir, and closedir. The dir function described above provides an alternative to this group of functions.

---

**Listing 9.31** *opendir*

```
<table border="1">
<tr>
    <th>Filename</th>
    <th>Size</th>
</tr>
<?php
    // open directory
    $myDirectory = opendir(".");

    // get each entry
    while($entryName = readdir($myDirectory))
    {
        print("<tr>");
        print("<td>$entryName</td>");
        print("<td align=\"right\">");
        print(filesize($entryName));
        print("</td>");
        print("</tr>\n");
    }

    // close directory
    closedir($myDirectory);
?>
</table>
```

---

### integer pclose(resource file)

The pclose function closes a file stream opened by popen. The return value is the integer returned by the underlying call to the C function wait4. Check your man page for description of this value.

### resource popen(string command, string mode)

The popen function (Listing 9.32) opens a pipe to an executing command that may be read from or written to as if it were a file. A file handle is returned that is appropriate for use with functions such as fgets. Pipes work in one direction only, which means you can't use update modes with popen. You may open a bidirectional pipe with proc_open.

When you open a pipe, you are executing a program in the local filesystem. As with the other functions that execute a command, you should consider both the high cost of starting a new process and the security risk if user input is included in the command argument. If you must pass user-supplied data to a command, pass the information through the escapeshellcmd function first.

---

**Listing 9.32**  *popen*

```php
<?php
    /*
    ** see who's logged in
    */
    $myPipe = popen('who', 'r');

    while(!feof($myPipe))
    {
        print(nl2br(fread($myPipe, 1024)));
    }

    pclose($myPipe);
?>
```

---

### string readdir(integer directory_handle)
The readdir function returns the name of the next file from a directory handle created by opendir, or FALSE when no entries remain. You can place readdir in the conditional expression of a while loop to get every entry in a directory. Keep in mind that . and .. are always present and will be returned. See closedir for an example of use.

### integer readfile(string filename, boolean use_include_path)
The file given is read and sent directly to the browser by the readfile function (Listing 9.33), and the number of bytes read is returned. If an error occurs, FALSE is returned. If the filename begins with http:// or ftp://, the file will be fetched using HTTP or FTP respectively. Otherwise, the file is opened in the local filesystem. If you need to send a compressed file to the browser, use readgzfile. If you'd rather read a file into a variable, use the file_get_contents function.

If you set the optional argument use_include_path to TRUE, PHP will search for the file in the default include path.

**Listing 9.33** *readfile*

```php
<?php
    print("Here is some data <br>\n");

    readfile("data.txt");
?>
```

### string readlink(string filename)

The `readlink` function (Listing 9.34) returns the path to which a symbolic link points. It returns FALSE on error. Another function that gets information about a link is `linkinfo`.

**Listing 9.34** *readlink*

```php
<?php
    print(readlink("/etc/rc"));
?>
```

### string realpath(string path)

The `realpath` function (Listing 9.35) returns a genuine, minimal path by following symbolic links, removing relational directories, and collapsing extra slashes. If the path does not exist, FALSE is returned.

**Listing 9.35** *realpath*

```php
<?php
    //prints /etc/rc.d/rc
    print(realpath('/usr/../etc/.////rc'));
?>
```

### boolean rename(string old_name, string new_name)

The `rename` function (Listing 9.36) changes the name of a file specified by the `old_name` argument to the name specified in the `new_name` argument. The new and old names may contain complete paths, which allow you to use `rename` to move files.

---

**Listing 9.36** *rename*

```php
<?php
    //move data.txt from local directory
    //to the temp directory
    rename("./data.txt", "/tmp/data.dat");
?>
```

---

### require(string filename)

The `require` function causes the PHP parser to open the given file and execute it. The file is treated as a normal PHP script. That is, text is sent directly to the browser unless PHP tags are used. PHP attempts to process `require` statements prior to executing any other code but can do so only if the path to the filename is static. If you use a variable to specify the file, PHP must wait until after it executes preceding code to execute the `require` statement. In either case, PHP executes a `require` statement only once. If called inside a loop, the code inserted by the `require` statement remains the same regardless of changes to variables used in the path.

You may also specify files by URL by starting them with `http://` or `ftp://`. PHP will fetch the file via the stated protocol and execute it as if it were in the local filesystem. Compare this function to `include`.

### include_once(string filename)

The `include_once` function is identical to `require` except that it will process a file only once per request. Any attempt to include the file a second time will result in silent failure.

### boolean rewind(resource file)

The `rewind` function (Listing 9.37) moves PHP's internal file pointer back to the beginning of the file. This is the same as using `fseek` to move to position zero.

---

**Listing 9.37** *rewind*

```php
<?php
    /*
    ** print a file, then print the first line again
    */
```

**Listing 9.37**  *rewind (cont.)*

```
// open a local file
$myFile = fopen("data.txt", "r");

while(!feof($myFile))
{
    // read a line from the file
    $myLine = fgetss($myFile, 255);
    print("$myLine <br>\n");
}

rewind($myFile);
$myLine = fgetss($myFile, 255);
print("$myLine <br>\n");

// close the file
fclose($myFile);
?>
```

### boolean rewinddir(integer handle)

The rewinddir function resets PHP's internal pointer to the beginning of a directory listing. It returns TRUE unless an error occurs, in which case it returns FALSE. The handle is an integer returned by opendir.

### boolean rmdir(string directory)

Use the rmdir function (Listing 9.38) to remove a directory. The directory must be empty. To remove a file, use unlink.

**Listing 9.38**  *rmdir*

```
<?php
    if(rmdir("/tmp/leon"))
    {
        print("Directory removed");
    }
    else
    {
        print("Directory not removed");
    }
?>
```

### array scandir(string path, boolean reverse_order)

The `scandir` function returns an array of files in the given path. By default, items are sorted alphabetically. You can reverse them with the optional `reverse_order` argument.

### set_file_buffer(resource file, integer size)

This function is now an alias to `stream_set_write_buffer`.

### string sha1_file(string filename)

The `sha1_file` function returns the SHA-1 (Secure Hash Algorithm 1) hash for the given file. These 160-bit hash keys are unique for files and are an alternative to MD5 hash keys.

### array stat(string filename)

The `stat` function executes C's `stat` function and returns an array. The array contains 13 elements, numbered starting at zero. If the filename argument points to a symbolic link, the array will reflect the file to which the link points. To get information about the link itself, use the `lstat` function. Table 9.6 lists the contents of the array.

### resource stream_context_create(array options)

The `stream_context_create` function creates a stream context used to configure and monitor streams. You may use this context for multiple streams you create with `fopen`. The optional `options` argument sets one or more options for the context. It must be an array of arrays. Each key must match a wrapper and point to an array of key/value pairs.

### array stream_context_get_options(resource context)

The `stream_context_get_options` function returns the options for the given context or stream.

### boolean stream_context_set_option(resource context, string wrapper, string option, string value)

The `stream_context_set_option` function sets a single option for a context or stream.

### boolean stream_context_set_params(resource context, array options)

The `stream_context_set_params` function sets parameters on the given context or stream. The `options` array should use parameter names for keys.

### boolean stream_filter_append(resource stream, string filter)

The `stream_filter_append` function adds a filter to the end of the list of filters for a stream.

### boolean stream_filter_prepend(resource stream, string filter)

The `stream_filter_prepend` function adds a filter to the beginning of the list of filters for a stream.

### array stream_get_filters()

The `stream_get_filters` function returns a list of available filters, including those you register.

### array stream_get_wrappers()

The `stream_get_wrappers` function returns a list of available wrappers, including those you register.

### array stream_get_meta_data(resource file)

The `stream_get_meta_data` function (Listing 9.39, Figure 9.2) returns an array describing the state of the open stream created by `fopen`, `fsockopen`, or `pfsockopen`. Table 9.7 describes the elements of the returned array.

**Table 9.7**　Array Returned by `stream_get_meta_data`

| Name | Description |
| --- | --- |
| `blocked` | TRUE if the stream is in blocking mode. |
| `eof` | TRUE if the stream has reached end-of-file. |
| `stream_type` | A string describing the stream type. |
| `timed_out` | TRUE if the stream aborted after waiting too long for data. |
| `unread_bytes` | The number of bytes left to read. |
| `wrapper_data` | An array of data related to the stream. |
| `wrapper_type` | A string describing the wrapper used. |

It's possible for the `eof` element to be TRUE while there are still unread bytes. You may wish to use `feof` instead.

**Listing 9.39** *stream_get_meta_data*

```php
<?php
    //connect to PHP site
    if(!($myFile = fopen("http://www.php.net/", "r")))
    {
        print("file could not be opened");
        exit;
    }

    //dump meta data
    print_r(stream_get_meta_data($myFile));

    // close the file
    fclose($myFile);
?>
```

```
Array
(
    [wrapper_data] => Array
        (
            [0] => HTTP/1.0 200 OK
            [1] => Date: Tue, 22 Oct 2002 21:11:36 GMT
            [2] => Server: Apache/1.3.26 (Unix) PHP/4.3.0-dev
            [3] => X-Powered-By: PHP/4.3.0-dev
            [4] => Last-Modified: Tue, 22 Oct 2002 20:48:31 GMT
            [5] => Content-Type: text/html
            [6] => Age: 4
            [7] => X-Cache: HIT from rs1.php.net
            [8] => Connection: close
        )

    [wrapper_type] => HTTP
    [stream_type] => socket
    [unread_bytes] => 1190
    [timed_out] =>
    [blocked] => 1
    [eof] =>
)
```

**Figure 9.2** Output from `stream_get_meta_data`.

### boolean stream_register_filter(string name, string class)

The `stream_register_filter` function (Listing 9.40) allows you to define a stream filter. You must supply the name of the filter and the name of a class that extends `php_user_filter`. Table 9.8 lists the methods you may include in the given class. If you do not implement a method, PHP uses the method in the parent.

Filters that change data character-by-character are easy to implement, probably needing only `read` and `write` methods. Filters that change the length of the data going in and out most likely require a buffer.

**Table 9.8**   Stream Protocol Filter Methods

| Method | Parameters | Returns |
| --- | --- | --- |
| flush | boolean closing | An integer containing the number of bytes flushed. |

PHP calls this method when the stream executes a buffer flush. The `closing` argument tells you whether or not the stream is in the process of closing. If you implement this method, be sure to call `parent::flush($closing)` at the end of your method.

| onclose | None | Nothing |

PHP calls this method when it shuts down the filter. It will call `flush` first.

| oncreate | None | Nothing |

PHP calls this method when the filter is registered.

| read | integer maximum | A string of the read bytes, the length not to exceed the given maximum. |

PHP calls this method when it reads from the stream. It should first get data by calling `parent::read($maximum)`. The maximum argument sets maximum number of bytes to return.

| write | string data | An integer telling the number of bytes in the data. |

PHP calls this method when the stream writes data. The data argument holds data to be written to the resource. After manipulating the data, call `parent::write($data)` to pass it along to the next filter or the wrapper. Returns the number of bytes in the data passed in, not the number of bytes in the output.

---

**Listing 9.40**   *stream_register_filter*

```php
<?php
    //define filter
    class caseChanger extends php_user_filter
    {
        function read($maximum)
        {
            //get data from stream
            $data = parent::read($maximum);

            //change to uppercase
            $data = ucwords($data);

            //return data
            return($data);
        }
    }

    //register filter
    stream_register_filter("corephp.cc", "caseChanger");

    //open stream
    $fp = fopen("/tmp/test.txt", "rb");

    //attach filter to the stream
    stream_filter_append($fp, "corephp.cc");

    //read contents
    $data = "";
    while(!feof($fp))
    {
        $data .= fgets($fp, 255);
    }

    //close stream
    fclose($fp);

    //show contents
    print($data);
?>
```

---

### boolean stream_register_wrapper(string protocol, string class)

The stream_register_wrapper function (Listing 9.41) allows you to implement a wrapper for a stream protocol. The second argument is the name of a class that implements a certain set of methods, described below. You may not override an existing stream protocol wrapper. Table 9.9 lists the methods expected in the given class.

**Table 9.9**    Stream Protocol Wrapper Methods

| Method | Parameters | Returns |
|---|---|---|
| stream_close | None | Nothing |
| This method closes the stream and is called by `fclose`. | | |
| stream_eof | None | TRUE if end-of-file reached, FALSE otherwise. |
| This method wraps calls to `feof`. | | |
| stream_flush | None | TRUE if the buffer flushes successfully, FALSE otherwise. |
| This method wraps calls to `fflush`. | | |
| stream_open | string path<br>The URL used in the `fopen` call.<br><br>string mode<br>The mode used in the `fopen` call.<br><br>integer options<br>Additional flags set by the call. If the STREAM_USE_PATH bit is set, the path is relative. If the STREAM_REPORT_ERRORS is set, you must raise errors yourself with `trigger_error`.<br><br>string opened_path<br>This parameter is a reference to a string in which you should place the full path to the opened resource. | TRUE if the resource opens successfully, FALSE if the open fails. |
| This method opens the stream and is called immediately after code uses your wrapper in a URL. | | |
| stream_read | integer count<br>The maximum number of bytes to return. | A string of the read bytes, the length not to exceed the given count. FALSE if no bytes remain. |
| This method returns a string of data read from the resource. You must not return more bytes than requested by the count argument. This method must also update its internal position counter to match the number of bytes returned. | | |

**Table 9.9** Stream Protocol Wrapper Methods *(cont.)*

| Method | Parameters | Returns |
|---|---|---|
| stream_seek | integer offset<br>The number of bytes to move the pointer, positive or negative.<br><br>integer from<br>An integer describing a relative starting point for the offset, as discussed in the fseek description. | TRUE if the move completes successfully, FALSE otherwise. |

This method wraps the fseek function.

| | | |
|---|---|---|
| stream_tell | None | An integer count of the current position within the resource. |

This method wraps the ftell function.

| | | |
|---|---|---|
| stream_write | string data<br>The data to be written to the resource. | An integer telling the number of bytes written. |

This method writes the given data to the resource. Returns the actual number of bytes written. This method must also update its internal position counter to match the number of bytes written.

**Listing 9.41** *stream_register_wrapper*

```php
<?php
    class MemoryStream
    {
        var $filename;
        var $filedata;
        var $position;

        function stream_open($path, $mode, $options, &$opened_path)
        {
            //break URL into parts
            $url = parse_url($path);

            //set the filename
            $this->filename = $url["host"];

            //just for kicks we'll set the opened path
            $opened_path = $this->filename;
```

**Listing 9.41**   *stream_register_wrapper (cont.)*

```php
        //start at zero
        $this->position = 0;

        //copy variable from global scope
        $this->filedata =
            $GLOBALS['MemoryStream'][$this->filename];

        //open was successful
        return(TRUE);
    }

    function stream_read($count)
    {
        //get data
        $data = substr($this->filedata, $this->position,
            $count);

        //move the pointer forward
        $this->position += strlen($data);

        return($data);
    }

    function stream_write($data)
    {
        //start writing at the current position, leaving
        //existing data if it stretches beyond the given data
        $this->filedata =
            substr($this->filedata, 0, $this->position) .
            $data .
            substr($this->filedata, $this->position
                + strlen($data));

        $this->position += strlen($data);

        return(strlen($data));
    }

    function stream_tell()
    {
        return($this->position);
    }
```

**Listing 9.41**   *stream_register_wrapper (cont.)*

```
function stream_eof()
{
    return($this->position >= strlen($this->filedata));
}

function stream_flush()
{
    //copy the entire set of data over
    //what's there globally
    $GLOBALS['MemoryStream'][$this->filename] =
        $this->filedata;

    return(TRUE);
}

function stream_close()
{
    $this->stream_flush();

    return(TRUE);
}

function stream_seek($offset, $from)
{
    switch($from)
    {
        case SEEK_SET:
            $position = $offset;
            break;

        case SEEK_CUR:
            $position += $offset;
            break;

        case SEEK_END:
            $position = strlen($this->filedata) + $offset;
            break;

        default:
            return false;
    }

    //check for impossible positions
    if(($position < 0) OR ($position >=
        strlen($this->filedata)))
```

| Listing 9.41 | *stream_register_wrapper (cont.)* |
| --- | --- |

```php
        {
            return(FALSE);
        }

        $this->position = $position;

        return(TRUE);
    }
}

$GLOBALS['MemoryStream']['test.txt'] = 'test test test test';

//register the new RAM Disk wrapper
if(!stream_register_wrapper('ram', 'MemoryStream'))
{
    print('Could not register RAM Disk wrapper.');
    exit;
}

//open file in RAM disk
if(!($fp = fopen('ram://test.txt', 'r+')))
{
    print('Could not open file.');
    exit;
}

//write three lines
fwrite($fp, "test 1\n");
fwrite($fp, "test 2\n");
fwrite($fp, "test 3\n");

//move pointer back to beginning
rewind($fp);

//read the contents
while(!feof($fp))
{
    print(fgets($fp) . '<br>');
}

//close
fclose($fp);
?>
```

**integer stream_select(array read, array write, array exception, integer timeout_seconds, integer timeout_microseconds)**

The `stream_select` function waits for changes to streams. PHP watches the streams given in the `read` array for new data coming in. PHP watches the streams given in the `write` array for being ready to accept more data. PHP watches the streams given in the `exception` argument for errors. If the number of seconds specified in the `timeout_seconds` argument passes, the function returns. Use the optional `timeout_microseconds` argument to specify a timeout less than 1 second.

The `stream_select` function returns the number of streams that changed or `FALSE` if an error occurred. If the call timed out, this function returns zero. It also modifies the given arrays so that they only include those streams that changed. If you have no streams of a particular type to watch, you may pass an empty array or a variable set to `NULL`.

**boolean stream_set_blocking(resource file, boolean mode)**

The `stream_set_blocking` function sets whether a stream blocks. If `mode` is `TRUE`, reads and writes to the stream will wait until the resource is available. If `mode` is `FALSE`, the call will return immediately.

**boolean stream_set_timeout(resource file, integer seconds, integer microseconds)**

The `stream_set_timeout` function (Listing 9.42) sets the time the PHP will wait for an operation on a stream to complete.

---

**Listing 9.42**   `stream_set_timeout`

```php
<?php
    //open connection to
    if(!$fp = fsockopen("localhost", 80))
    {
        exit();
    }

    //wait for 500 microseconds
    stream_set_timeout($fp, 0, 500);

    //send request for home page
    fputs($fp, "GET / HTTP/1.0\r\n\r\n");

    //attempt to read the first 1K
    print(fread($fp, 1024));

    fclose($fp);
?>
```

### integer stream_set_write_buffer(resource file, integer size)

Use `stream_set_write_buffer` (Listing 9.43) to set the size of the write buffer on a file stream. It requires a valid file handle as created by `fopen`, `fsockopen`, or `popen`. The `size` argument is a number of bytes, and if you set a buffer size of zero, no buffering will be used. You may only set the buffer size before making any reads or writes to the file stream. By default, file streams start with 8K buffers.

**Listing 9.43**  *stream_set_write_buffer*

```php
<?php
    // make sure the open was successful
    if(!($fp = fopen("/tmp/data.txt","w")))
    {
        print("file could not be opened");
        exit;
    }

    //use unbuffered writes
    stream_set_write_buffer($fp, 0);


    for($index=0; $index<10; $index++)
    {
        // write a line to the file
        fwrite($fp, "line $index\n");
    }

    // close the file
    fclose($fp);
?>
```

### boolean symlink(string source, string destination)

The `symlink` function (Listing 9.44) creates a symbolic link to the source argument with the name in the destination argument. To create a hard link, use the `link` function.

**Listing 9.44** *symlink*

```php
<?php
    //link moredata.txt to existing file data.txt
    if(symlink("data.txt", "moredata.txt"))
    {
        print("Symbolic link created");
    }
    else
    {
        print("Symbolic link not created");
    }
?>
```

### string tempnam(string path, string prefix)

The tempnam function creates a new file in the path given. The name of the file will be prefixed with the prefix argument. The implementation is different for each operating system. On Linux, six characters will be added to the filename to make it unique. The file is set to read/write mode for all users. The name of the file is returned.

### integer tmpfile()

The tmpfile function (Listing 9.45) opens a new temporary file and returns its file handle. This handle may be used in the same way as one returned by fopen using an update mode. When you close the file or your script ends, the file will be removed. This function is a wrapper for the C function of the same name. If for some reason a temporary file cannot be created, FALSE is returned.

**Listing 9.45** *tmpfile*

```php
<?php
    //open a temporary file
    $fp = tmpfile();

    //write 10K of random data
    //to simulate some process
    for($i=0; $i<10240; $i++)
    {
        //randomly choose a letter
        //from a range of printables
        fputs($fp, chr(rand(ord(' '), ord('z'))));
    }
```

---

**Listing 9.45**  *tmpfile (cont.)*

```
    //return to start of file
    rewind($fp);

    //dump and close file,
    //therefore deleting it
    fpassthru($fp);
?>
```

---

### boolean touch(string filename, integer time, integer atime)

The `touch` function (Listing 9.46) attempts to set the time the file was last modified to the given time, expressed in seconds since January 1, 1970. If the `time` argument is omitted, the current time is used. If the `atime` argument is present, the access time will be set with the given time. If the file does not exist, it will be created with zero length. This function is often used to create empty files.

To find out when a file was last modified, use `filemtime`. To find out when a file was last accessed, use `fileatime`.

---

**Listing 9.46**  *touch*

```php
<?php
    touch("data.txt");
?>
```

---

### integer umask(integer umask)

The `umask` function (Listing 9.47) returns the default permissions given files when they are created. If the optional `umask` argument is given, it sets the `umask` to a logical-AND (&) performed on the given integer and 0777. Under Windows this function does nothing and returns FALSE. To find out the permissions set on a particular file, use `fileperms`.

---

**Listing 9.47**  *umask*

```php
<?php
    printf("umask is %o", umask(0444));
?>
```

---

**boolean unlink(string filename)**

The `unlink` function (Listing 9.48) removes a file permanently. To remove a directory, use `rmdir`.

---

**Listing 9.48**   *unlink*

```php
<?php
    if(unlink("data2.txt"))
    {
        print("data2.txt deleted");
    }
    else
    {
        print("data2.txt could not be deleted");
    }
?>
```

---

**vfprintf(resource file, string format, array values)**

The `vfprintf` function operates similarly to `fprintf` except that values for format codes are passed in an array.

# 9.2  Compressed File Functions

The functions in this section use one of two compression libraries: zlib or bzip2. The zlib library is the same used by GNU compression tools, such as `gzip`, written by Jean-loup Gaill and Mark Adler. You can obtain more information and the library itself from the zlib home page `<http://www.cdrom.com/pub/infozip/zlib/>`. The bzip2 library was written by Julian Seward and powers the bzip2 command-line utility. You can read more about it on the bzip2 home page `<http://sources.redhat.com/bzip2/>`.

Most of the functions for reading and writing files are duplicated here, and they operate similarly. One difference is the lack of support for specifying files using HTTP or FTP protocol.

Functions that compress and decompress strings, which also rely on these two libraries, are described in Chapter 12.

### boolean bzclose(resource file)
This function closes a stream opened with bzopen.

### integer bzerrno(resource file)
This function returns the error number of the last error for the given stream opened with bzopen.

### array bzerror(resource file)
The bzerror function returns an array with two elements describing the last error for the given stream opened with bzopen. The errno element contains the error number and the errstr element contains the error description.

### string bzerrstr(resource file)
This function returns the error description of the last error for the given stream opened with bzopen.

### boolean bzflush(resource file)
The bzflush function flushes the contents of the write buffer for a stream opened with bzopen.

### resource bzopen(string filename, string mode)
The bzopen function opens a stream to a file compressed with the bzip2 library. The mode argument follows the same specification used by fopen, listed in Table 9.4. A resource handle to the stream is returned, or is FALSE on error.

### string bzread(resource file, integer length)
The bzread function reads from a compressed file opened with bzopen. The optional length argument sets a maximum string length returned. The default length is 1024 characters.

### integer bzwrite(resource file, string data, integer length)
The bzwrite function (Listing 9.49) writes a string into a file handle opened by bzopen. The optional length argument limits the string written to a certain length prior to compression.

**Listing 9.49**   *bzwrite*

```php
<?php
    $filename = '/tmp/test.bz2';

    //open file
    if(!($bz = bzopen($filename, 'w')))
    {
        print('Could not open file.');
        exit();
    }

    //write some text
    for($n=0; $n < 10; $n++)
    {
        bzwrite($bz, "Test Line $n\n");
    }

    //close file
    bzclose($bz);

    //open again in read mode
    if(!($bz = bzopen($filename, 'r')))
    {
        print('Could not open file.');
        exit();
    }

    //print each line
    while(!feof($bz))
    {
        print(nl2br(bzread($bz)));
    }

    //close file
    bzclose($bz);
?>
```

### boolean gzclose(resource file)

The gzclose function closes a file opened with gzopen. TRUE is returned if the file closed successfully. FALSE is returned if the file cannot be closed.

### boolean gzeof(resource file)

As you read from a compressed file, PHP keeps a pointer to the last place in the file you read. The gzeof function returns TRUE if you are at the end of the file.

### array gzfile(string filename, boolean use_include_path)

The `gzfile` function (Listing 9.50) reads an entire file into an array. The file is first uncompressed. Each line of the file is a separate element of the array, starting at zero. The optional `use_include_path` argument causes `gzfile` to search for the file within the include path specified in `php.ini`.

**Listing 9.50** *gzfile*

```php
<?php
    // open file and print each line
    foreach(gzfile("data.gz") as $line)
    {
        print("$line<br>\n");
    }
?>
```

### string gzgetc(resource file)

The `gzgetc` function (Listing 9.51) returns a single character from a compressed file. It expects a file handle as returned by `gzopen`.

**Listing 9.51** *gzgetc*

```php
<?php
    // open compressed file and print each character
    if($gz = gzopen("data.gz", "r"))
    {
        while(!gzeof($gz))
        {
            print(gzgetc($gz));
        }

        gzclose($gz);
    }
?>
```

### string gzgets(resource file, integer length)

The `gzgets` function (Listing 9.52) returns a string it reads from a compressed file specified by the file handle, which must have been created with `gzopen`. It will attempt to read as many characters as specified by the `length` argument less one (presumably this is PHP showing its C heritage). A linebreak is treated as a stopping point, as is the end of the file. Linebreaks are included in the return string.

**Listing 9.52** *gzgets*

```php
<?php
    // open file and print each line
    if($gz = gzopen("data.gz", "r"))
    {
        while(!gzeof($gz))
        {
            print(gzgets($gz, 255));
        }

        gzclose($gz);
    }
?>
```

**string gzgetss(resource file, integer length, string ignore)**
The gzgetss function (Listing 9.53) is in all respects identical to gzgets except that it attempts to strip any HTML or PHP code before returning a string. The optional ignore argument may contain tags to be ignored.

**Listing 9.53** *gzgetss*

```php
<?php
    // open file and print each line
    if($gz = gzopen("data.gz", "r"))
    {
        while(!gzeof($gz))
        {
            print(gzgetss($gz, 255));
        }

        gzclose($gz);
    }
?>
```

### integer gzopen(string filename, string mode, boolean use_include_path)

The `gzopen` function is similar in operation to the `fopen` function except that it operates on compressed files. If the `use_include_path` argument is TRUE, the include path specified in `php.ini` will be searched.

The mode argument accepts a few extra parameters compared to `fopen`. In addition to the modes listed in Table 9.4, you may specify a compression level and a compression strategy if you are creating a new file. Immediately following the write mode, you may place an integer between zero and nine that specifies the level of compression. Zero means no compression, and nine is maximum compression. After the compression level, you may use `h` to force Huffman encoding only, or `f` to optimize for filtered input. Filtered data is defined by the zlib source code as being small values of somewhat random distribution. In almost all cases the default settings are a good choice and the extra mode settings are unnecessary.

It is possible to open an uncompressed file with `gzopen`. Reads from the file will operate as expected. This can be convenient if you do not know ahead of time whether a file is compressed.

### boolean gzpassthru(resource file)

The `gzpassthru` function (Listing 9.54) prints the contents of the compressed file to the browser exactly like the `fpassthru` function does.

---

**Listing 9.54** *gzpassthru*

```php
<?php
    // open a compressed file
    if(!($myFile = gzopen("data.html.gz", "r")))
    {
        print("file could not be opened");
        exit;
    }

    // send the entire file to browser
    gzpassthru($myFile);
?>
```

---

### boolean gzputs(resource file, string output, integer length)

The `gzputs` function (Listing 9.55) writes data to a compressed file. It expects a file handle as returned by `gzopen`. It returns the number of bytes written if the write was successful, FALSE if it failed. The optional `length` argument specifies a maximum number of input bytes to accept. A side effect of specifying `length` is that the `magic_quotes_runtime` configuration setting will be ignored.

---

**Listing 9.55**   *gzputs*

```php
<?php
    // open file for writing
    // use maximum compress and force
    // Huffman encoding only
    if(!($gz = gzopen("data.gz","wb9h")))
    {
        print("file could not be opened");
        exit;
    }

    for($index=0; $index<10; $index++)
    {
        // write a line to the file
        gzputs($gz, "line $index\n");
    }

    // close the file
    gzclose($gz);
?>
```

---

### gzread

The `gzread` function is an alias to `gzgets`.

### boolean gzrewind(resource file)

The `gzrewind` function moves PHP's internal file pointer back to the beginning of a compressed file. It returns TRUE on success, FALSE if there is an error.

### integer gzseek(resource file, integer offset)

This function works exactly like `fseek` except that it operates on compressed files.

### integer gztell(resource file)

Given a valid file handle, `gztell` returns the offset of PHP's internal file pointer.

### gzwrite

The `gzwrite` function is an alias to `gzputs`.

### integer readgzfile(string filename, boolean use_include_path)

The `readgzfile` function (Listing 9.56) operates identically to the `readfile` function except that it expects the file to be compressed. The file is uncompressed on the fly and sent directly to the browser.

| Listing 9.56 | *readgzfile* |
|---|---|

```php
<?php
    //dump uncompressed contents of
    //data.gz to browser
    readgzfile("data.gz");
?>
```

# 9.3  Direct I/O

PHP supports lower level I/O than provided by the functions discussed earlier in this chapter. The file handles used by these functions are incompatible with those functions. Using Direct I/O for regular files is not interesting in most cases because the higher level functions are more convenient. Direct I/O becomes interesting when you wish to write to devices such as terminals, parallel ports, and serial ports. Keep in mind permission issues. Under normal circumstances, your Web server should not have permission to write directly to a serial port, for instance.

Sterling Hughes created the Direct I/O extension.

### dio_close(resource file)

The `dio_close` function closes an open file handle.

### resource dio_fcntl(resource file, integer command, integer additional_args)

The `dio_fcntl` function performs miscellaneous operations on an open file handle. The return value and expected type of the optional `additional_args` argument are determined by the command chosen from Table 9.10. Table 9.11 contains the elements that may appear in `additional_args`.

**Table 9.10**   `dio_fcntl` Commands

| Command | Description |
|---------|-------------|
| F_DUPFD | Find the lowest-numbered file descriptor greater than the one specified by `additional_args`, make it a copy of the given file handle, and return it. |
| F_GETLK | Get the status of a lock. An associate array is returned. |
| F_SETFL | Set the flags for file handle. Specify `O_APPEND`, `O_NONBLOCK`, or `O_ASYNC`. |
| F_SETLK | Attempt to set or clear the lock on the file. If another process holds the lock, `-1` is returned. |
| F_SETLKW | Attempt to set or clear the lock on the file. If another process holds the lock, wait until it gives it up. |

**Table 9.11**   `dio_fcntl` Argument Elements

| Key | Description |
|-----|-------------|
| length | Size of locked area. Set to `0` to go to the end of the file. |
| start | Starting offset. |
| type | Lock type. Valid values are `F_RDLCK`, `F_WRLCK`, and `F_UNLCK`. |
| wenth | Meaning of starting offset. Valid values are `SEEK_SET`, `SEEK_END`, and `SEEK_CUR`. |

### resource dio_open(string filename, integer flags, integer mode)

The `dio_open` function (Listing 9.57) opens a file and returns a file handle. The `flags` argument must include one of flags from Table 9.12. Optionally, you may combine these flags with any of those listed in Table 9.13 using the bitwise-OR operator ( `|` ). The optional `mode` argument sets the permissions for the file, as defined by `chmod`.

**Listing 9.57**   *dio_open*

```php
<?php
    //open file for appending, in synchronous mode
    $fp = dio_open('/tmp/data.txt',
        O_WRONLY | O_CREAT | O_APPEND | O_SYNC,
        0666);
```

**Listing 9.57** *dio_open (cont.)*

```
if($fp == -1)
{
    print('Unable to open file.');
    exit();
}

//write some random data
for($i=0; $i < 10; $i++)
{
    dio_write($fp, "Test: " . rand(1,100) . "\n");
}

//close
dio_close($fp);
?>
```

**Table 9.12**   dio_open Required Flags

| Flag | Description |
| --- | --- |
| O_RDONLY | Read only |
| O_RDWR | Read/Write |
| O_WRONLY | Write only |

**Table 9.13**   dio_open Optional Flags

| Flag | Description |
| --- | --- |
| O_APPEND | Open in append mode. |
| O_CREAT | Create the file if it doesn't exist. |
| O_EXCL | Cause dio_open to fail if O_CREAT is set and the file exists. |
| O_NDELAY | Alias for O_NONBLOCK. |
| O_NOCTTY | If the filename is a terminal device, it will not become the processes controlling terminal. |
| O_NONBLOCK | Start in nonblocking mode. |
| O_SYNC | Start in synchronous mode, which causes writes to block until data is written to the hardware. |
| O_TRUNC | If file exists and opened for write access, PHP truncates it to zero length. |

### string dio_read(resource file, integer length)

The dio_read function (Listing 9.58) returns a string read from an open file handle created by dio_open. The optional length argument specifies the number of bytes read. It defaults to 1024.

---

**Listing 9.58**   *dio_read*

```php
<?php
    //open /dev/random for reading
    $fp = dio_open('/dev/random', O_RDONLY);
    if($fp == -1)
    {
        print('Unable to open /dev/random');
        exit();
    }

    //read 4 bytes
    $data = dio_read($fp, 4);

    //covert raw binary into an integer
    $n = 0;
    for($i=0; $i < 4; $i++)
    {
        //get integer for this byte
        $p = ord(substr($data, $i, 1));

        //multiply it by the next power of 256
        $n += $p * pow(256, $i);
    }

    //print random number
    print($n);

    //close
    dio_close($fp);
?>
```

---

### dio_seek(resource file, integer position, integer from)

The dio_seek function moves the file pointer to the given position. The optional from argument may be SEEK_SET, SEEK_CUR, or SEEK_END, as described in relation to the fseek function.

### array dio_stat(resource file)

The `dio_stat` function returns an associative array that matches the data returned by the `stat` function. It requires a file handle created by `dio_open`.

### dio_tcsetattr(resource file, array options)

Use `dio_tcsetattr` to set terminal attributes for a file handle created with `dio_open`. Table 9.14 describes the options array.

**Table 9.14** `dio_tcsetattr` Options Array Elements

| Key | Description |
|---|---|
| baud | Set the baud rate. Valid values are 38400, 19200, 9600, 4800, 2400, 1800, 1200, 600, 300, 200, 150, 134, 110, 75, and 50. The default is 9600 baud. |
| bits | Set the number of data bits. Valid values are 8, 7, 6, and 5. The default is 8 data bits. |
| parity | Set the number of parity bits. Valid values are 0, 1, and 2. The default is 0. |
| stop | Set the number of stop bits. Valid values are 1 and 2. The default is 1. |

### boolean dio_truncate(resource file, integer length)

The `dio_truncate` function truncates a file to the given length. If the file is shorter than the given length, it is left to the operating system to decide if the file is left alone or padded with NULL characters.

### integer dio_write(resource file, string data, integer length)

The `dio_write` function writes the given data into an open file. If the optional `length` argument is set, it sets a maximum number of bytes written.

# 9.4 Debugging

The debugging functions help you figure out just what is going on with the inevitable broken script. Some of these functions make diagnostic information available to you inside your script. Others communicate with either a system log or a remote debugger. Practical approaches to debugging are addressed in Chapter 28.

**assert(boolean expression)**
**assert(string expression)**

The assert function (Listing 9.59) tests an expression. If the assertion is TRUE, no action is taken and the script continues. If the assertion is FALSE, behavior is dictated by the assertion options. By default, assertions are not active, which means they are simply ignored. Use assert_options to activate them.

Assertions are a nice way to add error checking to your code, especially paranoid checks that are useful during development but unneeded during production.

If the expression given assert is a string, PHP will evaluate it as it does with eval. This has the advantage of saving the time spent parsing the expression when assertions are turned off. It also has the advantage of making the expression available to a registered callback function.

---

**Listing 9.59** *assert*

```php
<?php
    //create custom assertion function
    function failedAssertion($file, $line, $expression)
    {
        print("On line $line, in file '$file' ");
        print("the following assertion failed:
            '$expression'<br>\n");
    }

    //turn on asserts
    assert_options(ASSERT_ACTIVE, TRUE);

    //bail on assertion failure
    assert_options(ASSERT_CALLBACK, "failedAssertion");

    //assert a false expression
    assert("1 == 2");
?>
```

---

**value assert_options(integer flag, value)**

Use assert_options to get and set assert flags. Table 9.15 lists the flags and their meanings. The previous value is returned. Most of the options expect a boolean because they are either on or off. The exception is the option for setting the callback function. This option expects the name of a function to be called when an assertion fails. This function will be called with three arguments: the filename, the line number, and the expression that evaluated as FALSE.

If you wish to register a class method for the callback, pass an array with two elements. The first is the name of the class, the second is the name of the method. To register that method of an object, pass a reference to the object as the first element.

Table 9.15 describes the options you can set with `assert`.

**Table 9.15** Assert Options

| Flag | Description |
|---|---|
| ASSERT_ACTIVE | Asserts are ignored unless activated with this option. |
| ASSERT_BAIL | Exits the script if assertion fails. FALSE by default. |
| ASSERT_CALLBACK | Registers a function to be called on failure. No function is registered by default. |
| ASSERT_QUIET_EVAL | Prints the expression passed to assert. FALSE by default. |
| ASSERT_WARNING | Prints a regular PHP warning message. TRUE by default. |

### boolean class_exists(string name)

The `class_exists` function (Listing 9.60) checks for the existence of a class.

**Listing 9.60** *class_exists*

```php
<?php
    class Counter
    {
        private $value;

        function Counter()
        {
            $this->value = 0;
        }

        function getValue()
        {
            return($this->value);
        }

        function increment()
        {
            $this->value++;
        }
    }
```

---

**Listing 9.60** *class_exists (cont.)*

```php
if(!class_exists('counter'))
{
    print('The counter class does not exist!');
    exit();
}

$c = new Counter;
$c->increment();
$c->increment();
print($c->getValue());
?>
```

---

### closelog()

The `closelog` function closes any connection to the system log. Calling it is optional, as PHP will close the connection for you when necessary. See `syslog` for an example of use.

### boolean connection_aborted()

Use `connection_aborted` (Listing 9.61) to test if a request for your script was aborted. The user may do this by clicking the stop button on the browser or closing the browser completely. Ordinarily, your script will stop executing when aborted. However, you may change this behavior with the `ignore_user_abort` function. You can also set abort handling using commands in `php.ini` or with an Apache directive. PHP can detect an abort only after it tries to send data to the browser.

---

**Listing 9.61** *connection_aborted*

```php
<?php
    //allow script continuation if aborted
    ignore_user_abort(TRUE);

    //fake a long task
    for($i=0; $i < 20; $i++)
    {
        print('Working...<br>');
        sleep(1);
    }
```

| Listing 9.61 | *connection_aborted (cont.)* |
|---|---|

```
   //check for abort
   if(connection_aborted())
   {
      //write to log that the process was aborted
      openlog("TEST", LOG_PID | LOG_CONS, LOG_USER);
      syslog(LOG_INFO, "The fake task has been aborted!");
      closelog();
   }
   else
   {
      print("Thanks for waiting!\n");
   }
?>
```

### integer connection_status()

The `connection_status` function (Listing 9.62) returns an integer describing the status of the connection to the browser. The integer uses bitfields to signal whether a connection was aborted or timed out. That is, binary digits are flipped on to signal either of the conditions. The first bit signals whether the script aborted. The second signals whether the script reached its maximum execution time. Rather than using 1 or 2, you can use the convenient constants `CONNECTION_ABORTED` and `CONNECTION_TIMEOUT`. There's also a constant named `CONNECTION_NORMAL`, which is set to zero, meaning no bitfields are turned on.

| Listing 9.62 | *connection_status* |
|---|---|

```
<?php
   function cleanUp()
   {
      $status = connection_status();

      $statusMessage = date("Y-m-d H:i:s");
      $statusMessage .= " Status was $status. ";

      if($status & CONNECTION_ABORTED)
      {
         $statusMessage .= "The script was aborted. ";
      }
```

**Listing 9.62** *connection_status (cont.)*

```
    if($status & CONNECTION_TIMEOUT)
    {
        $statusMessage .= "The script timed out. ";
    }

    $statusMessage .= "\n";

    //write status to log file
    error_log($statusMessage, 3, "/tmp/status.log");

    return(TRUE);
}

//set cleanUp to the shutdown function
register_shutdown_function("cleanUp");

set_time_limit(3);

//wait out the max execution time
while(TRUE)
{
    for($i=1; $i < 80; $i++)
    {
        print('x');
    }
    print('<br>');
}

print("Fake task finished.\n");
?>
```

### array debug_backtrace()

The debug_backtrace function (Listing 9.63) returns an array describing the call stack. Each element of the array is an array describing the calling function. The following elements are present in each array: file, line, function, and args. Class methods will also contain class and type elements, the latter being with :: or -> depending on whether the method executed statically or from an object respectively.

| Listing 9.63 | *debug_backtrace* |
|---|---|

```php
<?php
    function A()
    {
        print_r(debug_backtrace());
    }

    class B
    {
        function testB()
        {
            A();
        }
    }

    class C
    {
        function testC()
        {
            B::testB();
        }
    }

    $c = new C;
    $c->testC();

    B::testB();
?>
```

### debug_print_backtrace()

The `debug_print_backtrace` function prints call stack information rather than returning an array as `debug_backtrace` does.

### string debug_zval_dump(...)

The `debug_zval_dump` function (Listing 9.64) returns a string describing the internal Zend value of each argument. The arguments may be variables or literals. The description gives the type, the length for strings, the value, and the reference count.

| Listing 9.64 | *debug_zval_dump* |
|---|---|

```php
<?php
    //string(24) "/usr/local/apache/htdocs" refcount(2)
    debug_zval_dump($_SERVER["DOCUMENT_ROOT"]);
?>
```

### boolean error_log(string message, integer type, string destination, string extra_headers)

The `error_log` function (Listing 9.65) sends an error message to one of four places depending on the `type` argument. The values for the `type` argument are listed in Table 9.16. An alternative to `error_log` is the `syslog` function.

**Listing 9.65** `error_log`

```php
<?php
    //send log message via email to root
    error_log("The error_log is working", 1, "root", "");
?>
```

**Table 9.16** `error_log` Message Types

| Type | Description |
|------|-------------|
| 0 | Depending on the `error_log` configuration directive, the message is sent either to the system log or to a file. |
| 1 | The message is sent by email to the address specified by the `destination` argument. If the `extra_headers` argument is not empty, it is sent as headers to the email. |
| 3 | The message is appended to the file specified by the `destination` argument. |

### boolean extension_loaded(string extension)

Use `extension_loaded` (Listing 9.66) to test for the presence of an extension.

**Listing 9.66** `extension_loaded`

```php
<?php
    if(extension_loaded("mysql"))
    {
        print("mysql extension loaded");
    }
    else
    {
        print("mysql extension not loaded");
    }
?>
```

### boolean function_exists(string function)

Use `function_exists` (Listing 9.67) to test that a function is available, either natively or defined previously by PHP code. Note that it's possible for a function to exist and not be callable. You may wish to use `is_callable` instead.

---

**Listing 9.67** *function_exists*

```php
<?php
    $function = "date";
    if(function_exists($function))
    {
        print($function . " exists");
    }
?>
```

---

### object get_browser(string user_agent)

The `get_browser` function (Listing 9.68) works with the `browscap.ini` (browser capabilities) file to report the capabilities of a browser. The `user_agent` argument is the text a browser identifies itself with during an HTTP transaction. If you leave out this argument, PHP uses the user-agent request header. The argument is matched against all the browsers in the `browscap.ini` file. When a match occurs, each of the capabilities becomes a property in the object returned.

The location of the `browscap.ini` file is specified in `php.ini` using the `browscap` directive. If the directive is not used, or PHP can't match a browser to an entry in your `browscap.ini` file, no error will be produced. However, the returned object will have no properties.

Microsoft provides a `browscap.ini` file for use with its Web server, but it is not freely distributable. The best alternative is Gary Keith's Browser Capabilities Project <http://www.garykeith.com/>.

---

**Listing 9.68** *get_browser*

```php
<?php
    $browser = get_browser();
    print("You are using " . $browser->browser . "<br>\n");
    if($browser->javascript)
    {
        print("Your browser supports JavaScript.<br>\n");
    }
?>
```

---

### string get_cfg_var(string variable)

The `get_cfg_var` function (Listing 9.69) returns the value of the specified configuration variable. These are the variables specified in `php.ini` or in Apache's configuration files. You can get a report on all configuration information by calling the `phpinfo` function.

**Listing 9.69** `get_cfg_var`

```php
<?php
    print("Scripts are allowed to run " .
        get_cfg_var("max_execution_time") .
        " seconds");
?>
```

### string get_current_user()

The `get_current_user` function (Listing 9.70) returns the name of the user who owns the script being executed.

**Listing 9.70** `get_current_user`

```php
<?php
    print(get_current_user());
?>
```

### string getcwd()

The `getcwd` function (Listing 9.71) returns the name of the current working directory, including the full path.

**Listing 9.71** `getcwd`

```php
<?php
    print(getcwd());
?>
```

### array get_declared_classes()

The `get_declared_classes` function (Listing 9.72) returns an array of classes created by PHP, by extensions, or by your script.

| Listing 9.72 | *get_declared_classes,* *get_defined_constants,* *get_defined_functions, get_defined_vars* |
|---|---|

```php
<?php
    print("Classes\n");
    print_r(get_declared_classes());

    print("Constants\n");
    print_r(get_defined_constants());

    print("Functions\n");
    print_r(get_defined_functions());

    print("Variables\n");
    print_r(get_defined_vars());
?>
```

### array get_defined_constants()

The `get_defined_constants` function returns an array of all defined constants.

### array get_defined_functions()

The `get_defined_functions` function returns an array of available functions. The returned array contains two arrays indexed as `internal` and `user`.

### array get_defined_vars()

The `get_defined_vars` function returns an array of variables in the current scope.

### array get_extension_funcs(string extension)

Use `get_extension_funcs` to get an array of the names of functions created by an extension.

### string get_include_path()

The `get_include_path` function returns the current include path.

### array get_included_files()

The `get_included_files` function returns a list of files executed by PHP via `include`, `include_once`, `require`, and `require_once`. The currently executing file is included too.

### array get_loaded_extensions()

The `get_loaded_extensions` function returns an array of the names of the extensions available. This includes extensions compiled into PHP or loaded with `dl`. Another way to see this list is with `phpinfo`.

### integer getmygid()

Use `getmygid` to get the group ID of the owner of the executing script.

### array getopt(string options)

The `getopt` function (Listing 9.73) evaluates options passed to the PHP script on the command line. It uses the C function of the same name. At the time of writing, it only handled single-character options.

Pass a string of valid options for which you wish to check. Following the option with a colon requires the option to provide a value. Following the option with two colons makes a qualifying value optional. You may use letters and numbers for options.

The returned array uses the options for keys, which point to passed values if they exist. Options named more than once become arrays of values in the returned array.

---

**Listing 9.73** *getopt*

```php
<?php
    $option = getopt("a::");

    if(isset($option['a']))
    {
        print("Option a activated\n");

        if(is_array($option['a']))
        {
            print(count($option['a']) . " values:\n");

            foreach($option['a'] as $o)
            {
                if($o)
                {
                    print(" Value: $o\n");
                }
```

| Listing 9.73 | *getopt (cont.)* |
|---|---|

```
            else
            {
                print(" No value\n");
            }
        }
    }
    elseif($option['a'])
    {
        print("Value: {$option['a']}\n");
    }
    else
    {
        print("No value\n");
    }
}
?>
```

### get_required_files

This is an alias to `get_included_files`.

### array get_html_translation_table(integer table, integer quote_style)

Use `get_html_translation_table` (Listing 9.74) to get the table used by `htmlentities` and `htmlspecialchars`. Both arguments are optional. The `table` argument may be set to `HTML_ENTITIES` or `HTML_SPECIALCHARS` but defaults to the latter. The `quote_style` argument may be `ENT_COMPAT`, `ENT_QUOTES`, or `ENT_NOQUOTES`. It defaults to `ENT_COMPAT`.

| Listing 9.74 | *get_html_translation_table* |
|---|---|

```
<?php
    $trans = get_html_translation_table(HTML_ENTITIES);
    var_dump($trans);
?>
```

### integer get_magic_quotes_gpc()

The `get_magic_quotes_gpc` function (Listing 9.75) returns the `magic_quotes_gpc` directive setting, which controls whether quotes are escaped automatically in user-submitted data.

**Listing 9.75** `get_magic_quotes_gpc`

```php
<?php
    if(get_magic_quotes_gpc() == 1)
    {
        print("magic_quotes_gpc is on");
    }
    else
    {
        print("magic_quotes_gpc is off");
    }
?>
```

### integer get_magic_quotes_runtime()

The `get_magic_quotes_runtime` function (Listing 9.76) returns the `magic_quotes_runtime` directive setting, which controls whether quotes are escaped automatically in data retrieved from databases. You can use `set_magic_quotes_runtime` to change its value.

**Listing 9.76** `get_magic_quotes_runtime`

```php
<?php
    if(get_magic_quotes_runtime() == 1)
    {
        print("magic_quotes_runtime is on");
    }
    else
    {
        print("magic_quotes_runtime is off");
    }
?>
```

### integer getlastmod()

The `getlastmod` function (Listing 9.77) returns the date the executing script was last modified. The date is returned as a number of seconds since January 1, 1970. This is the same as calling `filemtime` on the current file.

**Listing 9.77** `getlastmod`

```php
<?php
    printf("This script was last modified %s",
        date("m/d/y", getlastmod()));
?>
```

### integer getmyinode()

The `getmyinode` function (Listing 9.78) returns the inode of the executing script. Under Windows zero is always returned. You can get the inode of any file using `fileinode`.

---

**Listing 9.78** *getmyinode*

```php
<?php
    print(getmyinode());
?>
```

---

### integer getmypid()

The `getmypid` function (Listing 9.79) returns the process identifier of the PHP engine.

---

**Listing 9.79** *getmypid*

```php
<?php
    print(getmypid());
?>
```

---

### integer getmyuid()

The `getmyuid` function (Listing 9.80) returns the user identifier of the owner of the script.

---

**Listing 9.80** *getmyuid*

```php
<?php
    print(getmyuid());
?>
```

---

### array getrusage(integer children)

The `getrusage` function (Listing 9.81) is a wrapper for the C function of the same name. It reports information about the resources used by the calling process. If the `children` argument is 1, the function will be called with the `RUSAGE_CHILDREN` constant. You may wish to read the man page for more information.

**Listing 9.81** *getrusage*

```php
<?php
    //show CPU time used
    $rusage = getrusage(1);
    print($rusage["ru_utime.tv_sec"] . " seconds used.");
?>
```

### boolean headers_sent(string file, integer line)

The headers_sent function (Listing 9.82) returns TRUE if HTTP headers have been sent. Headers must precede any content, so executing a print statement or placing text outside PHP tags will cause headers to be sent. Attempting to add headers to the stack after they're sent causes an error.

The optional file and line arguments will receive the name of the file and the line number where headers were sent.

**Listing 9.82** *headers_sent*

```php
<?php
    if(headers_sent($file, $line))
    {
        print("Headers were sent in $file on line $line<br>\n");
    }
    else
    {
        header("X-Debug: It's OK to send a header");
    }
?>
```

### string highlight_file(string filename, boolean return_instead)

The highlight_file function (Listing 9.83) prints a PHP script directly to the browser using syntax highlighting. HTML is used to emphasize parts of the PHP language in order to aid readability. If the optional return_instead argument is TRUE, PHP returns the HTML instead of printing it.

**Listing 9.83** *highlight_file*

```php
<?php
    //highlight this file
    highlight_file(__FILE__);
?>
```

### string highlight_string(string code, boolean return_instead)

The `highlight_string` function (Listing 9.84) prints a string of PHP code to the browser using syntax highlighting. If the optional `return_instead` argument is TRUE, PHP returns the HTML instead of printing it.

**Listing 9.84** *highlight_string*

```php
<?php
    //create some code
    $code = "<?php print(\"a string\"); ?>";

    //highlight sample code
    $source = highlight_string($code, TRUE);

    //show the HTML PHP uses to highlight code
    print(htmlentities($source));
?>
```

### array iconv_get_encoding(string type)

The `iconv_get_encoding` function returns the encoding types in use. The `type` argument may be `all`, `input_encoding`, `internal_encoding`, or `output_encoding`. If you set `type` to `all`, PHP returns an array with keys matching the three encoding types. If you fetch a single encoding type, PHP returns a string.

You may set `iconv` encodings with `iconv_set_encoding`. You may translate text with the `iconv` function or with the `ob_iconv_handler` output buffer handler.

### boolean is_callable(string function, boolean syntax, string name)
### boolean is_callable(array method, boolean syntax, string name)

Use `is_callable` (Listing 9.85) to test whether a function or object method is available for execution. You may pass a function name as a string or a two-element array that names an object method. The first element of the array must be the name of a class or an instance of the class. The second element must be a string containing the name of the method.

The optional `syntax` argument suppresses any checking for the function. In this mode, PHP checks on the syntax of the first argument only. The optional third argument receives the name of the function or method being tested. This is helpful when you want to report to the user about the function not being available.

**Listing 9.85** *is_callable*

```php
<?php
    //Call function if it's available
    function callIfPossible($f, $arg=FALSE)
    {
        //if no arguments, use empty array
        if($arg === FALSE)
        {
            $arg = array();
        }

        if(is_callable($f, FALSE, $callName))
        {
            call_user_func_array($f, $arg);
        }
        else
        {
            print("Unable to call $callName<br>");
        }
    }

    //functions for testing
    function a()
    {
        print('function a<br>');
    }

    class c
    {
        function m()
        {
            print('method m<br>');
        }
    }

    //built-in function
    callIfPossible('print_r', array('print_r<br>'));

    //not technically a function
    callIfPossible('print', array('print<br>'));

    //user function
    callIfPossible('a');

    //non-existent
    callIfPossible('b');
```

**Listing 9.85**  *is_callable (cont.)*

```
//method from a class
callIfPossible(array('c', 'm'));

//non-existent
callIfPossible(array('d', 'm'));

//method from an object
$C = new c;
callIfPossible(array($C, 'm'));

//non-existent
callIfPossible(array($C, 'x'));
?>
```

## boolean leak(integer bytes)

The `leak` function (Listing 9.86) purposely leaks memory. It is useful mostly for testing the garbage-collecting routines of PHP itself. You might also use it to simulate lots of memory usage if you are stress testing.

**Listing 9.86**  *leak*

```
<?php
    //leak 8 megs
    leak(8388608);
?>
```

## array localeconv()

The `localeconv` function returns an array describing the formatting performed by the current locale. It wraps the C function of the same name, so reading the man page may be helpful. You can change these by using `setlocale`. Table 9.17 lists the elements of the return array.

**Table 9.17**  `localeconv` Return Elements

| Name | Description |
| --- | --- |
| currency_symbol | Currency symbol, such as $. |
| decimal_point | Character used to for the decimal point, such as a period. |
| frac_digits | Number of fractional digits. |

**Table 9.17**   `localeconv` Return Elements *(cont.)*

| Name | Description |
|------|-------------|
| grouping | Array of numeric groupings. |
| int_curr_symbol | International currency symbol, such as USD. |
| int_frac_digits | Number of fractional digits. |
| mon_decimal_point | Decimal point character used in monetary figures. |
| mon_grouping | Array of numeric groupings used in monetary figures. |
| mon_thousands_sep | Character used to separate groups of thousands in monetary figures. |
| n_cs_precedes | Boolean for whether the currency symbol precedes a negative sign. |
| n_sep_by_space | Boolean for whether a space is inserted between a negative sign and a currency symbol. |
| n_sign_posn | 0   Parentheses surround the quantity and currency symbol.<br>1   Negative sign precedes the quantity and currency symbol.<br>2   Negative sign succeeds the quantity and currency symbol.<br>3   Negative sign immediately precedes the currency symbol.<br>4   Negative sign immediately succeeds the currency symbol. |
| negative_sign | Character used to denote a negative value, such as -. |
| p_cs_precedes | Boolean for whether the currency symbol precedes a positive sign. |
| p_sep_by_space | Boolean for whether a space is inserted between a positive sign and a currency symbol. |
| p_sign_posn | 0   Parentheses surround the quantity and currency symbol.<br>1   Positive sign precedes the quantity and currency symbol.<br>2   Positive sign succeeds the quantity and currency symbol.<br>3   Positive sign immediately precedes the currency symbol.<br>4   Positive sign immediately succeeds the currency symbol. |
| positive_sign | Character used to denote a positive value, such as +. |
| thousands_sep | Character used to separate groups of thousands, such as a comma. |

### string nl_langinfo(integer code)

The `nl_langinfo` function wraps the C function of the same name and offers more flexible access to the same information provided by `localeconv`. Reading the man page for `nl_langinfo` may be helpful. The codes in Table 9.18 are defined as constants.

**Table 9.18**　`nl_langinfo` Codes

| Code | Description |
|------|-------------|
| `ABDAY_[1-7]` | The abbreviated name of the day of the week, where `DAY_1` is Sunday. |
| `ABMON_[1-12]` | The abbreviated name of the month, where `MON_1` is January. |
| `CODESET` | The name of the character encoding used. |
| `CRNCYSTR` | The currency symbol, preceded by - if the symbol should appear before the value, + if the symbol should appear after the value, or . if the symbol should replace the radix character. |
| `DAY_[1-7]` | The name of the day of the week, where `DAY_1` is Sunday. |
| `D_FMT` | A string suitable for passing to `strftime` to represent a date. |
| `D_T_FMT` | A string suitable for passing to `strftime` to represent a date and time. |
| `MON_[1-12]` | The name of the month, where `MON_1` is January. |
| `NOEXPR` | A regular expression that represents a negative response to a yes/no question. |
| `RADIXCHAR` | The radix character, the character that separates whole numbers from decimal digits. |
| `THOUSEP` | The character used to separate thousands. |
| `T_FMT` | A string suitable for passing to `strftime` to represent a time. |
| `YESEXPR` | A regular expression that represents a positive response to a yes/no question. |

### openlog(string identifier, integer option, integer facility)

The `openlog` function begins a connection to the system log and calls C's `openlog` function. It is not strictly required to call `openlog` before using `syslog`, but it may be used to change the behavior of the `syslog` function. You may wish to refer to the man page for `openlog` for more details. On Windows emulation code is used to mimic UNIX functionality.

The `identifier` argument will be added to the beginning of any messages sent to the system log. Usually, this is the name of the process or task being performed.

The `option` argument is a bitfield that controls toggling of miscellaneous options. Use a logical-OR operator to combine the options you want. Table 9.19 lists the values available. Only the `LOG_PID` option has no effect under Windows.

**Table 9.19**   `openlog` Options

| Constant | Description |
| --- | --- |
| LOG_CONS | If a message can't be sent to the log, send it to the system console. |
| LOG_NDELAY | Open the log immediately. Do not wait for first call to `syslog`. |
| LOG_NOWAIT | Do not wait for child processes. The use of this flag is discouraged. |
| LOG_ODELAY | Delay opening log until the first call to `syslog`. This is TRUE by default. |
| LOG_PERROR | Log all messages to `stderr` as well. |
| LOG_PID | Add process identifier to each message. |

The `facility` argument sets a default value for the source of the error—that is, from which part of the system the report comes. The argument is ignored under Windows. Table 9.20 lists the facilities available. See `syslog` for an example of use.

**Table 9.20**   `openlog` Facilities

| Constant | Facility |
| --- | --- |
| LOG_AUTH | Authorization |
| LOG_AUTHPRIV | Authorization Privileges |
| LOG_CRON | Cron |
| LOG_DAEMON | Daemon |
| LOG_KERN | Kernel |
| LOG_LPR | Printer |
| LOG_MAIL | Mail |
| LOG_NEWS | News |
| LOG_SYSLOG | System Log |
| LOG_USER | User |
| LOG_UUCP | UNIX to UNIX Protocol |

### phpcredits(integer flags)

The `phpcredits` function prints information about the major contributors to the PHP project. If the optional `flags` argument is left out, all information will be provided. Otherwise, you may combine the flags listed in Table 9.21 to choose a specific set of information. The `PHP_FULL_PAGE` constant will cause the credits to be surrounded with tags for defining an HTML document.

You can also see this information by adding `?=PHPB8B5F2A0-3C92-11d3-A3A9-4C7B08C10000` to a request for a PHP script. This is similar to the technique described below for fetching the PHP or Zend logos.

**Table 9.21**   Flags for `phpcredits`

| Flag | Description |
| --- | --- |
| CREDITS_ALL | Print all credits and include HTML tags for creating a complete HTML document. |
| CREDITS_DOCS | Documentation team. |
| CREDITS_FULLPAGE | Include HTML tags for creating a complete HTML document. |
| CREDITS_GENERAL | General credits. |
| CREDITS_GROUP | Core developers. |
| CREDITS_MODULES | Module authors. |
| CREDITS_SAPI | Server API module authors. |

### boolean phpinfo(integer flags)

The `phpinfo` function sends a large amount of diagnostic information to the browser and returns `TRUE`. The `flags` argument is not required. By default, all information is returned. You may use the flags listed in Table 9.22 with bitwise-OR operators to choose specific information.

**Table 9.22**   Flags for `phpinfo`

| Flag | Description |
| --- | --- |
| INFO_CONFIGURATION | Configuration settings from `php.ini` and for the current script. |
| INFO_CREDITS | Credits as returned by `phpcredits`. |
| INFO_ENVIRONMENT | Environment variables. |

**Table 9.22** Flags for `phpinfo` *(cont.)*

| Flag | Description |
|---|---|
| INFO_GENERAL | Description of server, build date, line used to configure PHP for compilation, Server API, virtual directory support, path to `php.ini`, PHP API ID, extension ID, Zend Engine ID, debug build, thread safety, list of registered streams. |
| INFO_LICENSE | The PHP license. |
| INFO_MODULES | Extensions available. |
| INFO_VARIABLES | Predefined variables. |

Calling `phpinfo` is a good way to find out which environment variables are available to you.

### string php_ini_scanned_files()

The `php_ini_scanned_files` function returns a comma-separated list of configuration files parsed after `php.ini`. These are found in a path as defined by the `--with-config-file-scan-dir` option to PHP's `configure` script, which is used prior to compilation.

### string php_logo_guid()

The `php_logo_guid` function (Listing 9.87) returns a special code that when passed to a PHP script returns the PHP logo in GIF format. This is the logo shown on the page generated by `phpinfo`.

**Listing 9.87** `php_logo_guid`

```php
<?php
    //show PHP logo
    print('<img src="' . $_SERVER["PHP_SELF"] . '?=' .
        php_logo_guid() . '">');

    //show Zend log
    print('<img src="' . $_SERVER["PHP_SELF"] . '?=' .
        zend_logo_guid() . '">');
?>
```

### string php_sapi_name()

The `php_sapi_name` function returns the name of the Server API module used for the request.

### string php_uname()

Use `php_uname` to get information about the server that compiled PHP. This is the same information shown by the `phpinfo` function.

### string phpversion()

The `phpversion` function returns a string that describes the version of PHP executing the script.

### print_r(expression, boolean value)

The `print_r` function (Listing 9.88) prints the value of an expression. If the expression is a string, integer, or double, the simple representation of it is sent to the browser. If the expression is an object or array, special notation is used to show indices or property names. Arrays and objects are explored recursively. After showing an array, `print_r` will leave the internal pointer at the end of the array.

The formatting used by `print_r` is intended to be more readable than `var_dump`, which performs a similar function. It is usually helpful to use `print_r` inside PRE tags.

---

**Listing 9.88** *print_r*

```php
<?php
    //define some test variables
    $s = "an example string";
    $a = array("x", "y", "z", array(1, 2, 3));

    print('<pre>');

    //print a string
    print("\$s: ");
    print_r($s);
    print("\n");

    //print an array
    print("\$a: ");
    print_r($a);
    print("\n");

    print('</pre>');
?>
```

### register_tick_function(string function, …)

Use `register_tick_function` to execute a function with each PHP operation. You must supply the name of a function and then execute a block of code inside a `declare` statement that sets the `ticks` value. Optionally, you may supply any number of additional arguments, which PHP passes to the `callback` function. See Chapter 3 for a discussion of the `declare` statement.

This function offers a way to profile code. You can log the time on the microsecond clock to test how long each operation takes to execute. Keep in mind that many lines of code represent several operations.

Use `unregister_tick_function` to unregister a tick function.

### show_source

Use `show_source` as an alias to `highlight_file`.

### syslog(integer priority, string message)

The `syslog` function (Listing 9.89) adds a message to the system log. It is a wrapper for C's function of the same name. The `priority` is an integer that stands for how severe the situation is. Under UNIX the `priority` may cause the system to take special measures. Priorities are listed in Table 9.23.

**Table 9.23** `syslog` Priorities

| Constant | Priority | Description |
| --- | --- | --- |
| LOG_EMERG | Emergency | This is a panic situation, and the message may be broadcast to all users of the system. On Windows this is translated to a warning. |
| LOG_ALERT | Alert | This is a situation that demands being corrected immediately. It is translated into being an error on Windows. |
| LOG_CRIT | Critical | This is a critical condition that may be created by hardware errors. It is translated into being a warning on Windows. |
| LOG_ERR | Error | These are general error conditions. They are translated into warnings on Windows. |
| LOG_WARNING | Warning | These are warnings, less severe than errors. |
| LOG_NOTICE | Notice | A notice is not an error but requires more attention than an informational message. It is translated into a warning on Windows. |

**Table 9.23**  `syslog` Priorities *(cont.)*

| Constant | Priority | Description |
| --- | --- | --- |
| `LOG_INFO` | Information | Informational messages do not require that any special action be taken. |
| `LOG_DEBUG` | Debug | These messages are of interest only for debugging tasks. They are translated into warnings. |

Under Windows emulation code is used to simulate the UNIX functionality. Messages generated by the `syslog` function are added to the application log, which may be viewed with Event Viewer. The priority is used in two ways. First, it is translated into being an error, a warning, or information. This determines the icon that appears next to the message in Event Viewer. It is also used to fill the Category column. The Event column will always be set to 2000, and the User column will be set to null.

**Listing 9.89**  *syslog*

```php
<?php
    openlog("Core PHP", LOG_PID | LOG_CONS, LOG_USER);
    syslog(LOG_INFO, "The log has been tested");
    closelog();
?>
```

### trigger_error(string message, integer type)

Use `trigger_error` to cause PHP to report an error through its error-handling functionality. The first argument is the message displayed. The second argument is optional and may be set to `E_USER_ERROR`, `E_USER_WARNING`, or `E_USER_NOTICE`, which is the default.

### user_error

You may use `user_error` as an alias to `trigger_error`.

### var_dump(expression, ...)

The `var_dump` function (Listing 9.90) reports all information about a given variable. Information is printed directly to the browser. You may supply any number of variables separated by commas. The output of the command is well formatted, including indention for cases such as arrays containing other arrays. Arrays and objects are explored recursively.

The output of `var_dump` is more verbose but perhaps less readable than that of `print_r`.

---

**Listing 9.90**   *var_dump*

```php
<?php
    //define some test variables
    $s = "an example string";
    $a = array("x", "y", "z", array(1, 2, 3));

    print('<pre>');

    //print a string
    print("\$s: ");
    var_dump($s);
    print("\n");

    //print an array
    print("\$a: ");
    var_dump($a);
    print("\n");

    print('</pre>');
?>
```

---

**string var_export(expression, boolean return)**

The `var_export` function prints the PHP code for representing the given expression. If the optional `return` argument is TRUE, the string is returned instead. This function does not return usable information about objects. Compare this function to `var_dump`.

**integer version_compare(string version1, string version2, string operator)**

The `version_compare` function (Listing 9.91) compares two PHP version strings. Without the optional third argument, it returns -1, 0, or 1, depending on `version1` being less-than, equal-to, or greater-than `version2`. If you supply one of the operators shown in Table 9.24, `version_compare` returns TRUE or FALSE.

| Listing 9.91 | *version_compare* |
|---|---|

```php
<?php
    if(version_compare(PHP_VERSION, '5.0.10', '<'))
    {
        print('PHP version ' . PHP_VERSION . ' is too old.');
    }
    else
    {
        print('PHP version ' . PHP_VERSION . ' is new enough.');
    }
?>
```

**Table 9.24**   version_compare Operators

| Operator | Description |
|---|---|
| <, lt | Less than |
| <=, le | Less than or equal to |
| >, gt | Greater than |
| >=, ge | Greater than or equal to |
| ==, =, eq | Equal to |
| !=, <>, ne | Not equal to |

### unregister_tick_function(string name)

Use unregister_tick_function to unregister a tick function. See register_tick_function.

### string zend_logo_guid()

The zend_logo_guid function returns a special code that when passed to a PHP script returns the Zend logo in GIF format. This is the logo shown on the page generated by phpinfo.

### string zend_version()

Use zend_version (Listing 9.92) to get the version of the Zend library.

| Listing 9.92 | *zend_version* |
|---|---|

```php
<?php
    print(zend_version());
?>
```

**string zlib_get_coding_type()**

The `zlib_get_coding_type` function returns the name of the encoding type used for output compression.

# 9.5 POSIX

Kristian Koehntopp added a module to PHP to support the POSIX.1 standard, also known as IEEE 1003.1. This standard describes functionality provided to user processes by an operating system. A few functions in this section are not part of the standard, but are commonly available in System V or BSD UNIX systems.

Many of these functions are available only to the root user. PHP scripts are executed by the owner of the Web server process, which is usually a special user for just this purpose. Running the Web server as root is unusual and dangerous. Anyone able to view a PHP file through the Web server could have arbitrary control over the system. Keep in mind, however, that PHP can be compiled as a standalone executable. In this case it can be used like any other scripting engine.

These functions are wrappers for underlying C functions, usually named by the part after the `posix_` prefix. If you require detailed information, I suggest reading the man pages.

Listing 9.93 demonstrates many of the POSIX functions.

| Listing 9.93 | *Posix functions* |
| --- | --- |

```php
<?php
    print("Terminal Path Name: " . posix_ctermid() . "\n");
    print("Current Working Directory: " . posix_getcwd() . "\n");
    print("Effective Group ID: " . posix_getegid() . "\n");
    print("Effective User ID: " . posix_geteuid() . "\n");
    print("Group ID: " . posix_getgid() . "\n");

    $groupInfo = posix_getgrgid(posix_getgid());
    print("Group Name: " . $groupInfo['name'] . "\n");

    print("Supplementary Group IDs:" .
        implode(',', posix_getgroups()) . "\n");
    print("Login: " . posix_getlogin() . "\n");

    print("Process Group ID: " .
        posix_getpgid(posix_getpid()) . "\n");
    print("Current Process Group ID: " . posix_getpgrp() . "\n");
    print("Current Process ID: " . posix_getpid() . "\n");
    print("Parent Process ID: " . posix_getppid() . "\n");
```

| Listing 9.93 | *Posix functions (cont.)* |

```
    print("User Info (posix_getlogin): ");
    print_r(posix_getpwnam(posix_getlogin()));
    print("User Info (): ");
    print_r(posix_getpwuid(posix_geteuid()));

    print("Resource Limits: ");
    print_r(posix_getrlimit());

    print("SID: " . posix_getsid(posix_getpid()) . "\n");
    print("Real User ID: " . posix_getuid() . "\n");

    print("System Information: ");
    print_r(posix_uname());
?>
```

### string posix_ctermid()

The `posix_ctermid` function returns the terminal path name.

### integer posix_errno()

This function returns the last error created by a POSIX function.

### string posix_getcwd()

The `posix_getcwd` function returns the current working directory.

### integer posix_getegid()

The `posix_getegid` function returns the effective group ID of the calling process.

### integer posix_geteuid()

The `posix_geteuid` function returns the effective user ID for the process running the PHP engine.

### integer posix_getgid()

The `posix_getgid` function returns the ID of the current group.

### array posix_getgrgid(integer group)

The `posix_getgrgid` function returns an array describing access to the group database given the group number. The elements of the returned array are `gid`, `members`, `name`, and an entry of each member of the group.

### array posix_getgrnam(string group)

The `posix_getgrnam` function returns an array describing access to the group database given the group name. The elements of the returned array are `gid`, `members`, `name`, and an entry of each member of the group.

### array posix_getgroups()

The `posix_getgroups` function returns supplementary group IDs.

### string posix_getlogin()

Use `posix_getlogin` to get the login name of the user executing the PHP engine.

### integer posix_getpgid(integer pid)

The `posix_getpgid` function returns the group ID for the given process ID.

### integer posix_getpgrp()

The `posix_getpgrp` function returns the current process group ID.

### integer posix_getpid()

The `posix_getpid` function returns the process ID.

### integer posix_getppid()

The `posix_getppid` function returns the process ID of the parent process.

### array posix_getpwnam(string user)

The `posix_getpwnam` function returns an array describing an entry in the user database. The elements of the array are `dir`, `gecos`, `gid`, `name`, `passwd`, `shell`, and `uid`.

### array posix_getpwuid(integer user)

The `posix_getpwuid` function returns an array describing an entry in the user database based on a given user ID. The elements of the array are `dir`, `gecos`, `gid`, `name`, `passwd`, `shell`, and `uid`. These are the same elements returned by `posix_getpwnam`.

### array posix_getrlimit()

The `posix_getrlimit` function returns an array describing system resource usage. The array contains elements that begin with `hard` or `soft` followed by a space and one of the following limit names: `core`, `cpu`, `data`, `filesize`, `maxproc`, `memlock`, `openfiles`, `rss`, `stack`, `totalmem`, or `virtualmem`.

### integer posix_getsid()

The `posix_getsid` function returns the process group ID of the session leader.

### integer posix_getuid()

The `posix_getuid` function returns the user ID of the user executing the PHP engine.

### boolean posix_isatty(integer descriptor)

The `posix_isatty` function returns TRUE if the given file descriptor is a TTY.

### boolean posix_kill(integer process, integer signal)

The `posix_kill` function sends a signal to a process.

### boolean posix_mkfifo(string path, integer mode)

The `posix_mkfifo` function creates a FIFO file. The `mode` argument follows the same rules as `chmod`.

### boolean posix_setegid(integer group)

Use `posix_setegid` to change the effective group for the current process. Only the root user may switch groups.

### boolean posix_seteuid(integer user)

Use `posix_seteuid` to change the effective user for the current process. Only the root user may change the user ID.

### boolean posix_setgid(integer group)

Use `posix_setgid` to change the group for the current process. Only the root user may switch groups.

### integer posix_setpgid(integer process, integer group)

The `posix_setpgid` function puts the process into a process group.

### integer posix_setsid()

The `posix_setsid` function sets the current process as the session leader. The session ID is returned.

### boolean posix_setuid(integer user)

Use `posix_setuid` to change the user for the current process. Only the root user may change the user ID.

### string posix_strerror()

This function returns the description of the last error generated by a POSIX function.

### array posix_times()

The `posix_times` function returns an array of values on system clocks. The elements of the array are `cstime`, `cutime`, `stime`, `ticks`, and `utime`. Table 9.25 describes these elements. Typically, there are 1 million ticks in a second.

**Table 9.25**   Array Returned by `posix_times`

| Element | Description |
| --- | --- |
| cstime | The number of ticks spent by the operating system while executing child processes. |
| cutime | The number of ticks used by child processes. |
| stime | The number of ticks used by the operating system on behalf of the calling process. |
| ticks | The number of ticks since the system last rebooted. |
| utime | The number of ticks used by the CPU while executing user instructions. |

### string posix_ttyname(integer descriptor)

The `posix_ttyname` function returns the name of the terminal device.

### array posix_uname()

The `posix_uname` function returns an array of information about the system. The elements of the array are `machine`, `nodename`, `release`, `sysname`, and `version`.

# 9.6  Shell Commands

This section describes functions that interact with the command shell in some way. Some of them execute other programs, and two of them read or write to environment variables.

### string exec(string command, array output, integer return)

The exec function (Listing 9.94) attempts to execute the command argument as if you had typed it in the command shell. PHP sends nothing to the browser but returns the last line of output from the execution. If you supply the optional output argument, PHP adds each line of output to the output argument. If you supply the optional return argument, PHP sets it with the command's return value.

It is very dangerous to put any user-supplied information inside the command argument. Users may pass values in form fields that allow them to execute their own commands on your Web server. If you must execute a command based on user input, pass the information through the escapeshellcmd function.

Compare this function to passthru, shell_exec, and system.

---

**Listing 9.94** *exec*

```php
<?php
    // get directory list for the root of C drive
    $lastLine = exec("ls -l /", $allOutput, $returnValue);

    print("Last Line: $lastLine<br>\n");

    print("All Output:<br>\n");
    foreach($allOutput as $line)
    {
        print("$line<br>\n");
    }
    print("<br>\n");

    print("Return Value: $returnValue<br>\n");
?>
```

---

### string getenv(string variable)

The getenv function (Listing 9.95) returns the value of the given environment variable, or FALSE if there is an error. PHP places all environment variables into the _ENV array, so this function is useful only in those rare instances when environment variables change after a script begins executing. If you need to set the value of an environment variable, use putenv.

---

**Listing 9.95** *getenv*

```php
<?php
    print(getenv("PATH"));
?>
```

### string passthru(string command, integer return)

The `passthru` function is similar to `exec` and `system`. The `command` argument is executed as if you typed it in a command shell. If you provide the optional `return` argument, it will be set with the return value of the command. All output will be returned by the `passthru` function and sent to the browser. The output will be sent as binary data. This is useful in situations where you need to execute a shell command that creates some binary file, such as an image.

It is very dangerous to put any user-supplied information inside the command argument. Users may pass values in form fields that allow them to execute their own commands on your Web server. If you must allow this, pass the information through the `escapeshellcmd` function first.

Compare this function to `exec`, `shell_exec`, and `system`.

### integer proc_close(resource process)

Use `proc_close` to close a process opened with `proc_open`. It returns the value returned by the underlying file closure, which is usually 0 when the close completes successfully and 1 when an error occurs.

### array proc_get_status(resource process)

The `proc_get_status` function returns an array of information about the status of an open process. Table 9.26 describes the elements of this array.

**Table 9.26**  Process Status Array

| Element | Description |
| --- | --- |
| command | The name of the command executing. |
| exitcode | The return code of the command if it finishes normally. |
| pid | The process identifier. |
| running | TRUE if still running. |
| signaled | TRUE if terminated due to an uncaught signal. |
| stopped | TRUE if stopped. |
| stopsig | Signal number if stopped. |
| termsig | Signal number if terminated due to an uncaught signal. |

### boolean proc_nice(integer level)

The `proc_nice` function sets the priority of the current process. Unless the PHP script executes as the superuser, it may only decrease priority.

### resource proc_open(string command, array descriptor, array pipe)

The `proc_open` function (Listing 9.96) offers a powerful way to execute commands in the shell and manage input and output streams. The `command` argument is executed as if you typed it in the command shell.

The `descriptor` array instructs PHP where to send output for corresponding standard I/O. The keys to this array are valid file descriptor numbers. Keep in mind that all UNIX processes start with three standard file descriptors: `0` for `stdin`, `1` for `stdout`, and `2` for `sterr`. It is possible to use other file descriptor numbers for interprocess communication.

The values of the `descriptor` array should be a file handle created by `fopen` or an array describing a new stream PHP creates for you. The first element of this array is a string signifying type, `pipe` or `file`. If opening a pipe, supply a second argument to denote mode. If opening a file, supply a path and then a mode. Modes are the same as used by `fopen` and are shown in Table 9.4. Keep in mind that the modes are given from the perspective of the process. Therefore, opening a pipe with mode `r` will be for the process to read from, which means your script will write to it.

The `pipe` argument receives an array of open file handles. Use these handles exactly as if you had opened them with `fopen` or `popen`. When you finish with the process, be sure to close the open file handles, then close the process.

| Listing 9.96 | *proc_open* |
| --- | --- |

```php
<?php
    $descriptor = array(

        //process input (stdin)
        0=>array("pipe", "r"),

        //process output (stdout)
        1=>array("pipe", "w"),

        //error message sent to temporary file (stderr)
        2=>array("file", uniqid("/tmp/errors"), "w")
        );
```

| Listing 9.96 | *proc_open (cont.)* |
|---|---|

```php
//Execute CLI PHP
if(!($process = proc_open("php", $descriptor, $pipe)))
{
    print("Couldn't start process!");
    exit();
}

//Send PHP a short script
$script =
    "<?php\n" .
    "print('Core PHP<br>');\n" .
    "trigger_error('Testing stderr');\n" .
    "?>";
fwrite($pipe[0], $script);

//finished writing to pipe, so close it
fclose($pipe[0]);

//read output
while(!feof($pipe[1]))
{
    //send to browser
    print(fread($pipe[1], 128));
}

//close output pipe
fclose($pipe[1]);

//close process
proc_close($process);
?>
```

### integer proc_terminate(resource process, integer signal)

The `proc_terminate` function sends a signal to an open process. By default, the signal is `SIGTERM`. On Windows this function calls the C function `TerminateProcess`.

### putenv(string variable)

The `putenv` function sets the value of an environment variable. You must use syntax similar to that used by a command shell, as shown in Listing 9.97. To get the value of an environment variable, use `getenv` or use `phpinfo` to dump all environment variables.

---

**Listing 9.97**  *putenv*

```php
<?php
    putenv("PATH=/local/bin;.");
?>
```

---

### string shell_exec(string command)

The `shell_exec` function executes a command in the shell and returns the output as a string. It is very dangerous to put any user-supplied information inside the `command` argument. Users may pass values in form fields that allow them to execute their own commands on your Web server. If you must allow this, pass the information through the `escapeshellcmd` function first.

Compare this function to `exec`, `passthru`, and `system`.

### string system(string command, integer return)

The `system` function (Listing 9.98) behaves identically to C's `system` function. It executes the `command` argument, sends the output to the browser, and returns the last line of output. If the `return` argument is provided, it is set with the return value of the command. If you do not wish for the output to be sent to the browser, use the `exec` function.

It is very dangerous to put any user-supplied information inside the `command` argument. Users may pass values in form fields that allow them to execute their own commands on your Web server. If you must allow this, pass the information through the `escapeshellcmd` function first.

Compare this function to `exec`, `passthru`, and `shell_exec`.

---

**Listing 9.98**  *system*

```php
<?php
    // list files in directory
    print("<pre>");
    system("ls -l");
    print("</pre>");
?>
```

---

# 9.7  Process Control

The process control functions wrap UNIX functions for signal handling. They are appropriate for PHP CLI executable running on a UNIX operating system only. Signals are beyond the scope of this text but are a common topic in any relatively in-depth text on UNIX programming.

### integer pcntl_alarm(integer seconds)

The `pcntl_alarm` function sets up a SIGALRM signal after the given number of seconds. The operating system discards any previous alarm and returns the number of seconds left on it.

### boolean pcntl_exec(string path, array arguments, array environment)

The `pcntl_exec` function (Listing 9.99) executes a program. Set the optional `arguments` array with any number of arguments to pass on the command line. Set the `environment` argument with an associative array of environment variable definitions.

**Listing 9.99**  *pcntl_exec*

```php
<?php
    pcntl_exec('/bin/ls', array('-a'), array("COLUMNS"=>"40"));
?>
```

### integer pcntl_fork()

The `pcntl_fork` function (Listing 9.100) creates a child process. It returns the child's process ID to the parent. It returns zero to the child process.

**Listing 9.100**  *pcntl_fork*

```php
<?php
    //create child
    $pid = pcntl_fork();

    if($pid == 0)
    {
        //child process
        print(microtime() . " Child\n");
```

| Listing 9.100 | *pcntl_fork (cont.)* |
|---|---|

```
        //pretend to do some calculation
        for($i=0; $i < 10; $i++)
        {
            $x = pow($i, $i+1);
            print(microtime() . " Child working on $i\n");
        }

        exit(123);
    }
    elseif($pid > 0)
    {
        //parent process
        print(microtime() . " Parent\n");

        //wait for child
        pcntl_waitpid($pid, $status);

        if(pcntl_wifexited($status))
        {
            $retval = pcntl_wexitstatus($status);
            print(microtime() . " Parent gets $retval\n");
        }
    }
    else
    {
        print("Error: child not created!\n");
    }
?>
```

### boolean pcntl_signal(integer signal, string handler, boolean restart_syscalls)

The `pcntl_signal` function (Listing 9.101) registers a signal handler for the given signal. Choose a signal constant from Table 9.27. You may specify the handler by naming a function or by using a two-element array. The element may be the name of a class or an object. The second element should be the name of a method. You may also use `SIG_IGN` for the handler to ignore the specified signal. If you use `SIG_DFL` for the handler, PHP restores the default handler.

By default, PHP uses system call restarting. You may set the `restart_syscalls` argument to `FALSE` to change this behavior.

**Table 9.27**  Signal Constants

| SIGABRT | SIGCLD | SIGINT | SIGPOLL | SIGSTKFLT | SIGTSTP | SIGUSR2 |
|---------|--------|--------|---------|-----------|---------|---------|
| SIGALRM | SIGCONT | SIGIO | SIGPROF | SIGSTOP | SIGTTIN | SIGVTALRM |
| SIGBABY | SIGFPE | SIGIOT | SIGPWR | SIGSYS | SIGTTOU | SIGWINCH |
| SIGBUS | SIGHUP | SIGKILL | SIGQUIT | SIGTERM | SIGURG | SIGXCPU |
| SIGCHLD | SIGILL | SIGPIPE | SIGSEGV | SIGTRAP | SIGUSR1 | SIGXFSZ |

**Listing 9.101**  *pcntl_signal*

```php
<?php
    //define handler class
    class signal
    {
        function handle($signal)
        {
            if($signal == SIGHUP)
            {
                print("Caught HUP!\n");
            }
        }
    }

    //tell PHP to look signals
    declare(ticks=1);

    //register handler
    pcntl_signal(SIGHUP, array('signal', 'handle'));

    //generate a signal
    posix_kill(posix_getpid(), SIGHUP);
?>
```

### integer pcntl_waitpid(integer pid, integer status, integer options)

The `pcntl_waitpid` function halts execution of the parent process until the child process finishes. It returns the process ID of the terminated child. On error, it returns -1. If you use the WNOHANG option, it may return 0 if no children exist.

If you call this function with `pid` less than -1, PHP waits on a child process with a group ID that matches the absolute value of the `pid` argument. If you call this function with `pid` equal to -1, PHP waits for any child to terminate. If you call this function with `pid` equal to 0, PHP waits for any child with the same group ID.

PHP places a status identifier in the status argument. Use this value with any of the following functions: `pcntl_wexitstatus`, `pcntl_wifexited`, `pcntl_wifsignaled`, `pcntl_wifstopped`, `pcntl_wstopsig`, `pcntl_wtermsig`. This allows you to test for why the child process ended.

The `options` argument accepts two constants: WNOHANG and WUNTRACED. With WNOHANG, `pcntl_waitpid` returns immediately if no child has expired. With WUNTRACED, `pcntl_waitpid` returns for children that are stopped. You may combine these two with a bitwise-OR.

### integer pcntl_wexitstatus(integer status)

The `pcntl_wexitstatus` returns the exit value returned by the child status if it finished normally.

### boolean pcntl_wifexited(integer status)

This function tests the status set by `pcntl_waitpid`. It returns TRUE if the child process finished normally.

### boolean pcntl_wifsignaled(integer status)

This function tests the status set by `pcntl_waitpid`. It returns TRUE if the child process finished due to an uncaught signal.

### boolean pcntl_wifstopped(integer status)

This function tests the status set by `pcntl_waitpid`. It returns TRUE if the child process is stopped.

### integer pcntl_wstopsig(integer status)

This function tests the status set by `pcntl_waitpid`. It returns the signal that caused the child to stop if `pcntl_wifstopped` returns TRUE.

### boolean pcntl_wtermsig(integer status)

This function tests the status set by `pcntl_waitpid`. It returns the signal that caused the child to terminate if `pcntl_wifsignaled` returns TRUE.

# NETWORK I/O

# Chapter 10

The functions in this chapter allow you to communicate over a network. Compared to the network protocol wrappers used by PHP's file functions, the functions here operate at a lower level. This allows for greater flexibility and greater access to detail.

## 10.1  General Network I/O

The functions in this section offer general and simplified access to the Internet. Some of these functions talk to specific network services or return information about network services.

### checkdnsrr

You may use `checkdnsrr` as an alias to `dns_check_record`.

### boolean dns_check_record(string host, string type)

The `dns_check_record` function (Listing 10.1) checks DNS records for a host. The `type` argument defines the type of records for which to search. Valid types are listed in Table 10.1. If a type is not specified, `dns_check_record` checks for MX records. You may wish to read the man page for `named`, the Internet domain name server daemon.

**Listing 10.1** *dns_check_record*

```php
<?php
    if(dns_check_record("php.net", "MX"))
    {
        print("php.net is a mail exchanger");
    }
?>
```

**Table 10.1**   DNS Record Types

| Type | Description |
| --- | --- |
| A | IP address. |
| ANY | Any records. |
| CNAME | Canonical name. |
| MX | Mail exchanger. |
| NS | Name server. |
| SOA | Start of a zone of authority. |

### boolean dns_get_mx(string host, array mxhost, array weight)

The dns_get_mx function (Listing 10.2) gets mail-exchanger DNS records for a host. Hostnames will be added to the array specified by the mxhost argument. The optional weight array is assigned with the weight for each host. The return value signals whether the operation was successful. Chapter 24 contains an example of using dns_get_mx to verify an email address.

**Listing 10.2** *dns_get_mx*

```php
<?php
    //get mail-exchanger records for netscape.com
    dns_get_mx("netscape.com", $mxrecord, $weight);

    //display results
    foreach($mxrecord as $key=>$host)
    {
        print("$host - $weight[$key]<br>\n");
    }
?>
```

## array dns_get_record(string hostname, integer type, array authoritative, array additional)

The `dns_get_record` function returns an array of DNS Resource Records for the given host. Each element of the array is an associative array. Table 10.2 shows the possible elements of the returned array. The optional `type` argument controls which records to return. Table 10.3 describes available type constants. By default, PHP attempts to return records of any type, which you may specify by setting type to `DNS_ANY`. Depending on operating system, the default mode may not return all available records. The `DNS_ALL` mode forces returning all records. This function is not available on Windows.

The optional `authoritative` argument receives an array of records for the authoritative name server. The optional `additional` argument receives an array of additional records.

**Table 10.2**   Array Elements Returned by `dns_get_record`

| Element | Description |
| --- | --- |
| class | Class of record, which is always IN. |
| cpu | IANA CPU number. |
| expire | Expiration time in seconds. |
| host | Hostname. |
| ip | IPv4 address. |
| ipv6 | IPv6 address. |
| minimum-ttl | Minimum time-to-live in seconds. |
| mname | Domain name of the domain originator. |
| os | IANA OS number. |
| pri | Mail-exchanger priority. |
| refresh | Suggested refresh interval. |
| retry | Seconds to wait before a retry. |
| rname | Email address of the administrative contact. |
| serial | Serial number. |
| target | Target domain. |
| ttl | Time-to-live seconds left before refresh. |
| txt | Descriptive text. |
| type | Type of record. |

**Table 10.3**    Type Constants for `dns_get_record`

| Constant | Description |
| --- | --- |
| DNS_A | IPv4 address. |
| DNS_AAAA | IPv6 address. |
| DNS_ALL | Slower mode that returns all records. |
| DNS_ANY | Default mode that shows all records, depending on operating system. |
| DNS_CNAME | Canonical name. |
| DNS_HINFO | Host information. |
| DNS_MX | Mail exchanger. |
| DNS_NS | Name server. |
| DNS_PTR | Reverse domain pointer. |
| DNS_SOA | Start of authority. |
| DNS_TXT | Descriptive text. |

### integer fsockopen(string hostname, integer port, integer error_number, string error_description, double timeout)

The `fsockopen` function (Listing 10.3) begins a network connection as a file stream, returning a file descriptor suitable for use by `fputs`, `fgets`, and other file-stream functions discussed earlier in this chapter. A connection is attempted to the `hostname` at the given port. The `hostname` may also be a numerical IP address. The `hostname` may also be the path to a UNIX domain socket, in which case `port` should be set to 0. Some operating systems, specifically Windows, don't support UNIX domain sockets.

You may prefix host names with several qualifiers to change the protocol used for connections. Adding `udp://` will open a UDP connection. Adding `ssl://` or `tls://` will open an SSL or a TLS connection respectively, but only if PHP uses the OpenSSL extension.

If an error occurs, `FALSE` is returned and the optional `error_number` and `error_description` arguments are set. If the error number returned is zero, an error occurred before PHP tried to connect. This may indicate a problem initializing the socket.

The optional `timeout` argument will set the number of seconds PHP will wait for a connection to be established. You may specify fractions of a second as well if you wish. If you need to set a timeout for reads and writes, use `stream_set_timeout`. You can set several other options for the connection using the stream functions described in Chapter 9, such as setting the blocking mode shown in Listing 10.3.

The `pfsockopen` adds persistence to the `fsockopen` functionality.

---

**Listing 10.3** *fsockopen*

```php
<?php
    //tell browser not to render this
    header("Content-type: text/plain");

    //try to connect to Web server,
    //timeout after 60 seconds
    $fp = fsockopen("www.leonatkinson.com", 80,
        $error_number, $error_description,
        60);

    if($fp)
    {
        //set nonblocking mode
        stream_set_blocking($fp, FALSE);

        // tell server we want root document
        fputs($fp, "GET / HTTP/1.0\r\n");
        fputs($fp, "\r\n");

        while(!feof($fp))
        {
            //print next 4K
            print(fgets($fp, 4096));
        }

        //close connection
        fclose($fp);

    }
    else
    {
        //$connect was false
        print("An error occurred!<BR>\n");
        print("Number: $error_number<BR>\n");
        print("Description: $error_description<BR>\n");
    }
?>
```

### string gethostbyaddr(string ip_address)

The `gethostbyaddr` function (Listing 10.4) returns the name of the host specified by the numerical IP address. If the host cannot be resolved, the address is returned.

| Listing 10.4 | *gethostbyaddr* |
|---|---|

```php
<?php
    print(gethostbyaddr("216.218.178.111"));
?>
```

### string gethostbyname(string hostname)

The `gethostbyname` function (Listing 10.5) returns the IP address of the host specified by its name. It is possible a domain name resolves to more than one IP address. To get each one, use `gethostbynamel`.

| Listing 10.5 | *gethostbyname* |
|---|---|

```php
<?php
    print(gethostbyname("www.php.net"));
?>
```

### array gethostbynamel(string hostname)

The `gethostbynamel` function (Listing 10.6) returns a list of IP addresses that a given hostname resolves to.

| Listing 10.6 | *gethostbynamel* |
|---|---|

```php
<?php
    foreach(gethostbynamel("www.microsoft.com") as $host)
    {
        print("$host<br>\n");
    }
?>
```

### getmxrr

You may use `getmxrr` as an alias to `dns_get_mx`.

### integer getprotobyname(string name)

The `getprotobyname` function returns the number associated with a protocol.

### string getprotobynumber(integer protocol)

The `getprotobynumber` function (Listing 10.7) returns the name of a protocol given its number.

| Listing 10.7 | *getprotobyname* and *getprotobynumber* |

```php
<?php
    print("UDP is protocol " . getprotobyname('udp') . "<br>\n");
    print("Protocol 6 is " . getprotobynumber(6) . "<br>\n");
?>
```

### integer getservbyname(string service, string protocol)

The `getservbyname` function (Listing 10.8) returns the port used by a service. The `protocol` argument must be `tcp` or `udp`.

| Listing 10.8 | *getservbyname* and *getservbyport* |

```php
<?php
    //check which port ftp uses
    $port = getservbyname("ftp", "tcp");

    print("FTP uses port $port<br>\n");

    //check which service uses port 25
    $service = getservbyport(25, "tcp");

    print("Port 25 is $service<br>\n");
?>
```

### string getservbyport(integer port, string protocol)

The `getservbyport` function returns the name of the service that uses a specified port. The `protocol` argument must be `tcp` or `udp`.

### boolean mail(string recipient, string subject, string body, string headers, string parameters)

The `mail` function (Listing 10.9) sends email. Under UNIX it runs the `sendmail` shell command. Under Windows it makes a connection to an SMTP server. The mail is sent to the address specified in the `recipient` argument.

You may specify multiple recipients by separating them with commas. You must also provide a subject and a message body. Optionally, you may provide additional headers in the fourth argument. Separate each header with a carriage return (\r) and a newline character (\n). The fifth argument is passed to the sendmail shell command if PHP runs on UNIX. If the mail is sent successfully, mail returns TRUE.

On Windows, Date: and From: headers are added to the message automatically unless you supply them yourself.

There are a few directives in php.ini for configuring this function. For Windows, you can set the name of the SMTP host using the SMTP directive, and you can set the default From: header with the sendmail_from directive. It's valid to point to an SMTP server on the localhost. For UNIX, you may specify the path to your sendmail executable, which may have an acceptable default compiled in already. You can't set up PHP on UNIX to send mail directly to a remote SMTP host. You can configure sendmail to relay messages to a specific host, but the instructions are outside the scope of this text.

See Chapter 24 for an example that sends attachments.

---

**Listing 10.9**   *mail*

```php
<?php
    //define who is to receive the mail
    //(in this case, root of the localhost)
    $mailTo = "Admin <{$_SERVER["SERVER_ADMIN"]}>";

    //set the subject
    $mailSubject = "Testing Mail";

    //build body of the message
    $mailBody = "This is a test of PHP's mail function. ";
    $mailBody .= "It was generated by PHP version ";
    $mailBody .= phpversion();

    //add a from header
    $mailHeaders = "From: PHP Script".
        "<php@{$_SERVER["SERVER_NAME"]}>\r\n";

    //send mail
    if(mail($mailTo, $mailSubject, $mailBody, $mailHeaders))
    {
        print("Mail sent successfully.");
    }
    else
    {
        print("Mail failed!");
    }
?>
```

**integer pfsockopen(string hostname, integer port, integer error_number, string error_description, double timeout)**

The `pfsockopen` function operates identically to `fsockopen`, except that connections are cached. Connections opened with `pfsockopen` are not closed when a script terminates. They persist with the server process.

# 10.2 Sockets

The socket functions send information directly over the Internet Protocol. They operate at a much lower level compared to `fsockopen` and streams. Generally, they wrap C functions of the same name. If you have experience programming for sockets in C, these functions will be familiar. A full discussion of sockets programming is out of scope.

Use of these functions implies solving a problem that the higher level functions can't address. In other words, it makes little sense to use these functions to implement functionality provided by `fopen`. You may find them most useful when using PHP in a nontraditional way, such as starting an Internet daemon from the CLI (command-line interface) version of PHP.

**resource socket_accept(resource socket)**

Use `socket_accept` to accept an incoming connection, making your script a server. You must first create the socket, bind it to a name, and set it to listen on a port. In blocking mode, `socket_accept` will return only after accepting a connection. In nonblocking mode, it returns FALSE when no connections wait for acceptance. Otherwise, you get a new socket resource for reading and writing.

Listing 10.10 demonstrates a simple echo server. Start it from the CLI, and it will wait for connections from clients on port 12345.

| Listing 10.10 | *socket_accept* |
|---|---|

```php
<?php
    set_time_limit(0);

    //create the socket
    if(($socket = socket_create(AF_INET, SOCK_STREAM, 0)) < 0)
    {
        print("Couldn't create socket: " .
            socket_strerror(socket_last_error()) . "\n");
    }
```

**Listing 10.10**    *socket_accept (cont.)*

```php
//bind it to the given address and port
if(($error = socket_bind($socket,
    gethostbyname($_SERVER['HOSTNAME']), 12345)) < 0)
{
    print("Couldn't bind socket: " .
        socket_strerror(socket_last_error()) . "\n");
}

if(($error = socket_listen($socket, 5)) < 0)
{
    print("Couldn't list on socket: " .
        socket_strerror(socket_last_error()) . "\n");
}

while(TRUE)
{
    //wait for connection
    if(($accept = socket_accept($socket)) < 0)
    {
        print("Error while reading: " .
            socket_strerror($message) . "\n");
        break;
    }

    //send welcome message
    socket_write($accept, "Connection accepted\n");
    print(date('Y-m-d H:i:s') . " STATUS: Connection
        accepted\n");
    ob_flush();

    while(TRUE)
    {
        //read line from client
        if(FALSE === ($line = socket_read($accept, 1024)))
        {
            print("Couldn't read from socket: " .
                socket_strerror(socket_last_error()) . "\n");
            break 2;
        }

        if(!@socket_write($accept, "ECHO: $line"))
        {
            print(date('Y-m-d H:i:s') . " STATUS: Connection
                interrupted\n");
            break;
        }
```

**Listing 10.10** *socket_accept (cont.)*

```
        print(date('Y-m-d H:i:s') . " READ: $line");
        ob_flush();
    }

    socket_close($accept);
}
?>
```

## bool socket_bind(resource socket, string address, integer port)

The `socket_bind` function binds an address to a socket resource. The `socket` argument must be a resource returned by `socket_create`. The address must be an IP address or a path to a UNIX socket. For Internet sockets, you must supply a port.

## socket_clear_error(resource socket)

This function clears the error on a specific socket or, when called with no argument, for all sockets.

## socket_close(resource socket)

The `socket_close` function closes a socket and cleans up the memory associated with it.

## boolean socket_connect(resource socket, string address, integer port)

This function makes a client connection to a port or socket. You must supply a socket created by `socket_create`. The `address` argument is a path to a socket or an IP address. If the latter, you must supply a port number.

Listing 10.11 demonstrates the use of UDP sockets to fetch information about game servers.

**Listing 10.11** *socket_connect*

```php
<?php
    //create UDP socket
    if(($socket = socket_create(AF_INET, SOCK_DGRAM, SOL_UDP))
        < 0)
    {
        print("Couldn't create socket: " .
            socket_strerror(socket_last_error()) . "\n");
    }
```

**Listing 10.11**    *socket_connect (cont.)*

```
//timeout after 5 seconds
socket_set_option($socket, SOL_SOCKET,
    SO_RCVTIMEO, array('sec'=>5,'usec'=>0));

//connect to the RtCW master server
if(!socket_connect($socket, 'wolfmaster.idsoftware.com',
    27950))
{
    print("Couldn't connect: " .
        socket_strerror(socket_last_error()) . "\n");
}

//send request for servers
socket_write($socket, "\xFF\xFF\xFF\xFFgetservers\x00");

//get servers
$server = array();
while(FALSE !== ($line = @socket_read($socket, 4096)))
{
    //parse data
    for($i=22; ($i+5) < strlen($line); $i += 7)
    {
        $ip = ord(substr($line, $i+1, 1)) . '.' .
            ord(substr($line, $i+2, 1)) . '.' .
            ord(substr($line, $i+3, 1)) . '.' .
            ord(substr($line, $i+4, 1));

        $port = (ord(substr($line, $i+5, 1)) * 256) +
            ord(substr($line, $i+6, 1));

        $server[] = array('ip'=>$ip, 'port'=>$port);
    }
}

print("<h1>" . count($server) . " Servers</h1>\n");

//loop over servers, getting status
foreach($server as $s)
{
    print("<h1>{$s['ip']}:{$s['port']}</h1>\n");

    //connect to RtCW server
    if(!socket_connect($socket, $s['ip'], $s['port']))
    {
```

**Listing 10.11** *socket_connect (cont.)*

```php
        print("<p>\n" .
            socket_strerror(socket_last_error()) .
            "\n</p>\n");
        continue;
    }

    //send request for status
    socket_write($socket, "\xFF\xFF\xFF\xFFgetstatus\x00");

    //get status from server
    if(FALSE === ($line = @socket_read($socket, 1024)))
    {
        print("<p>\n" .
            socket_strerror(socket_last_error()) .
            "\n</p>\n");
        continue;
    }

    $part = explode("\n", $line);

    //settings are in second line separated by backslashes
    $setting = explode("\\", $part[1]);

    print("<h2>Configuration</h2>\n");
    print("<p>\n");
    for($s=1; $s < count($setting); $s += 2)
    {
        print("\t\t{$setting[$s]} = {$setting[$s+1]}<br>\n");
    }
    print("</p>\n");
    print("<h2>Players</h2>\n");
    $lastPlayer = count($part) - 1;
    for($p=2; $p < $lastPlayer; $p++)
    {
        $player = explode(" ", $part[$p]);
        print("{$player[2]} Score={$player[0]} " .
            "Ping={$player[1]}<br>\n");
    }
    print("</p>\n");

    ob_flush();
}

print("</table>\n");

socket_close($socket);
?>
```

### resource socket_create(integer family, integer socket_type, integer protocol)

The `socket_create` function initializes a framework for using the rest of the socket functions. The first argument is the protocol family, or domain. You must use `AF_INET` for Internet connections or `AF_UNIX` for UNIX socket connections. The second argument is the type of socket. Choose one from Table 10.4. Ordinarily, scripts use `SOCK_STREAM` for TCP and `SOCK_DGRAM` for UDP. The third argument specifies the protocol. Use `SOL_TCP` or `SOL_UDP` for TCP and UDP respectively. Alternatively, you can use `getprotobyname`.

**Table 10.4**   Socket Types

| Constant | Description |
| --- | --- |
| SOCK_DGRAM | Datagram socket. |
| SOCK_RAW | Raw-protocol interface. |
| SOCK_RDM | Reliably-delivered message. |
| SOCK_SEQPACKET | Sequenced packet socket. |
| SOCK_STREAM | Stream socket. |

### resource socket_create_listen(integer port, integer backlog)

Use `socket_create_listen` as a less complicated alternative to `socket_create` when you wish to create a socket for listening. The created socket will listen on all available interfaces for the given port. The optional `backlog` argument sets the maximum size of the queue for connections.

### boolean socket_create_pair(integer family, integer socket_type, integer protocol, array handles)

The `socket_create_pair` function (Listing 10.12) creates a pair of connected sockets. The first three arguments follow the description of `socket_create`. The `handles` argument is set to an array of the two socket resources. This function wraps C's `socketpair` function.

**Listing 10.12**   *socket_create_pair*

```php
<?php

    if(!socket_create_pair(AF_UNIX, SOCK_STREAM, 0, $socket))
    {
        print("Couldn't make sockets!\n");
        exit();
    }

    $child = pcntl_fork();
    if($child == -1)
    {
        print("Couldn't fork!\n");
        exit();
    }
    elseif($child > 0)
    {
        //parent
        socket_close($socket[0]);
        print("Parent: waiting for message\n");
        $message = socket_read($socket[1], 1024, PHP_NORMAL_READ);
        print("Parent: got message--$message\n");
        socket_write($socket[1], "Hello, Child Process!\n");
        pcntl_waitpid($child, $status);
    }
    else
    {
        //child
        socket_close($socket[1]);
        socket_write($socket[0], "Hello, Parent Process!\n");
        print("Child: waiting for message\n");
        $message = socket_read($socket[0], 1024, PHP_NORMAL_READ);
        print("Child: got message--$message\n");
        exit(0);
    }

?>
```

### value socket_get_option(resource socket, integer level, integer option)

The socket_get_option function (Listing 10.13) returns the value of one of the options given in Table 10.5. Additionally, you must provide a socket handle as created by socket_create and a level. To get values at the socket level, use SOL_SOCKET for the level argument. Otherwise, use the protocol, such as SOL_TCP for the TCP protocol. These options may be set with socket_set_option.

**Listing 10.13**  *socket_get_options*

```php
<?php
    $socket = socket_create(AF_INET, SOCK_STREAM, SOL_TCP);

    print('SO_BROADCAST: ' .
        socket_get_option($socket, SOL_SOCKET,
            SO_BROADCAST) . "<br>\n");
    print('SO_DEBUG: ' .
        socket_get_option($socket, SOL_SOCKET,
            SO_DEBUG) . "<br>\n");
    print('SO_DONTROUTE: ' .
        socket_get_option($socket, SOL_SOCKET,
            SO_DONTROUTE) . "<br>\n");
    print('SO_ERROR: ' .
        socket_get_option($socket, SOL_SOCKET,
            SO_ERROR) . "<br>\n");
    print('SO_KEEPALIVE: ' .
        socket_get_option($socket, SOL_SOCKET,
            SO_KEEPALIVE) . "<br>\n");
    print('SO_LINGER: ' .
        print_r(socket_get_option($socket, SOL_SOCKET,
            SO_LINGER), TRUE) . "<br>\n");
    print('SO_OOBINLINE: ' .
        socket_get_option($socket, SOL_SOCKET,
            SO_OOBINLINE) . "<br>\n");
    print('SO_RCVBUF: ' .
        socket_get_option($socket, SOL_SOCKET,
            SO_RCVBUF) . "<br>\n");
    print('SO_RCVLOWAT: ' .
        socket_get_option($socket, SOL_SOCKET,
            SO_RCVLOWAT) . "<br>\n");
    print('SO_RCVTIMEO: ' .
        print_r(socket_get_option($socket, SOL_SOCKET,
            SO_RCVTIMEO), TRUE) . "<br>\n");
    print('SO_REUSEADDR: ' .
        socket_get_option($socket, SOL_SOCKET,
            SO_REUSEADDR) . "<br>\n");
    print('SO_SNDBUF: ' .
        socket_get_option($socket, SOL_SOCKET,
            SO_SNDBUF) . "<br>\n");
    print('SO_SNDLOWAT: ' .
        socket_get_option($socket, SOL_SOCKET,
            SO_SNDLOWAT) . "<br>\n");
    print('SO_SNDTIMEO: ' .
        print_r(socket_get_option($socket, SOL_SOCKET,
            SO_SNDTIMEO), TRUE) . "<br>\n");
    print('SO_TYPE: ' .
        socket_get_option($socket, SOL_SOCKET,
            SO_TYPE) . "<br>\n");
?>
```

**Table 10.5** Socket Options

| Option | Description |
| --- | --- |
| SO_BROADCAST | Allow datagram sockets to send and receive broadcast packets. |
| SO_DEBUG | Enable socket debugging. Only root may enable this option. |
| SO_DONTROUTE | Disallow routing packets through a gateway. |
| SO_ERROR | Get and clear the last socket error. This option may not be set. |
| SO_KEEPALIVE | Enable keep-alive messages. |
| SO_LINGER | Blocks socket_close and socket_shutdown until all queued messages are sent or the timeout has expired. This option uses an array with two keys: l_onoff and l_linger. |
| SO_OOBINLINE | Place out-of-band data directly into receive buffer. |
| SO_RCVBUF | Limit receive buffer to a maximum number of bytes. |
| SO_RCVLOWAT | Delay passing data to the user until receiving a minimum number of bytes. |
| SO_RCVTIMEO | Delay reporting a timeout error while receiving until the given time passes. This option uses an array with two keys: sec and usec. |
| SO_REUSEADDR | Allow reuse of local addresses. |
| SO_SNDBUF | Limit send buffer to a maximum number of bytes. |
| SO_SNDLOWAT | Delay sending data to the protocol until receiving a minimum number of bytes. |
| SO_SNDTIMEO | Delay reporting a timeout error while sending until the given time passes. This option uses an array with two keys: sec and usec. |
| SO_TYPE | Get the socket type. This option may not be set. |

### boolean socket_getpeername(resource socket, string address, integer port)

Use socket_getpeername to get the address and port for the peer at the other side of a connection. If connected via a UNIX socket, the address is set with the path in the filesystem.

### boolean socket_getsockname(resource socket, string address, integer port)

The `socket_getsockname` function puts the name of the socket into the `address` argument and the `port` number into the port argument. It returns `FALSE` on failure.

### boolean socket_iovec_add(resource iovector, integer length)

The `socket_iovec_add` unction adds an I/O vector to the scatter/gather array.

### resource socket_iovec_alloc(integer count, ...)

The `socket_iovec_alloc` function returns a resource for handling a collection of I/O vectors. The first argument specifies the number of vectors. Following arguments specify the length of each vector.

### boolean socket_iovec_delete(resource iovector, integer position)

The `socket_iovec_delete` function removes the I/O vector at the given position.

### string socket_iovec_fetch(resource iovector, integer position)

The `socket_iovec_fetch` function returns the value of the specified vector in the I/O vector resource.

### boolean socket_iovec_free(resource iovector)

The `socket_iovec_free` function frees the memory used for an I/O vector resource.

### boolean socket_iovec_set(resource iovector, integer position, string value)

The `socket_iovec_set` sets the value of I/O vector at the given position.

### integer socket_last_error(resource socket)

The `socket_last_error` function returns the last error generated by a socket function. You may set the optional `socket` argument with a socket resource to get the last error for a specific connection. Table 10.6 lists the error codes returned. You may also use `socket_strerror` to get a description of the error. Use `socket_clear_error` to clear the error from the socket.

**Table 10.6**  Socket Errors

| Constant | Description |
| --- | --- |
| SOCKET_E2BIG | Argument list too long. |
| SOCKET_EACCES | Permission denied. |
| SOCKET_EADDRINUSE | Address already in use. |
| SOCKET_EADDRNOTAVAIL | Cannot assign requested address. |
| SOCKET_EADV | Advertise error. |
| SOCKET_EAFNOSUPPORT | Address family not supported by protocol. |
| SOCKET_EAGAIN | Resource temporarily unavailable. |
| SOCKET_EALREADY | Operation already in progress. |
| SOCKET_EBADE | Invalid exchange. |
| SOCKET_EBADF | Bad file descriptor. |
| SOCKET_EBADFD | File descriptor in bad state. |
| SOCKET_EBADMSG | Bad message. |
| SOCKET_EBADR | Invalid request descriptor. |
| SOCKET_EBADRQC | Invalid request code. |
| SOCKET_EBADSLT | Invalid slot. |
| SOCKET_EBUSY | Device or resource busy. |
| SOCKET_ECHRNG | Channel number out of range. |
| SOCKET_ECOMM | Communication error on send. |
| SOCKET_ECONNABORTED | Software caused connection abort. |
| SOCKET_ECONNREFUSED | Connection refused. |
| SOCKET_ECONNRESET | Connection reset by peer. |
| SOCKET_EDESTADDRREQ | Destination address required. |
| SOCKET_EDQUOT | Disk quota exceeded. |
| SOCKET_EEXIST | File exists. |
| SOCKET_EFAULT | Bad address. |

**Table 10.6**  Socket Errors *(cont.)*

| Constant | Description |
|---|---|
| SOCKET_EHOSTDOWN | Host is down. |
| SOCKET_EHOSTUNREACH | No route to host. |
| SOCKET_EIDRM | Identifier removed. |
| SOCKET_EINPROGRESS | Operation now in progress. |
| SOCKET_EINTR | Interrupted system call. |
| SOCKET_EINVAL | Invalid argument. |
| SOCKET_EIO | Input/output error. |
| SOCKET_EISCONN | Transport endpoint is already connected. |
| SOCKET_EISDIR | Is a directory. |
| SOCKET_EISNAM | Is a named type file. |
| SOCKET_EL2HLT | Level 2 halted. |
| SOCKET_EL2NSYNC | Level 2 not synchronized. |
| SOCKET_EL3HLT | Level 3 halted. |
| SOCKET_EL3RST | Level 3 reset. |
| SOCKET_ELNRNG | Link number out of range. |
| SOCKET_ELOOP | Too many levels of symbolic links. |
| SOCKET_EMEDIUMTYPE | Wrong medium type. |
| SOCKET_EMFILE | Too many open files. |
| SOCKET_EMLINK | Too many links. |
| SOCKET_EMSGSIZE | Message too long. |
| SOCKET_EMULTIHOP | Multihop attempted. |
| SOCKET_ENAMETOOLONG | Filename too long. |
| SOCKET_ENETDOWN | Network is down. |
| SOCKET_ENETRESET | Network dropped connection on reset. |
| SOCKET_ENETUNREACH | Network is unreachable. |

**Table 10.6**   Socket Errors *(cont.)*

| Constant | Description |
|---|---|
| SOCKET_ENFILE | Too many open files in system. |
| SOCKET_ENOANO | No anode. |
| SOCKET_ENOBUFS | No buffer space available. |
| SOCKET_ENOCSI | No CSI structure available. |
| SOCKET_ENODATA | No data available. |
| SOCKET_ENODEV | No such device. |
| SOCKET_ENOENT | No such file or directory. |
| SOCKET_ENOLCK | No locks available. |
| SOCKET_ENOLINK | Link has been severed. |
| SOCKET_ENOMEDIUM | No medium found. |
| SOCKET_ENOMEM | Cannot allocate memory. |
| SOCKET_ENOMSG | No message of desired type. |
| SOCKET_ENONET | Machine is not on the network. |
| SOCKET_ENOPROTOOPT | Protocol not available. |
| SOCKET_ENOSPC | No space left on device. |
| SOCKET_ENOSR | Out of streams resources. |
| SOCKET_ENOSTR | Device not a stream. |
| SOCKET_ENOSYS | Function not implemented. |
| SOCKET_ENOTBLK | Block device required. |
| SOCKET_ENOTCONN | Transport endpoint is not connected. |
| SOCKET_ENOTDIR | Not a directory. |
| SOCKET_ENOTEMPTY | Directory not empty. |
| SOCKET_ENOTSOCK | Socket operation on non-socket. |
| SOCKET_ENOTTY | Inappropriate ioctl for device. |
| SOCKET_ENOTUNIQ | Name not unique on network. |

**Table 10.6**   Socket Errors *(cont.)*

| Constant | Description |
| --- | --- |
| SOCKET_ENXIO | No such device or address. |
| SOCKET_EOPNOTSUPP | Operation not supported. |
| SOCKET_EPERM | Operation not permitted. |
| SOCKET_EPFNOSUPPORT | Protocol family not supported. |
| SOCKET_EPIPE | Broken pipe. |
| SOCKET_EPROTO | Protocol error. |
| SOCKET_EPROTONOSUPPORT | Protocol not supported. |
| SOCKET_EPROTOTYPE | Protocol wrong type for socket. |
| SOCKET_EREMCHG | Remote address changed. |
| SOCKET_EREMOTE | Object is remote. |
| SOCKET_EREMOTEIO | Remote I/O error. |
| SOCKET_ERESTART | Interrupted system call should be restarted. |
| SOCKET_EROFS | Read-only file system. |
| SOCKET_ESHUTDOWN | Cannot send after transport endpoint shutdown. |
| SOCKET_ESOCKTNOSUPPORT | Socket type not supported. |
| SOCKET_ESPIPE | Illegal seek. |
| SOCKET_ESRMNT | Srmount error. |
| SOCKET_ESTRPIPE | Streams pipe error. |
| SOCKET_ETIME | Timer expired. |
| SOCKET_ETIMEDOUT | Connection timed out. |
| SOCKET_ETOOMANYREFS | Too many references: Cannot splice. |
| SOCKET_EUNATCH | Protocol driver not attached. |
| SOCKET_EUSERS | Too many users. |
| SOCKET_EWOULDBLOCK | Resource temporarily unavailable. |
| SOCKET_EXDEV | Invalid cross-device link. |
| SOCKET_EXFULL | Exchange full. |

### boolean socket_listen(resource socket, integer backlog)

The `socket_listen` function waits for a connection from a client on the given socket. The optional `backlog` argument sets the size of the queue of waiting connection requests.

### string socket_read(resource socket, integer length, integer type)

The `socket_read` function reads the specified number of bytes from the given socket. It returns `FALSE` on error. By default, reads are binary-safe. You may make this mode explicit by setting the optional `type` argument to `PHP_BINARY_READ`. You may make PHP pay attention to linebreaks by setting `type` to `PHP_NORMAL_READ`.

### boolean socket_readv(resource socket, resource iovector)

The `socket_readv` function reads data into the `iovector` resource.

### integer socket_recv(resource socket, string buffer, integer length, integer flags)

The `socket_recv` function reads data into the given buffer. The `length` argument sets the maximum number of bytes received. Set the flags argument with `MSG_OOB` or `MSG_PEEK`. This function returns the number of bytes read.

### integer socket_recvfrom(resource socket, string buffer, integer length, string host, integer port)

The `socket_recvfrom` function reads data into the given buffer. The `length` argument sets the maximum number of bytes received. Set the `flags` argument with `MSG_OOB` or `MSG_PEEK`. PHP sets the host and port arguments with the appropriate values of the host sending the data.

### boolean socket_recvmsg(resource socket, resource iovector, array control, integer length, integer flags, string host, integer port)

The `socket_recvmsg` function reads data from a socket into an I/O vector resource. PHP sets the control argument to an associative array with three elements: `cmsg_level`, `cmsg_type`, and `cmsg_data`. The length argument gets the length of the ancillary data. The `flags` argument accepts values and returns values. At the time of writing, PHP doesn't implement all of the output constants. You may wish to refer to the `recvmsg` man page.

PHP sets the host and port arguments with the appropriate values of the host sending the data.

### integer socket_select(array read, array write, array exception, integer timeout_seconds, integer timeout_microseconds)

The `socket_select` function waits for changes to sockets. PHP watches the sockets given in the `read` array for new data coming in. PHP watches the streams given in the `write` array for being ready to accept more data. PHP watches the streams given in the `exception` argument for errors. If the number of seconds specified in the `timeout_seconds` argument passes, the function returns. Use the optional `timeout_microseconds` argument to specify a timeout less than 1 second.

The `socket_select` function returns the number of sockets that changed or FALSE if an error occurred. If the call timed out, this function returns zero. It also modifies the given arrays so that they include only those sockets that changed.

If you have no sockets of a particular type to watch, you may pass an empty array or a variable set to NULL.

### integer socket_send(resource socket, string buffer, integer length, integer flags)

The `socket_send` function writes data in the `buffer` argument into the given connection. You must specify the number of bytes from the buffer to write. You must also set the `flags` argument with NULL or a combination of the following constants: MSG_DONTROUTE and MSG_OOB. The number of bytes written is returned. FALSE is returned on error.

### boolean socket_sendmsg(resource socket, resource iovector, integer flags, string address, integer port)

The `socket_sendmsg` function attempts to send data through a socket. It is most appropriate for connectionless sockets. The `iovector` argument is a resource returned by `socket_iovec_alloc`. You must specify `flags` to be NULL, MSG_DONTROUTE, MSG_OOB, or a combination of the two constants. You must specify the address. Internet sockets require a port.

The `socket_sendmsg` function returns TRUE if it sends the data, but this does not guarantee delivery.

### integer socket_sendto(resource socket, string buffer, integer length, integer flags, string address, integer port)

The `socket_sendto` function attempts to send data in the `buffer` argument through a socket. It is most appropriate for connectionless sockets. You must specify `flags` to be NULL, MSG_DONTROUTE, MSG_OOB or a combination of the two constants. You must specify the address. Internet sockets require a port.

The socket_sendto function returns TRUE if it sends the data, but this does not guarantee delivery.

### boolean socket_set_block(resource socket)

The socket_set_block function sets the socket into blocking mode, the default mode. In blocking mode, I/O operations wait for requests to complete.

### boolean socket_set_nonblock(resource socket)

The socket_set_nonblock function sets the socket into nonblocking mode, the default mode. In nonblocking mode, I/O operations return immediately even if no data can be transmitted.

### boolean socket_set_option(resource socket, integer level, integer option, integer value)

The socket_set_option function sets an option on the given socket. The level argument should be a constant indicating the level at which the option applies. Valid values include SOL_SOCKET, SOL_TCP and SOL_UDP. The option argument should match one of the constants from Table 10.5.

### boolean socket_shutdown(resource socket, integer how)

The socket_shutdown function shuts down a socket for I/O. Set the how argument to 0 to stop receiving data. Set it to 1 to stop sending data. Set it to 2 to stop both.

### string socket_strerror(integer error)

The socket_strerror function returns the description of the given error number.

### integer socket_write(resource socket, string buffer, integer length)

The socket_write function writes data in the given buffer to a socket. Optionally, you may specify the number of bytes from the buffer to write with the length argument. Otherwise, PHP sends the entire buffer. This function is usually more convenient than socket_send.

### boolean socket_writev(resource socket, resource iovector)

The socket_writev function writes the given I/O vectors into a socket.

# 10.3  FTP

The functions in this section allow you to make connections to FTP servers. FTP is the File Transfer Protocol. While the file functions allow you to open and manipulate remote files by specifying a URL instead of a local path, these functions operate directly with the FTP protocol. They offer a greater degree of control. They also allow you to get a list of files on the server. The FTP functions were added to PHP by Andrew Skalski.

FTP operates in one of two modes, text or binary. In text mode, FTP attempts to translate line endings between different systems. Originally, PHP used the FTP_ASCII and FTP_IMAGE constants for choosing the mode. FTP_TEXT and FTP_BINARY were added for better readability.

Several new functions allow for nonblocking FTP transfers. This allows your script to execute code while the transfer continues in the background.

### boolean ftp_cdup(resource ftp)

The ftp_cdup function changes the working directory to the parent directory of the current working directory.

### boolean ftp_chdir(resource ftp, string directory)

The ftp_chdir function moves the working directory to the specified directory.

### boolean ftp_chmod(resource ftp, integer mode, string path)

The ftp_chmod function changes the permissions on a remote file.

### ftp_close(resource ftp)

The ftp_close function closes an FTP connection and frees the memory associated with it.

### resource ftp_connect(string host, integer port, integer timeout)

Use ftp_connect (Listing 10.14) to begin an FTP connection. The port argument is optional and defaults to 21. The timeout argument is optional and defaults to 90 seconds. This timeout applies to all FTP operations for the connection. An FTP resource identifier will be returned if the connection is successful; otherwise it returns FALSE. Use this resource with the rest of the FTP commands. Once you connect, you must log in before you can issue any commands.

**Listing 10.14** *ftp_connect*

```php
<?php
    //connect to server
    if(!($ftp = ftp_connect("www.leonatkinson.com")))
    {
        print("Unable to connect!<br>\n");
        exit();
    }

    print("Connected<br>\n");

    //log in
    if(!ftp_login($ftp, "anonymous", "corephp@"))
    {
        print("Unable to login!<br>\n");
        exit();
    }

    print("Logged in<br>\n");

    print("System Type: " . ftp_systype($ftp) . "<br>\n");
    print("Timeout: " .
        ftp_get_option($ftp, FTP_TIMEOUT_SEC) .
        " seconds<br>\n");

    //make sure passive mode is off
    ftp_pasv($ftp, FALSE);

    print("Working Directory: " . ftp_pwd($ftp) . "<br>\n");

    print("Raw List:<br>\n");
    foreach(ftp_rawlist($ftp, ".") as $line)
    {
        print("$line<br>\n");
    }
    print("<br>\n");

    if(!ftp_chdir($ftp, "pub/leon"))
    {
        print("Unable to go to the pub/leon directory!<br>\n");
    }

    print("Moved to pub/leon directory<br>\n");
```

**Listing 10.14** *ftp_connect (cont.)*

```
    print("Files:<br>\n");
    foreach(ftp_nlist($ftp, ".") as $filename)
    {
        print("$filename<br>\n");
    }
    print("<br>\n");

    if(!ftp_cdup($ftp))
    {
        print("Failed to move up a directory!<br>\n");
    }

    //close connection
    ftp_close($ftp);
?>
```

### boolean ftp_delete(resource ftp, string path)

The ftp_delete function removes a file on the remote server. The link argument is as returned by ftp_connect. The path argument is the path on the remote server to the file to be deleted. See ftp_put for an example of use.

### boolean ftp_exec(resource ftp, string command)

The ftp_exec function executes a command on the remote server. Most servers do not allow this functionality.

### boolean ftp_fget(resource ftp, resource file, string filename, integer mode, integer position)

The ftp_fget function (Listing 10.15) copies a remote file into an open file stream. You must create a file resource using fopen or a similar function to pass as the second argument. The mode argument should be set with one of two constants: FTP_TEXT or FTP_BINARY. These are sometimes referred to as text or binary modes. The optional position argument sets the position within the file to begin reading, allowing for resuming interrupted transfers.

| Listing 10.15 | ftp_fget |
| --- | --- |

```php
<?php
    //connect to server
    if(!($ftp = ftp_connect("www.leonatkinson.com")))
    {
        print("Unable to connect!<br>\n");
        exit();
    }

    //log in
    if(!ftp_login($ftp, "anonymous", "corephp@"))
    {
        print("Unable to login!<br>\n");
        exit();
    }

    //open local file for writing
    if(!$fp = fopen("/tmp/corephp3_examples.tar.gz", "w"))
    {
        print("Unable to open file!<br>\n");
        exit();
    }

    //save remote file in open file stream
    if(!ftp_fget($ftp, $fp, "/pub/leon/corephp3_examples.tar.gz",
        FTP_BINARY))
    {
        print("Unable to get remote file!<br>\n");
    }

    print("File downloaded!<br>\n");

    //close local file
    fclose($fp);

    //close connection
    ftp_close($ftp);
?>
```

### boolean ftp_fput(resource ftp, string remote, integer file, integer mode, integer position)

The ftp_fput function (Listing 10.16) creates a file on the remote server from the contents of an open file stream. The ftp argument is as returned by ftp_connect. The remote argument is the path to the file to be created on the remote server. The file argument is a file identifier as returned by fopen or a similar function. The mode argument should be FTP_TEXT or FTP_BINARY. The optional position argument sets the position within the file to begin writing, allowing for resuming interrupted transfers.

**Listing 10.16** *ftp_fput*

```php
<?php
    //connect to server
    if(!($ftp = ftp_connect("localhost")))
    {
        print("Unable to connect!<br>\n");
        exit();
    }

    //log in
    if(!ftp_login($ftp, "anonymous", "corephp@"))
    {
        print("Unable to login!<br>\n");
        exit();
    }

    //open local file
    if(!($fp = fopen("data.txt", "r")))
    {
        print("Unable to open local file!<br>\n");
        exit();
    }

    //write file to remote server
    if(!ftp_fput($ftp, "/pub/data.txt", $fp, FTP_TEXT))
    {
        print("Unable to upload file!<br>\n");
        exit();
    }

    print("File uploaded!<br>\n");

    //close local file
    fclose($fp);

    //close connection
    ftp_close($ftp);
?>
```

### boolean ftp_get(resource ftp, string local, string remote, integer mode, integer position)

Use ftp_get (Listing 10.17) to copy a file from the remote server to the local filesystem. The link argument is as returned by ftp_connect. The local and remote arguments specify paths. The mode argument should use FTP_TEXT or FTP_BINARY. The optional position argument sets the position within the file to begin reading, allowing for resuming interrupted transfers.

**Listing 10.17**   *ftp_get*

```php
<?php
    //connect to server
    if(!($ftp = ftp_connect("www.leonatkinson.com")))
    {
        print("Unable to connect!<br>\n");
        exit();
    }

    //log in
    if(!ftp_login($ftp, "anonymous", "corephp@"))
    {
        print("Unable to login!<br>\n");
        exit();
    }

    //save file to tmp directory
    ftp_get($ftp,
        "/tmp/data.bin",
        "/pub/leon/corephp3_examples.tar.gz",
        FTP_BINARY);

    print("File downloaded!<br>\n");

    //close connection
    ftp_close($ftp);
?>
```

### value ftp_get_option(resource ftp, integer option)

Use ftp_get_option to get one of the two options for an FTP connection. You must supply a resource created by ftp_connect. Available options are listed in Table 10.7.

**Table 10.7**  FTP Options

| Option | Description |
| --- | --- |
| FTP_AUTOSEEK | The autoseek functionality moves the local file pointer to the correct position when you use the `position` argument of `ftp_fget`, `ftp_fput`, `ftp_get` or `ftp_put`. This option is enabled by default. |
| FTP_TIMEOUT_SEC | This option defines the timeout used for FTP operations. |

### boolean ftp_login(resource ftp, string username, string password)

Once you make a connection to an FTP server, you must use `ftp_login` to identify yourself. All three arguments are required, even if you are logging in anonymously. See `ftp_connect` for an example of use.

### integer ftp_mdtm(resource ftp, string path)

The `ftp_mdtm` function (Listing 10.18) returns the last modification time for the file named in the `path` argument.

**Listing 10.18**  `ftp_mdtm`

```php
<?php
    //connect to server
    if(!($ftp = ftp_connect("www.leonatkinson.com")))
    {
        print("Unable to connect!<br>\n");
        exit();
    }

    //log in
    if(!ftp_login($ftp, "anonymous", "corephp@"))
    {
        print("Unable to login!<br>\n");
        exit();
    }

    print("Size: " .
        ftp_size($ftp, "/pub/leon/corephp3_examples.tar.gz") .
        "<br>\n");
```

**Listing 10.18** *ftp_mdtm (cont.)*

```
    print("Modified: " .
        date("Y-m-d",
            ftp_mdtm($ftp, "/pub/leon/corephp3_examples.tar.gz")) .
            "<BR>\n");

    //close connection
    ftp_close($ftp);
?>
```

### string ftp_mkdir(resource ftp, string directory)

The ftp_mkdir function (Listing 10.19) creates a directory on the remote
server. FALSE is returned if the directory cannot be created.

**Listing 10.19** *ftp_mkdir*

```
<?php
    //connect to server
    if(!($ftp = ftp_connect("localhost")))
    {
        print("Unable to connect!<br>\n");
        exit();
    }

    //log in
    if(!ftp_login($ftp, "leon", "corephp@"))
    {
        print("Unable to login!<br>\n");
        exit();
    }

    //create a new directory
    $result = ftp_mkdir($ftp, "corephp");
    if($result)
    {
        print("Created directory: $result<br>\n");
    }
    else
    {
        print("Unable to create corephp directory!<br>\n");
    }
```

| Listing 10.19 | `ftp_mkdir (cont.)` |
| --- | --- |

```
    //remove corephp directory
    if(!ftp_rmdir($ftp, "corephp"))
    {
        print("Unable to remove corephp directory!<br>\n");
    }

    //close connection
    ftp_close($ftp);
?>
```

### integer ftp_nb_continue(resource ftp)

Use `ftp_nb_continue` to continue a nonblocking transfer. The return value is an integer that matches one of the constants in Table 10.8.

**Table 10.8**   FTP Nonblocking Status

| Status | Description |
| --- | --- |
| FTP_FAILED | The transfer failed. |
| FTP_FINISHED | The transfer finished. |
| FTP_MOREDATA | The transfer has not finished yet. |

### integer ftp_nb_fget(resource ftp, resource file, string filename, integer mode, integer position)

The `ftp_nb_fget` function (Listing 10.20) operates exactly as `ftp_fget` except that it is nonblocking.

| Listing 10.20 | `ftp_nb_fget` |
| --- | --- |

```
<?php
    //connect to server
    if(!($ftp = ftp_connect("www.leonatkinson.com")))
    {
        print("Unable to connect!<br>\n");
        exit();
    }
```

**Listing 10.20**   *ftp_nb_fget (cont.)*

```php
//log in
if(!ftp_login($ftp, "anonymous", "corephp@"))
{
    print("Unable to login!<br>\n");
    exit();
}

//open local file for writing
if(!$fp = fopen("/tmp/corephp3_examples.tar.gz", "w"))
{
    print("Unable to open file!<br>\n");
    exit();
}

//save remote file in open file stream
$status = ftp_nb_fget($ftp, $fp,
    "/pub/leon/corephp3_examples.tar.gz", FTP_BINARY);

while($status == FTP_MOREDATA)
{
    print("Still downloading...");

    //fake some process
    usleep(100);

    $status = ftp_nb_continue($ftp);
}

if($status == FTP_FAILED)
{
    print("Unable to get remote file!<br>\n");
}
else
{
    print("File downloaded!<br>\n");
}

//close local file
fclose($fp);

//close connection
ftp_close($ftp);
?>
```

### integer ftp_nb_fput(resource ftp, string remote, integer file, integer mode, integer position)

The `ftp_nb_fput` function operates exactly as `ftp_fput` except that it is nonblocking.

### integer ftp_nb_get(resource ftp, string local, string remote, integer mode, integer position)

The `ftp_nb_get` function operates exactly as `ftp_get` except that it is nonblocking.

### integer ftp_nb_put(resource ftp, string remote, string local, integer mode, integer position)

The `ftp_nb_put` function operates exactly as `ftp_put` except that it is nonblocking.

### array ftp_nlist(resource ftp, string directory)

The `ftp_nlist` function returns an array of files in the specified directory.

### boolean ftp_pasv(resource ftp, boolean on)

Use `ftp_pasv` to turn passive mode on or off. It is off by default.

### boolean ftp_put(resource ftp, string remote, string local, integer mode, integer position)

The `ftp_put` function (Listing 10.21) copies a file from the local filesystem to the remote server. The `link` argument is as returned by `ftp_connect`. The `local` and `remote` arguments specify paths. The mode argument should be either `FTP_TEXT` or `FTP_BINARY`. The optional `position` argument sets the position within the file to begin writing, allowing for resuming interrupted transfers.

| Listing 10.21 | *ftp_put* |
|---|---|

```php
<?php
    //connect to server
    if(!($ftp = ftp_connect("localhost")))
    {
        print("Unable to connect!<br>\n");
        exit();
    }
```

**Listing 10.21** *ftp_put (cont.)*

```
//log in
if(!ftp_login($ftp, "anonymous", "corephp@localhost"))
{
    print("Unable to login!<br>\n");
    exit();
}

//copy local file to remote server
ftp_put($ftp, "/uploads/data.txt", "/tmp/data.txt", FTP_TEXT);

//remove remote file
ftp_delete($ftp, "/uploads/data.txt");

print("File uploaded!<br>\n");

//close connection
ftp_quit($ftp);
?>
```

### string ftp_pwd(resource ftp)

The ftp_pwd function returns the name of the current directory.

### boolean ftp_quit(resource ftp)

Use ftp_quit as an alias to ftp_close.

### ftp_raw(resource ftp, string command)

The ftp_raw function sends a command to the ftp server unaltered.

### array ftp_rawlist(resource ftp, string directory)

The ftp_rawlist returns the raw output of an ls -l command on the given directory.

### boolean ftp_rename(resource ftp, string original, string new)

The ftp_rename function changes the name of a file on the remote server.

### boolean ftp_rmdir(resource ftp, string directory)

Use ftp_rmdir to remove a directory.

### boolean ftp_set_option(resource ftp, integer option, value setting)

Use `ftp_set_option` to change the value of an option. Refer to Table 10.7 for a list of options.

### boolean ftp_site(resource ftp, string command)

The `ftp_site` function sends a SITE command, which varies by server. You may obtain a list of valid commands by sending `site help` during an interactive session.

### integer ftp_size(resource ftp, string path)

The `ftp_size` function returns the size of a remote file in bytes. If an error occurs, `-1` is returned.

### resource ftp_ssl_connect(string host, integer port, integer timeout)

Use `ftp_ssl_connect` to make an FTP connection over SSL. Otherwise, it operates exactly as `ftp_connect`. You must enable OpenSSL when compiling PHP to activate this function.

### string ftp_systype(resource ftp)

The `ftp_systype` function returns the system type of the remote FTP server.

## 10.4  Curl

Daniel Stenberg leads the Curl project, which aims to handle interpreting URLs and fetching data from them. PHP uses the Curl library to provide this functionality to your scripts. A typical session involves creating a Curl resource with `curl_init`, setting options with `curl_setopt`, and executing the request with `curl_exec`. Instead of a large set of functions, the Curl extension uses a small set of functions paired with a large set of constants used with `curl_setopt`.

You can learn more about Curl at its home page: <http://curl.haxx.se/>.

Recently, the Curl project added the so-called multi-interface. PHP includes support for these functions, but keep in mind their relative newness.

### void curl_close(resource curl)

Use `curl_close` to free the memory associated with the Curl resource.

### integer curl_errno(resource curl)

The `curl_errno` function returns the number of the last error generated for the given Curl resource. Table 10.9 shows the PHP constants that represent the error codes returned by `curl_errno`.

**Table 10.9**   Curl Error Codes

| Constant | Description |
|---|---|
| CURLE_ABORTED_BY_CALLBACK | Callback aborted operation. |
| CURLE_BAD_CALLING_ORDER | Incorrect function calling order. |
| CURLE_BAD_FUNCTION_ARGUMENT | Incorrect parameter to function. |
| CURLE_BAD_PASSWORD_ENTERED | Bad password entered. |
| CURLE_COULDNT_CONNECT | Couldn't connect to host. |
| CURLE_COULDNT_RESOLVE_HOST | Couldn't resolve host. |
| CURLE_COULDNT_RESOLVE_PROXY | Couldn't resolve proxy. |
| CURLE_FAILED_INIT | Initialization failure. |
| CURLE_FILE_COULDNT_READ_FILE | Couldn't read file. |
| CURLE_FTP_ACCESS_DENIED | Access denied during FTP operation. |
| CURLE_FTP_BAD_DOWNLOAD_RESUME | FTP download resume failed. |
| CURLE_FTP_CANT_GET_HOST | Cannot resolve FTP host. |
| CURLE_FTP_CANT_RECONNECT | Unable to reconnect to FTP server. |
| CURLE_FTP_COULDNT_GET_SIZE | FTP SIZE command failed. |
| CURLE_FTP_COULDNT_RETR_FILE | Couldn't retrieve file from FTP. |
| CURLE_FTP_COULDNT_SET_ASCII | Unable to select FTP ASCII mode. |
| CURLE_FTP_COULDNT_SET_BINARY | Unable to select FTP BINARY mode. |
| CURLE_FTP_COULDNT_STOR_FILE | FTP STOR command failed. |
| CURLE_FTP_COULDNT_USE_REST | FTP REST command failed. |
| CURLE_FTP_PORT_FAILED | FTP PORT command failed. |
| CURLE_FTP_QUOTE_ERROR | FTP QUOTE command error. |
| CURLE_FTP_USER_PASSWORD_INCORRECT | User/password incorrect for FTP connection. |
| CURLE_FTP_WEIRD_227_FORMAT | Unknown FTP 227 reply. |

**Table 10.9**    Curl Error Codes *(cont.)*

| Constant | Description |
| --- | --- |
| CURLE_FTP_WEIRD_PASS_REPLY | Unrecognized answer to FTP PASS. |
| CURLE_FTP_WEIRD_PASV_REPLY | Unrecognized answer to FTP PASV. |
| CURLE_FTP_WEIRD_SERVER_REPLY | Unrecognized FTP server reply. |
| CURLE_FTP_WEIRD_USER_REPLY | Unrecognized answer to FTP USER. |
| CURLE_FTP_WRITE_ERROR | FTP server reported write problems. |
| CURLE_FUNCTION_NOT_FOUND | LDAP function not found. |
| CURLE_HTTP_NOT_FOUND | HTTP page not found. |
| CURLE_HTTP_POST_ERROR | HTTP post error. |
| CURLE_HTTP_RANGE_ERROR | HTTP range error. |
| CURLE_LDAP_CANNOT_BIND | LDAP bind failed. |
| CURLE_LDAP_SEARCH_FAILED | LDAP search failed. |
| CURLE_LIBRARY_NOT_FOUND | LDAP library not found. |
| CURLE_MALFORMAT_USER | Username badly specified. |
| CURLE_OK | No error. |
| CURLE_OPERATION_TIMEOUTED | Operation timed out. |
| CURLE_OUT_OF_MEMORY | Out of memory. |
| CURLE_PARTIAL_FILE | Only a part of the file was transferred. |
| CURLE_READ_ERROR | Local read error. |
| CURLE_SSL_CONNECT_ERROR | SSL handshaking failed. |
| CURLE_SSL_PEER_CERTIFICATE | Unverified remote SSL certificate. |
| CURLE_TOO_MANY_REDIRECTS | Too many redirects. |
| CURLE_UNKNOWN_TELNET_OPTION | Unknown TELNET option specified. |
| CURLE_UNSUPPORTED_PROTOCOL | Unsupported protocol. |
| CURLE_URL_MALFORMAT | Malformed URL. |
| CURLE_URL_MALFORMAT_USER | Malformed URL in user. |
| CURLE_WRITE_ERROR | Local write error. |

### string curl_error(resource curl)
The curl_error function returns the description of the last error generated for the given Curl resource.

### boolean curl_exec(resource curl)
### string curl_exec(resource curl)
Use curl_exec (Listing 10.22) to execute the request. Depending on the CURLOPT_RETURNTRANSFER option, curl_exec returns a boolean or the data requested.

**Listing 10.22** *curl_exec*

```php
<?php
    if(!($curl = curl_init()))
    {
        print("Unable to initialize Curl resource!");
        exit();
    }

    //configure for a post request to php.net's search engine
    curl_setopt($curl, CURLOPT_URL,
        'http://www.php.net/search.php');
    curl_setopt($curl, CURLOPT_RETURNTRANSFER, TRUE);
    curl_setopt($curl, CURLOPT_POST, TRUE);
    curl_setopt($curl, CURLOPT_POSTFIELDS,
        'lang=en_US&pattern=Zend API&show=nosource');

    //make request
    $results = curl_exec($curl);

    print("<pre>");
    print(htmlentities($results));
    print("</pre>");
?>
```

### string curl_getinfo(resource curl, integer info)
Use curl_getinfo (Listing 10.23) to retrieve information about a Curl request. Table 10.10 lists constants for use with the info argument.

**Table 10.10**    Curl Request Information

| Constant | Description |
| --- | --- |
| CURLINFO_CONNECT_TIME | The time spent making the connection. |
| CURLINFO_CONTENT_LENGTH_DOWNLOAD | The value of the HTTP Content-length header. |
| CURLINFO_CONTENT_LENGTH_UPLOAD | The size of the upload file. |
| CURLINFO_CONTENT_TYPE | The value of the HTTP Content-type header. |
| CURLINFO_EFFECTIVE_URL | The effective URL used for the last request. |
| CURLINFO_FILETIME | If Curl can determine the modification time of the requested file, this will be set with a UNIX timestamp. Curl returns –1 if it fails to get the modification time. |
| CURLINFO_HEADER_SIZE | The number of bytes in all HTTP requests. |
| CURLINFO_HTTP_CODE | The HTTP code returned by the server. |
| CURLINFO_NAMELOOKUP_TIME | A double describing the number of seconds needed to resolve the hostname. |
| CURLINFO_PRETRANSFER_TIME | A double describing the number of seconds elapsed until just before the transfer begins. |
| CURLINFO_REDIRECT_COUNT | The number of redirects. |
| CURLINFO_REDIRECT_TIME | A double describing the number of seconds needed for all redirect steps. |
| CURLINFO_REQUEST_SIZE | The size of the HTTP request. |
| CURLINFO_SIZE_DOWNLOAD | Total bytes downloaded. |
| CURLINFO_SIZE_UPLOAD | Total bytes uploaded. |
| CURLINFO_SPEED_DOWNLOAD | The speed of all downloads in bytes per second. |
| CURLINFO_SPEED_UPLOAD | The speed of all uploads in bytes per second. |
| CURLINFO_SSL_VERIFYRESULT | The result of verifying the peer in an SSL request. |
| CURLINFO_STARTTRANSFER_TIME | The time spent starting the transfer. |
| CURLINFO_TOTAL_TIME | A double describing the number of seconds needed to complete the transfer, excluding the connection time. |

**Listing 10.23**   *curl_getinfo*

```php
<?php
    //get Zend home page
    $curl = curl_init('http://www.zend.com/');
    curl_setopt($curl, CURLOPT_RETURNTRANSFER, TRUE);
    curl_exec($curl);

    //dump information about the
    print("CURLINFO_CONNECT_TIME: " .
        curl_getinfo($curl, CURLINFO_CONNECT_TIME) .
        '<br>');
    print("CURLINFO_CONTENT_LENGTH_DOWNLOAD: " .
        curl_getinfo($curl, CURLINFO_CONTENT_LENGTH_DOWNLOAD) .
        '<br>');
    print("CURLINFO_CONTENT_LENGTH_UPLOAD: " .
        curl_getinfo($curl, CURLINFO_CONTENT_LENGTH_UPLOAD) .
        '<br>');
    print("CURLINFO_CONTENT_TYPE: " .
        curl_getinfo($curl, CURLINFO_CONTENT_TYPE) .
        '<br>');
    print("CURLINFO_EFFECTIVE_URL: " .
        curl_getinfo($curl, CURLINFO_EFFECTIVE_URL) .
        '<br>');
    print("CURLINFO_FILETIME: " .
        curl_getinfo($curl, CURLINFO_FILETIME) .
        '<br>');
    print("CURLINFO_HEADER_SIZE: " .
        curl_getinfo($curl, CURLINFO_HEADER_SIZE) .
        '<br>');
    print("CURLINFO_HTTP_CODE: " .
        curl_getinfo($curl, CURLINFO_HTTP_CODE) .
        '<br>');
    print("CURLINFO_NAMELOOKUP_TIME: " .
        curl_getinfo($curl, CURLINFO_NAMELOOKUP_TIME) .
        '<br>');
    print("CURLINFO_PRETRANSFER_TIME: " .
        curl_getinfo($curl, CURLINFO_PRETRANSFER_TIME) .
        '<br>');
    print("CURLINFO_REDIRECT_COUNT: " .
        curl_getinfo($curl, CURLINFO_REDIRECT_COUNT) .
        '<br>');
    print("CURLINFO_REDIRECT_TIME: " .
        curl_getinfo($curl, CURLINFO_REDIRECT_TIME) .
        '<br>');
    print("CURLINFO_REQUEST_SIZE: " .
        curl_getinfo($curl, CURLINFO_REQUEST_SIZE) .
        '<br>');
```

**Listing 10.23**    *curl_getinfo (cont.)*

```php
print("CURLINFO_SIZE_DOWNLOAD: " .
    curl_getinfo($curl, CURLINFO_SIZE_DOWNLOAD) .
    '<br>');
print("CURLINFO_SIZE_UPLOAD: " .
    curl_getinfo($curl, CURLINFO_SIZE_UPLOAD) .
    '<br>');
print("CURLINFO_SPEED_DOWNLOAD: " .
    curl_getinfo($curl, CURLINFO_SPEED_DOWNLOAD) .
    '<br>');
print("CURLINFO_SPEED_UPLOAD: " .
    curl_getinfo($curl, CURLINFO_SPEED_UPLOAD) .
    '<br>');
print("CURLINFO_SSL_VERIFYRESULT: " .
    curl_getinfo($curl, CURLINFO_SSL_VERIFYRESULT) .
    '<br>');
print("CURLINFO_STARTTRANSFER_TIME: " .
    curl_getinfo($curl, CURLINFO_STARTTRANSFER_TIME) .
    '<br>');
print("CURLINFO_TOTAL_TIME: " .
    curl_getinfo($curl, CURLINFO_TOTAL_TIME) .
    '<br>');
?>
```

### resource curl_init(string url)

Use `curl_init` to create a Curl resource handle. The optional `url` argument sets the `CURLOPT_URL` option.

### integer curl_multi_add_handle(resource multi, resource curl)

The `curl_multi_add_handle` function adds an ordinary Curl resource to a multiresource stack. It returns a status code.

### curl_multi_close(resource multi)

The `curl_multi_close` function closes a Curl multiresource. It calls Curl's `curl_multi_cleanup` function.

### integer curl_multi_exec(resource multi)

The `curl_multi_exec` function reads and writes data on all sockets in the multiresource stack. It calls Curl's `curl_multi_perform` function.

### string curl_multi_getcontent(resource multi)

The `curl_multi_getcontent` function returns content read from the multiresource.

### array curl_multi_info_read(resource multi)

The `curl_multi_info_read` function returns an array of information about a multiresource.

### resource curl_multi_init()

The `curl_multi_init` function returns a resource pointing to the multi-interface.

### integer curl_multi_remove_handle(resource multi, resource curl)

The `curl_multi_remove_handle` function removes an ordinary Curl resource from a multiresource stack. It returns a status code.

### curl_multi_select(resource multi, integer timeout)

The `multi_select` function executes a C library `select` call on the set of Curl resources in the multiresource stack. The optional timeout argument is passed through to `select`.

### boolean curl_setopt(resource curl, string option, value setting)

The `curl_setopt` function configures a Curl connection prior to execution with `curl_exec`. You must supply a Curl resource handle as created by `curl_init`. Choose one of the options from Table 10.11.

**Table 10.11** Curl Options

| Option | Description |
| --- | --- |
| CURLOPT_BINARYTRANSFER | Use CURLOPT_BINARYTRANSFER with CURLOPT_RETURNTRANSFER to make sure the return value is binary safe. |
| CURLOPT_CAINFO | Set CURLOPT_CAINFO with the path to a file holding one or more certificates used for verifying the peer. You must pair this option with CURLOPT_SSL_VERIFYPEER. |
| CURLOPT_CAPATH | Set x with the path to a directory containing certificates used for verifying the peer. You must pair this option with CURLOPT_SSL_VERIFYPEER. |

**Table 10.11**   Curl Options *(cont.)*

| Option | Description |
| --- | --- |
| CURLOPT_CLOSEPOLICY | Use CURLOPT_CLOSEPOLICY to set the policy for closing connections when the connection is full. Set this option to CURLCLOSEPOLICY_LEAST_RECENTLY_USED or CURLCLOSEPOLICY_OLDEST. |
| CURLOPT_CONNECTTIMEOUT | Set CURLOPT_CONNECTTIMEOUT to the maximum number of seconds to wait while making a connection. |
| CURLOPT_COOKIE | Use CURLOPT_COOKIE to pass cookies in the request. Specify cookies as a string with the equal sign separating cookie name from value and semicolons separating cookies. For example, cookie1=valueA;cookie1=valueB sets two cookies named cookie1 and cookie2. |
| CURLOPT_COOKIEFILE | Set CURLOPT_COOKIEFILE to the path to a file used to pass cookies for requests. The file may follow the format used by Netscape Navigator or normal HTTP header format. |
| CURLOPT_COOKIEJAR | Set CURLOPT_COOKIEJAR with the path to a file used for saving cookies. Curl saves any cookies it receives during the request in this file. You may then use this file with CURLOPT_COOKIEFILE. |
| CURLOPT_CRLF | If TRUE, Curl converts UNIX newlines into carriage return/linefeed pairs. |
| CURLOPT_CUSTOMREQUEST | Use CURLOPT_CUSTOMREQUEST to send an alternative command during an HTTP request. Set it with the command only, not the entire request string. |
| CURLOPT_DNS_CACHE_TIMEOUT | Curl keeps a cache of hostname lookups. Set CURLOPT_DNS_CACHE_TIMEOUT to the number of seconds to keep a name in the cache. |
| CURLOPT_DNS_USE_GLOBAL_CACHE | If TRUE, Curl shares a cache of hostname lookups. This option is not thread-safe. |
| CURLOPT_EGDSOCKET | Set CURLOPT_EGDSOCKET with the path to the Entropy Gathering Daemon socket. Curl uses this to seed the random number generator used for SSL. |

**Table 10.11** Curl Options *(cont.)*

| Option | Description |
|--------|-------------|
| CURLOPT_FAILONERROR | If TRUE, HTTP response codes greater than 300 to cause a silent error instead of returning whatever page the server returns. |
| CURLOPT_FILE | Set CURLOPT_FILE with an open file stream to send output into the file instead of out to the browser. |
| CURLOPT_FILETIME | If TRUE, Curl attempts to get the modification time of the requested file. |
| CURLOPT_FOLLOWLOCATION | If TRUE, Curl follows redirection headers returned by HTTP servers. |
| CURLOPT_FORBID_REUSE | If TRUE, Curl closes the connection after completing the request, forbidding its reuse. |
| CURLOPT_FRESH_CONNECT | If TRUE, Curl makes a fresh connection regardless of having an appropriate connection in the cache. |
| CURLOPT_FTPAPPEND | If TRUE, Curl appends to an FTP upload instead of overwriting. |
| CURLOPT_FTPLISTONLY | If TRUE, Curl returns a list of files in an FTP directory. |
| CURLOPT_FTPPORT | The CURLOPT_FTPPORT option sets the configuration for an FTP POST command, which requests a connection from the server. Set this option to an IP address, hostname, network interface name, or – to use the default address. |
| CURLOPT_FTP_USE_EPSV | Curl uses the EPSV command during passive FTP transfers by default. Set this option to FALSE to stop the use of EPSV. |
| CURLOPT_HEADER | If TRUE, Curl includes the headers in the output. |
| CURLOPT_HEADERFUNCTION | Set CURLOPT_HEADERFUNCTION with the name of a function that Curl calls for each received HTTP header. The function must accept two arguments, the Curl resource and a string containing a complete header. |

**Table 10.11**    Curl Options *(cont.)*

| Option | Description |
| --- | --- |
| CURLOPT_HTTPGET | If TRUE, Curl uses GET method for HTTP transfers. This may be useful only when reusing a Curl resource. |
| CURLOPT_HTTPHEADER | Set CURLOPT_HTTPHEADER with an array of HTTP headers to send during the request. |
| CURLOPT_HTTPPROXYTUNNEL | If TRUE, Curl tunnels all requests through a proxy. |
| CURLOPT_HTTP_VERSION | Use CURLOPT_HTTP_VERSION to force Curl to use a particular HTTP protocol version. Set the option to CURL_HTTP_VERSION_NONE to allow Curl to choose. Set the option to CURL_HTTP_VERSION_1_0 to force HTTP/1.0. Set the option to CURL_HTTP_VERSION_1_1 to force HTTP/1.1. |
| CURLOPT_INFILE | Setting CURLOPT_INFILE with an open file stream causes Curl to read input from the file. |
| CURLOPT_INFILESIZE | Use CURLOPT_INFILESIZE to specify the size of an uploaded file. |
| CURLOPT_INTERFACE | Set CURLOPT_INTERFACE to the name of the interface used. You may use the interface name, host name, or IP address. |
| CURLOPT_KRB4LEVEL | For FTP transfers, you may set the Kerberos security level with the CURLOPT_KRB4LEVEL option. Set the option value with one of the following strings: clear, safe, confidential, private. Alternatively, setting the string to FALSE will disable Kerberos security. |
| CURLOPT_LOW_SPEED_LIMIT | Use CURLOPT_LOW_SPEED_LIMIT to set the lower limit for transfer speeds, specified in bytes per second. If the transfer speed falls below this limit for the number of seconds given by CURLOPT_LOW_SPEED_TIME, Curl aborts the transfer. |
| CURLOPT_LOW_SPEED_TIME | Use CURLOPT_LOW_SPEED_TIME together with CURLOPT_LOW_SPEED_LIMIT to enforce a lower transfer speed limit. |

**Table 10.11**  Curl Options *(cont.)*

| Option | Description |
| --- | --- |
| CURLOPT_MAXCONNECTS | The CURLOPT_MAXCONNECTS option sets the size of the connection cache. |
| CURLOPT_MAXREDIRS | Set CURLOPT_MAXREDIRS to the maximum number of redirects to follow. |
| CURLOPT_MUTE | If TRUE, PHP generates no browser output when executing Curl functions. |
| CURLOPT_NETRC | If TRUE, Curl looks in ~/.netrc for user authentication. |
| CURLOPT_NOBODY | If TRUE, Curl excludes the body from the output. |
| CURLOPT_NOPROGRESS | If FALSE, Curl shows a progress indicator. This option is TRUE by default. |
| CURLOPT_PASSWDFUNCTION | Set CURLOPT_PASSWDFUNCTION to the name of a function for handling password requests. The function should accept three arguments: the Curl resource, the password prompt sent by the server, and a reference into which you place the password. The function should return zero if successful and nonzero if an error occurs. Set this option to FALSE to restore the default functionality. |
| CURLOPT_PORT | Use CURLOPT_PORT to set the port number used for the request. |
| CURLOPT_POST | If TRUE, Curl makes an HTTP POST request using application/x-www-form-urlencoded encoding. |
| CURLOPT_POSTFIELDS | Pass a string containing the complete post data with the CURLOPT_POSTFIELDS option. Format the post fields exactly as you would get fields. For example, apple=1&ball=red&cat=45.56 would send three post fields named apple, ball, and cat respectively. |
| CURLOPT_POSTQUOTE | Set CURLOPT_POSTQUOTE with an array of FTP commands executed after the main request. |
| CURLOPT_PROXY | Set this option to the proxy server. |

**Table 10.11**   Curl Options *(cont.)*

| Option | Description |
|---|---|
| CURLOPT_PROXYUSERPWD | Use CURLOPT_PROXYUSERPWD to set the username and password required by the proxy server. Use the username:password format. |
| CURLOPT_PUT | If TRUE, Curl executes an HTTP PUT request. You must set CURLOPT_INFILE and CURLOPT_INFILESIZE. |
| CURLOPT_QUOTE | Set CURLOPT_QUOTE with an array of FTP commands executed prior to the main request. |
| CURLOPT_RANDOM_FILE | Set CURLOPT_RANDOM_FILE with the path to a file Curl will read for seeding the SSL random number generator. |
| CURLOPT_RANGE | Use CURLOPT_RANGE to set the range header sent to the HTTP server. Pass a string containing beginning and ending byte offsets separated by a hyphen. Multiple ranges may be separated by commas, 100-150,233-502, for example. You can read more about ranges in the HTTP 1.1 specification. |
| CURLOPT_READFUNCTION | Set CURLOPT_READFUNCTION with the name of a function for sending data to the peer. The function should accept two arguments, the Curl resource and a string reference. Copy data into the string reference and return the number of bytes. Returning zero signals the end of the file. |
| CURLOPT_REFERER | Use CURLOPT_REFERER to set the Referer field passed in HTTP requests. |
| CURLOPT_RESUME_FROM | Use CURLOPT_RESUME_FROM to resume a transfer. Specify an offset in bytes. |
| CURLOPT_RETURNTRANSFER | Ordinarily, Curl sends the results of commands directly to the browser. Set CURLOPT_RETURNTRANSFER to TRUE to get results a return value from curl_exec. |
| CURLOPT_SSLCERT | Set CURLOPT_SSLCERT with the path to an SSL certificate in PEM (Privacy Enhanced Mail) format. |

**Table 10.11**  Curl Options *(cont.)*

| Option | Description |
| --- | --- |
| CURLOPT_SSLCERTPASSWD | Set CURLOPT_SSLCERTPASSWD to the password needed to read the SSL certificate specified by CURLOPT_SSLCERT. |
| CURLOPT_SSLENGINE | Set this option with the name of the SSL engine used for the private key. |
| CURLOPT_SSLENGINE_DEFAULT | Set this option with the name of the SSL engine used for most cases, excluding private keys. |
| CURLOPT_SSLKEY | Set CURLOPT_SSLKEY with the path to a private key. The default type is PEM and can be changed with CURLOPT_SSLKEYTYPE. |
| CURLOPT_SSLKEYPASSWD | Set CURLOPT_SSLKEYPASSWD with the password necessary to use the private key specified by CURLOPT_SSLKEY. |
| CURLOPT_SSLKEYTYPE | Set CURLOPT_SSLKEYTYPE with the type of private key specified by CURLOPT_SSLKEY. Pass the type as one of the following strings: PEM, DER, ENG. |
| CURLOPT_SSLVERSION | Use CURLOPT_SSLVERSION to enforce SSL version 2 or 3. Ordinarily, Curl can guess the appropriate protocol version. |
| CURLOPT_SSL_CIPHER_LIST | Use CURLOPT_SSL_CIPHER_LIST to set the list of ciphers to use for SSL connections. Use colons to separate cipher names. The default list is set when compiling OpenSSL. |
| CURLOPT_SSL_VERIFYHOST | Set CURLOPT_SSL_VERIFYHOST to 1 if you wish Curl to verify the common name on the SSL certificate. Set it to 2 to ensure it matches the host name. |
| CURLOPT_SSL_VERIFYPEER | If TRUE, Curl will attempt to verify the identity of the peer using the certificates specified by CURLOPT_CAINFO. |
| CURLOPT_STDERR | Set CURLOPT_STDERR with an open file stream to redirect error messages. |

**Table 10.11**    Curl Options *(cont.)*

| Option | Description |
| --- | --- |
| CURLOPT_TIMECONDITION | Use `CURLOPT_TIMECONDITION` to enforce a condition on the transfer based on the last modification time of the remote file. Use `CURLOPT_TIMEVALUE` to set the time value used for this condition. Use `TIMECOND_IFMODSINCE` to require the file to be modified since the given time. Use `TIMECOND_ISUNMODSINCE` to require the file to be unmodified since the given time. |
| CURLOPT_TIMEOUT | The `CURLOPT_TIMEOUT` option holds the maximum time in seconds that a Curl operation may execute. |
| CURLOPT_TIMEVALUE | Use `CURLOPT_TIMEVALUE` to set the time in standard UNIX timestamp format used by `CURLOPT_TIMECONDITION`. |
| CURLOPT_TRANSFERTEXT | If `TRUE`, Curl makes FTP transfers in ASCII mode and LDAP in text instead of HTML. |
| CURLOPT_UPLOAD | If `TRUE`, Curl makes an HTTP upload. You must set `CURLOPT_INFILE` and `CURLOPT_INFILESIZE`. |
| CURLOPT_URL | Set `CURLOPT_URL` to the URL to execute. You may also set this option with `curl_init`. |
| CURLOPT_USERAGENT | Use `CURLOPT_USERAGENT` to set the `User-agent` field passed in HTTP requests. |
| CURLOPT_USERPWD | Use `CURLOPT_USERPWD` to set the username and password required by a connection. Use the `username:password` format. |
| CURLOPT_VERBOSE | If `TRUE`, Curl reports verbose status messages. |
| CURLOPT_WRITEFUNCTION | Set `CURLOPT_WRITEFUNCTION` with the name of a function for receiving data from the connection. The function should accept two arguments, the Curl resource and a string of data. The function must return the number of bytes processed. If this return value does not match the number of bytes passed in, Curl signals an error. |
| CURLOPT_WRITEHEADER | Set `CURLOPT_WRITEHEADER` with an open file stream that will receive the headers. The option value should be a resource as returned by `fopen`. |

**string curl_version()**

Use `curl_version` to get the version of the underlying Curl library.

# 10.5 SNMP

SNMP, the Simple Network Management Protocol, is a protocol for Internet network management. It was first described in RFC 1089. One place to start learning about SNMP is SNMP Research at `<http://www.snmp.com/>`. To use these functions under UNIX, you must have the UCD SNMP libraries. You can find them at `<http://www.net-snmp.org/>`.

### boolean snmp_get_quick_print()

The `snmp_get_quick_print` function returns the status of the UCD SNMP library's `quick_print` setting. The `quick_print` setting controls how verbose object values are. By default, `quick_print` is `FALSE`, and values include types and other information. The UCD SNMP manual provides more information.

### snmp_set_quick_print(boolean on)

The `snmp_set_quick_print` function sets the value of the UCD SNMP library's `quick_print` setting. See the description of `snmp_get_quick_print` for a brief description of the `quick_print` setting.

### string snmpget(string host, string community, string object, integer timeout, integer retries)

The `snmpget` function (Listing 10.24) returns the value of the specified object. The host may be numerical or named. You must also specify the community and the object. Optionally, you may supply a timeout in seconds and a number of times to retry a connection.

---

**Listing 10.24** *snmpget*

```php
<?php
    //find out how long the system has been up
    //should return something like
    //Timeticks: (586731977) 67 days, 21:48:39.77
    if($snmp = snmpget("test.net-snmp.org",
        "demopublic", "system.sysUpTime.0"))
    {
```

| Listing 10.24 | *snmpget (cont.)* |
|---|---|

```
        print($snmp);
    }
    else
    {
        print("snmpget failed!");
    }
?>
```

### boolean snmpset(string host, string community, string object, string type, string value, integer timeout, integer retries)

The snmpset function (Listing 10.25) sets the value of the specified object. The host may be numerical or named. You must also specify the community and the object. The type argument is a one-character string. Table 10.12 lists valid types. Optionally, you may supply a timeout in seconds and a number of times to retry a connection.

**Table 10.12** SNMP Types

| Type | Description |
|---|---|
| a | IP address. |
| d | Decimal string. |
| i | Integer. |
| o | Object ID. |
| s | String. |
| t | Time ticks. |
| u | Unsigned integer. |
| x | Hex string. |
| D | Double. |
| F | Float. |
| I | Signed 64-bit integer. |
| U | Unsigned 64-bit integer. |

Listing 10.25 *snmpset*

```php
<?php
    //show current value of the demo string
    $snmp = snmpget("test.net-snmp.org",
        "demopublic", "ucdDemoPublicString.0");
    print("$snmp (original value)<br>\n");

    //set it to something else
    snmpset("test.net-snmp.org",
        "demopublic", "ucdDemoPublicString.0",
        "s", "Core PHP Programming");

    //see current value of the demo string
    $snmp = snmpget("test.net-snmp.org",
        "demopublic", "ucdDemoPublicString.0");
    print("$snmp (new value)<br>\n");
?>
```

### array snmpwalk(string host, string community, string object, integer timeout, integer retries)

The snmpwalk function (Listing 10.26) returns an array of all objects in the tree that starts at the specified object. You can use an empty string for the object parameter to get all objects. Optionally, you may supply a timeout in seconds and a number of times to retry a connection.

**Listing 10.26**  *snmpwalk*

```php
<?php
    //get all the SNMP objects
    $snmp = snmpwalk("test.net-snmp.org", "demopublic", "");

    print_r($snmp);
?>
```

# DATA

**Topics in This Chapter**

- Data Types, Constants, and Variables
- Arrays
- Objects and Classes
- User Defined Functions

# Chapter

The functions in this chapter manipulate data. They check the values of variables. They transform one type of data into another. They also deal with arrays. You may find it useful to turn back to Chapter 2 and read the discussion on data types and variables.

## 11.1  Data Types, Constants, and Variables

These functions check the status of a variable, change its type, or return a value as a particular data type.

### value constant(string name)
Use `constant` (Listing 11.1) to fetch the value of a constant. This offers the ability to specify a constant with a variable.

Listing 11.1 *constant*

```php
<?php
    function getDatabaseProperty($property)
    {
        return(constant("DATABASE_$property"));
    }

    define("DATABASE_HOST", "localhost");
    define("DATABASE_USER", "httpd");
    define("DATABASE_PASSWORD", "");
    define("DATABASE_NAME", "freetrade");

    print(getDatabaseProperty('HOST'));
?>
```

### boolean ctype_alnum(string text)

The `ctype_alnum` function tests whether every character in the given string is in the set of all digits and letters, uppercase and lowercase. An empty string matches this set.

### boolean ctype_alpha(string text)

The `ctype_alpha` function tests whether every character in the given string is in the set of all letters, uppercase and lowercase. An empty string matches this set.

### boolean ctype_cntrl(string text)

The `ctype_cntrl` function tests whether every character in the given string is a control character. An empty string matches this set.

### boolean ctype_digit(string text)

The `ctype_digit` function tests whether every character in the given string is a digit. An empty string passes this test.

### boolean ctype_graph(string text)

The `ctype_graph` function tests whether every character in the given string has a graphical representation. An empty string passes this test.

### boolean ctype_lower(string text)

The `ctype_lower` function tests whether every character in the given string is in the set of lowercase letters. An empty string matches this set.

### boolean ctype_print(string text)

The `ctype_print` function tests whether every character in the given string is printable, including spaces and tabs. An empty string passes this test.

### boolean ctype_punct(string text)

The `ctype_punct` function tests whether every character in the given string is in the set of punctuation characters. An empty string matches this set.

### boolean ctype_space(string text)

The `ctype_space` function tests whether every character in the given string is in the set of space characters, which includes tabs and linefeeds. An empty string matches this set.

### boolean ctype_upper(string text)

The `ctype_upper` function tests whether every character in the given string is in the set of uppercase letters. An empty string matches this set.

### boolean ctype_xdigit(string text)

The `ctype_xdigit` function tests whether every character in the given string is in the set of hexadecimal digits. An empty string matches this set.

### boolean define(string name, value, boolean non_case_sensitive)

The `define` function (Listing 11.2) creates a constant, which is essentially a variable that may be set only once. The `value` argument may be a string, integer, double, or boolean. It may not be an array or object. The `non_case_sensitive` argument is optional. By default, constants are case sensitive, which is the same as with variables.

If the constant cannot be created for some reason, `FALSE` will be returned. If you wish to check that a constant is defined, use the `defined` function.

It is customary to name constants using all uppercase letters, as is the practice in C. This makes them stand out among other identifiers.

Because PHP allows for unquoted string literals, it is possible to write code that uses constants that do not exist yet produces no error. When you are using constants to hold strings to be displayed on the page, this is simply an annoyance, because you can see the error right away. When used for values not displayed, it can be a frustrating source of bugs. If you discover a constant mysteriously evaluating to zero, check that you defined the constant. PHP creates an `E_NOTICE` level error message if you use an undefined constant.

Listing 11.2    *define*

```php
<?php
    /*
    ** Database variables
    */
    define("DATABASE_HOST", "localhost");
    define("DATABASE_USER", "httpd");
    define("DATABASE_PASSWORD", "");
    define("DATABASE_NAME", "freetrade");

    print("Connecting to " . DATABASE_HOST . "<br>\n");
?>
```

### boolean defined(string constantname)

The `defined` function (Listing 11.3) returns TRUE if a constant exists and FALSE otherwise.

Listing 11.3    *defined*

```php
<?php
    define("THERMOSTAT","72 degrees");
    if(defined("THERMOSTAT"))
    {
        print("THERMOSTAT is " . THERMOSTAT);
    }
?>
```

### double doubleval(expression)

The `doubleval` function (Listing 11.4) returns its argument as a double. Chapter 2 discusses converting between data types. Related functions are `strval` and `intval`. It is an error to pass an array or object to `doubleval`.

Listing 11.4    *doubleval*

```php
<?php
    $myNumber = "13.1cm";
    print(doubleval($myNumber));
?>
```

### boolean empty(variable)

The empty function returns FALSE if the variable has been given a value or TRUE if the variable has never been on the left side of a set operator. In other words, it tests that the variable has been set with a value other than NULL. It returns the opposite value of isset.

### floatval

Use floatval as an alias for doubleval.

### string get_resource_type(resource handle)

The get_resource_type function returns a string describing the type of resource of the handle argument.

### boolean import_request_variables(string types, string prefix)

The import_request_variables function (Listing 11.5) creates variables in the global scope from submitted form fields. This matches the functionality of the register_globals directive in php.ini. The types argument should be a string containing one or more of the following letters: G, P, C. These import get variables, post variables, and cookies respectively. The order of the letters specifies the order in which variables of different types and duplicate names overwrite each other. You may use lowercase letters if you wish.

The prefix argument is optional but causes an E_NOTICE error if left out. PHP adds the prefix to the form field names when creating the global variables.

**Listing 11.5**   *import_request_variables*

```php
<?php
    import_request_variables('GP', 'form_');

    if(isset($form_message))
    {
        print("Text: $form_message<br>");
    }
?>
<form>
<input type="text" name="message">
<input type="submit">
</form>
```

### integer intval(expression, integer base)

The `intval` function (Listing 11.6) returns its argument as an integer. The optional `base` argument instructs `intval` to use a numerical base other than 10. Chapter 2 discusses converting between types.

---

**Listing 11.6** *intval*

```php
<?php
    //drop extraneous stuff after decimal point
    print(intval("13.5cm") . "<BR>\n");

    //convert from hex
    print(intval("EE", 16));
?>
```

---

### boolean is_array(expression)

The `is_array` function (Listing 11.7) returns TRUE if the expression is an array; otherwise FALSE is returned.

---

**Listing 11.7** *is_array*

```php
<?php
    $colors = array("red", "blue", "green");
    if(is_array($colors))
    {
        print("colors is an array");
    }
?>
```

---

### boolean is_bool(expression)

Use `is_bool` to test whether an expression is a boolean.

### boolean is_double(expression)

The `is_double` function (Listing 11.8) returns TRUE if the expression is a double and FALSE otherwise.

**Listing 11.8**  *is_double*

```php
<?php
    $Temperature = 15.23;
    if(is_double($Temperature))
    {
        print("Temperature is a double");
    }
?>
```

### boolean is_finite(expression)

The is_finite function returns TRUE if the expression is a finite number and FALSE otherwise. In this context, finite means that the value fits within the boundaries of floating-point numbers for the platform.

### is_float

The is_float function is an alias for the is_double function.

### boolean is_infinite(expression)

The is_infinite function returns TRUE if the expression is an infinite number and FALSE otherwise. In this context, infinite means that the value falls outside the boundaries of floating-point numbers for the platform.

### is_int

The is_int function is an alias for the is_integer function.

### boolean is_integer(expression)

The is_integer function (Listing 11.9) returns TRUE if the expression is an integer, FALSE otherwise.

**Listing 11.9**  *is_integer*

```php
<?php
    $PageCount = 2234;
    if(is_integer($PageCount))
    {
        print("$PageCount is an integer");
    }
?>
```

### is_long

The is_long function is an alias for the is_integer function.

### boolean is_nan(expression)

The is_nan function (Listing 11.10) returns TRUE if the given expression is not a number. Some mathematic functions generate this value when given nonsense values.

**Listing 11.10**    *is_nan*

```php
<?php
    if(is_nan(asin(2)))
    {
        print("This is not a number.");
    }
?>
```

### boolean is_null(expression)

Use is_null to test whether the given express is NULL. Refer to Chapter 2 for a discussion of the NULL type.

### boolean is_numeric(expression)

Use is_numeric (Listing 11.11) to test an expression for being a number or a string that would covert to a number with no extra characters.

**Listing 11.11**    *is_numeric*

```php
<?php
    function testNumeric($n)
    {
        if(is_numeric($n))
        {
            print("'$n' is numeric<br>");
        }
        else
        {
            print("'$n' is not numeric<br>");
        }
    }
```

**Listing 11.11**  *is_numeric (cont.)*

```
//numeric
testNumeric(3);
testNumeric('4');
testNumeric(4e+5);
testNumeric(0xDE);
testNumeric('0xDE');
testNumeric(0667);

//not numeric
testNumeric('3 fish');
testNumeric('4e+5');
?>
```

### boolean is_object(expression)

The `is_object` function (Listing 11.12) returns TRUE if the expression is an object and FALSE otherwise.

**Listing 11.12**  *is_object*

```
<?php
    class widget
    {
        var $name;
        var $length;
    }

    $thing = new widget;

    if(is_object($thing))
    {
        print("thing is an object");
    }
?>
```

### boolean is_real(expression)

The `is_real` function is an alias for the `is_double` function.

### boolean is_resource(variable)

This function returns TRUE if the given variable is a resource, such as the return value of `fopen`.

## boolean is_scalar(expression)

Use `is_scalar` (Listing 11.13) to test whether an express is a scalar, which in this context means a single value as compared to aggregate value. The `is_scalar` function returns FALSE when given a NULL value.

---

**Listing 11.13**   *is_scalar*

```php
<?php
    function testScalar($s)
    {
        if(is_scalar($s))
        {
            print("'$s' is scalar<br>");
        }
        else
        {
            print(print_r($s, TRUE) . " is not scalar<br>");
        }
    }

    class c { }

    //scalar
    testScalar(TRUE);
    testScalar(1234);
    testScalar(1.234);
    testScalar('a string');

    //not scalar
    testScalar(array(1,2,3,4));
    testScalar(new c);
    testScalar(fopen('/tmp/test', 'w'));
    testScalar(NULL);
?>
```

---

## boolean is_string(expression)

The `is_string` function (Listing 11.14) returns TRUE if the expression is a string and FALSE otherwise.

**Listing 11.14** *is_string*

```php
<?php
    $Greeting = "Hello";
    if(is_string($Greeting))
    {
        print("Greeting is a string");
    }
?>
```

### boolean isset(variable)

The `isset` function (Listing 11.15) returns TRUE if the variable has been given a value or FALSE if the variable has never been on the left side of a set operator. In other words, it tests that the variable has been set with a value. This complements the `is_null` function.

**Listing 11.15** *isset*

```php
<?php
    if(isset($Name))
    {
        print("Your Name is $Name");
    }
    else
    {
        print("I don't know your name");
    }
?>
```

### boolean settype(variable, string type)

The `settype` function (Listing 11.16) changes the type of a variable. The type is written as a string and may be one of the following: `array`, `bool`, `double`, `float`, `int`, `integer`, `null`, `object`, `string`. If the type could not be set, FALSE is returned.

**Listing 11.16** *settype*

```php
<?php
    $myValue = 123.45;
    settype($myValue, "integer");
    print($myValue);
?>
```

### string strval(expression)

The `strval` function (Listing 11.17) returns its argument as a string.

| Listing 11.17 | *strval* |
|---|---|

```php
<?php
    $myNumber = 13;
    print(strval($myNumber));
?>
```

### unset(variable)

The `unset` function (Listing 11.18) destroys a variable, causing all memory associated with the variable to be freed. You may accomplish the same effect by setting the variable to NULL.

| Listing 11.18 | *unset* |
|---|---|

```php
<?php
    $list= array("milk", "eggs", "sugar");

    unset($list);

    if(!isset($list))
    {
        print("list has been cleared and has ");
        print(count($list));
        print(" elements");
    }
?>
```

# 11.2  Arrays

The functions in this section operate on arrays. Some of them sort the arrays; some of them help you find and retrieve values from arrays. Chapter 5 discusses arrays in depth.

**array array(...)**

The array function (Listing 11.19) takes a list of values separated by commas and returns an array. This is especially useful for creating one-off arrays to be passed to functions. Elements will be added to the array as if you used empty square brackets, which means they are numbered consecutively starting at zero. You may use the => operator to specify index values.

**Listing 11.19** *array*

```php
<?php
    //create an array
    $myArray = array(
        "Name"=>"Leon Atkinson",
        "Profession"=>array("Programmer", "Author"),
        "Residence"=>"Martinez, California"
        );
?>
```

**array array_change_key_case(array data, integer case)**

Use array_change_key_case to change the keys in an array to all uppercase or all lowercase. You may use CASE_LOWER or CASE_UPPER for the optional case argument. By default, this function coverts keys to lowercase. Any nonalphabetic characters used in keys are unaffected.

Keep in mind that since array keys are case-sensitive, this function may return an array with fewer elements than given in the data argument. When two keys become identical due to change in case, PHP keeps the element that appears last in the array. Listing 11.20 and Figure 11.1 demonstrate this behavior.

**Listing 11.20** *array_change_key_case*

```php
<?php
    $location = array('Leon Atkinson'=>'home',
        'john villarreal'=>'away',
        'leon atkinson'=>'away',
        'Carl porter'=>'home',
        'Jeff McKillop'=>'away',
        'Rick Marazzani'=>'away',
        'bob dibetta'=>'away',
        'Joe Tully'=>'home'
        );

    print_r(array_change_key_case($location, CASE_UPPER));
?>
```

```
Array
(
    [LEON ATKINSON] => away
    [JOHN VILLARREAL] => away
    [CARL PORTER] => home
    [JEFF MCKILLOP] => away
    [RICK MARAZZANI] => away
    [BOB DIBETTA] => away
    [JOE TULLY] => home
)
```

**Figure 11.1**  `array_change_key_case` output.

### array array_chunk(array data, integer size, boolean preserve_keys)

The `array_chunk` function (Listing 11.21) splits the elements of the given array into subarrays of the given size. The optional `preserve_keys` argument preserves the original keys. Otherwise, the subarrays use integers starting with zero for keys. See Figure 11.2.

**Listing 11.21**  *array_chunk*

```php
<?php
    //set available players
    $players = array(
        'Leon Atkinson',
        'John Villarreal',
        'Carl Porter',
        'Jeff McKillop',
        'Rick Marazzani',
        'Bob Dibetta',
        'Joe Tully',
        'John Foster'
        );

    //shuffle players
    srand(time());
    shuffle($players);

    //divide players into two teams
    $teams = array_chunk($players, count($players)/2);

    print_r($teams);
?>
```

```
Array
(
    [0] => Array
        (
            [0] => Jeff McKillop
            [1] => Carl Porter
            [2] => Rick Marazzani
            [3] => Joe Tully
        )

    [1] => Array
        (
            [0] => John Foster
            [1] => Bob Dibetta
            [2] => John Villarreal
            [3] => Leon Atkinson
        )

)
```

**Figure 11.2** `array_chunk` output.

### array array_combine(array keys, array values)

The `array_combine` function returns an array that uses the elements of the first array for keys that point to the elements given in the second array. If the arrays do not have the same number of elements, PHP generates an error.

### array array_count_values(array data)

The `array_count_values` function (Listing 11.22) returns counts for each distinct value in the `data` argument. The returned array is indexed by the values of the `data` argument. Although the example below uses an array of numbers, `array_count_values` will count the appearance of elements that contain any data type.

**Listing 11.22** *array_count_values*

```php
<?php
    //generate random numbers between 1 and 5
    $sample_size = 100;
    srand(time());
    for($i=0; $i<$sample_size; $i++)
    {
        $data[] = rand(1,5);
    }
```

**Listing 11.22**   *array_count_values (cont.)*

```
//count elements
$count = array_count_values($data);

//sort by keys
ksort($count);

//print out totals
foreach($count as $number=>$count)
{
    print("$number: $count (" .
        (100 * $count/$sample_size) .
        "%)<br>\n");
}
?>
```

### array array_diff(array data, array comparison, ...)

The `array_diff` function (Listing 11.23) returns an array containing the elements in the first argument that are not in any of the following arguments. The keys in the first array are preserved. Two elements are considered identical if their string representation is the same, meaning `"123"` equals `123.00` in this context. See Figure 11.3.

You can find the intersection of two arrays with `array_intersect`.

**Listing 11.23**   *array_diff*

```
<?php
    $a = array(1,2,3,4,5,6,7,8);
    $b = array(2,6);
    $c = array(8,1,5,6);

    print_r(array_diff($a, $b, $c));
    print_r(array_intersect($a, $b, $c));
?>
```

```
Array
(
    [2] => 3
    [3] => 4
    [6] => 7
)
Array
(
    [5] => 6
)
```

**Figure 11.3**  `array_diff` output.

### array array_diff_assoc(array data, array comparison, ...)

The `array_diff_assoc` function (Listing 11.24) returns an array containing the elements in the first argument and not in any of the following arguments, just as with `array_diff`. In addition to values being identical, keys must match. Otherwise, functionality matches `array_diff`. See Figure 11.4.

The `array_intersect_assoc` function complements this function.

**Listing 11.24**  *array_diff_assoc*

```php
<?php
    $a = array(
        1=>'apple',
        2=>'ball',
        3=>'cat',
        4=>'dog',
        'ape'=>'banana'
        );

    $b = array(
        2=>'apple',
        'ape'=>'banana'
        );

    $c = array(
        3=>'cat',
        2=>'ball',
        'cat'=>'ball',
        'ape'=>'banana'
        );

    print_r(array_diff_assoc($a, $b, $c));
    print_r(array_intersect_assoc($a, $b, $c));
?>
```

```
Array
(
    [1] => apple
    [4] => dog
)
Array
(
    [ape] => banana
)
```

**Figure 11.4** `array_diff_assoc` output.

### array array_fill(integer start, integer number, value)

Use `array_fill` (Listing 11.25, Figure 11.5) to create an array of the given size filled out with the same value. The keys are numeric and start with the value passed as the `start` argument. Be careful if you pass an object for the filler value. PHP passes objects in function calls by reference, not by value. Consequently, using an object for this function's third argument will create an array of references to the same object. If you wish to create copies of the object, use the `__clone` method. You can read more about objects in Chapter 6.

**Listing 11.25** *array_fill*

```php
<?php
    print_r(array_fill(100, 3, 'filler'));
?>
```

```
Array
(
    [100] => filler
    [101] => filler
    [102] => filler
)
```

**Figure 11.5** `array_fill` output.

### array array_filter(array data, string function)

The `array_filter` function (Listing 11.26) removes elements from an array based on a callback function, preserving keys. The callback function should accept a single value and return a boolean. It should return TRUE if the value should appear in the returned array.

**Listing 11.26** *array_filter*

```php
<?php
    function is_square($n)
    {
        $s = sqrt($n);
        return(intval($s) == $s);
    }

    $a = range(2, 100);

    foreach(array_filter($a, 'is_square') as $n)
    {
        print("$n<br>");
    }
?>
```

**array array_flip(array data)**

The `array_flip` function (Listing 11.27) returns the `data` argument with the keys and values exchanged. Values must be valid keys—that is, integers or strings. Otherwise, PHP generates a warning and skips that element. Multiple occurrences of a value, will overwrite each other as they become keys. See Figure 11.6.

**Listing 11.27** *array_flip*

```php
<?php
    $colors = array("red", "blue", "green");
    print_r(array_flip($colors));
?>
```

```
Array
(
    [red] => 0
    [blue] => 1
    [green] => 2
)
```

**Figure 11.6** `array_flip` output.

### array array_intersect(array data, array comparison, …)

The `array_intersect` function returns an array containing the elements that appear in every given array. The keys are preserved. Two elements are considered identical if their string representation is the same, meaning `"123"` equals `123.00` in this context.

You can find the difference of two or more arrays with `array_diff`.

### array array_intersect_assoc(array data, array comparison, …)

The `array_intersect_assoc` function returns an array containing the elements common to every array passed as an argument, just as with `array_intersect`. In addition to values being identical, keys must match. The `array_diff_assoc` function complements this function.

### boolean array_key_exists(key, array data)

The `array_key_exists` tests for the existence of a key in the given array.

### array array_keys(array data, string value)

The `array_keys` function (Listing 11.28) returns an array of the keys used in the `data` array. If the optional `value` argument is supplied, only the subset of indices that point to the given element value are returned.

---

**Listing 11.28**  *array_keys*

```php
<?php
    //create random test data with 0 or 1
    srand(time());
    for($i=0; $i<10; $i++)
    {
        $data[] = rand(0,1);
    }

    //print out the keys to 1's
    foreach(array_keys($data, 1) as $key)
    {
        print("$key<br>\n");
    }
?>
```

---

### array array_map(string function, array data, …)

Use `array_map` (Listing 11.29) to apply a callback function to every element of the data argument. PHP calls the given function with each element of the array. You can pass any number of additional arrays to this function, and PHP uses their elements for the callback function. This implies that the callback should accept as many arguments as arrays passed. See Figure 11.7.

**Listing 11.29** *array_map*

```php
<?php
    $a = array(1, 2, 3);
    $b = array(4, 5, 6);
    $c = array(7, 8);

    function add($n1, $n2)
    {
        return($n1 + $n2);
    }

    //each each element
    print_r(array_map('add', $a, $b));

    //combine arrays into map
    print_r(array_map(NULL, $a, $b, $c));
?>
```

```
Array
(
    [0] => 5
    [1] => 7
    [2] => 9
)
Array
(
    [0] => Array
        (
            [0] => 1
            [1] => 4
            [2] => 7
        )

    [1] => Array
        (
            [0] => 2
            [1] => 5
            [2] => 8
        )

    [2] => Array
        (
            [0] => 3
            [1] => 6
            [2] =>
        )
)
```

**Figure 11.7** array_map output.

It is possible to call this function with a NULL callback function, in which case PHP will create an array of arrays from the submitted arrays. The first element will be an array of the first elements from each array, and so on.

If any of the arrays are shorter than the rest, PHP fills them in with NULL values.

### array array_merge(array data, array data, ...)

The array_merge function (Listing 11.30) takes two or more arrays and returns a single array containing all elements. Elements indexed by integers are added to the new array one at a time, in most cases renumbering them. Elements indexed by strings retain their index values and are added as they are encountered in the input arrays. They may replace previous values. If you are unsure of the indices used in the merged arrays, you can use array_values to make sure all values are indexed by an integer.

---

**Listing 11.30**  *array_merge*

```php
<?php
    //set up an array of color names
    $colors = array("red", "blue", "green");
    $more_colors = array("yellow", "purple", "orange");

    //merge arrays
    print_r(array_merge($colors, $more_colors));
?>
```

---

### array array_merge_recursive(array data, array data, ...)

The array_merge_recursive function (Listing 11.31) operates like array_merge except that it merges elements with string keys into subarrays. See Figure 11.8.

**Listing 11.31** *array_merge_recursive*

```php
<?php
    $robot1 = array(
        'name'=>'Avenger',
        'weapon'=>array(
            'Machine Gun',
            'Laser'),
        'motivation'=>'tires'
        );

    $robot2 = array(
        'name'=>'Assassin',
        'weapon'=>'Machine Gun',
        'motivation'=>array(
            'tires',
            'wings'
            )
        );

    print_r(array_merge_recursive($robot1, $robot2));
?>
```

```
Array
(
    [name] => Array
        (
            [0] => Avenger
            [1] => Assassin
        )

    [weapon] => Array
        (
            [0] => Machine Gun
            [1] => Laser
            [2] => Machine Gun
        )

    [motivation] => Array
        (
            [0] => tires
            [1] => tires
            [2] => wings
        )

)
```

**Figure 11.8** array_merge_recursive output.

### boolean array_multisort(array data, integer direction, …)

The `array_multisort` function (Listing 11.32) sorts arrays together, as if the arrays were columns in a table. The `data` argument is an array, and the `direction` argument is one of two constants: `SORT_ASC` or `SORT_DESC`. These stand for ascending and descending respectively. If left out, the direction defaults to ascending order, which is smallest to largest. You may specify any number of arrays, but you must alternate between arrays and sort order constants as you do.

The way `array_multisort` works is similar to the way a relational database sorts the results of a join. The first element of each array is joined into a virtual row, and all elements in a row move together. The arrays are sorted by the first array. In the case where elements of the first array repeat, rows are sorted on the second row. Sorting continues as necessary.

| Listing 11.32 | *array_multisort* |
|---|---|

```php
<?php
    //create data
    $color = array("green", "green", "blue", "white", "white");
    $item = array("dish soap", "hand soap", "dish soap", "towel",
        "towel");
    $dept = array("kitchen", "bathroom", "kitchen", "kitchen",
        "bathroom");
    $price = array(2.50, 2.25, 2.55, 1.75, 3.00);

    //sort by department, item name, color, price
    array_multisort($dept, SORT_ASC,
        $item, SORT_ASC,
        $color, SORT_ASC,
        $price, SORT_DESC);

    //print sorted list
    for($i=0; $i < count($item); $i++)
    {
        print("$dept[$i] $item[$i] $color[$i] $price[$i]<br>\n");
    }
?>
```

### array array_pad(array data, integer size, value padding)

The `array_pad` function (Listing 11.33) adds elements to an array until it has the number of elements specified by the `size` argument. If the array is long enough already, no elements are added. Otherwise, the `padding` argument is used for the value of the new elements. If the `size` argument is positive, padding is added to the end of the array. If the `size` argument is negative, padding is added to the beginning.

**Listing 11.33** *array_pad*

```php
<?php
    //create test data
    $data = array(1,2,3);

    //add "start" to beginning of array
    $data = array_pad($data, -4, "start");

    //add "end" to end of array twice
    print_r(array_pad($data, 6, "end"));
?>
```

### value array_pop(array stack)

The `array_pop` function (Listing 11.34) returns the last element of an array, removing it from the array as well. The `array_push` function complements it, and `array_shift` and `array_unshift` add and remove elements from the beginning of an array.

**Listing 11.34** *array_pop, array_push*

```php
<?php
    //set up an array of color names
    $colors = array("red", "blue", "green");

    $lastColor = array_pop($colors);

    //prints "green"
    print($lastColor . "\n");

    //shows that colors contains red, blue
    print_r($colors);

    //push two more items on the stack
    array_push($colors, "purple", "yellow");

    //shows that colors contains red, blue, purple, yellow
    print_r($colors);
?>
```

**boolean array_push(array stack, expression entry, ...)**

The `array_push` function adds one or more values to the end of an array. It treats the array as a stack. Use `array_pop` to remove elements from the stack. The `array_shift` and `array_unshift` functions to add and remove elements to the beginning of an array.

**array array_rand(array data, integer quantity)**

The `array_rand` function (Listing 11.35) returns a number of randomly chosen keys from an array. The optional `quantity` argument defaults to one, in which case this function returns one key. Otherwise, the function returns an array of keys.

---

**Listing 11.35** *array_rand*

```php
<?php
    //set up an array of color names
    $colors = array("red", "blue", "green");

    //seed random number generator
    srand(time());

    //choose one
    print($colors[array_rand($colors)] . "\n");

    //choose two
    print_r(array_rand($colors, 2));
?>
```

---

**value array_reduce(array data, string function, value initial)**

The `array_reduce` function (Listing 11.36) converts an array into a single value by repeatedly submitting pairs of values to a callback function. By default, PHP submits the first two elements to the callback function, which must return a value. PHP then calls the callback function with this value and the next element of the array. If you supply a value for the optional `initial` argument, PHP uses it for the first value when first calling the callback.

---

**Listing 11.36** *array_reduce*

```php
<?php
    //set up an array of color names
    $colors = array(0xFF99FF, 0xCCFFFF, 0xFFFFEE);

    function maskColors($c1, $c2)
    {
```

| Listing 11.36 | *array_reduce (cont.)* |

```
        return($c1 & $c2);
    }

    $color = array_reduce($colors, 'maskColors', 0xFFFFFF);
    $colorHTML = sprintf('#%X', $color);

    print('<table><tr>' .
        "<td bgcolor=\"$colorHTML\">$colorHTML</td>".
        '</tr></table>');
?>
```

### array array_reverse(array data, boolean preserve_keys)

The array_reverse function (Listing 11.37) returns the data argument with the elements in reverse order. The elements are not sorted in any way. They are simply in the opposite order. If you set the optional preserve_keys argument to TRUE, PHP keeps the key values. See Figure 11.9.

| Listing 11.37 | *array_reverse* |

```
<?php
    $data = array(3, 1, 2, 7, 5);

    print_r(array_reverse($data));
    print_r(array_reverse($data, TRUE));
?>
```

```
Array
(
    [0] => 5
    [1] => 7
    [2] => 2
    [3] => 1
    [4] => 3
)
Array
(
    [4] => 5
    [3] => 7
    [2] => 2
    [1] => 1
    [0] => 3
)
```

**Figure 11.9** array_reverse output.

**value array_search(value query, array data, boolean check_type)**

The `array_search` function (Listing 11.38) returns the key of the element in data that matches `query` or `FALSE` if not found. If `check_type` is `TRUE`, PHP only matches if the types match as well.

**Listing 11.38** *array_search*

```php
<?php
    $data = array(3, 1, 2, 7, 5);

    if(FALSE !== ($key = array_search(3, $data, TRUE)))
    {
        print("Found 3 at element $key");
    }
    else
    {
        pring("Not found");
    }
?>
```

**value array_shift(array stack)**

The `array_shift` function (Listing 11.39) returns the first element of an array, removing it as well. This allows you to treat the array like a stack. The `array_unshift` function adds an element to the beginning of an array. Use `array_pop` and `array_push` to perform the same actions with the end of the array. Each shift operation changes the key values appropriately.

**Listing 11.39** *array_shift, array_unshift*

```php
<?php
    //set up an array of color names
    $colors = array("red", "blue", "green");

    $firstColor = array_shift($colors);

    //print "red"
    print($firstColor . "\n");

    //dump colors (0=>blue, green)
    print_r($colors);

    array_unshift($colors, "purple", "yellow");

    //dump colors (0=>purple, yellow, blue, green)
    print_r($colors);
?>
```

### array array_slice(array data, integer start, integer stop)

The `array_slice` function (Listing 11.40) returns part of an array, starting with the element specified by the `start` argument. If you specify a negative value for `start`, the starting position will be that many elements before the last element. The optional `stop` argument allows you to specify how many elements to return or where to stop returning values. A positive value is treated as a maximum number of elements to return. A negative `stop` is used to count backward from the last element to specify the element at which to stop.

Compare this function to `array_merge` and `array_splice`.

**Listing 11.40**   *array_slice*

```php
<?php
    //set up an array of color names
    $colors = array("red", "blue", "green",
        "purple", "cyan", "yellow");

    //get a new array consisting of a slice
    //from "green" to "cyan"
    print_r(array_slice($colors, 2, 3));
?>
```

### array_splice(array data, integer start, integer length, array insert_data)

The `array_splice` function (Listing 11.41) removes part of an array and inserts another in its place. The array passed is altered in place, not returned. Starting with the element specified by the `start` argument, PHP removes the number of elements specified by the `length` argument. If you leave out `length`, removal continues to the end of the array. If `length` is negative, it references a stopping point from the end of the array backward. If you wish to insert but not remove elements, use a length of zero.

In place of any removed elements, the array passed as the `insert_data` argument is inserted if it is supplied. Declaring it is optional, as you may wish simply to remove some elements. If you wish to insert a single element into the array, you may use a single value instead.

Compare this function to `array_merge` and `array_slice`.

---

| Listing 11.41 | *array_splice* |

```php
<?php
    //set up an array of color names
    $colors = array("red", "blue", "green",
        "yellow", "orange", "purple");
    print_r($colors);

    //remove green
    array_splice($colors, 2, 1);
    print_r($colors);

    //insert "pink" after "blue"
    array_splice($colors, 2, 0, "pink");
    print_r($colors);

    //insert "cyan" and "black" between
    //"orange" and "purple"
    array_splice($colors, 4, 0, array("cyan", "black"));
    print_r($colors);
?>
```

---

### value array_sum(array data)

Use `array_sum` (Listing 11.42) to get the sum of every element of an array.

---

| Listing 11.42 | *array_sum* |

```php
<?php
    $data = array(1, 2, 3, 4.0, 5.6, 'nothing');

    //print 15.6
    print(array_sum($data));
?>
```

---

### array array_unique(array data)

The `array_unique` function (Listing 11.43) returns the given array with duplicates removed, preserving the keys and keeping the first key encountered.

**Listing 11.43** *array_unique*

```php
<?php
    $colors = array(
        "red"=>"FF0000",
        "blue"=>"0000FF",
        "green"=>"00FF00",
        "purple"=>"FF00FF",
        "violet"=>"FF00FF"
        );

    //removes "violet"
    print_r(array_unique($colors));
?>
```

### boolean array_unshift(array stack, expression entry, ...)

The `array_unshift` function adds one or more values to the beginning of an array, as if the array were a stack. Use `array_shift` to remove an element from the beginning of an array. Compare this function to `array_pop` and `array_push`, which operate on the end of the array.

### array array_values(array data)

The `array_values` function (Listing 11.44) returns just the array elements, reindexed with integers. See Figure 11.10.

**Listing 11.44** *array_values*

```php
<?php
    $UserInfo = array("First Name"=>"Leon",
        "Last Name"=>"Atkinson",
        "Favorite Language"=>"PHP");

    print_r(array_values($UserInfo));
?>
```

```
Array
(
    [0] => Leon
    [1] => Atkinson
    [2] => PHP
)
```

**Figure 11.10** array_values output.

## boolean array_walk(array data, string function, value extra)

The `array_walk` function (Listing 11.45) executes the specified function on each element of the given array. By default, PHP passes two arguments to the callback function: the value and the key respectively. If you set the optional `extra` argument, PHP passes it as a third argument. You may define the first argument of the function to accept a reference if you wish to modify the element value in place.

---

**Listing 11.45**  *array_walk*

```php
<?php
    //set up an array of color names
    $colors = array("red", "blue", "green");

    function printElement($value)
    {
        print("$value\n");
    }

    function printElement2($value, $key, $extra)
    {
        print("$key: $value ($extra)\n");
    }

    array_walk($colors, "printElement");
    array_walk($colors, "printElement2", "user data");
?>
```

---

## boolean array_walk_recursive(array data, string function, value extra)

The `array_walk_recursive` function operates like `array_walk` with the added feature that it traverses subarrays recursively. This allows PHP to explore multidimensional arrays.

## arsort(array unsorted_array, integer comparison)

The `arsort` function sorts an array in reverse order by its values. The indices are moved along with the values. This sort is intended for associative arrays. The optional `comparison` argument sets the method for comparing elements. See Table 11.1 for valid comparison methods. By default, PHP uses `SORT_REGULAR`.

**Table 11.1**   Comparison Methods for Sorting Functions

| Method | Description |
|---|---|
| SORT_NUMERIC | Compare as numbers. |
| SORT_REGULAR | Compare mixed types as string, compare all numbers numerically. |
| SORT_STRING | Compare as strings. |

### asort(array unsorted_array, integer comparison)

The `asort` function sorts an array by its values. The indices are moved along with the values. This sort is intended for associative arrays. The optional `comparison` argument sets the method for comparing elements. See Table 11.1 for valid comparison methods. By default, PHP uses SORT_REGULAR.

### array compact(...)

The `compact` function (Listing 11.46) returns an array containing the names and values of variables named by the arguments. Any number of arguments may be passed, and they may be single string values or arrays of string values. Arrays containing other arrays will be recursively explored. The variables must be in the current scope; otherwise, PHP silently ignores them. This function complements `extract`, which creates variables from an array. See Figure 11.11.

**Listing 11.46**   *compact*

```php
<?php
    //create some variables
    $name = "Leon";
    $language = "PHP";
    $color = "blue";
    $city = "Martinez";

    //get variables as array
    $variable = compact("name",
        array("city", array("language", "color")));

    //print out all the values
    print_r($variable);
?>
```

```
Array
(
    [name] => Leon
    [city] => Martinez
    [language] => PHP
    [color] => blue
)
```

**Figure 11.11**    compact output.

### integer count(variable array)

The count function (Listing 11.47) returns the number of elements in an array. If the variable has never been set, count returns zero. If the variable is not an array, count returns 1. Despite this added functionality, you should use the isset and is_array functions to determine the nature of a variable.

**Listing 11.47**    *count*

```php
<?php
    $colors = array("red", "green", "blue");
    print(count($colors));
?>
```

### value current(array data)

The current function (Listing 11.48) returns the value of the current element pointed to by PHP's internal pointer. Each array maintains a pointer to one of the elements of an array. By default, it points to the first element added to the array until it is moved by a function such as next or reset.

**Listing 11.48**    *current*

```php
<?php
    //create test data
    $colors = array("red", "green", "blue");

    //loop through array using current
    for(reset($colors); $value = current($colors); next($colors))
    {
        print("$value\n");
    }
?>
```

### array each(array arrayname)

The each function returns a four-element array that represents the next value from an array. The four elements of the returned array (0, 1, key, and value) refer to the key and value of the current element. You may refer to the key with 0 or key, and to get the value use 1 or value. You may traverse an entire array by repeatedly using list and each, as in the example below.

Historically, this function preceded the foreach statement. During that time, it was common to use the idiom shown in Listing 11.49, looping over an array with each and list called in a while loop. Today, foreach offers a better choice.

**Listing 11.49** *each*

```php
<?php
    //create test data
    $colors = array("red", "green", "blue");

    //loop through array using each
    //output will be like "0 = red"
    reset($colors);
    while(list($key, $value) = each($colors))
    {
        print("$key = $value\n");
    }
?>
```

### value end(array arrayname)

The end function (Listing 11.50) moves PHP's internal array pointer to the array's last element and returns it. The reset function moves the internal pointer to the first element.

**Listing 11.50** *end*

```php
<?php
    $colors = array("red", "green", "blue");

    //print blue twice
    print(end($colors) . "\n");
    print(current($colors) . "\n");
?>
```

### array explode(string delimiter, string data, integer limit)

The `explode` function (Listing 11.51) creates an array from a string. The `delimiter` argument divides the `data` argument into elements but is not included in the resulting strings in the new array. The optional `limit` argument limits the total number of elements, in which case the last element may contain a longer string containing delimiters.

This function is safe for use with binary strings. The `implode` function will convert an array into a string.

---

**Listing 11.51**    *explode*

```php
<?php
    //convert tab-delimited list into an array
    $data = "red\tgreen\tblue";
    $colors = explode("\t", $data);

    //print out the values
    foreach($colors as $key=>$val)
    {
        print("$key: $val\n");
    }
?>
```

---

### integer extract(array variables, integer mode, string prefix)

The `extract` function (Listing 11.52) creates variables in the local scope based on elements in the `variables` argument and returns a count of variables extracted. Elements not indexed by strings are ignored. The optional `mode` argument controls whether variables overwrite existing variables or are renamed to avoid a collision. The valid modes are listed in Table 11.2. If left out, `EXTR_OVERWRITE` mode is assumed. The `prefix` argument is required only if `EXTR_PREFIX_SAME` or `EXTR_PREFIX_ALL` modes are chosen. If used, the `prefix` argument and an underscore are added to the name of the extracted variable.

---

**Listing 11.52**    *extract*

```php
<?php
    $new_variables = array('Name'=>'Leon', 'Language'=>'PHP');

    $Language = 'English';
```

**Listing 11.52** *extract (cont.)*

```
extract($new_variables, EXTR_PREFIX_SAME | EXTR_REFS,
        "collision");

//print extracted variables
print("$Name\n");
print("$collision_Language\n");
?>
```

**Table 11.2** extract Modes

| Mode | Description |
|------|-------------|
| EXTR_IF_EXISTS | Extract variables only if they exist in the current scope. |
| EXTR_OVERWRITE | Overwrite any variables with the same name. |
| EXTR_PREFIX_ALL | Prefix all variables. |
| EXTR_PREFIX_IF_EXISTS | Extract variables with prefixes added only if the non-prefixed variable exists. |
| EXTR_PREFIX_INVALID | Prefix variables that otherwise would be ignored due to keys that start with numbers. |
| EXTR_PREFIX_SAME | Add prefix to variables with same name. |
| EXTR_REFS | Extract variables as references. You may combine this flag with any of the others using a bitwise-OR ( | ). |
| EXTR_SKIP | Skip any variables with the same name. |

Compare this function to compact, which creates an array based on variables in the local scope.

### boolean in_array(value query, array data, boolean strict)

The in_array function (Listing 11.53) returns TRUE if the query argument is an element of the data argument. The optional strict argument requires that query and the element be of the same type. You may pass an array for the query argument.

**Listing 11.53**  *in_array*

```php
<?php
    //create test data
    $colors = array("red", "green", "blue");

    //test for the presence of green
    if(in_array("green", $colors))
    {
        print("Yes, green is present!");
    }
?>
```

### string implode(string delimiter, array data)

The `implode` function (Listing 11.54) transforms an array into a string. The elements are concatenated with the optional `delimiter` string separating them. To perform the reverse functionality, use `explode`.

**Listing 11.54**  *implode*

```php
<?php
    $colors = array("red", "green", "blue");

    //red,green,blue
    print(implode($colors, ","));
?>
```

### join

You may use `join` as an alias to the implode function.

### value key(array arrayname)

The `key` function (Listing 11.55) returns the index of the current element. Use `current` to find the value of the current element. If PHP's internal array pointer moves past the end of the array, `key` returns NULL.

| Listing 11.55 | *key* |
| --- | --- |

```php
<?php
    $colors = array(
        "FF0000"=>"red",
        "00FF00"=>"green",
        "0000FF"=>"blue");

    for(reset($colors); (NULL !== ($key=key($colors)));
        next($colors))
    {
        print("$key is $colors[$key]\n");
    }
?>
```

### boolean krsort(array data, integer comparison)

The `krsort` function (Listing 11.56) sorts an array by its keys in reverse order—that is, largest values first. The element values are moved along with the keys. This is mainly for the benefit of associative arrays, since arrays indexed by integers can easily be traversed in order of their keys.

The optional `comparison` argument sets the method for comparing elements. See Table 11.1 for valid comparison methods. By default, PHP uses `SORT_REGULAR`.

| Listing 11.56 | *krsort* |
| --- | --- |

```php
<?php
    $colors = array(
        "red"=>"FF0000",
        "green"=>"00FF00",
        "blue"=>"0000FF");

    // sort an array by its keys
    krsort($colors);

    print_r($colors);
?>
```

### boolean ksort(array data, integer comparison)

The `ksort` function (Listing 11.57) sorts an array by its keys, or index values. The element values are moved along with the keys. This is mainly for the benefit of associative arrays, since arrays indexed by integers can easily be traversed in order of their keys.

The optional `comparison` argument sets the method for comparing elements. See Table 11.1 for valid comparison methods. By default, PHP uses `SORT_REGULAR`.

**Listing 11.57**    *ksort*

```php
<?php
    $colors = array(
        "red"=>"FF0000",
        "green"=>"00FF00",
        "blue"=>"0000FF");

    // sort an array by its keys
    ksort($colors);

    print_r($colors);
?>
```

### list(...)

The `list` function (Listing 11.58) treats a list of variables as if they were an array. It may only be used on the left side of an assignment operator. It considers only elements indexed by integers. This function is useful for translating a returned array directly into a set of variables.

**Listing 11.58**    *list*

```php
<?php
    $colors = array("red", "green", "blue");

    //put first two elements of returned array
    //into key and value, respectively
    list($key, $value) = each($colors);

    print("$key: $value\n");
?>
```

**value max(array arrayname)**

**value max(...)**

The max function (Listing 11.59) returns the largest value from all the array elements. If all values are strings, then the values will be compared as strings. If any of the values is a number, only the integers and doubles will be compared numerically. The alternate version of the max function takes any number of arguments and returns the largest of them. With this use, you must supply at least two values. To find the minimum value, use min.

**Listing 11.59** *max*

```php
<?php
    $colors = array("red"=>"FF0000",
        "green"=>"00FF00",
        "blue"=>"0000FF");

    //prints FF0000
    print(max($colors) . "\n");

    //prints 13
    print(max("hello", "55", 13) . "\n");

    //prints 17
    print(max(1, 17, 3, 5.5) . "\n");
?>
```

**value min(array arrayname)**

**value min(...)**

The min function (Listing 11.60) returns the smallest value from all the array elements. If all values are strings, then the values will be compared as strings. If any of the values is a number, only the integers and doubles will be compared numerically. The alternate version of the min function takes any number of arguments and returns the smallest of them. You must supply at least two values.

**Listing 11.60** *min*

```php
<?php
    $colors = array("red"=>"FF0000",
        "green"=>"00FF00",
        "blue"=>"0000FF");
```

---

**Listing 11.60**   *min (cont.)*

```
//prints 0000FF
print(min($colors) . "\n");

//prints 13
print(min("hello", "55", 13) . "\n");

//prints 1
print(min(1, 17, 3, 5.5) . "\n");
?>
```

---

### natcasesort(array data)

The natcasesort function sorts an array the way a person might, ignoring case. That is, uppercase and lowercase values appear together.

### natsort(array data)

The natsort function (Listing 11.61) sorts an array in a natural order, as described by Martin Pool on his Web site <http://www.naturalorder-sort.org/>. This sorting method pays attention to numbers embedded in strings and recognizes that abc2 ought to come before abc12. See Figure 11.12.

---

**Listing 11.61**   *natcasesort, natsort*

```
<?php
    $files = array(
        'Picture12.jpg',
        'picture3.jpg',
        'Picture1.jpg',
        'Picture7.jpg',
        'picture11.jpg',
        'Picture2.jpg'
        );

    natsort($files);
    print_r($files);

    natcasesort($files);
    print_r($files);

    sort($files);
    print_r($files);
?>
```

---

```
Array
(
    [2] => Picture1.jpg
    [5] => Picture2.jpg
    [3] => Picture7.jpg
    [0] => Picture12.jpg
    [1] => picture3.jpg
    [4] => picture11.jpg
)
Array
(
    [2] => Picture1.jpg
    [5] => Picture2.jpg
    [1] => picture3.jpg
    [3] => Picture7.jpg
    [4] => picture11.jpg
    [0] => Picture12.jpg
)
Array
(
    [0] => Picture1.jpg
    [1] => Picture12.jpg
    [2] => Picture2.jpg
    [3] => Picture7.jpg
    [4] => picture11.jpg
    [5] => picture3.jpg
)
```

**Figure 11.12**  `natcasesort, natsort` output.

### value next(array arrayname)

The `next` function (Listing 11.62) moves PHP's array pointer forward one element and returns it. If the pointer is already at the end of the array, FALSE is returned.

**Listing 11.62** *next*

```php
<?php
    $colors = array("red", 0, "green", 43, "blue", 5);
    $c = current($colors);
    do
    {
        print("$c\n");
    }
    while(FALSE !== ($c = next($colors)))
?>
```

### pos
You may use pos as an alias to the current function.

### value prev(array arrayname)
The prev function (Listing 11.63) operates similarly to the next function, except that it moves backward through the array. The internal pointer to the array is moved back one element, and the value at that position is returned. If the pointer is already at the beginning, FALSE is returned.

**Listing 11.63**   *prev*

```php
<?php
    $colors = array("red", 0, "green", 43, "blue", 5);
    $c = end($colors);
    do
    {
        print("$c\n");
    }
    while(FALSE !== ($c = prev($colors)))
?>
```

### array range(integer start, integer stop, integer step)
Use range (Listing 11.64) to create an array containing every integer or character between the first argument and the second, inclusive. The optional step argument can skip over elements. If using characters with range, PHP considers only the first character of the given string and orders them according to their ASCII values.

**Listing 11.64**   *range*

```php
<?php
    //13, 14, 15, 16, 17, 18, 19
    print_r(range(13, 19));

    //15, 14, 13, 12
    print_r(range(15, 12));

    //x, y, z
    print_r(range('x', 'z'));

    //1, 4, 7, 10
    print_r(range(1, 10, 3));
?>
```

### value reset(array arrayname)

Use the `reset` function (Listing 11.65) to move an array's internal pointer to the first element. The element in the first position is returned. Use `end` to set the pointer to the last element.

Listing 11.65 *reset*

```php
<?php
    //create test data
    $colors = array("red", "green", "blue");

    //move internal pointer
    next($colors);

    //set internal pointer to first element
    reset($colors);

    //show which element we're at (red)
    print(current($colors));
?>
```

### rsort(array unsorted_array, integer comparison)

The `rsort` function (Listing 11.66) sorts an array in reverse order. As with other sorting functions, the presence of string values will cause all values to be treated as strings, and the elements will be sorted alphabetically. If all the elements are numbers, they will be sorted numerically. The difference between `rsort` and `arsort` is that `rsort` discards any key values and reassigns elements with key values starting at zero. Chapter 15 discusses sorting in depth.

The optional `comparison` argument sets the method for comparing elements. See Table 11.1 for valid comparison methods. By default, PHP uses `SORT_REGULAR`.

Listing 11.66 *rsort*

```php
<?php
    //create test data
    $colors = array("one"=>"orange", "two"=>"cyan",
        "three"=>"purple");

    //sort and discard keys
    rsort($colors);

    //show array
    print_r($colors);
?>
```

### shuffle(array data)

The `shuffle` function (Listing 11.67) randomly rearranges the elements in an array. The `srand` function may be used to seed the random number generator, but as with the `rand` function, a seed based on the current time will be used if you do not.

**Listing 11.67** *shuffle*

```php
<?php
    //create test data
    $numbers = range(1, 10);

    //rearrange
    shuffle($numbers);

    //print out all the values
    print_r($numbers);
?>
```

### sizeof

This is an alias for the `count` function.

### sort(array unsorted_array, integer comparison)

The `sort` function (Listing 11.68) sorts an array by element values from lowest to highest. If any element is a string, all elements will be converted to strings for the purpose of comparison, which will be made alphabetically. If all elements are numbers, they will be sorted numerically. Like `rsort`, `sort` discards key values and reassigns elements with key values starting at zero. Chapter 15 discusses sorting in depth.

The optional `comparison` argument sets the method for comparing elements. See Table 11.1 for valid comparison methods. By default, PHP uses `SORT_REGULAR`.

**Listing 11.68** *sort*

```php
<?php
    //create test data
    $colors = array("one"=>"orange", "two"=>"cyan",
        "three"=>"purple");
```

**Listing 11.68** *sort (cont.)*

```
    //sort and discard keys
    sort($colors);

    //show array
    print_r($colors);
?>
```

### uasort(array unsorted_array, string comparison_function)

The uasort function (Listing 11.69) sorts an array using a custom comparison function. The index values, or keys, move along with the element values, similar to the behavior of the asort function.

The comparison function must return a signed integer. If it returns zero, then two elements are considered equal. If a negative number is returned, the two elements are considered to be in order. If a positive number is returned, the two elements are considered to be out of order.

**Listing 11.69** *uasort*

```
<?php
    //duplicate normal ordering
    function compare($left, $right)
    {
        return($left - $right);
    }

    //create test data
    $some_numbers = array(
        "red"=>6,
        "green"=>4,
        "blue"=>8,
        "yellow"=>2,
        "orange"=>7,
        "cyan"=>1,
        "purple"=>9,
        "magenta"=>3,
        "black"=>5);

    //sort using custom compare
    uasort($some_numbers, "compare");

    //show sorted array
    print_r($some_numbers);
?>
```

### uksort(array unsorted_array, string comparison_function)

The uksort function (Listing 11.70) sorts an array using a custom comparison function. Unlike usort, the array will be sorted by the index values, not the elements. The comparison function must return a signed integer. If it returns zero, then two indices are considered equal. If a negative number is returned, the two indices are considered to be in order. If a positive number is returned, the two indices are considered to be out of order.

**Listing 11.70** *uksort*

```php
<?php
    //duplicate normal ordering
    function compare($left, $right)
    {
        return($left - $right);
    }

    //create test data
    srand(time());
    for($i=0; $i<10; $i++)
    {
        $data[rand(1,100)] = rand(1,100);
    }

    //sort using custom compare
    uksort($data, "compare");

    //show sorted array
    print_r($data);
?>
```

### usort(array unsorted_array, string compare_function)

The usort function (Listing 11.71) sorts an array by element values using a custom comparison function. It also reindexes the array starting from zero. The function must return a signed integer. If it returns zero, then two elements are considered equal. If a negative number is returned, the two elements are considered to be in order. If a positive number is returned, the two elements are considered to be out of order.

---

**Listing 11.71**   *usort*

```php
<?php
    //duplicate normal ordering
    function compare($left, $right)
    {
        return($left - $right);
    }

    //create test data
    srand(time());
    for($i=0; $i<10; $i++)
    {
        $data[rand(1,100)] = rand(1,100);
    }

    //sort using custom compare
    usort($data, "compare");

    //show sorted array
    print_r($data);
?>
```

---

# 11.3  Objects and Classes

These functions return information about objects and classes.

### string get_class(object variable)

The get_class function (Listing 11.72) returns the name of the class for the given object. From within a class method, you may use the __CLASS__ constant to get the same value. Note that PHP always returns class names in all lowercase.

---

**Listing 11.72**   *get_class*

```php
<?php
    class animal
    {
        var $name;
    }

    $gus = new animal;

    print("Gus is of type " . get_class($gus) . "<br>\n");
?>
```

---

**array get_class_methods(string class)**

**array get_class_methods(object instance)**

The `get_class_methods` function (Listing 11.73) returns an array of the names of the methods for the given class. You may give the class name or an instance of the class.

**Listing 11.73** *get_class_methods*

```php
<?php
    class dog
    {
        var $name="none";
        var $sound="woof!";

        function speak()
        {
            print($this->sound);
        }
    }

    $gus = new dog;
    $gus->name = "Gus";

    foreach(get_class_methods($gus) as $method)
    {
        print("$method<br>\n");
    }
?>
```

**array get_class_vars(string class)**

The `get_class_vars` function (Listing 11.74) returns an array containing properties of a class and their default values. Compare this function to `get_object_vars`.

**Listing 11.74** *get_class_vars, get_object_vars*

```php
<?php
    class animal
    {
        var $name="none";
        var $age=0;
        var $color="none";
    }
```

---

**Listing 11.74** *get_class_vars, get_object_vars (cont.)*

```php
    $gus = new animal;
    $gus->name = "Gus";
    $gus->age = 7;
    $gus->color = "black and tan";

    print("<b>get_class_vars</b><br>\n");
    foreach(get_class_vars("animal") as $key=>$val)
    {
        print("$key=$val<br>\n");
    }

    print("<br>\n");

    print("<b>get_object_vars</b><br>\n");
    foreach(get_object_vars($gus) as $key=>$val)
    {
        print("$key=$val<br>\n");
    }
?>
```

---

### array get_object_vars(object data)

The `get_object_vars` function returns an array describing the properties of an object and their values. See `get_class_vars` for an example of use.

### string get_parent_class(object variable)
### string get_parent_class(string class)

The `get_parent_class` function (Listing 11.75) returns the name of the parent class for an object or class.

---

**Listing 11.75** *get_parent_class*

```php
<?php
    class animal
    {
        var $name;
    }

    class dog extends animal
    {
        var $owner;
    }
```

| Listing 11.75 | *get_parent_class (cont.)* |
|---|---|

```
$gus = new dog;
$gus->name = "Gus";

//Gus is of type dog, which is of type animal
print("$gus->name is of type " .
    get_class($gus) . ", which is of type ".
    get_parent_class($gus) . "<BR>\n");
?>
```

### boolean is_a(object instance, string class)

The is_a function (Listing 11.76) returns TRUE if the given object is a member of the named class or its parents.

| Listing 11.76 | *is_a* |
|---|---|

```
<?php
    class Fruit
    {
        var $color;
    }

    class Apple extends Fruit
    {
        var $variety;
    }

    $a = new Apple;

    //true
    if(is_a($a, 'Fruit'))
    {
        $a->color = 'yellow';
    }

    //true
    if(is_a($a, 'Apple'))
    {
        $a->variety = 'Fuji';
    }
```

| Listing 11.76 | *is_a (cont.)* |

```
    //false
    if(is_a($a, 'Vegetable'))
    {
        $a->vitamin = 'E';
    }

    print_r($a);
?>
```

### boolean is_subclass_of(object instance, string class)

Use is_subclass_of to test if an object is a subclass of the named class.

### boolean method_exists(object variable, string method)

The method_exists function (Listing 11.77) returns TRUE when the named method exists in the specified object.

| Listing 11.77 | *method_exists* |

```
<?php
    class animal
    {
        var $name;
    }

    class dog extends animal
    {
        var $owner;

        function speak()
        {
            print("woof!");
        }
    }

    $gus = new dog;
    $gus->name = "Gus";

    if(method_exists($gus, "speak"))
    {
        $gus->speak();
    }
?>
```

# 11.4  User Defined Functions

These functions support using and creating your own functions.

### value call_user_func(string function, ...)

Use `call_user_func` (Listing 11.78) to execute a function you've defined. The function argument names the function. Arguments to be passed to the function follow. This allows you to determine the function you wish to call at runtime.

You may use this function to call a method on a class or object by passing an array for the function name. The first element of the array should be the name of the class or the object. The second element should be the method name.

---

**Listing 11.78**  *call_user_func*

```php
<?php
    function addThree($a, $b, $c)
    {
        return($a + $b + $c);
    }

    function multiplyThree($a, $b, $c)
    {
        return($a + $b + $c);
    }

    class mathClass
    {
        function subtractThree($a, $b, $c)
        {
            return($a - $b - $c);
        }
    }

    //call first function
    $f = 'addThree';
    print(call_user_func($f, 1, 2, 3) . '<br>');

    //call second function
    $f = 'multiplyThree';
    print(call_user_func($f, 4, 5, 6) . '<br>');
```

---

**Listing 11.78**   *call_user_func (cont.)*

```
//call method on class
$f = array('mathClass', 'subtractThree');
print(call_user_func($f, 10, 5, 2) . '<br>');

//call method on object
$m = new mathClass;
$f = array($m, 'subtractThree');
print(call_user_func($f, 7, 2, 1) . '<br>');
?>
```

---

### value call_user_func_array(string function, array parameters)

This function works exactly like `call_user_func` except that it expects the parameters as an array.

### string create_function(string arguments, string code)

The `create_function` function creates a function and returns a unique name. These are called anonymous functions. This allows for functions that depend on information known only at runtime. Although you could store the name of this new function in a variable and call it later, `create_function` is perhaps most useful for defining simple lambda-style callback functions. Listing 11.79 shows an example of this idea.

---

**Listing 11.79**   *create_function*

```
<?php
    $data = array('carrot', 'apple', 'banana');

    //add underscore to each end and make all letters uppercase
    array_walk($data, create_function('&$v',
        '$v = "_" . strtoupper($v) . "_";'));

    print_r($data);
?>
```

---

### eval(string phpcode)

The `eval` function (Listing 11.80) attempts to execute the phpcode argument as if it were a line in your PHP script. As with all strings, double quotes will cause the string to be evaluated for embedded strings and other special characters, so you may wish to use single quotes or escape dollar signs with backslashes.

In some ways, eval is like include or require. Beyond the obvious difference that eval works on strings instead of files, eval starts in a mode where it expects PHP code. If you need to switch to a mode where plain HTML is passed directly to the browser, you will need to insert a closing PHP tag (?>). Why would you ever want to execute eval on a string that contained plain HTML? Probably because the code was stored in a database.

Be extremely careful when calling eval on any string that contains data that at any time came from form variables. This includes database fields that were originally set through a form. When possible, use nested $ operators instead of eval.

| Listing 11.80 | *eval* |
|---|---|

```php
<?php
    //Simulation of using eval
    //on data from a database
    $code_from_database = '<b><?php print(date("Y-m-d")); ?></b>';
    eval("?>" . $code_from_database);
?>
```

### value func_get_arg(integer argument)

The func_get_arg function (Listing 11.81) allows you to get by number an argument passed to a function you write. The first argument will be number zero. This allows you to write functions that take any number of arguments. The return value might be any type, matching the type of the argument being fetched. The func_num_args function returns the number of arguments available.

Chapter 4 discusses functions, including writing functions that accept an unlimited number of arguments.

| Listing 11.81 | *func_get_arg* |
|---|---|

```php
<?php
    /*
    ** Function concat
    ** Input: any number of strings
    ** Output: string
    ** Description: input strings are put together in
    ** order and returned as a single string.
    */
```

**Listing 11.81**   *func_get_arg (cont.)*

```php
function concat()
{
    //start with empty string
    $data = "";

    //loop over each argument
    for($i=0; $i < func_num_args(); $i++)
    {
        //add current argument to return value
        $data .= func_get_arg($i);
    }

    return($data);
}

//prints "OneTwoThree"
print(concat("One", "Two", "Three"));
?>
```

### array func_get_args()

Use `func_get_args` (Listing 11.82) to get an array containing all the arguments passed to the function. The elements of the array will be indexed with integers, starting with zero. This provides an alternative to using `func_get_arg` and `func_num_args`.

**Listing 11.82**   *func_get_args*

```php
<?php
    /*
    ** Function gcd
    ** Input: any number of integers
    ** Output: integer
    ** Description: Returns the greatest common
    ** denominator from the input.
    */
    function gcd()
    {
        /*
        ** start with the smallest argument and try every
        ** value until we get to 1, which is common to all
        */
```

**Listing 11.82**   *func_get_args (cont.)*

```php
$start = 2147483647;
foreach(func_get_args() as $arg)
{
    if(abs($arg) < $start)
    {
        $start = abs($arg);
    }
}

for($i=$start; $i > 1; $i--)
{
    //assume we will find a gcd
    $isCommon = TRUE;

    //try each number in the supplied arguments
    foreach(func_get_args() as $arg)
    {
        //if $arg divided by $i produces a
        //remainder, then we don't have a gcd
        if(($arg % $i) != 0)
        {
            $isCommon = FALSE;
        }
    }

    //if we made it through the previous code
    //and $isCommon is still TRUE, then we found
    //our gcd
    if($isCommon)
    {
        break;
    }
}

    return($i);
}

//prints 5
print(gcd(10, 20, -35));
?>
```

### integer func_num_args()

The func_num_args function returns the number of arguments passed to a function. See the description of func_get_arg for an example of use.

# ENCODING AND DECODING

**Topics in This Chapter**

- Strings
- String Comparison
- Encoding and Decoding
- Compression
- Encryption
- Hashing
- Spell Checking
- Regular Expressions
- Character Set Encoding

# Chapter 12

The functions for transforming text can be put into three general categories: functions that make arbitrary changes to strings, functions that transform strings according to special rules, and functions that evaluate strings and return a number or a boolean. Among the transformative functions are functions for encrypting text and compressing text. Among the evaluative functions are those for checking spelling, creating hashes, and pattern matching.

## 12.1 Strings

For the most part, the string functions create strings from other strings or report the properties of a string.

> **array count_chars(string data, integer mode)**
> **string count_chars(string data, integer mode)**
> The count_chars function (Listing 12.1) analyzes a string by the characters present. The mode argument controls the return value as described in Table 12.1. See Figure 12.1.

**Table 12.1**   `count_chars` Modes

| Mode | Description |
| --- | --- |
| 0 | Returns an array indexed by ASCII codes. Each element is set with the count for that character. |
| 1 | Returns an array indexed by ASCII codes. Only characters with positive counts appear in the array. |
| 2 | Returns an array indexed by ASCII codes. Only characters with zero counts appear in the array. |
| 3 | Returns a string containing each character appearing in the input string. |
| 4 | Returns a string containing all characters not appearing in the input string. |

**Listing 12.1**   *count_chars*

```php
<?php
    //print counts for characters found
    foreach(count_chars("Core PHP", 1) as $key=>$value)
    {
        print("$key: $value\n");
    }

    //print list of characters found
    print("Characters: '" . count_chars("Core PHP", 3) . "'\n");
?>
```

```
32: 1
67: 1
72: 1
80: 2
101: 1
111: 1
114: 1
Characters: ' CHPeor'
```

**Figure 12.1**   `count_chars` output.

### string sprintf(string format, ...)

The `sprintf` function (Listing 12.2) operates identically to the `printf` function except that instead of sending the assembled string to the browser, it returns the string. See the description of `printf` for a detailed discussion. This function offers an easy way to control the representation of numbers. Ordinarily, PHP may print a double with no fraction; this function allows you to format them with any number of digits after the decimal point.

**Listing 12.2** *sprintf*

```php
<?php
    $x = 3.00;

    //print $x as PHP default
    print($x . "\n");

    //format value of $x so that
    //it show two decimals after
    //the decimal point
    $s = sprintf("%.2f", $x);
    print($s . "\n");
?>
```

### value sscanf(string text, string format, ...)

The `sscanf` function parses a string in the same way `fscanf` parses a line of input from a file. That is, it attempts to break it into variables according to the `format` argument. If you give only two arguments, `sscanf` returns an array. Otherwise, it attempts to place the values in the supplied list of variable references.

Chapter 9 contains a description of `fscanf`, including available format codes.

### strchr

This function is an alias to `strstr`.

### integer strcspn(string text, string set)

The `strcspn` function (Listing 12.3) returns the position of the first character in the `text` argument that is part of the `set` argument. Compare this function to `strspn`.

**Listing 12.3** *strcspn*

```php
<?php
    $text = "red cabbage";
    $set = "abc";
    $position = strcspn($text, $set);

    // prints 'red '
    print("'" . substr($text, 0, $position) . "'");
?>
```

### integer stripos(string data, string substring, integer offset)

The `stripos` function returns the position of the `substring` argument in the `data` argument. It operates like the `strpos` function described in this chapter except it ignores letter case.

### string stristr(string text, string substring)

The `stristr` function (Listing 12.4) is a case-insensitive version of `strstr`, described in this chapter. A portion of the `text` argument is returned starting from the first occurrence of the `substring` argument to the end.

| Listing 12.4 | *stristr* |
| --- | --- |

```php
<?php
  $text = "Although he had help, Leon is the author of this book.";
  print("Looking for 'leon': " . stristr($text, "leon"));
?>
```

### integer strlen(string text)

Use the `strlen` function (Listing 12.5) to get the length of a string. It is binary-safe.

| Listing 12.5 | *strlen* |
| --- | --- |

```php
<?php
  $text = "a short string";
  print("'$text' is " . strlen($text) . " characters long.");
?>
```

### string str_pad(string text, integer length, string padding, integer mode)

Use `str_pad` (Listing 12.6) to expand a string to a certain length. You may set the optional `padding` argument with a string used for padding. Otherwise, PHP pads with spaces. The optional `mode` argument controls where PHP places padding. Use `STR_PAD_RIGHT` to place padding on the right, `STR_PAD_LEFT` to place padding on the left, and `STR_PAD_BOTH` to pad both sides. By default, PHP pads on the right.

**Listing 12.6** *str_pad*

```php
<?php
    //prints 'abc        '
    print("'" . str_pad("abc", 10) . "'\n");

    //prints xyzxyzxabc
    print(str_pad("abc", 10, "xyz", STR_PAD_LEFT) . "\n");

    //print ***Core PHP***
    print(str_pad("Core PHP", 14, "*", STR_PAD_BOTH) . "\n");
?>
```

### integer strpos(string data, string substring, integer offset)

The strpos function (Listing 12.7) returns the position of the substring argument in the data argument. If the substring argument is not a string, it will be treated as an ASCII code. If the substring appears more than once, the position of the first occurrence is returned. If the substring doesn't exist at all, then FALSE is returned. The optional offset argument instructs PHP to begin searching after the specified position. Positions are counted starting with zero.

This function is a good alternative to ereg when you are searching for a simple string. It carries none of the overhead involved in parsing regular expressions. It is safe for use with binary strings. If you wish to search for a string with no regard to case, use stristr.

**Listing 12.7** *strpos*

```php
<?php
    $text = "Hello, World!";

    //check for a space
    if(strpos($text, 32))
    {
        print("There is a space in '$text'\n");
    }

    //find where in the string World appears
    print("World is at position " . strpos($text, "World") . "\n");
?>
```

### strrchr

This is an alias for `strrpos`.

### string str_repeat(string text, integer count)

The `str_repeat` function (Listing 12.8) returns a string consisting of the `text` argument repeated the number of times specified by the `count` argument.

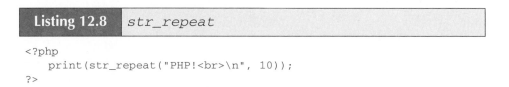

**Listing 12.8**  *str_repeat*

```php
<?php
    print(str_repeat("PHP!<br>\n", 10));
?>
```

### integer strripos(string text, string character)

The `strripos` function returns the last occurrence of the second argument in the first argument, ignoring case. Compare it to `strrpos`, which only finds letters that match case.

### integer strrpos(string text, string character)

The `strrpos` function operates similarly to `strpos`. It returns the last occurrence of the second argument in the first argument. However, only the first character of the second argument is used. This function offers a very neat way of chopping off the last part of a path, as in Listing 12.9.

**Listing 12.9**  *strrpos*

```php
<?php
    //set test string
    $path = "/usr/local/apache";

    //find last slash
    $pos = strrpos($path, "/");

    //print everything after the last slash
    print(substr($path, $pos+1));
?>
```

### integer strspn(string text, string set)

The `strspn` function (Listing 12.10) returns the position of the first character in the `text` argument that is not part of the set of characters in the `set` argument. Compare this function to `strcspan`.

**Listing 12.10**  *strspn*

```php
<?php
    $text = "cabbage";
    $set = "abc";
    $position = strspn($text, $set);

    //prints 'cabba'
    print(substr($text, 0, $position));
?>
```

### string strstr(string text, string substring)

The `strstr` function returns the portion of the `text` argument from the first occurrence of the `substring` argument to the end of the string. If `substring` is not a string, it is assumed to be an ASCII code. ASCII codes are listed in Appendix B.

An empty string is returned when `substring` is not found in `text`. You can use it as a faster alternative to `ereg` if you test for an empty string, as in Listing 12.11. The `stristr` function is a case-insensitive version of this function. This function is binary-safe.

**Listing 12.11**  *strstr*

```php
<?php
    $text = "Although this is a string, it's not very long.";
    if(strstr($text, "it") != "")
    {
        print("The string contains 'it'.<br>\n");
    }
?>
```

### string strtok(string line, string separator)

The strtok function (Listing 12.12) pulls tokens from a string. The line argument is split up into tokens separated by any of the characters in the separator string. The first call to strtok must contain two arguments. Subsequent calls are made with just the separator argument, unless you wish to begin tokenizing another string. Chapter 16 discusses this function in depth, including alternatives like ereg.

**Listing 12.12**    *strtok*

```php
<?php
    // create a demo string
    $line = "leon\tatkinson\tleon@clearink.com";

    // loop while there are still tokens
    for($token = strtok($line, "\t");
        $token != "";
        $token = strtok("\t"))
    {
        print("token: $token<br>\n");
    }
?>
```

### integer str_word_count(string text, integer mode)
### array str_word_count(string text, integer mode)

Use str_word_count (Listing 12.13) to count words in a string of text. A word is defined as being a series of alphabetic characters that may contain ' or - characters. By default, PHP returns an integer. The str_word_count function returns an array of the words found when mode is 1. When mode is 2, it returns an associative array in which the words are keys and the values are the positions of the words in the text. See Figure 12.2.

**Listing 12.13**    *str_word_count*

```php
<?php
    $text = "\"That can't be right,\" said the half-elf.";

    print(str_word_count($text) . "\n");
    print_r(str_word_count($text, 1));
    print_r(str_word_count($text, 2));
?>
```

```
7
Array
(
    [0] => That
    [1] => can't
    [2] => be
    [3] => right
    [4] => said
    [5] => the
    [6] => half-elf
)
Array
(
    [1] => That
    [6] => can't
    [12] => be
    [15] => right
    [23] => said
    [28] => the
    [32] => half-elf
)
```

**Figure 12.2** `str_word_count` output.

### string substr(string text, integer start, integer length)

Use the `substr` function (Listing 12.14) to extract a substring from the `text` argument. A string is returned that starts with the character identified by the `start` argument, counting from zero. If `start` is negative, counting will begin at the last character of the `text` argument instead of the first and work backward.

The `length` argument or the end of the string determines the number of characters returned. If `length` is negative, the returned string will end as many characters from the end of the string. In any case, if the combination of `start` and `length` calls for a string of negative length, a single character is returned. This function is safe for use with binary strings.

**Listing 12.14** *substr*

```php
<?php
    $text = "My dog's name is Angus.";

    //print Angus
    print(substr($text, 17, 5));
?>
```

### integer substr_count(string text, string substring)

The substr_count function (Listing 12.15) returns a count of the substring argument in the text argument.

---

**Listing 12.15**   *substr_count*

```php
<?php
    $text = 'How much wood would a woodchuck chuck, ' .
        'if a woodchuck could chuck wood?';

    //prints 4
    print(substr_count($text, 'wood'));
?>
```

---

### array token_get_all(string text)

The token_get_all function (Listing 12.16) parses PHP code and returns an array with one element for each token. The element may be a string or a two-element array containing a token identifier and the token itself. You can use token_name to get a textual name for the token. See Figure 12.3.

---

**Listing 12.16**   *token_get_all, token_name*

```php
<?php
    $code = '<?php$a = 3;?>';

    foreach(token_get_all($code) as $c)
    {
        if(is_array($c))
        {
            print(token_name($c[0]) . ": '" . htmlentities($c[1]) .
                "'<br>\n");
        }
        else
        {
            print("$c<br>\n");
        }
    }
?>
```

---

```
T_OPEN_TAG: '<?php'
T_VARIABLE: '$a'
T_WHITESPACE: ' '
=
T_WHITESPACE: ' '
T_LNUMBER: '3'
;
T_CLOSE_TAG: '?>'
```

**Figure 12.3** `token_get_all`, `token_name` output.

### string token_name(integer token)

The `token_name` function returns a name for a token identifier as returned by `token_get_all`.

### string vsprintf(string format, array arguments)

The `vsprintf` function works exactly like `sprintf` except that you pass arguments in an array.

## 12.2 String Comparison

These functions compare one string to another. They all return integers. A negative integer means the first string comes before the second. Zero means the strings are equal. A positive number means the first string comes after the second. You may consider the hashing functions described later in this function for comparing strings.

### integer strcasecmp(string first, string second)

The `strcasecmp` function (Listing 12.17) operates identically to `strcmp` except that it treats uppercase and lowercase as identical.

**Listing 12.17** `strcasecmp`

```php
<?php
    $first = "abc";
    $second = "aBc";

    if(strcasecmp($first, $second) == 0)
    {
        print("strings are equal");
    }
```

| Listing 12.17 | *strcasecmp (cont.)* |
|---|---|

```
    else
    {
        print("strings are not equal");
    }
?>
```

### integer strcmp(string first, string second)

The `strcmp` function (Listing 12.18) compares the first string to the second string. Comparisons are made by ASCII values. This function is safe for comparing binary data.

| Listing 12.18 | *strcmp* |
|---|---|

```
<?php
    $first = "abc";
    $second = "xyz";

    if(strcmp($first, $second) == 0)
    {
        print("strings are equal");
    }
    else
    {
        print("strings are not equal");
    }
?>
```

### integer strcoll(string first, string second)

The `strcoll` function compares two strings as with `strcmp` except that it considers the ordering of characters defined by the locale. If locale is C or POSIX, it duplicates the `strcmp` function's output. This function is not binary safe. That is, if either string contains a NULL character (ASCII 0), PHP will not compare the entire string.

### integer strnatcasecmp(string first, string second)

The `strnatcasecmp` function compares two strings using the method used by `strnatcmp`, described next, except that it ignores case.

### integer strnatcmp(string first, string second)

The `strnatcmp` function compares two strings in a natural order, as described by Martin Pool on his Web site `<http://www.naturalordersort.org/>`. This sorting method pays attention to numbers embedded in strings and recognizes that `abc2` ought to come before `abc12`. It returns a number less than zero if the first string is less than the second. It returns zero if they are equal. It returns a number greater than zero if the first string is greater than the second string.

### integer strncasecmp(string first, string second, integer length)

Use `strncasecmp` to compare the first parts of two strings. PHP compares the strings, character by character, until comparing the number of characters specified by `length` or reaching the end of one of the strings. PHP treats letters of different case as equal. If `first` and `second` are equal, PHP returns zero. If `first` comes before `second`, PHP returns a negative number. If `second` comes before `first`, PHP returns a positive number.

### integer strncmp(string first, string second, integer length)

The `strncmp` function compares the first parts of two strings. PHP compares the strings, character by character, until comparing the number of characters specified by `length` or reaching the end of one of the strings. PHP considers order based on ASCII value. If `first` and `second` are equal, PHP returns zero. If `first` comes before `second`, PHP returns a negative number. If `second` comes before `first`, PHP returns a positive number.

### string strpbrk(string text, string list)

The `strpbrk` function returns the substring of the given text after it finds one of the characters in the given list. This function wraps the C function of the same name.

## 12.3 Encoding and Decoding

The functions in this section transform data from one form to another. This includes stripping certain characters, substituting some characters for others, and translating data into some encoded form.

### string addcslashes(string text, string characters)

The `addcslashes` function returns the `text` argument after escaping characters in the style of the C programming language. Briefly, this means special characters are replaced with codes, such as `\n` replacing a newline character, and other characters outside ASCII 32–126 are replaced with backslash octal codes.

The optional `characters` argument may contain a list of characters to be escaped, which overrides the default of escaping all special characters. The characters are specified with octal notation. You may specify a range using two periods as in Listing 12.19.

**Listing 12.19**   *addcslashes*

```php
<?php
    $s = addcslashes($s, "\0..\37");
?>
```

### string addslashes(string text)

The `addslashes` function (Listing 12.20) returns the `text` argument with backslashes preceding characters that have special meaning in database queries. These are single quotes ( ' ), double quotes ( " ), and backslashes themselves ( \ ).

**Listing 12.20**   *addslashes*

```php
<?php
    // add slashes to text
    $phrase = addslashes("I don't know");

    // build query
    $Query = "SELECT * ";
    $Query .= "FROM comment ";
    $Query .= "WHERE text like '%$phrase%'";

    print($Query);
?>
```

### string base64_decode(string data)

The `base64_decode` function (Listing 12.21) translates data from MIME base64 encoding into 8-bit data. Base64 encoding is used for transmitting data across protocols, such as email, where raw binary data would otherwise be corrupted.

**Listing 12.21**   *base64_decode*

```php
<?php
    $data = "VGhpcyBpcyBhIAptdWx0aS1saW5lIG1lc3NhZ2UK";
    print(base64_decode($data));
?>
```

### string base64_encode(string text)

The base64_encode function (Listing 12.22) converts text to a form that will pass through 7-bit systems uncorrupted, such as email.

**Listing 12.22**   *base64_encode*

```php
<?php
    $text = "This is a \nmulti-line message\n";
    print(base64_encode($text));
?>
```

### string basename(string path, string suffix)

The basename function (Listing 12.23) returns only the filename part of a path. Directories are understood to be strings of numbers and letters separated by slash characters (/). When running on Windows, backslashes (\) are used as well. If you supply the optional suffix argument, PHP will remove it from the end of the string if it appears.

The flip side to this function is dirname, which returns the directory.

**Listing 12.23**   *basename*

```php
<?php
    $path="/usr/local/scripts/test.php";

    //test.php
    print(basename($path) . "<br>\n");

    //test
    print(basename($path, '.php') . "<br>\n");
?>
```

### string bin2hex(string data)

The `bin2hex` function (Listing 12.24) returns the `data` argument with each byte replaced by its hexadecimal representation. The numbers are returned in little-endian style. That is, the first digit is most significant.

---

**Listing 12.24**  *bin2hex*

```php
<?php
    //print book title in hex
    //436f726520504850205072616d6d696e67
    print(bin2hex("Core PHP Programming"));
?>
```

---

### string chop(string text)

Use `chop` as an alias for `rtrim`.

### string chr(integer ascii_code)

Use `chr` to get the character for an ASCII code. This function is helpful for situations in which you need to use a nonprinting character that has no backslash code or in which the backslash code is ambiguous. Imagine a script that writes to a formatted text file. Ordinarily, you would use `\n` for an end-of-line marker. But the behavior may be different when your script is moved from Windows to Linux, because Windows uses a carriage return followed by a linefeed. If you wish to enforce that each line end with a linefeed only, you can use `chr(10)`, as in (Listing 12.25).

Of course, you may always use a backslash code to specify an ASCII code, as listed in Appendix A and discussed in Chapter 2. Another alternative to `chr` is `sprintf`. The `%c` code stands for a single character, and you may specify an ASCII value for the character. Additionally, some functions, such as `ereg_replace`, accept integers that are interpreted as ASCII codes.

If you need the ASCII code for a character, use `ord`. Appendix B lists ASCII codes.

| Listing 12.25 | *chr* |
|---|---|

```php
<?php
    //open a test file
    $fp = fopen("data.txt", "w");

    //write a couple of records that have
    //linefeeds for end markers
    fwrite($fp, "data record 1" . chr(10));
    fwrite($fp, "data record 2" . chr(10));

    //close file
    fclose($fp);
?>
```

### string chunk_split(string data, integer length, string marker)

The chunk_split function (Listing 12.26) returns the data argument after inserting an end-of-line marker at regular intervals. By default, a carriage return and a linefeed are inserted every 76 characters. Optionally, you may specify a different length and a different marker string.

Sascha Schumann added this function specifically to break base64 codes up into 76-character chunks. Although ereg_replace can mimic this functionality, chunk_split is faster. It isn't appropriate for breaking prose between words. That is, it isn't intended for performing a soft wrap.

| Listing 12.26 | *chunk_split* |
|---|---|

```php
<?php
    $encodedData = chunk_split(base64_encode($rawData));
?>
```

### string convert_cyr_string(string text, string from, string to)

Use convert_cyr_string (Listing 12.27) to convert a string in one Cyrillic character set to another. The from and to arguments are single-character codes listed in Table 12.2.

**Table 12.2** `convert_cyr_string` Codes

| Code | Description |
| --- | --- |
| a,d | x-cp866 |
| i | iso8859-5 |
| k | koi8-r |
| m | x-mac-cyrillic |
| w | windows-1251 |

**Listing 12.27** *convert_cyr_string*

```php
<?php
    $new = convert_cyr_string($old, "a", "w");
?>
```

### string dirname(string path)

The `dirname` function (Listing 12.28) returns only the directory part of a path. The trailing slash is not included in the return value. Directories are understood to be separated by slashes (/). On Windows, backslashes (\) may be used too. If you need to get the filename part of a path, use `basename`. If the given path contains only a filename, this function returns a single period.

**Listing 12.28** *dirname*

```php
<?php
    $path = "/usr/local/bin/ls";

    //prints /usr/local/bin
    print(dirname($path));
?>
```

### string escapeshellarg(string argument)

The `escapeshellarg` function (Listing 12.29) adds a backslash before any characters that may cause trouble in a shell command and wraps the entire argument in single quotes.

**Listing 12.29**   *escapeshellarg*

```php
<?php
    $arg = escapeshellarg("potentially; bad text $ ' }");

    print("Trying echo $arg<br>\n");

    system("echo $arg");
?>
```

### string escapeshellcmd(string command)

The `escapeshellcmd` function (Listing 12.30) adds a backslash before any characters that may cause trouble in a shell command. This function should be used to filter user input before it is used in `exec` or `system`. Table 12.3 lists characters escaped by `escapeshellcmd`.

**Table 12.3**   Characters Escaped by `escapeshellcmd`

| Character | Description |
| --- | --- |
| & | Ampersand |
| ; | Semicolon |
| ` | Left Tick |
| ' | Single Quote |
| " | Double Quote |
| \| | Vertical Bar |
| * | Asterisk |
| ? | Question Mark |
| ~ | Tilde |
| < | Left Angle Bracket |
| > | Right Angle Bracket |
| ^ | Caret |
| ( | Left Parenthesis |
| ) | Right Parenthesis |

**Table 12.3**  Characters Escaped by `escapeshellcmd` *(cont.)*

| Character | Description |
|-----------|-------------|
| [ | Left Square Bracket |
| ] | Right Square Bracket |
| { | Left Curly Brace |
| } | Right Curly Brace |
| $ | Dollar Sign |
| \ | Backslash |
| ASCII 10 | Linefeed |
| ASCII 255 | |

**Listing 12.30**  *escapeshellcmd*

```php
<?php
    $cmd = escapeshellcmd("echo 'potentially; bad text'");

    print("Trying $cmd<br>\n");

    system($cmd);
?>
```

### string hebrev(string text, integer length)

Unlike English, Hebrew text reads right to left, which makes working with strings inconvenient at times. The `hebrev` function reverses the orientation of Hebrew text but leaves English alone. Hebrew characters are assumed to be in the ASCII range 224 through 251, inclusive. The optional `length` argument specifies a maximum length per line. Lines that exceed this length are broken.

### string hebrevc(string text, integer length)

The `hebrevc` function operates exactly like `hebrev` except that `br` tags are inserted before end-of-line characters.

### string htmlentities(string text, integer quote_style, string character_set)

The `htmlentities` function (Listing 12.31) returns the `text` argument with certain characters translated into HTML entities.

The optional `quote_style` argument controls how PHP converts single quotes ( ' ) and double quotes ( " ). Use one of the constants described in Table 12.4. It defaults to `ENT_COMPAT`. The optional `character_set` controls the table of entities used. It defaults to the ISO-8859-1 standard.

**Table 12.4** Quote Styles

| Constant | Description |
|----------|-------------|
| ENT_COMPAT | Convert double quotes only. |
| ENT_NOQUOTES | Do not convert quotes. |
| ENT_QUOTES | Convert both single quotes and double quotes. |

The `nl2br` function is similar: It translates line breaks to `br` tags. You can use `strip_tags` to remove HTML tags altogether.

**Listing 12.31** *htmlentities*

```
<?php
    $text = "Use <HTML> to begin a document.";
    print(htmlentities($text));
?>
```

### string html_entity_decode(string text, integer quote_style, string character_set)

The `html_entity_decode` function performs the reverse operation of the `htmlentities` function. It converts entities into single characters. The optional `quote_style` argument controls how PHP converts single quotes ( ' ) and double quotes ( " ). Use one of the constants described in Table 12.4. It defaults to `ENT_COMPAT`. The optional `character_set` argument controls the table of entities used. It defaults to the ISO-8859-1 standard.

### string htmlspecialchars(string text, integer quote_style, string character_set)

The `htmlspecialchars` function works like `htmlentities` except that a smaller set of entities is used. They are `amp`, `quot`, `lt`, and `gt`.

### integer ip2long(string address)

The `ip2long` function takes an IP address and returns an integer. This allows you to compress a 16-byte string into a 4-byte integer. Use `long2ip` to reverse the process.

### string long2ip(integer address)

Use `long2ip` to get the textual representation of an IP address. Use `ip2long` to reverse the process.

### string ltrim(string text, string strip)

The `ltrim` function (Listing 12.32) returns the `text` argument with any leading whitespace removed. If you wish to remove whitespace on the end of the string, use `rtrim`. If you wish to remove whitespace from the beginning and end, use `trim`. Whitespace includes spaces, tabs, and other nonprintable characters, including nulls (ASCII 0).

The optional `strip` argument overrides the set of whitespace characters with any list of characters you provide. You may also provide a range of characters using two periods. For example, `a..f` would trim all lowercase letters from `a` to `f`.

---

**Listing 12.32**   *ltrim*

```php
<?php
    $text = "     Leading whitespace";
    print("'" . ltrim($text) . "'");
?>
```

---

### string money_format(string format, double money)

The `money_format` function (Listing 12.33) wraps C's `strfmon` function. It returns a monetary value formatted according to the locale and the `format` argument. The format string should contain a single code that stands for the number. Other characters are passed through unchanged. Format codes start with `%` and end with `n`. Between these two characters, you may place one of the flags from Table 12.5.

**Table 12.5** `money_format` Codes

| Flag | Description |
| --- | --- |
| = | Use this flag to specify a padding character. For example, =* uses asterisks. By default, numbers are padded with spaces. |
| ^ | This flag disables grouping of digits. |
| ( | This flag wraps negative values in parentheses. |
| + | This flag represents the default behavior of preceding negative values with – and positive values with nothing. |
| ! | This flag suppresses the currency symbol. |
| – | This flag uses left justification instead of right justification. |

Immediately following any format codes, you may place an integer for the minimum width of the entire monetary value, padded out with spaces. Following that, you may place a # and a left precision. If there are fewer digits than required, the padding character specified by the = is used. Finally, you may place a period and a right precision. If there are more digits than requested, they are rounded.

**Listing 12.33** *money_format*

```php
<?php
    //[      **1234.57]
    print(money_format("[%=*15#6.2n]", 1234.567));
?>
```

### string nl2br(string text)

The `nl2br` function (Listing 12.34) inserts `<br />` before every newline in the text argument and returns the modified text.

**Listing 12.34** *nl2br*

```php
<?php
    $text = "line1\nline2\nline3\n";
    print(nl2br($text));
?>
```

### string number_format(double value, integer precision, string decimal, string thousands)

The number_format function (Listing 12.35) returns a formatted representation of the value argument as a number with commas inserted to separate thousands. The optional precision argument specifies the number of digits after the decimal point, which by default is zero. The optional decimal and thousands arguments must be used together. They override the default use of periods and commas for decimal points and thousands separators.

---

**Listing 12.35** *number_format*

```php
<?php
    $test_number = 123456789.123456789;

    //add commas, drop any fraction
    print(number_format($test_number) . "<br>\n");

    //add commas and limit to two digit precision
    print(number_format($test_number, 2) . "<br>\n");

    //format for Germans
    print(number_format($test_number, 2, ",", ".") . "<br>\n");
?>
```

---

### integer ord(string character)

The ord function (Listing 12.36) returns the ASCII code of the first character in the character argument. This function allows you to deal with characters by their ASCII values, which often can be more convenient than using backslash codes, especially if you wish to take advantage of the order of the ASCII table. Refer to Appendix B for a complete table of ASCII codes. If you need to find the character associated with an ASCII code, use the chr function.

---

**Listing 12.36** *ord*

```php
<?php
    /*
    ** Decompose a string into its ASCII codes.
    ** Test for codes below 32 because these have
    ** special meaning and we may not want to
    ** print them.
    */
```

**Listing 12.36**    *ord (cont.)*

```
$text = "Line 1\nLine 2\n";

print("ASCII Codes for '$text'<br>\n");

print("<table>\n");

for($i=0; $i < strlen($text); $i++)
{
    print("<tr>");

    print("<th>");
    if(ord($text[$i]) > 31)
    {
        print($text[$i]);
    }
    else
    {
        print("(unprintable)");
    }
    print("</th> ");

    print("<td>");
    print(ord($text[$i]));
    print("</td>");

    print("</tr>\n");
}

print("</table>\n");
?>
```

### string pack(string format, ...)

The `pack` function (Listing 12.37) takes inspiration from the Perl function of the same name. It allows you to put data in a compact format that is readable on all platforms. Format codes in the first argument match with the arguments that follow it. The codes determine how the values are stored. An optional number, called the repeat count, may follow the format code. It specifies how many of the following arguments to use. The repeat count may also be *, which matches the remaining arguments. Some of the codes use the repeat count differently. Table 12.6 lists all the format codes and how they use the repeat count.

A string with the packed data is returned. Note that it will be in a binary form, unsuitable for printing. In the example below, I've printed out each byte of the packed data as hexadecimal codes.

**Table 12.6**   pack Codes

| Code | Data Type | Description |
| --- | --- | --- |
| a | String | Repeat count is the number of characters to take from the string. If there are fewer characters in the string than specified by the repeat count, spaces are used to pad it out. |
| A | String | Repeat count is the number of characters to take from the string. If there are fewer characters in the string than specified by the repeat count, nulls (ASCII 0) are used to pad it out. |
| c | Integer | The integer will be converted to a signed character. |
| C | Integer | The integer will be converted to an unsigned character. |
| d | Double | The double will be stored in double-width floating-point format. Depending on your operating system, this is probably 8 bytes. |
| f | Double | The double will be converted to a single-width floating-point format. Depending on your operating system, this is probably 4 bytes. |
| h | String | The ASCII value of each character of the argument will be saved as two characters representing the ASCII code in hexadecimal, big-endian. The repeat count denotes the number of characters to take from the input. |
| H | String | The ASCII value of each character of the argument will be saved as two characters representing the ASCII code in hexadecimal, little-endian. The repeat count denotes the number of characters to take from the input. |
| i | Integer | The argument will be saved as an unsigned integer. Typically, this is 4 bytes. |
| I | Integer | The argument will be saved as a signed integer. Typically, this is 4 bytes, with one bit used for sign. |
| l | Integer | The argument is saved as an unsigned long, which is usually 8 bytes. |
| L | Integer | The argument is saved as a signed long, which is usually 8 bytes with one bit used for sign. |
| n | Integer | The argument is saved as an unsigned short, which is 2 bytes. The value is saved in a way that allows for safe unpacking on both little-endian and big-endian machines. |

**Table 12.6**  pack Codes *(cont.)*

| Code | Data Type | Description |
|------|-----------|-------------|
| N | Integer | The argument is saved as an unsigned long, which is 8 bytes. The value is saved in a way that allows for safe unpacking on both little-endian and big-endian machines. |
| s | Integer | The argument is saved as an unsigned short, which is usually 2 bytes. |
| S | Integer | The argument is saved as a signed short, which is usually 2 bytes with one bit used for sign. |
| v | Integer | The argument is saved as an unsigned short in little-endian order. |
| V | Integer | The argument is saved as an unsigned long in little-endian order. |
| x | None | This format directive doesn't match with an argument. It writes a null byte. |
| X | None | This format directive causes the pointer to the packed string to back up 1 byte. |
| @ | None | This format directive moves the pointer to the absolute position specified by its repeat count. The empty space is padded with null bytes. |

**Listing 12.37**  *pack, unpack*

```php
<?php
    //create some packed data
    $packedData = pack("ca10n", 65, "hello", 1970);

    //display ASCII code for each character
    for($i=0; $i<strlen($packedData); $i++)
    {
        print("0x" . dechex(ord($packedData[$i])) . " ");
    }
    print("\n");

    //unpack the data
    $data = unpack("cOne/a10Two/nThree", $packedData);

    //show all elements of the unpacked array
    print_r($data);
?>
```

### parse_str(string query, array fields)

The `parse_str` function (Listing 12.38) parses the `query` argument as if it were an HTTP GET query. Without the optional `fields` argument, PHP creates a variable in the current scope for each field in the query. With the `fields` argument, PHP sets it with an array of the fields.

You may wish to use this function on the output of `parse_url`.

**Listing 12.38** *parse_str*

```php
<?php
    $query = "name=Leon&occupation=Web+Engineer";
    parse_str($query, $fields);
    print_r($fields);
?>
```

### array parse_url(string query)

The `parse_url` function (Listing 12.39) breaks a URL into an associative array with the following elements: `fragment`, `host`, `pass`, `path`, `port`, `query`, `scheme`, `user`. The query is not evaluated as with the `parse_str` function. See Figure 12.4.

**Listing 12.39** *parse_url*

```php
<?php
    $query = "http://leon:secret@www.leonatkinson.com:80" .
        "/test/test.php3?" .
        "name=Leon&occupation=Web+Engineer";
    print_r(parse_url($query));
?>
```

```
Array
(
    [scheme] => http
    [host] => www.leonatkinson.com
    [port] => 80
    [user] => leon
    [pass] => secret
    [path] => /test/test.php3
    [query] => name=Leon&occupation=Web+Engineer
)
```

**Figure 12.4** `parse_url` output.

### array pathinfo(string path)

The `pathinfo` function (Listing 12.40) breaks a path into an array with three parts: `basename`, `dirname`, `extension`. This combines the functionality of `basename` and `dirname`. See Figure 12.5.

---

**Listing 12.40**   *pathinfo*

```php
<?php
    print_r(pathinfo('/usr/local/apache/htdocs/index.php'));
?>
```

---

```
Array
(
    [dirname] => /usr/local/apache/htdocs
    [basename] => index.php
    [extension] => php
)
```

**Figure 12.5**   `pathinfo` output.

### string quoted_printable_decode(string text)

The `quoted_printable_decode` function (Listing 12.41) converts a quoted string into 8-bit binary form. Quoted-printable is a method of encoding binary strings for email, as described in RFC 2045. Generally, characters that could be problematic can be replaced with a = followed by their hexadecimal ASCII code.

This function performs the same function as `imap_qprint` but does not require the IMAP extension.

---

**Listing 12.41**   *quoted_printable_decode*

```php
<?php
    $command = "Line 1=0ALine 2=0A";
    print(quoted_printable_decode($command));
?>
```

---

### string quotemeta(string command_text)

The `quotemeta` function returns the `command_text` argument with back-slashes preceding special characters. These characters are listed in Table 12.7.

Compare this function to `addslashes` and `escapeshellcmd`. If your intention is to ensure that user data will cause no harm when placed within a shell command, use `escapeshellcmd`.

The `quotemeta` function may be adequate for assembling PHP code passed to `eval`. Notice in (Listing 12.42) how characters with special meaning inside double quotes are escaped by `quotemeta`, thus defeating an attempt at displaying the `password` variable.

**Table 12.7**   Meta Characters

| Character | Description |
| --- | --- |
| . | Period |
| \ | Backslash |
| + | Plus |
| * | Asterisk |
| ? | Question Mark |
| [ | Left Square Bracket |
| ] | Right Square Bracket |
| ^ | Caret |
| ( | Left Parenthesis |
| ) | Right Parenthesis |
| $ | Dollar Sign |

**Listing 12.42**   *quotemeta*

```php
<?php
    //simulate user input
    $input = '$password';

    //assemble safe PHP command
    $cmd = '$text = "' . quotemeta($input) . '";';

    //execute command
    eval($cmd);

    //print new value of $text
    print($text);
?>
```

### string rawurldecode(string url_text)

The `rawurldecode` function (Listing 12.43) returns the `url_text` string translated from URL format into plain text. It reverses the action of `rawurlencode`. This function is safe for use with binary data. The `urldecode` function is not.

---

**Listing 12.43** *rawurldecode*

```php
<?php
    print(rawurldecode("mail%20leon%40example.com"));
?>
```

---

### string rawurlencode(string url_text)

The `rawurlencode` function (Listing 12.44) returns the `url_text` string translated into URL format. This format uses percent signs (`%`) to specify characters by their ASCII code, as required by the HTTP specification. This allows you to pass information in a URL that includes characters that have special meaning in URLs, such as the ampersand (`&`). This is discussed in detail in RFC 1738.

This function is safe for use with binary data. Compare this to `urlencode`, which is not.

---

**Listing 12.44** *rawurlencode*

```php
<?php
    print(rawurlencode("mail leon@clearink.com"));
?>
```

---

### string rtrim(string text, string strip)

The `rtrim` function (Listing 12.45) returns the `text` argument with any trailing whitespace removed. If you wish to remove both trailing and leading whitespace, use the `trim` function. If you wish to remove leading whitespace only, use `ltrim`. Whitespace includes spaces, tabs, and other nonprintable characters, including nulls (ASCII 0).

The optional `strip` argument overrides the set of whitespace characters with any list of characters you provide. You may also provide a range of characters using two periods. For example, `a..f` would trim all lowercase letters from `a` to `f`.

---

**Listing 12.45** *rtrim*

```php
<?php
    print("\"" .
        rtrim("This has whitespace        ") .
        "\"");
?>
```

---

### string serialize(value)

Use serialize (Listing 12.46) to transform a value into an ASCII string that later may be turned back into the same value using the unserialize function. The serialized value may be stored in a file or a database for retrieval later. In fact, this function offers a great way to store complex data structures in a database without writing any special code.

PHP is capable of serializing all data types except resources. When serializing objects, PHP attempts to execute a method named __sleep if it exists. Use this method to prepare the object for serialization if necessary.

---

**Listing 12.46** *serialize*

```php
<?php
    //simulate a shopping basket as
    //a multi-dimensional array
    $Basket = array(
        array("soap", 1.59),
        array("bread", 0.99),
        array("milk", 1.29)
        );

    //serialize array
    $data = serialize($Basket);

    //print out the data, just for fun
    print($data . "<br>\n");

    //unserialize the data
    $recoveredBasket = unserialize($data);

    //show the contents
    print("Unserialized:<br>\n");
    print_r($recoveredBasket);
?>
```

---

### string sql_regcase(string regular_expression)

The `sql_regcase` function (Listing 12.47) translates a case-sensitive regular expression into a case-insensitive regular expression. This is unnecessary for use with PHP's built-in regular expression functions but can be useful when creating regular expressions for external programs such as databases.

**Listing 12.47** `sql_regcase`

```php
<?php
    //print [Mm][Oo][Zz][Ii][Ll][Ll][Aa]
    print(sql_regcase("Mozilla"));
?>
```

### str_ireplace(string target, string replacement, string text)

The `str_ireplace` function attempts to replace all occurrences of `target` in `text` with `replacement`. It operates like `str_replace` except that it ignores letter case.

### string str_replace(string target, string replacement, string text)

The `str_replace` function (Listing 12.48) attempts to replace all occurrences of `target` in `text` with `replacement`. This function is safe for replacing strings in binary data. It's also a much faster alternative to `ereg_replace`. Note that `str_replace` is case-sensitive.

The three arguments may also be arrays. When `text` is an array, PHP replaces strings in each element and returns an array. When `target` is an array, PHP searches for each term in order, making replacements. When using an array of targets and a string for replacement, the string replaces each match. When using an array of targets and an array of replacements, elements are matched by position. PHP uses an empty string for extra elements in `target`.

Compare this function to `str_ireplace`.

**Listing 12.48** `str_replace`

```php
<?php
    $text = "Search results with keywords highlighted.";
    print(str_replace("keywords", "<b>keywords</b>", $text) .
'<br>');
?>
```

### string str_rot13(string text)

Use `str_rot13` (Listing 12.49) to perform ROT13 encoding, sometimes called Caesarean code. This encoding method treats the alphabet as a circular list and replaces each letter with the letter 13 spaces away. This method is extremely weak from a cryptographic perspective but is common for placing spoilers in plain text.

**Listing 12.49** *str_rot13*

```php
<?php
    $text = "Ybbx sbe n frperg qbbe haqre gur cyngsbez.";
    print(str_rot13($text));
?>
```

### string str_shuffle(string text)

The `str_shuffle` function (Listing 12.50) randomizes the characters in a string.

**Listing 12.50** *str_shuffle*

```php
<?php
    //prints something like bgvhsdxejnrmoyqatcluzkiwfp
    print(str_shuffle("abcdefghijklmnopqrstuvwxyz"));
?>
```

### array str_split(string text, integer length)

The `str_split` function converts a string into an array. By default, the elements of the array hold one character in the given string. You may set the optional `length` argument to a number greater than one in order to break the string into larger chunks.

### string strip_tags(string text, string ignore)

The `strip_tags` function (Listing 12.51) attempts to remove all SGML tags from the `text` argument. This includes HTML and PHP tags. The optional `ignore` argument may contain tags to be left alone. This function uses the same algorithm used by `fgetss`. If you want to preserve tags, you may wish to use `htmlentities`.

**Listing 12.51** *strip_tags*

```php
<?php
    //create some test text
    $text = "<p><b>Paragraph One</b></p><p>Paragraph Two</p>";

    //strip out all tags except paragraph and break
    print(strip_tags($text, "<p><br>"));
?>
```

### string stripcslashes(string text)

The stripcslashes function (Listing 12.52) complements addcslashes. It removes backslash codes that conform to the C style. See addcslashes for more details.

**Listing 12.52** *stripcslashes*

```php
<?php
    //create some test text
    $text = "Line 1\x0ALine 2\x0A";

    //convert backslashes to actual characters
    print(stripcslashes($text));
?>
```

### string stripslashes(string text)

The stripslashes function (Listing 12.53) returns the text argument with backslash encoding removed. It complements addslashes.

**Listing 12.53** *stripslashes*

```php
<?php
    $text = "Leon\'s Test String";

    print("Before: $text<br>\n");
    print("After: " . stripslashes($text) . "<br>\n");
?>
```

### string strrev(string text)

The strrev function (Listing 12.54) returns the text argument in reverse order.

| Listing 12.54 | *strrev* |
|---|---|

```php
<?php
    //prints gfedcba
    print(strrev("abcdefg"));
?>
```

### string strtolower(string text)

The strtolower function (Listing 12.55) returns the text argument with all letters changed to lowercase. Other characters are unaffected. Locale affects which characters are considered letters, and you may find that letters with accents and umlauts are being ignored. You may overcome this by using setlocale. Similar functions are strtoupper, ucfirst, and ucwords.

| Listing 12.55 | *strtolower, strtoupper, ucfirst, ucwords* |
|---|---|

```php
<?php
    //core php programming
    print(strtolower("coRe pHP prOGraMMing") . "<br>");

    //CORE PHP PROGRAMMING
    print(strtoupper("coRe pHP prOGraMMing") . "<br>");

    //CoRe pHP prOGraMMing
    print(ucfirst("coRe pHP prOGraMMing") . "<br>");

    //CoRe PHP PrOGraMMing
    print(ucwords("coRe pHP prOGraMMing") . "<br>");
?>
```

### string strtoupper(string text)

The strtoupper function returns the text argument with all letters changed to uppercase. Other characters are unaffected. Locale affects which characters are considered letters, and you may find that letters with accents and umlauts are being ignored. You may overcome this by using setlocale. Similar functions are strtolower, ucfirst, and ucwords.

**string strtr(string text, string original, string translated)**
**string strtr(string text, array replacement)**

When passed three arguments, the `strtr` function (Listing 12.56) returns the `text` argument with characters matching the second argument changed to those in the third argument. If `original` and `translated` aren't the same length, the extra characters are ignored.

When called with two arguments, the second argument must be an associative array. The indices specify strings to be replaced, and the values specify replacement text. If a substring matches more than one index, the longer substring will be used. The process is not iterative. That is, once substrings are replaced, they are not further matched. This function is safe to use with binary strings.

---

**Listing 12.56**   `strtr`

```php
<?php
    $text = "Wow!  This is neat.";
    $original = "!.";
    $translated = ".?";

    // turn sincerity into sarcasm
    print(strtr($text, $original, $translated));
?>
```

---

**string substr_replace(string text, string replacement, integer start, integer length)**

Use `substr_replace` (Listing 12.57) to replace one substring with another. Unlike `str_replace`, which searches for matches, `substr_replace` simply removes a length of text and inserts the `replacement` argument. The arguments operate similarly to `substr`. The `start` argument is an index into the `text` argument with the first character numbered as zero. If `start` is negative, counting will begin at the last character of the `text` argument instead of the first.

The number of characters replaced is determined by the optional `length` argument or the ends of the string. If `length` is negative, the returned string will end as many characters from the end of the string. In any case, if the combination of `start` and `length` calls for a string of negative length, a single character is removed.

**Listing 12.57**  *substr_replace*

```php
<?php
    $text = "My dog's name is Angus.";

    //replace Angus with Gus
    print(substr_replace($text, "Gus", 17, 5));
?>
```

### string trim(string text, string strip)

The `trim` function (Listing 12.58) strips whitespace from both the beginning and end of a string. Compare this function to `ltrim` and `rtrim`. Whitespace includes spaces, tabs, and other nonprintable characters, including nulls (ASCII 0).

The optional `strip` argument overrides the set of whitespace characters with any list of characters you provide. You may also provide a range of characters using two periods. For example, `a..f` would trim all lowercase letters from `a` to `f`.

**Listing 12.58**  *trim*

```php
<?php
    $text = "     whitespace     ";
    print("\"" . trim($text) . "\"");
?>
```

### string ucfirst(string text)

Use the `ucfirst` function to capitalize the first character of a string. Similar functions are `strtolower`, `strtoupper`, and `ucwords`. As with these other functions, your locale determines which characters are considered letters.

### string ucwords(string text)

Use the `ucwords` function to capitalize every word in a string. Similar functions are `strtolower`, `strtoupper`, and `ucfirst`. As with these other functions, your locale determines which characters are considered letters.

### array unpack(string format, string data)

The `unpack` function transforms data created by the `pack` function into an associative array. The `format` argument follows the same rules used for `pack` except that each element is separated by a slash to allow them to be named. These names are used as the keys in the returned associative array. See the pack example.

### value unserialize(string data)

Use unserialize to transform serialized data back into a PHP value. The description of serialize has an example of the entire process. When unserializing an object, PHP attempts to call the __wakeup method if it exists.

The unserialize_callback_func directive in php.ini sets a function called when unserializing an object of an unknown class. This may allow you to define the class first, perhaps by using include_once. This callback function should take a single argument, the name of the class.

### string urldecode(string url_text)

The urldecode function returns the url_text string translated from URL format into plain text. It is not safe for binary data.

### string urlencode(string url_text)

The urlencode function returns the url_text string translated into URL format. This format uses percent signs (%) to specify characters by their ASCII code. This function is not safe for use with binary data.

### string wordwrap (string text, integer width, string break, integer cut)

The wordwrap function (Listing 12.59) wraps text at 75 columns by inserting linebreaks between words. The optional width argument overrides the default width. The optional break argument sets the string used for linebreaks.

In the case of words longer than the defined width, PHP allows the line to exceed the width. This may be overridden by setting the optional cut argument to 1, in which case PHP inserts a linebreak in the middle of the word.

---

**Listing 12.59** *wordwrap*

```php
<?php
    $text = "Core PHP Programming";

    //Core PHP
    //Programming
    print(wordwrap($text, 8) . "\n\n");
```

| Listing 12.59 | *wordwrap (cont.)* |
|---|---|

```
//Core PHP
//Programm
//ing
print(wordwrap($text, 8, "\n", 1));
?>
```

# 12.4 Compression

These functions compress and decompress strings using the bzip2 or gzip libraries. There are functions described in Chapter 9 for reading and writing to compressed files.

### string bzcompress(string data, integer blocksize, integer workfactor)

Use `bzcompress` (Listing 12.60) to compress a string using the bzip2 library. The optional `blocksize` argument may be set with an integer from 1 to 9, with 9 being the highest compression. By default, `blocksize` is 4. The optional `workfactor` argument influences how `bzcompress` handles long strings of repetitive sequences. It should be an integer from 0 to 250.

| Listing 12.60 | *bzcompress, bzdecompress* |
|---|---|

```php
<?php
    $text = "Core PHP Programming";

    $bzText = bzcompress($text, 9);
    print(bin2hex($bzText) . "<br>");

    print(bzdecompress($bzText) . "<br>");
?>
```

### string bzdecompress(string data, boolean small)

Use `bzdecompress` to uncompress data compressed with the bzip2 algorithm. When the optional `small` argument is TRUE, PHP uses an alternative decompression routine that limits the use of memory at the expense of slower performance.

### string gzcompress(string data, integer level)

Use gzcompress (Listing 12.61) to compress a string using the zlib algorithm. The optional level argument sets the level of compression from 1 to 9, with 9 being the highest compression. This is not the same as gzip compression used by gzencode. Use gzuncompress to uncompress the output of this function.

**Listing 12.61**   *gzcompress, gzuncompress*

```php
<?php
    $text = "Core PHP Programming";

    $gzText = gzcompress($text, 9);
    print(bin2hex($gzText) . "<br>");

    print(gzuncompress($gzText) . "<br>");
?>
```

### string gzdeflate(string data, integer level)

The gzdeflate function (Listing 12.62) compresses data using the deflate algorithm. The optional level argument sets the level of compression from 0 to 9, with 9 being the highest compression. Use gzinflate to uncompress the data.

**Listing 12.62**   *gzdeflate, gzinflate*

```php
<?php
    $text = "Core PHP Programming";

    $gzText = gzdeflate($text, 9);
    print(bin2hex($gzText) . "<br>");

    //strip first 10 bytes (header) and last 4 bytes (checksum)
    print(gzinflate($gzText) . "<br>");
?>
```

### string gzencode(string data, integer level, integer mode)

The gzencode function compresses data with the gzip library. The optional level argument sets the level of compression from 0 to 9, with 9 being the highest compression. The third argument forces the method for compression.

Use FORCE_GZIP for gzip mode, which is the default. Use FORCE_DEFLATE for standard zlib mode.

The return value includes the gzip header and a trailing checksum. If you wish to uncompress the data with gzinflate, you must strip these, as in Listing 12.63.

| Listing 12.63 | *gzencode* |
| --- | --- |

```php
<?php
    $text = "Core PHP Programming";

    $gzText = gzencode($text, 9);
    print(bin2hex($gzText) . "<br>");

    //strip first 10 bytes (header) and last 4 bytes (checksum)
    print(gzinflate(substr($gzText, 10, -4)) . "<br>");
?>
```

### string gzinflate(string data, integer length)
Use gzinflate to uncompress data compressed with the deflate algorithm. The optional length argument sets a maximum length for the uncompressed data.

### string gzuncompress(string data, integer length)
Use gzuncompress to uncompress data compressed with gzcompress. The optional length argument sets a maximum size for the uncompressed data.

## 12.5 Encryption

Encryption is the process of transforming information to and from an unreadable format. Some algorithms simply scramble text; others allow for reversing the process. PHP offers a wrapper to C's crypt function plus an extension that wraps the mcrypt library.

The mcrypt functions rely on a library of the same name written by Nikos Mavroyanopoulos, which provides an advanced system for encrypting data. The URI for the project is <http://mcrypt.hellug.gr/>. Sascha Schumann added mycrypt functionality to PHP. Derick Rethans added support for the new API introduced in mcrypt 2.4.4.

Cryptography is a topic beyond the scope of this text. Some concepts discussed in this section require familiarity with advanced cryptographic theories. A great place to start learning about cryptography is the FAQ file for the sci.crypt Usenet newsgroup. The URI is `<http://www.faqs.org/faqs/cryptography-faq/>`. Another resource is a book Prentice Hall publishes called *Cryptography and Network Security: Principles and Practice* by William Stallings.

### string crypt(string text, string salt)

The `crypt` function (Listing 12.64) encrypts a string using C's `crypt` function, which usually uses standard DES encryption but depends on your operating system. The `text` argument is returned encrypted. The `salt` argument is optional. PHP will create a random `salt` value if one is not provided. You may wish to read the man page on `crypt` to gain a better understanding.

Note that data encrypted with the `crypt` function cannot be decrypted. The function is usually used to encrypt a password that is saved for when authorization is necessary. At that time, the password is asked for, encrypted, and compared to the previously encrypted password.

Depending on your operating system, alternatives to DES encryption may be available. The `salt` argument is used to determine which algorithm to use. A two-character salt is used for standard DES encryption. A nine-character salt specifies extended DES. A 12-character salt specifies MD5 encryption. And a 16-character salt specifies the blowfish algorithm.

When PHP is compiled, available algorithms are incorporated. The following constants will hold TRUE or FALSE values that you can use to determine the availability of the four algorithms: CRYPT_STD_DES, CRYPT_EXT_DES, CRYPT_MD5, CRYPT_BLOWFISH.

---

**Listing 12.64**   `crypt`

```php
<?php
    $password = "secret";

    if(CRYPT_MD5)
    {
        $salt = "leonatkinson";
        print("Using MD5: ");
    }
    else
    {
        $salt = "cp";
        print("Using Standard DES: ");
    }

    print(crypt($password, $salt));
?>
```

### string mcrypt_create_iv(integer size, integer source)

Use `mcrypt_create_iv` to create an initialization vector. The size should match the encryption algorithm and should be set using `mcrypt_get_block_size`.

The source argument can be one of three constants. `MCRYPT_DEV_RANDOM` uses random numbers from `/dev/random`. `MCRYPT_DEV_URANDOM` uses random numbers from `/dev/urandom`. `MCRYPT_RAND` uses random numbers from the `rand` function.

### string mcrypt_decrypt(string cipher, string key, string data, string mode, string iv)

Use `mcrypt_decrypt` (Listing 12.65) to decrypt data. The `cipher` argument should be one of the ciphers listed in Table 12.8. The `key` argument is a secret key used to decrypt the `data` argument. The `mode` argument should be one of the modes in Table 12.9. The optional `iv` argument is an initialization vector necessary for some algorithms and modes.

**Listing 12.65**  *mcrypt_decrypt*

```php
<?php
    //set up test data
    $message = "This message is sensitive.";
    $key = "secret";

    //encrypt message
    $code = @mcrypt_encrypt(MCRYPT_BLOWFISH, $key, $message,
        MCRYPT_MODE_ECB);

    //pring decrypted message
    print(@mcrypt_decrypt(MCRYPT_BLOWFISH, $key, $code,
        MCRYPT_MODE_ECB));
?>
```

**Table 12.8**  Encryption Algorithms

| Cipher | Description |
| --- | --- |
| MCRYPT_3DES | Triple-DES |
| MCRYPT_ARCFOUR | RC4 |
| MCRYPT_ARCFOUR_IV | RC4 with initialization vector |
| MCRYPT_BLOWFISH | Blowfish |

**Table 12.8**  Encryption Algorithms *(cont.)*

| Cipher | Description |
| --- | --- |
| MCRYPT_CAST_128 | CAST with 128-bit keys |
| MCRYPT_CAST_256 | CAST with 256-bit keys |
| MCRYPT_CRYPT | Algorithm used by crypt |
| MCRYPT_DES | DES |
| MCRYPT_GOST | GOST, the Soviet encryption algorithm |
| MCRYPT_IDEA | IDEA (International Data Encryption Algorithm) |
| MCRYPT_LOKI97 | LOKI97, which uses 128-bit blocks |
| MCRYPT_MARS | IBM's MARS cipher |
| MCRYPT_PANAMA | Panama |
| MCRYPT_RC2 | RC2 |
| MCRYPT_RC6 | RC6 |
| MCRYPT_RIJNDAEL_128 | Rijndael with 128-bit keys |
| MCRYPT_RIJNDAEL_192 | Rijndael with 192-bit keys |
| MCRYPT_RIJNDAEL_256 | Rijndael with 256-bit keys |
| MCRYPT_SAFER128 | SAFER (Secure and Fast Encryption Routine) with 128-bit keys |
| MCRYPT_SAFER64 | SAFER with 64-bit keys |
| MCRYPT_SAFERPLUS | SAFER+ |
| MCRYPT_SERPENT | Serpent |
| MCRYPT_SKIPJACK | Skipjack, the cipher used by the Clipper chip |
| MCRYPT_THREEWAY | 3-Way |
| MCRYPT_TRIPLEDES | Triple-DES |
| MCRYPT_TWOFISH | Twofish |
| MCRYPT_WAKE | WAKE |
| MCRYPT_XTEA | xTEA, the expansion of The Tiny Encryption Algorithm |

**Table 12.9**  Encryption Modes

| Mode | Name |
|------|------|
| MCRYPT_MODE_ECB | Electronic codebook |
| MCRYPT_MODE_CBC | Cipher block chaining |
| MCRYPT_MODE_CFB | Cipher feedback |
| MCRYPT_MODE_OFB | Output feedback, 8-bit |
| MCRYPT_MODE_NOFB | Output feedback, variable block size |
| MCRYPT_MODE_STREAM | Stream |

### string mcrypt_enc_get_algorithms_name(resource mcrypt)

The mcrypt_enc_get_algorithms_name function returns the name of the algorithm used by the open resource.

### integer mcrypt_enc_get_block_size(resource mcrypt)

Use mcrypt_enc_get_block_size to get the block size used by the open resource.

### integer mcrypt_enc_get_iv_size(resource mcrypt)

Use mcrypt_enc_get_iv_size to get the size of the initialization vector used by the open resource.

### integer mcrypt_enc_get_key_size(resource mcrypt)

Use mcrypt_enc_get_key_size to get the maximum key size allowed by the open resource.

### string mcrypt_enc_get_modes_name(resource mcrypt)

Use mcrypt_enc_get_modes_name to get the name of the mode used by the open resource.

### array mcrypt_enc_get_supported_key_sizes(resource mcrypt)

Use mcrypt_enc_get_supported_key_sizes to get an array of supported key sizes used by the open resource.

### boolean mcrypt_enc_is_block_algorithm(resource mcrypt)

Use mcrypt_enc_is_block_algorithm to test whether the algorithm of the open resource is a block cipher.

## boolean mcrypt_enc_is_block_algorithm_mode(resource mcrypt)

Use `mcrypt_enc_is_block_algorithm_mode` to test whether the mode used by the given resource supports block ciphers.

## boolean mcrypt_enc_is_block_mode(resource mcrypt)

Use `mcrypt_enc_is_block_mode` to test whether the mode used by the given resource outputs blocks.

## boolean mcrypt_enc_self_test(resource mcrypt)

Use `mcrypt_enc_self_test` to test the algorithm used by the given resource.

## string mcrypt_encrypt(string cipher, string key, string data, string mode, string iv)

Use `mcrypt_encrypt` to encrypt data. The `cipher` argument should be one of the ciphers listed in Table 12.8. The `key` argument is a secret key used to encrypt the `data` argument. The `mode` argument should be one of the modes in Table 12.9. The optional `iv` argument is an initialization vector necessary for some algorithms and modes.

## string string mcrypt_generic(resource mcrypt, string data)

Use `mcrypt_generic` (Listing 12.66) to encrypt data. PHP pads the data with NULL characters to ensure the data length is a multiple of the block size. Before using this function, you must initialize the resource with `mcrypt_generic_init`.

**Listing 12.66** `mcrypt_generic`

```php
<?php
    $message = "This message is sensitive.";

    //open cipher
    $mcrypt = mcrypt_module_open(MCRYPT_3DES, NULL,
        MCRYPT_MODE_ECB, NULL);

    //make initialization vector
    $iv = mcrypt_create_iv(mcrypt_enc_get_iv_size($mcrypt),
        MCRYPT_DEV_RANDOM);

    //make key, use md5 to make sure key is long enough
    $key = substr(md5('secret'), 0,
        mcrypt_enc_get_key_size($mcrypt));
```

| Listing 12.66 | *mcrypt_generic (cont.)* |

```
//init for encryption
mcrypt_generic_init($mcrypt, $key, $iv);

//encrypt
$code = mcrypt_generic($mcrypt, $message);

//clean up
mcrypt_generic_deinit($mcrypt);

//init for decryption
mcrypt_generic_init($mcrypt, $key, $iv);

//decrypt
print(mdecrypt_generic($mcrypt, $code));

//clean up
mcrypt_generic_deinit($mcrypt);

//close module
mcrypt_module_close($mcrypt);
?>
```

### boolean mcrypt_generic_deinit(resource mcrypt)

Use `mcrypt_generic_deinit` to free the memory used by the `mcrypt` resource created by `mcrypt_generic_init`.

### integer mcrypt_generic_init(resource mcrypt, string key, string iv)

Use `mcrypt_generic_init` to initialize the resource with a key and initialization vector so you can call `mcrypt_generic` or `mdecrypt_generic`.

### integer mcrypt_get_block_size(integer algorithm)

Use `mcrypt_get_block_size` to find the block size for a given encryption algorithm. Use one of the constants listed in Table 12.8.

### string mcrypt_get_cipher_name(integer algorithm)

Use `mcrypt_get_cipher_name` to get the name of an encryption algorithm. Use one of the constants listed in Table 12.8.

**integer mcrypt_get_iv_size(resource mcrypt)**
**integer mcrypt_get_iv_size(string cipher, string mode)**
Use `mcrypt_get_iv_size` to get the length of the initialization vector required by the open module. Alternatively, you may specify a cipher and mode using the constants described in Table 12.8 and Table 12.9.

**integer mcrypt_get_key_size(resource mcrypt)**
**integer mcrypt_get_key_size(string cipher, string mode)**
Use `mcrypt_get_key_size` to find the key size for the open module. Alternatively, you may specify a cipher and mode using the constants described in Table 12.8 and Table 12.9.

**array mcrypt_list_algorithms(string path)**
The `mcrypt_list_algorithms` function returns an array of ciphers usable by the mcrypt functions. The optional `path` argument looks for modules in a directory other than the default, which is usually `/usr/local/lib/libmcrypt`.

**array mcrypt_list_modes(string path)**
The `mcrypt_list_modes` function returns an array of modes usable by the mcrypt functions. The optional `path` argument looks for modules in a directory other than the default, which is usually `/usr/local/lib/libmcrypt`.

**boolean mcrypt_module_close(resource mcrypt)**
Use `mcrypt_module_close` to close a `mcrypt` resource.

**integer mcrypt_module_get_algo_block_size(string algorithm, string path)**
The `mcrypt_module_get_algo_block_size` function returns the block size for the given algorithm, specified by one of the constants from Table 12.8. The optional `path` argument looks for modules in a directory other than the default, which is usually `/usr/local/lib/libmcrypt`.

**integer mcrypt_module_get_algo_key_size(string algorithm, string path)**
The `mcrypt_module_get_algo_key_size` function returns the maximum key size for the given algorithm, specified by one of the constants from Table 12.8. The optional `path` argument looks for modules in a directory other than the default, which is usually `/usr/local/lib/libmcrypt`.

### array mcrypt_module_get_supported_key_sizes(string algorithm, string path)

The `mcrypt_module_get_supported_key_sizes` function returns an array of valid key sizes for the given algorithm, specified by one of the constants from Table 12.8. The optional `path` argument looks for modules in a directory other than the default, which is usually `/usr/local/lib/libmcrypt`.

### boolean mcrypt_module_is_block_algorithm(string algorithm, string path)

The `mcrypt_module_is_block_algorithm` function returns TRUE if the given algorithm, specified by one of the constants from Table 12.8, is a block algorithm. The optional `path` argument looks for modules in a directory other than the default, which is usually `/usr/local/lib/libmcrypt`.

### boolean mcrypt_module_is_block_algorithm_mode(string mode, string path)

The `mcrypt_module_is_block_algorithm_mode` function returns TRUE if the given mode, specified by one of the constants from Table 12.9, supports block algorithms. The optional `path` argument looks for modules in a directory other than the default, which is usually `/usr/local/lib/libmcrypt`.

### boolean mcrypt_module_is_block_mode(string mode, string path)

The `mcrypt_module_is_block_mode` function returns TRUE if the given mode, specified by one of the constants from Table 12.9, outputs blocks. The optional `path` argument looks for modules in a directory other than the default, which is usually `/usr/local/lib/libmcrypt`.

### resource mcrypt_module_open(string algorithm, string algorithm_path, string mode, string mode_path)

Use `mcrypt_module_open` to create an `mcrypt` resource. Set the `algorithm` argument with a value from Table 12.8. If you wish to override the path used for mcrypt cipher modules, set the `algorithm_path` argument. Set the `mode` argument with a value from Table 12.9. The `mode_path` argument overrides the path to the mcrypt mode modules.

### boolean mcrypt_module_self_test(string algorithm, string path)

The `mcrypt_module_self_test` function tests a cipher module. The optional `path` argument looks for modules in a directory other than the default, which is usually `/usr/local/lib/libmcrypt`.

### string mdecrypt_generic(resource mcrypt, string data)

Use `mdecrypt_generic` to decrypt data using an open resource.

# 12.6 Hashing

Hashing is the process of creating an index for a value using the value itself. The index is called a hash. Sometimes hashes are unique to values, but not always. Hashes can be used to make fast lookups, a method that PHP uses for keeping track of variables. Other times hashes are used like encryption. If the hashes of two strings match, you can assume the two strings match, as long as hash values are unique. In this way, you can check passwords without ever decrypting the original password.

Some of the functions in this section are built into PHP. The others are part of Sascha Shumann's Mhash library. This library presents a universal interface to many hashing algorithms. Visit the home site to learn more about it <http://schumann.cx/mhash/>.

### integer crc32(string data)
The crc32 function (Listing 12.67) returns the 32-bit cyclic redundancy checksum for the given data. Typically, this hash helps verify that transmitted data remains unaltered.

---

**Listing 12.67**  *crc32*

```php
<?php
    $message = "Who is John Galt?";
    $crc = 1847359068;

    if(crc32($message) == $crc)
    {
        print("The message is unaltered");
    }
    else
    {
        print("The CRC does not match");
    }
?>
```

---

### integer ezmlm_hash(string address)
The ezmlm function calculates the hash for an email address used by EZMLM, which is a mailing list manager.

### integer ftok(string path, string project)

The `ftok` function wraps the C function of the same name. It returns a hash for a given path and project identifier. The `project` argument should be a single character. The return value is a System V IPC key. Keys are the same regardless of alternate paths if they are to the same file.

Keys returned by this function are appropriate for use with the semaphore functions described in Chapter 19.

### integer levenshtein(string first, string second)
### integer levenshtein(string first, string second, integer insert, integer replace, integer delete)

Use `levenshtein` to find the *Levenshtein distance* between two strings of 255 characters or less. The return value is the minimum number of changes to the first string needed to transform it into the second. A change is defined as the addition, removal, or change to a single character.

The simple version of this function takes two strings. Alternatively, you may supply costs for performing inserts, replacements, and deletions, respectively.

You may read more about the Levenshtein distance algorithm at `<http://www.merriampark.com/ld.htm>`.

### string md5(string text)

The `md5` function (Listing 12.68) produces a hash as described by RFC 1321. The function takes a string of any length and returns a 32-character identifier. It is theorized that the algorithm for the `md5` function will produce unique identifiers for all strings.

---

**Listing 12.68**   *md5*

```php
<?php
    //bebcd5657c9c3d62f9e22f2e0730868a
    print(md5("Who is John Galt?"));
?>
```

---

### string metaphone(string word)

Use `metaphone` (Listing 12.69) to produce a string that describes how a word sounds when spoken. This function is similar to `soundex`; however, it knows about how groups of letters are pronounced in English. Therefore, it is more accurate. Compare this function to `soundex` and `similar_text`.

The metaphone algorithm, invented by Lawrence Philips, was first described in *Computer Language* magazine. You may find a discussion of metaphone hosted by the Aspell project at SourceForge <http://aspell.sourceforge.net/metaphone/>.

**Listing 12.69** *metaphone*

```php
<?php
    print("Atkinson encodes as " . metaphone("Atkinson"));
?>
```

### string mhash(integer hash, string data)

Use `mhash` (Listing 12.70) to get a hash for a string. Hashing algorithms available at the time of writing are shown in Table 12.10. Refer to the Mhash documentation for more information about each algorithm.

**Table 12.10** Mhash Algorithms

| | | |
|---|---|---|
| MHASH_ADLER32 | MHASH_HAVAL192 | MHASH_SHA1 |
| MHASH_CRC32 | MHASH_HAVAL224 | MHASH_SHA256 |
| MHASH_CRC32B | MHASH_HAVAL256 | MHASH_TIGER |
| MHASH_GOST | MHASH_MD4 | MHASH_TIGER128 |
| MHASH_HAVAL128 | MHASH_MD5 | MHASH_TIGER160 |
| MHASH_HAVAL160 | MHASH_RIPEMD160 | |

**Listing 12.70** *mhash*

```php
<?php
    $hash = array(
        MHASH_ADLER32, MHASH_CRC32, MHASH_CRC32B, MHASH_GOST,
        MHASH_HAVAL128, MHASH_HAVAL160, MHASH_HAVAL192,
        MHASH_HAVAL224, MHASH_HAVAL256, MHASH_MD4, MHASH_MD5,
        MHASH_RIPEMD160, MHASH_SHA1, MHASH_SHA256, MHASH_TIGER,
        MHASH_TIGER128, MHASH_TIGER160);
```

| Listing 12.70 | *mhash (cont.)* |
|---|---|

```
//try each hash algorithm
foreach($hash as $h)
{
    $name = mhash_get_hash_name($h);
    $size = mhash_get_block_size($h);
    $key = bin2hex(mhash($h, "Who is John Galt?"));

    print("$name ($size): $key<br>\n");
}
?>
```

### integer mhash_get_block_size(integer hash)

The `mhash_get_block_size` function returns the block size used for a hash algorithm.

### string mhash_get_hash_name(integer hash)

The `mhash_get_hash_name` function returns the name for a particular hash identifier.

### string mhash_keygen_s2k(integer hash, string password, string salt, integer length)

The `mhash_keygen_s2k` function generates a key using one of the hash algorithms from Table 12.10. This complies with the Salted S2K algorithm described by RFC 2440.

### string sha1(string data)

The `sha1` function returns the hash according to the U.S. Secure Hash Algorithm 1, described by RFC 3174.

### int similar_text(string left, string right, reference percentage)

The `similar_text` function (Listing 12.71) compares two strings and returns the number of characters they have in common. If present, the variable specified for the `percentage` argument will receive the percentage similarity. Compare this function to `metaphone` and `soundex`.

The algorithm used for `similar_text` is taken from a book by Ian Oliver called *Programming Classics: Implementing the World's Best Algorithms*. It's published by Prentice Hall, and you can find out more about it on the Prentice Hall PTR Web site <http://www.phptr.com/ptrbooks/ptr_0131004131.html>.

**Listing 12.71** `similar_text`

```php
<?php
    //create two strings
    $left = "Leon Atkinson";
    $right = "Vicky Atkinson";

    //test to see how similar they are
    $i = similar_text($left, $right, $percent);

    //print results
    print($i . " shared characters<br>\n");
    print($percent . "% similar<br>\n");
?>
```

### string soundex(string text)

The `soundex` function (Listing 12.72) returns an identifier based on how a word sounds when spoken. Similar-sounding words will have similar or identical soundex codes. The soundex code is four characters and starts with a letter. Compare this function to the `similar_text` and the `metaphone` functions.

The soundex algorithm is described by Donald Knuth in Volume 3 of *The Art of Computer Programming*.

**Listing 12.72** `soundex`

```php
<?php
    print(soundex("lion") . "<br>" . soundex("lying"));
?>
```

# 12.7 Spell Checking

PHP offers spell checking through the Pspell library, which is a replacement for the older Aspell library.

### integer pspell_add_to_personal(integer configuration, string word)

The `pspell_add_to_personal` function (Listing 12.73) adds a word to a personal dictionary. You must supply a configuration link as created by `pspell_new_config`.

---

**Listing 12.73** *pspell_add_to_personal*

```php
<?php
    //create a configuration link
    $config = pspell_config_create("en");

    //set path to personal words
    pspell_config_personal($config, "/tmp/custom.pws");

    //load dictionary
    $new_config = pspell_new_config($config);

    //add word to dictionary
    pspell_add_to_personal($new_config, "Leon");

    //save personal dictionary
    pspell_save_wordlist($new_config);
?>
```

---

### integer pspell_add_to_session(integer configuration, string word)

Use `pspell_add_to_session` to add a word to the session.

### boolean pspell_check(integer dictionary, string word)

The `pspell_check` function (Listing 12.74) checks the spelling of a word.

---

**Listing 12.74** *pspell_check*

```php
<?php
    //open dictionary
    $dictionary = pspell_new("en");

    if(pspell_check($dictionary, "Leon"))
    {
        print('Yes');
    }
    else
    {
        print('No');
    }
?>
```

---

### integer pspell_clear_session(integer dictionary)

Use `pspell_clear_session` to clear the words in the current session.

### integer pspell_config_create(string language, string spelling, string jargon, string encoding)

The `pspell_config_create` function loads a dictionary and returns an identifier. You must supply a language in the form of a two-letter code, optionally followed by an underscore and a two-letter country code.

The `spelling` argument chooses between options for languages that use alternate spellings. For example, valid English values are `american`, `british`, and `canadian`.

The `jargon` argument chooses among dictionaries containing jargon. For example, using `medical` includes jargon used by the medical community.

The `encoding` argument sets the encoding used for words. These correspond to `.map` files in the pspell installation. For example, using `iso8859-1` uses the `iso8859-1.map` file.

This function allows you to set certain parameters before fully initializing a spell-checking session. After setting options, you must call `pspell_new_config`. Rather than calling these two functions, you may call `pspell_new`.

### integer pspell_config_ignore(integer configuration, integer length)

Use `pspell_config_ignore` and PHP will ignore words that are less than the given length.

### integer pspell_config_mode(integer configuration, integer mode)

Use `pspell_config_mode` to set the mode in which pspell operates. The default is `PSPELL_NORMAL` mode. In `PSPELL_FAST` mode, pspell returns fewer suggestions. In `PSPELL_BAD_SPELLERS` mode, pspell returns more suggestions.

### integer pspell_config_personal(integer configuration, string path)

The `pspell_config_personal` function sets the path to a personal dictionary. Words are checked from this dictionary in addition to the one defined by `pspell_config_create`. You may also add to this dictionary with `pspell_add_to_personal`.

### integer pspell_config_repl(integer configuration, string path)

The `pspell_config_repl` function sets the path to a personal set of replacement pairs, which help pspell make suggestions for misspelled words.

### integer pspell_config_runtogether(integer configuration, boolean runtogether)

The `pspell_config_runtogether` function controls whether pspell considers a word misspelled if it looked like two valid words with no space between them. For example, pspell considers `spellcheck` a misspelling unless run-together words are allowed.

### integer pspell_new(string language, string spelling, string jargon, string encoding, integer mode)

The `pspell_new` function opens a dictionary and initializes pspell for spell checking. You are required to supply a language, but may optionally supply values for the `spelling`, `jargon`, and `encoding` arguments. All four arguments are as described above with regard to `pspell_config_create`. The optional `mode` argument is as described above with regard to `pspell_config_mode`.

### integer pspell_new_config(integer configuration)

Use `pspell_new_config` (Listing 12.75) to initialize pspell after loading a dictionary and setting configuration options. The configuration option should be a value returned by `pspell_config_create`.

---

**Listing 12.75**  *pspell_new_config*

```php
<?php
    $text = "Here's some text to spellcheck. Is abcd a word?";

    //create configuration framework
    $config = pspell_config_create("en", "american", "medical");

    //skip words less than 5 letters long
    pspell_config_ignore($config, 5);

    //activate fast mode
    pspell_config_mode($config, PSPELL_FAST);

    //set path to personal dictionary
    pspell_config_personal($config, "/tmp/personal.pws");

    //set path to personal replacement pairs
    pspell_config_repl ($config, "/tmp/personal.repl");
```

| Listing 12.75 | *pspell_new_config (cont.)* |
|---|---|

```
//allow run-together words
pspell_config_runtogether($config, TRUE);


//initialize session
$pspell_link = pspell_new_config($config);

foreach(str_word_count($text, 1) as $word)
{
    if(!pspell_check($pspell_link, $word))
    {
        print("$word is unrecognized.");
    }
}
?>
```

### integer pspell_new_personal(string personal, string language, string spelling, string jargon, string encoding, integer mode)

The `pspell_new_personal` function loads a standard dictionary and a personal dictionary, and then initializes pspell for spell checking. The path to the personal dictionary and the language are required. The other arguments are not. Refer to the descriptions of `pspell_config_create` and `pspell_config_mode` for descriptions of the arguments.

### integer pspell_save_wordlist(integer dictionary)

Use `pspell_save_wordlist` to save a personal dictionary. See the description of `pspell_add_to_personal` to see an example of use.

### integer pspell_store_replacement(integer dictionary, string misspelling, string correction)

Use `pspell_store_replacement` to set a replacement pair for an open dictionary. PHP uses this pair to make suggestions on subsequent checks. If you use `pspell_config_repl`, you can save replacements to a file.

### array pspell_suggest(integer dictionary, string word)

The `pspell_suggest` function (Listing 12.76) returns an array of suggestions for a misspelled word.

---

**Listing 12.76**    *pspell_suggest*

```php
<?php
    $dictionary = pspell_new ("en");

    $word = "instantiayt";

    if(!pspell_check($dictionary, $word))
    {
        foreach(pspell_suggest($dictionary, $word) as $suggestion)
        {
            print("$suggestion<br>");
        }
    }
?>
```

---

# 12.8  Regular Expressions

Regular expressions offer a powerful way to test strings for the presence of patterns. They use a language all their own to describe patterns, a language that consists mostly of symbols. PHP offers two types of functions for regular expressions: native and Perl-compatible. You may wish to turn to Chapter 22, which describes regular expressions in detail.

Andrei Zmievski added support to PHP for Perl-compatible regular expressions. Expressions are surrounded by delimiters, which are usually / or | characters, but can be any printable character other than a number, letter, or backslash. After the second delimiter, you may place one or more modifiers. These are letters that change the way the regular expression is interpreted. There are a few very specific differences between PHP's Perl-compatible regular expressions and those in Perl 5. They are narrow enough that you probably won't run into them, and they may not make much sense without explaining regular expressions in detail. If you're curious, read the excellent notes in the PHP manual available online *<http://www.php.net/manual/html/ref.pcre.html>*.

### boolean ereg(string pattern, string text, array matches)

The ereg function (Listing 12.77) evaluates the pattern argument as a regular expression and attempts to find matches in the text argument. If the optional matches argument is supplied, each match will be added to the array. TRUE is returned if at least one match is made; otherwise, FALSE is returned.

The first element in the matches array, with an index of zero, will contain the match for the entire regular expression. Subsequent elements of matches will contain the matches for subexpressions. These are the expressions enclosed in parentheses in the example.

**Listing 12.77**   *ereg*

```php
<?php
    //show User Agent
    print("User Agent: {$_SERVER['HTTP_USER_AGENT']}<br>\n");

    //try to parse User Agent
    if(ereg("^(.+)/([0-9])\.([0-9]+)",
        $_SERVER['HTTP_USER_AGENT'], $matches))
    {
        print("Full match: $matches[0]<br>\n");
        print("Browser: $matches[1]<br>\n");
        print("Major Version: $matches[2]<br>\n");
        print("Minor Version: $matches[3]<br>\n");
    }
    else
    {
        print("User Agent not recognized");
    }
?>
```

### string ereg_replace(string pattern, string replacement, string text)

Use ereg_replace (Listing 12.78) to replace substrings within the text argument. Each time the pattern matches a substring within the text argument, it is replaced with the replacement argument. The text argument is unchanged, but the altered version is returned.

If the pattern contains subexpressions in parentheses, the replacement argument may contain a special code for specifying which subexpression to replace. The form is to use two backslashes followed by a single digit, zero through nine. Zero matches the entire expression; one through nine each match the first nine subexpressions respectively. Subexpressions are numbered left to right, which accounts for nested subexpressions.

---

**Listing 12.78** *ereg_replace*

```php
<?php
    // swap newlines for break tags
    $text = "line1\nline2\nline3\n";
    print(ereg_replace("\n", "<br>", $text));

    print("<hr>\n");

    //mix up these words
    $text = "one two three four";
    print(ereg_replace("([a-z]+) ([a-z]+) ([a-z]+) ([a-z]+)",
        "\\4 \\2 \\1 \\3", $text));
?>
```

---

### boolean eregi(string pattern, string text, array matches)

The eregi function operates identically to ereg with the exception that letters are matched with no regard for uppercase or lowercase.

### string eregi_replace(string pattern, string replacement, string text)

The eregi_replace function operates identically to ereg_replace with the exception that letters are matched with no regard for uppercase or lowercase.

### array fnmatch(string pattern, string filename, integer flags)

The fnmatch function (Listing 12.79) checks whether a filename matches a pattern. The pattern conforms to the patterns accepted by a command shell for filename patterns.

The optional flags argument changes the behavior of the check. FNM_NOESCAPE causes PHP to ignore backslash escape codes. FNM_PATHNAME causes PHP to match slashes literally. That is, they don't match wildcards. FNM_PERIOD causes PHP to match leading periods exactly.

---

**Listing 12.79** *fnmatch*

```php
<?php
    if(fnmatch('php-[4-5].?.*', "php-5.1.2.tar.gz"))
    {
        print('yes');
    }
    else
    {
        print('no');
    }
?>
```

## array preg_grep(string pattern, array data)

The `preg_grep` function compares the elements of the `data` argument that match the given pattern.

## boolean preg_match(string pattern, string text, array matches, integer flags)

The `preg_match` function (Listing 12.80) is the Perl-compatible equivalent of `ereg`. It evaluates the pattern argument as a regular expression and attempts to find matches in the text argument. If the optional `matches` argument is supplied, each match will be added to the array. TRUE is returned if at least one match is made, FALSE otherwise.

The first element in the `matches` array, with an index of zero, will contain the match for the entire regular expression. Subsequent elements of `matches` will contain the matches for subexpressions. These are the expressions enclosed in parentheses in the example.

You may set the optional `flags` argument with PREG_OFFSET_CAPTURE to have `preg_match` return the offset for every match.

---

**Listing 12.80** *preg_match*

```php
<?php
    // show User Agent
    print("User Agent: {$_SERVER['HTTP_USER_AGENT']}<br>\n");

    // try to parse User Agent
    if(preg_match("/^(.+)\/([0-9])\.([0-9]+)/",
        $_SERVER['HTTP_USER_AGENT'], $matches))
    {
        print("Full match: $matches[0]<br>\n");
        print("Browser: $matches[1]<br>\n");
        print("Major Version: $matches[2]<br>\n");
        print("Minor Version: $matches[3]<br>\n");
    }
    else
    {
        print("User Agent not recognized");
    }
?>
```

## integer preg_match_all (string pattern, string text, array matches, integer order)

The `preg_match_all` function (Listing 12.81) operates similarly to `preg_match`. A pattern is evaluated against the `text` argument, but instead of stopping when a match is found, subsequent matches are sought. The `matches` argument is required and will receive a two-dimensional array. The method for filling this array is determined by the `order` argument. It may be set with two constants, either `PREG_PATTERN_ORDER`, the default, or `PREG_SET_ORDER`. You may combine this flag with `PREG_OFFSET_CAPTURE`. The number of matches against the full pattern is returned.

If `PREG_PATTERN_ORDER` is used, the first element of the `matches` array will contain an array of all the matches against the full pattern. The other elements of the array will contain arrays of matches against subpatterns.

If `PREG_SET_ORDER` is used, each element of the `matches` array contains an array organized like those created by `preg_match`. The first element is the entire matching string. Each subsequent element contains the match against the subpattern for that match.

If `PREG_OFFSET_CAPTURE` is used, the offset for each match is also returned.

| Listing 12.81 | *preg_match_all* |
| --- | --- |

```php
<?php
   //create test data
   $paragraph = "This is a <b>short</b> paragraph. Some ";
   $paragraph .= "<b>words</b> and <b>some phrases</b> ";
   $paragraph .= "are surround by <b>bold</b> tags. ";

   /*
   ** use PREG_PATTERN_ORDER to find bold words
   */
   preg_match_all("|<[^>]+>(.*)</[^>]+>|", $paragraph,
      $match, PREG_PATTERN_ORDER);

   //print full matches
   print("<b>Subpattern matches</b>:<br>\n");
   for($i=0; $i < count($match[0]); $i++)
   {
      print(htmlentities($match[0][$i]) . "<br>\n");
   }
```

**Listing 12.81** *preg_match_all (cont.)*

```
print("<b>Subpattern matches</b>:<br>\n");
for($i=0; $i < count($match[1]); $i++)
{
    print(htmlentities($match[0][$i]) . "<br>\n");
}

/*
** use PREG_SET_ORDER to find bold words
*/
preg_match_all("|<[^>]+>(.*)</[^>]+>|", $paragraph,
    $match, PREG_SET_ORDER);

foreach($match as $m)
{
    print(htmlentities($m[0]));

    for($i=1; $i < count($m); $i++)
    {
        print(" (".htmlentities($m[$i]).")");
    }

    print("<br>\n");
}
?>
```

### string preg_quote(string text, string delimiter)

The `preg_quote` function returns `text` with backslashes inserted before characters that have special meaning to the functions in this section. The special characters are

```
. \ + * ? [ ^ ] $ ( ) { } = ! < > | :
```

The optional `delimiter` argument sets the delimiter you are using, making sure PHP escapes it as well.

### string preg_replace(string pattern, string replacement, string text, integer limit)

The `preg_replace` function (Listing 12.82) is the Perl-compatible equivalent to `ereg_replace`. Each time the pattern matches a substring within the text argument, it is replaced with the `replacement` argument. The `text` argument is unchanged, but the altered version is returned.

If the pattern contains subexpressions in parentheses, the `replacement` argument may contain a special code for specifying which subexpression to replace. The form is to use two backslashes followed by a single digit, zero through nine. Zero matches the entire expression; one through nine each match the first nine subexpressions respectively. Subexpressions are numbered left to right, which accounts for nested subexpressions.

The optional `limit` argument sets a maximum number of replacements.

---

**Listing 12.82**   *preg_replace*

```php
<?php
    // swap newlines for break tags
    $text = "line1\nline2\nline3\n";
    print(preg_replace("|\n|", "<br>", $text));

    print("<hr>\n");

    //mix up these words
    $text = "one two three four";
    print(preg_replace("|([a-z]+) ([a-z]+) ([a-z]+) ([a-z]+)|",
        "\\4 \\2 \\1 \\3", $text));
?>
```

---

**string preg_replace_callback(string pattern, string callback, string text, integer limit)**
**string preg_replace_callback(string pattern, array callback, string text, integer limit)**

The `preg_replace_callback` function (Listing 12.83) operates like `preg_replace` except that instead of making static replacements, PHP passes matches to a function that returns an appropriate replacement. If you wish to use a class method for the callback function, use an array that contains two elements. The first element should be the name of the class or an instantiated object. The second element should be the name of the method.

---

**Listing 12.83**   *preg_replace_callback*

```php
<?php
    function rotateColor($match)
    {
        static $color = 0;
        static $colorList = array(0=>'red','blue','green');
```

---

**Listing 12.83**  *preg_replace_callback (cont.)*

```
    $text = "<span style=\"color:{$colorList[$color]}\">" .
        implode($match) .
        "</span>";

    $color++;

    return($text);
}

//color each match with rotating colors
$text = "line1\nline2\nline3\n";
print(preg_replace_callback("|line[0-9]|", 'rotateColor',
    $text));
?>
```

---

### array preg_split(string pattern, string text, integer limit, integer flags)

The preg_split function (Listing 12.84) returns an array of substrings from the text argument. The pattern argument will be used as a field delimiter. The optional limit argument sets the maximum number of elements to return. The optional flags argument changes the behavior of preg_split. With the PREG_SPLIT_NO_EMPTY flag, only non-empty matches are returned. With the PREG_SPLIT_DELIM_CAPTURE flag, subpatterns in parentheses are captured as well instead of being discarded. With the PREG_SPLIT_OFFSET_CAPTURE flag, the offset of each match is included in the return value.

This function is equivalent to split.

---

**Listing 12.84**  *preg_split*

```
<?php
    $paragraph = "This is a short paragraph. Each ";
    $paragraph .= "sentence will be extracted by ";
    $paragraph .= "the preg_split function. As a ";
    $paragraph .= "result, you will be amazed!";

    $sentence = preg_split("/[\.\!\?]/", $paragraph);

    for($index = 0; $index < count($sentence); $index++)
    {
        print("$index. {$sentence[$index]}<br>\n");
    }
?>
```

---

**array split(string pattern, string text, integer limit)**

The `split` function (Listing 12.85) returns an array of substrings from the `text` argument. The `pattern` argument will be used as a field delimiter. The optional `limit` argument sets the maximum number of elements to return. There is no case-insensitive version of `split`.

Compare this function to `explode`, which uses a simple string to delimit substrings. Regular expression processing is slower than straight string matching, so use `explode` when you can.

---

**Listing 12.85**   *split*

```php
<?php
    $paragraph = "This is a short paragraph. Each ";
    $paragraph .= "sentence will be extracted by ";
    $paragraph .= "the split function. As a ";
    $paragraph .= "result, you will be amazed!";

    $sentence = split("[\.\!\?]", $paragraph);

    for($index = 0; $index < count($sentence); $index++)
    {
        print("$index. {$sentence[$index]}<br>\n");
    }
?>
```

---

**array spliti(string pattern, string text, integer limit)**

The `spliti` function is a case-insensitive version of `split`. It is identical in all other ways.

# 12.9  Character Set Encoding

Historically, computers have represented textual data as strings of characters. Each character is a single byte, which allows for 256 different characters. This is more than enough for English speakers and was adapted for people speaking most European languages. Asian languages, however, do not fit neatly into 256 characters. To cope with a larger range of characters, we have multibyte encoding. Instead of a single byte, these encodings use multiple bytes to represent one visual character.

PHP scripts are written in standard, single-byte ASCII, but it's possible to embed strings of multibyte text in a script. Unfortunately, PHP's text manipulation functions assume single-byte encoding. A string encoded to use two bytes per character seems twice as long to *strlen* than it does when printed. The solution is the multibyte string extension.

Rui Hirokawa and Tsukada Takuya added multibyte support to PHP.

### string iconv(string from, string to, string text)

The `iconv` function (Listing 12.86) converts a string from one character set to another. This function becomes available with the iconv extension, which also includes an output buffer handler described in Chapter 8.

| Listing 12.86 | *iconv* |
|---|---|

```php
<?php
    print(iconv("ISO-8859-1","ISO-8859-15",
        "Core PHP Programming"));
?>
```

### string mb_convert_case(string text, integer mode, string encoding)

Use `mb_convert_case` (Listing 12.87) to change the case of letters in the given text. Use one of the modes from Table 12.11. The optional encoding argument overrides the default encoding.

Unlike conventional functions, such as `strtolower`, this function understands how to change the case of letters with accents and other decorations. You can also use `mb_strtolower` and `mb_strtoupper`.

**Table 12.11**   `mb_convert_case` Modes

| Mode | Description |
|---|---|
| MB_CASE_LOWER | Convert all letters to lowercase. |
| MB_CASE_TITLE | Make first letter of each word uppercase and all other letters lowercase. |
| MB_CASE_UPPER | Convert all letters to uppercase. |

> **Listing 12.87** `mb_convert_case`

```php
<?php
    $text = "Jedes Jahr PHP gewinnt größere Popularität!";
    print(mb_convert_case($text, MB_CASE_LOWER) . '<br>');
    print(mb_convert_case($text, MB_CASE_TITLE) . '<br>');
    print(mb_convert_case($text, MB_CASE_UPPER) . '<br>');
?>
```

### string mb_convert_encoding(string text, string target, array source)

The `mb_convert_encoding` function converts a string from one encoding to another. The optional third argument defaults to PHP's internal encoding. Otherwise, you may set it to one or more encoding identifiers separated by commas. You may use `auto` as a shortcut for `ASCII`, `JIS`, `UTF-8`, `EUC-JP`, and `SJIS`. You may also specify the `source` argument as an array.

### string mb_convert_kana(string text, string option, array encoding)

The `mb_convert_kana` function translates Japanese text between various alphabets. The `option` argument controls the translation. Table 12.12 shows available options. If left out, `option` defaults to `KV`. The optional `source` argument sets the encoding used for the source text. It defaults to PHP's default encoding.

**Table 12.12** `mb_convert_kana` Options

| Option | Description |
| --- | --- |
| a, A | Convert zen-kaku alphabets and numbers to han-kaku. Converted characters include U+0021 through U+007E, excluding U+0022, U+0027, U+005C, and U+007E. |
| C | Convert zen-kaku hira-gana to zen-kaku kata-kana. |
| c | Convert zen-kaku kata-kana to zen-kaku hira-gana. |
| H | Convert han-kaku kata-kana to zen-kaku hira-gana. |
| h | Convert zen-kaku hira-gana to han-kaku kata-kana. |
| K | Convert han-kaku kata-kana to zen-kaku kata-kana. |
| k | Convert zen-kaku kata-kana to han-kaku kata-kana. |

**Table 12.12**   `mb_convert_kana` Options *(cont.)*

| Option | Description |
|--------|-------------|
| N | Convert han-kaku numbers to zen-kaku. |
| n | Convert zen-kaku numbers to han-kaku. |
| R | Convert han-kaku letters to zen-kaku. |
| r | Convert zen-kaku letters to han-kaku. |
| S | Convert han-kaku whitespace to zen-kaku (U+0020 through U+3000). |
| s | Convert zen-kaku whitespace to han-kaku (U+3000 through U+0020). |
| V | Collapse voiced sound notations and convert them into a character. Use this option with K or H. |

### string mb_convert_variables(string target, array source, …)

The `mb_convert_variables` function (Listing 12.88) converts the contents of variables from one encoding to another. The `source` argument may be an array of possible encoding identifiers or a comma-separated list. The function returns the encoding used to convert the variables. You may supply one or more variables starting with the third argument. The values of the variables are changed in place.

**Listing 12.88**   `mb_convert_variables`

```php
<?php
    $text1 = "Every year PHP wins larger popularity!";
    $text2 = "Jedes Jahr PHP gewinnt größere Popularität!";
    $encoding = mb_convert_variables(
        mb_internal_encoding(),
        "ASCII,UTF-8",
        $text1, $text2);

    print("Text was encoded as $encoding.<br>");
?>
```

### string mb_decode_mimeheader(string text)

Use `mb_decode_mimeheader` (Listing 12.89) to convert the text of a MIME header to the default encoding.

**Listing 12.89**   *mb_decode_mimeheader*

```php
<?php
    print(mb_decode_mimeheader(
        '=?UTF-7?Q?Gro+AN=38-er=20Affe?='));
?>
```

### string mb_decode_numericentity(string text, array conversion, array encoding)

The `mb_decode_numericentity` function (Listing 12.90) decodes HTML numeric entity codes. The `conversion` argument defines a conversion map. PHP looks for blocks of four elements in this array that have the following meaning: starting code, ending code, offset, and mask. The starting and ending codes should match the beginning and ending of a range of characters. If an entity matches the range, PHP applies the offset before decoding it. For example, an offset of 1 changes 65 to 66, or A to B. PHP converts the entity based on a bitwise-AND of the entity code and the mask. For example, a mask of 0xFF applied to entity 321 results in A because 321 & 0xFF equals 65.

**Listing 12.90**   *mb_decode_numericentity*

```php
<?php
    print(mb_decode_numericentity(
        '&#65;&#66;&#67;&#32;&#49;&#50;&#51;',
        array(0x00, 0xFF, 0x00, 0xFF)));
?>
```

### string mb_detect_encoding(string text, array encoding)

The `mb_detect_encoding` function (Listing 12.91) returns the detected encoding used for the given text. The optional `encoding` argument may define a set of encoding methods to try in order. You may specify this argument as a string of comma-separated encoding identifiers or as an array.

**Listing 12.91**   *mb_detect_encoding*

```php
<?php
    print(mb_detect_encoding('groß',
        array('ASCII','UTF-8','EUC-JP')));
?>
```

### array mb_detect_order(array encoding)

The `mb_detect_order` function returns an array describing the encoding methods PHP uses when detecting the encoding used for a string, such as with the `mb_detect_encoding` function. You may change this value by supplying an array or comma-separated list for the `encoding` argument.

### string mb_encode_mimeheader(string text, string encoding, string method, string linefeed)

Use `mb_encode_mimeheader` (Listing 12.92) to encode a string for use with a MIME header. The optional `encoding` argument sets the encoding used for the given text. It defaults to ISO-2022-JP. The optional `method` argument should be B for base64 or Q for Quoted-Printable. The optional `linefeed` argument defaults to a carriage return followed by a linefeed character.

---

**Listing 12.92**   *mb_encode_mimeheader*

```php
<?php
    print(mb_encode_mimeheader('Großer Affe', 'UTF-7', 'Q') .
        " <corephp@leonatkinson.com>");
?>
```

---

### string mb_encode_numericentity(string text, array conversion, string encoding)

Use `mb_encode_numericentity` (Listing 12.93) to convert a set of characters to HTML numeric entities. It performs the reverse of the `mb_decode_numericentity`. Refer to that function for a description of the conversion array.

---

**Listing 12.93**   *mb_encode_numericentity*

```php
<?php
    print(mb_encode_numericentity("ABC 123", array(0x00, 0xFF,
        0x00, 0xFF)));
?>
```

---

### string mb_http_input(string type)

The `mb_http_input` function returns the encoding used for the given HTTP input type. Use G for GET, P for POST, or C for cookies. You may leave out the type to get the encoding for the last type processed. If no processing occurs, this function returns FALSE.

### string mb_http_output(string encoding)

The mb_http_output function operates in two modes. If called without the encoding argument, it returns the current encoding used for output. If called with the encoding argument, it attempts to set the output encoding and returns a boolean. PHP converts all output from the internal encoding to the output encoding. By default, PHP uses no output encoding.

### string mb_internal_encoding(string encoding)

The mb_internal_encoding function operates in two modes. If called without the encoding argument, it returns the current encoding used for internal strings. If called with the encoding argument, it attempts to set the internal encoding and returns a boolean. By default, PHP uses no internal encoding.

### string mb_language(string language)

Use mb_language to get or set the language assumed by mb_send_mail. If called with no argument, mb_language returns the current setting. Otherwise, it sets the language and returns a boolean.

Table 12.13 shows valid languages. You may specify them with the full name or the abbreviation. The table also shows the character set and encoding used by mb_send_mail.

**Table 12.13**     mb_language Languages

| Language | Abbreviation | Character Set | Encoding |
|----------|--------------|---------------|----------|
| English | en | ISO-8859-1 | Quoted-Printable |
| German | de | ISO-8859-15 | Quoted-Printable |
| Japanese | ja | ISO-2022-JP | Base64 |
| Korean | ko | ISO-2022-KR | Base64 |
| neutral |  | UTF-8 | Base64 |
| Russian | ru | KOI8-R | Quoted-Printable |
| Simplified Chinese | zh-cn | HZ | Base64 |
| Traditional Chinese | zh-tw | BIG-5 | Base64 |
| universal | uni | UTF-8 | Base64 |

### string mb_output_handler(string contents, integer status)

Use mb_output_handler (Listing 12.94) together with ob_start to perform encoding conversion on all output. Translation will be made from the internal encoding to the external encoding if two conditions are met: if the Content-type header begins with text/ and if you have set the output encoding to anything other than pass.

| Listing 12.94 | *mb_output_handler* |
| --- | --- |

```php
<?php
    //set output encoding
    mb_http_output('sjis-win');

    //begin output buffering
    ob_start('mb_output_handler');
?>
<html>
<head>
<title>mb_output_handler</title>
</head>
<body>
<?php
    print("At this point ");
    print(mb_strlen(ob_get_contents()));
    print(" characters are in the buffer.<br>\n");
?>
</body>
</html>
<?php
    //send appropriate content type (Shift_JIS)
    header("Content-type: text/html; charset=" .
        mb_preferred_mime_name('sjis-win'));

    //dump the contents
    ob_end_flush();
?>
```

### boolean mb_parse_str(string query, array results)
The mb_parse_str function offers a multibyte alternative to parse_str. In addition to converting variables in the given query, it also detects the encoding used and converts the data to the internal encoding.

### string mb_preferred_mime_name(string encoding)
Use mb_preferred_mime_name to fetch an appropriate charset value matching the given encoding for use with a MIME Content-type header.

### boolean mb_send_mail(string to, string subject, string body, string headers, string parameters)

The `mb_send_mail` function sends mail in the same way the `mail` function sends mail except that it encodes the message body and sets headers accordingly.

### string mb_strcut(string text, integer start, integer length, string encoding)

Use `mb_strcut` (Listing 12.95) to take a portion of a string. You must supply a string of text and the number of the first character to include. Characters are numbered from zero. The optional `length` argument limits the number of characters returned instead of returning the rest of the string, as in the default. The optional `encoding` argument may specify the encoding used by the given string, overriding the default internal encoding.

| Listing 12.95 | mb_strcut, mb_strimwidth, mb_strlen, mb_strpos, mb_strrpos |
|---|---|

```php
<?php
    $text = "Jedes Jahr PHP gewinnt größere Popularität!";

    print(mb_strcut($text, 23, 7, 'ISO-8859-15') . '<br>');
    print(mb_strimwidth($text, 23, 7, 'X', 'ISO-8859-15') .
        '<br>');
    print(mb_strlen($text, 'ISO-8859-15') . '<br>');
    print(mb_strpos($text, 'PHP', 0, 'ISO-8859-15') . '<br>');
    print(mb_strrpos($text, ' P', 'ISO-8859-15') . '<br>');
?>
```

### string mb_strimwidth(string text, integer start, integer width, string marker, string encoding)

The `mb_strimwidth` function takes a portion of a string strictly limited to the given width. The optional `marker` argument replaces characters at the end of the string. For example, given a string `abcd`, a width of four, and a marker `123`, `mb_strimwidth` returns `a123`. If the length of `marker` exceeds `width`, PHP returns the entire marker. The optional `encoding` argument may specify the encoding used by the given string, overriding the default internal encoding.

### integer mb_strlen(string text, string encoding)

Use `mb_strlen` to get the number of characters in a multibyte character string. The optional `encoding` argument may specify the encoding used by the given string, overriding the default internal encoding.

### integer mb_strpos(string data, string substring, integer offset, string encoding)

Use `mb_strpos` as a multibyte alternative to `strpos`; it returns the position of the first occurrence of the `substring` argument in the `data` argument. The optional `offset` argument instructs PHP to begin searching after the specified position. Counting begins with zero. The optional `encoding` argument may specify the encoding used by the given string, overriding the default internal encoding.

### integer mb_strrpos(string data, string substring, string encoding)

Use `mb_strrpos` to find the position of the last occurrence of `substring` in `data`, both multibyte strings. Counting begins with zero. The optional `encoding` argument may specify the encoding used by the given string, overriding the default internal encoding.

### string mb_strtolower(string text, string encoding)

The `mb_strtolower` function converts the given string to lowercase with respect to multibyte character strings. The optional `encoding` argument may specify the encoding used by the given string, overriding the default internal encoding.

Compare this function to `mb_convert_case`.

### string mb_strtoupper(string text, string encoding)

The `mb_strtoupper` function converts the given string to uppercase with respect to multibyte character strings. The optional `encoding` argument may specify the encoding used by the given string, overriding the default internal encoding.

Compare this function to `mb_convert_case`.

### integer mb_strwidth(string text, string encoding)

The `mb_strwidth` function returns the width of a multibyte character string. This is not the same value returned by `mb_strlen`. It is a measure of visual width.

### boolean mb_substitute_character(integer character)

Use mb_substitute_character (Listing 12.96) to get or set the substitution character used when a character in a converted string does not appear in the target encoding. When called with no argument, this function returns the integer value of the Unicode character used for substitutions. When called with an integer value, it sets the substitution character and returns a boolean. You may also use two special strings for the character argument. If you use none, PHP removes nonmatching characters. If you use long, PHP inserts the Unicode representation for the character, such as U+1234.

---

**Listing 12.96**   *mb_substitute_character*

```php
<?php
    //show default substitution character
    $c = mb_substitute_character();
    printf("0x%X = %c<br>", $c, $c);

    //set and show substitution character
    mb_substitute_character(0x3013);
    $c = mb_substitute_character();
    printf("0x%X = %c<br>", $c, $c);

    //test substitution with character value
    mb_substitute_character('long');
    print(mb_convert_encoding('Großer Affe', 'ASCII'));
?>
```

---

### string mb_substr(string text, integer start, integer length, string encoding)

Use mb_substr as an alias to mb_strcut.

### integer mb_substr_count(string text, string substring, string encoding)

The mb_substr_count function emulates substr_count for multibyte strings.

# MATH

**Topics in This Chapter**

- Common Math
- Random Numbers
- Arbitrary-Precision Numbers

# Chapter 13

The math functions fall into three categories: common mathematical operations, random numbers, and special functions for handling numbers of arbitrary precision.

## 13.1 Common Math

The functions in this section offer most of the common mathematical operations that are part of arithmetic, geometry, and trigonometry. Most of these functions work on either doubles or integers. The return type will be the same as the argument. Unless a specific type is called for, I've written "number" to indicate that either an integer or a double is expected.

### number abs(number value)

The abs function (Listing 13.1) returns the absolute value of a number. This is the number itself if it's positive or the number multiplied by negative one (–1) if negative.

| Listing 13.1 | *abs* |
|---|---|

```php
<?php
    //prints 13
    print(abs(-13));
?>
```

### double acos(double value)

The `acos` function (Listing 13.2) returns the arc cosine of the `value` argument. Trying to find the arc cosine of a value greater than one or less than negative one is undefined.

**Listing 13.2** *acos, asin, atan, atanh*

```php
<?php
    print("<table border=\"1\">\n");
    print("<tr>" .
        "<th>x</th>" .
        "<th>acos(x)</th>" .
        "<th>asin(x)</th>" .
        "<th>atan(x)</th>" .
        "<th>atanh(x)</th>" .
        "</tr>\n");

    for($index = -1; $index <= 1; $index += 0.25)
    {
        print("<tr>\n" .
            "<td>$index</td>\n" .
            "<td>" . acos($index) . "</td>\n" .
            "<td>" . asin($index) . "</td>\n" .
            "<td>" . atan($index) . "</td>\n" .
            "<td>" . atanh($index) . "</td>\n" .
            "</tr>\n");
    }

    print("</table>\n");
?>
```

### double acosh(double value)

Use `acosh` (Listing 13.3) to find the inverse hyperbolic cosine of the given value.

**Listing 13.3** *acosh, asinh*

```php
<?php
    print("<table border=\"1\">\n");
    print("<tr>" .
        "<th>x</th>" .
        "<th>acosh(x)</th>" .
        "<th>asinh(x)</th>".
        "</tr>\n");
```

Listing 13.3    *acosh, asinh (cont.)*

```
for($index = 1; $index <= 10; $index++)
{
    print("<tr>\n" .
        "<td>$index</td>\n" .
        "<td>" . acosh($index) . "</td>\n" .
        "<td>" . asinh($index) . "</td>\n" .
        "</tr>\n");
}

print("</table>\n");
?>
```

### double asin(double value)

The `asin` function returns the arc sine of the `value` argument. Trying to find the arc sine of a value greater than one or less than negative one is undefined.

### double asinh(double value)

Use `asinh` to find the inverse hyperbolic sine of the given value.

### double atan(double value)

The `atan` function returns the arc tangent of the `value` argument.

### double atan2(double x, double y)

The `atan2` function (Listing 13.4) returns the angle portion in radians of the polar coordinate specified by the Cartesian coordinates.

Listing 13.4    *atan2*

```
<?php
    //print 0.40489178628508
    print(atan2(3, 7));
?>
```

### double atanh(double value)

The `atanh` function finds the inverse hyperbolic tangent of the given value.

### string base_convert(string value, int base, int new_base)

The `base_convert` function (Listing 13.5) converts a number from one base to another. Some common bases have their own functions.

**Listing 13.5** *base_convert*

```php
<?php
    //convert hex CC to decimal
    print(base_convert("CC", 16, 10));
?>
```

### integer bindec(string binary_number)

The `bindec` function (Listing 13.6) returns the integer value of a binary number written as a string. The binary numbers are little-endian, which means the least significant bit is to the right. PHP ignores any digits in the input other than 0 and 1.

**Listing 13.6** *bindec*

```php
<?php
    print(bindec("11010010110101001010"));
?>
```

### integer ceil(double value)

The `ceil` function (Listing 13.7) returns the ceiling of the argument, which is the smallest integer greater than the argument.

**Listing 13.7** *ceil*

```php
<?php
    //print 14
    print(ceil(13.2));
?>
```

### double cos(double angle)

The `cos` function (Listing 13.8) returns the cosine of an angle expressed in radians.

**Listing 13.8** *cos*

```php
<?php
    //prints 1
    print(cos(2 * pi()));
?>
```

## double cosh(double value)

The cosh function (Listing 13.9) returns the hyperbolic cosine of the given number.

**Listing 13.9**   *cosh, sinh, tanh*

```php
<?php
    print("<table border=\"1\">\n");
    print("<tr>" .
        "<th>x</th>" .
        "<th>cosh(x)</th>" .
        "<th>sinh(x)</th>".
        "<th>tanh(x)</th>".
        "</tr>\n");

    for($index = -4; $index <= 4; $index++)
    {
        print("<tr>\n" .
            "<td>$index</td>\n" .
            "<td>" . cosh($index) . "</td>\n" .
            "<td>" . sinh($index) . "</td>\n" .
            "<td>" . tanh($index) . "</td>\n" .
            "</tr>\n");
    }

    print("</table>\n");
?>
```

## string decbin(integer value)

The decbin function (Listing 13.10) returns a binary representation of an integer as a string.

**Listing 13.10**   *decbin, dechex, decoct*

```php
<?php
    //prints 11111111
    print(decbin(255) . "<br>");

    //prints ff
    print(dechex(255) . "<br>");

    //prints 377
    print(decoct(255) . "<br>");
?>
```

### string dechex(integer value)

The `dechex` function returns the hexadecimal representation of the `value` argument as a string.

### string decoct(integer value)

The `decoct` function returns the octal representation of the `value` argument as a string.

### double deg2rad(double angle)

The `deg2rad` function (Listing 13.11) returns the radians that correspond to the `angle` argument, specified in degrees.

---

**Listing 13.11**    *deg2rad*

```php
<?php
    //prints 1.5707963267949
    print(deg2rad(90));
?>
```

---

### double exp(double power)

The `exp` function (Listing 13.12) returns the natural logarithm base raised to the power of the argument.

---

**Listing 13.12**    *exp*

```php
<?php
    //prints 20.085536923188
    print(exp(3));
?>
```

---

### double expm1(double power)

The `expm1` function (Listing 13.13) returns the natural logarithm base raised to the power of the argument minus 1. This function calculates values to a higher precision than `exp` when the given power is close to zero.

**Listing 13.13**   *expm1*

```php
<?php
    //1.1051709180756
    print(exp(0.1));

    print('<br>');

    //0.10517091807565
    print(expm1(0.1));
?>
```

### integer floor(double value)

The `floor` function (Listing 13.14) returns the floor of the argument, which is the integer part of the argument.

**Listing 13.14**   *floor*

```php
<?php
    //prints 13
    print(floor(13.2));
?>
```

### double fmod(double x, double y)

The `fmod` function (Listing 13.15) returns the floating-point modulo of `x` divided by `y`. This value is defined as `x = i * y + r`, where `i` is the integer result of division and `r` is the remainder.

**Listing 13.15**   *fmod*

```php
<?php
    $x = 9.87;
    $y = 1.24;
    $i = intval($x / $y);
    $r = fmod($x, $y);

    //9.87 = 7 * 1.24 + 1.19
    print("$x = $i * $y + $r");
?>
```

### integer hexdec(string hexadecimal_number)

The `hexdec` function (Listing 13.16) converts a string that represents a hexadecimal number into an integer. Preceding the number with "0x" is optional.

| Listing 13.16 | *hexdec* |
| --- | --- |

```php
<?php
    //255
    print(hexdec("FF"));
    print("<br>\n");

    //32685
    print(hexdec("0x7FAD"));
    print("<br>\n");
?>
```

### double hypot(double x, double y)

The `hypot` function (Listing 13.17) returns the length of the hypotenuse of a right triangle given the two other sides using the Pythagorean theorem.

| Listing 13.17 | *hypot* |
| --- | --- |

```php
<?php
    //sqrt(39*39 + 52*52) == 65
    print(hypot(39,52));
?>
```

### double log(double value, double base)

The `log` function (Listing 13.18) returns the natural logarithm of the `value` argument. The optional `base` argument allows for logarithms of other bases.

| Listing 13.18 | *log, log1p, log10* |
| --- | --- |

```php
<?php
    //prints 3.0022112396517
    print(log(20.13) . "<br>");

    //prints 2.732730436951
    print(log(20.13, 3) . "<br>");
```

**Listing 13.18** *log, log1p, log10 (cont.)*

```
    //prints 0.00099950033308353
    print(log1p(0.001) . "<br>");

    //prints 3.2494429614426
    print(log10(1776) . "<br>");
?>
```

### double log1p(double value)

The `log1p` function returns the natural logarithm of 1 plus the given value. Like `expm1`, this function returns values with better accuracy when given numbers very close to zero.

### double log10(double value)

The `log10` function returns the decimal logarithm of its argument.

### integer octdec(string octal_number)

The `octdec` function (Listing 13.19) returns the integer value of a string representing an octal number.

**Listing 13.19** *octdec*

```
<?php
    //prints 497
    print(octdec("761"));
?>
```

### double pi()

The `pi` function (Listing 13.20) returns the approximate value of pi. Alternatively, you may use the `M_PI` constant.

**Listing 13.20** *pi*

```
<?php
    //prints 3.1415926535898
    print(pi() . "<br>");

    //prints 3.1415926535898
    print(M_PI . "<br>");
?>
```

### double pow(double base, double power)

Use the pow function (Listing 13.21) to raise the base argument to the power indicated by the second argument.

**Listing 13.21**    *pow*

```php
<?php
    //print 32
    print(pow(2, 5));
?>
```

### double rad2deg(double angle)

The rad2deg function (Listing 13.22) returns the degrees that correspond to the radians specified in the angle argument.

**Listing 13.22**    *rad2deg*

```php
<?php
    //print 90.00021045915
    print(rad2deg(1.5708));
?>
```

### double round(double value, integer precision)

The round function (Listing 13.23) returns the argument rounded to the nearest integer. The optional precision argument allows you to round to a number of digits to the right of the decimal point.

**Listing 13.23**    *round*

```php
<?php
    //prints 1
    print(round(1.4) . "<br>");

    //prints 1
    print(round(1.5) . "<br>");

    //prints 2
    print(round(1.6) . "<br>");

    //prints 1.6
    print(round(1.61, 1) . "<br>");
?>
```

### double sin(double angle)

The `sin` function (Listing 13.24) returns the sine of the angle. The angle is assumed to be in radians.

| Listing 13.24 | *sin* |
|---|---|

```php
<?php
    //prints 1
    print(sin(0.5 * M_PI));
?>
```

### double sinh(double value)

The `sinh` function returns the hyperbolic sine of the given value.

### double sqrt(double value)

Use `sqrt` (Listing 13.25) to find the square root of a number.

| Listing 13.25 | *sqrt* |
|---|---|

```php
<?php
    //prints 9
    print(sqrt(81.0));
?>
```

### double tan(double angle)

The `tan` function (Listing 13.26) returns the tangent of an angle. The angle is expected to be expressed in radians.

| Listing 13.26 | *tan* |
|---|---|

```php
<?php
    //prints 1.5574077246549
    print(tan(1));
?>
```

### double tanh(double value)

The `tanh` function returns the hyperbolic tangent of the given value.

# 13.2 Random Numbers

The following functions help you generate pseudorandom numbers. There are wrappers for the randomizing functions offered by your operating system, and there are functions based on the Mersenne Twister algorithm. The Mersenne Twister functions are faster and return numbers with a much better distribution suitable for cryptographic applications. The algorithm was developed by Makoto Matsumoto and Takuji Nishimura. You can read more about it on their Web page `<http://www.math.keio.ac.jp/~matumoto/emt.html>`. Pedro Melo refactored an implementation by Shawn Cokus in order to add support to PHP.

Pseudorandom number generators need seeding. Traditionally, the program seeds the generator itself, but PHP can handle this task. For the illusion of really random numbers, you should seed with data from a source that changes often. The microsecond clock is a good start. PHP does a great job of seeding, so you shouldn't worry about it in most cases. A seed will reliably produce the same sequence of pseudorandom numbers, which can be useful in certain situations.

### integer getrandmax()

The `getrandmax` function (Listing 13.27) returns the maximum random number that may be returned by the `rand` function.

**Listing 13.27**   *getrandmax*

```php
<?php
    print(getrandmax());
?>
```

### integer mt_getrandmax()

The `mt_getrandmax` function (Listing 13.28) returns the maximum random number that may be returned by the `mt_rand` function.

**Listing 13.28**   *mt_getrandmax*

```php
<?php
    print(mt_getrandmax());
?>
```

## double lcg_value()

The `lcg_value` function returns a number between 0 and 1 using an algorithm called a linear congruential generator, or LCG. This is a common method for generating pseudorandom numbers. The generator is seeded with the process identifier.

## integer mt_rand(integer min, integer max)

The `mt_rand` function (Listing 13.29) uses the Mersenne Twister algorithm to return a number between the two optional arguments, inclusive. If left out, zero and the integer returned by the `mt_getrandmax` function will be used. Use `mt_srand` to seed the Mersenne Twister random number generator.

**Listing 13.29** *mt_rand*

```php
<?php
    //get ten random numbers from 1 to 100
    for($index = 0; $index < 10; $index++)
    {
        print(mt_rand(1, 100) . "<br>");
    }
?>
```

## mt_srand(integer seed)

The `mt_srand` function seeds the Mersenne Twister random number generator.

## integer rand(integer lowest, integer highest)

The `rand` function (Listing 13.30) returns a number between the two optional arguments, inclusive. If you leave out the arguments, zero and the integer returned by the `getrandmax` function will be used. Use the `srand` function to seed the random number generator.

**Listing 13.30** *rand*

```php
<?php
    //get ten random numbers from -100 to 100
    for($index = 0; $index < 10; $index++)
    {
        print(rand(-100, 100) . "<br>");
    }
?>
```

**srand(integer seed)**

The srand function seeds the random number generator.

**string uniqid(string prefix, boolean use_lcg)**

The uniqid function (Listing 13.31) joins the prefix argument to a random series of numbers and letters, which are generated based on the system clock. The prefix may be up to 114 characters long and the unique string is always 13 characters long.

If the optional use_lcg argument is TRUE, nine additional characters will be added to the end of the return string These characters are generated by the same algorithm used by the lcg_value function: a period followed by eight digits. Because the lcg_value function seeds itself with the process ID, turning on this flag may not actually add much randomness.

Compare this function to tempnam, discussed in Chapter 9.

| Listing 13.31 | *uniqid* |
|---|---|

```php
<?php
    print(uniqid("data"));
?>
```

# 13.3  Arbitrary-Precision Numbers

Doubles are usually sufficiently precise for any numerical analysis you may wish to perform. However, PHP offers a way to work with numbers of much higher precision. The functions in this section use strings to store very long floating-point numbers. They each use a scale value that is the number of digits to the right of the decimal point. The scale argument that appears in all of the functions is optional and will override the default scale. The bcscale function, described in Chapter 15, sets the default scale.

These functions are part of the bcmath extension. They are part of the binary distribution for Windows, but they are not activated by default for other operating systems. If PHP reports these functions as being unrecognized, you may need to recompile PHP using the --enable-bcmath option.

PHP also supports an extension for GNU MP, also known as GMP. At the time of writing, the PHP extension supports only integers. You can read more about GMP at the home site <http://www.swox.com/gmp/>.

Listing 13.32 demonstrates the arbitrary-precision number functions.

---

**Listing 13.32**   *Arbitrary-precision number functions*

```php
<?php
    //11.1111111000
    print(bcadd("1.234567890", "9.87654321", 10) . '<br>');

    //1, that is, the first is larger than the second
    print(bccomp("12345","1.111111111111", 10) . '<br>');

    //0.1250075946
    print(bcdiv("12345", "98754", 10) . '<br>');

    //121134
    print(bcmod("66394593", "133347") . '<br>');

    //8853519792771
    print(bcmul("66394593", "133347", 10) . '<br>');

    //292683432083423203645857
    print(bcpow("66394593", "3", 10) . '<br>');

    //35.1364056215
    print(bcsqrt("1234.567", 10) . '<br>');

    //1146
    print(bcsub("1234.4842", "88.6674") . '<br>');
?>
```

### string bcadd(string left, string right, integer scale)
The `bcadd` function adds `left` to `right`.

### integer bccomp(string left, string right, integer scale)
The `bccomp` function compares `left` to `right`. If they are equal, zero is returned. If `left` is less than `right`, −1 is returned. If `left` is greater than `right`, 1 is returned.

### string bcdiv(string left, string right, integer scale)
Use `bcdiv` to divide `left` by `right`.

### string bcmod(string left, string right)
The `bcmod` function finds the modulus of the division of `left` by `right`.

### string bcmul(string left, string right, integer scale)
Use `bcmul` to multiply the `left` argument and the `right` argument.

### string bcpow(string value, string exponent, integer scale)

The `bcpow` function raises the `value` argument to the power of the `exponent` argument. If the exponent is not an integer, the fractional part will be chopped off.

### string bcpowmod(string value, string exponent, string mod, integer scale)

The `bcpowmod` function returns the value of a number raised to the power of another reduced by a modulus.

### string bcsqrt(string value, integer scale)

The `bcsqrt` function returns the square root of the `value` argument.

### string bcsub(string left, string right, integer scale)

Use the `bcsub` function to subtract the `right` argument from the `left` argument.

# TIME
# AND DATE

**Topics in This Chapter**

- Time and Date
- Alternative Calendars

# Chapter 14

The functions in this chapter describe time-related functions. Most of PHP's time and date functions are standard for any programming language. They allow you to get the current date in several formats. The calendar functions manipulate dates in various calendars, including ancient and obscure calendars.

## 14.1 Time and Date

All the time functions work off the UNIX epoch, which is January 1, 1970. Dates are expressed as seconds since the epoch. This makes it easy to refer to dates with integers. When a function calls for seconds since the epoch, I've referred to it as a timestamp.

Windows accepts timestamps from zero to the largest 32-bit integer, which corresponds to January 19, 2038. UNIX allows for negative timestamps, which stretch back to December 13, 1901.

### boolean checkdate(integer month, integer day, integer year)

The checkdate function (Listing 14.1) returns TRUE if a date is valid, and FALSE otherwise. A day is considered valid if the year is between 0 and 32767, the month is between 1 and 12, and the day is within the allowable days for that month. This function takes leap years into consideration.

**Listing 14.1**    *checkdate*

```php
<?php
    if(checkdate(2,18,1970))
    {
        print("It is a good day");
    }
?>
```

### string date(string format, integer timestamp)

The date function (Listing 14.2) returns a string describing the date of the timestamp according to the format argument. Letters in the format argument are replaced with parts of the date or time. Any characters not understood as codes pass unchanged. You can pass any character by preceding it with a backslash. Format codes are listed in Table 14.1.

**Table 14.1**    date Format Codes

| Code | Description |
|------|-------------|
| a | am or pm |
| A | AM or PM |
| B | Swatch Beat time |
| d | Day of the month with leading zeroes |
| D | Day of the week as a three-letter abbreviation |
| F | Name of the month |
| g | Hour from 1 to 12 (no leading zeroes) |
| G | Hour from 0 to 23 (no leading zeroes) |
| h | Hour from 01 to 12 |
| H | Hour from 00 to 23 |
| i | Minutes |
| I | 1 if daylight savings time |
| j | Day of the month with no leading zeroes |
| l | Day of the week |
| L | 1 if leap year, 0 otherwise |

**Table 14.1** `date` Format Codes *(cont.)*

| Code | Description |
|------|-------------|
| m | Month number from 01 to 12 |
| M | Abbreviated month name (Jan, Feb, ...) |
| n | Month number from 1 to 12 (no leading zeroes) |
| O | Difference in Greenwich Mean Time (+0800) |
| r | RFC822 formatted date |
| s | Seconds 00 to 59 |
| S | Ordinal suffix for day of the month (1st, 2nd, 3rd) |
| t | Number of days in the month |
| T | Time zone, dependent on OS |
| U | Seconds since the epoch |
| w | Day of the week from 0 (Sunday) to 6 (Saturday) |
| W | Week number of year using ISO 8601 standard |
| y | Year as two digits |
| Y | Year as four digits |
| z | Day of the year from 0 to 365 |
| Z | Time zone offset in seconds (-43,200 to 43,200) |

The `timestamp` argument is optional. If left out, the current time will be used. The timestamp is interpreted as being in local time.

**Listing 14.2** *date*

```php
<?php
    //prints something like
    //04:01 PM Tuesday December 17th, 2002
    print(date("h:i A l F dS, Y"));
?>
```

### integer date_sunrise(integer timestamp, integer format, double latitude, double longitude, double zenith, double offset)

The `date_sunrise` function returns the time of sunrise on the date of the given timestamp. The optional format argument may be set to SUNFUNCS_RET_ TIMESTAMP, SUNFUNCS_RET_STRING, or SUNFUNCS_RET_DOUBLE. The first constant causes PHP to return the number of seconds after midnight the sun rises. The second constant causes PHP to return a string with the time on the 24-hour clock. This is the default return format. The third constant returns the timestamp for sunrise on that day.

You may optionally set the latitude, longitude, zenith, and offset from GMT. If you do not set these, PHP uses defaults defined in `php.ini` for the first three. The configuration directives are `date.default_latitude`, `date.default_ longitude`, and `date.sunset_zenith`. PHP can figure the time zone from the operating system.

### integer date_sunset(integer timestamp, integer format, double latitude, double longitude, double zenith, double offset)

The `date_sunset` function returns the time of sunset on the date of the given timestamp. Its arguments match those of `date_sunrise`.

### array getdate(integer timestamp)

The `getdate` function (Listing 14.3) returns an associative array with information about the given date. This array is described in Table 14.2. The `timestamp` argument is the number of seconds since January 1, 1970. If left out, the current time is used.

**Table 14.2** Elements in `getdate` Array

| Element | Description |
| --- | --- |
| hours | Hour in 24-hour format |
| mday | Day of the month |
| minutes | Minutes for the hour |
| mon | Month as a number |
| month | Full name of the month |
| seconds | Seconds for the minute |
| wday | Day of the week as a number from 0 to 6 |
| weekday | Name of the day of the week |

**Table 14.2**   Elements in `getdate` Array *(cont.)*

| Element | Description |
|---------|-------------|
| yday | Day of the year as a number |
| year | Year |
| 0 | Timestamp |

**Listing 14.3**   *getdate*

```php
<?php
    $d = getdate();
    print("Timestamp {$d[0]} is {$d['mon']}-{$d['mday']}-".
        "{$d['year']}");
?>
```

### array gettimeofday()

The `gettimeofday` function (Listing 14.4) returns an associative array containing information about the current time. This is a direct interface to the C function of the same name. The elements of the returned array are listed in Table 14.3.

**Table 14.3**   Elements of the Array Returned by `gettimeofday`

| Element | Meaning |
|---------|---------|
| sec | Seconds |
| usec | Microseconds |
| minuteswest | Minutes West of Greenwich |
| dsttime | Type of DST correction |

**Listing 14.4**   *gettimeofday*

```php
<?php
    $t = gettimeofday();
    print("{$t['sec']} {$t['usec']} {$t['minuteswest']}".
        "{$t['dsttime']}");
?>
```

### string gmdate(string format, integer timestamp)

The gmdate function (Listing 14.5) operates identically to the date function except that Greenwich Mean Time is returned instead of the time for the local time zone.

**Listing 14.5**    *gmdate*

```php
<?php
    print("Local: " . date("h:i A l F dS, Y") . "<br>");
    print("GMT: " . gmdate("h:i A l F dS, Y") . "<br>");
?>
```

### integer gmmktime(integer hour, integer minute, integer second, integer month, integer day, integer year)

The gmmktime function operates identically to mktime except that it returns a timestamp for Greenwich Mean Time rather than the local time zone.

### string gmstrftime(string format, integer timestamp)

The gmstrftime function operates identically to strftime except that the timestamp is considered Greenwich Mean Time. The same format codes defined in Table 14.5 are used in the format argument.

### integer idate(string format, integer timestamp)

The idate function returns the integer value for a format code from Table 14.1. If you don't supply the optional timestamp argument, PHP uses the current time.

### array localtime(integer timestamp, boolean associative)

The localtime function wraps the C function of the same name. It returns an array of information about the local time. By default, it returns an array indexed by integers. If associative is set to TRUE, it uses associative keys. Table 14.4 shows these keys.

**Table 14.4**    Elements of the Array Returned by localtime

| Integer Key | Associative Key | Description |
| --- | --- | --- |
| 0 | tm_sec | Seconds |
| 1 | tm_min | Minutes |
| 2 | tm_hour | Hour |

**Table 14.4**   Elements of the Array Returned by `localtime` *(cont.)*

| Integer Key | Associative Key | Description |
|---|---|---|
| 3 | tm_mday | Day of the month |
| 4 | tm_mon | Month of the year, January being 0 |
| 5 | tm_year | Years since 1900 |
| 6 | tm_wday | Day of the week |
| 7 | tm_yday | Day of the year |
| 8 | tm_isdst | 1 if daylight savings time is in effect |

### string microtime()

The `microtime` function (Listing 14.6) returns a string with two numbers separated by a space. The first number is microseconds on the system clock. The second is the number of seconds since January 1, 1970.

**Listing 14.6**   *microtime*

```php
<?php
    //print microtime
    print("Start: ". microtime() . "<br>");

    //sleep for a random time
    usleep(rand(100,5000));

    //print microtime
    print("Stop: " . microtime() . "<br>");
?>
```

### integer mktime(integer hour, integer minute, integer second, integer month, integer day, integer year, integer daylight_savings_time)

The `mktime` function (Listing 14.7) returns a timestamp for a given date, the number of seconds since January 1, 1970. All the arguments are optional and, if left out, the appropriate value for the current time will be used. The `daylight_savings_time` argument should be 1 (yes), 0 (no) or –1 (let PHP guess). If an argument is out of range, `mktime` will account for the surplus or deficit by modifying the other time units. For example, using 13 for the `month` argument is equivalent to January of the following year. This makes `mktime` an effective tool for adding arbitrary time to a date.

**Listing 14.7** *mktime*

```php
<?php
    print("Fifty Hours from Now: " .
        date("h:i A l F dS, Y", mktime(date("h")+50)) . "<br>");
?>
```

### sleep(integer seconds)

The `sleep` function (Listing 14.8) causes execution to pause for the given number of seconds.

**Listing 14.8** *sleep*

```php
<?php
    print(microtime() . '<br>');
    sleep(3);
    print(microtime() . '<br>');
?>
```

### string strftime(string format, integer timestamp)

The `strftime` function (Listing 14.9) returns a date in a particular format. If the optional `timestamp` argument is left out, the current time will be used. Language-dependent strings will be set according to the current locale, which may be changed with the `setlocale` function. The format string may contain codes that have special meaning and begin with a percentage sign. Other characters are passed through unchanged. See Table 14.5 for a list of format codes.

**Table 14.5**  Codes Used by `strftime`

| Code | Description |
| --- | --- |
| %a | Abbreviated weekday name |
| %A | Full weekday name |
| %b | Abbreviated month name |
| %B | Full month name |
| %c | Preferred date and time representation |
| %C | Century number |
| %d | Two-digit day of the month with zero-fill |
| %D | Shortcut for %m/%d/%y |

**Table 14.5**   Codes Used by `strftime` *(cont.)*

| Code | Description |
|------|-------------|
| `%e` | Day of the month with space-fill |
| `%g` | The two-digit year corresponding to the ISO 8601:1988 week number |
| `%G` | The four-digit year corresponding to the ISO 8601:1988 week number |
| `%h` | Alias to `%b` |
| `%H` | Hour on the 24-hour clock with zero-fill |
| `%I` | Hour on the 12-hour clock |
| `%j` | Three-digit day of the year with zero-fill |
| `%m` | Month number from 1 to 12 |
| `%M` | Minutes |
| `%n` | Newline character |
| `%p` | Equivalent representation of a.m. or p.m. |
| `%r` | Time on 12-hour clock |
| `%R` | Time on 24-hour clock |
| `%S` | Seconds |
| `%t` | Tab character |
| `%T` | Shortcut for `%H:%M:%S` |
| `%u` | Weekday number, with 1 being Monday |
| `%U` | Week number with week one starting with the first Sunday of the year |
| `%V` | The ISO 8601:1988 week number |
| `%W` | Week number with week one starting with the first Monday of the year |
| `%w` | Day of the week as a number with Sunday being 0 |
| `%x` | Date representation preferred by locale |
| `%X` | Time representation preferred by locale |
| `%y` | Two-digit year with zero-fill |
| `%Y` | Four-digit year |
| `%Z` | Time zone |
| `%%` | A `%` character |

**Listing 14.9** *strftime*

```php
<?php
    //prints something like
    //Wednesday, Wed Dec 18 09:04:22 2002
    print(strftime("%A, %c"));
?>
```

### integer strtotime(string date, integer now)

The strtotime function (Listing 14.10) attempts to parse a string containing date and time, returning the timestamp for it. If partial information is provided in the date argument, the missing information will be drawn from the now argument. You may leave out the now argument to use the current time.

**Listing 14.10** *strtotime*

```php
<?php
    //create a reason description
    //of a date
    $time = "Feb 18, 1970 3AM";

    //get its timestamp
    $ts = strtotime($time);

    //print it to verify that it worked
    print(date("h:i A l F dS, Y", $ts));
?>
```

### integer time()

Use time (Listing 14.11) to get the current timestamp.

**Listing 14.11** *time*

```php
<?php
    print(time());
?>
```

### usleep(integer microseconds)

The `usleep` function (Listing 14.12) causes execution to pause for the given number of microseconds. There are a million microseconds in a second.

---

**Listing 14.12**   `usleep`

```php
<?php
    print(microtime() . '<br>');
    usleep(30);
    print(microtime() . '<br>');
?>
```

---

## 14.2  Alternative Calendars

PHP offers a powerful way to convert dates from one calendar system to another. In order to do this, you must first convert a date into a Julian Day Count. You then convert that integer back into a date according to another calendar.

These functions require the calendar extension. You may load it dynamically, or compile it into PHP.

### integer cal_days_in_month(integer calendar, integer month, integer year)

The `cal_days_in_month` function (Listing 14.13) returns the number of days in a month for a given calendar's month and year. Use one of the constants in Table 14.6 to specify the calendar.

**Table 14.6**   Calendar Type Constants

| Constant | Description |
| --- | --- |
| CAL_FRENCH | French Republican Calendar |
| CAL_GREGORIAN | Gregorian Calendar |
| CAL_JEWISH | Jewish Calendar |
| CAL_JULIAN | Julian Calendar |

---

**Listing 14.13** `cal_days_in_month`

```php
<?php
   //prints 30
   print(cal_days_in_month(CAL_FRENCH, 1, 1));
?>
```

---

### array cal_from_jd(integer julian_day, integer calendar)

The `cal_from_jd` function returns an array describing a given Julian Day Count in the given calendar. Use one of the constants in Table 14.6 to specify the calendar. Table 14.7 describes the elements in the returned array. Use this function as an alternative to `jdtofrench`, `jdtogregorian`, `jdtojewish`, and `jdtojulian`.

**Table 14.7**  Array Returned by `cal_from_jd`

| Element | Description |
|---|---|
| date | Date formatted as MM/DD/YYYY |
| month | Month number |
| day | Day |
| year | Year |
| dow | Day of the week number |
| abbrevdayname | Abbreviated day of the week |
| dayname | Day of the week |
| abbrevmonth | Abbreviated month name |
| monthname | Month name |

### array cal_info(integer calendar)

The `cal_info` function returns information about the given calendar, specified with one of the constants in Table 14.6. Table 14.8 describes the returned array.

**Table 14.8**   Array Returned by `cal_info`

| Element | Description |
| --- | --- |
| `months` | An array of month names indexed by number |
| `abbrevmonths` | An array of abbreviated month names indexed by number |
| `maxdaysinmonth` | The maximum number of days in any month |
| `calname` | The name of the calendar |
| `calsymbol` | The name of the constant used for the calendar |

### integer cal_to_jd(integer calendar, integer month, integer day, integer year)

The `cal_to_jd` function converts a date for the given calendar to a Julian Day Count. Use this function as an alternate to `frenchtojd`, `gregoriantojd`, `jewishtojd`, and `juliantojd`.

### integer easter_date(integer year)

Use `easter_date` (Listing 14.14) to get the timestamp for midnight on Easter for a given year. You may leave out the year to find Easter for the current year.

**Listing 14.14**   *easter_date*

```php
<?php
    print(easter_date(2000));
?>
```

### integer easter_days(integer year, integer method)

The `easter_days` function (Listing 14.15) returns the number of days after March 21 on which Easter falls for the given year. You may leave out the year to use the current year. The optional `method` argument may be set with the constants in Table 14.9.

**Table 14.9**   `easter_days` Methods

| |
| --- |
| `CAL_EASTER_DEFAULT` |
| `CAL_EASTER_ROMAN` |
| `CAL_EASTER_ALWAYS_GREGORIAN` |
| `CAL_EASTER_ALWAYS_JULIAN` |

| Listing 14.15 | *easter_days* |
|---|---|

```php
<?php
    print(easter_days(2003, CAL_EASTER_DEFAULT) . '<br>');
    print(easter_days(2003, CAL_EASTER_ROMAN) . '<br>');
    print(easter_days(2003, CAL_EASTER_ALWAYS_GREGORIAN) .
        '<br>');
    print(easter_days(2003, CAL_EASTER_ALWAYS_JULIAN) . '<br>');
?>
```

### integer frenchtojd(integer month, integer day, integer year)

The `frenchtojd` function returns the Julian Day Count for the given French Republican calendar date.

### integer gregoriantojd(integer month, integer day, integer year)

The `gregoriantojd` function returns the Julian Day Count for the given Gregorian date.

### value jddayofweek(integer julian_day, integer mode)

The `jddayofweek` function returns either an integer or a string, depending on the mode. Modes are listed in Table 14.10.

**Table 14.10** Calendar Day Modes

| Mode | Description |
|---|---|
| 0 | Returns the day of the week as a number from zero to 6, zero being Sunday. |
| 1 | Returns the day of the week as a name using the English name from the Gregorian calendar. |
| 2 | Returns the abbreviated name of the day of the week using the English name from the Gregorian calendar. |

### string jdmonthname(integer julian_day, integer mode)

The `jdmonthname` function returns the name of the month for a particular day. The `mode` argument specifies which calendar to draw month names from. Modes are listed in Table 14.11.

**Table 14.11** `jdmonthname` Modes

| Mode | Calendar |
|------|----------|
| 0 | Gregorian, abbreviated |
| 1 | Gregorian, full |
| 2 | Julian, abbreviated |
| 3 | Julian, full |
| 4 | Jewish |
| 5 | French Republican |

**string jdtofrench(integer julian_day)**

The `jdtofrench` function returns the date on the French Republican calendar for a Julian Day Count.

**string jdtogregorian(integer julian_day)**

Use the `jdtogregorian` function to convert a Julian Day Count to a Gregorian date.

**string jdtojewish(integer julian_day)**

The `jdtojewish` function returns the Jewish calendar date for the given Julian Day Count.

**string jdtojulian(integer julian_day)**

Use the `jdtojulian` function to get the Julian date for a Julian Day Count.

**integer jdtounix(integer julian_day)**

The `jdtounix` function returns a timestamp for the given Julian Day Count if the date falls within dates in the UNIX epoch. It returns FALSE, otherwise.

**integer jewishtojd(integer month, integer day, integer year)**

The `jewishtojd` function returns a Julian Day Count for the given Jewish calendar date.

**integer juliantojd(integer month, integer day, integer year)**

Use the `juliantojd` function to get the Julian Day Count for a Julian calendar date.

**integer unixtojd(integer timestamp)**

The `unixtojd` function returns the Julian Day Count given a UNIX timestamp.

# CONFIGURATION

**Topics in This Chapter**

- Configuration Directives
- Configuration

# Chapter 15

This chapter describes method for configuring the behavior of PHP. You may accomplish this by setting configuration directives or by executing functions. Configuration directives are set in `php.ini`, Apache `.htaccess` files or with the `set_ini` function. Chapter 1 discusses configuration basics.

## 15.1 Configuration Directives

Configuration directives change the behavior of PHP. PHP looks for these directives in `php.ini`. PHP looks for this file in three locations, in the following order: the current directory, the path set in the `PHPRC` environment variable, or in a standard path compiled into PHP. On UNIX, this path is `/usr/local/lib`. On Windows, it's the main system directory, usually `C:\WINDOWS` or `C:\WINNT`. A typical installation uses a single `php.ini` file, kept in this last path.

If you use the Apache Web server, you may override `php.ini` settings with `.htaccess` and `httpd.conf` files. You may use one of four Apache commands to set a PHP directive. Write the Apache command followed by the PHP directive name followed by the appropriate value. Use space to separate the three parts. For a PHP directive that may be on or off, use either `php_admin_flag` or `php_flag`. For a PHP directive that expects an arbitrary value, use `php_admin_value` or `php_value`. The two admin commands may appear only in `httpd.conf` and may not be overridden in an `.htaccess` file.

The `set_ini` function allows you to change most directives within a script. Because this function executes after PHP's initialization, some directives have no meaning in the context of a script. A description of `set_ini` appears later in this chapter.

Table 15.1 describes configuration directives available in a typical PHP installation. Extensions can add directives, so your list may not match this list exactly. Setting a directive that PHP doesn't recognize is not an error. It's just ignored.

You may set any directive in `php.ini`. Some will have no effect if set during runtime with `ini_set`.

**Table 15.1**    Configuration Directives

| Directive | Type | Default Value | ini_set | .htaccess | httpd.conf |
|---|---|---|---|---|---|
| allow_call_time_pass_reference | Flag | On | No | Yes | Yes |
| allow_url_fopen | Flag | On | Yes | Yes | Yes |
| allow_webdav_methods | Flag | NULL | No | Yes | Yes |
| always_populate_raw_post_data | Flag | Off | Yes | Yes | Yes |
| arg_separator.input | Value | & | No | Yes | Yes |
| arg_separator.output | Value | & | Yes | Yes | Yes |
| asp_tags | Flag | Off | No | Yes | Yes |
| assert.active | Flag | On | Yes | Yes | Yes |
| assert.bail | Flag | Off | Yes | Yes | Yes |
| assert.callback | Value | NULL | Yes | Yes | Yes |
| assert.quiet_eval | Flag | Off | Yes | Yes | Yes |
| assert.warning | Flag | On | Yes | Yes | Yes |
| auto_append_file | Value | NULL | No | Yes | Yes |
| auto_detect_line_endings | Flag | Off | Yes | Yes | Yes |
| auto_prepend_file | Value | NULL | No | Yes | Yes |
| browscap | Value | NULL | No | No | Yes |
| child_terminate | Flag | Off | Yes | Yes | Yes |
| com.allow_dcom | Flag | Off | No | No | Yes |

**Table 15.1**   Configuration Directives *(cont.)*

| Directive | Type | Default Value | ini_set | .htaccess | httpd.conf |
|---|---|---|---|---|---|
| com.autoregister_casesensitive | Flag | On | No | No | Yes |
| com.autoregister_typelib | Flag | Off | No | No | Yes |
| com.autoregister_verbose | Flag | Off | No | No | Yes |
| com.typelib_file | Value | NULL | No | No | Yes |
| crack.default_dictionary | Value | NULL | No | No | Yes |
| dbx.colnames_case | Value | unchanged | No | No | No |
| default_charset | Value | SAPI_DEFAULT_CHARSET | Yes | Yes | Yes |
| default_mimetype | Value | SAPI_DEFAULT_MIMETYPE | Yes | Yes | Yes |
| default_socket_timeout | Value | 60 | Yes | Yes | Yes |
| define_syslog_variables | Flag | Off | Yes | Yes | Yes |
| disable_functions | Value | NULL | No | No | Yes |
| display_errors | Flag | On | Yes | Yes | Yes |
| display_startup_errors | Flag | Off | Yes | Yes | Yes |
| doc_root | Value | NULL | No | No | Yes |
| docref_ext | Value | NULL | Yes | Yes | Yes |
| docref_root | Value | http://www.php.net/ | Yes | Yes | Yes |
| enable_dl | Flag | On | No | No | Yes |
| engine | Flag | On | Yes | Yes | Yes |
| error_append_string | Value | NULL | Yes | Yes | Yes |
| error_log | Value | NULL | Yes | Yes | Yes |
| error_prepend_string | Value | NULL | Yes | Yes | Yes |
| error_reporting | Value | NULL | Yes | Yes | Yes |
| exif.decode_jis_intel | Value | JIS | Yes | Yes | Yes |
| exif.decode_jis_motorola | Value | JIS | Yes | Yes | Yes |

**Table 15.1** Configuration Directives *(cont.)*

| Directive | Type | Default Value | ini_set | .htaccess | httpd.conf |
|---|---|---|---|---|---|
| exif.decode_unicode_intel | Value | UCS-2LE | Yes | Yes | Yes |
| exif.decode_unicode_motorola | Value | UCS-2BE | Yes | Yes | Yes |
| exif.encode_jis | Value | NULL | Yes | Yes | Yes |
| exif.encode_unicode | Value | ISO-8859-15 | Yes | Yes | Yes |
| expose_php | Flag | On | No | No | Yes |
| extension | Value | NULL | No | No | Yes |
| extension_dir | Value | usr/local/lib/php/ extensions/no-debug-non-zts-20020429 on UNIX or c:\php4\extensions on Windows | No | No | Yes |
| extname.global_string | Value | foobar | Yes | Yes | Yes |
| extname.global_value | Value | 42 | Yes | Yes | Yes |
| file_uploads | Flag | On | No | No | Yes |
| gpc_order | Value | GPC | Yes | Yes | Yes |
| highlight.bg | Value | HL_BG_COLOR | Yes | Yes | Yes |
| highlight.comment | Value | HL_COMMENT_COLOR | Yes | Yes | Yes |
| highlight.default | Value | HL_DEFAULT_COLOR | Yes | Yes | Yes |
| highlight.html | Value | HL_HTML_COLOR | Yes | Yes | Yes |
| highlight.keyword | Value | HL_KEYWORD_COLOR | Yes | Yes | Yes |
| highlight.string | Value | HL_STRING_COLOR | Yes | Yes | Yes |
| html_errors | Flag | On | No | No | Yes |
| iconv.input_encoding | Value | ICONV_INPUT_ENCODING | Yes | Yes | Yes |
| iconv.internal_encoding | Value | ICONV_INTERNAL_ENCODING | Yes | Yes | Yes |
| iconv.output_encoding | Value | ICONV_OUTPUT_ENCODING | Yes | Yes | Yes |
| ignore_repeated_errors | Flag | Off | Yes | Yes | Yes |

**Table 15.1** Configuration Directives *(cont.)*

| Directive | Type | Default Value | ini_set | .htaccess | httpd.conf |
|---|---|---|---|---|---|
| ignore_repeated_source | Flag | Off | Yes | Yes | Yes |
| ignore_user_abort | Flag | Off | Yes | Yes | Yes |
| implicit_flush | Flag | Off | No | Yes | Yes |
| include_path | Value | PHP_INCLUDE_PATH | Yes | Yes | Yes |
| java.class.path | Value | NULL | Yes | Yes | Yes |
| java.home | Value | NULL | Yes | Yes | Yes |
| java.library | Value | jvm.dll | Yes | Yes | Yes |
| java.library.path | Value | NULL | Yes | Yes | Yes |
| last_modified | Flag | Off | Yes | Yes | Yes |
| ldap.max_links | Value | -1 | No | No | Yes |
| log_errors | Flag | Off | Yes | Yes | Yes |
| log_errors_max_len | Value | 1024 | Yes | Yes | Yes |
| magic_quotes_gpc | Flag | On | No | Yes | Yes |
| magic_quotes_runtime | Flag | Off | Yes | Yes | Yes |
| magic_quotes_sybase | Flag | Off | Yes | Yes | Yes |
| max_execution_time | Value | 30 | Yes | Yes | Yes |
| max_input_time | Value | -1 | No | Yes | Yes |
| mbstring.detect_order | Value | NULL | Yes | Yes | Yes |
| mbstring.encoding_translation | Flag | Off | No | Yes | Yes |
| mbstring.func_overload | Flag | Off | No | No | Yes |
| mbstring.http_input | Value | NULL | Yes | Yes | Yes |
| mbstring.http_output | Value | NULL | Yes | Yes | Yes |
| mbstring.internal_encoding | Value | NULL | Yes | Yes | Yes |
| mbstring.language | Value | neutral | No | Yes | Yes |

**Table 15.1** Configuration Directives *(cont.)*

| Directive | Type | Default Value | ini_set | .htaccess | httpd.conf |
|---|---|---|---|---|---|
| mbstring.substitute_character | Value | NULL | Yes | Yes | Yes |
| mcrypt.algorithms_dir | Value | NULL | Yes | Yes | Yes |
| mcrypt.modes_dir | Value | NULL | Yes | Yes | Yes |
| memory_limit | Value | 8M | Yes | Yes | Yes |
| mime_magic.magicfile | Value | /usr/share/misc/magic.mime | No | No | Yes |
| mssql.allow_persistent | Flag | On | No | No | Yes |
| mssql.batchsize | Flag | Off | Yes | Yes | Yes |
| mssql.connect_timeout | Value | 5 | Yes | Yes | Yes |
| mssql.datetimeconvert | Flag | On | Yes | Yes | Yes |
| mssql.max_links | Value | -1 | No | No | Yes |
| mssql.max_persistent | Value | -1 | No | No | Yes |
| mssql.max_procs | Value | 25 | Yes | Yes | Yes |
| mssql.min_error_severity | Value | 10 | Yes | Yes | Yes |
| mssql.min_message_severity | Value | 10 | Yes | Yes | Yes |
| mssql.textlimit | Value | -1 | Yes | Yes | Yes |
| mssql.textsize | Value | -1 | Yes | Yes | Yes |
| mssql.timeout | Value | 60 | Yes | Yes | Yes |
| mysql.allow_persistent | Flag | On | No | No | Yes |
| mysql.connect_timeout | Value | -1 | No | No | No |
| mysql.default_host | Value | NULL | Yes | Yes | Yes |
| mysql.default_password | Value | NULL | Yes | Yes | Yes |
| mysql.default_port | Value | NULL | Yes | Yes | Yes |
| mysql.default_socket | Value | NULL | Yes | Yes | Yes |
| mysql.default_user | Value | NULL | Yes | Yes | Yes |

**Table 15.1** Configuration Directives *(cont.)*

| Directive | Type | Default Value | ini_set | .htaccess | httpd.conf |
|---|---|---|---|---|---|
| mysql.max_links | Value | -1 | No | No | Yes |
| mysql.max_persistent | Value | -1 | No | No | Yes |
| mysql.trace_mode | Flag | Off | Yes | Yes | Yes |
| odbc.allow_persistent | Flag | On | No | No | Yes |
| odbc.check_persistent | Flag | On | No | No | Yes |
| odbc.defaultbinmode | Flag | On | Yes | Yes | Yes |
| odbc.defaultlrl | Value | 4096 | Yes | Yes | Yes |
| odbc.max_links | Value | -1 | No | No | Yes |
| odbc.max_persistent | Value | -1 | No | No | Yes |
| open_basedir | Value | NULL | No | No | Yes |
| output_buffering | Flag | Off | No | Yes | Yes |
| output_handler | Value | NULL | No | Yes | Yes |
| pfpro.defaulthost | Value | test-payflow.verisign.com | Yes | Yes | Yes |
| pfpro.defaultport | Value | 443 | Yes | Yes | Yes |
| pfpro.defaulttimeout | Value | 30 | Yes | Yes | Yes |
| pfpro.proxyaddress | Value | NULL | Yes | Yes | Yes |
| pfpro.proxylogon | Value | NULL | Yes | Yes | Yes |
| pfpro.proxypassword | Value | NULL | Yes | Yes | Yes |
| pfpro.proxyport | Value | NULL | Yes | Yes | Yes |
| pgsql.allow_persistent | Flag | On | No | No | Yes |
| pgsql.auto_reset_persistent | Flag | Off | No | No | Yes |
| pgsql.ignore_notice | Flag | Off | Yes | Yes | Yes |
| pgsql.log_notice | Flag | Off | Yes | Yes | Yes |
| pgsql.max_links | Value | -1 | No | No | Yes |

**Table 15.1** Configuration Directives *(cont.)*

| Directive | Type | Default Value | ini_set | .htaccess | httpd.conf |
|---|---|---|---|---|---|
| pgsql.max_persistent | Value | -1 | No | No | Yes |
| post_max_size | Value | 8M | No | No | Yes |
| precision | Value | 14 | Yes | Yes | Yes |
| register_argc_argv | Flag | On | No | Yes | Yes |
| register_globals | Flag | Off | No | Yes | Yes |
| report_memleaks | Flag | On | Yes | Yes | Yes |
| report_zend_debug | Flag | On | Yes | Yes | Yes |
| safe_mode | Flag | Off | No | No | Yes |
| safe_mode_allowed_env_vars | Value | PHP_ | No | No | Yes |
| safe_mode_exec_dir | Flag | On | No | No | Yes |
| safe_mode_gid | Flag | Off | No | No | Yes |
| safe_mode_include_dir | Value | NULL | No | No | Yes |
| safe_mode_protected_env_vars | Value | LD_LIBRARY_PATH | No | No | Yes |
| sendmail_from | Value | NULL | Yes | Yes | Yes |
| sendmail_path | Value | sendmail -t -i | No | No | Yes |
| session.auto_start | Flag | Off | Yes | Yes | Yes |
| session.bug_compat_42 | Flag | On | Yes | Yes | Yes |
| session.bug_compat_warn | Flag | On | Yes | Yes | Yes |
| session.cache_expire | Value | 180 | Yes | Yes | Yes |
| session.cache_limiter | Value | nocache | Yes | Yes | Yes |
| session.cookie_domain | Value | NULL | Yes | Yes | Yes |
| session.cookie_lifetime | Flag | Off | Yes | Yes | Yes |
| session.cookie_path | Value | / | Yes | Yes | Yes |
| session.cookie_secure | Value | NULL | Yes | Yes | Yes |

**Table 15.1**   Configuration Directives *(cont.)*

| Directive | Type | Default Value | ini_set | .htaccess | httpd.conf |
|---|---|---|---|---|---|
| session.entropy_file | Value | NULL | Yes | Yes | Yes |
| session.entropy_length | Flag | Off | Yes | Yes | Yes |
| session.gc_dividend | Value | 100 | Yes | Yes | Yes |
| session.gc_maxlifetime | Value | 1440 | Yes | Yes | Yes |
| session.gc_probability | Flag | On | Yes | Yes | Yes |
| session.name | Value | PHPSESSID | Yes | Yes | Yes |
| session.referer_check | Value | NULL | Yes | Yes | Yes |
| session.save_handler | Value | files | Yes | Yes | Yes |
| session.save_path | Value | /tmp | Yes | Yes | Yes |
| session.serialize_handler | Value | php | Yes | Yes | Yes |
| session.use_cookies | Flag | On | Yes | Yes | Yes |
| session.use_only_cookies | Flag | Off | Yes | Yes | Yes |
| session.use_trans_sid | Flag | On | No | Yes | Yes |
| short_open_tag | Value | DEFAULT_SHORT_OPEN_TAG | No | Yes | Yes |
| SMTP | Value | localhost | Yes | Yes | Yes |
| smtp_port | Value | 25 | Yes | Yes | Yes |
| sql.safe_mode | Flag | Off | No | No | Yes |
| sybct.allow_persistent | Flag | On | No | No | Yes |
| sybct.hostname | Value | NULL | Yes | Yes | Yes |
| sybct.max_links | Value | -1 | No | No | Yes |
| sybct.max_persistent | Value | -1 | No | No | Yes |
| sybct.min_client_severity | Value | 10 | Yes | Yes | Yes |
| sybct.min_server_severity | Value | 10 | Yes | Yes | Yes |
| sysvshm.init_mem | Value | 10000 | No | Yes | Yes |

**Table 15.1**   Configuration Directives *(cont.)*

| Directive | Type | Default Value | ini_set | .htaccess | httpd.conf |
|---|---|---|---|---|---|
| track_errors | Flag | Off | Yes | Yes | Yes |
| unserialize_callback_func | Value | NULL | Yes | Yes | Yes |
| upload_max_filesize | Value | 2M | No | No | Yes |
| upload_tmp_dir | Value | NULL | No | No | Yes |
| url_rewriter.tags | Value | a=href,area=href, frame=src, form=fakeentry | Yes | Yes | Yes |
| user_agent | Value | NULL | Yes | Yes | Yes |
| user_dir | Value | NULL | No | No | Yes |
| variables_order | Value | NULL | Yes | Yes | Yes |
| xbithack | Flag | Off | Yes | Yes | Yes |
| xmlrpc_error_number | Flag | Off | Yes | Yes | Yes |
| xmlrpc_errors | Flag | Off | No | No | Yes |
| y2k_compliance | Flag | Off | Yes | Yes | Yes |
| zlib.output_compression | Flag | Off | No | Yes | Yes |
| zlib.output_compression_level | Value | -1 | Yes | Yes | Yes |
| zlib.output_handler | Value | NULL | Yes | Yes | Yes |

### allow_call_time_pass_reference
Historically, PHP supported passing variable references to functions by prepending an ampersand (&) in the call. This behavior was abandoned for using ampersands in function definitions. If this directive is on, PHP issues a warning when you force a reference in a function call. If off, PHP issues an error.

### allow_url_fopen
This directive activates the use of URLs in fopen calls and similar functions.

## allow_webdav_methods

When activated, this directive causes PHP to process WebDAV requests. If you wish to process the contents of the request, be sure to turn on `always_populate_raw_post_data`.

## always_populate_raw_post_data

PHP sets a global variable named `HTTP_RAW_POST_DATA` when this directive is on and the request includes `Post` method data.

## arg_separator.input

This directive sets the characters used by PHP to separate fields in an HTTP request. For example, `x = 1 & y = 2` uses ampersands, as is the usual case. PHP uses each character you supply to this directive as a possible field separator.

## arg_separator.output

When PHP generates URLs, it uses the value of this directive to separate field values.

## asp_tags

This directive controls whether PHP allows `<%` and `%>` for surrounding code.

## assert.active

This controls whether you may use the `assert` function. Common wisdom suggests that if you use assertions, you keep this value on while developing a site and off when the application runs in production.

## assert.bail

This controls whether PHP stops executing a script if an assertion fails.

## assert.callback

Set this directive to the name of a user-defined function to be called when an assertion fails.

## assert.quiet_eval

If this directive is on, PHP turns off error reporting before testing an assertion, then restores error reporting afterwards.

## assert.warning

If this directive is on, PHP creates a warning for every failed assertion.

### auto_append_file

Set this directive with the path to a PHP script that PHP executes when a requested script finished unless the script ends in error or by the `exit` function.

### auto_detect_line_endings

If this directive is on, PHP will automatically detect appropriate line endings of a file read with `fgets` or `file`.

### auto_prepend_file

Set this directive with the path to a PHP script that PHP executes before a requested script.

### browscap

Set this directive with the path to a `browscap.ini` file.

### child_terminate

This directive is for Apache on UNIX only. If turned on, PHP will terminate Apache's child process after finishing the request. This may be useful for PHP scripts that use large amounts of memory that won't return to the operating system until the child process ends.

### com.allow_dcom

If this directive is turned on, PHP allows calls to distributed COM objects in the COM extension.

### com.autoregister_casesensitive

If this directive is turned on, PHP constants registered in the COM extension are case-sensitive.

### com.autoregister_typelib

If this directive is turned on, PHP automatically registers constants when you call `com_load`.

### com.autoregister_verbose

If this directive is turned on, PHP shows warnings when registering COM constants with duplicate names.

### com.typelib_file

Set this directive with the path to a file containing GUIDs, IIDs, or filenames of files with TypeLibs used by the COM extension.

### crack.default_dictionary

Use this directive to set the path to a default dictionary used by the crack extension.

### dbx.colnames_case

This directive controls how the DBX extension changes column names returned by queries. The value should be `unchanged`, `lowercase`, or `uppercase`. Respectively, these make PHP leave the column names unchanged, convert to all lowercase, or convert to all uppercase.

### default_charset

Use this directive to set the character set sent in the HTTP Content-type header.

### default_mimetype

Use this directive to set the MIME type sent in the HTTP Content-type header.

### default_socket_timeout

Set this directive to the number of seconds to wait before a socket stream aborts.

### define_syslog_variables

If this directive is turned on, PHP automatically creates the syslog variables you can create manually with `define_syslog_variables`.

### disable_functions

Set this directive with a comma-separated list of functions to disable.

### display_errors

If this directive is turned on, PHP sends error messages to the browser. Common wisdom suggests that error messages be on during development and off after a site goes live.

### display_startup_errors

If turned on, PHP sends errors encountered during startup to the browser.

### doc_root

Use this directive to force a document root. This is recommended when running PHP as a CGI.

### docref_ext

If the `html_errors` directive is on, PHP error messages contain references to the online PHP manual. PHP constructs the links by adding an extension to the function name. This directive sets the extension.

### docref_root

This directive sets the path to the PHP manual used when `html_errors` is on.

### enable_dl

When this directive is turned on, PHP allows loading extensions with `dl`.

### engine

This directive allows you to turn off the PHP engine in Apache.

### error_append_string

Use this directive to append a string to the end of every error message PHP generates. You can use it to decorate error messages with HTML.

### error_log

Set this directive with a path to which PHP will write all error messages. You must turn on error logging with `log_errors`.

### error_prepend_string

Use this directive to print a string before every error message.

### error_reporting

Use this directive to set which errors are reported by PHP when `display_errors` is on. Use the constants in Table 15.2 to set the types of errors PHP reports. You may use bitwise operators to combine these constants, if you wish. For example, you may activate all errors messages except for notices by using `E_ALL & ~E_NOTICE & ~E_USER_NOTICE`.

Constants are not available in `httpd.conf` and `.htaccess`. If you wish to change error reporting in these files, use the numeric values and do the math by hand.

**Table 15.2** Error Levels

| Constant | Numeric Value | Description |
|---|---|---|
| E_ALL | 2047 | All errors and warnings |
| E_COMPILE_ERROR | 64 | Fatal compile-time errors |
| E_COMPILE_WARNING | 128 | Compile-time warnings |
| E_CORE_ERROR | 16 | Fatal initialization errors |
| E_CORE_WARNING | 32 | Initialization warnings |
| E_ERROR | 1 | Fatal runtime errors |
| E_NOTICE | 8 | Runtime notices |
| E_PARSE | 4 | Parse errors |
| E_USER_ERROR | 256 | User-generated error |
| E_USER_NOTICE | 1024 | User-generated notice |
| E_USER_WARNING | 512 | User-generated warning |
| E_WARNING | 2 | Runtime warnings |

### exif.decode_jis_intel
Use this directive to set the character set used to decode exif messages for Intel byte-order JIS messages.

### exif.decode_jis_motorola
Use this directive to set the character set used to decode exif messages for Motorola byte-order JIS messages.

### exif.decode_unicode_intel
Use this directive to set the character set used to decode exif messages for Intel byte-order UNICODE messages.

### exif.decode_unicode_motorola
Use this directive to set the character set used to decode exif messages for Motorola byte-order UNICODE messages.

### exif.encode_jis
Use this directive to set the character set used to encode JIS exif messages.

### exif.encode_unicode

Use this directive to set the character set used to encode UNICODE exif messages.

### expose_php

Use this directive to control whether PHP adds its signature to the `Server` header. For example, Apache might identify itself as `Apache/1.3.26 (Unix) PHP/5.0.0 mod_ssl/2.8.10 OpenSSL/0.9.6b`. Letting people know you have PHP installed is not a security issue, but it is a way to help promote PHP. One way to judge the popularity of a Web technology is by counting responses by Web servers.

### extension

Use this directive to load an extension. Repeat this directive to load multiple extensions.

### extension_dir

Use this directive to set the path where PHP looks for extensions. Paths are relative to the location of the PHP executable. For example, using `./` on a typical Windows install would cause PHP to look for extensions in the directory where you installed `php.exe`. It's better to use an absolute path, such as `C:\php5\extensions`.

### file_uploads

Use this directive to control whether PHP scripts can accept HTTP uploads.

### highlight.bg

This directive allows you to set the background color used for syntax highlighting.

### highlight.comment

This directive allows you to set the color used for comments for syntax highlighting.

### highlight.default

This directive allows you to set the default code color used for syntax highlighting.

### highlight.html

This directive allows you to set the color used for HTML for syntax highlighting.

### highlight.keyword

This directive allows you to set the color used for PHP keywords for syntax highlighting.

### highlight.string

This directive allows you to set the color used for string literals for syntax highlighting.

### html_errors

Use this directive to control whether PHP decorates error messages with HTML and links to the online manual or not.

### iconv.input_encoding

Use this directive to set the input encoding used by the iconv extension.

### iconv.internal_encoding

Use this directive to set the internal encoding used by the iconv extension.

### iconv.output_encoding

Use this directive to set the output encoding used by the iconv extension.

### ignore_repeated_errors

When this directive is on, PHP ignores duplicate errors generated by the same line of source. For example, a bug inside a loop will often generate a page full of the same error message. This directive helps keep the page short.

### ignore_repeated_source

This directive has meaning only when `ignore_repeated_errors` is on. It forces PHP to ignore any error message that matches a previous error message, regardless of file or line number.

### ignore_user_abort

When this directive is on, PHP continues to execute a script after a client aborts the connection.

### implicit_flush

Use this directive to force PHP to flush the output buffer with every print operation. This includes blocks of HTML outside of PHP tags. For performance reasons, it's best to leave this directive off during production.

### include_path

Use this directive to set the directories in which PHP looks for files when you use `include` and similar statements. For UNIX, separate any number of paths with colons, such as `.:/usr/local/lib/php/myincludes`. For Windows, use semicolons, such as `.;C:\php\includes`.

### java.class.path

Use this directive to set the path containing your compiled classes, including PHP's `php_java.jar`. On Windows, this could be `C:\php5\extensions\php_java.jar`, depending on where you installed PHP.

### java.home

Set this directive to the JDK binaries path. On Windows, this could be `C:\j2sdk1.4.1_01\jre\bin`, depending on where you installed Java.

### java.library

Set this directive with the path to the JVM library. On Windows, this could be `C:\j2sdk1.4.1_01\jre\bin\client\jvm.dll`, depending on where you installed Java.

### java.library.path

Set this directive with the path to the Java extension. On Windows, this could be `C:\PHP4\extensions`, depending on where you installed PHP.

### last_modified

If this directive is on, PHP uses the modification time of the requested script in the HTTP `Last-modified` header. Otherwise, the header is not sent.

### ldap.max_links

Use this directive to set the maximum number of links the LDAP extension follows. Setting it to –1 imposes no limit.

### log_errors

Use this directive to make PHP write errors to a file. Set the path to the error log with `error_log`.

### log_errors_max_len

This directive sets a maximum length for error messages written to a file. Use a value of 0 to impose no limit.

**magic_quotes_gpc**

When this directive is on, PHP adds backslashes to quote characters in user input.

**magic_quotes_runtime**

When this directive is on, PHP adds backslashes to quote characters data from external sources, such as databases.

**magic_quotes_sybase**

When this directive is on, PHP uses `''` instead of `\'` when escaping single quotes.

**max_execution_time**

This directive controls how many seconds PHP allows a script to execute before halting it.

**max_input_time**

This directive controls how many seconds PHP spends parsing input data before halting.

**mbstring.detect_order**

This directive sets the order in which the mbstring extension detects character sets.

**mbstring.encoding_translation**

When this directive is turned on, PHP detects input encoding and translates text into internal encoding.

**mbstring.func_overload**

This directive expects a bitfield that controls whether the mbstring extension overloads any of three groups of functions with its own set. Use 1 for overloading mail. Use 2 for overloading string functions. Use 4 to overload regular expression functions. Add numbers together to overload more than one group.

**mbstring.http_input**

Set this directive with the encoding for user input.

**mbstring.http_output**

Set this directive with the encoding for text sent to the browser.

### mbstring.internal_encoding
Set this directive with the encoding used internally.

### mbstring.language
Use this directive to set the default language used by the mbstring extension. This directive also sets the appropriate internal encoding.

### mbstring.substitute_character
Use this directive to set the character used to substitute for characters that can't be translated.

### mcrypt.algorithms_dir
Set this directive with the path to mcrypt algorithms, such as `/usr/local/lib/libmcrypt`.

### mcrypt.modes_dir
Set this directive with the path to mcrypt modes.

### memory_limit
Use this directive to set the maximum amount of memory PHP allocates before halting. You can specify the value in bytes, suffix the value with K for kilobytes, or suffix the value with M for megabytes.

### mime_magic.magicfile
Use this directive to set the path to the file used for detecting the MIME type of a file.

### mssql.allow_persistent
When this directive is on, PHP uses persistent connections for MS SQL Server.

### mssql.batchsize
This directive allows you to limit the number of records fetched in an MS SQL Server query.

### mssql.connect_timeout
Set this directive with the number of seconds to wait to establish a connection to MS SQL Server.

### mssql.datetimeconvert
If this directive is on, PHP converts MS SQL Server datetime columns into a regular format: Year-Month-Day Hour:Minute:Second.

### mssql.max_links

This directive sets the maximum number of connections to MS SQL Servers.

### mssql.max_persistent

This directive sets the maximum number of persistent connections to MS SQL Servers.

### mssql.max_procs

This directive sets the maximum number of processes for MS SQL Server connections.

### mssql.min_error_severity

This directive sets the minimum severity of error generated by MS SQL Server connections.

### mssql.min_message_severity

This directive sets the minimum severity of messages generated by MS SQL Server connections.

### mssql.textlimit

This directive sets the maximum value for MS SQL Server's SET TEXTSIZE statement or the `mssql.textsize` directive.

### mssql.textsize

This directive sets the maximum length of a field returned in a MS SQL Server query.

### mssql.timeout

This directive set the maximum number of seconds PHP waits for a MS SQL Server query to finish.

### mysql.allow_persistent

When this directive is on, PHP uses persistent connections for MySQL.

### mysql.connect_timeout

This directive sets the maximum number of seconds PHP waits to make a connection to MySQL.

### mysql.default_host

This directive sets the default MySQL host.

### mysql.default_password
This directive sets the default MySQL password.

### mysql.default_port
This directive sets the default MySQL port.

### mysql.default_socket
This directive sets the default MySQL socket path.

### mysql.default_user
This directive sets the default MySQL user.

### mysql.max_links
This directive sets the maximum number of connections to MySQL.

### mysql.max_persistent
This directive sets the maximum number of persistent connections to MySQL.

### mysql.trace_mode
This directive activates warnings generated by MySQL.

### odbc.allow_persistent
When this directive is on, PHP uses persistent connections for ODBC.

### odbc.check_persistent
When this directive is on, PHP checks that a persistent connection is still good.

### odbc.defaultbinmode
When this directive is set to 0, PHP sends binary data straight to the browser. When it's 1, it returns binary data unchanged. When it's 2, PHP returns a string of hexadecimal numbers.

### odbc.defaultlrl
This directive sets a limit on the number of bytes returned from a `longvarbinary` column. If you set it to 0, PHP sends the entire column directly to the browser.

### odbc.max_links
Use this directive to set the maximum number of connections to an ODBC database. Use –1 to set no limit.

### odbc.max_persistent

Use this directive to set the maximum number of persistent connections to an ODBC database.

### open_basedir

The `open_basedir` directive sets a top-level directory for PHP. Scripts cannot access directives above this base directory.

### output_buffering

The `output_buffering` directive may be set to `on` or `off`, or you may set it with a buffer size.

### output_handler

Use this directive to set the output buffering handler.

### pfpro.defaulthost

Use this directive to set the default host for PayFlow connections.

### pfpro.defaultport

Use this directive to set the default port for PayFlow connections.

### pfpro.defaulttimeout

Use this directive to set the maximum number of seconds to wait for a PayFlow connection.

### pfpro.proxyaddress

Use this directive to set the proxy address for PayFlow connections.

### pfpro.proxylogon

Use this directive to set the logon identifier for the PayFlow proxy.

### pfpro.proxypassword

Use this directive to set the password for the PayFlow proxy.

### pfpro.proxyport

Use this directive to set the PayFlow proxy port number.

### pgsql.allow_persistent

When this directive is on, PHP uses persistent connections for PostgreSQL.

### pgsql.auto_reset_persistent

When this directive is on, PHP checks that a persistent connection is still good.

### pgsql.ignore_notice

When turned on, this directive tells PHP to ignore notices from the PostgreSQL server.

### pgsql.log_notice

When turned on, this directive tells PHP to log notices from the PostgreSQL server.

### pgsql.max_links

Use this directive to set the maximum number of connections to a PostgreSQL database. Use –1 to set no limit.

### pgsql.max_persistent

Use this directive to set the maximum number of persistent connections to a PostgreSQL database.

### post_max_size

Use this directive to set a maximum size for data send via the POST method.

### precision

Use this directive to set the number of significant digits shown for floating-point numbers.

### register_argc_argv

When on, this directive instructs PHP to create the `argc` and `argv` variables.

### register_globals

When `register_globals` is on, PHP creates a global variable for every form field and cookie. Generally, this is considered a security risk because users can send variables that override other global variables. Use the `$_REQUEST` array instead.

### report_memleaks

When compiled in debug mode, PHP displays warnings about memory leaks when this directive is on.

### report_zend_debug

When compiled in debug mode, PHP displays debug information about the Zend Engine when this directive is on.

### safe_mode

This directive controls whether or not PHP operates in safe mode.

### safe_mode_allowed_env_vars

When safe mode is active, this directive restricts access to environment variables that begin with a given set of prefixes. Set this directive with any number of prefixes separated with commas.

### safe_mode_exec_dir

When safe mode is active, PHP scripts may only execute shell commands that are in the given path.

### safe_mode_gid

In safe mode, PHP allows access to files owned by the user running the script. When `safe_mode_gid` is on, PHP only requires the group to match.

### safe_mode_include_dir

In safe mode, PHP scripts may bypass UID or GID restrictions if including files from the path given by this directive.

### safe_mode_protected_env_vars

Set this directive with a list of environment variables that may not be set when in safe mode.

### sendmail_from

For Win32 systems, this directive sets the value of the `From` header sent with the `mail` function.

### sendmail_path

For UNIX systems, this directive sets the path to the `sendmail` executable. You may include parameters too.

### session.auto_start

When this directive is on, PHP starts a session for every request.

### session.bug_compat_42

This directive controls whether PHP allows the bug that appeared in PHP 4.2 and earlier that allowed creating variables in the global scope even when `register_globals` is off.

### session.bug_compat_warn

When this directive is on, PHP issues a warning if a script exploits the bug from PHP 4.2 and earlier that allows creation of global variables when `register_globals` is off.

### session.cache_expire

Use this directive to set the lifetime for document.

### session.cache_limiter

This directive may be blank or set to one of the following strings: `nocache`, `private`, `private_no_expire`, `public`. This controls how the session handler attempts to control caching of pages. See Chapter 8's discussion of `session_cache_limiter` for a description of these options.

### session.cookie_domain

Use this directive to set the domain for the session identifier cookie.

### session.cookie_lifetime

Use this directive to set the lifetime of the session identifier cookie.

### session.cookie_path

Use this directive to set the path of the session identifier cookie.

### session.cookie_secure

Use this directive to set whether the session identifier cookie requires a secure connection.

### session.entropy_file

Set this directive with the path to a file for providing extra randomness to the process of creating a session identifier. Typically, this would be `/dev/random` or `/dev/urandom`.

### session.entropy_length

Set this directive with the number of bytes to read from the file specified by `session.entropy_file`.

### session.gc_dividend

Use this directive with `session.gc_probability` to set the chance that PHP performs garbage collection on sessions. PHP calculates the chance as `session.gc_probability / session.gc_dividend`.

### session.gc_maxlifetime

If a session records no activity for the given number of seconds, PHP nominates it for garbage collection. When using the files handler, this directive may not work on Win32 or when using subdirectories.

### session.gc_probability

Use this directive with `session.gc_dividend` to set the chance that PHP performs garbage collection on sessions.

### session.name

Use this directive to set the name of the cookie or form field used for the session identifier.

### session.referer_check

Set this directive with a substring that must appear in the `Referer` header.

### session.save_handler

This directive sets the handler for sessions.

### session.save_path

This directive sets the path used by the session handler. For the files handler, this is a path in the file system for keeping session files. In this case, you may prefix the path with an integer and a semicolon. This causes PHP to split sessions between subdirectories. You must create these subdirectories yourself.

### session.serialize_handler

Use this directive to set the handler PHP uses to serialize session data.

### session.use_cookies

When this directive is on, PHP uses cookies to pass the session identifier between client and server.

### session.use_only_cookies

When this directive is on, PHP uses cookies exclusively to pass the session identifier.

### session.use_trans_sid

When turned on, this directive causes PHP to alter URLs in your documents to include the session identifier.

### short_open_tag

Use this directive to control whether PHP recognizes the short opening tag, (<?).

### SMTP

For Win32 systems only, this directive points to the host that accepts outgoing mail.

### smtp_port

This directive allows you to change the port used for outgoing SMTP mail on Win32 systems.

### sql.safe_mode

When `sql.safe_mode` is on, PHP does not allow scripts to set the host, username, or password for MySQL connections.

### sybct.allow_persistent

When this directive is on, PHP uses persistent connections for Sybase.

### sybct.hostname

Set this directive to the default Sybase database server host.

### sybct.max_links

Use this directive to set the maximum number of connections to a Sybase database. Use –1 to set no limit.

### sybct.max_persistent

Use this directive to set the maximum number of persistent connections to a Sybase database.

### sybct.min_client_severity

Use this directive to set the minimum severity for client messages reported as PHP warnings.

### sybct.min_server_severity

Use this directive to set the minimum severity for server messages reported as PHP warnings.

### sysvshm.init_mem
Use this directive to set the default number of bytes allocated by `shm_attach`.

### track_errors
If this directive is on, PHP stores the last error message in the global variable `php_errormsg`.

### unserialize_callback_func
Use this directive to set a function PHP calls when unserializing an object of a class it doesn't recognize. The function accepts a single argument, the name of the class. This allows you to define the class just in time.

### upload_max_filesize
This directive allows you to set the maximum size for uploaded files.

### upload_tmp_dir
Use this directive to set the path used to store uploaded files.

### url_rewriter.tags
This directive sets the tags and attributes that PHP alters to include session identifiers. Set it with a comma-separated list of tag/attribute pairs. Separate the tag from the attribute with an equal sign (`=`).

### user_agent
When making HTTP connections with fopen wrappers, PHP uses this directive for the `User-agent` header.

### user_dir
When a script uses a path like `/~username`, PHP uses this directive to find the appropriate directory.

### variables_order
Use this directive to set the order in which PHP creates entries in `_REQUEST` and variables in the global scope when `register_globals` is on. The value should be letters EGPCS, which stand for environment, GET, POST, Cookie, and System respectively. Data sources are processed from left to right, with duplicate names overwriting previous values.

### xbithack
This directive applies to Apache only. When it's on and a text/html file has its execute bit set, the file is parsed as a PHP script.

### xmlrpc_error_number

Set this directive with the value for `faultCode` passed in XML-RPC error messages when `xmlrpc_errors` is on.

### xmlrpc_errors

When this directive is on, PHP returns error messages as valid XML-RPC.

### y2k_compliance

This directive controls whether dates sent in HTTP headers are Y2K-compliant.

### zlib.output_compression

This directive allows you to turn on transparent output compression. In addition to being on or off, you can set this directive with a buffer size.

### zlib.output_compression_level

This directive sets the compression level used by the zlib compression library.

### zlib.output_handler

This directive allows you to specify additional output handlers that run before output passes through zlib compression.

## 15.2  Configuration

The following functions affect the operation of PHP. Some of them alter configuration variables. Others cause a script to stop executing for a period.

### boolean bcscale(integer scale)

The `bcscale` function (Listing 15.1) sets the default scale for the functions that perform math on arbitrary-precision numbers. The scale is the number of digits after the decimal point. See the section on arbitrary-precision numbers in Chapter 13.

| Listing 15.1 | *bcscale* |
|---|---|

```php
<?php
    //use ten digits
    bcscale(10);
?>
```

### clearstatcache()

Calling C's `stat` function (Listing 15.2) may take a considerable amount of time. To increase performance, PHP caches the results of each call. When you use a function that relies on `stat`, the information from the cache is returned. If information about a file changes often, you may need to clear the stat cache.

The functions that use the stat cache are `fileatime`, `filectime`, `filegroup`, `fileinode`, `filemtime`, `fileowner`, `fileperms`, `filesize`, `filetype`, `file_exists`, `is_dir`, `is_executable`, `is_file`, `is_link`, `is_readable`, `is_writable`, `lstat`, `stat`.

**Listing 15.2**   *clearstatcache*

```php
<?php
    //make sure info isn't cached
    clearstatcache();

    //get size of this file
    print(filesize(__FILE__));
?>
```

### define_syslog_variables()

The `define_syslog_variables` function (Listing 15.3) emulates the configuration directive of the same name. It causes the constants for use with the system log to be created as variables. The functions that interact with the system log are `closelog`, `openlog`, and `syslog`.

**Listing 15.3**   *define_syslog_variables*

```php
<?php
    define_syslog_variables();
?>
```

### boolean dl(string extension)

Use the `dl` function to load a dynamic extension module. The function returns FALSE if the module could not be loaded. The path to these modules is set in `php.ini`, so you need type only the name of the module file. On UNIX, these end in `.so`. On Windows, they end in `.dll`.

The `dl` function does not function when PHP executes as a module to a multi-threaded Web server such as Apache2. If you use loadable extensions, it's best to load them inside `php.ini` with the `extension` directive.

### integer error_reporting(integer level)

The `error_reporting` function (Listing 15.4) sets the level of error reporting and returns the previous value. The `level` argument is a bitfield. Use the bitwise-OR operator ( | ) to put together the type of error reporting you would like. This function mirrors the directive of the same name. Refer to Table 15.2 for error level codes.

---

**Listing 15.4**    *error_reporting*

```php
<?php
    //start with all but notices
    error_reporting(E_ALL & ~E_NOTICE);

    //empty variable, but no notice
    print($empty_variable);

    //add notices to current setting
    error_reporting(error_reporting() | E_NOTICE);

    //empty variable, notice message
    print($empty_variable);
?>
```

---

### string get_include_path()

The `get_include_path` function returns the current setting for the `include_path` directive.

### boolean iconv_set_encoding(string type, string character_set)

Use the `iconv_set_encoding` function to set encoding used by the iconv extension for one of three types: `input_encoding`, `internal_encoding`, `output_encoding`. You can get the current character set with `iconv_get_encoding`.

### boolean ignore_user_abort(boolean ignore)

Calling `ignore_user_abort` (Listing 15.5) with a TRUE value for the `ignore` argument will cause PHP to continue executing even when the remote client abruptly closes the connection. The previous setting is returned. You may call `ignore_user_abort` with no argument, in which case no change is made.

| Listing 15.5 | *ignore_user_abort* |
|---|---|

```php
<?php
    function fakeProcess($name)
    {
        print("Start of fake process.<br>");
        flush();
        sleep(10);
        print("End of fake process.<br>");

        //write message to log
        $statusMessage = date("Y-m-d H:i:s") .
            " Fake process $name completed\n";
        error_log($statusMessage, 3, "/tmp/status.log");
    }

    //finish script even if user
    //aborts execution
    ignore_user_abort(TRUE);

    fakeProcess("one");

    //allow aborts again
    ignore_user_abort(FALSE);

    fakeProcess("two");
?>
```

### ini_alter

This is an alias to ini_set.

### string ini_get(string directive)

The ini_get function (Listing 15.6) returns the value of one of the directives described earlier in this chapter.

| Listing 15.6 | *ini_get* |
|---|---|

```php
<?php
    //see what SMTP is now
    print(ini_get("SMTP") . "<br>");

    //change to bogus value
    ini_alter("SMTP", "mail.corephp.com");
    print(ini_get("SMTP") . "<br>");
```

---

| Listing 15.6 | *ini_get (cont.)* |
|---|---|

```
    //return to original
    ini_restore("SMTP");
    print(ini_get("SMTP") . "<br>");
?>
```

---

### array ini_get_all(string extension)

The `ini_get_all` function (Listing 15.7) returns an array listing the current settings for configuration directives. The optional extension argument limits the list to directives for a single extension. The returned array contains one element for each directive. The element values are arrays themselves with three entries: `access`, `global_value`, `local_value`. The access level is a bitfield. The first bit is set if you can set the directive in a script. The second bit (2) is set if you can set the directive in `.htaccess` files. The third bit (4) is set if you can set the directive in `httpd.conf`. You can always set a directive in `php.ini`.

---

| Listing 15.7 | *ini_get_all* |
|---|---|

```
<table>
<tr>
<td>Directive</td>
<td>Global</td>
<td>Local</td>
<td>Changeable Here</td>
</tr>
<?php
    foreach(ini_get_all('mysql') as $directive=>$setting)
    {
        print("<tr>");
        print("<td>$directive</td>");
        print("<td>{$setting['global_value']}</td>");
        print("<td>{$setting['local_value']}</td>");

        print("<td>");
        if($setting['access'] & 1)
        {
            print("Yes");
        }
```

| Listing 15.7 | `ini_get_all` (cont.) |
|---|---|

```
    else
    {
        print("No");
    }
    print("</td>");

    print("</tr>\n");
    }
?>
</table>
```

### ini_restore(string directive)

The `ini_restore` function returns the named directive to the value in the `php.ini` file. See `ini_get` for an example of use.

### string ini_set(string directive, string value)

Use `ini_set` to override the value of one of the directives described earlier in this chapter. The setting is for your script only. The file itself is not changed. Keep in mind that some directives may not be set at the script level.

### restore_include_path()

The `restore_include_path` function sets the `include_path` directive to its original value after you've changed it with `set_include_path` or `ini_set`.

### register_shutdown_function(string function)

Use `register_shutdown_function` (Listing 15.8) to cause PHP to execute a function after it has parsed the entire script, including anything outside PHP tags. The shutdown function will also be executed in the event of an error, timeout, or user abort.

Keep in mind that the shutdown function may be called after the connection to the browser has been shut down, in which case using `print` makes little sense. In other words, this isn't a good way to debug.

You may register more than one shutdown function. PHP executes each shutdown function in the order you register them.

**Listing 15.8** `register_shutdown_function`

```php
<?php
    function shutdown()
    {
        error_log('Script terminated', 3, "/tmp/status.log");
    }

    register_shutdown_function("shutdown");
?>
```

### restore_error_handler()

After changing the error handler with `set_error_handler`, the `restore_error_handler` restores the previous error handler.

### restore_exception_handler()

After changing the exception handler with `set_exception_handler`, the `restore_exception_handler` restores the previous error handler.

### string set_error_handler(string function)
### string set_error_handler(array function)

The `set_error_handler` function (Listing 15.9) sets a function that PHP calls when an error occurs and returns the name of the previous error handler, if one existed. PHP calls the error handler with five arguments: error number, description, file path, line number, and context. This last argument is a copy of the GLOBALS array. Alternatively, you may supply a class or object method for the error handler. In this case, use an array with two elements. The first element must be the name of a class or an object. The second element should be the name of the method.

When you set a custom error handler, PHP ignores the `error_reporting` directive and calls your function for every error, warning or notice. If you wish to ignore classes of errors, you must check the value returned by `error_reporting` and react accordingly.

If you wish to restore the default error handler, you can use `restore_error_handler` or you can call `set_error_handler` with NULL.

**Listing 15.9**   *set_error_handler*

```php
<?php
    function handleError($error, $description, $file, $line,
        $context)
    {
        switch($error)
        {
            case E_USER_ERROR:
                $type = "Error";
                $color = "red";
                break;

            case E_WARNING:
            case E_USER_WARNING:
                $type = "Warning";
                $color = "yellow";
                break;

            case E_NOTICE:
            case E_USER_NOTICE:
                $type = "Notice";
                $color = "blue";
                break;

            default:
                $type = "Other Error";
        }

        print("<table border=\"1\"><tr><td bgcolor=\"$color\">" .
            "$type: $description in $file on line $line " .
            "({$context["_SERVER"]["REMOTE_ADDR"]})<br>" .
            "</tr></td></table>");
    }

    //switch to our custom handler
    set_error_handler('handleError');
    trigger_error("Custom error handler", E_USER_WARNING);

    //show PHP's default handler
    restore_error_handler();
    trigger_error("PHP's default error handler", E_USER_WARNING);
?>
```

### set_exception_handler(string function)
### set_exception_handler(array function)

The `set_exception_handler` function sets a function that PHP calls when an exception occurs and returns the name of the previous exception handler. Alternatively, you may supply a class or object method for the error handler. In this case, use an array with two elements. The first element must be the name of a class or an object. The second element should be the name of the method.

### boolean set_include_path(string path)

The `set_include_path` function (Listing 15.10) sets the `include_path` directive. You can also set this directive with `ini_set`.

**Listing 15.10** *set_include_path*

```php
<?php
    //prints something like .:/usr/local/lib/php
    print(get_include_path() . "<br>");

    set_include_path("/home/leon/library");
    print(get_include_path() . "<br>");

    restore_include_path();
    print(get_include_path() . "<br>");
?>
```

### integer set_magic_quotes_runtime(boolean setting)

Use `set_magic_quotes_runtime` (Listing 15.11) to change whether quotes are escaped in data pulled from a database. The original value is returned.

**Listing 15.11** *set_magic_quotes_runtime*

```php
<?php
    //turn off magic_quotes_runtime
    set_magic_quotes_runtime(0);
?>
```

### string setlocale(string category, string locale, ...)

The `setlocale` function (Listing 15.12) modifies the locale information for PHP and returns the new locale specification. FALSE is returned if an error occurs. The locale determines things such as whether to use a comma or a period in floating-point numbers. Locale does not affect how you write PHP scripts, only the output of some functions.

**Listing 15.12** `set_locale`

```php
<?php
    print("Changing to Russian: ");
    print(setlocale(LC_ALL, "russian", "ru_RU.cp1251",
        "ru_RU.koi8r"));
    print("<br>\nDos vedanya!");
?>
```

If the `category` argument is an empty string, the values for the categories will be set from environment variables. If the category argument is zero, the current setting will be returned. Otherwise, choose a category from Table 15.3.

**Table 15.3** Categories for `setlocale`

| Category | Description |
| --- | --- |
| LC_ALL | All aspects of locale |
| LC_COLLATE | Comparison of strings |
| LC_CTYPE | Conversion and classification of characters |
| LC_MONETARY | Monetary formatting |
| LC_NUMERIC | Number separation |
| LC_TIME | Time formatting |

Location codes differ with operation systems. In general, they take the form of `language_country`—that is, a language code followed by an optional underscore and a country code. If you are using Windows, Visual C's help file lists all the languages and countries. You may list multiple location codes to allow PHP to choose the preferred locale.

### set_time_limit(integer seconds)

Use `set_time_limit` (Listing 15.13) to override the default time a script is allowed to run, which is usually set to 30 seconds inside `php.ini`. If this limit is reached, an error occurs and the script stops executing. Setting the seconds argument to zero causes the time limit to be disabled. Each time the `set_time_limit` function is called, the counter is reset to zero. This means that calling `set_time_limit(30)` gives you a fresh 30 seconds of execution time.

Seconds PHP spends waiting during a call to `sleep` or `system` do not count towards the limit.

**Listing 15.13**  `set_time_limit`

```php
<?php
  // allow this script to run forever
  set_time_limit(0);
?>
```

# IMAGES
# AND GRAPHICS

**Topics in This Chapter**

- Analyzing Images
- Creating Images

# Chapter 16

Most of the functions described in this chapter require the gd extension or the `exif` extension. The functions from the `gd` extension begin with image, have no underscores, and require the GD library. The `exif` functions begin with `exif_`.

Other functions in this chapter require the GD library plus one or more additional supporting libraries. For example, in order to read and write JPEG images, you need the JPEG library. Consequently, these functions may not be available to you, depending on how PHP was compiled.

The GD library was created at Boutell.com, a company that has contributed several Open Source tools to the Web community. The library historically supported GIF image creation, but in 1999 this functionality was pulled in favor of PNG format files. The compression algorithm used in GIF creation is patented, which means permission must be granted to software authors who use it. PNG, on the other hand, is an open specification. It also happens to be technically superior to GIF. Support for PNG was added to the fourth generations of the two most popular browsers, Netscape Navigator and Microsoft Internet Explorer, so using PNG is feasible. In early 2000 support for JPEG and WBMP images was added to GD.

In 2002, the GD library lacked attention, while interest from the PHP community continued. In order to keep fixes and improvements flowing, the PHP developers decided to branch the GD library and include it in the PHP project. Although some development occurs in the original GD project, PHP's version includes more functionality. You have the option of not using the built-in version of GD, but there's little reason to do so at the time of writing.

The GD library's home on the Web is <http://www.boutell.com/gd/>. The URL for PNG's home page is <http://www.libpng.org/pub/png/>.

Chapter 25 makes use of the functions in this chapter to explore some practical applications.

# 16.1 Analyzing Images

These functions read information from images.

### integer exif_imagetype(string file)

The exif_imagetype function reads the first few bytes of an image file and returns the type as an integer. Table 16.1 lists image types recognized. If PHP cannot determine the type, it returns FALSE.

**Table 16.1** Image Types

| Constant | Description | File Extension |
|---|---|---|
| IMAGETYPE_BMP | Windows Bitmap | .bmp |
| IMAGETYPE_GIF | Graphic Interchange Format | .gif |
| IMAGETYPE_IFF | Interchange Format Files | .iff |
| IMAGETYPE_JB2 | Joint Bi-level Image Experts Group | .jb2 |
| IMAGETYPE_JP2 | JPEG 2000 | .jp2 |
| IMAGETYPE_JPC | JPEG 2000 | .jpc |
| IMAGETYPE_JPEG | Joint Photographic Experts Group | .jpg |
| IMAGETYPE_JPX | JPEG 2000 | .jpx |
| IMAGETYPE_PNG | Portable Network Graphics | .png |
| IMAGETYPE_PSD | Adobe Photoshop | .psd |
| IMAGETYPE_SWC | MacroMedia Flash | .swc |
| IMAGETYPE_SWF | MacroMedia Flash | .swf |
| IMAGETYPE_TIFF_II | Tagged Image File Format (Intel byte order) | .tff |
| IMAGETYPE_TIFF_MM | Tagged Image File Format (Motorola byte order) | .tff |

### array exif_read_data(string file, string sections, boolean create_arrays, boolean read_thumbnail)

The `exif_read_data` function (Listing 16.1) reads EXIF headers from a JPEG or TIFF image file and returns an array that uses the header names for keys. The optional `sections` argument may be a comma-delimited list of sections that must be present in the file. Table 16.2 lists them. The optional `create_arrays` argument controls whether PHP organizes header values into subarrays named after sections. The optional `read_thumbnail` argument controls where PHP reads the thumbnail.

**Table 16.2** EXIF Sections

| Section | Description |
| --- | --- |
| ANY_TAG | Include any information that has a tag. |
| COMMENT | Include comment headers. |
| COMPUTED | Include computed sizes. |
| EXIF | Include extra information within the IFD0 section provided by some digital cameras. |
| FILE | Include filename, size, creation date, SectionsFound. |
| IFD0 | Include all IFD0 tags. |
| THUMBNAIL | Include the thumbnail. |

---

**Listing 16.1**  *exif_read_data*

```php
<?php
   $file = 'waterfall.jpg';
   if(exif_imagetype($file) == IMAGETYPE_JPEG)
   {
      $exif = exif_read_data($file, "COMPUTED,IFD0", TRUE);

      print("<img src=\"$file\" " .
         "{$exif['COMPUTED']['html']} " .
         "border=\"0\"><br>" .
         "Picture taken {$exif['IFD0']['DateTime']} " .
         "with a {$exif['IFD0']['Make']} " .
         "{$exif['IFD0']['Model']}<br>");
```

**Listing 16.1**     *exif_read_data (cont.)*

```
    }
    else
    {
        print('Incorrect image type');
    }
?>
```

### string exif_thumbnail(string file, reference width, reference height, reference type)

The `exif_thumbnail` function (Listing 16.2) extracts the thumbnail from a JPEG or TIFF file if it exists. The optional `width` and `height` arguments receive integers for the width and height respectively. The optional `type` argument receives one of the image types from Table 16.1.

**Listing 16.2**     *exif_thumbnail*

```
<?php
    $file = 'waterfall.jpg';
    $thumbnail = exif_thumbnail($file, $width, $height, $type);

    if($thumbnail !== FALSE)
    {
        header("Content-type: " . image_type_to_mime_type($type));
        print($image);
    }
?>
```

### array getimagesize(string file, array image_info)

The `getimagesize` function (Listing 16.3) returns a four-element array that tells you the image size of the given filename. The contents of this array are listed in Table 16.3. Image type corresponds to the types shown in Table 16.1.

**Table 16.3**   Array Elements for `getimagesize`

| Element | Description |
| --- | --- |
| 0 | Width in pixels |
| 1 | Height in pixels |
| 2 | Image Type |

**Table 16.3**   Array Elements for `getimagesize` *(cont.)*

| Element | Description |
|---------|-------------|
| 3 | String like `height=150 width=200`, usable in `img` tag |
| bits | Bits per sample for jpegs |
| channels | Samples per pixel for jpegs |
| mime | MIME type |

The optional `image_info` argument will be set with additional information from the file. At the time of this writing, this array is set with APP markers 0–15 from JPEG files. One of the most common is APP13, which is an International Press Telecommunications Council (IPTC) block. These blocks are used to communicate information about electronic media released to news agencies. They are stored in binary form, so to decode them, you must use the `iptcparse` function. You can find out more about the IPTC at their Web site: `<http://www.iptc.org/>`.

**Listing 16.3**    *getimagesize*

```php
<?php
    $file = "php.jpg";
    $size = getimagesize($file, $info);
    $iptc = iptcparse($info['APP13']);

    //show headline from IPTC headers
    print("<h1>{$iptc['2#105'][0]}</h1>");

    //show image, use IPTC caption for alt text
    print("<img src=\"$file\" {$size[3]} alt=".
        "\"{$iptc['2#120'][0]}\"><br>\n");
?>
```

**string iptcembed(string iptc, string file, integer spool)**
The `iptcembed` function adds IPTC blocks to JPEG files. By default, the blocks are added to the file, and the modified file is returned. The `spool` argument allows you to change this behavior. If the `spool` flag is 1 or 2, then the modified JPEG will be sent directly to the browser. If the `spool` flag is 2, the JPEG will not be returned as a string.

### array iptcparse(string iptc_block)

The `iptcparse` function takes an IPTC block and returns an array containing all the tags in the block.

### array image_type_to_mime_type(int imagetype)

The `image_type_to_mime_type` function returns a MIME type suitable for a `Content-type` header based on one of the image type constants in Table 16.1.

### read_exif_data

You may use `read_exif_data` as an alias to exif_read_data.

# 16.2  Creating Images

All the functions in this section require the GD library. If you haven't compiled it as part of your PHP module, either load it automatically by editing `php3.ini` or use the `dl` function. Some of these functions also require other libraries, which allow you to use font files.

To get started, you can use either `imagecreate` to start with a blank graphic or a function such as `imagecreatefrompng` to load a PNG from a file. Coordinates in these functions treat $(0, 0)$ as the top left corner and refer to pixels. Likewise, any size arguments refer to pixels.

When creating images with these functions, you can't simply decide to output an image in the middle of a script that outputs HTML. You must create a separate script that sends a Content-type header. All the examples illustrate this idea.

For functions that use fonts, there are five built-in fonts numbered 1, 2, 3, 4, and 5. You may also load fonts, which will always have identifiers greater than five.

The image functions use colors that must be allocated first with one of the color allocation functions, such as `imagecolorallocate`. These functions give you an index into the palette. In addition, you can use a few constants if you wish to paint with brushes or tiles. See the descriptions of `imagesetbrush`, `imagesetstyle`, and `imagesettile` for more information.

### array gd_info()

The `gd_info` function returns an array describing which parts of the GD library are available. Table 16.4 describes the elements of the array.

**Table 16.4** Information Returned by `gd_info`

| Element | Description |
| --- | --- |
| GD Version | Text describing the GD library used |
| FreeType Support | Boolean for whether FreeType functions are active |
| FreeType Linkage | Text describing how FreeType functions were activated |
| T1Lib Support | Boolean for whether Type 1 font functions are active |
| GIF Read Support | Boolean for whether `imagecreatefromgif is active` |
| GIF Create Support | Boolean for whether `imagegif is active` |
| JPG Support | Boolean for whether JPEG functions are active |
| PNG Support | Boolean for whether PNG functions are active |
| WBMP Support | Boolean for whether Wireless Bitmap functions are active |
| XBM Support | Boolean for whether XBM functions are active |

### image2wbmp(resource image, string file, integer threshold)

The `image2wbmp` function outputs an image in Wireless Bitmap format to the browser. If the optional file argument is set, the file is saved to a file instead. The optional `threshold` argument sets the threshold for when a pixel is converted to black or white. Keep in mind that WBMP files are monochrome.

Use the `imagewmp` function as an alternative.

### boolean imagealphablending(resource image, boolean blending_mode)

This `imagealphablending` function controls whether or not drawing in true color images occurs in blending mode. In blending mode pixels drawn on an image are blended with existing pixels. Alpha blending works only for true color images.

### boolean imagearc(resource image, integer center_x, integer center_y, integer width, integer height, integer start, integer end, integer color)

Use `imagearc` (Listing 16.4) to draw a section of an ellipse. The first argument specifies a valid image. The ellipse is centered at `center_x` and `center_y`. The height and width are set by the respective arguments in pixels. The start and end points of the curve are given in degrees. Zero degrees is at 3 o'clock and proceeds counterclockwise. Figure 16.1 shows the output of Listing 16.4.

| Listing 16.4 | *imagearc* |
| --- | --- |

```php
<?php
    /*
    ** cut out a circular view of an image
    */

    //attempt to open image, suppress error messages
    if(!($image = @imagecreatefrompng("leonatkinson.png")))
    {
        //error, so create an error image and exit
        $image = imagecreate(200,200);
        $colorWhite = imagecolorallocate($image, 255, 255, 255);
        $colorBlack = imagecolorallocate($image, 0, 0, 0);
        imagefill($image, 0, 0, $colorWhite);
        imagestring($image, 4, 10, 10, "Couldn't load image!",
            $colorBlack);
        header("Content-type: image/png");
        imagepng($image);
        exit();
    }

    //make sure we're in palette mode so that transparency works
    imagetruecolortopalette($image, FALSE, 32);

    //create a color to be transparent, hopefully
    //not already in the image
    $colorMagenta = imagecolorallocate($image, 255, 0, 255);

    //draw a circle
    imagearc($image,
        70, 140,
        120, 120,
        0, 360,
        $colorMagenta);

    //fill outside of circle with Magenta
    imagefilltoborder($image, 0, 0,$colorMagenta, $colorMagenta);

    //turn magenta transparent
    imagecolortransparent($image, $colorMagenta);

    //send image to browser
    header("Content-type: image/png");
    imagepng($image);
?>
```

**Figure 16.1**   imagearc output.

### imageantialias(resource image, boolean antialias)

The imageantialias function (Listing 16.5) controls a flag on images that tells PHP whether to apply antialiasing when drawing. Your image should be in true color mode, although you can later convert the image to palette mode with imagetruecolortopalette. Output is shown in Figure 16.2.

**Listing 16.5**   *imageantialias*

```php
<?php
    $image = imagecreatetruecolor(200,200);
    $colorWhite = imagecolorallocate($image, 255, 255, 255);
    $colorRed = imagecolorallocate($image, 255, 0, 0);
    $colorBlue = imagecolorallocate($image, 0, 0, 255);

    imagefill($image, 0, 0, $colorWhite);

    //make antialiased red line
    imageantialias($image, TRUE);
    imageline($image, 10, 10, 150, 130, $colorRed);

    //make non-antialiased blue line
    imageantialias($image, FALSE);
    imageline($image, 20, 10, 160, 130, $colorBlue);

    header("Content-type: image/png");
    imagepng($image);
?>
```

**Figure 16.2** `imageantialias` output.

### boolean imagechar(resource image, integer font, integer x, integer y, string character, integer color)

The `imagechar` function (Listing 16.6) draws a single character at the given pixel. The font argument can be a loaded font or one of the five built-in fonts. The character will be oriented horizontally—that is, left to right. The *x* and *y* coordinates refer to the top left corner of the letter. Output is shown in Figure 16.3.

| Listing 16.6 | *imagechar, imagecharup* |
|---|---|

```php
<?php
    //create white rectangle
    $image = imagecreate(125,100);
    $colorBlack = imagecolorallocate($image, 0, 0, 0);
    $colorWhite = imagecolorallocate($image, 255,255,255);
    imagefill($image, 0, 0, $colorWhite);

    //draw a horizontal C in each built-in font
    imagechar($image, 1, 0, 0, "C", $colorBlack);
    imagechar($image, 2, 20, 20, "C", $colorBlack);
    imagechar($image, 3, 40, 40, "C", $colorBlack);
    imagechar($image, 4, 60, 60, "C", $colorBlack);
    imagechar($image, 5, 80, 80, "C", $colorBlack);
```

| Listing 16.6 | *imagechar, imagecharup (cont.)* |
|---|---|

```
//draw a vertical M in each built-in font
imagecharup($image, 1, 10, 10, "M", $colorBlack);
imagecharup($image, 2, 30, 30, "M", $colorBlack);
imagecharup($image, 3, 50, 50, "M", $colorBlack);
imagecharup($image, 4, 70, 70, "M", $colorBlack);
imagecharup($image, 5, 90, 90, "M", $colorBlack);

//send image
header("Content-type: image/png");
imagepng($image);
?>
```

**Figure 16.3**   imagechar, imagecharup output.

### boolean imagecharup(resource image, integer font, integer x, integer y, string character, integer color)

The imagecharup function operates identically to imagechar except that the character is oriented vertically, bottom to top.

### integer imagecolorallocate(resource image, integer red, integer green, integer blue)

The imagecolorallocate function (Listing 16.7) allocates a color in the given image. The color is specified by the amount of red, green, and blue. An identifier is returned for referring to this color in other functions. Figure 16.4 shows the output of Listing 16.7.

| Listing 16.7 | *imagecolorallocate* |
|---|---|

```php
<?php
    //create white square
    $image = imagecreate(200,200);
    $colorWhite = imagecolorallocate($image, 255,255,255);
    $colorRed = imagecolorallocate($image, 255, 0, 0);
    $colorGreen = imagecolorallocate($image, 0, 255, 0);
    $colorBlue = imagecolorallocate($image, 0, 0, 255);
    imagefill($image, 0, 0, $colorWhite);

    //make red circle
    imagearc($image, 50, 50, 100, 100, 0, 360, $colorRed);
    imagefilltoborder($image, 50, 50, $colorRed, $colorRed);

    //make green circle
    imagearc($image, 100, 50, 100, 100, 0, 360, $colorGreen);
    imagefilltoborder($image, 100, 50, $colorGreen, $colorGreen);

    //make blue circle
    imagearc($image, 75, 75, 100, 100, 0, 360, $colorBlue);
    imagefilltoborder($image, 75, 75, $colorBlue, $colorBlue);

    //send image
    header("Content-type: image/png");
    imagepng($image);
?>
```

**Figure 16.4**  imagecolorallocate output.

### integer imagecolorallocatealpha (resource image, integer red, integer green, integer blue, integer alpha)

The imagecolorallocatealpha function operates like imagecolorallocate except that it allows you to set the alpha level as well.

### integer imagecolorat(resource image, integer x, integer y)

The imagecolorat function (Listing 16.8) returns the index of the color at the specified pixel. Palette-based images have a palette of arbitrary colors referred to by integers.

**Listing 16.8**   *imagecolorat*

```php
<?php
    //attempt to open image, suppress error messages
    if(!($image = @imagecreatefrompng("leonatkinson.png")))
    {
        //error, so create an error image and exit
        $image = imagecreate(200,200);
        $colorWhite = imagecolorallocate($image, 255, 255, 255);
        $colorBlack = imagecolorallocate($image, 0, 0, 0);
        imagefill($image, 0, 0, $colorWhite);
        imagestring($image, 4, 10, 10, "Couldn't load image!",
            $colorBlack);
        header("Content-type: image/png");
        imagepng($image);
        exit();
    }

    //get RGB value of color at (50,50)
    $rgb = imagecolorat($image, 50, 50);
    $rgb = strtoupper(
        dechex(($rgb >> 0xF) & 0xFF) .
        dechex(($rgb >> 0x8) & 0xFF) .
        dechex($rgb & 0xFF));

    //write the RGB value into image
    $colorBlack = imagecolorallocate($image, 0, 0, 0);;
    imagestring($image, 5, 10, 10, "#$rgb", $colorBlack);

    //switch to palette mode
    imagetruecolortopalette($image, FALSE, 16);

    //get index of the color at (50,50)
    $colorIndex = imagecolorat($image, 50, 50);

    //change that color to red
    imagecolorset($image, $colorIndex, 255, 0, 0);

    //send image
    header("Content-type: image/png");
    imagepng($image);
?>
```

### integer imagecolorclosest(resource image, integer red, integer green, integer blue)

The `imagecolorclosest` function (Listing 16.9) returns the index of the color in the given image closest to the given color. Colors are treated as three-dimensional coordinates, and closeness is defined as the distance between two points.

| Listing 16.9 | *imagecolorclosest, imagecolorexact, imagecolorresolve, imagecolorsforindex* |
|---|---|

```php
<?php
    /*
    ** Compare closest color to real color
    */

    //attempt to open image, suppress error messages
    if(!($image = @imagecreatefromjpeg("waterfall.jpg")))
    {
        //error, so create an error image and exit
        $image = imagecreate(200,200);
        $colorWhite = imagecolorallocate($image, 255, 255, 255);
        $colorBlack = imagecolorallocate($image, 0, 0, 0);
        imagefill($image, 0, 0, $colorWhite);
        imagestring($image, 4, 10, 10, "Couldn't load image!",
            $colorBlack);
        header("Content-type: image/png");
        imagepng($image);
        exit();
    }

    //convert true color to 128 color palette
    imagetruecolortopalette($image, FALSE, 128);

    //move up to a 256 color palette
    //so we have room for allocation
    imagetruecolortopalette($image, FALSE, 256);

    //find index of color closest to pure green
    $closestColor = imagecolorclosest($image, 0, 255, 0);

    //draw block of color
    imagefilledrectangle($image, 0, 0, 199, 99, $closestColor);
```

| Listing 16.9 | *imagecolorclosest, imagecolorexact, imagecolorresolve, imagecolorsforindex (cont.)* |
| --- | --- |

```
//allocate inverse so we can print RGB values
$rgb = imagecolorsforindex($image, $closestColor);
$inverseColor = imagecolorallocate($image,
    ~$rgb['red'], ~$rgb['green'], ~$rgb['blue']);
imagestring($image, 4, 10, 10,
    "{$rgb['red']}, {$rgb['green']}, {$rgb['blue']}",
    $inverseColor);

//try to get exactly pure green
$exactColor = imagecolorexact($image, 0, 255, 0);
if($exactColor == -1)
{
    //if not found, use black
    $exactColor = imagecolorallocate($image, 0, 0, 0);
}

//draw block of color
imagefilledrectangle($image, 0, 100, 199, 199, $exactColor);

//if pure green doesn't exist, allocate it
$resolveColor = imagecolorresolve($image, 0, 255, 0);

//draw block of color
imagefilledrectangle($image, 0, 200, 199, 299, $resolveColor);

//send image
header("Content-type: image/png");
imagepng($image);
?>
```

### integer imagecolorclosestalpha(resource image, integer red, integer green, integer blue, integer alpha)

The `imagecolorclosestalpha` function operates identically to `imagecolorclosest` except that it also accounts for the alpha channel.

### integer imagecolorclosesthwb(resource image, integer hue, integer white, integer black)

The `imagecolorclosesthwb` function finds the color in the image closest to the color given by hue, white level, and black level, otherwise known as HWB. Do not confuse this with the so-called HSV (Hue-Saturation-Value) method for describing colors. The HWB method was first described by Alvy Ray Smith and

Eric Ray Lyons in "HWB—A More Intuitive Hue-Based Color Model," an article that appeared in the *Journal of Graphics Tools* in 1996.

### imagecolordeallocate(resource image, integer color)

The `imagecolordeallocate` deallocates a color in an image. It does not change the pixels of that color in the image; it merely removes the color from the list available to you for drawing.

### resource imagecolorexact(resource image, integer red, integer green, integer blue)

Use the `imagecolorexact` function to find the index of the color in the given image that matches the given color exactly. If the color doesn't exist, negative one (−1) is returned.

### integer imagecolorexactalpha(resource image, integer red, integer green, integer blue, integer alpha)

The `imagecolorexactalpha` function operates identically to `imagecolorexact` except that it also accounts for the alpha channel.

### boolean imagecolormatch(resource truecolor_image, resource palette_image)

The `imagecolormatch` function adjusts the palette for the given palette image argument to match colors used in the true color version. This function can improve the quality of an image converted to a small palette with `imagetruecolortopalette`.

### integer imagecolorresolve(resource image, integer red, integer green, integer blue)

The `imagecolorresolve` function returns a color identifier based on a specified color. If the color does not exist in the image's palette, it will be added. In the event that the color cannot be added, an identifier for the closest color will be returned.

### integer imagecolorresolvealpha(resource image, integer red, integer green, integer blue, integer alpha)

The `imagecolorresolvealpha` function operates identically to `imagecolorresolve` except that it also accounts for the alpha channel.

## boolean imagecolorset(resource image, integer index, integer red, integer green, integer blue)

The `imagecolorset` function sets the color at the given index to the specified color. This function works only for palette images. See Listing 16.8 for an example of use.

## array imagecolorsforindex(resource image, integer index)

The `imagecolorsforindex` function returns an associative array with the `red`, `green`, and `blue` elements of the color for the specified color index. See Listing 16.9 for an example of use.

## resource imagecolorstotal(resource image)

The `imagecolorstotal` function (Listing 16.10) returns the number of colors in the given image.

---

**Listing 16.10**  *imagecolorstotal, imageistruecolor*

```php
<?php
    //attempt to open image, suppress error messages
    if(!($image = @imagecreatefrompng("leonatkinson.png")))
    {
        //error, so print error message
        print("Couldn't load image!");
    }

    if(imageistruecolor($image))
    {
        print("This image is true color.");
    }
    else
    {
        print("Total Colors: " . imagecolorstotal($image));
    }
?>
```

---

## resource imagecolortransparent(resource image, integer color)

The `imagecolortransparent` function (Listing 16.11) sets the given color as transparent. The `color` argument is as returned by the `imagecolorallocate` functions. The image must be in palette mode. You may call this function without the second argument to fetch the transparent color.

| Listing 16.11 | *imagecolortransparent* |
|---|---|

```php
<?php
    //create red square
    $image = imagecreate(200,200);
    $colorRed = imagecolorallocate($image, 255, 0, 0);
    $colorBlue = imagecolorallocate($image, 0, 0, 255);
    imagefill($image, 0, 0, $colorRed);

    //draw a smaller blue square
    imagefilledrectangle($image, 30, 30, 70, 70, $colorBlue);

    //make blue transparent
    imagecolortransparent($image, $colorBlue);

    //send image
    header("Content-type: image/png");
    imagepng($image);
?>
```

### boolean imagecopy(resource destination, resource source, integer destination_x, integer destination_y, integer source_x, integer source_y, integer src_width, integer src_height)

The imagecopy function (Listing 16.12) copies a portion of a source image into a destination image. This function does not respect transparency when the source image is in true color mode. Use imagecopymerge instead. Output is shown in Figure 16.5.

| Listing 16.12 | *imagecopy* |
|---|---|

```php
<?php
    $picture = "leonatkinson.png";

    //create yellow rectangle 20 pixels bigger than picture
    $size = getimagesize($picture);
    $image = imagecreatetruecolor($size[0] + 20, $size[1] + 20);
    $colorYellow = imagecolorallocate($image, 255, 255, 128);
    imagefill($image, 0, 0, $colorYellow);

    //attempt to open picture, suppress error messages
    if(!($image2 = @imagecreatefrompng($picture)))
    {
```

**Listing 16.12** *imagecopy (cont.)*

```
        //error, so create an error image and exit
        $image = imagecreate(200,200);
        $colorWhite = imagecolorallocate($image, 255, 255, 255);
        $colorBlack = imagecolorallocate($image, 0, 0, 0);
        imagefill($image, 0, 0, $colorWhite);
        imagestring($image, 4, 10, 10, "Couldn't load image!",
            $colorBlack);
        header("Content-type: image/png");
        imagepng($image);
        exit();
    }

    //drop picture into yellow rectangle
    imagecopy($image, $image2, 10, 10, 0, 0, $size[0], $size[1]);

    //send image
    header("Content-type: image/png");
    imagepng($image);
?>
```

**Figure 16.5** imagecopy output.

**boolean imagecopymerge(resource destination, resource source, integer destination_x, integer destination_y, integer source_x, integer source_y, integer src_width, integer src_height, integer opacity)**

The imagecopymerge function (Listing 16.13) copies one image into another and allows you to set how opaque the copied image is during the copy. The opacity should be between 0, where the copied image doesn't show, and 100, which duplicates the functionality of imagecopy. Output is shown in Figure 16.6.

This function respects transparency for true color and palette images. If you wish to layer an image with transparent pixels over another image without any blending, use this function with opacity set to 100.

| Listing 16.13 | *imagecopymerge* |
| --- | --- |

```php
<?php
    $picture = "leonatkinson.png";

    //create yellow rectangle 20 pixels bigger than picture
    $size = getimagesize($picture);
    $image = imagecreatetruecolor($size[0] + 20, $size[1] + 20);
    $colorYellow = imagecolorallocate($image, 255, 255, 128);
    imagefill($image, 0, 0, $colorYellow);

    //attempt to open picture, suppress error messages
    if(!($image2 = @imagecreatefrompng($picture)))
    {
        //error, so create an error image and exit
        $image = imagecreate(200,200);
        $colorWhite = imagecolorallocate($image, 255, 255, 255);
        $colorBlack = imagecolorallocate($image, 0, 0, 0);
        imagefill($image, 0, 0, $colorWhite);
        imagestring($image, 4, 10, 10, "Couldn't load image!",
            $colorBlack);
        header("Content-type: image/png");
        imagepng($image);
        exit();
    }

    //drop picture into yellow rectangle at 50% opacity
    imagecopymerge($image, $image2, 10, 10, 0, 0, $size[0],
        $size[1], 50);

    //send image
    header("Content-type: image/png");
    imagepng($image);
?>
```

**Figure 16.6** `imagecopymerge` output.

**boolean imagecopymergegray(resource destination, resource source, integer destination_x, integer destination_y, integer source_x, integer source_y, integer src_width, integer src_height, integer opacity)**

The `imagecopymergegray` function operates identically to `imagecopymerge` except that PHP first converts the source image to grayscale. This preserves the hue information in the destination image.

**boolean imagecopyresampled(resource destination, resource source, integer destination_x, integer destination_y, integer source_x, integer source_y, integer destination_width, integer destination_height, integer source_width, integer source_height)**

The `imagecopyresampled` function (Listing 16.14) copies a portion of an image into another image, optionally resizing it and resampling for better clarity. Compare the output of this function with that of `imagecopyresized`.

| Listing 16.14 | *imagecopyresample* |
| --- | --- |

```php
<?php
    function makeThumbnail($source, $destination, $width, $height)
    {
        //load source image
        if(!($sourceImage = @imagecreatefromjpeg($source)))
        {
            //error, so create an error image and exit
            $image = imagecreate($width, $height);
            $colorWhite = imagecolorallocate($image,
                255, 255, 255);
            $colorBlack = imagecolorallocate($image, 0, 0, 0);
            imagefill($image, 0, 0, $colorWhite);
            imagestring($image, 1, 1, 10, "Failed!", $colorBlack);
            imagepng($image, $destination);
            return(FALSE);
        }

        //make destination
        $destinationImage = imagecreatetruecolor($width, $height);

        //copy source into destination,
        //resampling and possibly distorting
        imagecopyresampled($destinationImage, $sourceImage,
            0, 0, 0, 0, $width, $height,
            imagesx($sourceImage), imagesy($sourceImage));

        //save image
        imagepng($destinationImage, $destination);
    }

    makeThumbnail("waterfall.jpg", "waterfall_thumb.jpg", 64, 64);
?>
<h1>Original</h1>
<img src="waterfall.jpg" border="0">

<h1>Thumbnail</h1>
<img src="waterfall_thumb.jpg" border="0">
```

**resource imagecopyresized(integer destination, integer source, integer destination_x, integer destination_y, integer source_x, integer source_y, integer destination_width, integer destination_height, integer source_width, integer source_height)**

The imagecopyresized function (Listing 16.15) copies a portion of the source image into the destination image. If the destination width and height are different than the source width and height, the clip will be stretched or shrunk. It is possible to copy and paste into the same image, but if the destination and source overlap, there will be unpredictable results. Output is shown in Figure 16.7.

**Listing 16.15**    *imagecopyresized*

```php
<?php
    //create yellow square
    $image = imagecreatetruecolor(200,200);
    $colorYellow = imagecolorallocate($image, 255, 255, 128);
    imagefill($image, 0, 0, $colorYellow);

    //attempt to open image, suppress error messages
    if(!($image2 = @imagecreatefrompng("leonatkinson.png")))
    {
        //error, so create an error image and exit
        $image = imagecreate(200,200);
        $colorWhite = imagecolorallocate($image, 255, 255, 255);
        $colorBlack = imagecolorallocate($image, 0, 0, 0);
        imagefill($image, 0, 0, $colorWhite);
        imagestring($image, 4, 10, 10, "Couldn't load image!",
            $colorBlack);
        header("Content-type: image/png");
        imagepng($image);
        exit();
    }

    //drop image2 into image, and stretch or squash it
    imagecopyresized($image, $image2, 10, 10, 0, 0,
        180, 180, imagesx($image2), imagesy($image2));

    //send image
    header("Content-type: image/png");
    imagepng($image);
?>
```

**Figure 16.7** `imagecopyresized` output.

### resource imagecreate(integer width, integer height)

The `imagecreate` function returns an image identifier of the specified width and height. The image will be in palette mode.

### resource imagecreatefromgd(string file)

Use this function to create an image resource from a GD image file.

### resource imagecreatefromgd2(string file)

Use this function to create an image resource from a GD image file stored in GD2 format.

### resource imagecreatefromgd2part(string file, integer x, integer y, integer width, integer height)

The `imagecreatefromgd2part` function creates an image resource from a rectangular section of a GD2 image file.

### resource imagecreatefromgif(string file)

The `imagecreatefromgif` function returns an image resource from a GIF image file.

### resource imagecreatefromjpeg(string file)

Use `imagecreatefromjpeg` to load a JPEG image from a file.

### resource imagecreatefrompng(string file)

Use `imagecreatefrompng` to load a PNG image from a file.

### resource imagecreatefromstring(string file)

The `imagecreatefromstring` function (Listing 16.16) creates an image resource from a string. The string should contain the equivalent of the contents from an image file. PHP detects the image format.

**Listing 16.16**   *imagecreatefromstring*

```php
<?php
    //open JPEG
    $image = imagecreatefromstring(file_get_contents
        ("waterfall.jpg"));

    //send PNG image
    header("Content-type: image/png");
    imagepng($image);
?>
```

### resource imagecreatefromwbmp(string file)

Use `imagecreatefromwbmp` to load a Wireless Bitmap image from a file.

### resource imagecreatefromxbm(string file)

Use `imagecreatefromxbm` to load an XBM image from a file.

### resource imagecreatefromxpm(string file)

Use `imagecreatefromxpm` to load an XPM image from a file.

### resource imagecreatetruecolor(integer width, integer height)

The `imagecreatetruecolor` function creates an image in true color mode.

### boolean imagedestroy(resource image)

Use the `imagedestroy` function to clear memory associated with the specified image. Most of the time you will not need this function. PHP will clean up when your script ends.

### imageellipse(resource image, integer center_x, integer center_y, integer width, integer height, integer color)

The `imageellipse` function (Listing 16.17) draws an ellipse into the given image. The ellipse is centered at `center_x` and `center_y`. To create a circle, set the `width` and `height` arguments equal to each other. The color must be an index returned by one of the color allocation functions. Output is shown in Figure 16.8.

| Listing 16.17 | *imagearc, imageellipse,* *imagefilledarc, imagefilledellipse* |
|---|---|

```php
<?php
    $image = imagecreatetruecolor(175,50);
    $colorWhite = imagecolorallocate($image, 255, 255, 255);
    $colorRed = imagecolorallocate($image, 255, 0, 0);
    $colorBlue = imagecolorallocate($image, 0, 0, 255);

    imagefill($image, 0, 0, $colorWhite);

    imagearc($image, 25, 25, 30, 30, 90, 270, $colorRed);

    imageellipse($image, 60, 25, 40, 20, $colorBlue);

    imagefilledarc($image, 105, 25, 30, 30, 90, 270,
        $colorRed, IMG_ARC_PIE);

    imagefilledellipse($image, 145, 25, 40, 20, $colorBlue);

    header("Content-type: image/png");
    imagepng($image);
?>
```

**Figure 16.8**  imagearc, imageellipse, imagefilledarc, imagefilledellipse output.

### boolean imagefill(resource image, integer x, integer y, integer color)

The imagefill function performs a flood fill at the given point with the given color. The color argument must be as returned by imagecolorallocate. Starting at the given point, pixels are changed to the specified color. The coloring spreads out, continuing until a color different from the one at the specified point is encountered. See the description of imagearc for an example of use. See imagefilltoborder for an alternative.

**boolean imagefilledarc(resource image, integer center_x, integer center_y, integer width, integer height, integer start, integer end, integer color, integer style)**

Use `imagefilledarc` (Listing 16.18) to draw a section of an ellipse and fill it with the given color. The first argument specifies a valid image. The ellipse is centered at `center_x` and `center_y`. The start and end points of the curve are given in degrees. Zero degrees is at 3 o'clock and proceeds counterclockwise.

The `style` argument is a bitfield that controls which part of the arc PHP draws. See Table 16.5.

**Table 16.5** Filled Arc Styles

| Style | Description |
| --- | --- |
| IMG_ARC_CHORD | Draw the straight line connecting the ends of the arc |
| IMG_ARC_EDGED | Draw the edge of the arc |
| IMG_ARC_NOFILL | Do not fill the arc |
| IMG_ARC_PIE | Fill the arc |

**Listing 16.18** *imagefilledarc*

```php
<?php
    $image = imagecreatetruecolor(140,50);
    $colorWhite = imagecolorallocate($image, 255, 255, 255);
    $colorRed = imagecolorallocate($image, 255, 0, 0);
    $colorBlue = imagecolorallocate($image, 0, 0, 255);

    imagefill($image, 0, 0, $colorWhite);

    //draw solid half-circle
    imagefilledarc($image, 20, 25, 30, 30, 90, 270,
        $colorRed, IMG_ARC_PIE);

    //draw outlined half-circle
    imagefilledarc($image, 60, 25, 30, 30, 90, 270,
        $colorBlue, IMG_ARC_EDGED | IMG_ARC_NOFILL);

    //draw just the line connecting the two ends of the arc
    imagefilledarc($image, 100, 25, 30, 30, 90, 180,
        $colorRed, IMG_ARC_CHORD | IMG_ARC_NOFILL);

    header("Content-type: image/png");
    imagepng($image);
?>
```

### boolean imagefilledellipse(resource image, integer center_x, integer center_y, integer width, integer height, integer color)

The `imagefilledellipse` function operates identically to `imageellipse` except that it fills the ellipse with the given color.

### boolean imagefilledpolygon(resource image, array points, integer number, integer color)

The `imagefilledpolygon` function (Listing 16.19) creates a polygon with its inside filled with the specified color. The `points` argument is an array of x and y values for each point: Each point uses two array elements. The number argument reports how many points to use from the array. Output is shown in Figure 16.9.

| Listing 16.19 | *imagefilledpolygon* |
|---|---|

```php
<?php
    //create red square
    $image = imagecreate(100,100);
    $colorRed = imagecolorallocate($image, 255, 0, 0);
    $colorBlack = imagecolorallocate($image, 0, 0, 0);
    imagefill($image, 0, 0, $colorRed);

    //set up three points of the triangle
    $points = array(50, 10, 10, 90, 90, 90);

    //draw triangle
    imagefilledpolygon($image,
        $points, count($points)/2,
        $colorBlack);

    //send image
    header("Content-type: image/png");
    imagepng($image);
?>
```

**Figure 16.9** `imagefilledpolygon` output.

**boolean imagefilledrectangle(resource image, integer top_left_x, integer top_left_y, integer bottom_right_x, integer bottom_right_y, integer color)**

The `imagefilledrectangle` function (Listing 16.20) draws a filled rectangle based on the top left and bottom right corners. Output is shown in Figure 16.10.

---

**Listing 16.20**   *imagefilledrectangle*

```php
<?php
    //create green square
    $image = imagecreate(200,200);
    $colorGreen = imagecolorallocate($image, 128, 255, 128);
    $colorBlack = imagecolorallocate($image, 0, 0, 0);
    imagefill($image, 0, 0, $colorGreen);

    //draw a black rectangle
    imagefilledrectangle($image,
        10, 10, 90, 90,
        $colorBlack);

    //send image
    header("Content-type: image/png");
    imagepng($image);
?>
```

---

**Figure 16.10**   `imagefilledrectangle` output.

### boolean imagefilltoborder(resource image, integer x, integer y, integer border_color, integer color)

The `imagefilltoborder` function will flood-fill an area bounded by the `border_color` argument. The flood fill will begin at the given coordinate. See Listing 16.4 for an example.

### boolean imagefilter(resource image, integer filter, ...)

The `imagefilter` function (Listing 16.21) applies a filter to a given image. Use one of the filters shown in Table 16.6. Some filters require extra arguments, as described in the table. The exact nature of these filters is beyond the scope of this text. You may find more information in discussions about digital image filtering, especially those about Adobe PhotoShop or GIMP.

**Table 16.6**  Filters

| Filter | Description |
|---|---|
| IMG_FILTER_BRIGHTNESS | This filter allows you to adjust the brightness up or down. It expects an argument that should range from –255 to 255. |
| IMG_FILTER_COLORIZE | The colorize filter adds or subtracts color from every pixel of the image. It expects three arguments for red, green, and blue. These values should range from –255 to 255, with negative value subtracting color. For example, using –255 for the first argument removes all red from every pixel. |
| IMG_FILTER_CONTRAST | This filter adjusts the contrast of the image. It expects an argument that should range from –255 to 255. Negative values reduce contrast. |
| IMG_FILTER_EDGEDETECT | This filter detects edges and sets other areas to gray. |
| IMG_FILTER_EMBOSS | This filter attempts to make the image look as if it's embossed. |
| IMG_FILTER_GAUSSIAN_BLUR | This filter applies a Gaussian blur. |
| IMG_FILTER_GRAYSCALE | The grayscale filter converts the image to monochrome. |
| IMG_FILTER_MEAN_REMOVAL | The mean removal filter attempts to remove anomalies in the image. |
| IMG_FILTER_NEGATE | The negate filter changes the image to the negative. |
| IMG_FILTER_SELECTIVE_BLUR | This filter offers an alternative blurring technique to Gaussian blur. |
| IMG_FILTER_SMOOTH | This filter smoothes differences in adjacent pixels. |

**Listing 16.21** *imagefilter*

```php
<?php
    $picture = "leonatkinson.png";

    //shows the effect of the filter
    function showPicture(&$image, $file, $title)
    {
        //write filter name into image
        $colorBlack = imagecolorallocate($image, 0, 0, 0);
        imagestring($image, 5, 10, 10, $title, $colorBlack);

        //write image to a file
        imagepng($image, $file);

        //clean up memory
        imagedestroy($image);

        //print image tag
        print("<img src=\"$file\">");
    }

    //Reduce Brightness
    $image = imagecreatefrompng($picture);
    imagefilter($image, IMG_FILTER_BRIGHTNESS, -128);
    showPicture($image, "brightness_$picture", "Brightness");

    //Colorize
    $image = imagecreatefrompng($picture);
    imagefilter($image, IMG_FILTER_COLORIZE, 100, 128, -64);
    showPicture($image, "colorize_$picture", "Colorize");

    //Increase contrast
    $image = imagecreatefrompng($picture);
    imagefilter($image, IMG_FILTER_CONTRAST, 60);
    showPicture($image, "contrast_$picture", "Contrast");

    //Edge
    $image = imagecreatefrompng($picture);
    $outputFile = "edge_$picture";
    imagefilter($image, IMG_FILTER_EDGEDETECT);
    showPicture($image, "edge_$picture", "Detect Edges");

    //Emboss
    $image = imagecreatefrompng($picture);
    imagefilter($image, IMG_FILTER_EMBOSS);
    showPicture($image, "emboss_$picture", "Emboss");
```

**Listing 16.21**    *imagefilter (cont.)*

```php
//Blur
$image = imagecreatefrompng($picture);
imagefilter($image, IMG_FILTER_GAUSSIAN_BLUR);
showPicture($image, "blur_$picture", "Gaussian Blur");

//Convert to grayscale
$image = imagecreatefrompng($picture);
imagefilter($image, IMG_FILTER_GRAYSCALE);
showPicture($image, "grayscale_$picture", "Grayscale");

//Mean Removal
$image = imagecreatefrompng($picture);
imagefilter($image, IMG_FILTER_MEAN_REMOVAL);
showPicture($image, "mean_$picture", "Mean Removal");

//Get negative
$image = imagecreatefrompng($picture);
imagefilter($image, IMG_FILTER_NEGATE);
showPicture($image, "negate_$picture", "Negative");

//Selective blur
$image = imagecreatefrompng($picture);
imagefilter($image, IMG_FILTER_SELECTIVE_BLUR);
showPicture($image, "selective_$picture", "Selective blur");

//Smooth
$image = imagecreatefrompng($picture);
imagefilter($image, IMG_FILTER_SMOOTH, 123);
showPicture($image, "smooth_$picture", "Smooth");
?>
```

### resource imagefontheight(integer font)

The imagefontheight function (Listing 16.22) returns the height in pixels of the specified font, which may be a built-in font (1–5) or a font loaded with imagefontload.

**Listing 16.22**   *imagefontheight, imagefontwidth*

```php
<?php
    $Text = "Core PHP Programming";
    $Font = 5;
    $Width = imagefontwidth($Font) * strlen($Text);
    $Height = imagefontheight($Font);

    //create green square
    $image = imagecreate($Width, $Height);
    $colorGreen = imagecolorallocate($image, 128, 255, 128);
    $colorBlack = imagecolorallocate($image, 0, 0, 0);
    imagefill($image, 0, 0, $colorGreen);

    //add text in black
    imagestring($image, $Font, 0, 0, $Text, $colorBlack);

    //send image
    header("Content-type: image/jpeg");
    imagejpeg($image);
?>
```

### resource imagefontwidth(integer font)

The `imagefontwidth` function returns the width in pixels of the specified font, which may be a built-in font (1–5) or a font loaded with `imagefontload`. See `imagefontheight` for an example.

### array imageftbbox(integer size, integer angle, string font, string text, array extra)

The `imageftbbox` function returns an array describing the bounding box produced by `imagefttext`. It operates like `imagettfbbox` except that it uses FreeType 2 library.

### imagefttext(resource image, integer point_size, integer angle, integer x, integer y, integer color, string fontfile, string text, array extra)

The `imagefttext` function uses the FreeType 2 library to draw text with a TrueType font. It operates exactly like `imagettftext`.

### boolean imagegammacorrect(resource image, double original, double new)

The `imagegammacorrect` function (Listing 16.23) changes the gamma for an image. Video display hardware is given a gamma rating that describes relatively how bright images appear. Identical images appear lighter on Macintosh hardware than on the typical Windows machine. PHP adjusts each color in the palette of the image to the new gamma.

| Listing 16.23 | *imagegammacorrect* |
|---|---|

```php
<?php
    //attempt to open image, suppress error messages
    if(!($image = @imagecreatefromjpeg("waterfall.jpg")))
    {
        //error, so create an error image and exit
        $image = imagecreate(200,200);
        $colorWhite = imagecolorallocate($image, 255, 255, 255);
        $colorBlack = imagecolorallocate($image, 0, 0, 0);
        imagefill($image, 0, 0, $colorWhite);
        imagestring($image, 4, 10, 10, "Couldn't load image!",
            $colorBlack);
        header("Content-type: image/jpeg");
        imagejpeg($image);
        exit();
    }

    //adjust gamma, display
    imagegammacorrect($image, 2.2, 1.571);

    //send image
    header("Content-type: image/jpeg");
    imagejpeg($image);
?>
```

### boolean imagegd(resource image, string file)

The imagegd function either sends an image to the browser or writes it to a file in GD format. This format is unique to the GD library. It is not compressed and not recognized by browsers. It may be helpful to keep images in GD format if you use them often to construct larger images.

### boolean imagegd2(resource image, string file)

The imagegd2 function either sends an image to the browser or writes it to a file in GD2 format. This format is special to the GD library. The contents are compressed but organized for random access, which means you can keep a large amalgamated image on disk and retrieve smaller parts with the imagecreatefromgd2 function.

### boolean imagegif(resource image, string file)

This function allows for creating GIF files, but it's only available with very old versions of the GD library.

### boolean imageinterlace(resource image, boolean on)

Use `imageinterlace` to set an image as interlaced or not. If the change is successful, `TRUE` is returned.

Interlaced images are stored so that they appear progressively rather than all at once. JPEGs marked as interlaced are called progressive JPEGs. When viewing an image over a slow connection, a progressive JPEG will appear to slowly come into focus. An interlaced PNG will show alternating lines first in the same situation.

### boolean imageistruecolor(resource image)

The `imageistruecolor` function returns `TRUE` if the given image is in true color mode.

### boolean imagejpeg(resource image, string file, integer quality)

The `imagejpeg` function either sends an image to the browser or writes it to a file. If a filename is provided, a JPEG file is created. Otherwise, the image is sent directly to the browser. The optional `quality` argument determines the compression level used in the image and should range from 0 (lowest quality) to 10 (highest quality).

### imagelayereffect(resource image, integer effect)

This function sets the method used when copying images. Use this function as an alternative to `imagealphablending`. Table 16.7 lists valid values for the `effect` argument.

**Table 16.7** Layer Effects

| Effect | Description |
| --- | --- |
| IMG_EFFECT_ALPHABLEND | This mode works like calling `imagealphablending(TRUE)`. |
| IMG_EFFECT_NORMAL | This mode works like alpha blending but can handle transparent backgrounds. |
| IMG_EFFECT_OVERLAY | This mode works like an overlay method available in most graphics programs. |
| IMG_EFFECT_REPLACE | This mode works like calling `imagealphablending(FALSE)`. |

**boolean imageline(resource image, integer start_x, integer start_y, integer end_x, integer end_y, integer color)**
The `imageline` function draws a line from the starting point to the ending point. By default, PHP creates a solid line. You may draw a dashed line by setting the line style with `imagesetstyle` and the special color `IMG_COLOR_STYLED`. You can draw lines with brushes with imagesetstyle and `IMG_COLOR_STYLEDBRUSH`. Listing 16.24 demonstrates these techniques, and output is shown in Figure 16.11.

| Listing 16.24 | *imageline* |
|---|---|

```php
<?php
    /*
    ** create cyan square canvas
    */
    $image = imagecreate(200,200);
    $colorCyan = imagecolorallocate($image, 128, 255, 255);
    $colorBlack = imagecolorallocate($image, 0, 0, 0);
    imagefill($image, 0, 0, $colorCyan);

    /*
    ** draw solid line
    */
    imageline($image, 50, 0, 200, 150, $colorBlack);

    /*
    ** draw dashed line
    */
    $styleDashed = array_merge(array_fill(0, 4, $colorBlack),
        array_fill(0, 4, IMG_COLOR_TRANSPARENT));
    imagesetstyle($image, $styleDashed);
    imageline($image, 0, 0, 200, 200, IMG_COLOR_STYLED);

    /*
    ** draw dotted line using brush
    */

    //make a dot brush
    $dot = imagecreate(10, 10);
    $dotColorBlack = imagecolorallocate($dot, 0, 0, 0);
    $dotColorTransparent = imagecolorallocate($dot, 255, 0, 255);
    imagecolortransparent($dot, $dotColorTransparent);
    imagefill($dot, 0, 0, $dotColorTransparent);
    imagefilledellipse($dot, 4, 4, 5, 5, $dotColorBlack);
    imagesetbrush($image, $dot);
```

**Listing 16.24** *imageline (cont.)*

```
//set line style
$styleDotted = array_merge(array_fill(0, 1, $colorBlack),
    array_fill(0, 9, IMG_COLOR_TRANSPARENT));
imagesetstyle($image, $styleDotted);

//draw dotted line
imageline($image, 0, 50, 150, 200, IMG_COLOR_STYLEDBRUSHED);

/*
** show image
*/
header("Content-type: image/png");
imagepng($image);
?>
```

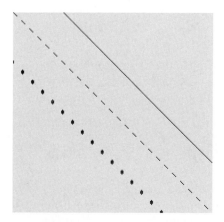

**Figure 16.11** imageline output.

### resource imageloadfont(string file)

The imageloadfont function loads a font and returns a font identifier that may be used with the other font functions. The fonts are stored as bitmaps in a special, architecture-dependent format. Table 16.8 shows the structure of a font file for systems that use 32-bit integers.

Keep in mind your ability to use TrueType and PostScript fonts, which offer much better quality. The five built-in fonts are convenient, but these other popular font formats offer better quality.

**Table 16.8**    Font File Format

| Position | Length | Description |
|---|---|---|
| 0 | 4 | Number of characters in the font. |
| 4 | 4 | ASCII value of first character. |
| 8 | 4 | Width in pixels for each character. |
| 12 | 4 | Height in pixels for each character. |
| 16 | variable | Each pixel uses 1 byte, so this field should be the product of the number of characters, the width, and the height. |

### boolean imagepalettecopy(resource destination, resource source)

The `imagepalettecopy` function replaces the palette in the destination image with the palette of the source image.

### boolean imagepng(resource image, string file)

The `imagepng` function either sends an image to the browser or writes it to a file. If a filename is provided, a PNG file is created. Otherwise, the image is sent directly to the browser. This latter method is used in most of the examples in this section.

### boolean imagepolygon(resource image, array points, integer number, integer color)

The `imagepolygon` function (Listing 16.25) behaves identically to the `imagefilledpolygon` function with the exception that the polygon is not filled. The `points` argument is an array of integers, two for each point of the polygon. A line will be drawn from each point in succession and from the last point to the first point. Output is shown in Figure 16.12.

**Listing 16.25**    *imagepolygon*

```php
<?php
    //create red square
    $image = imagecreate(100,100);
    $colorPink = imagecolorallocate($image, 0xFF, 0xCC, 0xCC);
    $colorBlack = imagecolorallocate($image, 0, 0, 0);
    imagefill($image, 0, 0, $colorPink);
```

| Listing 16.25 | *imagepolygon (cont.)* |
|---|---|

```
//set up three points of the triangle
$points = array(50, 10, 10, 90, 90, 90);

//draw triangle
imagepolygon($image,
    $points, count($points)/2,
    $colorBlack);

//send image
header("Content-type: image/png");
imagepng($image);
?>
```

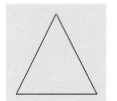

**Figure 16.12**  imagepolygon output.

### array imagepsbbox(string text, integer font_identifier, integer size, integer spacing, integer leading, double angle)

The imagepsbbox function returns an array containing a pair of coordinates that specify a bounding box that would surround a theoretical string of text. The first two numbers are the x and y values of the lower-left corner. The second pair of numbers specify the upper-right corner.

The font_identifier is an integer returned by imagepsloadfont. The size argument is in pixels. The spacing argument controls vertical spacing between lines of text. The leading argument controls horizontal spacing between characters. Both are expressed in units of 1/1000th of an em-square and are added to the default spacing or leading for a font. They may be positive or negative. The angle argument specifies a number of degrees to rotate from normal left-to-right orientation.

### imagepsencodefont(string file)

Use imagepsencodefont to change the encoding vector used to match ASCII characters to PostScript font images. By default, PostScript fonts only have characters for the first 127 ASCII values.

### imagepsextendfont(integer font_identifier, double extension_factor)

The `imagepsextendfont` function (Listing 16.26) stretches or compresses a PostScript font. The normal width of the font will be multiplied by the `extension_factor`. See `imagepscopyfont` for an example. Multiple calls to this function are not cumulative; they just change the extension. If you want to set the font back to normal width, use a factor of one. Output is shown in Figure 16.13.

---

**Listing 16.26**   *imagepsextendfont, imagepsslantfont*

```php
<?php
    //set parameters for text
    $font_file = "/usr/share/fonts/default/Type1/n0190031.pfb";
    $size = 20;
    $angle = 0;
    $text = "PHP";
    $antialias_steps = 16;
    $spacing = 0;
    $leading = 0;

    //create red square
    $image = imagecreate(100, $size*3);
    $colorYellow = imagecolorallocate($image, 0xFF, 0xFF, 0xCC);
    $colorBlack = imagecolorallocate($image, 0, 0, 0);
    imagefill($image, 10, 10, $colorYellow);

    //Load font
    if(!($myFont = imagepsloadfont($font_file)))
    {
        print("Unable to load font!");
        exit();
    }

    //write normal text
    imagepstext($image, $text, $myFont, $size,
        $colorBlack, $colorYellow,
        0, $size-1, $spacing, $leading,
        $angle, $antialias_steps);

    //make extended font
    $myFontExtended = imagepsloadfont($font_file);
    imagepsextendfont($myFontExtended, 1.5);
```

**Listing 16.26** *imagepsextendfont, imagepsslantfont (cont.)*

```
//write extended text
imagepstext($image, $text, $myFontExtended, $size,
    $colorBlack, $colorYellow,
    0, ($size*2)-1, $spacing, $leading,
    $angle, $antialias_steps);

//make slanted font
$myFontSlanted = imagepsloadfont($font_file);
imagepsslantfont($myFontSlanted, 1.5);

//write slanted text
imagepstext($image, $text, $myFontSlanted, $size,
    $colorBlack, $colorYellow,
    0, ($size*3)-1, $spacing, $leading,
    $angle, $antialias_steps);

//unload fonts
imagepsfreefont($myFont);
imagepsfreefont($myFontExtended);
imagepsfreefont($myFontSlanted);

//send image
header("Content-type: image/png");
imagepng($image);
?>
```

**Figure 16.13** `imagepsextendfont, imagepsslantfont` output.

### imagepsfreefont(integer font_identifier)

The `imagepsfreefont` function removes a PostScript font from memory. Generally, you do not need to do this. PHP will unload fonts when your script ends.

### resource imagepsloadfont(string file)

Use `imagepsloadfont` to load a PostScript font. A font identifier will be returned for use with the other PostScript functions. If the load fails, FALSE is returned.

### imagepsslantfont(integer font_identifier, double slant_factor)

Use `imagepsslantfont` to pitch the font forward or backwards. Sometimes this is referred to as italics. The `font_identifier` is an integer returned by `imagepsloadfont`. The `slant_factor` operates similarly to the `extension_factor` in the `imagepsextendfont` function. Values greater than one will cause the top of the font to pitch to the right. Values less than one will cause the top of the font to pitch to the left.

### array imagepstext(resource image, string text, integer font_identifier, integer size, integer foreground, integer background, integer x, integer y, integer spacing, integer leading, double angle, integer antialias_steps)

The `imagepstext` function (Listing 16.27) draws a string of text into an image using a PostScript font. The image argument is an integer as returned by `imagecreate`, `imagecreatefrompng`, or a similar function. The `font_identifier` argument is a value returned by the `imagepsloadfont` function. The `size` argument specifies the height in number of pixels. The `foreground` and `background` arguments are color identifiers. The background color is used for antialiasing. The bounding box is not flooded with this color.

The x and y arguments specify the bottom left corner from where to begin drawing. The `spacing` argument controls vertical spacing between lines of text. The `leading` argument controls horizontal spacing between characters. Both are expressed in units of 1/1000th of an em-square and are added to the default spacing or leading for a font. They may be positive or negative. The `angle` argument specifies a number of degrees to rotate from normal left-to-right orientation. The `antialias_steps` argument specifies how many colors to use when antialiasing, or smoothing. Two values are valid: 4 and 16. The last four arguments are optional.

The returned array contains two pairs of coordinates specifying the lower-left corner and upper-right corner of the bounding box, respectively.

---

**Listing 16.27**   *imagepstext*

```php
<?php
    /*
    ** Draw text over a photograph using a PostScript font
    */

    //set parameters for text
    $image = "waterfall.jpg";
```

**Listing 16.27**  *imagepstext (cont.)*

```
$font_file = "/usr/share/fonts/default/Type1/n0190031.pfb";
$size = 100;
$angle = 0;
$text = "Waterfall";
$antialias_steps = 16;
$spacing = 0;
$leading = 0;

//Load font
if(!($myFont = imagepsloadfont($font_file)))
{
    print("Unable to load font!");
    exit();
}

//get bounding box
$Box = imagepsbbox($text, $myFont, $size, $spacing, $leading,
    $angle);

//load photograph
$image = imagecreatefromjpeg($image);

//set up text color
$colorText = imagecolorallocate($image, 0x00, 0xFF, 0x00);
$colorClearText = imagecolorresolvealpha($image, 0x00, 0xFF,
    0x00, 0xFF);
$colorShadow = imagecolorresolvealpha($image, 0x00, 0x00,
    0x00, 0x50);
$colorClearShadow = imagecolorresolvealpha($image, 0x00, 0x00,
    0x00, 0xFF);

imagelayereffect($image, IMG_EFFECT_NORMAL);

//make soft drop shadow
imagepstext($image, $text, $myFont, $size,
    $colorShadow, $colorClearShadow,
    55, $Box[3]+55, $spacing, $leading,
    $angle, $antialias_steps);

//write the text
imagepstext($image, $text, $myFont, $size,
    $colorText, $colorClearText,
    50, $Box[3]+50, $spacing, $leading,
    $angle, $antialias_steps);
```

| Listing 16.27 | *imagepstext (cont.)* |
|---|---|

```
//unload font
imagepsfreefont($myFont);

//send image
header("Content-type: image/png");
imagepng($image);
?>
```

### imagerectangle(resource image, integer top_left_x, integer top_left_y, integer bottom_right_x, integer bottom_right_y, integer color)

The imagerectangle function (Listing 16.28) draws a rectangle based on the top left and bottom right corners. The inside of the rectangle will not be filled as it is with the imagefilledrectangle function. Output is shown in Figure 16.14.

| Listing 16.28 | *imagerectangle* |
|---|---|

```
<?php
    //create green square
    $image = imagecreate(200,200);
    $colorGreen = imagecolorallocate($image, 128, 255, 128);
    $colorBlack = imagecolorallocate($image, 0, 0, 0);
    imagefill($image, 0, 0, $colorGreen);

    //draw a black rectangle
    imagerectangle($image,
        10, 10, 90, 90,
        $colorBlack);

    //send image
    header("Content-type: image/png");
    imagepng($image);
?>
```

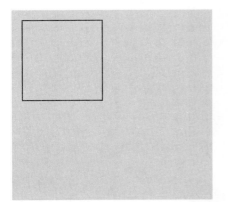

**Figure 16.14**   imagerectangle output.

### resource imagerotate(resource image, double angle, integer background)

The imagerotate function (Listing 16.29) returns a new image with the source image rotated by the given angle. Positive values for the angle argument rotate the image counterclockwise. The background argument specifies a color used for filling in areas uncovered when you rotate by angles that aren't multiples of 90. Output is shown in Figure 16.15.

**Listing 16.29**   *imagerotate*

```php
<?php
    //create green square
    $image = imagecreatetruecolor(200,200);
    $colorGreen = imagecolorallocate($image, 128, 255, 128);
    $colorBlack = imagecolorallocate($image, 0, 0, 0);
    imagefill($image, 0, 0, $colorGreen);

    //draw a black rectangle
    imagerectangle($image,
        10, 10, 90, 90,
        $colorBlack);

    //rotate 35 degrees and replace
    $image = imagerotate($image, 35, $colorBlack);

    //show image
    header("Content-type: image/png");
    imagepng($image);
?>
```

**Figure 16.15** `imagerotate` output.

### imagesavealpha(resource image, boolean on)

The `imagesavealpha` function sets whether PHP saves alpha levels when it writes an image to disk.

### boolean imagesetbrush(resource image, resource brush)

Use `imagesetbrush` (Listing 16.30) to set the brush used for drawing. The brush is an image itself. To draw with it, use `IMG_COLOR_BRUSHED` or `IMG_COLOR_STYLEDBRUSHED` instead of an allocated color. The former constant paints the brush for each pixel. The latter constant paints according to a style you set with `imagesetstyle`. Output is shown in Figure 16.16.

---

**Listing 16.30** *imagesetbrush*

```php
<?php
    //create black canvas
    $image = imagecreate(100,100);
    $colorBlack = imagecolorallocate($image, 0, 0, 0);
    imagefill($image, 0, 0, $colorBlack);

    //make a brush with transparent background
    $brush = imagecreate(20, 20);
```

---

**Listing 16.30** *imagesetbrush (cont.)*

```
$brushColorTransparent = imagecolorallocate($brush, 255, 0,
    255);
imagecolortransparent($brush, $brushColorTransparent);
imagefill($brush, 0, 0, $brushColorTransparent);

//draw three diagonal dots
$brushColorRed = imagecolorallocate($brush, 255, 0, 0);
$brushColorYellow = imagecolorallocate($brush, 255, 255, 0);
$brushColorBlue = imagecolorallocate($brush, 0, 0, 255);
imagefilledellipse($brush, 5, 5, 5, 5, $brushColorRed);
imagefilledellipse($brush, 10, 10, 5, 5, $brushColorYellow);
imagefilledellipse($brush, 15, 15, 5, 5, $brushColorBlue);

//set the brush
imagesetbrush($image, $brush);

//draw triangle with brush
$points = array(50, 10, 10, 90, 90, 90);
imagepolygon($image,
    $points, count($points)/2,
    IMG_COLOR_BRUSHED);

//show image
header("Content-type: image/png");
imagepng($image);
?>
```

---

**Figure 16.16** imagesetbrush output.

### boolean imagesetpixel(resource image, integer x, integer y, integer color)

The imagesetpixel function (Listing 16.31) sets a single pixel to the specified color.

**Listing 16.31**   *imagesetpixel*

```php
<?php
    //create black canvas
    $image = imagecreate(100, 100);
    $colorBlack = imagecolorallocate($image, 0, 0, 0);
    imagefill($image, 0, 0, $colorBlack);

    $dotColor = array(
        imagecolorallocate($image, 255, 0, 0),
        imagecolorallocate($image, 0, 255, 0),
        imagecolorallocate($image, 255, 255, 0),
        imagecolorallocate($image, 0, 0, 255),
        imagecolorallocate($image, 0, 255, 255),
        imagecolorallocate($image, 255, 0, 255)
        );
    $lastColor = count($dotColor) - 1;

    //draw 10000 random black dots
    srand(time());
    for($i=0; $i < 10000; $i++)
    {
        $color = $dotColor[rand(0, $lastColor)];
        imagesetpixel($image, rand(0, 99), rand(0, 99), $color);
    }

    //send image
    header("Content-type: image/png");
    imagepng($image);
?>
```

### boolean imagesetstyle(resource image, array style)

The imagesetstyle function sets a pattern PHP uses to draw lines. The style array should be an array of colors, each element representing a single pixel. You may use the IMG_COLOR_TRANSPARENT constant to represent a pixel not to be drawn. This constant applies only to styles.

After defining the line style, you may draw with the style by using the IMG_COLOR_STYLED and IMG_COLOR_STYLEDBRUSHED constants. The latter draws with a brush instead of single pixels.

### boolean imagesetthickness(resource image, integer pixels)

Use imagesetthickness (Listing 16.32) to set the width of lines. PHP paints the lines with a line of pixels of the given width and one pixel high, rotating the line to be perpendicular to the current angle. This produces good results for straight lines. Curved lines may appear jagged because it's hard to produce exact angles with digital images. Figure 16.17 demonstrates this effect. You may avoid this by painting with a round brush.

---

**Listing 16.32**   *imagesetthickness*

```php
<?php
    //create red square
    $image = imagecreate(300,100);
    $colorPink = imagecolorallocate($image, 0xFF, 0xCC, 0xCC);
    $colorBlack = imagecolorallocate($image, 0, 0, 0);
    imagefill($image, 0, 0, $colorPink);

    imagesetthickness($image, 10);

    //set up three points of the triangle
    $points = array(50, 10, 10, 90, 90, 90);

    //draw triangle
    imagepolygon($image,
        $points, count($points)/2,
        $colorBlack);

    //draw ellipse
    imageellipse($image, 150, 50, 80, 50, $colorBlack);

    //draw rectangle
    imagerectangle($image,
        210, 10, 290, 90,
        $colorBlack);

    //send image
    header("Content-type: image/png");
    imagepng($image);
?>
```

---

**Figure 16.17**   imagesetthickness output.

### boolean imagesettile(resource image, resource tile)

The imagesettile function (Listing 16.33) sets a tile instead of a solid color used for filling areas. The tile argument should be an image resource as returned by one of the image creation functions. After setting the tile, use the IMG_COLOR_TILED instead of an allocated color. Transparent colors in the tile will allow anything behind the fill pattern to show through.

**Listing 16.33** *imagesettile*

```php
<?php
    $image = imagecreatetruecolor(200,200);
    $colorYellow = imagecolorresolve($image, 255, 255, 128);
    imagefill($image, 0, 0, $colorYellow);

    //load a tile
    $tile = imagecreatefromjpeg("woodtile.jpg");
    imagesettile($image, $tile);

    //set up three points of the triangle
    $points = array(100, 10, 10, 190, 190, 190);

    //draw triangle
    imagefilledpolygon($image,
        $points, count($points)/2,
        IMG_COLOR_TILED);

    //create a grid tile
    $grid = imagecreate(32, 32);
    $gridColorBlack = imagecolorallocate($grid, 0x00, 0x00, 0x00);
    $gridColorTransparent = imagecolorallocate($grid,
        0xFF, 0x00, 0xFF);
    imagecolortransparent($grid, $gridColorTransparent);
    imagefill($grid, 0, 0, $gridColorTransparent);

    imagesetthickness($grid, 5);
    imageline($grid, 0, 0, 31, 0, $gridColorBlack);
    imageline($grid, 0, 0, 0, 31, $gridColorBlack);

    imagesettile($image, $grid);

    //paint grid over entire image
    imagefilledrectangle($image, 0, 0, 199, 199, IMG_COLOR_TILED);

    //send image
    header("Content-type: image/png");
    imagepng($image);
?>
```

**boolean imagestring(resource image, integer font, integer x, integer y, string text, integer color)**

The `imagestring` function (Listing 16.34) draws the given text at the specified point. The top left part of the string will be at the specified point. The font argument may be a built-in font or one loaded by `imageloadfont`.

The good thing about this function is that it's always available. It's handy for debugging. The `imagepstext` and `imagettftext` function produce better-looking text.

**Listing 16.34** *imagestring, imagestringup*

```php
<?php
   //create yellow square
   $image = imagecreate(150, 150);
   $colorYellow = imagecolorallocate($image, 255, 255, 128);
   $colorBlack = imagecolorallocate($image, 0, 0, 0);
   imagefill($image, 0, 0, $colorYellow);

   //draw text horizontally
   imagestring($image, 5, 10, 10, "Hello World!", $colorBlack);

   //draw text vertically
   imagestringup($image, 5, 10, 140, "Hello World!",
      $colorBlack);

   //send image
   header("Content-type: image/png");
   imagepng($image);
?>
```

**boolean imagestringup(resource image, integer font, integer x, integer y, string text, integer color)**

The `imagestringup` function draws a string oriented vertically instead of horizontally. Otherwise, it works identically to `imagestring`.

**resource imagesx(resource image)**

The `imagesx` function (Listing 16.35) returns the width in pixels of the specified image.

| Listing 16.35 | *imagesx, imagesy* |

```php
<?php
    /*
    ** Put a rectangle in the center of any image
    */

    //attempt to open image, suppress error messages
    if(!($image = @imagecreatefromjpeg("waterfall.jpg")))
    {
        //error, so create an error image and exit
        $image = imagecreate(200,200);
        $colorWhite = imagecolorallocate($image, 255, 255, 255);
        $colorBlack = imagecolorallocate($image, 0, 0, 0);
        imagefill($image, 0, 0, $colorWhite);
        imagestring($image, 4, 10, 10, "Couldn't load image!",
            $colorBlack);
        header("Content-type: image/jpeg");
        imagejpeg($image);
    }

    //find center
    $centerX = intval(imagesx($image)/2);
    $centerY = intval(imagesy($image)/2);

    $colorGreen = imagecolorallocate($image, 0, 255, 0);

    //draw a green rectangle in center
    imagefilledrectangle($image,
        ($centerX-15), ($centerY-15),
        ($centerX+15), ($centerY+15),
        $colorGreen);

    //send image
    header("Content-type: image/png");
    imagepng($image);
?>
```

### resource imagesy(resource image)

The imagesy function returns the height in pixels of the specified image.

### boolean imagetruecolortopalette(resource image, boolean dither, integer colors)

The `imagetruecolortopalette` function converts a true color image to one that uses a set number of colors. The dither argument specifies whether PHP should use dithering to approximate colors. The `colors` argument sets the maximum number of colors in the palette.

### array imagettfbbox(integer point_size, integer angle, string font, string text)

The `imagettfbbox` function returns an array of points that describe a bounding box around text to be drawn by the `imagettftext` function. The points are relative to the leftmost point on the baseline. The array elements correspond to the lower-left, lower-right, upper-right, and upper-left corners, in that order, as shown in Table 16.9.

This function may not be available, depending on the libraries available when PHP was compiled.

**Table 16.9**   Array Returned by `imagettfbbox`

| Array Pair | Corner |
| --- | --- |
| 0, 1 | Lower-Left |
| 2, 3 | Lower-Right |
| 4, 5 | Upper-Right |
| 6, 7 | Upper-Left |

### boolean imagettftext(resource image, integer point_size, integer angle, integer x, integer y, integer color, string font, string text)

The `imagettftext` function (Listing 16.36) uses a TrueType font to draw a string of text. The x and y arguments refer to the leftmost position of the baseline. The text will radiate from that point at the given angle, which should be from 0 to 360. An angle of zero represents normal right-to-left text. The font argument is the full path to a `.ttf` file. Output is shown in Figure 16.18.

This function may not be available, depending on the libraries available when PHP was compiled.

**Listing 16.36**    *imagettfbbox, imagettftext*

```php
<?php
    /*
    ** Draw text using a TrueType font
    ** Also, draw a box behind the text.
    */

    //set parameters for text
    $size = 40;
    $angle = 45;
    $startX = 30;
    $startY = 90;
    $font = "c:\windows\fonts\comic.ttf";

    //create red square
    $image = imagecreate(100, 100);
    $colorYellow = imagecolorallocate($image, 0xFF, 0xFF, 0x99);
    $colorGray = imagecolorallocate($image, 0xCC, 0xCC, 0xCC);
    $colorBlack = imagecolorallocate($image, 0, 0, 0);
    imagefill($image, 10, 10, $colorYellow);


    //get bounding box
    $Box = imagettfbbox($size, $angle, $font, "PHP");

    //move bounding box to starting point (100,100)
    for($index = 0; $index < count($Box); $index += 2)
    {
        $Box[$index] += $startX;
        $Box[$index+1] += $startY;
    }

    //draw bounding box
    imagefilledpolygon($image, $Box, count($Box)/2, $colorGray);

    //write the text
    $Box = imagettftext($image, $size, $angle,
        $startX, $startY, $colorBlack,
        $font, "PHP");

    //send image
    header("Content-type: image/png");
    imagepng($image);
?>
```

**Figure 16.18**   `imagettfbbox`, `imagettftext` output.

### integer imagetypes()

The `imagetypes` function (Listing 16.37) returns a bitfield set with the types of images supported by the version of PHP executing the script. Use the constants shown in Table 16.10 to test for the availability of an image file format.

**Table 16.10**   Image Type Constants

| | |
|---|---|
| IMG_GIF | IMG_PNG |
| IMG_JPEG | IMG_WBMP |
| IMG_JPG | IMG_XPM |

**Listing 16.37**   *imagetypes*

```php
<?php
    $types = imagetypes();

    print("Supported Output Image Types:<br>");

    if($types & IMG_GIF)
    {
        print('GIF<br>');
    }

    if($types & IMG_JPEG)
    {
        print('JPEG<br>');
    }

    if($types & IMG_PNG)
    {
        print('PNG<br>');
    }
```

| Listing 16.37 | *imagetypes (cont.)* |
|---|---|

```
if($types & IMG_WBMP)
{
    print('WBMP<br>');
}

if($types & IMG_XPM)
{
    print('XPM<br>');
}
?>
```

### boolean imagewbmp(resource image, string file, integer foreground)

The imagewbmp function either sends an image to the browser or writes it to a file. If a filename is provided, a WAP (Wireless Application Protocol) bitmap file is created. Otherwise, the image is sent directly to the browser. The optional foreground argument should be set with the index for a color to be considered the foreground color in WBMP files.

### jpeg2wbmp(string jpeg_file, string wbmp_file, integer height, integer width, integer threshold)

The jpeg2wbmp function reads a JPEG file and writes a WBMP file. The optional threshold argument sets the threshold for when a pixel is converted to black or white. Keep in mind that WBMP files are monochrome.

### png2wbmp(string png_file, string wbmp_file, integer height, integer width, integer threshold)

The jpeg2wbmp function reads a PNG file and writes a WBMP file. The optional threshold argument sets the threshold for when a pixel is converted to black or white. Keep in mind that WBMP files are monochrome.

# DATABASE

**Topics in This Chapter**

- DBM-Style Database Abstraction
- DBX
- LDAP
- MySQL
- ODBC
- Oracle
- Postgres
- Sybase and Microsoft SQL Server

# Chapter 17

PHP offers support for many databases. Open Source relational databases are well represented, as are many commercial products. If native support for a database doesn't exist, it's likely you may use ODBC with an appropriate driver. Chapter 23 discusses strategies for using databases with PHP-powered sites.

Most of the functions in this section rely on an extension module. These may be loaded either in the `php.ini` file or the `dl` function but most likely are compiled into PHP.

While this chapter describes the PHP functions that communicate with various systems, it does not pursue introducing the intricacies of all the systems. I can't possibly include a full tutorial on SQL within this book. If you have chosen a database for integration with PHP, I assume you will take the time to learn about that database. I am a big fan of MySQL and wrote a book about it in 2001: *Core MySQL*.

## 17.1 DBM-Style Database Abstraction

The DBA functions abstract communications with databases that conform to the style of Berkeley DB database systems. Rather than storing relational records, a DBM database simply stores key/value pairs. This is similar to an associative array.

The functions in this section replace a set of functions that allow just one type of DBM database. These new functions allow for choosing the underlying system from within your PHP code rather than compiling PHP for a single DBM implementation.

You choose a type of database when you open a connection, and the rest of the functions perform accordingly. Sascha Schumann added these functions to PHP.

### dba_close(resource connection)

The `dba_close` function closes a link to a database. The `connection` argument is an integer returned by the `dba_open` or `dba_popen` functions. If you choose not to close a database connection, PHP will close it for you.

### boolean dba_delete(string key, resource connection)

The `dba_delete` function (Listing 17.1) removes an entry from a database. You must supply both the key and a valid connection to a database, as supplied by `dba_open` or `dba_popen`. The success of the deletion is returned as a boolean.

| **Listing 17.1** | *Interfacing with a DBM-style database* |
| --- | --- |

```php
<?php
    // open database in write mode
    if(($db = dba_popen('inventory', 'w', 'gdbm')) === FALSE)
    {
        print('Could not open database!');
        exit();
    }

    if(dba_exists('3', $db))
    {
        //item 3 exists, set inventory to 150
        dba_replace('3', '150', $db);
        print("Replaced inventory for item 3<br>");
    }
    else
    {
        //item 3 doesn't exists, insert it
        dba_insert('3', '150', $db);
        print("Inserted inventory for item 3<br>");
    }

    if(dba_exists('4', $db))
    {
        // remove item 4
        dba_delete('4', $db);
        print("Removed item 4<br>");
    }
```

| Listing 17.1 | *Interfacing with a DBM-style database (cont.)* |
|---|---|

```
else
{
    dba_insert('4', '500', $db);
    print("Inserted inventory for item 4<br>");
}

//sync database
dba_sync($db);

//get all the records
for($key = dba_firstkey($db);
    $key !== FALSE;
    $key = dba_nextkey($db))
{
    print("$key = " . dba_fetch($key, $db) . "<br>");
}


// close database
dba_close($db);
?>
```

### boolean dba_exists(string key, resource connection)

The `dba_exists` function tests for the presence of a key. The `connection` argument must be an integer returned by the `dba_open` or `dba_popen` functions. The description of `dba_delete` has an example of using `dba_exists`.

### string dba_fetch(string key, resource connection)
### string dba_fetch(string key, integer skip, resource connection)

Use the `dba_fetch` function to retrieve a record given its key. Only CDB databases support the second form that includes the optional `skip` argument; it specifies the number of duplicate records to skip. The `connection` argument should be a resource returned by `dba_open` or `dba_popen`.

### string dba_firstkey(resource connection)

The `dba_firstkey` function returns the first key in the database. If the database is empty, `FALSE` will be returned. As the example for `dba_delete` shows, `dba_firstkey` and `dba_nextkey` may be used to traverse the entire database.

### array dba_handlers()

The `dba_handlers` function returns the list of database types supported.

### boolean dba_insert(string key, string value, resource connection)

Use `dba_insert` to add a record to the database. The success of the insert is returned. Trying to insert a record that already exists is not allowed. If you need to update a record, use `dba_replace`.

### array dba_list()

The `dba_list` function returns an array of open DBA databases. The keys of the array are unique integers that represent the resources, but they aren't usable as resources themselves.

### string dba_nextkey(resource connection)

The `dba_nextkey` function returns the next key from the database. When there are no keys left, FALSE is returned.

### resource dba_open(string filename, string mode, string type, …)

Use `dba_open` to establish a connection to a DBM-style database. A positive integer is returned if the open is successful; FALSE is returned if it fails. The `filename` argument is simply the path to a database. The `mode` argument can be one of four characters that control input and output of data. Table 17.1 lists the four modes.

The `type` argument chooses the underlying database engine. Table 17.2 describes the four types. You may also supply any number of optional arguments that will be passed directly to the underlying engine. Generally, the second character controls locking. A lowercase `l` instructs the engine to implement locking using a `.lck` file. A `d` instructs the engine to lock the database file itself. A hyphen (-) suspends locking. Locking is cooperative, which means all scripts must specify the same locking method. You may also add a `t` as the third argument to test.

When your script finishes executing, the database connection closes automatically. You may choose to close it sooner with `dba_close`, and this may save some small amount of memory. Contrast this function to `dba_popen`, which attempts to reuse links.

### boolean dba_optimize(resource connection)

Use `dba_optimize` to optimize a database, which usually consists of eliminating gaps between records created by deletes. This function returns TRUE on success. Some underlying engines do not support optimizations, in which case this function will have no effect.

**Table 17.1** DBA Open Modes

| Mode | Description |
|------|-------------|
| c | If the database doesn't exist, it will be created. Reads and writes may be performed. |
| n | If the database doesn't exist, it will be created. If it does exist, all records will be deleted. Reads and writes may be performed. |
| r | Only reads may be performed. |
| w | Reads and writes may be performed. If the file does not exist, an error occurs. |

**Table 17.2** DBA Database Engine Codes

| Code | Description |
|------|-------------|
| cdb<br>cdb_make | CDB is a package for creating constant databases—that is, databases that are created and read from only. This offers a performance advantage with the tradeoff that none of the writing functions work. To download the software, visit <http://cr.yp.to/cdb.html>. PHP includes a bundled version of CDB, which allows inserting rows, but not updating. |
| db2<br>db3<br>db4 | These codes stand for a database package developed by Sleepycat Software, which is based on the original Berkeley source code. In fact, the founders wrote the original DBM at Berkeley. You can get more information and download software at their Web site: <http://www.sleepycat.com/>. |
| dbm | This code represents the original style of DBM database as developed at Berkeley. |
| flatfile | This code allows reading from files created with PHP's deprecated DBM functions. |
| gdbm | The GNU Database Manager is the result of a project by GNU. You can download gdbm from the GNU FTP server <ftp://ftp.gnu.org/gnu/gdbm>. |
| ndbm | This code stands for a newer version of the DBM standard with fewer restrictions than DBM. |

### resource dba_popen(string filename, string mode, string type, ...)

The dba_popen function behaves identically to dba_open with one difference: Connections are not closed. They remain with the process until the process ends. When you call dba_popen, it first tries to find an existing connection.

Failing that, it will create a new connection. You never call `dba_close` on a connection returned by `dba_popen`.

Since the links are pooled on a per-process basis, this functionality offers no benefit when using PHP as a standalone executable. When using PHP as an Apache module, there may be some small performance benefit due to the way Apache uses child processes.

### boolean dba_replace(string key, string value, resource connection)

Use `dba_replace` to update the value of an existing record. As with the other DBA functions, a valid link as returned by `dba_open` or `dba_popen` should be used for the `connection` argument. See the description of `dba_insert` for an example using `dba_replace`.

### boolean dba_sync(resource connection)

The `dba_sync` function will synchronize the view of the database in memory and its image on the disk. As you insert records, they may be cached in memory by the underlying engine. Other processes reading from the database will not see these new records until synchronization.

## 17.2  DBX

The DBX extension provides a simple, universal interface to several relational databases. This disallows some special features of each database with the benefit of easily switching database servers. Of course, differences in the SQL the database server understands must be addressed in your scripts. There are alternatives to this extension written in PHP, including the one in PEAR. Listing 17.2 demonstrates the use of the DBX functions.

Marc Boeren added the DBX extension to PHP.

| Listing 17.2 | *Using DBX* |
| --- | --- |

```php
<?php
    function myDBX_Order($a, $b)
    {
        return(dbx_compare($a, $b, "ID", DBX_CMP_ASC |
            DBX_CMP_NUMBER));
    }
```

**Listing 17.2**    *Using DBX (cont.)*

```php
//connect to MySQL server
if(!($db = dbx_connect(
    DBX_MYSQL,
    'localhost',
    'ft3',
    'freetrade', '',
    DBX_PERSISTENT)))
{
    print("Unable to connect to database");
    exit();
}

//select from item table
$result = dbx_query($db,
    'SELECT ID, Name from item',
    DBX_RESULT_ASSOC | DBX_COLNAMES_UNCHANGED);

if($result == FALSE)
{
    print("Error: " . dbx_error($db));
    exit();
}

//sort result set
dbx_sort($result, 'myDBX_Order');

print('<table border="1">');

print('<tr>');
for($c=0; $c < $result->cols; $c++)
{
    print("<th>{$result->info['name'][$c]}</th>");
}
print('</tr>');

for($r=0; $r < $result->rows; $r++)
{
    print('<tr>');
    for($c=0; $c < $result->cols; $c++)
    {
        print("<td>{$result->data[$r][$c]}</td>");
    }
    print('</tr>');
}
print('</table>');
?>
```

### boolean dbx_close(object link)

The dbx_close closes a connection to a database. The link argument should be an object returned by dbx_connect.

### integer dbx_compare(array left, array right, string key, integer flags)

The dbx_compare function compares two rows, mostly for the benefit of the dbx_sort function. If the rows are equal, it returns 0. If the left argument comes after the right argument, it returns 1. Otherwise, it returns –1. The left and right arguments should be row arrays created by dbx_query. The key argument names the column used for comparison.

Optionally, you may set the flags argument in order to control the direction of the comparison and type of comparison. Combine the flags shown in Table 17.3 with a bitwise-OR operator. By default, comparisons are made with the native types in ascending order.

**Table 17.3** DBX Comparison Flags

| Flag | Description |
| --- | --- |
| DBX_CMP_ASC | Ascending order |
| DBX_CMP_DESC | Descending order |
| DBX_CMP_NATIVE | Use native types |
| DBX_CMP_NUMBER | Convert and compare as numbers |
| DBX_CMP_TEXT | Compare as strings |

### object dbx_connect(string module, string host, string database, string user, string password, integer persistent)

The dbx_connect function connects to a database server and returns an object used by the other DBX functions. The first argument specifies the database server type. Set it with one of the constants or strings from Table 17.4. The host argument typically specifies an Internet host that runs the database server. The database argument specifies the name of the database, similar to SQL's USE statement. The user and password arguments set login parameters. The optional persistent argument may be set with DBX_PERSISTENT, in which case PHP attempts to reuse connections between script executions.

The returned object contains three properties. The handle property is a resource for the connection. The module property matches the module specified in the first argument to `dbx_connect`. The `database` property matches the database argument to `dbx_connect`.

**Table 17.4**   DBX Connection Constants

| Database | Constant | String |
|---|---|---|
| Frontbase | DBX_FBSQL | fbsql |
| Microsoft SQL Server | DBX_MSSQL | mssql |
| MySQL | DBX_MYSQL | mysql |
| Oracle OCI8 | DBX_OCI8 | oci8 |
| ODBC | DBX_ODBC | odbc |
| PostgreSQL | DBX_PGSQL | pgsql |
| Sybase CT | DBX_SYBASECT | sybase_ct |

### string dbx_error(object link)

The `dbx_error` function returns a string describing the last error produced by the database module used by the given connection.

### string dbx_escape_string(object link, string text)

The `dbx_escape_string` function escapes special characters in the given text according to the capabilities of the database module, preparing the text for placement inside an SQL statement as a string literal.

### object dbx_query(object link, string query, integer flags)

The `dbx_query` function executes a query on an open connection, returning an object containing the result set. The result set object will contain four or five properties. The optional `flags` argument allows you to control aspects of the result set. Available options are shown in Table 17.5.

The result set's `handle` property is a connection resource, the same contained in the object returned by `dbx_connect`. The `info` property contains two arrays, `name` and `type`. These are arrays that give the name and type, respectively, of columns in the result set. The `data` property is an array of rows in the result set. Each element of this array is an array of the column values. An integer references each column value. Optionally, the column name may reference the value as well. The `rows` and `cols` properties contain counts for rows and columns in the result set.

By default, `dbx_query` includes all information and leaves column names unchanged. Specifying `DBX_RESULT_INDEX` removes both column information and column names. Specifying `DBX_RESULT_ASSOC` automatically activates `DBX_RESULT_INFO`.

**Table 17.5**   DBX Query Flags

| Flag | Description |
|------|-------------|
| DBX_COLNAMES_LOWERCASE | Convert column names to lowercase. |
| DBX_COLNAMES_UNCHANGED | Leave column names unchanged. |
| DBX_COLNAMES_UPPERCASE | Convert column names to uppercase. |
| DBX_RESULT_ASSOC | Reference column values with column names. |
| DBX_RESULT_INDEX | Reference column values with column numbers. |
| DBX_RESULT_INFO | Include information about column in the `info` property. |

### boolean dbx_sort(object result, string comparison_function)

The `dbx_sort` function sorts a result set returned by `dbx_query` using the function named by `comparison_function`. Typical use of this function involves defining your own wrapper of `dbx_compare`, as shown in Listing 17.2.

Sorting results within the SQL statement is faster, so use this functionality only when necessary.

## 17.3  LDAP

LDAP is an acronym for Lightweight Directory Access Protocol. It is a universal method of storing directory information and is a partial implementation of the X.500 standard. LDAP was first described in RFC 1777 and RFC 1778.

Through TCP/IP, clients can access a centralized address book containing contact information, public encryption keys, and similar information. Many servers are live on the Internet. Dante, a nonprofit organization, maintains a list of LDAP servers organized by country at `<http://www.dante.net/np/pdi.html>`. A full discussion of LDAP is beyond the scope of this book, but abundant information can be found on the Web. A good starting point is the OpenLDAP project at `<http://www.openldap.org/>`.

The functions in this section require either compiling LDAP support into the PHP module or loading an extension module with dl. The LDAP module is the result of collaboration by Amitay Isaacs, Rasmus Lerdorf, Gerrit Thomson, and Eric Warnke.

### boolean ldap_add(resource connection, string dn, array entry)

The ldap_add function (Listing 17.3) adds entries to the specified DN (distinguished name) at the object level. The entry argument is an array of the attribute values. If an attribute can have multiple values, the array element should be an array itself. See the mail attribute in Listing 17.3. If you wish to add attributes at the attribute level, use ldap_mod_add.

---

**Listing 17.3**   `ldap_add`

```php
<?php
    //connect to LDAP server
    if(!($ldap=ldap_connect("localhost")))
    {
        die("Could not connect to LDAP server!");
    }

    //set login DN
    $dn="cn=Manager,dc=leonatkinson,dc=com";

    //attempt to bind to DN using password
    if(!ldap_bind($ldap, $dn, "secret"))
    {
        die("Unable to bind to '$dn'!");
    }

    // create entry
    $entry["cn"]="Barry Bat";
    $entry["objectClass"]="inetOrgPerson";
    $entry["sn"]="Barry";
    $entry["mail"][0] = "barry@example.com";
    $entry["mail"][1] = "bat@example.com";
    $entry["initials"]="BB";
    $entry["homePhone"]="123-123-1234";
    $entry["mobile"]="123-123-1234";

    //create new entry's DN
    $dn = "cn=Barry Bat,dc=leonatkinson,dc=com";
```

| Listing 17.3 | *ldap_add (cont.)* |
|---|---|

```
//add entry
if(ldap_add($ldap, $dn, $entry))
{
    print("Entry Added!");
}
else
{
    print("Add failed!");
}

//close connection
ldap_close($ldap);
?>
```

### boolean ldap_bind(resource connection, string dn, string password)

Use `ldap_bind` to bind to a directory. Use the optional `dn` and `password` arguments to identify yourself. Servers typically require authentication for any commands that change the contents of the directory.

### boolean ldap_close(resource connection)

The `ldap_close` function closes the connection to the directory server.

### boolean ldap_compare(resource connection, string dn, string attribute, string value)

The `ldap_compare` function compares an entry to the given value.

### integer ldap_connect(string host, integer port)

The `ldap_connect` function returns an LDAP connection identifier, or `FALSE` when there is an error. Both arguments are optional. With no arguments, `ldap_connect` returns the identifier of the current open connection. If the `port` argument is omitted, port 389 is assumed.

### integer ldap_count_entries(resource connection, integer result)

The `ldap_count_entries` function returns the number of entries in the specified result set. The `result` argument is a result identifier returned by `ldap_read`.

### boolean ldap_delete(resource connection, string dn)

The `ldap_delete` function (Listing 17.4) removes an entry from the directory.

| Listing 17.4 | *ldap_delete* |
| --- | --- |

```php
<?php
    // connect to LDAP server
    if(!($ldap=ldap_connect("localhost")))
    {
        die("Unable to connect to LDAP server!");
    }

    //set login DN
    $dn="cn=Manager,dc=leonatkinson,dc=com";

    //attempt to bind to DN using password
    if(!ldap_bind($ldap, $dn, "secret"))
    {
        die("Unable to bind to '$dn'!");
    }

    //delete entry from directory
    $dn="cn=Barbara J Jensen,dc=leonatkinson,dc=com";
    if(ldap_delete($ldap, $dn))
    {
        print("Entry Deleted!");
    }
    else
    {
        print("Delete failed!");
    }

    //close connection
    ldap_close($ldap);
?>
```

### string ldap_dn2ufn(string dn)

The ldap_dn2ufn translates a DN into a more user-friendly form, with type specifiers stripped.

### integer ldap_errno(resource connection)

The ldap_errno function returns the error number for the last error on a connection.

### string ldap_error(resource connection)

The ldap_error function returns a description of the last error on a connection.

### string ldap_err2str(integer error)

Use ldap_err2str to convert an error number to a textual description.

### array ldap_explode_dn(string dn, boolean attributes)

The ldap_explode_dn function (Listing 17.5) splits a DN returned by ldap_get_dn into an array. Each element is a relative distinguished name, or RDN. The array contains an element indexed by count that is the number of RDNs. The attributes argument specifies whether values are returned with their attribute codes.

| Listing 17.5 | ldap_explode_dn |
| --- | --- |

```php
<?php
    //set test DN
    $dn = "cn=Leon Atkinson, o=PHP Community, c=US";

    $rdn = ldap_explode_dn($dn, FALSE);

    for($index = 0; $index < $rdn["count"]; $index++)
    {
        print("$rdn[$index] <BR>\n");
    }
?>
```

### string ldap_first_attribute(resource connection, integer result, integer pointer)

The ldap_first_attribute function returns the first attribute for a given entry. The pointer argument must be passed as a reference. This variable stores a pointer in the list of attributes. The ldap_get_attributes function is probably more convenient.

### resource ldap_first_entry(resource connection, integer result)

The ldap_first_entry function returns an entry identifier for the first entry in the result set. This integer is used in the ldap_next_entry function. Use ldap_get_entries to retrieve all entries in an array.

### resource ldap_first_reference(resource connection, resource result)

The ldap_first_reference function returns the first reference from a result set.

### boolean ldap_free_result(integer result)

Use `ldap_free_result` to clear any memory used for a result returned by `ldap_read` or `ldap_search`.

### array ldap_get_attributes(resource connection, resource result)

Use `ldap_get_attributes` to get a multidimensional array of all the attributes and their values for the specified result identifier. Attributes may be referenced by their names or by a number. The `count` element specifies the number of elements. Multivalue attributes have a `count` element as well, and each element is referenced by number. This function allows you to browse a directory, discovering attributes you may not have known existed.

### string ldap_get_dn(integer ldap, resource result)

The `ldap_get_dn` function returns the DN for the specified result.

### array ldap_get_entries(resource connection, resource result)

The `ldap_get_entries` function returns a three-dimensional array containing every entry in the result set. An associative element, `count`, returns the number of entries in the array. Each entry is numbered from zero. Each entry has a `count` element and a `dn` element. The attributes for the entry may be referenced by name or by number. Each attribute has its own `count` element and a numbered set of values.

### boolean ldap_get_option(resource connection, integer option, reference value)

The `ldap_get_option` function sets the `value` argument with the value of the option specified by the `option` argument. Use one of the options from Table 17.6. Use `ldap_set_option` to change the value of an option.

**Table 17.6**  LDAP Options

| Option | Description |
| --- | --- |
| LDAP_OPT_CLIENT_CONTROLS | The list of default controls for the client. |
| LDAP_OPT_DEREF | Dereference mode, set with a constant from Table 17.7. |
| LDAP_OPT_ERROR_NUMBER | Error number. |
| LDAP_OPT_ERROR_STRING | Error message. |
| LDAP_OPT_HOST_NAME | Host name. |

**Table 17.6** LDAP Options *(cont.)*

| | |
|---|---|
| LDAP_OPT_MATCHED_DN | The matched DN. |
| LDAP_OPT_PROTOCOL_VERSION | The protocol version used for communication with the server. |
| LDAP_OPT_REFERRALS | Automatically follow referrals. |
| LDAP_OPT_RESTART | Restart automatically if a query aborts. |
| LDAP_OPT_SERVER_CONTROLS | The list of default controls for the server. |
| LDAP_OPT_SIZELIMIT | Maximum number of entries returned in a search, list or read. |
| LDAP_OPT_TIMELIMIT | Maximum number of seconds spent querying the server. |

### array ldap_get_values(resource connection, resource entry, string attribute)

The `ldap_get_values` function (Listing 17.6) returns an array of every value for a given attribute. The values will be treated as strings. Use `ldap_get_values_len` if you need to get binary data.

**Listing 17.6** *ldap_get_values*

```php
<?php
    //connect to LDAP server
    if(!($ldap=ldap_connect("localhost")))
    {
        die("Could not connect to LDAP server!");
    }

    //set up search criteria
    $dn = "cn=Barry Bat,dc=leonatkinson,dc=com";
    $filter = "sn=*";
    $attributes = array("mail");

    //perform search
    if(!($result = ldap_read($ldap, $dn, $filter, $attributes)))
    {
        die("Nothing Found!");
    }

    $entry = ldap_first_entry($ldap, $result);
    $values = ldap_get_values($ldap, $entry, "mail");
```

| Listing 17.6 | *ldap_get_values (cont.)* |
|---|---|

```
    print($values["count"] . " Values:<ol>\n");

    for($index=0; $index < $values["count"]; $index++)
    {
        print("<li>{$values[$index]}</li>\n");
    }

    print("</ol>\n");

    ldap_free_result($result);
?>
```

### integer ldap_get_values_len(resource connection, resource_entry, string attribute)

This function operates identically to `ldap_get_values` except that it works with binary entries.

### integer ldap_list(resource connection, string dn, string filter, array attributes, boolean attributes_only, integer size_limit, integer time_limit, integer dereference)

The `ldap_list` function (Listing 17.7) returns all objects at the level of the given DN. The `attributes` argument is optional. If given, it limits results to objects containing the specified attributes.

The optional `attributes_only` argument causes `ldap_list` to return only attributes. The optional `size_limit` and `time_limit` limit, respectively, the number of entries returned or the number of seconds spent fetching results. The optional `dereference` argument controls how references are resolved. Use a constant from Table 17.7 for this argument.

**Table 17.7** LDAP Options

| Dereference Mode | Description |
|---|---|
| LDAP_DEREF_ALWAYS | Always dereference. |
| LDAP_DEREF_FINDING | Dereference when locating the base DN but not otherwise. |
| LDAP_DEREF_NEVER | Never dereference, which is the default. |
| LDAP_DEREF_SEARCHING | Dereference while searching but not otherwise. |

---

**Listing 17.7**    *ldap_list*

```php
<?php
   /*
   ** ldap_list example
   ** This script explores the organizational units at
   ** the University of Michigan.  Links are created
   ** to explore units within units.
   */
   $self = $_SERVER['PHP_SELF'];
   $dn = $_REQUEST['dn'];
   if(!isset($_REQUEST['dn']))
   {
       $dn = "o=University of Michigan, c=US";
   }

   print("<b>Search DN:</b> $dn<br>\n");

   //connect to LDAP server
   if(!($ldap=ldap_connect("ldap.itd.umich.edu")))
   {
       die("Could not connect to LDAP server!");
   }

   $filter = "objectClass=*";
   $attributes = array("ou", "cn");

   //perform search
   if(!($result = ldap_list($ldap, $dn, $filter, $attributes)))
   {
       die("Nothing Found!");
   }

   $entries = ldap_get_entries($ldap, $result);

   for($index = 0; $index < $entries["count"]; $index++)
   {
       if(isset($entries[$index]["ou"]))
       {
          print("<a href=\"$self?dn=" .
             $entries[$index]["dn"]."\">");
          print($entries[$index]["ou"][0]);
          print("</a>");
       }
```

**Listing 17.7**    *ldap_list (cont.)*

```
        else
        {
            print($entries[$index]["cn"][0]);
        }              (

        print("<br>\n");
    }

    ldap_free_result($result);

    // close connection
    ldap_close($ldap);
?>
```

### boolean ldap_mod_add(resource connection, string dn, array entry)

The `ldap_mod_add` function adds attributes to a DN at the attribute level. Compare this to `ldap_add`, which adds attributes at the object level.

### boolean ldap_mod_del(resource connection, string dn, array entry)

Use `ldap_mod_del` to remove attributes from a DN at the attribute level. Compare this to `ldap_delete`, which removes attributes at the object level.

### boolean ldap_mod_replace(resource connection, string dn, array entry)

The `ldap_mod_replace` function replaces entries for a DN at the attribute level. Compare this to `ldap_modify`, which replaces attributes at the object level.

### boolean ldap_modify(resource connection, string dn, array entry)

The `ldap_modify` function modifies an entry. Otherwise, it behaves identically to `ldap_add`.

### string ldap_next_attribute(resource connection, integer entry, reference pointer)

The `ldap_next_attribute` function (Listing 17.8) is used to traverse the list of attributes for an entry.

| Listing 17.8 | `ldap_next_attribute` |
|---|---|

```php
<?php
    //connect to LDAP server
    if(!($ldap=ldap_connect("ldap.itd.umich.edu")))
    {
        die("Could not connect to LDAP server!");
    }

    // list organizations in the US
    $dn = "o=University of Michigan, c=US";
    $filter = "objectClass=*";

    //perform search
    if(!($result = ldap_list($ldap, $dn, $filter)))
    {
        die("Nothing Found!");
    }

    // get all attributes for first entry
    $entry = ldap_first_entry($ldap, $result);

    $attribute = ldap_first_attribute($ldap, $entry, $pointer);
    while($attribute)
    {
        print("$attribute<br>\n");
        $attribute = ldap_next_attribute($ldap, $entry, $pointer);
    }

    ldap_free_result($result);
?>
```

### integer ldap_next_entry(resource connection, resource entry)

The `ldap_next_entry` function (Listing 17.9) returns the next entry in a result set. Use `ldap_first_entry` to get the first entry in a result set.

**Listing 17.9**   `ldap_next_entry`

```php
<?php
    //connect to LDAP server
    if(!($ldap=ldap_connect("ldap.itd.umich.edu")))
    {
        die("Could not connect to LDAP server!");
    }

    // list organizations in the US
    $dn = "o=University of Michigan, c=US";
    $filter = "objectClass=*";

    //perform search
    if(!($result = ldap_list($ldap, $dn, $filter)))
    {
        die("Nothing Found!");
    }

    //get each entry
    $entry = ldap_first_entry($ldap, $result);
    do
    {
        //dump all attributes for each entry
        $attribute = ldap_get_attributes($ldap, $entry);
        print("<pre>");
        print_r($attribute);
        print("</pre>\n");
        print("<hr>\n");
    }
    while($entry = ldap_next_entry($ldap, $entry));

    ldap_free_result($result);
?>
```

**resource ldap_next_reference(resource connection, resource entry)**

The `ldap_next_reference` function returns the next entry in a result set.

**boolean ldap_parse_reference(resource connection, resource entry, reference referrals)**

The `ldap_parse_reference` function fills the `referrals` array with the references for the given entry.

## boolean ldap_parse_result(resource connection, resource result, reference error_number, reference dn, reference error_message, reference referrals)

The `ldap_parse_result` function fetches information about the given result. The `error_number` argument receives the error number generated. The optional `dn` argument receives the matched DN. The optional `error_message` argument receives a textual error message. The optional `referrals` argument is set with an array of referrals.

## integer ldap_read(resource connection, string dn, string filter, array attributes, boolean attributes_only, integer size_limit, integer time_limit, integer dereference)

The `ldap_read` function functions similarly to `ldap_list` and `ldap_search`. Arguments are used in the same manner, but `ldap_read` searches only in the base DN. The optional `attributes_only` argument causes `ldap_list` to return only attributes. The optional `size_limit` and `time_limit` limit, respectively, the number of entries returned or the number of seconds spent fetching results. The optional `dereference` argument controls how references are resolved. Use a constant from Table 17.7 for this argument.

## boolean ldap_rename(resource connection, string dn, string new_dn, string parent, boolean delete)

The `ldap_rename` function renames an existing entry identified by the `dn` argument. You must also specify the new parent with the `parent` argument. Setting the `delete` argument to TRUE causes PHP to delete the original DN.

## integer ldap_search(resource connection, string dn, string filter, array attributes, boolean attributes_only, integer size_limit, integer time_limit, integer dereference)

The `ldap_search` function (Listing 17.10) behaves similarly to `ldap_list` and `ldap_read`. The difference is that it finds matches from the current directory down into every subtree. The `attributes` argument is optional and specifies a set of attributes that all matched entries must contain.

The optional `attributes_only` argument causes `ldap_search` to return only attributes. The optional `size_limit` and `time_limit` limit, respectively, the number of entries returned or the number of seconds spent fetching results. The optional `dereference` argument controls how references are resolved. Use a constant from Table 17.7 for this argument.

**Listing 17.10** *ldap_search*

```php
<?php
    /*
    ** Function: compareEntry
    ** This function compares two entries for
    ** the purpose of sorting.
    */
    function compareEntry($left, $right)
    {
        $ln = strcmp($left["last"], $right["last"]);
        if($ln == 0)
        {
            return(strcmp($left["full"],
                $right["full"]));
        }
        else
        {
            return($ln);
        }
    }

    //connect to LDAP server
    if(!($ldap=ldap_connect("ldap.itd.umich.edu")))
    {
        die("Could not connect to LDAP server!");
    }

    //set up search criteria
    $dn = "ou=People, o=University of Michigan, c=US";
    $filter = "sn=Atkinson*";
    $attributes = array("cn", "sn");

    //perform search
    if(!($result = ldap_search($ldap, $dn, $filter, $attributes)))
    {
        die("Nothing Found!");
    }

    //get all the entries
    $entry = ldap_get_entries($ldap, $result);

    print("There are " . $entry["count"] . " people.<br>\n");

    //pull names out into array so we can sort them
    $person = array();
```

| Listing 17.10 | *ldap_search (cont.)* |
|---|---|

```
for($i=0; $i < $entry["count"]; $i++)
{
    $person[$i]["full"] = $entry[$i]["cn"][0];
    $person[$i]["last"] = $entry[$i]["sn"][0];
}

//sort by last name, then first name using
//compareEntry (defined above)
usort($person, "compareEntry");

//loop over each entry
for($i=0; $i < $entry["count"]; $i++)
{
    print("{$person[$i]["last"]} ".
        "({$person[$i]["full"]})<br>\n");
}

//free memory used by search
ldap_free_result($result);
?>
```

### boolean ldap_set_option(resource connection, integer option, value)

The `ldap_set_option` sets the value of an LDAP option. Use one of the constants from Table 17.6.

### boolean ldap_sort(resource connection, resource result, string filter)

The `ldap_sort` function sorts a result set according to the order of the attributes given in the filter, then by the values of those attributes.

### boolean ldap_start_tls(resource connection)

The `ldap_start_tls` function starts Transport Security Layer (TSL) communication with the server.

### boolean ldap_unbind(resource connection)

The `ldap_unbind` function is an alias for `ldap_close`.

# 17.4 MySQL

MySQL is a relational database with a license that allows you to use it cost-free for most noncommercial purposes. It shares many features with mSQL because it was originally conceived as a faster, more flexible replacement. Indeed, MySQL has delivered on these goals. It easily outperforms even commercial databases. Not surprisingly, MySQL is the database of choice for many PHP developers.

To find out more about MySQL as well as obtain source code and binaries, visit the Web site at <http://www.mysql.com/>. There are plenty of mirrors to aid your download speed. If you're looking for a printed text on MySQL, please consider *Core MySQL*.

The MySQL extension was written by Zeev Suraski.

### integer mysql_affected_rows(resource connection)

The `mysql_affected_rows` function (Listing 17.11) returns the number of rows affected by the last query made to the specified database connection link. If the `connection` argument is omitted, the last opened connection is assumed. If the last query was an unconditional DELETE, zero will be returned. If you want to know how many rows a SELECT statement returns, use `mysql_num_rows`.

| Listing 17.11 | *mysql_affected_rows* |
|---|---|

```php
<?php
    //connect to server as freetrade user, no password
    $db = mysql_connect("localhost", "freetrade", "");

    //select the 'ft3' database
    mysql_select_db("ft3", $db);

    //update some invoices
    $Query = "UPDATE invoice " .
        "SET Active = 'Y' " .
        "WHERE ID < 100 ";
    $dbResult = mysql_query($Query, $db);

    //let user know how many rows were updated
    $AffectedRows = mysql_affected_rows($db);
    print("$AffectedRows rows updated.<br>");

    //close connection
    mysql_close($db);
?>
```

### string mysql_client_encoding(resource connection)

The `mysql_client_encoding` function returns the character set used by the connection. If you omit the `connection` resource, PHP returns the character set used by the last used connection.

### boolean mysql_close(resource connection)

Use `mysql_close` to close the connection to a database created with `mysql_connect`. Use of this function is not strictly necessary, as all nonpersistent links are closed automatically when the script finishes. The `connection` argument is optional, and when it's left out, the connection last opened is closed.

### resource mysql_connect(string host, string user, string password, boolean new_link, integer flags)

The `mysql_connect` function begins a connection to a MySQL database at the specified host. If the database is on a different port, follow the hostname with a colon and a port number. You may alternatively supply a colon and the path to a socket if connecting to localhost. This might be written as `:/tmp/mysql.sock`. All the arguments are optional and will default to localhost, the name of the user executing the script, an empty string, no new link, and no flags respectively. The user executing the script is typically `nobody`, the Web server.

Connections are automatically closed when a script finishes execution, though they may be closed earlier with `mysql_close`. If you attempt to open a connection that is already open, a second connection will not be made. The identifier of the previously open connection will be returned. If you wish to force a new connection, set the `new_link` argument to `TRUE`.

The `flags` argument may be a combination of the constants shown in Table 17.8.

If PHP cannot establish a connection, this function returns `FALSE`.

**Table 17.8**    MySQL Connection Options

| Option | Description |
| --- | --- |
| MYSQL_CLIENT_COMPRESS | Compress communication between client and server. |
| MYSQL_CLIENT_IGNORE_SPACE | This instructs the MySQL server to ignore spaces after function names. |
| MYSQL_CLIENT_INTERACTIVE | Use the interactive timeout instead of the normal timeout. |
| MYSQL_CLIENT_SSL | Encrypt communication between client and server using SSL. |

### boolean mysql_data_seek(resource result, integer row)

The mysql_data_seek function (Listing 17.12) moves the internal row pointer of a result set to the specified row, with rows counting from zero. Use this function with mysql_fetch_row to jump to a specific row. The result argument must have been returned from mysql_query or a similar function.

**Listing 17.12**   *mysql_data_seek*

```php
<?php
    //connect to server as freetrade user, no password
    $dbLink = mysql_pconnect("localhost", "freetrade", "");

    //select the 'ft3' database
    mysql_select_db("ft3", $dbLink);

    //get states from tax table
    $Query = "SELECT State FROM tax ";
    $dbResult = mysql_query($Query, $dbLink);

    //jump to fifth row
    mysql_data_seek($dbResult, 4);

    //get row
    $row = mysql_fetch_row($dbResult);

    //print state name
    print($row[0]);
?>
```

### string mysql_db_name(integer result, integer row, string field)

This function is intended to pull results from a call to mysql_db_list. Instead, execute a SHOW DATABASES statement with mysql_query.

### integer mysql_errno(resource connection)

The mysql_errno function (Listing 17.13) returns the error number of the last database action. If the optional connection identifier is left out, the last connection you used will be assumed.

---

| Listing 17.13 | *mysql_errno, mysql_error* |
| --- | --- |

```php
<?php
    //connect to server as freetrade user, no password
    $dbLink = mysql_connect("localhost", "freetrade", "");

    //select the 'ft3' database
    mysql_select_db("ft3", $dbLink);

    //try to execute a bad query (missing fields)
    $Query = "SELECT FROM tax ";
    if(!($dbResult = mysql_query($Query, $dbLink)))
    {
        // get error and error number
        $errno = mysql_errno($dbLink);
        $error = mysql_error($dbLink);

        print("ERROR $errno: $error<br>\n");
    }
?>
```

### string mysql_error(resource connection)

Use `mysql_error` to get the textual description of the error for the last database action. If the optional link identifier is left out, the last connection will be assumed.

### string mysql_escape_string(string text)

The `mysql_escape_string` function escapes special characters in a text string, making it ready for placement inside single quotes. Compare this function to `mysql_real_escape_string`, which pays attention to the encoding character set.

### array mysql_fetch_array(resource result, integer type)

The `mysql_fetch_array` function (Listing 17.14) returns an array that represents all the fields for a row in the result set. Each call produces the next row until no rows are left, in which case FALSE is returned. By default, each field value is stored twice: once indexed by offset starting at zero and once indexed by the name of the field. This behavior can be controlled with the `type` argument. If the MYSQL_NUM constant is used, PHP indexes elements by field numbers only. If the MYSQL_ASSOC constant is used, PHP indexes elements by field names only. You can also use MYSQL_BOTH to force the default.

Compare this function to `mysql_fetch_object` and `mysql_fetch_row`.

**Listing 17.14** *mysql_fetch_array*

```php
<?php
    //connect to server as freetrade user, no password
    $dbLink = mysql_connect("localhost", "freetrade", "");

    //select the 'ft3' database
    mysql_select_db("ft3", $dbLink);

    //get rates from tax table
    $Query = "SELECT State, Rate " .
        "FROM tax " .
        "LIMIT 10";
    $dbResult = mysql_query($Query, $dbLink);

    // get each row
    while($row = mysql_fetch_array($dbResult, MYSQL_ASSOC))
    {
        // print state and rate
        print("{$row["State"]} = {$row["Rate"]}<br>\n");
    }
?>
```

### array mysql_fetch_assoc(resource result)

The mysql_fetch_assoc is equivalent to calling mysql_fetch_array with the MYSQL_ASSOC type.

### object mysql_fetch_field(resource result, integer field)

Use the mysql_fetch_field function (Listing 17.15) to get information about a field in a result set. Fields are numbered starting with zero. The return value is an object with properties described in Table 17.9.

If the field argument is left out, the next field in the set will be returned. This behavior allows you to loop through each field easily.

**Table 17.9** Properties of mysql_fetch_field Object

| Property | Description |
| --- | --- |
| blob | TRUE if the column is a blob |
| max_length | Maximum length |
| multiple_key | TRUE if the column is a nonunique key |

**Table 17.9**    Properties of `mysql_fetch_field` Object *(cont.)*

| Property | Description |
|---|---|
| name | Name of the column |
| not_null | TRUE if the column cannot be null |
| numeric | TRUE if the column is numeric |
| primary_key | TRUE if the column is a primary key |
| table | Name of the table or alias used |
| type | Type of the column |
| unique_key | TRUE if the column is a unique key |
| unsigned | TRUE if the column is unsigned |
| zerofill | TRUE if the column is zero-filled |

**Listing 17.15**    *mysql_fetch_field*

```php
<?php
    //connect to server as freetrade user, no password
    $dbLink = mysql_connect("localhost", "freetrade", "");

    //select the 'ft3' database
    mysql_select_db("ft3", $dbLink);

    //get everything from address table
    $Query = "SELECT * " .
        "FROM address a, user u " .
        "WHERE u.Address = a.ID ";
    $dbResult = mysql_query($Query, $dbLink);

    // get description of each field
    while($Field = mysql_fetch_field($dbResult))
    {
        print("$Field->table, $Field->name, $Field->type<br>\n");
    }
?>
```

### array mysql_fetch_lengths(resource result)

Use `mysql_fetch_lengths` to get an array of the lengths for each of the fields in the last row fetched. This can be helpful if columns contain binary data since embedded NULL characters will break `strlen`.

### object mysql_fetch_object(resource result)

The `mysql_fetch_object` function (Listing 17.16) is similar to `mysql_fetch_array` and `mysql_fetch_row`. Instead of an array, it returns an object. Each field in the result set is a property in the returned object. Each call to `mysql_fetch_object` returns the next row, or FALSE if there are no rows remaining. This allows you to call `mysql_fetch_object` in the test condition of a while loop to get every row.

---

**Listing 17.16**    *mysql_fetch_object*

```php
<?php
    //connect to server as freetrade user, no password
    $dbLink = mysql_connect("localhost", "freetrade", "");

    //select the 'ft3' database
    mysql_select_db("ft3", $dbLink);

    //get unique cities from address table
    $Query = "SELECT DISTINCT City, StateProv " .
        "FROM address ";
    $dbResult = mysql_query($Query, $dbLink);

    // get each row
    while($row = mysql_fetch_object($dbResult))
    {
        // print name
        print("$row->City, $row->StateProv<br>");
    }
?>
```

---

### array mysql_fetch_row(resource result)

The `mysql_fetch_row` function (Listing 17.17) returns an array that represents all the fields for a row in the result set. Each call produces the next row until no rows are left, in which case FALSE is returned. Each field value is indexed numerically, starting with zero. Compare this function to `mysql_fetch_array` and `mysql_fetch_object`. There isn't much difference in performance between these three functions.

**Listing 17.17** `mysql_fetch_row`

```php
<?php
    //connect to server as freetrade user, no password
    $dbLink = mysql_connect("localhost", "freetrade", "");

    //select the 'ft3' database
    mysql_select_db("ft3", $dbLink);

    //get unique cities from address table
    $Query = "SELECT City, StateProv " .
        "FROM address ";
    $dbResult = mysql_query($Query, $dbLink);

    //get each row
    while($row = mysql_fetch_row($dbResult))
    {
        // print city, state
        print("$row[0], $row[1]<br>");
    }
?>
```

### string mysql_field_flags(resource result, integer field)

Use `mysql_field_flags` to get a description of the flags on the specified field. The flags are returned in a string and separated by spaces. The flags you can expect are `auto_increment`, `binary`, `blob`, `enum`, `multiple_key`, `not_null`, `primary_key`, `timestamp`, `unique_key`, `unsigned`, and `zerofill`. Some of these flags may be available only in the newest versions of MySQL.

### integer mysql_field_len(resource result, integer field)

Use `mysql_field_len` to get the maximum number of characters to expect from a field. The fields are numbered from zero.

### string mysql_field_name(resource result, integer field)

Use `mysql_field_name` to get the name of a column. The `field` argument is an offset numbered from zero.

### boolean mysql_field_seek(resource result, integer field)

The `mysql_field_seek` function (Listing 17.18) moves the internal field pointer to the specified field. PHP numbers fields starting with zero. The next call to `mysql_fetch_field` will get information from this field.

**Listing 17.18** `mysql_field_seek`

```php
<?php
    //connect to server as freetrade user, no password
    $dbLink = mysql_connect("localhost", "freetrade", "");

    //select the 'ft3' database
    mysql_select_db("ft3", $dbLink);

    // get everything from address table
    $Query = "SELECT * " .
        "FROM address ";
    $dbResult = mysql_query($Query, $dbLink);

    //skip to second field
    mysql_field_seek($dbResult, 1);

    //get description of each field
    while($Field = mysql_fetch_field($dbResult))
    {
        print("$Field->table, $Field->name, $Field->type<br>");
    }
?>
```

### string mysql_field_table(resource result, integer field)

The `mysql_field_table` function returns the name of the table for the specified field. PHP numbers fields starting with zero. If an alias is used, the alias is returned.

### string mysql_field_type(resource result, integer field)

Use `mysql_field_type` to get the type of a particular field in the result set.

### boolean mysql_free_result(resource result)

Use `mysql_free_result` to free any memory associated with the specified result set. This is not strictly necessary, as this memory is automatically freed when a script finishes executing.

### string mysql_get_client_info()

The `mysql_get_client_info` function returns a string describing the version of the client library compiled into PHP.

### string mysql_get_host_info(resource connection)

The `mysql_get_host_info` function returns a string describing the type of connection, in the form `localhost via UNIX socket`.

### integer mysql_get_proto_info(resource connection)

This function returns the protocol version used for the given connection.

### string mysql_get_server_info(resource connection)

This function returns the version of MySQL running on the server.

### string mysql_info(resource connection)

The `mysql_info` function returns a string describing the results of certain statements: `ALTER TABLE`, `INSERT`, `LOAD DATA INFILE`, `UPDATE`. For other statements, this function returns an empty string. Call this function immediately after `mysql_query`.

### integer mysql_insert_id(resource connection)

After inserting into a table with an `auto_increment` field, the `mysql_insert_id` function (Listing 17.19) returns the ID assigned to the inserted row. If the `connection` argument is left out, the most recent connection will be used.

You can also get this value with MySQL's `LAST_INSERT_ID` function. This may be necessary in the situation where an `auto_increment` column exceeds the maximum value of a PHP integer.

---

**Listing 17.19** *mysql_insert_id*

```php
<?php
    //connect to server as freetrade user, no password
    $dbLink = mysql_connect("localhost", "freetrade", "");

    //select the 'ft3' database
    mysql_select_db("ft3", $dbLink);

    //insert a row
    $Query = "INSERT INTO user (Login, Password) " .
        "VALUES('leon', 'secret') ";
    $dbResult = mysql_query($Query, $dbLink);

    //get id
    print("ID is " . mysql_insert_id($dbLink));
?>
```

### integer mysql_list_dbs(resource connection)

The `mysql_list_dbs` function queries the server for a list of databases. It returns a result pointer that may be used with `mysql_fetch_row` and similar functions. Instead of using this function, use a SHOW DATABASES statement with `mysql_query`.

### integer mysql_list_fields(string database, string table, resource connection)

The `mysql_list_fields` function (Listing 17.20) returns a result pointer to a query on the list of fields for a specified table. The result pointer may be used with any of the functions that get information about columns in a result set: `mysql_field_flags`, `mysql_field_len`, `mysql_field_name`, `mysql_field_type`. The `connection` argument is optional.

---

**Listing 17.20**  *mysql_list_fields*

```php
<?php
    //connect to server
    $dbLink = mysql_connect("localhost", "freetrade", "");

    //get list of fields
    $dbResult = mysql_list_fields("ft3", "invoice", $dbLink);

    //start HTML table
    print("<table>\n");
    print("<tr>\n");
    print("<th>Name</th>\n");
    print("<th>Type</th>\n");
    print("<th>Length</th>\n");
    print("<th>Flags</th>\n");
    print("</tr>\n");

    //loop over each field
    for($i = 0; $i < mysql_num_fields($dbResult); $i++)
    {
        print("<tr>\n");

        print("<td>" . mysql_field_name($dbResult, $i) . "</td>\n");
        print("<td>" . mysql_field_type($dbResult, $i) . "</td>\n");
        print("<td>" . mysql_field_len($dbResult, $i) . "</td>\n");
        print("<td>" . mysql_field_flags($dbResult, $i) .
            "</td>\n");
```

**Listing 17.20**   *mysql_list_fields (cont.)*

```
    print("</tr>\n");
}

//close HTML table
print("</table>\n");
?>
```

### resource mysql_list_processes(resource connection)

This function returns a result identifier for a query of processes on the server. Instead, use a SHOW PROCESSLIST statement with mysql_query.

### integer mysql_list_tables(string database, resource connection)

Use mysql_list_tables to get a result pointer to a list of tables for a specified database. Instead, use a SHOW TABLES statement with mysql_query.

### integer mysql_num_fields(resource result)

The mysql_num_fields function returns the number of fields in a result set.

### integer mysql_num_rows(resource result)

The mysql_num_rows function returns the number of rows in a result set.

### integer mysql_pconnect(string host, string user, string password, integer flags)

The mysql_pconnect function operates like mysql_connect except that the connection will be persistent. That is, it won't be closed when the script ends. The connection will last as long as the server process lasts, so that if a connection is attempted later from the same process, the overhead of opening a new connection will be avoided. The flags argument may be a combination of the constants shown in Table 17.8.

A link identifier is returned. This identifier is used in many of the other functions in this section.

### boolean mysql_ping(resource connection)

The mysql_ping function returns TRUE if the connection with the server remains open. Use this function in scripts that run for a long time without using an open connection. You can test whether the server shut down the connection for inactivity and reconnect if necessary.

### resource mysql_query(string query, resource connection, nteger result_mode)

Use `mysql_query` to execute a query. If the `connection` argument is omitted, the last connection made is used. If there has been no previous connection, PHP will connect to the local host. The optional `result_mode` argument controls whether PHP buffers the result set, which is the default. Use `MYSQL_STORE_RESULT` to emphasize the default. Use `MYSQL_USE_RESULT` to fetch rows in unbuffered mode. See `mysql_unbuffered_query`.

If the query performs an insert, delete, or update, a boolean value will be returned, indicating success or failure. Select queries return a result identifier.

### string mysql_real_escape_string(string text, resource connection)

The `mysql_real_escape_string` function escapes a string, making it ready for placement inside single quotes in an SQL statement. This function accommodates the character encoding used on the server.

### string mysql_result(resource result, integer row, string field)

The `mysql_result` function returns the value of the specified field in the specified row. The `field` argument may be a number, in which case it is considered a field offset. It may also be the name of a column, either with the table name or without. It could also be an alias. In general, this function is very slow. It's better to use `mysql_fetch_row` or a similar function.

### boolean mysql_select_db(string database, resource connection)

Use `mysql_select_db` to select the default database. You may also use an SQL `USE` statement to select the default database.

### array mysql_stat(resource connection)

The `mysql_stat` function returns an array with information about the server status. Instead, use a `SHOW STATUS` statement with `mysql_query`.

### integer mysql_thread_id(resource connection)

This function returns the thread ID used for the given connection.

### resource mysql_unbuffered_query(string query, resource connection, integer result_mode)

The `mysql_unbuffered_query` function executes a query exactly as `mysql_query` does except that it defaults to unbuffered mode. In unbuffered mode, PHP reads from the result set only as necessary instead of reading the entire result set into memory. The downside to this mode is that if you execute another query on the same connection, the remainder of the result set is lost. However, it definitely conserves memory. This may be helpful with queries that return huge result sets, but keep in mind that you can limit the number of rows in a result set with the LIMIT clause.

# 17.5  ODBC

Open Database Connectivity (ODBC) has become an industry standard for communicating with a database. The model is simple. Client software is designed to use an ODBC API. Vendors write drivers that implement this API on the client side and talk natively to their database on the server side. This allows application developers to write one application that can communicate with many different databases simply by changing the driver, which is an external file.

ODBC uses SQL as its language for communicating with any database, even when the database isn't relational. Microsoft offers drivers that allow you to query text files and Excel workbooks. A good place to start learning more about ODBC is Microsoft's Developer's Network site: <http://msdn.microsoft.com/>.

Microsoft has offered free ODBC drivers for some time, but only for its operating systems. ODBC drivers for UNIX are harder to come by. Most database manufacturers offer drivers, and there are third parties, like Intersolv, that sell optimized drivers for both Windows and UNIX platforms.

Most of the databases with native support in PHP can also be accessed via ODBC. There are also numerous databases that can be accessed only via ODBC by PHP, such as Solid and Empress.

Stig Bakken, Andreas Karajannis, and Frank Kromann have contributed to the creation of the ODBC extension.

### boolean odbc_autocommit(resource connection, boolean on)
The odbc_autocommit function (Listing 17.21) sets whether queries are automatically committed when executed. By default, it is on. The connection argument is an integer returned by the odbc_connect or odbc_pconnect functions. This function has to be used intelligently, as not all ODBC drivers support commits and rollbacks.

**Listing 17.21**   *odbc_autocommit*

```php
<?php
    //connect to database
    $Link = odbc_connect("inventory", "guest", "guest");

    //turn off auto-commit
    odbc_autocommit($Link, FALSE);
?>
```

### boolean odbc_binmode(resource result, integer mode)

Use `odbc_binmode` (Listing 17.22) to set the way binary columns return data for a result set. When binary data are returned by the driver, each byte is represented by hexadecimal codes. By default, PHP will convert these codes into raw binary data. If you have to use the `odbc_longreadlen` function to set the maximum length of long data to anything other than zero, then the modes in Table 17.10 apply. If the maximum read length is zero, the data are always converted to raw binary data.

**Table 17.10**   Binary Column Modes

| Mode | Description |
| --- | --- |
| ODBC_BINMODE_PASSTHRU | Pass through as binary data. |
| ODBC_BINMODE_RETURN | Return as hexadecimal codes. |
| ODBC_BINMODE_CONVERT | Return with data converted to a string. |

**Listing 17.22**   *odbc_binmode*

```php
<?php
    //get a GIF from a database and send it to browser

    //connect to database
    $Connection = odbc_connect("inventory", "admin", "secret");

    //execute query
    $Query = "SELECT Data " .
        "FROM Picture " .
        "WHERE ID=2 ";

    $Result = odbc_do($Connection, $Query);
```

**Listing 17.22** *odbc_binmode (cont.)*

```
    //make sure binmode is set for binary pass through
    odbc_binmode($Result, ODBC_BINMODE_PASSTHRU);

    //make sure longreadlen mode
    //is set for echo to browser
    odbc_longreadlen($Result, 0);

    //get the first row, ignore the rest
    odbc_fetch_row($Result);

    //send header so browser knows it's a gif
    header("Content-type: image/gif");

    //get the picture
    odbc_result($Result, 1);
?>
```

### odbc_close(resource connection)

Use odbc_close (Listing 17.23) to close a connection to a database. If there are open transactions for the connection, an error will be returned and the connection will not be closed.

**Listing 17.23** *odbc_close*

```
<?php
    //connect to database
    $Link = odbc_connect("inventory", "guest", "guest");

    // execute query
    $Query = "SELECT CategoryName, Room, Description,
        PurchasePrice ";
    $Query .= "FROM [Household Inventory] ";

    $Result = odbc_do($Link, $Query);

    //loop over results
    while(odbc_fetch_row($Result))
    {
        print(odbc_result($Result, 1) . ", ");
        print(odbc_result($Result, 2) . ", ");
        print(odbc_result($Result, 3) . ", ");
        print(odbc_result($Result, 4) . "<br>");
    }

    //close connection
    odbc_close($Link);
?>
```

### odbc_close_all()

The `odbc_close_all` function (Listing 17.24) closes every connection you have open to ODBC data sources. Like `odbc_close`, it will report an error if you have an open transaction on one of the connections.

**Listing 17.24**   *odbc_close_all*

```php
<?php
    //connect to database three times
    $Connection1 = odbc_connect("inventory", "guest", "guest");
    $Connection2 = odbc_connect("inventory", "guest", "guest");
    $Connection3 = odbc_connect("inventory", "guest", "guest");

    //close all the connections
    odbc_close_all();
?>
```

### resource odbc_columnprivileges(resource connection, string catalog, string schema, string table, string column)

The `odbc_columnprivileges` function (Listing 17.25) returns information about a table's columns and privileges. Use the return value with any of the row-fetching functions. ODBC drivers are not required to implement the C API call behind this function, `SQLColumnPrivileges`. So, calling this function with a nonsupporting driver may generate an error or simply return no results.

The `catalog` and `schema` arguments have different meanings depending on the driver. The `column` argument may contain `%` and `_` wildcards. Use `%` alone to get the entire list. The other arguments may not contain wildcards.

The returned result set contains the following columns: TABLE_QUALIFIER, TABLE_OWNER, TABLE_NAME, GRANTOR, GRANTEE, PRIVILEGE, IS_GRANTABLE.

**Listing 17.25**   *odbc_columnprivileges*

```php
<?php
    //connect to database
    $Link = odbc_connect("SQLServer-Local", "dbo", "secret");

    $Result = odbc_columnprivileges($Link, "Store", "dbo",
        "Items","%");
```

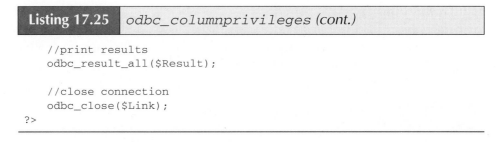

**Listing 17.25**  *odbc_columnprivileges (cont.)*

```
    //print results
    odbc_result_all($Result);

    //close connection
    odbc_close($Link);
?>
```

### resource odbc_columns(resource connection, string catalog, string schema, string table, string column)

The `odbc_columns` function (Listing 17.26) returns a result set describing the columns in a table. Use the return value with any of the row-fetching functions. The `catalog` and `schema` arguments have different meanings depending on the driver. The `schema`, `table`, and `column` arguments may contain % and _ wildcards. The `catalog` argument may not contain wildcards.

The returned result set contains the following columns: TABLE_CAT, TABLE_SCHEM, TABLE_NAME, COLUMN_NAME, DATA_TYPE, TYPE_NAME, COLUMN_SIZE, BUFFER_LENGTH, DECIMAL_DIGITS, NUM_PREC_RADIX, NULLABLE, REMARKS, COLUMN_DEF, SQL_DATA_TYPE, SQL_DATTIME_SUB, CHAR_OCTET_LENGTH, ORDINAL_POSITION, IS_NULLABLE.

**Listing 17.26**  *ODBC functions returning metadata*

```php
<?php
    /*
    ** This script tests the functions that return meta data.
    ** Note the slightly tricky use of the ternary operator.
    */

    $catalog = "ft3";
    $schema = "";

    //connect to database
    $Link = odbc_connect("mysql-galt", "leon", "");

    print("<h1>odbc_columns</h1>");
    $Result = @odbc_columns($Link, "", "", "item");
    $Result ? odbc_result_all($Result) : print('Unsupported');
```

**Listing 17.26**  *ODBC functions returning metadata (cont.)*

```php
    print("<h1>odbc_foreignkeys</h1>");
    $Result = @odbc_foreignkeys($Link, $catalog, $schema, "user");
    $Result ? odbc_result_all($Result) : print('Unsupported');

    print("<h1>odbc_gettypeinfo</h1>");
    $Result = @odbc_gettypeinfo($Link);
    $Result ? odbc_result_all($Result) : print('Unsupported');

    print("<h1>odbc_primarykeys</h1>");
    $Result = @odbc_primarykeys(Link, $catalog, $schema, "user");
    $Result ? odbc_result_all($Result) : print('Unsupported');

    print("<h1>odbc_procedurecolumns</h1>");
    $Result = @odbc_procedurecolumns($Link);
    $Result ? odbc_result_all($Result) : print('Unsupported');

    print("<h1>odbc_procedures</h1>");
    $Result = @odbc_procedures($Link);
    $Result ? odbc_result_all($Result) : print('Unsupported');

    print("<h1>odbc_specialcolumns</h1>");
    $Result = @odbc_specialcolumns($Link, $catalog, $schema,
        "user", SQL_SCOPE_SESSION, SQL_NULLABLE);
    $Result ? odbc_result_all($Result) : print('Unsupported');

    print("<h1>odbc_statistics</h1>");
    $Result = @odbc_statistics($Link, $catalog, $schema,
        "user", SQL_INDEX_ALL, SQL_QUICK);
    $Result ? odbc_result_all($Result) : print('Unsupported');

    print("<h1>odbc_tableprivileges</h1>");
    $Result = @odbc_tableprivileges($Link, $catalog, $schema,
        "%");
    $Result ? odbc_result_all($Result) : print('Unsupported');

    print("<h1>odbc_tables</h1>");
    $Result = @odbc_tables($Link, $catalog, $schema, "%");
    $Result ? odbc_result_all($Result) : print('Unsupported');

    //close connection
    odbc_close($Link);
?>
```

### boolean odbc_commit(resource connection)

Use `odbc_commit` to commit all pending actions for the specified connection. If automatic commit is turned on, as is default, this function has no effect. Also, make sure your driver supports transactions before using this function.

### resource odbc_connect(string dsn, string user, string password, integer cursor_type)

Use `odbc_connect` to connect to an ODBC data source. A connection identifier is returned, which is used by most of the other functions in this section. The `user` and `password` arguments are required, so if your driver does not require them, pass empty strings.

The optional `cursor_type` argument forces the use of a particular cursor so that you may avoid problems with some ODBC drivers. For example, using the `SQL_CUR_USE_ODBC` constant for cursor type may avoid problems with calling stored procedures or getting row numbers. Use one of the following constants for `cursor_type`: `SQL_CUR_DEFAULT`, `SQL_CUR_USE_DRIVER`, `SQL_CUR_USE_IF_NEEDED`, `SQL_CUR_USE_ODBC`.

### string odbc_cursor(resource result)

Use `odbc_cursor` to fetch the name of a cursor for a result set.

### array odbc_data_source(resource connection, integer type)

Use the `odbc_data_source` function (Listing 17.27) to get a list of available ODBC data sources. First, open a connection with a valid data source, then call `odbc_data_source` with the type argument set to `SQL_FETCH_FIRST`. Follow that with calls with type set to `SQL_FETCH_NEXT` until the function returns `FALSE`.

The returned array has two elements: `server` and `description`. The first element is the name of the data source, otherwise known as a DSN.

Some drivers return a warning when fetching after the last entry. Prefix the function call with an at symbol (`@`) to suppress these from showing in the browser.

**Listing 17.27** *odbc_data_source*

```php
<?php
    //connect to database
    $Link = odbc_connect("mysql-galt", "leon", "");

    //get list of data sources
    $d = @odbc_data_source($Link, SQL_FETCH_FIRST);
    while($d !== FALSE)
    {
        print("<b>{$d['server']}:</b> {$d['description']}<br>\n");
        $d = @odbc_data_source($Link, SQL_FETCH_NEXT);
    }

    //close connection
    odbc_close($Link);
?>
```

### integer odbc_do(resource connection, string query)

Use `odbc_do` as an alias to `odbc_exec`.

### string odbc_error(resource connection)

The `odbc_error` function returns a six-digit number describing the current error state for the last active database link. You may optionally specify an open link.

### string odbc_errormsg(resource connection)

The `odbc_errormsg` function returns a message describing the current error state for the last active database link. You may optionally specify an open link.

### integer odbc_exec(resource connection, string query)

Use `odbc_exec` to execute a query on a connection. A result identifier is returned and is used in many of the other functions for fetching result data.

### integer odbc_execute(resource result, array parameters)

The `odbc_execute` function executes a prepared statement. The `result` argument is an identifier returned by `odbc_prepare`. The `parameters` argument is an array passed by reference and will be set with the value of the result columns. PHP considers parameters wrapped in single quotes as paths to files. In this case, PHP reads from or writes to the files. See `odbc_prepare` for an example of use.

### integer odbc_fetch_into(resource result, array fields, integer row)

The `odbc_fetch_into` function (Listing 17.28) fetches a row from a result set and places it in the `fields` argument. It returns the number of columns in the row. The `row` argument may be omitted, in which case the next row in the set is returned.

---

**Listing 17.28** *odbc_fetch_into*

```php
<?php
    //connect to database
    $Link = odbc_connect("mysql-galt", "leon", "");

    //switch to freetrade database
    odbc_do($Link, "USE ft3");

    // execute query
    $Query = "SELECT Name, SalePrice " .
        $Query .= "FROM sku ";

    $Result = odbc_do($Link, $Query);

    while(odbc_fetch_into($Result, $field))
    {
        print($field[0] . ": $" .
            number_format($field[1], 2) . "<br>");
    }

    odbc_close($Link);
?>
```

---

### boolean odbc_fetch_row(resource result, integer row)

Use `odbc_fetch_row` to get a row of data from a result set. The data for the row is stored in internal memory, ready to be retrieved with the `odbc_result` function. The `row` argument is optional and, if left out, the next available row will be returned. FALSE will be returned when there are no more rows in the result set. See the `odbc_result` function for an example of use.

### integer odbc_field_len(resource result, integer field)

Use `odbc_field_len` (Listing 17.29) to get the length of a field in a result set. Fields are numbered starting with 1.

## Listing 17.29 `odbc_field_len`

```php
<?php
    //connect to database
    $Link = odbc_connect("mysql-galt", "leon", "");

    //switch to freetrade database
    odbc_do($Link, "USE ft3");

    // execute query
    $Query = "SELECT * " .
        $Query .= "FROM sku ";

    $Result = odbc_do($Link, $Query);

    print("<table border=\"1\">\n");
    print("<tr>\n");
    print("<th>Number</th>");
    print("<th>Name</th>");
    print("<th>Type</th>");
    print("<th>Length</th>");
    print("<th>Precision</th>");
    print("<th>Scale</th>");
    print("</tr>\n");

    $cols = odbc_num_fields($Result);
    for($c=1; $c <= $cols; $c++)
    {
        print("<tr>\n");
        print("<td>$c</td>");
        print("<td>".odbc_field_name($Result, $c)."</td>");
        print("<td>".odbc_field_type($Result, $c)."</td>");
        print("<td>".odbc_field_len($Result, $c)."</td>");
        print("<td>".odbc_field_precision($Result, $c)."</td>");
        print("<td>".odbc_field_scale($Result, $c)."</td>");
        print("</tr>\n");
    }
    print("</table>\n");

    //close connection
    odbc_close($Link);
?>
```

### string odbc_field_name(resource result, integer field)

Use `odbc_field_name` to get the name of a field in a result set. Fields are numbered starting with 1.

### integer odbc_field_num(resource result, string name)

The `odbc_field_num` function returns the number of the named column in the result set.

### string odbc_field_precision(resource result, integer field)

Use `odbc_field_precision` to get the precision of a field in a result set. Fields are numbered starting with 1.

### string odbc_field_scale(resource result, integer field)

Use `odbc_field_scale` to get the scale of a field in a result set. Fields are numbered starting with 1.

### string odbc_field_type(resource result, integer field)

Use `odbc_field_type` to get the type of a field in a result set. Fields are numbered starting with 1.

### resource odbc_foreignkeys(resource connection, string primary_catalog, string primary_schema, string primary_table, string foreign_catalog, string foreign_schema, string foreign_table)

The `odbc_foreignkeys` function returns a result set describing foreign keys if the database server supports them. PHP requires all arguments, but you may supply empty strings. Some drivers do not use the catalog and schema values.

The values returned by this function depend on whether you provide a value for `primary_table` or `foreign_table`. If you give only a value for `primary_table`, the result set contains that primary key for that table and any foreign keys that point to it. If you give only a value for `foreign_table`, the result set contains all the foreign keys in that table and the primary keys to which they point. If you specify both `primary_table` and `foreign_table`, the result set contains only the foreign key in the foreign table that points to the primary key in the primary table.

The result set contains the following columns: `DELETE_RULE`, `FKCOLUMN_NAME`, `FKTABLE_CAT`, `FKTABLE_NAME`, `FKTABLE_SCHEM`, `FK_NAME`, `KEY_SEQ`, `PKCOLUMN_NAME`, `PKTABLE_CAT`, `PKTABLE_NAME`, `PKTABLE_SCHEM`, `PK_NAME_DEFERABILITY`, `UPDATE_RULE`.

### boolean odbc_free_result(resource result)

Use `odbc_free_result` to free the memory associated with the result set. This is not strictly necessary, but it's a good idea if you are worried about running out of memory. If autocommit is disabled and you free a result set before calling `odbc_commit`, the database driver performs a transaction rollback.

### resource odbc_gettypeinfo(resource connection)

The `odbc_gettypeinfo` function returns a result set describing the types supported by the data source. The result set contains the following columns: `TYPE_NAME`, `DATA_TYPE`, `COLUMN_SIZE`, `LITERAL_PREFIX`, `LITERAL_SUFFIX`, `CREATE_PARAMS`, `NULLABLE`, `CASE_SENSITIVE`, `SEARCHABLE`, `UNSIGNED_ATTRIBUTE`, `FIXED_PREC_SCALE`, `AUTO_UNIQUE_VALUE`, `LOCAL_TYPE_NAME`, `MINIMUM_SCALE`, `MAXIMUM_SCALE`, `SQL_DATATYPE`, `SQL_DATETIME_SUB`, `NUM_PREC_RADIX`, `INTERVAL_PRECISION`.

### boolean odbc_longreadlen(resource result, integer length)

Use `odbc_longreadlen` to set the maximum length for values of any columns of type long. This includes binary columns such as `longvarbinary`. By default, the maximum length is zero, which has the special meaning of causing fetched columns to be echoed to the browser. Any other positive number will cause returned values to be truncated to the specified length.

Note that it is not always apparent that a field is considered to be a long by the ODBC driver. For example, a memo column in Microsoft Access is a long. Column contents appearing in the wrong place in an HTML page is a sign of fetching a long where you didn't expect it. One strategy to avoid these problems is to always call `longreadlen`.

### boolean odbc_next_result(resource result)

The `odbc_next_result` function advances the row pointer in the result set.

### integer odbc_num_fields(resource result)

Use `odbc_num_fields` to find the number of fields in the result set.

### integer odbc_num_rows(resource result)

The `odbc_num_rows` function returns the number of rows in the result set or the number of rows affected by a DELETE or INSERT if the driver supports it. Some drivers do not support returning the number of rows in a result set and return –1 instead.

### resource odbc_pconnect(string dsn, string user, string password)

The `odbc_pconnect` function operates similarly to `odbc_connect`. A connection is attempted to the specified Data Source Name (DSN) and a connection identifier is returned. The connection should not be closed with `odbc_close`.

It will persist as long as the Web server process. The next time a script executes `odbc_pconnect`, PHP will first check for existing connections.

### integer odbc_prepare(resource connection, string query)

The `odbc_prepare` function (Listing 17.30) parses a query and prepares it for execution. A result identifier that may be passed to `odbc_execute` is returned. Preparing statements can be more efficient than making the driver reparse statements. This is usually the case where you have many rows to insert into the same table. To specify a value to be filled in later, use a question mark.

---

**Listing 17.30**   *odbc_execute, odbc_prepare*

```php
<?php
    //connect to database
    $Link = odbc_connect("mysql-galt", "leon", "");

    //use the freetrade database
    odbc_do($Link, "USE ft3");

    //prepare query for inserting new SKUs for item 1
    $Query = "INSERT INTO sku (Item, Name, SalePrice) ";
    $Query .= "VALUES(1, ?, ?) ";
    $Result = odbc_prepare($Link, $Query);

    //insert these rows
    //2003 Calendar, 20.00
    //2004 Calendar, 20.50
    //2005 Calendar, 21.00
    for($index = 2003; $index <= 2005; $index++)
    {
        $values[0] = "$index Calendar";
        $values[1] = 20.00 + (0.50 * ($index-2000));

        odbc_execute($Result, $values);
    }

    //dump all SKUs for item 1
    $Query = "Select ID, Name, SalePrice " .
        "FROM sku " .
        "WHERE Item = 1";
    $Result = odbc_do($Link, $Query);

    odbc_result_all($Result, 'border="1"');

    //close connection
    odbc_close($Link);
?>
```

### resource odbc_primarykeys(resource connection, string catalog, string schema, string table)

Use this function to get a result set describing the columns that make up the primary key of the given table. Not all ODBC drivers support the `catalog` and `schema` arguments, in which case you may pass an empty string. The result set contains the following columns: TABLE_QUALIFIER, TABLE_OWNER, TABLE_NAME, COLUMN_NAME, KEY_SEQ, PK_NAME.

### resource odbc_procedurecolumns(resource connection, string catalog, string schema, string table, string column)

Use this function to get a result set describing stored procedures. Not all ODBC drivers support the `catalog` and `schema` arguments, in which case you may pass an empty string. Other than the database link, all arguments are optional. The result set contains the following columns:
PROCEDURE_QUALIFIER, PROCEDURE_OWNER, PROCEDURE_NAME, COLUMN_NAME, COLUMN_TYPE, DATA_TYPE, TYPE_NAME, PRECISION, LENGTH, SCALE, RADIX, NULLABLE, REMARKS.

### resource odbc_procedures(resource connection, string catalog, string schema, string procedure)

Use this function to get a result set describing stored procedures. Not all ODBC drivers support the `catalog` and `schema` arguments, in which case you may pass an empty string. Other than the database link, all arguments are optional. The result set contains the following columns:
PROCEDURE_QUALIFIER, PROCEDURE_OWNER, PROCEDURE_NAME, NUM_INPUT_PARAMS, NUM_OUTPUT_PARAMS, NUM_RESULT_SETS, REMARKS, PROCEDURE_TYPE.

### string odbc_result(resource result, string field)

Use `odbc_result` (Listing 17.31) to get the value of a field for the current row. Fields may be referenced by number or name. If using numbers, start counting fields with 1. If you specify a field by name, do not include the table name.

This function is affected by the settings controlled by `odbc_binmode` and `odbc_longreadlen`. An important fact to keep in mind is that while in most cases the value of the field will be returned, fields that contain long data will be echoed to the browser instead by default. Use `odbc_longreadlen` to change this behavior.

| Listing 17.31 | `odbc_result` |
|---|---|

```php
<?php
    //connect to database
    $Link = odbc_connect("mysql-galt", "leon", "");

    //switch to ft3 database
    odbc_do($Link, "USE ft3");

    //dump all SKUs
    $Query = "Select Name, SalePrice " .
        "FROM sku ";
    $Result = odbc_do($Link, $Query);

    while(odbc_fetch_row($Result))
    {
        $name = odbc_result($Result, 1);
        $price = odbc_result($Result, 2);
        print("$name: $price<br>\n");
    }

    //close connection
    odbc_close($Link);
?>
```

### integer odbc_result_all(resource result, string format)

The `odbc_result_all` function will dump all the rows for a result set to the browser. The number of rows is returned. The dumped rows are formatted in a table. The fields are printed in a header row with TH tags. The optional `format` argument will be inserted inside the initial table tag so that you may set table attributes.

### boolean odbc_rollback(resource connection)

Use `odbc_rollback` to abandon all pending transactions. By default all queries are automatically committed, but this behavior may be modified with `odbc_autocommit`. Not all databases support transactions.

### integer odbc_setoption(integer id, integer function, integer option, integer parameter)

The `odbc_setoption` function changes the configuration of the ODBC driver for an entire connection or a single result set. Its purpose is to allow access to any ODBC setting in order to avoid problems with buggy ODBC drivers. To use this function, you ought to understand ODBC in greater detail than the average user does. You will need to know the values of the various options available to you.

The id argument is either a connection identifier or a result set identifier. Since `odbc_setoption` wraps two C API functions, `SQLSetConnectOption` and `SQLSetStmtOption`, you must specify which to use with the `function` argument. The `option` argument is an integer that identifies one of the many options available on the ODBC driver. The `parameter` argument is the value to use with the option.

### resource odbc_specialcolumns(resource connection, integer type, string catalog, string schema, string table, integer scope, integer nullable)

The `odbc_specialcolumns` function has two modes, one that returns the set of columns that uniquely identifies a row and one that returns the set of columns that update automatically with updates to other columns in the table. You may choose between these rows by setting the `type` argument to `SQL_BEST_ROWID` for the first mode or to `SQL_ROWVER` for the second. Not all ODBC drivers support the `catalog` and `schema` arguments, in which case you may pass an empty string.

The `scope` argument controls the scope of the query and may be set with any of three constants. `SQL_SCOPE_CURROW` specifies that the result is good for the current row only. `SQL_SCOPE_SESSION` specifies that the result is good for the entire session. `SQL_SCOPE_TRANSACTION` specifies that the results are good for the current transaction only.

The `nullable` argument specifies whether to return rows that allow NULL values. Use `SQL_NULLABLE` to allow them or `SQL_NO_NULLS` to disallow them.

The result set contains the following columns: SCOPE, COLUMN_NAME, DATA_TYPE, TYPE_NAME, PRECISION, LENGTH, SCALE, PSEUDO_COLUMN.

### resource odbc_statistics (resource connection, string catalog, string schema, string table, integer unique, integer reserved)

The `odbc_statistics` function returns a result set containing statistics about a table and its indexes. Not all ODBC drivers support the `catalog` and `schema` arguments, in which case you may pass an empty string. The `unique` argument controls the type of indexes to include. Only unique indexes are included if you set `unique` to `SQL_INDEX_UNIQUE`. PHP includes all indexes if you set `unique` to `SQL_INDEX_ALL`.

The `reserved` argument controls fetching of the CARDINALITY and PAGES columns in the result set. Set `reserved` to `SQL_ENSURE` to fetch the statistics unconditionally. Set `reserved` to `SQL_QUICK` to fetch these values only if the server has them ready to send. Some ODBC drivers are capable of returning data using the `SQL_QUICK` mode only.

The result set contains the following columns: `TABLE_QUALIFIER`, `TABLE_OWNER`, `TABLE_NAME`, `NON_UNIQUE`, `INDEX_QUALIFIER`, `INDEX_NAME`, `TYPE`, `SEQ_IN_INDEX`, `COLUMN_NAME`, `COLLATION`, `CARDINALITY`, `PAGES`, `FILTER_CONDITION`.

### resource odbc_tableprivileges(resource connection, string catalog, string schema, string table)

The `odbc_tableprivileges` function returns a result set describing tables and their privileges. Not all ODBC drivers support the `catalog` and `schema` arguments, in which case you may pass an empty string. The `table` argument is a pattern matching table names in the database. Use the `%` and `_` wildcard characters.

The result contains the following columns: `TABLE_QUALIFIER`, `TABLE_OWNER`, `TABLE_NAME`, `GRANTOR`, `GRANTEE`, `PRIVILEGE`, `IS_GRANTABLE`.

### resource odbc_tables(resource connection, string catalog, string schema, string table, string types)

The `odbc_tables` function returns a result set describing tables in the given catalog. Not all ODBC drivers support the `catalog` and `schema` arguments, in which case you may pass an empty string. The `catalog` and `table` arguments are patterns that allow you to use the `%` and `_` wildcard characters. Set the `types` argument with one of the following strings: `ALIAS`, `GLOBAL TEMPORARY`, `LOCAL TEMPORARY`, `SYNONYM`, `SYSTEM TABLE`, `TABLE`, `VIEW`.

The result contains the following columns: `TABLE_CAT`, `TABLE_SCHEM`, `TABLE_NAME`, `TABLE_TYPE REMARKS`.

# 17.6  Oracle

Oracle is one of the most popular relational databases in the world. It is an industrial-strength engine preferred by large corporations using databases of exceeding complexity. Oracle database administrators are scarce and command high salaries. A full explanation of working with Oracle is far beyond the scope of this text. Fortunately, you will find many books about Oracle for sale as well as free documentation on the Oracle Web site. Try the following URL `<http://otn.oracle.com/documentation/oracle9i.html>`.

PHP supports two generations of Oracle libraries, Version 7 and Version 8. The functions that use Oracle 7 begin with `ora_`, such as `ora_logon`. The functions that work with Oracle 8 begin with `oci`, such as `ocilogon`. The Oracle 8 library supports connecting to older Oracle databases. In previous editions, I've included descriptions of the older functions, but enough time has passed that it seems unlikely many people are still forced to use the older library.

Thies Arntzen, Stig Bakken, Mitch Golden, Andreas Karajannis, and Rasmus Lerdorf contributed to the Oracle 7 extension. Oracle 8 support was added to PHP by Thies Arntzen and Stig Bakken.

Oracle provides the option of installing a sample database. The login is `scott` and the password is `tiger`. The examples in this section take advantage of this feature.

### boolean ocibindbyname (resource statement, string placeholder, reference variable, integer length, integer type)

The `ocibindbyname` function (Listing 17.32) binds an Oracle placeholder to a PHP variable. You must supply a valid statement identifier as created by `ociparse`, the name of the placeholder, a reference to a PHP variable, and the maximum length of the bind data. You may use a value of –1 to use the length of the variable passed as the `variable` argument.

The optional `type` argument specifies a data type and is necessary if you wish to bind to an abstract data type. Use one of the following constants to set the data type: OCI_B_BLOB, OCI_B_CFILE, OCI_B_CLOB, OCI_B_FILE, OCI_B_ROWID. Make sure you use `ocinewdescriptor` before binding to an abstract data type. You also need to use –1 for the `length` argument.

Listing 17.33 and Listing 17.34 demonstrate using `ocibindbyname` with a stored procedure.

---

**Listing 17.32**   *ocibindbyname*

```php
<?php
    //set-up data to insert
    $NewEmployee = array(
        array(8001, 'Smith', 'Clerk', 30),
        array(8002, 'Jones', 'Analyst', 20),
        array(8003, 'Atkinson', 'President', 40)
        );

    //connect to database
    $Link = ocilogon("scott", "tiger");

    //assemble query
    $Query = "INSERT INTO emp " .
        "(EMPNO, ENAME, JOB, HIREDATE, DEPTNO) " .
        "VALUES (:empno, :ename, :job, SYSDATE, :deptno ) ";
```

**Listing 17.32** *ocibindbyname (cont.)*

```
//parse query
$Statement = ociparse($Link, $Query);

//create descriptor the abstract data type
$RowID = ocinewdescriptor($Link, OCI_D_ROWID);

//bind input and output variables
ocibindbyname($Statement, ":empno", $EmployeeNumber, 32);
ocibindbyname($Statement, ":ename", $EmployeeName, 32);
ocibindbyname($Statement, ":job", $Job, 32);
ocibindbyname($Statement, ":deptno", $DeptNo, 32);

//loop over each new employee
foreach($NewEmployee as $e)
{
    //set column values
    $EmployeeNumber = $e[0];
    $EmployeeName = $e[1];
    $Job = $e[2];
    $DeptNo = $e[3];

    //execute query, do not automatically commit
    ociexecute($Statement, OCI_DEFAULT);
}

//free the statement
//ocifreestatement($Statement);

//assemble query for getting contents
$Query = "SELECT EmpNo, EName, Job, HireDate, DName " .
    "FROM emp JOIN dept ON (emp.DeptNo = dept.DeptNo)";

//parse query
$Statement = ociparse($Link, $Query);

//execute query, make sure keep autocommit off
ociexecute($Statement, OCI_DEFAULT);

//fetch each row
while(ocifetchinto($Statement, $Columns,
    OCI_NUM | OCI_RETURN_NULLS | OCI_RETURN_LOBS))
{
    print(implode(",", $Columns) . "<br>\n");
}

//free the statement
ocifreestatement($Statement);
```

**Listing 17.32** *ocibindbyname (cont.)*

```
    //undo the inserts
    //Normally, you won't do this, if we undo the inserts
    //each time, we can run the example over and over
    ocirollback($Link);

    //close connection
    ocilogoff($Link);
?>
```

**Listing 17.33** *Procedure for fetching employee name*

```
CREATE OR REPLACE PROCEDURE get_emp_name (
    emp_number IN   emp.Empno%TYPE,
    emp_name OUT emp.Ename%TYPE) AS
BEGIN
    SELECT Ename
        INTO emp_name
        FROM emp
        WHERE Empno = emp_number;
END;
```

**Listing 17.34** *ocibindbyname and stored procedures*

```
<?php
    //open connection
    $Connection = ocilogon("scott", "tiger");

    //create statement that calls a stored procedure
    $Query = "BEGIN get_emp_name(7499, :emp_name); END;";
    $Statement = ociparse($Connection, $Query);

    //bind placeholder to name
    ocibindbyname($Statement, ":emp_name", $EmployeeName, 32);

    //execute statement
    ociexecute($Statement);

    print($EmployeeName);

    //free memory for statement
    ocifreestatement($Statement);

    //close connection
    ocilogoff($Connection);
?>
```

### boolean ocicancel(resource statement)

Use the `ocicancel` function if you wish to stop reading from a cursor.

### boolean ocicollappend(object collection, string value)

The `ocicollappend` function adds a value to a collection.

### boolean ocicollassign(object collection, object collection2)

The `ocicollassign` function assigns a collection from another collection.

### boolean ocicollassignelem(object collection, integer index, string value)

The `ocicollassignelem` function assigns the given value to the collection at the given index.

### string ocicollgetelem(object collection, integer index)

The `ocicollgetelem` function returns the value of the collection entry at the given index.

### integer ocicollmax(object collection)

Use the `ocicollmax` function to get the maximum value of a collection. For arrays, this value is the maximum length.

### integer ocicollsize(object collection)

Use `ocicollsize` to get the size of the collection.

### boolean ocicolltrim(object collection, integer number)

The `ocicolltrim` function removes the given number of elements from the end of the collection.

### boolean ocicolumnisnull(resource statement, value column)

Use `ocicolumnisnull` to test whether a column is null. You may specify columns by number, in which case columns are numbered starting with 1. Alternatively, you may specify columns by name.

### string ocicolumnname(resource statement, integer column)

The `ocicolumnname` function returns the name of a column given the column number. You may specify columns by number, in which case columns are numbered starting with 1, or you may specify columns by name.

**integer ocicolumnprecision(resource statement, value column)**

Use `ocicolumnprecision` to get the precision of the given column. You may specify columns by number, in which case columns are numbered starting with 1, or you may specify columns by name.

**integer ocicolumnscale(resource statement, value column)**

Use `ocicolumnscale` to get the precision of the given column. You may specify columns by number, in which case columns are numbered starting with 1, or you may specify columns by name.

**integer ocicolumnsize(resource statement, value column)**

The `ocicolumnsize` function returns the size of a column. You may specify columns by number, in which case columns are numbered starting with 1, or you may specify columns by name.

**string ocicolumntype(resource statement, value column)**

Use `ocicolumntype` to get the type of the specified column. You may specify columns by number, in which case columns are numbered starting with 1, or you may specify columns by name. The name of the type will be returned if it is one of the following: BFILE, BLOB, CHAR, CLOB, DATE, LONG RAW, LONG, NUMBER, RAW, REFCURSOR, ROWID, VARCHAR. Otherwise, an integer code representing the data type will be returned.

**integer ocicolumntyperaw(resource statement, value column)**

The `ocicolumtyperaw` function returns the raw Oracle type number for the given column. You may specify the column by name or number. If by number, keep in mind that columns are numbered beginning with 1.

**boolean ocicommit(resource connection)**

The `ocicommit` function commits all previous statements executed on the connection. By default, statements are committed when executed. You can override this functionality when you call `ociexecute` with OCI_DEFAULT.

**boolean ocidefinebyname(resource statement, string column, reference variable, integer type)**

The `ocidefinebyname` function (Listing 17.35) associates a column with a PHP variable. When the statement is executed, the value of the column will be copied into the variable. The `statement` argument must be an integer returned by `ociparse`. The column name must be written in uppercase; otherwise, Oracle will not recognize it. Unrecognized column names do not produce errors.

The `type` argument appears to be necessary only if you are attaching to an abstract data type, such as a `ROWID`. Abstract data types require `ocinewdescriptor` be used prior to `ocidefinebyname`. If the `type` argument is left out, the variable will be set as a null-terminated string.

---

**Listing 17.35**    *ocidefinebyname*

```php
<?php
    //connect to database
    $Link = ocilogon("scott", "tiger");

    //assemble query
    $Query = "SELECT ENAME, HIREDATE " .
        "FROM emp " .
        "WHERE JOB='CLERK' ";

    //parse query
    $Statement = ociparse($Link, $Query);

    //associate two columns with variables
    ocidefinebyname($Statement, "ENAME", $EmployeeName);
    ocidefinebyname($Statement, "HIREDATE", $HireDate);

    //execute query
    ociexecute($Statement);

    //fetch each row
    while(ocifetch($Statement))
    {
        print("$EmployeeName was hired $HireDate<br>\n");
    }

    //free the statement
    ocifreestatement($Statement);

    //close connection
    ocilogoff($Link);
?>
```

---

### array ocierror(resource identifier)

The `ocierror` function returns an associative array describing the last error generated by Oracle. You may set the optional `identifier` argument with a statement resource or a connection resource to get an error from a particular step in the query execution process.

If no error has occurred, this function returns FALSE. Otherwise, the returned array contains two elements: code and message.

### boolean ociexecute(resource statement, integer mode)

Use ociexecute to execute a statement. The mode argument is optional. It controls whether the statement will be committed after execution. By default, OCI_COMMIT_ON_EXECUTE is used. If you do not wish to commit the transaction immediately, use OCI_DEFAULT. Every time you call ociexecute, PHP sets the autocommit flag. If you have a series of statements you wish to execute without committing, be sure to use OCI_DEFAULT for each of them.

### boolean ocifetch(resource statement)

The ocifetch function (Listing 17.36) prepares the next row of data to be read with ociresult. When no rows remain, FALSE is returned.

---

**Listing 17.36**  *ocifetch*

```php
<?php
    //connect to database
    $Link = ocilogon("scott", "tiger");

    //check that we made the connection
    if($Error = ocierror())
    {
        die('<p style="color: red">Connection Failed--' .
            $Error["message"] . "</p>");
    }

    //assemble query
    $Query = "SELECT * FROM emp ";

    //parse query
    $Statement = ociparse($Link, $Query);

    //execute query
    ociexecute($Statement);

    //check that the query executed successfully
    if($Error = ocierror($Statement))
    {
        die('<p style="color: red">Execution Failed--' .
            $Error["message"] .
            "</p>");
    }
```

**Listing 17.36**    *ocifetch (cont.)*

```
//start HTML table
print("<table border=\"1\">\n");

//build headers from column information
print("<tr>\n");
for($i=1; $i <= ocinumcols($Statement); $i++)
{
    print("<th>" .
        ocicolumnname($Statement, $i) . "<br>" .
        ocicolumntype($Statement, $i) .
        "(" . ocicolumnsize($Statement, $i) . ")<br>" .
        ocicolumnprecision($Statement, $i) . "<br> " .
        ocicolumnscale($Statement, $i) .
        "</th>\n");
}
print("</tr>\n");

//fetch each row
while(ocifetch($Statement))
{
    print("<tr>\n");

    //loop over each column
    for($i=1; $i <= ocinumcols($Statement); $i++)
    {
        //print a line like "<td>SMITH</td>"
        print("<td>");
        if(ocicolumnisnull($Statement, $i))
        {
            print("(null)");
        }
        else
        {
            print(ociresult($Statement, $i));
        }
        print("</td>\n");
    }

    print("</tr>\n");
}

//close table
print("</table>\n");

//free the statement
ocifreestatement($Statement);

//close connection
ocilogoff($Link);
?>
```

### boolean ocifetchinto(resource statement, reference data, integer mode)

Use ocifetchinto (Listing 17.37) to get the next row of data from an executed statement and place it in an array. The data argument will contain an array that by default will be indexed by integers starting with 1. The optional mode argument controls how PHP indexes the array. You may add the constants listed in Table 17.11 to get the features you desire.

**Table 17.11** Constants for Use with ocifetchinto

| Constant | Description |
| --- | --- |
| OCI_ASSOC | Return columns indexed by name. |
| OCI_NUM | Return columns indexed by number. |
| OCI_RETURN_LOBS | Return values of LOBs instead of descriptors. |
| OCI_RETURN_NULLS | Create elements for null columns. |

**Listing 17.37** *ocifetchinto*

```php
<?php
    //connect to database
    $Link = ocilogon("scott", "tiger");

    //assemble query
    $Query = "SELECT * " .
        "FROM emp ";

    //parse query
    $Statement = ociparse($Link, $Query);

    //execute query
    ociexecute($Statement);

    //start HTML table
    print('<table border="1">');

    //fetch each row
    while(ocifetchinto($Statement, $Column,
        OCI_NUM | OCI_RETURN_NULLS | OCI_RETURN_LOBS))
    {
```

| Listing 17.37 | *ocifetchinto (cont.)* |
|---|---|

```
        print("<tr><td>" .
            implode('</td><td>', $Column) .
            "</td></tr>\n");
    }

    //close table
    print("</table>\n");

    //free the statement
    ocifreestatement($Statement);

    //close connection
    ocilogoff($Link);
?>
```

### integer ocifetchstatement(resource statement, reference data)

The `ocifetchstatement` function (Listing 17.38) places an array with all the result data in the `data` argument and returns the number of rows. The `data` array is indexed by the names of the columns. Each element is an array itself, indexed by integers starting with zero. Each element in this subarray corresponds to a row.

| Listing 17.38 | *ocifetchstatement* |
|---|---|

```
<?php
    //connect to database
    $Link = ocilogon("scott", "tiger");

    //assemble query
    $Query = "SELECT * " .
        "FROM emp ";

    //parse query
    $Statement = ociparse($Link, $Query);

    //execute query
    ociexecute($Statement);

    print('<table border="1">');

    //fetch all rows into array
    $RowCount = ocifetchstatement($Statement, $Data);
```

**Listing 17.38** *ocifetchstatement (cont.)*

```
print("$RowCount Rows<br>");

foreach($Data as $Column)
{
    print("<tr><td>" .
        implode('</td><td>', $Column) .
        "</td></tr>\n");

}

print("</table>\n");

//free the statement
ocifreestatement($Statement);

//close connection
ocilogoff($Link);
?>
```

### boolean ocifreecollection(object collection)
The `ocifreecollection` function frees the memory reserved by a collection.

### boolean ocifreecursor(integer cursor)
Use `ocifreecursor` to free the memory associated with a cursor you created with `ocinewcursor`.

### boolean ocifreedesc(object lob)
The `ocifreedesc` function frees the memory reserved by a large object descriptor.

### boolean ocifreestatement(resource statement)
Use `ocifreestatement` to free the memory associated with a statement. The `statement` argument is an integer returned by `ociparse`.

### ociinternaldebug(boolean on)
The `ociinternaldebug` function controls whether debugging information is generated. The debugging output will be sent to the browser. It is off by default, of course.

### string ociloadlob(object lob)
The `ociloadlob` function returns the contents of a large object.

### boolean ocilogoff(integer link)
Use `ocilogoff` to close a connection.

### integer ocilogon(string user, string password, string sid)

The `ocilogon` function establishes a connection to an Oracle database. The identifier it returns is used to create statements, cursors, and descriptors. The `user` and `password` arguments are required. The optional `sid` argument specifies the server; if it is left out, the `ORACLE_SID` environment variable will be used.

If you attempt to create a second connection to the same database, you will not really get another connection. This means that commits or rollbacks affect all statements created by your script. If you want a separate connection, use `ocinlogon` instead.

### boolean ocinewcollection(resource connection, string tdo, string schema)

The `ocinewcollection` function creates a new collection. You must supply a TDO (type descriptor object). Optionally, you may specify a schema.

### integer ocinewcursor(integer link)

Use `ocinewcursor` to create a cursor. The cursor identifier that is returned is similar to a statement identifier. Use `ocifreecursor` to free the memory associated with a cursor. You can use a cursor to get the data returned by a stored procedure, as shown in Listing 17.40. Listing 17.39 is the package used in Listing 17.40.

To use a cursor, first create it with `ocinewcursor`. Parse a query that contains a placeholder, and bind the placeholder to the cursor. Execute the statement, then execute the cursor. Now you may read from the cursor in the same way you read from an executed statement.

---

**Listing 17.39**  *Oracle package using reference cursors*

```
CREATE OR REPLACE PACKAGE emp_data AS
    TYPE EmpCurTyp IS REF CURSOR RETURN emp%ROWTYPE;
    PROCEDURE open_emp_cv (
        emp_number IN emp.empno%TYPE,
        emp_cv IN OUT EmpCurTyp);
END emp_data;

CREATE OR REPLACE PACKAGE BODY emp_data AS
    PROCEDURE open_emp_cv (
        emp_number IN emp.empno%TYPE,
        emp_cv IN OUT EmpCurTyp) IS
```

**Listing 17.39**    *Oracle package using reference cursors (cont.)*

```
BEGIN
    OPEN emp_cv FOR SELECT *
        FROM emp
        WHERE empno = emp_number;
END open_emp_cv;
END emp_data;
```

**Listing 17.40**    *ocinewcursor*

```php
<?php
    //open connection
    $Connection = ocilogon("scott", "tiger");

    //create cursor
    $Cursor = ocinewcursor($Connection);

    //create statement that calls a stored procedure
    $Query = "BEGIN emp_data.open_emp_cv(7902, :myrow); END;";
    $Statement = ociparse($Connection, $Query);

    //bind placeholder to cursor
    ocibindbyname($Statement, ":myrow", $Cursor, -1, OCI_B_CURSOR);

    //execute statement
    ociexecute($Statement);

    //execute cursor
    ociexecute($Cursor);

    //get row from cursor
    while(ocifetchinto($Cursor, $Column,
        OCI_NUM | OCI_RETURN_NULLS))
    {
        print(implode(',', $Column) . "<br>\n");
    }

    //free memory for statement
    ocifreestatement($Statement);

    //free row
    ocifreecursor($Cursor);

    //close connection
    ocilogoff($Connection);
?>
```

### string ocinewdescriptor(resource connection, integer type)

The `ocinewdescriptor` function allocates memory for descriptors and LOB locators. The type defaults to being a file, but you may specify `OCI_D_FILE`, `OCI_D_LOB`, or `OCI_D_ROWID`. See `ocibindbyname` for an example of use.

### integer ocinlogon(string user, string password, string sid)

The `ocinlogon` function establishes a unique connection to an Oracle database. The identifier it returns is used to create statements, cursors, and descriptors. The `user` and `password` arguments are required. The optional `sid` argument specifies the server, and if left out, the `ORACLE_SID` environment variable will be used.

Compare this function to `ocilogon` and `ociplogon`.

### integer ocinumcols(resource statement)

The `ocinumcols` function returns the number of columns in a statement.

### integer ociparse(resource connection, string query)

The `ociparse` function creates a statement from a query. It requires a valid connection identifier.

### integer ociplogon(string user, string password, string sid)

The `ociplogon` function establishes a persistent connection to an Oracle database. These connections exist as long as the server process. When you request a persistent connection, you may get a connection that already exists, thus saving the overhead of establishing a connection.

The returned identifier is used to create statements, cursors, and descriptors. The `user` and `password` arguments are required. The optional `sid` argument specifies the server, and if left out, the `ORACLE_SID` environment variable will be used.

Compare this function to `ocilogon` and `ocinlogon`.

### string ociresult(resource statement, value column)

Use `ociresult` to get the value of a column on the current row. The column may be identified by number or name. Columns are numbered starting with 1. Results are returned as strings, except in the case of LOBs, ROWIDs, and FILEs. See `ocifetch` for an example of use.

## boolean ocirollback(resource connection)

Use `ocirollback` to issue a rollback operation on the given connection. By default, calls to `ociexecute` are committed automatically, so be sure to override this functionality if you wish to use `ocirollback`.

Keep in mind that if you used `ocilogon` or `ociplogon` to get more than one connection, they may not be unique. Therefore, issuing a rollback will affect all statements. To avoid this situation, use `ocinlogon` instead.

## integer ocirowcount(resource statement)

The `ocirowcount` function returns the number of rows affected by an update, insert, or delete.

## boolean ocisavelob(object lob)

The `ocisavelob` function writes the PHP instance of a large object into the database.

## boolean ocisavelobfile(object lob)

The `ocisavelobfile` function saves a large object file.

## string ociserverversion(resource connection)

Use `ociserverversion` to get a string describing the version of the server for a connection.

## integer ocisetprefetch(resource statement, integer size)

The `ocisetprefetch` function sets the size of a buffer that Oracle uses to prefetch results into. The `size` argument will be multiplied by 1024 to set the actual number of bytes.

## string ocistatementtype(resource statement)

Use `ocistatementtype` to get a string that describes the type of the statement. The types you can expect are ALTER, BEGIN, CREATE, DECLARE, DELETE, DROP, INSERT, SELECT, UNKNOWN, and UPDATE.

## boolean ociwritelobtofile(object lob, string filename, integer start, integer length)

The `ociwritelobtofile` function writes a large object to a file in the file system. The optional `start` and `length` arguments cause PHP to write only a portion of the large object.

# 17.7 Postgres

Postgres was originally developed at the University of California, Berkeley. It introduced many of the advanced object-relational concepts becoming popular in commercial databases. PostgreSQL is the most current incarnation of Postgres. It implements almost all of the SQL specification. Best of all, it's free.

As with other sections in this chapter, the descriptions of the functions can't stand alone. You will have to study PostgreSQL to fully understand how it works. More information may be found at the official PostgreSQL Web site at `<http://www.postgresql.org/>`.

Zeev Suraski wrote the original PostgreSQL extension. Jouni Ahto added support for large objects.

### integer pg_affected_rows(resource result)

The `pg_affected_rows` function (Listing 17.41) returns the number of instances affected by the last query. This includes DELETE, INSERT, and UPDATE statements, but not SELECT statements.

---

**Listing 17.41**  *pg_affected_rows*

```php
<?php
    //connect to database
    $Link = pg_connect("host=localhost " .
        "dbname=freetrade " .
        "user=freetrade " .
        "password=freetrade");

    //discount prices by 5%
    $Query = "UPDATE sku " .
        "SET SalePrice = ListPrice * 0.95 " .
        "WHERE ListPrice > 30.00 ";

    //execute query
    if(!($Result = pg_query($Link, $Query)))
    {
        print("Failed: " . pg_last_error($Link));
    }

    //tell user how many rows were inserted
    print(pg_affected_rows($Result) . " rows updated.<br>");

    //close connection
    pg_close($Link);
?>
```

### boolean pg_cancel_query(resource connection)

The `pg_cancel_query` stops an asynchronous query created with `pg_send_query`.

### string pg_client_encoding (resource connection)

The `pg_client_encoding` function returns a string representing the encoding used on the client.

### boolean pg_close(resource connection)

Use `pg_close` to close a connection to a PostgreSQL database created with `pg_connect`. Using this function is not strictly necessary, as PHP closes open connections when a script ends.

### resource pg_connect(string options)

The `pg_connect` function returns a connection identifier to a PostgreSQL database. The `options` string follows a format defined by PostgreSQL. This string should be `option=value` pairs separated by spaces. Available options include `dbname`, `host`, `options`, `password`, `port`, `tty`, and `user`. If you set the host option, PHP will connect to the database using TCP/IP. Otherwise, it connects via a socket.

If you attempt to connect a second time with the same set of options, PHP will return the same connection resource instead of creating a new connection. If you wish to use persistent connections, use `pg_pconnect` instead.

### boolean pg_connection_busy(resource connection)

Use `pg_connection_busy` to check whether an asynchronous query has finished. It returns `TRUE` until the query finishes. Use `pg_send_query` to begin an asynchronous query.

### boolean pg_connection_reset(resource connection)

The `pg_connection_reset` function resets a connection, which may be necessary after an error.

### integer pg_connection_status(resource connection)

The `pg_connection_status` tests the status of a connection. The return value matches `PGSQL_CONNECTION_OK` or `PGSQL_CONNECTION_BAD`.

### array pg_convert(resource connection, string table, array row, integer option)

The `pg_convert` function checks and prepares a row of data for insertion into the named table. The `data` array must be an associative array with keys matching columns in the table. PHP checks that the values can convert to the types defined in the table. The `option` argument may be set with the following constants: PGSQL_CONV_FORCE_NULL, PGSQL_CONV_IGNORE_DEFAULT, PGSQL_CONV_IGNORE_NOT_NULL.

This function returns the converted array, or FALSE if the conversion fails.

### boolean pg_copy_from(resource connection, string table, array rows, string delimiter, string null_as)

The pg_copy_from function (Listing 17.42) executes a COPY statement to insert the given set of rows into the named table. The SQL statement appears as COPY "…" FROM STDIN DELIMITERS '[tab]' WITH NULL AS ''. PHP formats the given rows into a string suitable for the statement. Optionally, you may override the defaults for delimiters (tab) and nulls (empty string). The rows array should consist of strings representing rows with fields separated by the delimiter character.

**Listing 17.42**   *pg_copy_from, pg_copy_to*

```php
<?php
    //connect to database
    $Link = pg_connect(" " .
        "dbname=freetrade " .
        "user=freetrade " .
        "password=freetrade");

    //get contents of the fee table
    $rows = pg_copy_to($Link, 'fee');

    //make new set of rows based on the old ones
    $count = count($rows);
    for($r=0; $r < $count; $r++)
    {
        $columns = explode("\t", $rows[$r]);

        //add 100 to the ID
        //(naively assuming no key problems)
        $columns[0] += 100;

        //add "New" to the name
        $columns[1] = "New " . $columns[1];

        $rows[$r] = implode("\t", $columns);
    }

    //show the new rows going in
    print_r($rows);

    //insert new rows
    pg_copy_from($Link, 'fee', $rows);
?>
```

### array pg_copy_to(resource connection, string table, string delimiter, string null_as)

The pg_copy_to function returns the contents of the named table by executing a COPY statement. The SQL statement appears as COPY "..." FROM STDOUT DELIMITERS '[tab]' WITH NULL AS ''. The returned array consists of formatted strings. Optionally, you may override the defaults for delimiters (tab) and nulls (empty string).

### string pg_dbname(resource connection)

Use pg_dbname to get the name of the current database.

### integer pg_delete(resource connection, string table, array conditions, integer options)

The pg_delete function (Listing 17.43) assembles and executes a DELETE statement against the given table. The conditions argument should be a set of column=value pairs for use in the WHERE clause. PHP does not require the options argument. If you set options, PHP passes the conditions through the pg_convert function using the given options.

**Listing 17.43**  *pg_delete*

```php
<?php
    $c = pg_delete($Link, 'fee', array('id'=>'101'));
    print("$c rows deleted");
?>
```

### boolean pg_end_copy(resource connection)

Use the pg_end_copy function with pg_put_line to signal your finishing of an inserted record.

### string pg_escape_bytea(string text)

The pg_escape_bytea function returns binary data prepared for use in a query for a BYTEA column by escaping special characters.

### string pg_escape_string(string text)

The pg_escape_string function returns binary data prepared for use in a query by escaping special characters. You may use this function instead of addslashes.

### array pg_fetch_all(resource result)

The `pg_fetch_all` function (Listing 17.44) returns the entire result set. PHP indexes each row with an integer, starting with zero. Each element is an array indexed by column name.

**Listing 17.44** *pg_fetch_all*

```php
<?php
    //connect to database
    $Link = pg_connect(" " .
        "dbname=freetrade " .
        "user=freetrade " .
        "password=freetrade");

    //get all SKUs
    $Query = "SELECT ID, Name " .
        "FROM sku ";

    //execute the query
    $Result = pg_query($Link, $Query);

    //get the entire result set
    $Row = pg_fetch_all($Result);

    print_r($Row);
?>
```

### array pg_fetch_array(resource result, integer row, integer type)

The `pg_fetch_array` function (Listing 17.45) returns an array containing every field value for the given row. Optionally, you may leave out the row number to fetch the next row.

PHP indexes the values by number, starting with zero, and by column name. Each call to `pg_fetch_array` returns the next row, or FALSE when no rows remain. You may control the returned array by setting the optional `type` argument with one of the following constants: PGSQL_ASSOC, PGSQL_BOTH, PGSQL_NUM. With PGSQL_ASSOC, PHP indexes with column names only. With PGSQL_NUM, PHP indexes with numbers only.

Compare this function to `pg_fetch_assoc` and `pg_fetch_row`.

**Listing 17.45** *pg_fetch_array*

```php
<?php
    //connect to database
    $Link = pg_connect(" " .
        "dbname=freetrade " .
        "user=freetrade " .
        "password=freetrade");

    //get all SKUs
    $Query = "SELECT ID, Name " .
        "FROM item ";

    //execute the query
    $Result = pg_query($Link, $Query);

    //loop over each row
    while($Row = pg_fetch_array($Result))
    {
        print("{$Row['id']} = {$Row['name']}<br>\n");
    }
?>
```

### array pg_fetch_assoc(resource result, integer row)

The pg_fetch_assoc function returns an array containing every field value for the given row. Optionally, you may leave out the row number to fetch the next row. PHP indexes the values by column name.

Compare this function to pg_fetch_array and pg_fetch_row.

### object pg_fetch_object(resource result, integer row)

The pg_fetch_object function (Listing 17.46) returns an object with a property for every field. Each property is named after the field name. Each call to pg_fetch_object returns the next row, or FALSE when no rows remain.

Compare this function to pg_fetch_array.

**Listing 17.46** *pg_fetch_object*

```php
<?php
    //connect to database
    $Link = pg_connect(" " .
        "dbname=freetrade " .
        "user=freetrade " .
        "password=freetrade");
```

---

**Listing 17.46**  *pg_fetch_object (cont.)*

```
//get all SKUs
$Query = "SELECT ID, Name " .
    "FROM item ";

//execute the query
$Result = pg_query($Link, $Query);

//loop over each row
while($Row = pg_fetch_object($Result))
{
    print("$Row->id = $Row->name<br>\n");
}
?>
```

---

### string pg_fetch_result(resource result, integer row, value field)

Use `pg_fetch_result` (Listing 17.47) to get the value of a specific field in a result set. Rows and fields are numbered from zero, but fields may also be specified by name.

---

**Listing 17.47**  *pg_fetch_result*

```
<?php
    //connect to database
    $Link = pg_connect(" " .
        "dbname=freetrade " .
        "user=freetrade " .
        "password=freetrade");

    //print information about connection
    print("Connection established<br>\n");
    print("Host: " . pg_host($Link) . "<br>\n");
    print("Port: " . pg_port($Link) . "<br>\n");
    print("Database: " . pg_dbname($Link) . "<br>\n");
    print("Options: " . pg_options($Link) . "<br>\n");
    print("<br>\n");

    //create query
    $Query = "SELECT * " .
        "FROM session ";
```

**Listing 17.47** *pg_fetch_result (cont.)*

```
//execute query
if(!($Result = pg_query($Link, $Query)))
{
    print("Could not execute query: ");
    print(pg_last_error($Link));
    print("<br>\n");
    exit;
}


// print each row in a table
print("<table border=\"1\">\n");

// print header row
print("<tr>\n");

for($Field=0; $Field < pg_num_fields($Result); $Field++)
{
    print("<th>");

    print(pg_field_name($Result, $Field) . "<br>");
    print(pg_field_type($Result, $Field));
    print("(" . pg_field_size($Result, $Field) . ")");

    print("</th>\n");
}
print("</tr>\n");

//loop through rows
for($Row=0; $Row < pg_num_rows($Result); $Row++)
{
    print("<tr>\n");

    for($Field=0; $Field < pg_num_fields($Result); $Field++)
    {
        print("<td>");

        if(pg_field_is_null($Result, $Row, $Field))
        {
            print("NULL");
        }
        else
        {
            print(pg_fetch_result($Result, $Row, $Field));
        }
```

---

**Listing 17.47** *pg_fetch_result (cont.)*

```
        print("</td>\n");
    }

    print("</tr>\n");
}

print("</table>\n");

// free the result and close the connection
pg_freeresult($Result);
pg_close($Link);
?>
```

---

### array pg_fetch_row(resource result, integer row)

The `pg_fetch_row` function returns the values of all the fields in a row. The fields are indexed by their field number, starting with zero. Each call to `pg_fetch_row` returns the next row, or FALSE when no rows remain. Compare this function to `pg_fetch_array` and `pg_fetch_assoc`.

### boolean pg_field_is_null(resource result, integer row, value field)

The `pg_field_is_null` function returns TRUE if the specified field is NULL. Fields are counted from zero.

### string pg_field_name(resource result, integer field)

The `pg_field_name` function returns the name of the field in the result set specified by the field number, which starts counting at zero.

### integer pg_field_num(resource result, string field)

The `pg_field_num` function returns the number of the field given its name. Numbering begins with 0. If an error occurs, negative one (–1) is returned.

### integer pg_field_prtlen(resource result, integer row, value field)

The `pg_field_prtlen` function returns the printed length of a particular field value. You may specify the field either by number, starting at zero, or by name.

### integer pg_field_size(resource result, value field)

The `pg_field_size` function returns the size of the field, which may be specified by name or number. Fields are numbered from zero.

### string pg_field_type(resource result, value field)

The pg_field_type function returns the type of the specified field. The field argument may be a number or a name. Fields are numbered starting with zero.

### boolean pg_free_result(resource result)

The pg_free_result function frees any memory associated with the result set. Ordinarily, it is not necessary to call this function, as all memory will be cleared when the script ends.

### array pg_get_notify(resource connection, integer type)

The pg_get_notify function (Listing 17.48) returns an array describing the first notification in the queue. You must execute a LISTEN statement on the connection to receive notifications. This function returns FALSE when there are no notifications.

The returned array contains two associative keys: message and pid. The first contains the name used for the notification. The second contains the process ID of the client that created the notification. You can use pg_get_pid to compare this process ID with your own process ID, allowing you to skip messages you generate yourself.

---

**Listing 17.48** *pg_get_notify, pg_get_pid*

```php
<?php
    //connect to database
    $Link = pg_connect(" " .
        "dbname=freetrade " .
        "user=freetrade " .
        "password=freetrade");

    //listen for notifications
    $Query = "LISTEN corephp";
    pg_query($Link, $Query);

    //generate two notifications
    $Query = "NOTIFY corephp";
    pg_query($Link, $Query);
    pg_query($Link, $Query);

    while($n = pg_get_notify($Link))
    {
        print("Message: {$n['message']}<br>");
        if($n['pid'] == pg_get_pid($Link))
        {
            print("(This script created the notification)<br>");
        }
    }
?>
```

### pg_get_pid(resource connection)

Use `pg_get_pid` to get the process ID of the current script.

### resource pg_get_result(resource connection)

The `pg_get_result` function returns a result resource for an asynchronous query executed with `pg_send_query`.

### string pg_host(resource connection)

The `pg_host` function returns the name of the host for the connection.

### boolean pg_insert(resource connection, string table, array data, integer options)

The `pg_insert` function assembles and executes an INSERT statement for the given table. The `data` argument should be an array of column values indexed by column name. PHP does not require the `options` argument. If you set `options`, PHP passes the conditions through the `pg_convert` function using the given options.

### string pg_last_error(resource connection)

The `pg_last_error` function returns a description of the last error generated by the given connection. If you leave out the connection resource, PHP uses the last connection. Compare this function to `pg_result_error`. To test a connection, use `pg_connection_status`.

### string pg_last_notice(resource connection)

The `pg_last_notice` function gets the last notice returned by the PostgreSQL server. Notices are not the same as messages generated by NOTIFY statements.

### integer pg_last_oid(resource result)

The `pg_last_oid` function (Listing 17.49) returns the object ID (OID) of the last row inserted into a table if the last call to `pg_query` was an INSERT statement. The OID is an internal identifier unique to every row in the database, not the table's primary key. You can identify the new row with the OID, however, as shown in Listing 17.49. Negative one (−1) is returned if there is an error.

Listing 17.49 *pg_last_oid*

```php
<?php
    //connect to database
    $Link = pg_connect(" " .
        "dbname=freetrade " .
        "user=freetrade " .
        "password=freetrade");


    //insert a row into a table using a sequence
    $Query = "INSERT INTO fee (name) " .
        "VALUES ('Gift Wrap')";
    $Result = pg_query($Link, $Query);

    if(!$Result)
    {
        print("Insert failed");
        exit();
    }

    $oid = pg_last_oid($Result);
    print("Row inserted as OID $oid<br>");

    //get the primary key value
    $Query = "SELECT id FROM fee WHERE OID=$oid ";
    $Result = pg_query($Link, $Query);
    $Rows = pg_fetch_all($Result);
    $id = $Rows[0]['id'];
    print("ID column set to $id<br>");
?>
```

### boolean pg_lo_close(resource lob)
The pg_lo_close function closes a large object. The lob argument is a
resource returned by pg_lo_open.

### integer pg_lo_create(resource connection)
The pg_lo_create function (Listing 17.51) creates a LOB and returns the
OID. Listing 17.50 is the SQL for creating a table for storing images. Postgre-
SQL creates the object with both read and write access.

---

**Listing 17.50** *Table for uploaded images*

```sql
CREATE TABLE image (
    name VARCHAR(255),
    mime VARCHAR(255),
    object_id OID NOT NULL,
    PRIMARY KEY(name)
);
```

---

**Listing 17.51** *Using PostgreSQL large objects*

```php
<?php
    //connect to database
    $Link = pg_connect(" " .
        "dbname=freetrade " .
        "user=freetrade " .
        "password=freetrade");

    /*
    ** Insert an image as a lob
    */

    //start transaction
    pg_query($Link, "BEGIN");

    //create the large object
    $oid = pg_lo_create($Link);

    //create new row in image table
    $Query = "INSERT INTO image (name, mime, object_id) " .
        "VALUES ('leonatkinson.png', 'image/png', $oid)";
    pg_query($Link, $Query);

    //read the image and write it into the lob
    $image = file_get_contents("leonatkinson.png");
    $lob = pg_lo_open($Link, $oid, "w");
    pg_lo_write($lob, $image);
    pg_lo_close($lob);

    pg_query($Link, "COMMIT");
```

| Listing 17.51 | *Using PostgreSQL large objects (cont.)* |
|---|---|

```
/*
** get lob image
*/

//start transaction
pg_query($Link, "BEGIN");

//get OID and MIME type
$Query = "SELECT object_id, mime " .
    "FROM image " .
    "WHERE name = 'leonatkinson.png' ";
$Result = pg_query($Link, $Query);
$oid = pg_fetch_result($Result, 0, 0);
$mime = pg_fetch_result($Result, 0, 1);

//send image to browser
$lob = pg_lo_open($Link, $oid, "w");
header("Content-type: $mime");
pg_lo_read_all($lob);
pg_lo_close($lob);

pg_query($Link, "COMMIT");
?>
```

### boolean pg_lo_export(resource lob, string path, resource connection)

The pg_lo_export function writes a large object to a file specified by path. The optional connection argument defaults to the last connection used by the script.

### resource pg_lo_import(resource connection, string path)

The pg_lo_import function creates a large object from a file. This function returns a resource for the large object.

### integer pg_lo_open(resource connection, resource lob, string mode)

The pg_lo_open function opens a large object. The object argument is a valid large OID, and the mode may be one of r, w, rw. A file identifier is returned. You must close the large object with pg_lo_close.

### string pg_lo_read(resource lob, integer length)

The `pg_lo_read` function returns the large object as a string. The `length` argument specifies a maximum length to return.

### pg_lo_read_all(resource lob)

The `pg_lo_read_all` function reads an entire large object and sends it directly to the browser.

### boolean pg_lo_seek(resource lob, integer offset, integer start)

The `pg_lo_seek` function moves the internal pointer to the large object, just as `fseek` moves a normal file pointer. Use `PGSQL_SEEK_CUR`, `PGSQL_SEEK_END`, or `PGSQL_SEEK_SET` for the optional `start` argument.

### integer pg_lo_tell(resource lob)

The `pg_lo_tell` function returns the position of the internal pointer to the open large object, just as `ftell` returns the pointer to a normal file.

### pg_lo_unlink(resource lob, resource object)

Use `pg_lo_unlink` to delete a large object.

### pg_lo_write(resource lob, string buffer)

The `pg_lo_write` function writes the named buffer to the large object.

### array pg_meta_data(resource connection, string table)

The `pg_meta_data` function returns an array describing the named table by executing a query from the `pg_attribute`, `pg_class`, and `pg_type` tables. The returned array contains an array of column definitions indexed by column name. The column definitions are arrays containing the following keys: `num`, `type`, `len`, `not_null`, `has_default`.

### integer pg_num_fields(resource result)

The `pg_num_fields` function returns the number of fields in the result set.

### integer pg_num_rows(resource result)

Use `pg_num_rows` to get the number of rows in the result set.

### string pg_options(resource connection)

The `pg_options` function returns the options used when the connection was opened.

### integer pg_pconnect(string host, string port, string options, string tty, string database)

The pg_pconnect function operates identically to pg_connect except that a persistent connection is created. This connection will last as long as the server process does, so it may be recycled. This saves the overhead time of opening a connection.

### boolean pg_ping(resource connection)

The pg_ping function returns TRUE if a connection to a database server is still valid. This may be necessary for scripts that run for a long time.

### integer pg_port(resource connection)

The pg_port function returns the port number used in the pg_connect function.

### boolean pg_put_line(resource connection, string data)

The pg_put_line function (Listing 17.52) writes a record to the server after you execute a COPY statement. After sending one or more records, use this function to send \. to signal the end of the data. Then, call pg_end_copy. Compare this function to pg_copy_from.

| Listing 17.52 | pg_put_line |
|---|---|

```php
<?php
    //connect to database
    $Link = pg_connect(" " .
        "dbname=freetrade " .
        "user=freetrade " .
        "password=freetrade");

    $data = array(
        "1001\tPackaging\n",
        "1002\tHandling\n",
        "1003\tGift Wrap\n");

    //begin the copy
    pg_query($Link, "COPY fee FROM stdin");

    //insert each row
    foreach($data as $r)
    {
        pg_put_line($Link, $r);
    }

    //end the copy with a \.
    pg_put_line($Link, "\\.\n");

    pg_end_copy($Link);
?>
```

### resource pg_query(resource connection, string query)

The pg_query function executes a query on the given connection and returns a result identifier.

### string pg_result_error(resource result)

The pg_result_error function returns a description of the last error for the given result set.

### array pg_result_seek(resource connection, integer offset)

The pg_result_seek function moves the internal row pointer to a specified row and returns it.

### integer pg_result_status(resource result)

The pg_result_status function returns the status of a result set. The return value will match one of the constants in Table 17.12.

**Table 17.12**   Constants for Use with pg_result_status

| | |
|---|---|
| PGSQL_BAD_RESPONSE | PGSQL_EMPTY_QUERY |
| PGSQL_COMMAND_OK | PGSQL_FATAL_ERROR |
| PGSQL_COPY_FROM | PGSQL_NONFATAL_ERROR |
| PGSQL_COPY_TO | PGSQL_TUPLES_OK |

### array pg_select(resource connection, string table, array conditions, integer option)

The pg_select function executes a SELECT statement and returns matching rows. The conditions argument should be a set of column=value pairs for use in the WHERE clause. PHP does not require the options argument. If you set options, PHP passes the conditions through the pg_convert function using the given options.

### boolean pg_send_query(resource connection, string query)

The pg_send_query function starts an asynchronous query. Your script may continue executing while the server completes the operation. To fetch the results, use pg_get_result, but first you must check that the query has finished by getting a FALSE return value from pg_connection_busy.

### integer pg_set_client_encoding(resource connection, string encoding)

Use `pg_set_client_encoding` to set the encoding used by the client. Choose one of the encoding strings described in the PostgreSQL manual. The return value will be zero for success or negative one (`-1`) for failure.

### boolean pg_trace(string path, string mode, resource connection)

The `pg_trace` function causes communication between your client script and the PostgreSQL server to be logged to a file. The `mode` argument should match the modes used by `fopen` and similar functions.

### string pg_tty(resource connection)

The `pg_tty` function returns the tty name used for debugging and supplied with the `pg_connect` function.

### string pg_unescape_bytea(string text)

The `pg_unescape_bytea` function decodes the output received when selecting a BYTEA column.

### boolean pg_untrace(resource connection)

Use `pg_untrace` to halt logging started with `pg_trace`.

### long pg_update(resource connection, string table, array conditions, array data, integer option)

The `pg_update` function assembles and executes an UPDATE statement for the given table. The `conditions` argument should be a set of `column=value` pairs for use in the WHERE clause. The `data` argument should be an array of column values indexed by column name. PHP does not require the `options` argument. If you set `options`, PHP passes the conditions through the `pg_convert` function using the given options.

# 17.8  Sybase and Microsoft SQL Server

Sybase offers an industrial-strength database that stands out among other big competitors such as Oracle, Informix, and IBM's DB2. Unlike these other databases, Sybase is more available to developers with small budgets because of partnerships with application vendors.

Microsoft's SQL Server is a dressed-up version of Sybase. In fact, PHP's Sybase functions are able to connect to SQL Server databases. For the sake of code readability, there are function aliases for all the Sybase functions that start with `mssql_` instead of `sybase_`, but I've left them out of the reference to save space. Table 17.13 lists all `mssql_` aliases.

**Table 17.13** ■ MSSQL Functions

| | |
|---|---|
| mssql_affected_rows | mssql_get_last_message |
| mssql_close | mssql_min_client_severity |
| mssql_connect | mssql_min_server_severity |
| mssql_data_seek | mssql_num_fields |
| mssql_deadlock_retry_count | mssql_num_rows |
| mssql_fetch_array | mssql_pconnect |
| mssql_fetch_assoc | mssql_query |
| mssql_fetch_field | mssql_result |
| mssql_fetch_object | mssql_select_db |
| mssql_fetch_row | mssql_set_message_handler |
| mssql_field_seek | mssql_unbuffered_query |
| mssql_free_result | |

When support for Sybase is compiled for PHP, one of two libraries may be used. One is the older DB-Library. The other is its replacement, Client-Library. These two libraries are not compatible with each other, so PHP has special code to adapt either of them into a single set of functions. Consequently, some of these functions are present when using DB-Library and not when using Client-Library. Also, it is possible to compile PHP for Windows using an MSSQL library. This library is really just the DB-Library, but the PHP extension creates only `mssql_` functions. It also contains three functions unavailable in the Sybase extension: `mssql_field_length`, `mssql_field_name`, and `mssql_field_type`.

Sybase's home page is <http://www.sybase.com/>. If you want to learn more about the two libraries, check out the online documentation <http://www.sybase.com/support/manuals/>.

Tom May and Zeev Suraski both contributed to the Sybase extensions.

### integer sybase_affected_rows(resource connection)

Use sybase_affected_rows (Listing 17.53) to get the number of rows affected by the last DELETE, INSERT, or UPDATE statement on a given connection. If the optional connection argument is left out, the most recently opened connection will be used. Note that this function is not useful for determining the number of rows returned by a SELECT statement.

---

**Listing 17.53**   *sybase_affected_rows*

```php
<?php
    //connect
    $Link = @sybase_connect('falcon', 'leon', 'corephp');

    //use the "sample" database
    @sybase_select_db("sample", $Link);

    //update some rows
    $Query = "UPDATE item " .
        "SET Price = Price * 0.90 " .
        "WHERE Price > 1.00 ";
    $Result = sybase_query($Query, $Link);

    //get number of rows changed
    $RowsChanged = sybase_affected_rows($Link);

    print("$RowsChanged prices updated.<br>\n");

    //close connection
    sybase_close($Link);
?>
```

---

### boolean sybase_close(resource connection)

The sybase_close function closes a connection to a database. Its use is not strictly necessary, since PHP will close connections for you when your script ends. You can leave out the connection argument, and the last connection to be opened will be closed.

### integer sybase_connect(string server, string user, string password, string character_set)

The sybase_connect function returns a connection identifier based on the server, user, and password arguments. The server must be a valid server name as defined in the interfaces file. Connections created with sybase_connect will be closed automatically when your script completes. Compare this function with sybase_pconnect.

The optional `character_set` argument sets the character set.

### boolean sybase_data_seek(integer result, integer row)

The `sybase_data_seek` function (Listing 17.54) moves the internal row pointer for a result to the specified row. Rows are numbered starting with zero. Use this function with `sybase_fetch_array`, `sybase_fetch_object`, or `sybase_fetch_row` to move arbitrarily among the result set.

---

**Listing 17.54**    *sybase_data_seek, sybase_fetch_row*

```php
<?php
    //connect
    $Link = @sybase_connect('falcon', 'leon', 'corephp');

    //use the "sample" database
    @sybase_select_db("sample", $Link);

    //get all items
    $Query = "SELECT ID, Name, Price " .
        "FROM item ";

    $Result = sybase_query($Query, $Link);

    //jump to third row
    sybase_data_seek($Result, 2);

    print("<table border=\"1\">\n");

    //get rows
    while($Row = sybase_fetch_row($Result))
    {
        print("<tr>\n");
        print("<td>" . $Row[0] . "</td>\n");
        print("<td>" . $Row[1] . "</td>\n");
        print("<td>" . $Row[2] . "</td>\n");
        print("</tr>\n");
    }

    print("</table>\n");

    //close connection
    sybase_close($Link);
?>
```

### sybase_deadlock_retry_count(integer retries)

The `sybase_deadlock_retry_count` function sets the number of retries when encountering a deadlock. By default, PHP retries on deadlock forever. You can specify this behavior by setting `retries` to -1. Setting it to zero tells PHP never to retry.

You may also set this value in `php.ini`.

### array sybase_fetch_array(integer result)

The `sybase_fetch_array` function returns an array that contains the values of all the fields for the next row. Each call to `sybase_fetch_array` gets the next row in the result set, or returns FALSE if no rows remain.

Each field is returned in two elements. One is indexed by the field number, starting with zero. The other is indexed by the name of the field. Compare this function to `sybase_fetch_assoc` and `sybase_fetch_row`.

### array sybase_fetch_assoc(integer result)

The `sybase_fetch_assoc` function (Listing 17.55) returns an array that contains the values of all the fields for the next row. Each call to `sybase_fetch_assoc` gets the next row in the result set, or returns FALSE if no rows remain.

Each field is returned indexed by the name of the field. If a result contains more than one column with the same name, PHP adds a number to the end of the index. For example, if you have three columns named Price, the returned row contains Price, Price1, and Price2.

Compare this function to `sybase_fetch_array` and `sybase_fetch_row`.

---

**Listing 17.55**   *sybase_fetch_assoc, sybase_fetch_field*

```php
<?php
    //connect
    $Link = @sybase_connect('falcon', 'leon', 'corephp');

    //use the "sample" database
    @sybase_select_db("sample", $Link);

    //get all items
    $Query = "SELECT ID, Name, Price " .
        "FROM item ";

    $Result = sybase_query($Query, $Link);
```

**Listing 17.55**   *sybase_fetch_assoc, sybase_fetch_field (cont.)*

```
print("<table border=\"1\">\n");

print("<tr>\n");
while($Field = sybase_fetch_field($Result))
{
    print("<th>" .
        "$Field->name $Field->type($Field->max_length)<br>" .
        "Numeric: " . ($Field->numeric ? 'YES' : 'NO') . "<br>" .
        "Source: $Field->column_source" .
        "</th>\n");
}
print("</tr>\n");

//get rows
while($Row = sybase_fetch_assoc($Result))
{
    print("<tr>" .
        "<td>{$Row['ID']}</td>" .
        "<td>{$Row['Name']}</td>" .
        "<td>{$Row['Price']}</td>" .
        "</tr>\n");
}

print("</table>\n");

//close connection
sybase_close($Link);
?>
```

### object sybase_fetch_field(integer result, integer field)

The `sybase_fetch_field` function returns an object that describes a field in the result set. The `field` argument is optional. If left out, the next field is returned. The object contains the properties described in Table 17.14.

**Table 17.14**   `sybase_fetch_field` Object Properties

| Property | Description |
| --- | --- |
| column_source | The name of the table the column belongs to. |
| max_length | The maximum size of the field. |
| name | Name of the column. |

**Table 17.14** `sybase_fetch_field` Object Properties *(cont.)*

| Property | Description |
|----------|-------------|
| numeric | If the column is numeric, this property will be 1. |
| type | An approximate description of the type. |

### object sybase_fetch_object(integer result)

The `sybase_fetch_object` function (Listing 17.56) returns an object with a property for each of the fields in the next row. Each call to `sybase_fetch_object` gets the next row in the result set, or returns FALSE if no rows remain. Compare this function to `sybase_fetch_array`.

**Listing 17.56** *sybase_fetch_object*

```php
<?php
    //connect
    $Link = @sybase_connect('falcon', 'leon', 'corephp');

    //use the "sample" database
    @sybase_select_db("sample", $Link);

    //get all items
    $Query = "SELECT ID, Name, Price " .
        "FROM item ";

    $Result = sybase_query($Query, $Link);

    print("<table border=\"1\">\n");

    //get rows
    while($Row = sybase_fetch_object($Result))
    {
        print("<tr>" .
            "<td>$Row->ID</td>" .
            "<td>$Row->Name</td>" .
            "<td>$Row->Price</td>" .
            "</tr>\n");
    }

    print("</table>\n");

    //close connection
    sybase_close($Link);
?>
```

### array sybase_fetch_row(integer result)

The `sybase_fetch_row` function returns an array of all the field values for the next row. The fields are indexed by integers starting with zero. Each call to `sybase_fetch_row` gets the next row in the result set, or returns FALSE if no rows remain. Compare this function to `sybase_fetch_array` and `sybase_fetch_assoc`.

### boolean sybase_field_seek(integer result, integer field)

The `sybase_field_seek` function moves the internal field pointer to the specified field. Fields are numbered starting with zero. If you leave out the `field` argument, the internal pointer will be moved to the next field. This is the same internal pointer used by `sybase_fetch_field`.

### boolean sybase_free_result(integer result)

The `sybase_free_result` function frees memory associated with a result set. It is not strictly necessary to call this function. All memory is freed when a script finishes executing.

### string sybase_get_last_message()

The `sybase_get_last_message` function returns the last message from the Sybase database. This function is not available if you're using Client-Library.

### sybase_min_client_severity(integer severity)

This function is available only when using Client-Library. It sets the minimum severity for messages sent from the client interface to be turned into PHP error messages.

### sybase_min_error_severity(integer severity)

Use `sybase_min_error_severity` to set the minimum severity level for errors to be turned into PHP error messages. This function is available only when using DB-Library.

### sybase_min_message_severity(integer severity)

Use `sybase_min_message_severity` to set the minimum severity level for messages to be turned into PHP error messages. This function is available only when using DB-Library.

### sybase_min_server_severity(integer severity)

This function is available only when using Client-Library. It sets the minimum level for messages from the server interface to cause PHP error messages to be generated.

### integer sybase_num_fields(integer result)

The `sybase_num_fields` function returns the number of fields in the given result set.

### integer sybase_num_rows(integer result)

The `sybase_num_rows` function returns the number of rows in a result set.

### integer sybase_pconnect(string server, string username, string password)

The `sybase_pconnect` function is identical to `sybase_connect` except that connections created with this function persist after the script ends. The connection lasts as long as the server process does, so if the process executes another PHP script, the connection will be reused. Connections created with `sybase_pconnect` should not be closed with `sybase_close`.

### integer sybase_query(string query, resource connection)

The `sybase_query` function (Listing 17.58) executes a query on the given connection and returns a result identifier. This is used by many of the other functions in this section. If the `connection` argument is left out, the last opened connection is used.

Aside from ordinary queries, you may invoke stored procedures just as you would from the `isql` command shell. Access the result set in the same way you would get a result set from a `SELECT` statement. Unfortunately, PHP's interface allows for only one result set. If you call a stored procedure that returns multiple results, you have access to the last result set only.

Listing 17.57 shows a simple stored procedured used by Listing 17.58.

---

**Listing 17.57**   *Simple Sybase stored procedure*

```
CREATE PROCEDURE dbo.add_numbers (@a int, @b int)
AS
BEGIN
    SELECT @a + @b
END
```

---

**Listing 17.58**   *Calling a Sybase stored procedure*

```php
<?php
    //connect
    $Link = @sybase_connect('falcon', 'leon', 'corephp');

    //use the "sample" database
    @sybase_select_db("sample", $Link);

    //execute the add_numbers stored procedure
    $Query = "exec add_numbers 2, 3";

    $Result = sybase_query($Query, $Link);

    //get result, which we assume is the
    //first column in the first row
    print(sybase_result($Result, 0, 0));

    //close connection
    sybase_close($Link);
?>
```

---

### string sybase_result(integer result, integer row, value field)

The `sybase_result` function returns the value of a particular field, identified by row and field. The `field` argument may be an integer or the name of a field. Fields and rows are numbered starting with zero. If performance is an issue, considering using `sybase_fetch_row`, which is much faster.

### boolean sybase_select_db(string database, resource connection)

The `sybase_select_db` function selects the database to use on the database server. If the `connection` argument is omitted, the last connection created will be used. See `sybase_fetch_array` for an example.

### boolean sybase_set_message_handler(string function)
### boolean sybase_set_message_handler(array method)

Use `sybase_set_message_handler` (Listing 17.59) to intercept messages generated by the server. You may set the handler by naming a function or an object method. In the latter case, you may specify the method of an instantiated object or the static method of a class by providing an array with two elements. The first element is the instance or class name. The second element is the method name.

The handler receives five arguments in the following order: message number, severity, state, line number, and description. The first four are integers. The last is a string. If the function returns FALSE, PHP generates an ordinary error message.

**Listing 17.59** *sybase_set_message_handler*

```php
<?php
    function handleSybaseError($message, $severity, $state, $line,
        $text)
    {
        //report bad table names
        if($message == 208)
        {
            return(FALSE);
        }

        //silently log the error
        error_log("Sybase Error $message " .
            "Severity:$severity State:$state Line:$line $text",
            3, "C:/tmp/sybase_error.log");
        return(TRUE);
    }

    //register the handler
    sybase_set_message_handler("handleSybaseError");

    //connect
    $Link = @sybase_connect('falcon', 'leon', 'corephp');

    //use the "sample" database
    @sybase_select_db("sample", $Link);

    //try a bad query just so we can see
    //what happens when an error occurs
    $Query = "SELECT FROM item ";

    if(!($Result = sybase_query($Query, $Link)))
    {
        print("The query failed!");
    }

    //close connection
    sybase_close($Link);
?>
```

### resource sybase_unbuffered_query(string query, resource connection)

The `sybase_unbuffered_query` function executes a query and returns a result resource. Unlike `sybase_query`, this function does not pull the entire result set into memory. Instead, it reads one row at a time. This allows for handling huge result sets without huge amounts of dedicated memory. The downside is that you may not execute another query on the connection until you finish reading from the result set or you free the result set with `sybase_free_result`. You also can't get a true reading of the number of rows until you've fetched them all.

# OBJECT LAYERS

**Topics in This Chapter**

- COM
- CORBA
- Java

# Chapter

The functions in this chapter allow you to interface with external object layers. Generally, PHP instantiates an object from another environment and thereafter treats it as a native object. COM and CORBA are two competing standards for packaging reusable functionality into objects that any programming language may use. Java is a programming language, but to PHP it appears as another system with external objects.

## 18.1 COM

The component object model (COM) is a framework that allows sharing of executable modules without recompiling. If you have used Windows for any time at all, you are aware of dynamic-link libraries (DLLs), collections of functions a program can load on demand. Many programs can share a DLL. Unfortunately, DLLs that work well with some programming languages don't work at all with others. COM seeks to solve this problem. COM objects are accessible by C++, Visual Basic, PHP, and many other programming languages.

A tutorial on COM is beyond the scope of this text, of course. Microsoft's list of "noteworthy" books about COM is relatively long <http://www.microsoft.com/com/tech/com.asp>. However, you could keep busy just reading the articles online. You might read *Dr. GUI's Gentle Guide to COM* first <http://www.microsoft.com/com/news/drgui.asp>.

You have two options for using a COM object in PHP. In the first method, you load it with com_load. After that, you can invoke methods with com_invoke, and you can get and set properties with com_propget and com_propset. This method has limitations. In the second method, you instantiate the object with new COM. You then treat the object as any other PHP object.

Zeev Suraski added COM support to PHP.

### object COM::COM(string module, string server, integer code_page)

Use the COM class (Listing 18.1) to create a COM object in your script. The constructor requires the name of the COM module only, which should use the ProgID. Optionally, you may load a remote object by specifying the Internet address of the COM module with the optional server argument. In that case, remember to activate DCOM in php.ini. The optional code_page argument may be set with one of the following constants: CP_ACP, CP_MACCP, CP_OEMCP, CP_SYMBOL, CP_THREAD_ACP, CP_UTF7, CP_UTF8.

| Listing 18.1 | *COM::COM* |
| --- | --- |

```php
<?php
    //create ADO object
    $adodb = new COM("ADODB.Connection");

    //connect to same MS Access file
    $adodb->Open("PROVIDER=MSDASQL; " .
        "DRIVER={Microsoft Access Driver (*.mdb)}; " .
        "DBQ=C:\Program Files\Microsoft Office" .
        "\Office\Samples\inventry.mdb");

    //execute a Query
    $recordset = $adodb->Execute(
        "SELECT * FROM [Household Inventory]");

    //get the number of columns
    $columns = $recordset->Fields->Count();

    //print table headers
    print('<table border="1"><tr>');
    for($c=0; $c < $columns; $c++)
    {
        $f = $recordset->Fields($c);
        print("<th>$f->Name</th>");
    }
    print("</tr>\n");
```

| Listing 18.1 | COM::COM (cont.) |
|---|---|

```
//print each row
while(!$recordset->EOF)
{
    print("<tr>");

    for($c=0; $c < $columns; $c++)
    {
        $f = $recordset->Fields($c);
        print("<td>$f->Value</td>");
    }

    print("\n");
    $recordset->MoveNext();

    print("</tr>\n");
}
print("</table>\n");

//clean up
$recordset->Close();
$adodb->Close();

$recordset->Release();
$adodb->Release();

$recordset = null;
$adodb = null;
?>
```

### integer com_addref(object com)

The com_addref function increments the reference counter and returns the new count.

### boolean com_event_sink(object com, object sink_object, string interface)

The com_event_sink function (Listing 18.2) connects COM events to a PHP handler object. The optional interface argument sets the event interface used.

| Listing 18.2 | *com_event_sink, com_message_pump* |
|---|---|

```php
<?php
    class MSIE_EventHandler
    {
        var $quit = FALSE;

        function NavigateComplete2($d, $url)
        {
            print(date("H:i:s") .
                " NavigateComplete2 $url\n");
        }

        function OnQuit()
        {
            $this->quit = TRUE;
        }
    }

    //allow this to run forever
    set_time_limit(0);

    //open MS Internet Explorer
    $msie = new COM("internetexplorer.application");

    //create event handler
    $sink = new MSIE_EventHandler();

    //register sink
    com_event_sink($msie, $sink, "DWebBrowserEvents2");

    //show the browser
    $msie->Visible = true;

    while(!$sink->quit)
    {
        //get messages once per second
        com_message_pump(1000);
    }

    $msie = null;
?>
```

### value com_get(resource com, string property)

The com_get function returns the value of a property on a COM object.

### value com_invoke(object com, string method, argument, argument, ...)

The `com_invoke` function invokes a method on a COM object. You must specify a valid COM resource and the name of a method. If the method takes arguments, you list them after the method name.

### boolean com_isenum(object com)

The `com_isenum` function returns TRUE if the given COM object has an `IEnumVariant` interface.

### object com_load(string module, string server, integer code_page)

The `com_load` function (Listing 18.3) loads the named COM object and returns a resource identifier to be used by the other COM functions. The module is named by its ProgID. The optional `server` argument allows you to specify a remote server by Internet address. The optional `code_page` argument may be set with one of the following constants: CP_ACP, CP_MACCP, CP_OEMCP, CP_SYMBOL, CP_THREAD_ACP, CP_UTF7, CP_UTF8.

FALSE is returned if the load fails.

---

**Listing 18.3**  `com_load`

```php
<?php
    //open Word
    $word = com_load("word.application");

    //if it's not visible, make it visible
    $visible = com_get($word, "Visible");

    if(!$visible)
    {
        //make it visible
        com_set($word, "Visible", 1);
    }

    //wait a couple of seconds just so we can see it
    sleep(2);

    //increment the reference counter
    print("Ref: " . com_addref($word) . "<br>");

    //close Word
    com_invoke($word, "Quit");
```

| Listing 18.3 | *com_load (cont.)* |
|---|---|

```
    //release and free memory
    com_release($word);
    $word = NULL;
?>
```

### boolean com_load_typelib(string typelib_name, integer case_insensitive)

Use `com_load_typelib` to load a type library. The `case_insensitive` argument is optional.

### boolean com_message_pump(integer milliseconds)

The `com_message_pump` function processes COM events. Use it together with `com_event_sink`. In most contexts, it's best to set the number of milliseconds PHP waits between polling for new messages with the optional `milliseconds` argument. It defaults to zero. If you check for messages in a busy loop, be sure to pick a reasonable time to wait between polling, or your script will consume large amounts of CPU time just looping.

### boolean com_print_typeinfo(object com, string dispinterface, boolean want_sink)
### boolean com_print_typeinfo(string typelib, string dispinterface, boolean want_sink)

The `com_print_typeinfo` function (Listing 18.4) prints a skeleton class for handling the events of a given COM object and interface.

| Listing 18.4 | *com_print_typeinfo* |
|---|---|

```
<?php
    $msie = new COM("internetexplorer.application");
    com_print_typeinfo($msie, "DWebBrowserEvents2", TRUE);
?>
```

### com_propget

Use `com_propget` as an alias for `com_get`.

### com_propput

Use `com_propput` as an alias for `com_set`.

**com_propset**

Use `com_propset` as an alias for `com_set`.

**integer com_release(object com)**

The `com_release` function decrements the reference counter for the given COM object.

**boolean com_set(object com, string property, value data)**

The `com_set` function changes the value of a property.

# 18.2 CORBA

The Common Object Request Broker Architecture (CORBA) is a standard by the Object Management Group that allows applications on disparate platforms to communicate. The best place to start learning about CORBA is `<http://www.corba.org/>`.

Support for CORBA in PHP was originally contained in an extension named Satellite. You can still get this implementation from the PECL repository, but its use is discouraged in favor of a new extension named Universe. At the time of writing, Universe is not part of the PHP distribution, but you can download it from `<http://universe-phpext.sourceforge.net/>`. Universe relies on the MICO implementation on Linux `<http://www.mico.org/>`, another free project.

The relative newness of this extension at the time of writing makes it hard to describe its operation. Existing functions may change or disappear. Certainly, new functions will appear.

David Eriksson wrote the Universe extension.

**UniverseObject::UniverseObject(string ior)**

The essence of the Universe extension (Listing 18.5) is the `UniverseObject` class. This class allows you to instantiate a CORBA object in a PHP script. In order to create a CORBA object, you must know its Interoperable Object Reference (IOR). This long string uniquely identifies the object stored on a remote server. After creating the instance of `UniverseObject`, you may access properties and methods as you do with any other object.

**Listing 18.5**    *Using Universe*

```php
<?php
    //define IOR
    $ior = "IOR:000000000000000f49444c3a" .
        "52616e646f6d3a312e30000000000001" .
        "0000000000000005000010000000016" .
        "706c616e7874792e6473672e63732e74" .
        "63642e69650006220000002c3a5c706c" .
        "616e7874792e6473672e63732e746364" .
        "2e69653a52616e646f6d3a303a3a4952" .
        "3a52616e646f6d00";

    //instantiate object
    $corba = new UniverseObject($ior);

    //get a random number
    $value = $obj->lrand48();
    print("Random number: $value<br>");

    //get IOR
    print("IOR: " . universe_object_to_string($corba) . "<br>");

?>
```

**string universe_object_to_string(object corba)**
Use this function to fetch the IOR for a given CORBA object.

# 18.3  Java

In 1999 Sam Ruby added support to allow PHP to use Java objects. Java is Sun Microsystem's object-oriented language intended to be platform-independent. Java is very popular, and you won't have any trouble finding books, Web sites, and free source code. Perhaps the best place to get information about Java used on Web servers is the Java Apache Project <http://java.apache.org/>.

The Java extension creates a class called Java. You can use the `new` operator to instantiate any Java class in your class path. An object is returned that can be treated like any other PHP object. Its properties and methods match the Java class.

## object Java::Java(string class, ...)

To create a Java object, call this constructor with the name of a class. If the constructor allows for arguments, add them after the class name. See Listing 18.6.

---

**Listing 18.6**    *Using Java*

```php
<?php
    /*
    ** Adapted from Sam Ruby's example
    */

    //get version of Java
    $system = new Java("java.lang.System");
    print("Java version: " .
        $system->getProperty("java.version") .
        "<br>\n");

    //print formatted date
    $formatter = new Java("java.text.SimpleDateFormat",
        "EEEE, MMMM dd, yyyy 'at' h:mm:ss a zzzz");
    print($formatter->format(new Java("java.util.Date")) .
        "<br>\n");
?>
```

---

## java_last_exception_clear()

The `java_last_exception_clear` function clears the last exception.

## object java_last_exception_get()

The `java_last_exception_get` function (Listing 18.7) returns a Java exception object for the last exception generated.

---

**Listing 18.7**    *java_last_exception_clear, java_last_exception_get*

```php
<?php
    $a = new Java('java.lang.String', 'PHP');

    //show contents of the String
    print($a->toString() . "<br>");

    //let an exception pass through
    $b = $a->substring(5, 6);
```

| Listing 18.7 | *java_last_exception_clear,*<br>*java_last_exception_get (cont.)* |
| --- | --- |

```
//hide warning and capture exception
$b = @$a->substring(5, 6);
$e = java_last_exception_get();
if($e)
{
    print("Caught Exception: " .
        $e->toString() . "<br>");
}
java_last_exception_clear();
?>
```

# MISCELLANEOUS

**Topics in This Chapter**

- Apache
- IMAP
- MnoGoSearch
- OpenSSL
- System V Messages
- System V Semaphores
- System V Shared Memory

# Chapter 19

The functions in this section do not fit neatly into any other section of the functional reference. They are not available by default when compiling PHP, and most of them require extra libraries. While none are essential to building PHP scripts, some are quite useful in the right context. Because you may not be familiar with all the technologies in this chapter, I've attempted to give a brief synopsis and links to Web sites where you can learn more.

## 19.1 Apache

The functions in this section are available only when PHP is compiled as a module for the Apache Web server.

### boolean apache_child_terminate()

The `apache_child_terminate` function instructs Apache to terminate the child process executing the PHP script when the request finishes. This applies only when Apache runs in multiprocess mode, which is normal behavior for Apache 1.3.x and optional for Apache 2.x. Ordinarily, Apache terminates child processes after a set number of requests, but you may wish to terminate early when your PHP script uses a large amount of memory. Processes allocate heap space as necessary but do not release it until shutdown. Terminating the processes early returns the memory to the pool immediately. This may improve performance.

The `child_terminate` directive controls whether you may call this function.

### array apache_get_modules()

The `apache_get_modules` function returns an array of modules compiled into Apache. PHP indexes the modules by integers starting with zero.

### string apache_get_version()

The `apache_get_version` function returns the header that Apache sends in the response header in order to identify itself. This includes the version of Apache and some modules.

### object apache_lookup_uri(string uri)

The `apache_lookup_uri` function evaluates a URI, or Universal Resource Identifier, and returns an object containing properties describing the URI. This function is a wrapper for a function that's part of the Apache Web server's API: `sub_req_lookup_uri`. The exact meaning of the returned object's properties is beyond this text. They mirror the properties of Apache's `request_rec` structure. The `sub_req_lookup_uri` function is contained in Apache's `http_request.c` source file, and the comments there may satisfy the truly curious. Table 19.1 lists the properties of the returned object.

**Table 19.1** Properties of the Object Returned by `apache_lookup_uri`

| | | |
|---|---|---|
| `allowed` | `filename` | `request_time` |
| `args` | `handler` | `send_bodyct` |
| `boundary` | `method` | `status` |
| `byterange` | `no_cache` | `status_line` |
| `bytes_sent` | `no_local_copy` | `the_request` |
| `clength` | `path_info` | `uri` |
| `content_type` | | |

### string apache_note(string name, string value)

The `apache_note` function allows you to fetch and set values in Apache's note table. The current value of the named entry is returned. If the optional `value` argument is present, then the value of the entry will be changed to the supplied value. The notes table exists for the duration of the request made to the

Apache Web Server and is available to any modules activated during the request. This function allows you to communicate with other Apache modules.

One possible use of this functionality is the passing of information to the logging module. For example, you could write a session identifier to a note and then add that note to a log generated by Apache. This would allow identifying each request with a specific session.

This function is a wrapper for the `table_get` and `table_set` functions that are part of the Apache API.

### array apache_request_headers()

The `apache_request_headers` function returns every header sent by the browser, indexed by name. Some of these are turned into environment variables, which are then made available as variables inside your PHP script. Since this function relies on the Apache API, it is available only when you run PHP as an Apache module.

### array apache_response_headers()

The `apache_response_headers` function returns every header sent by the server, indexed by name.

### boolean apache_setenv(string variable, string value, boolean walk_to_top)

The `apache_setenv` function sets the value of an Apache subprocess environment variable. If you set the optional `walk_to_top` to `TRUE`, PHP walks to the top of the request records first. This may be helpful if you've arrived at the script through a redirect.

### array getallheaders()

This is an alias to `apache_request_headers`.

### boolean virtual(string filename)

The `virtual` function is equivalent to writing `<!-- #include virtual filename-->`, which is an Apache subrequest. You may wish to refer to the Apache documentation to learn more.

If you need to execute an external PHP script, use the `include` or `require` statements instead.

# 19.2 IMAP

IMAP is the Internet Message Access Protocol. It was developed in 1986 at Stanford University; however, it has been overshadowed by less sophisticated mail protocols, such as POP (Post Office Protocol). IMAP allows the user to manipulate mail on the server as if it existed locally.

PHP implements IMAP 4, the latest incarnation described in RFC 1730. More information may be obtained at <http://www.imap.org/>, the IMAP Connection.

### string imap_8bit(string text)

The `imap_8bit` function converts an 8-bit string into a quote-printable string.

### array imap_alerts()

The `imap_alerts` function returns all the alerts generated by IMAP functions as an array and clears the stack of alerts.

### integer imap_append(resource imap, string mailbox, string message, string flags)

The `imap_append` function (Listing 19.1) appends a message to a mailbox using IMAP's APPEND command. The `imap` argument is a resource returned by `imap_open`. The `flags` argument is optional. See Section 2.3.2 of RFC 2060 for a discussion of flags.

This function may be useful for copying messages from one server to another or for keeping sent messages in a folder. You can move messages between folders with `imap_mail_copy`.

| Listing 19.1 | *imap_append* |
|---|---|

```php
<?php
    $imap = imap_open("{clearink.com}INBOX", "jsmith", "secret");
    if(!$imap)
    {
        print("Connection to IMAP server failed!");
    }

    //append a test message to in-box
    imap_append($imap, "{localhost}INBOX",
        "From: jsmith@example.com\r\n" .
        "To: jsmith@example.com \r\n" .
```

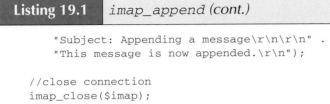

```
        "Subject: Appending a message\r\n\r\n" .
        "This message is now appended.\r\n");

    //close connection
    imap_close($imap);
?>
```

### string imap_base64(string text)

Use `imap_base64` to decode base64 text. This routine is part of the IMAP extension; `base64_decode` is a built-in PHP function that offers the same functionality.

### string imap_binary(string text)

Use `imap_binary` to convert an 8-bit string into a base64 string.

### string imap_body(resource imap, integer message, integer flags)

The `imap_body` function (Listing 19.2) returns the body of the specified message. The optional `flags` argument is a bit field that accepts the constants listed in Table 19.2. You can use the | operator to combine them.

**Table 19.2** `imap_body` Flags

| Constant | Description |
|---|---|
| FT_INTERNAL | Return the body using local line-end characters instead of CRLF. |
| FT_NOT | Do not fetch header lines. |
| FT_PEEK | Do not mark this message being read. |
| FT_PREFETCHTEXT | Fetch the text when getting the header. |
| FT_UID | The message argument is a UID. |

| Listing 19.2 | *imap_body* |
| --- | --- |

```php
<?php
    //connect to IMAP server
    $imap = imap_open("{example.com}INBOX", "leon", "secret");
    if(!$imap)
    {
        print("Connection to IMAP server failed!");
    }

    //get the number of messages in the INBOX
    $check = imap_check($imap);
    print("$check->Nmsgs messages<br>\n");

    for($n=1; $n <= $check->Nmsgs; $n++)
    {
        $body = imap_body($imap, $n, FT_INTERNAL | FT_PEEK);
        print("<hr>\n$body\n");
    }

    //close connection
    imap_close($imap);
?>
```

### object imap_bodystruct(resource imap, integer message, integer section)

The `imap_bodystruct` function returns an object describing the structure of a body section. The object will contain the following properties: `bytes`, `description`, `disposition`, `dparameters`, `encoding`, `id`, `ifdescription`, `ifdisposition`, `ifdparameters`, `ifid`, `ifparameters`, `ifsubtype`, `lines`, `parameters`, `subtype`, `type`. The elements such as `ifsubtype` that begin with `if` are booleans that signal whether the similarly named elements are present.

### object imap_check(resource imap)

The `imap_check` function (Listing 19.3) returns information about the current mailbox in the form of an object. Table 19.3 lists the properties of the object. If the connection has timed out, `FALSE` is returned.

**Table 19.3**  Return Elements for `imap_check`

| Property | Description |
|----------|-------------|
| Date | Date of the most recent message |
| Driver | Driver being used |
| Mailbox | Name of the mailbox |
| Nmsgs | Number of messages |
| Recent | Number of recent messages |

**Listing 19.3**  *imap_check*

```php
<?php
    //connect to IMAP server
    $imap = imap_open("{example.com}INBOX", "leon", "secret");
    if(!$imap)
    {
        print("Connection to IMAP server failed!");
    }

    //get the number of messages in the INBOX
    $check = imap_check($imap);
    print("$check->Nmsgs messages<br>\n");
    print("$check->Recent new messages<br>\n");
    print("Most Recent Message: $check->Date<br>\n");

    for($n=1; $n <= $check->Nmsgs; $n++)
    {
        $header = imap_headerinfo($imap, $n);
        $body = imap_body($imap, $n, FT_INTERNAL | FT_PEEK);
        print("<hr>\n");

        $to = array();
        foreach($header->to as $t)
        {
            $to[] = "$t->personal <$t->mailbox@$t->host>";
        }
        $to = implode(",", $to);

        $from = array();
        foreach($header->from as $f)
        {
```

| Listing 19.3 | *imap_check (cont.)* |
|---|---|

```
        $from[] = "$f->personal <$f->mailbox@$f->host>";
    }
    $from = implode(",", $from);


    print(
        "Date: $header->date<br>\n" .
        "To: " . htmlentities($to) . "<br>" .
        "From: " . htmlentities($from) . "<br>\n" .
        "Subject: $header->subject<br>\n" .
        "<br>\n" .
        nl2br(htmlentities($body)) . "<br>\n");
    }

    //close connection
    imap_close($imap);
?>
```

### string imap_clearflag_full(resource imap, string sequence, string flag, integer options)

The `imap_clearflag_full` function (Listing 19.4) deletes a flag on a sequence of messages. The `options` argument, if supplied, may be set to `ST_UID`, which signals that the `sequence` argument contains UIDs instead of message numbers.

| Listing 19.4 | *imap_clearflag_full* |
|---|---|

```
<?php
    //connect to IMAP server
    $imap = imap_open("{news.example.com/nntp:119}alt.fan.devo",
        "leon@example.com", "secret");
    if(!$imap)
    {
        print("Connection to NNTP server failed!");
    }

    //set first 3 messages as unread
    imap_clearflag_full($imap, "1,2,3", "\\Seen");

    //close connection
    imap_close($imap);
?>
```

### boolean imap_close(resource imap, integer flags)

Use imap_close to close a connection to a mailbox. The imap argument is an integer returned by imap_open. The optional flags argument may be set to CL_EXPUNGE, which will delete all messages marked for deletion.

### boolean imap_createmailbox(resource imap, string mailbox)

Use imap_createmailbox (Listing 19.5) to create a mailbox.

| Listing 19.5 | *imap_createmailbox, imap_deletemailbox* |
|---|---|

```php
<?php
    //connect to IMAP server
    $imap = imap_open("{mail.example.com}INBOX", "leon",
        "secret");
    if(!$imap)
    {
        print("Connection to IMAP server failed!<br>");
        foreach(imap_errors() as $e)
        {
            print_r("$e<br>");
        }
        exit();
    }

    //create mailbox
    imap_createmailbox($imap, "PHP List");

    //delete mailbox
    imap_deletemailbox($imap, "PHP List");

    //close connection
    imap_close($imap);
?>
```

### boolean imap_delete(resource imap, integer message)

The imap_delete function (Listing 19.6) marks a message for deletion. Use imap_expunge to cause the message to be permanently deleted. Alternatively, you can use the CL_EXPUNGE flag when you call imap_close.

| Listing 19.6 | *imap_delete* |
|---|---|

```php
<?php
    // delete message number 3
    $imap = imap_open("{mail.example.com}INBOX",
        "leon", "password");
    imap_delete($imap, 3);
    imap_close($imap);
?>
```

### boolean imap_deletemailbox(resource imap, string mailbox)

The `imap_deletemailbox` function deletes the named mailbox.

### array imap_errors()

Use `imap_errors` to get an array of all errors generated by IMAP functions, removing them from an internal stack. You can use `imap_last_error` to get just the last error.

### boolean imap_expunge(resource imap)

Use `imap_expunge` to remove all messages marked for deletion.

### string imap_fetchbody(resource imap, integer message, integer part, integer flags)

The `imap_fetchbody` function gets a specific part of a multipart message. If the part is encoded with base64 or is quoted-printable, you must decode it in your script. The optional `flags` argument accepts the flags described in Table 19.2. It may be easier to use `imap_fetchstructure`.

### string imap_fetchheader(resource imap, integer message, integer flags)

Use `imap_fetchheader` to get the complete RFC 822 header text for a message. The optional `flags` argument accepts the flags described in Table 19.2.

### array imap_fetch_overview(resource imap, string sequence, integer options)

The `imap_fetch_overview` function returns an array of objects for the given sequence of messages. Each object describes the headers for one of the messages.

## object imap_fetchstructure(resource imap, integer message, integer flags)

The `imap_fetchstructure` returns an object with information about the specified message. Table 19.4 lists the properties of this object. The optional `flags` argument accepts the `FT_UID` constant described in Table 19.2.

**Table 19.4**  `imap_fetchstructure` Properties

| Property | Description |
|---|---|
| Type | The type, matching one of the following:<br>TYPETEXT<br>TYPEMULTIPART<br>TYPEMESSAGE<br>TYPEAPPLICATION<br>TYPEAUDIO<br>TYPEIMAGE<br>TYPEVIDEO<br>TYPEOTHER |
| Encoding | The encoding, matching one of the following:<br>ENC7BIT<br>ENC8BIT<br>ENCBINARY<br>ENCBASE64<br>ENCQUOTEDPRINTABLE<br>ENCOTHER |
| ifsubtype | TRUE if subtype is set |
| subtype | MIME subtype |
| ifdescription | TRUE if description is set |
| description | Description header |
| ifid | TRUE if id is set |
| lines | Number of lines |
| bytes | Total bytes |
| ifdisposition | TRUE if disposition is set |
| disposition | Disposition header |
| ifdparameters | TRUE if dparameters is set |
| dparameters | Array of disposition objects |

**Table 19.4**    `imap_fetchstructure` Properties *(cont.)*

| Property | Description |
|---|---|
| ifparameters | TRUE if parameters is set |
| parameters | Array of parameter objects |
| parts | Object for each part of a multipart message using the same structure |

### array imap_getmailboxes(resource imap, string reference, string pattern)

The `imap_getmailboxes` function (Listing 19.7) returns detailed information about mailboxes in the form of an array of objects. The `reference` argument is an IMAP server in the normal form: `{server:port}`. The `pattern` argument controls which mailboxes are returned. An asterisk (`*`) matches all mailboxes, and a percentage symbol (`%`) matches all mailboxes at a particular level.

The returned objects contain three properties: `name`, `delimiter`, and `attributes`, a bitfield that may be tested against the constants listed in Table 19.5.

**Table 19.5**    Constants in the `attributes` Property

| Constant | Description |
|---|---|
| LATT_NOINFERIORS | The mailbox contains no other mailboxes. |
| LATT_NOSELECT | The mailbox is a container only and cannot be opened. |
| LATT_MARKED | The mailbox is marked. |
| LATT_UNMARKED | The mailbox is unmarked. |

**Listing 19.7**    *imap_getmailboxes*

```php
<?php
    $host = "{news.example.com/nntp:119}";

    //connect to IMAP server
    $imap = imap_open($host,
        "leon@example.com", "secret", OP_HALFOPEN);

    //grab a list of all the comp.lang newsgroups
    $group = imap_getmailboxes($imap, $host, "comp.lang.*");
```

| Listing 19.7 | *imap_getmailboxes (cont.)* |

```
foreach($group as $g)
{
    print(str_replace($host, '', $g->name) . "<br>");
}

//close connection
imap_close($imap);
?>
```

### array imap_get_quota(resource imap, string root)

The `imap_get_quota` function (Listing 19.8) returns an array describing quota limits and usage for a given user. It may be run by the mail administrator only. The `root` argument should name a mail account in the form `user.jsmith`.

| Listing 19.8 | *imap_get_quota* |

```
<?php
    $imap = imap_open("{mail.example.com}",
        "mailadmin", "secret", OP_HALFOPEN);

    $quota = imap_get_quota($imap, "user.leon");

    foreach($quota as $k=>$v)
    {
        print("$k {$v['usage']} {$v['limit']}<br>");
    }

    imap_close($imap);
?>
```

### array imap_get_quotaroot(resource imap, string root)

The `imap_get_quotaroot` function returns quota limits and usage for your own account. The `root` argument should name a mailbox, such as INBOX. It returns an array in the same form returned by `imap_get_quota`.

### array imap_getsubscribed(resource imap, string reference, string pattern)

This function returns subscribed mailboxes. The `reference` and `pattern` arguments are optional.

### imap_header

The `imap_header` function is an alias for `imap_headerinfo`.

### object imap_headerinfo(resource imap, integer message, integer from_length, integer subject_length, string default_host)

The `imap_headerinfo` function returns an object with properties matching message headers. The `from_length` and `subject_length` arguments are optional. These values govern the `fetchfrom` and `fetchsubject` properties respectively.

Table 19.6 lists the possible properties of the returned object. Some properties depend on whether the message is mail or news.

**Table 19.6**   `imap_header` Properties

| Property | Description |
| --- | --- |
| `Answered` | Set to `A` if the message is flagged as answered. |
| `Bcc` | Array of objects describing the `Bcc` header with the following properties: `adl`, `host`, `mailbox`, `personal`. |
| `Bccaddress` | The complete text of the `Bcc` header. |
| `Cc` | Array of objects describing the `Cc` header with the following properties: `adl`, `host`, `mailbox`, `personal`. |
| `Ccaddress` | The complete text of the `Cc` header. |
| `Date` | Message date in the following form: Thu, 23 Jan 2003 09:55:17 -0800 |
| `Deleted` | Set to `D` if the message is marked for deletion. |
| `Draft` | Set to `X` if the message is a draft. |
| `Flagged` | Set to `F` if the message is flagged. |
| `followup_to` | The complete text of the `Followup-To` header. |
| `From` | Array of objects describing the `From` header with the following properties: `adl`, `host`, `mailbox`, `personal`. |
| `Fromaddress` | The complete text of the `From` header. |
| `in_reply_to` | The complete text of the `In-Reply-To` header. |
| `MailDate` | The mailing date in the following form: 23-Jan-2003 09:55:09 -0800 |

**Table 19.6** `imap_header` Properties *(cont.)*

| Property | Description |
|---|---|
| `message_id` | The `Message-ID` header. |
| `Msgno` | The message number. |
| `Recent` | Set to `R` if the message is recent. Set to `N` if the message is flagged as answered. |
| `References` | The complete text of the `References` header. |
| `Remail` | The complete text of the `Remail` header. |
| `reply_to` | Array of objects describing the `reply-to` header with the following properties: `adl`, `host`, `mailbox`, `personal`. |
| `reply_toaddress` | The complete text of the `Reply-To` header. |
| `return_path` | Array of objects describing the `Return-Path` header with the following properties: `adl`, `host`, `mailbox`, `personal`. |
| `return_pathaddress` | The complete text of the `Return-Path` header. |
| `Sender` | Array of objects describing the `Sender` header with the following properties: `adl`, `host`, `mailbox`, `personal`. |
| `Senderaddress` | The complete text of the `Sender` header. |
| `Size` | The size of the message. |
| `Subject` | The complete text of the `Subject` header. |
| `To` | Array of objects describing the `To` header with the following properties: `adl`, `host`, `mailbox`, `personal`. |
| `Toaddress` | The complete text of the `To` header. |
| `Udate` | The message date represented as a UNIX timestamp. |
| `Unseen` | Set to `U` if the message is unread and not recent. |

### array imap_headers(resource imap)

The `imap_headers` function returns an array of strings, with one element per message. Each string summarizes the headers for the message.

### string imap_last_error()

Use `imap_last_error` to get the last error generated by an `IMAP` function.

### array imap_list(resource imap)

Use `imap_list` to get the name of every mailbox in an array.

### imap_list_full

The `imap_list_full` function is an alias to `imap_getmailboxes`.

### imap_listmailbox

The `imap_listmailbox` function is an alias to `imap_list`.

### imap_listsubscribed

Use `imap_listsubscribed` as an alias to `imap_lsub`.

### array imap_lsub(resource imap)

The `imap_lsub` function returns a list of subscribed mailboxes.

### boolean imap_mail(string to, string subject, string message, string headers, string cc, string bcc, string return_path)

The `imap_mail` function is an alternative to the `mail` function. The optional `cc` and `bcc` arguments may contain a list of comma-separated addresses. The `return_path` argument sets the `Return-Path` header.

### string imap_mail_compose(array envelope, array body)

The `imap_mail_compose` function (Listing 19.9) returns a MIME message given arrays describing the envelope and body. The `envelope` argument may contain the following elements: `bcc`, `cc`, `custom_headers`, `date`, `from`, `in_reply_to`, `message_id`, `remail`, `reply_to`, `return_path`, `subject`, `to`. The `body` argument should contain an array of arrays that may contain the following elements: `bytes`, `charset`, `contents.data`, `description`, `disposition`, `disposition.type`, `encoding`, `id`, `lines`, `md5`, `subtype`, `type`, `type.parameters`.

To send a composed message, send the output of this function to the headers argument of `imap_mail` or `mail`. Keep in mind that these functions set the value of the `To` and `Subject` headers. Including them in the MIME envelope will result in duplicate headers. You may also send the message by passing the message off to an external process, such as `sendmail`.

**Listing 19.9** `imap_mail_compose`

```php
<?php
    //assemble envelope
    $envelope = array(
        'from'=>'leon@example.com',
        'return_path'=>'leon@example.com'
        );

    //grab logo
    $logo = file_get_contents("/image/logo.gif");

    //assemble body
    $body = array(

        //first part should be multipart/mixed
        array(
            'type'=>TYPEMULTIPART,
            'subtype'=>'mixed'
            ),

        //add a plain text message
        array(
            'type'=>TYPETEXT,
            'subtype'=>'plain',
            'contents.data'=>"Here's a message for you."
            ),

        //add an image
        array(
            'type'=>TYPEIMAGE,
            'subtype'=>'gif',
            'encoding'=>ENCBASE64,
            'contents.data'=>chunk_split(base64_encode($logo)),
            'description'=>'logo.gif'
            )
        );

    //compose MIME headers
    $mime = imap_mail_compose($envelope, $body);

    //show user the raw MIME
    print(nl2br($mime));

    //send the message
    imap_mail('leon@example.com', 'MIME Test', '', $mime);
?>
```

### boolean imap_mail_copy(resource imap, string list, string mailbox, integer flags)

The `imap_mail_copy` function (Listing 19.10) copies messages into another mailbox. The list of messages can be a list of messages or a range. If listing messages, separate them with commas. If giving a range, separate the beginning and ending numbers with a colon. You may use an asterisk in place of the end of the range to stand for the last message in the mailbox.

The optional `flags` argument is a bitfield that may be set with `CP_UID`, which specifies that the list contains UIDs, or `CP_MOVE`, which instructs the function to delete the original messages after copying. This last functionality may be accomplished with the `imap_mail_move` function.

---

**Listing 19.10**   *imap_mail_copy*

```php
<?php
    //delete messages 1 through 10
    $imap = imap_open("{mail.example.com}INBOX", "leon",
        "password");
    imap_mail_copy($imap, "INBOX.php", "1:10");
    imap_close($imap);
?>
```

---

### boolean imap_mail_move(resource imap, string list, string mailbox, integer flags)

The `imap_mail_move` function moves messages from the current mailbox to a new mailbox. The original messages are marked for deletion. The list can be a comma-separated list of messages or a range. If giving a range, separate the beginning and ending numbers with a colon. You may use an asterisk in place of the end to stand for the last message.

The optional `flags` argument is a bitfield that may be set with `CP_UID`, which specifies that the list contains UIDs.

### object imap_mailboxmsginfo(resource imap)

Use `imap_mailboxmsginfo` to return information about the current mailbox. The object will have the properties listed in Table 19.7.

**Table 19.7** Properties for `imap_mailboxmsginfo`

| | |
|---|---|
| Date | Recent |
| Driver | Size |
| Mailbox | Unread |
| Nmsgs | Recent |

### array imap_mime_header_decode(string text)

RFC 2047 defines the method for encoding MIME headers using non-ASCII character sets. This function decodes these headers into an array of objects containing two elements: `charset` and `text`. Each block of encoded text becomes an object in the array.

### integer imap_msgno(resource imap, integer uid)

The `imap_msgno` function returns the message number based on a UID. To get the UID based on message number, use `imap_uid`.

### integer imap_num_msg(resource imap)

The `imap_num_msg` function returns the number of messages in the current mailbox.

### integer imap_num_recent(resource imap)

The `imap_num_recent` function returns the number of recent messages in the current mailbox.

### integer imap_open(string mailbox, string username, string password, integer flags)

Use `imap_open` to begin a connection to a mail server. The `mailbox` argument requires a special format. It should begin with a hostname enclosed in curly braces. Although optional, you should add a colon and port number immediate after the host name. Leaving it out causes PHP to delay making the connection.

By default, this function opens a connection to an IMAP server. You can connect to a POP3 server by adding `/pop3` after the hostname and port. You can connect to a Usenet news server by adding `/nntp` to the end. You may also connect to IMAP and POP servers using SSL. Table 19.8 summarizes server connection strings.

After the host and outside the curly braces, you may specify an IMAP mailbox or NNTP newsgroup.

This function returns a resource representing the connection to the server. Use this identifier with the IMAP functions that require an IMAP resource.

The optional `flags` argument is a bitfield that uses the constants listed in Table 19.9.

**Table 19.8**    IMAP Server Strings

| Connection Type | Connection String |
| --- | --- |
| IMAP | `{mail.example.com:143}INBOX` |
| IMAP over SSL | `{mail.example.com:993/ssl}INBOX` |
| IMAP over SSL with self-signed certificate | `{mail.example.com:993/ssl/novalidate-cert}INBOX` |
| POP3 | `{mail.example.com:110/pop3}` |
| POP3 over SSL | `{mail.example.com:995/pop3/ssl}` |
| POP3 over SSL with self-signed certificate | `{mail.example.com:995/pop3/ssl/novalidate-cert}` |
| NNTP | `{news.example.com:119/nntp}` |

**Table 19.9**    Constants Used by `imap_open`

| Constant | Description |
| --- | --- |
| `CL_EXPUNGE` | Clean out messages marked for deletion on close. |
| `OP_ANONYMOUS` | Don't use `.newsrc` file if connecting to an NNTP server. |
| `OP_DEBUG` | Debug protocol negotiations. |
| `OP_EXPUNGE` | Expunge connections. |
| `OP_HALFOPEN` | Open connection, but not an IMAP or NNTP mailbox. |
| `OP_PROTOTYPE` | Return driver prototype; for internal use only. |
| `OP_READONLY` | Open in read-only mode. |
| `OP_SECURE` | Don't do nonsecure authentication. |
| `OP_SHORTCACHE` | Use short caching. |
| `OP_SILENT` | Don't pass up events. |

## boolean imap_ping(resource imap)

The `imap_ping` function checks the stream to makes sure it is still alive. If new mail has arrived, it will be detected when this function is called.

## integer imap_popen(string mailbox, string username, string password, integer flags)

The `imap_popen` function opens a persistent connection to an IMAP server. This connection is not closed until the calling process ends, so it may be reused by many page requests. At the time of this writing, the code behind this function was unfinished.

## string imap_qprint(string text)

The `imap_qprint` function converts a quote-printable string into an 8-bit string.

## imap_rename

You may use `imap_rename` as an alias for `imap_renamemailbox`.

## boolean imap_renamemailbox(resource imap, string old_name, string new_name)

The `imap_renamemailbox` function changes the name of a mailbox.

## boolean imap_reopen(resource imap, string username, string password, integer flags)

Use `imap_reopen` to open a connection that has died. Its operation is identical to `imap_open`.

## array imap_rfc822_parse_adrlist(string address, string host)

The `imap_rfc_parse_adrlist` function parses an email address given a default host and returns an array of objects. Each object has the following properties: `mailbox`, `host`, `personal`, `adl`. The `mailbox` property is the name before the @. The `host` property is the destination machine or domain. The `personal` property is the name of the recipient. The `adl` property is the source route, the chain of machines the mail will travel, if the address is specified in that style. As the name of the function suggests, this function implements addresses according to RFC 822.

## object imap_rfc822_parse_headers(string text, string default_host)

The `imap_rfc822_parse_headers` function parses raw mail headers and returns an object similar to the object returned by `imap_headerinfo`.

### string imap_rfc822_write_address(string mailbox, string host, string personal_info)

The `imap_rfc822_write_address` returns an email address. As its name suggests, this function implements addresses according to RFC 822.

### imap_scan

You may use `imap_scan` as an alias for `imap_scanmailbox`.

### array imap_scanmailbox(resource imap, string fragment)

The `imap_scanmailbox` function returns an array of mailbox names that contain the given fragment.

### array imap_search(resource imap, string criteria, integer flags)

Use `imap_search` to get a list of message numbers based on search criteria. It wraps the use of IMAP SEARCH statement defined in RFC 1176.

The `criteria` argument is a list of search codes separated by spaces. Table 19.10 summarizes these strings. Some of them take an argument, which must always be surrounded by double quotes. The optional `flags` argument may be set to SE_UID to cause UIDs to be returned instead of message numbers.

**Table 19.10**   `imap_search` Criteria Codes

| Criteria | Description |
| --- | --- |
| ALL | All messages in the mailbox. |
| ANSWERED | Messages with the \ANSWERED flag set. |
| BCC "string" | Messages containing the specified string in the Bcc field. |
| BEFORE "date" | Messages whose date is earlier than the specified date. |
| BODY "string" | Messages containing the specified string in the body. |
| CC "string" | Messages containing the specified string in the Cc field. |
| DELETED | Messages with the \DELETED flag set. |
| FLAGGED | Messages with the \FLAGGED flag set. |
| FROM "string" | Messages containing the specified string in the From field. |
| KEYWORD "flag" | Messages with the specified flag set. |
| NEW | Messages that have the \RECENT flag set but not the \SEEN flag. |

**Table 19.10** `imap_search` Criteria Codes *(cont.)*

| Criteria | Description |
| --- | --- |
| `OLD` | Messages that do not have the `\RECENT` flag set. |
| `ON "date"` | Messages whose date matches the specified date. |
| `RECENT` | Messages that have the `\RECENT` flag set. |
| `SEEN` | Messages that have the `\SEEN` flag set. |
| `SINCE "date"` | Messages whose date is after the specified date. |
| `SUBJECT "string"` | Messages containing the specified string in the `Subject` field. |
| `TEXT "string"` | Messages containing the specified string. |
| `TO "string"` | Messages containing the specified string in the `To` field. |
| `UNANSWERED` | Messages that do not have the `\ANSWERED` flag set. |
| `UNDELETED` | Messages that do not have the `\DELETED` flag set. |
| `UNFLAGGED` | Messages that do not have the `\FLAGGED` flag set. |
| `UNKEYWORD "flag"` | Messages that do not have the specified flag set. |
| `UNSEEN` | Messages that do not have the `\SEEN` flag set. |

### boolean imap_setacl(resource imap, string mailbox, string user, string access)

The `imap_setacl` function sets the access control list for the given mailbox. It wraps the `SETACL` IMAP command, as defined in RFC 2086. Only a mail administrator may execute this function. The `mailbox` argument should take the form of `user.leon`. The access string should be a combination of the codes in Table 19.11.

**Table 19.11** ACL Codes

| Code | Name | Rights |
| --- | --- | --- |
| `A` | Administer | Set access for other users. |
| `c` | Create | Create new mailboxes. |
| `d` | Delete | Delete messages. |
| `i` | Insert | Append and copy messages. |

**Table 19.11**   ACL Codes *(cont.)*

| Code | Name | Rights |
|------|------|--------|
| l | Lookup | The mailbox shows in searches. |
| p | Post | Send mail to submission address for mailbox. |
| r | Read | Allow reading from mailbox. |
| s | Seen/Unseen | Mark a message as being seen or unseen. |
| w | Write | Change information about messages (excluding deleted and seen flags). |

### string imap_setflag_full(resource imap, string sequence, string flag, string options)

The `imap_setflag_full` function sets a flag on a sequence of messages. The `options` argument, if supplied, may be set to `ST_UID`, which signals that the `sequence` argument contains UIDs instead of message numbers.

### boolean imap_set_quota(resource imap, string root, integer limit)

The `imap_set_quota` function sets the quota for the given account. Only a mail administrator may execute this function. The `mailbox` argument should take the form of `user.leon`.

### array imap_sort(resource imap, integer criteria, integer reverse, integer options, string search)

Use the `imap_sort` function to get a sorted list of message numbers based on sort criteria. The `criteria` argument must be one of the constants defined in Table 19.12. If the `reverse` argument is set to 1, the sort order will be reversed. The `options` argument is a bitfield that may be set with `SE_UID`, specifying that UIDs are used, or `SE_NOPREFETCH`, which will stop messages from being prefetched. The `search` argument may be set with same search criteria accepted by `imap_search`.

**Table 19.12**  Criteria Constants for `imap_sort`

| Constant | Description |
|----------|-------------|
| SORTARRIVAL | Arrival date |
| SORTDATE | Message date |
| SORTFROM | First mailbox in `from:` line |
| SORTSIZE | Size of message |
| SORTSUBJECT | Message subject |
| SORTCC | First mailbox in `cc:` line |
| SORTO | First mailbox in `to:` line |

### object imap_status(resource imap, string mailbox, integer options)

The `imap_status` function returns an object with properties describing the status of a mailbox. The only property guaranteed to exist is `flags`, which tells you which other properties exist. You choose the properties to generate with the `options` argument. Constants to use for `options` are listed in Table 19.13.

**Table 19.13**  `imap_status` Options

| Constant | Description |
|----------|-------------|
| SA_ALL | Turns on all properties |
| SA_MESSAGES | Number of messages in mailbox |
| SA_RECENT | Number of recent messages |
| SA_QUOTA | Disk space used by mailbox |
| SA_QUOTA_ALL | Disk space used by all mailboxes |
| SA_UIDNEXT | Next UID to be used |
| SA_UIDVALIDITY | Flag for the validity of UID data |
| SA_UNSEEN | Number of new messages |

### boolean imap_subscribe(resource imap, string mailbox)

Use `imap_subscribe` to subscribe to a mailbox.

### array imap_thread(resource imap, integer options)

The `imap_thread` function (Listing 19.11) returns the list of messages for the open mailbox, organized by thread. On the backend, it uses IMAP's THREAD command and the REFERENCES algorithm. The optional `options` argument accepts the same search flags used by `imap_search`.

The returned array is one-dimensional and represents the tree of threads. Each element of the array uses a key in the form `node.property`, where `node` is the number of one of the nodes in the tree and property is one of three strings: `num`, `next`, `branch`. The `num` property is the message number, suitable for fetching headers or body. The `next` property is the node number of the next message in the thread. A value of zero signifies the last message in the local thread. The `branch` property stands for the end of a branch and the next node will belong one level up. If the value of the `branch` property is zero, the sub-tree continues. A non-zero branch value points to the next message in the list, which starts a new thread.

---

**Listing 19.11**  *imap_thread*

```php
<?php
    //connect to IMAP server
    $imap = imap_open(
        "{news.example.com:119/nntp}alt.fan.henry-rollins",
        "leon@example.com", "secret");

    //get threads
    $thread = imap_thread($imap);

    foreach($thread as $id=>$val)
    {
        list($node, $property) = explode(".", $id);

        if($property == 'num')
        {
            $header = imap_headerinfo($imap, $val);
            print("<ul>\n" .
                "<li>" .
                $header->Subject .
                " by " . htmlentities($header->fromaddress) .
                "</li>\n");
        }
        elseif($property == 'branch')
        {
            print "</ul>\n";
        }
    }
?>
```

**integer imap_uid(resource imap, integer message)**

The `imap_uid` function returns the UID for the given message. To get the message number based on UID, use `imap_msgno`.

**boolean imap_undelete(resource imap, integer message)**

The `imap_undelete` function removes the deletion mark on a message.

**boolean imap_unsubscribe(resource imap, string mailbox)**

Use `imap_unsubscribe` to unsubscribe to a mailbox.

**string imap_utf7_decode(string data)**

The `imap_utf7_decode` function takes UTF-7 encoded text and returns plaintext.

**string imap_utf7_encode(string data)**

The `imap_utf7_encode` function returns UTF-7 encoded text.

**string imap_utf8(string text)**

The `imap_utf8` function converts the given text to UTF-8.

# 19.3  MnoGoSearch

MnoGoSearch is a Web site search engine, formerly known as UdmSearch. It works by following links on a Web site to build a database of keywords. Although you may use it by itself, it can be more convenient to access the engine directly from PHP.

You can find more information about MnoGoSearch at the home site: `<http://www.mnogosearch.ru/>`. Listing 19.12 demonstrates use of the MnoGoSearch functions.

**Listing 19.12**    *Using MnoGoSearch*

```php
<?php
    if(!isset($_REQUEST['query']))
    {
        $_REQUEST['query'] = '';
    }
```

| Listing 19.12 | *Using MnoGoSearch (cont.)* |
| --- | --- |

```php
if(!isset($_REQUEST['page']))
{
    $_REQUEST['page'] = 0;
}

//connect to search engine
$agent = udm_alloc_agent('mysql://user@localhost/mnogo/');

//only return English documents
udm_add_search_limit($agent, UDM_LIMIT_LANG, 'en');

//ignore words of 2 or less letters
udm_set_agent_param($agent, UDM_PARAM_MIN_WORD_LEN, 3);

//return 10 results per page
udm_set_agent_param($agent, UDM_PARAM_PAGE_SIZE, 10);

//jump to specified page
udm_set_agent_param($agent, UDM_PARAM_PAGE_NUM,
    $_REQUEST['page']);

//get results
$result = udm_find($agent, $_REQUEST['query']);

$matches = udm_get_res_param($result, UDM_PARAM_FOUND);
$rows = udm_get_res_param($result, UDM_PARAM_NUM_ROWS);
$first = udm_get_res_param($result, UDM_PARAM_FIRST_DOC);
$last = udm_get_res_param($result, UDM_PARAM_LAST_DOC);
$rating = udm_get_res_param($result, UDM_PARAM_LAST_DOC);

print("$matches matches<br>");
$pages = ceil($matches/10);

//links to each page
for($p=0; $p < $pages; $p++)
{
    if($p == $_REQUEST['page'])
    {
        print(($p+1) . " ");
    }
    else
    {
        print("<a href=\"{$_SERVER['PHP_SELF']}?" .
            "query={$_REQUEST['query']}&amp;page=$p\">" .
            ($p+1) . "</a> ");
    }
```

**Listing 19.12** *Using MnoGoSearch (cont.)*

```
    }
    print("<br><br>\n");

    for($i=0; $i < $rows; $i++)
    {
        print("<a href=\"" .
            udm_get_res_field($result, $i, UDM_FIELD_URL) .
            "\">" . udm_get_res_field($result, $i,
            UDM_FIELD_TITLE) . "</a><br>" .
            udm_get_res_field($result, $i, UDM_FIELD_TEXT) .
            "<br><br>");
    }

    udm_free_res($result);
    udm_free_agent($agent);
?>
<form action="<?php=$_SERVER['PHP_SELF']?>">
<input type="text" name="query"
value="<?php=$_REQUEST['query']?>">
<input type="submit">
</form>
```

### boolean udm_add_search_limit(resource agent, integer limit, string value)

The `udm_add_search_limit` function sets one of the limits on search results. You must supply a resource as returned by `udm_alloc_agent`. The `limit` argument should match one of the constants in Table 19.14. You should read the MnoGoSearch manual for information about categories and tags.

**Table 19.14** MnoGoSearch Search Limits

| Limit | Description |
| --- | --- |
| UDM_LIMIT_CAT | Return results for the given category only. |
| UDM_LIMIT_DATE | Return results whose modification date is before or after a given date. The value should be < or > followed by a UNIX timestamp. |
| UDM_LIMIT_LANG | Return documents in the given language, specified by two-letter code. |
| UDM_LIMIT_TAG | Return results for the given tag only. |
| UDM_LIMIT_URL | Return results only for pages whose URL matches the given pattern, using % and _ wildcard characters. |

### resource udm_alloc_agent(string address, string mode)

The `udm_alloc_agent` function returns a resource used for communicating with the search engine. The `address` argument specifies database connection information. The optional `mode` argument controls how the search engine stores words.

The `address` argument takes the following form: `type://user:password@host:port/database/`. The user, password, and port parts are optional. If you use MnoGoSearch's built-in database, you can leave the address blank. For other databases, use one of the following types: `ibase`, `msql`, `mssql`, `mysql`, `oracle`, `pgsql`, `solid`.

The mode argument can be one of four values: `single`, `multi`, `crc`, `crc-multi`. See Chapter 5 of the MnoGoSearch manual for a description of these modes.

### integer udm_api_version()

Use `udm_api_version` to get the version of the MnoGoSearch API compiled into the PHP extension.

### array udm_cat_list(resource agent, string category)

The `udm_cat_list` function returns all category values of the same level as the given category code. The returned array contains two elements for each category. The first element is the category code. The second element is the category name.

### array udm_cat_path(resource agent, string category)

The `udm_cat_path` function returns an array tracing the path from the root of the category tree to the given category code. The returned array contains two elements for leaf: the category code and the category name.

### boolean udm_check_charset(resource agent, string charset)

The `udm_check_charset` function checks whether MnoGoSearch recognizes the given character set.

### boolean udm_check_stored(resource agent, resource store, string document_id)

The `udm_check_stored` function checks whether the document cache daemon recognizes the named document.

### boolean udm_clear_search_limits(resource agent)

The `udm_clear_search_limits` function resets the search limits for the given connection.

### boolean udm_close_stored(resource agent, resource store)

The `udm_close_stored` function closes a connection to the document cache daemon.

### integer udm_crc32 (resource agent, string text)

The `udm_crc32` function returns the CRC32 checksum for the given string.

### integer udm_errno(resource agent)

The `udm_errno` function returns the error number for the given connection or zero if no error occurred.

### string udm_error(resource agent)

The `udm_error` function returns the error description for the given connection or an empty string if no error occurred.

### resource udm_find(resource agent, string query)

The `udm_find` function executes the given query and returns a result resource. Use `udm_get_res_field` to get each result.

### boolean udm_free_agent(resource agent)

Use `udm_free_agent` to end a connection to the search engine.

### boolean udm_free_ispell_data(resource agent)

The `udm_free_ispell_data` function frees memory allocated by `udm_load_ispell_data`.

### boolean udm_free_res(resource result)

The `udm_free_res` function frees memory used by a result resource.

### integer udm_get_doc_count(resource agent)

The `udm_get_doc_count` function returns the total number of documents in the index.

### string udm_get_res_field(resource result, integer row, integer field)

Use `udm_get_res_field` to get the value of a field in the search results. Specify the field with one of the constants in Table 19.15.

**Table 19.15** MnoGoSearch Result Fields

| Field | Description |
| --- | --- |
| UDM_FIELD_CATEGORY | Category code |
| UDM_FIELD_CONTENT | MIME type |
| UDM_FIELD_CRC | CRC32 checksum |
| UDM_FIELD_DESC | Description from the meta tag |
| UDM_FIELD_KEYWORDS | Keywords from the meta tag |
| UDM_FIELD_MODIFIED | Last modification time as UNIX timestamp |
| UDM_FIELD_ORDER | The number of the document in the result set |
| UDM_FIELD_RATING | Rating |
| UDM_FIELD_SIZE | Size |
| UDM_FIELD_TEXT | The first few lines of the document |
| UDM_FIELD_TITLE | Title |
| UDM_FIELD_URL | URL |
| UDM_FIELD_URLID | Unique ID |

### string udm_get_res_param(resource result, integer parameter)

The udm_get_res_param function returns the value of one of the parameters of a result set. Use one of the constants in Table 19.16 for the parameter argument.

**Table 19.16** MnoGoSearch Output Parameters

| Parameter | Description |
| --- | --- |
| UDM_PARAM_FIRST_DOC | The number of the first document on current page |
| UDM_PARAM_FOUND | The number of matches in the result set |
| UDM_PARAM_LAST_DOC | The number of the last document on the current page |
| UDM_PARAM_NUM_ROWS | The number of matches on the current page |
| UDM_PARAM_SEARCHTIME | The number of seconds spend executing the search |
| UDM_PARAM_WORDINFO | Information about query words found in the index |

### boolean udm_load_ispell_data(integer agent, integer source, string option1, string option2, boolean sort)

The `udm_load_ispell_data` function loads ISpell-related data. Use a constant from Table 19.17 for the `source` argument. The meaning of the other three arguments change depending on the constant chosen. The `sort` argument sorts the words in the dictionary.

**Table 19.17**    ISpell Loading Options

| Source | Description |
|---|---|
| UDM_ISPELL_TYPE_AFFIX | Load an affix file. The `option1` argument should be a two-letter language code. The `option2` argument should be the path to the affix file. |
| UDM_ISPELL_TYPE_DB | Load dictionary from an SQL database. Set `option1` and `option2` to blank strings. |
| UDM_ISPELL_TYPE_SERVER | Load from a spell server. Set `option1` to the host running the server. Set `option2` to an empty string. |
| UDM_ISPELL_TYPE_SPELL | Load a dictionary file. The `option1` argument should be a two-letter language code. The `option2` argument should be the path to the dictionary file. |

### resource udm_open_stored(resource agent, string address)

The `udm_open_stored` function opens a connection to the document cache server running on the specified server.

### boolean udm_set_agent_param(resource agent, integer parameter, string value)

The `udm_set_agent_param` function sets a parameter on an open agent resource. Choose one of the parameters from Table 19.18.

**Table 19.18**    MnoGoSearch Input Parameters

| Parameter | Description |
|---|---|
| UDM_PARAM_CACHE_MODE | Enable or disable caching of search results. Set the `value` argument to `UDM_CACHE_DISABLED` or `UDM_CACHE_ENABLED`. |
| UDM_PARAM_CHARSET | Set the local character set. |
| UDM_PARAM_CROSS_WORDS | Enable or disable cross words. Set the `value` argument to `UDM_CROSS_WORDS_DISABLED` or `UDM_CROSS_WORDS_ENABLED`. |

**Table 19.18**   MnoGoSearch Input Parameters *(cont.)*

| Parameter | Description |
|---|---|
| UDM_PARAM_ISPELL_PREFIXES | Enable or disable the matches on queries that differ by a prefix. This parameter requires loading of an ISpell dictionary. Set the value argument to UDM_PREFIXES_DISABLED or UDM_PREFIXES_ENABLED. |
| UDM_PARAM_MIN_WORD_LEN | Set minimum word length. |
| UDM_PARAM_PAGE_NUM | Choose result page, counting from zero. |
| UDM_PARAM_PAGE_SIZE | Set number of results per page. |
| UDM_PARAM_PHRASE_MODE | Enable or disable phrase searching. Set the value argument to UDM_PHRASE_DISABLED or UDM_PHRASE_ENABLED. |
| UDM_PARAM_SEARCH_MODE | Set the search mode. Set the value argument to UDM_MODE_ALL, UDM_MODE_ANY, UDM_MODE_BOOL, UDM_MODE_PHRASE. |
| UDM_PARAM_STOPFILE | Set the path to the stop words file. |
| UDM_PARAM_STOPTABLE | Set the name of a stop words table. |
| UDM_PARAM_TRACK_MODE | Enable or disable query tracking. Set the value argument to UDM_TRACK_DISABLED or UDM_TRACK_ENABLED. |
| UDM_PARAM_VARDIR | Set the path to MnoGoSearch's var directory. |
| UDM_PARAM_WEIGHT_FACTOR | Set weight factors for parts of the document. The value should be a string of five hexadecimal digits. The digits represent the weight of matches against URL, body, title, keyword, and description, in that order. |
| UDM_PARAM_WORD_MATCH | Set the word match mode. Use one of the following constants for the value argument: UDM_MATCH_BEGIN, UDM_MATCH_END, UDM_MATCH_SUBSTR, UDM_MATCH_WORD. |

# 19.4  OpenSSL

The OpenSSL extension wraps a subset of the functions in the OpenSSL library, allowing you to perform public key cryptography. They allow you to make and verify signatures, and they allow you to encrypt and decrypt data.

Public key cryptography uses a pair of keys: One key encrypts data and the other decrypts it. Compare this to simple encryption schemes that use the same password to encrypt and decrypt. With two keys, the owner can keep one key private while making the other public. Anyone can use the public key to encrypt data for the holder of the private key. Without the private key, the data remains unreadable.

This extension allows you to refer to keys in several ways. One way is with a resource generated by one of the key-reading functions, such as `openssl_get_publickey`. Alternatively, you can supply a string containing the key or a string containing the path to a file containing the key. In these two cases, the key must be in PEM (privacy-enhanced mail) format. For private keys requiring a passphrase, you must specify an array containing the key and the passphrase. Be sure to begin paths with `file://` so that PHP understands it's a path and not a key.

### boolean openssl_csr_export(resource csr, string output, boolean terse)

The `openssl_csr_export` function puts a CSR (Certificate Signing Request) into the `output` argument. The optional `terse` argument controls whether the output includes extra, human-readable comments. It defaults to TRUE, meaning it does not include comments.

### boolean openssl_csr_export_to_file(resource csr, string path, boolean terse)

The `openssl_csr_export_to_file` function (Listing 19.13) writes a CSR to the specified path. The optional `terse` argument controls whether the output includes extra, human-readable comments. It defaults to TRUE, meaning it does not include comments.

---

**Listing 19.13**   *openssl_csr_export_to_file*

```php
<?php
    //setup distinguished name
    $dn = array(
        "countryName"=>"US",
        "stateOrProvinceName"=>"California",
        "organizationName"=>"Example Company, Inc.",
        "commonName"=>"example.com",
        "emailAddress"=>"leon@example.com");

    //setup configuration
    $config = array(
        'private_key_bits'=>1024);
```

| Listing 19.13 | *openssl_csr_export_to_file (cont.)* |
|---|---|

```
//make new key
$privatekey = openssl_pkey_new();
openssl_pkey_export_to_file($privatekey, 'example.pem',
    'corephp');

//make certificate signing request
$csr = openssl_csr_new($dn, $privatekey, $config);
openssl_csr_export_to_file($csr, 'example.csr', FALSE);

//make self-signed certificate
$certificate = openssl_csr_sign($csr, NULL, $privatekey, 45);
openssl_x509_export_to_file($certificate, 'example.crt');
?>
```

### resource openssl_csr_new(array dn, resource privatekey, array config, array extra)

The `openssl_csr_new` function returns a CSR given an array describing the DN (distinguished name) and a private key. The `dn` argument must be an array with keys matching attributes required by the certificate authority. The optional `config` argument can be an array that controls the configuration of the CSR. Use the configuration parameters from Table 19.19. Use the optional `extra` argument to include extra attributes.

**Table 19.19**  Configuration Keys for `openssl_csr_new`

| Configuration | Description |
|---|---|
| `digest_alg` | Override `default_md` in `opennssl.cnf`. |
| `encrypt_key` | Override `encrypt_key` in `opennssl.cnf`. |
| `private_key_bits` | Override `default_bits` in `opennssl.cnf`. |
| `private_key_type` | Set the private key type. Set with `OPENSSL_KEYTYPE_DH`, `OPENSSL_KEYTYPE_DSA` or `OPENSSL_KEYTYPE_RSA` (default). |
| `req_extensions` | Override `req_extensions` in `opennssl.cnf`. |
| `x509_extensions` | Override `x509_extensions` in `opennssl.cnf`. |

### resource openssl_csr_sign(resource csr, resource ca, resource privatekey, integer days)

The `openssl_csr_sign` function signs a CSR. You may set `ca` to NULL to produce a self-signed certificate. The `days` argument sets the number of days the certificate is valid.

### string openssl_error_string()

The `openssl_error_string` function returns a description of the last error or FALSE if no error occurred. PHP keeps errors in a stack, which allows you to call this function multiple times to fetch each error in reverse order.

### openssl_free_key

Use `openssl_free_key` as an alias to `openssl_pkey_free`.

### openssl_get_privatekey

Use `openssl_get_privatekey` as an alias to `openssl_pkey_get_private`.

### openssl_get_publickey

Use `openssl_get_publickey` as an alias to `openssl_pkey_get_public`.

### boolean openssl_open(string sealed_data, string opened_data, string envelope, value privatekey)

The `openssl_open` function opens a sealed message and writes the clear text into the `opened_data` argument.

### boolean openssl_pkcs7_decrypt(string encrypted, string clear, resource certificate, resource key)

Use `openssl_pkcs7_decrypt` to decrypt an S/MIME message. The `encrypted` and `clear` arguments are paths to files.

### boolean openssl_pkcs7_encrypt(string clear, string encrypted, resource certificate, array headers, long flags)

Use `openssl_pkcs7_encrypt` to encrypt an S/MIME message. The `clear` argument is the path to a clear text message. The `encrypted` argument is the path to where PHP writes the encrypted message. Set the `certificate` argument with a single certificate or an array of certificates if there are multiple recipients. The `headers` argument is an array of headers to be prepended to the encrypted data. The array may be indexed by integers, in which case each element is a complete header, or indexed by header name.

The optional `flags` argument changes aspects of the encryption. Combine constants in Table 19.20 with logical-OR operators.

**Table 19.20**   S/MIME Constants

| Constant | Description |
| --- | --- |
| PKCS7_BINARY | Write encrypted message in binary format rather than ordinary MIME text. |
| PKCS7_DETACHED | When signing a message, use cleartext signing with the MIME type multipart/signed. |
| PKCS7_NOATTR | Suppress inclusion of attributes. |
| PKCS7_NOCERTS | Suppress inclusion of signer's certificate. |
| PKCS7_NOCHAIN | Suppress chaining of certificates. |
| PKCS7_NOINTERN | Do not look for certificates in the included message. |
| PKCS7_NOSIGS | Do not verify the signatures on a message. |
| PKCS7_NOVERIFY | Do not verify the signer's certificate of a signed message. |
| PKCS7_TEXT | Add text/plain Content-type headers to encrypted messages. Strip Content-type headers from decrypted output. |

### boolean openssl_pkcs7_sign(string clear, string signed, resource certificate, resource key, array headers, integer flags, string extra_certificates)

The openssl_pkcs7_sign function signs an S/MIME message. PHP reads the message from the file specified by the clear argument and writes the signed message to the file specified by the signed argument. The headers argument is an array of headers to be prepended to the encrypted data. The array may be indexed by integers, in which case each element is a complete header, or indexed by header name.

The optional flags argument changes aspects of the encryption. Combine constants in Table 19.20 with logical-OR operators. It defaults to PKCS7_DETACHED.

The optional extra_certificates argument may be the path to a collection of extra certificates to include.

### boolean openssl_pkcs7_verify(string file, long flags, string certificates, array ca, string extra_certificates)

The openssl_pkcs7_verify function verifies an S/MIME message in a file. The flags argument can be set with the constants in Table 19.20.

Set the optional `certificates` argument with the path to a file into which PHP writes the certificates of the signers. The optional `ca` argument should be an array of paths to files or directories containing certificate authority certificates. The optional `extra_certificates` argument may specify the path to a collection of untrusted certificates.

### boolean openssl_pkey_export(resource key, string output, string passphrase, array config)

The `openssl_pkey_export` function writes the PEM version of the given key into the `output` argument. The optional `config` argument can be an array that controls the configuration of the key. Use the configuration parameters from Table 19.19.

### boolean openssl_pkey_export_to_file(resource key, string file, string passphrase, array config_args)

The `openssl_pkey_export_to_file` function writes the PEM version of the given key into the specified file. The optional `config` argument can be an array that controls the configuration of the key. Use the configuration parameters from Table 19.19.

### openssl_pkey_free(resource key)

The `openssl_pkey_free` function frees memory used by a key resource.

### resource openssl_pkey_get_private(string key, string passphrase)

The `openssl_pkey_get_private` function creates a key resource from a string or a file. The `passphrase` argument is optional.

### resource openssl_pkey_get_public(resource certificate)

The `openssl_pkey_get_public` function creates a key resource from a certificate. You may specify the certificate by a resource, as returned by `openssl_x509_read`, or from a PEM file.

### resource openssl_pkey_new(array config)

The `openssl_pkey_new` argument returns a key resource. The optional `config` argument can be an array that controls the configuration of the key. Use the configuration parameters from Table 19.19.

### boolean openssl_private_decrypt(string data, string decrypted, resource key, integer padding)

The `openssl_private_decrypt` function (Listing 19.14) decrypts a message with a private key. The optional `padding` argument defaults to `OPENSSL_PKCS1_PADDING`. You may also set it with one of the following constants: `OPENSSL_SSLV23_PADDING`, `OPENSSL_PKCS1_OAEP_PADDING`, `OPENSSL_NO_PADDING`.

| Listing 19.14 | *openssl_private_decrypt, openssl_public_encrypt* |
|---|---|

```php
<?php
    /*
    ** Simulate a private message
    */

    //someone encrypts message with public key
    $message = "This message is for you only.";
    openssl_public_encrypt($message, $encrypted,
        "file://example.crt");


    //recipient uses private key to decrypt
    openssl_private_decrypt($encrypted, $clear,
        array("file://example.pem", 'corephp'));
    print("Decrypted message: $clear<br>");
?>
```

### boolean openssl_private_encrypt(string data, string encrypted, resource key, integer padding)

The `openssl_private_encrypt` function encrypts a message with a private key. The optional `padding` argument defaults to `OPENSSL_PKCS1_PADDING`. You may also set it with one of the following constants: `OPENSSL_SSLV23_PADDING`, `OPENSSL_PKCS1_OAEP_PADDING`, `OPENSSL_NO_PADDING`.

### boolean openssl_public_decrypt(string data, string decrypted, resource key, integer padding)

The `openssl_public_decrypt` function (Listing 19.15) decrypts a message with a public key. The optional `padding` argument defaults to `OPENSSL_PKCS1_PADDING`. You may also set it with one of the following constants: `OPENSSL_SSLV23_PADDING`, `OPENSSL_PKCS1_OAEP_PADDING`, `OPENSSL_NO_PADDING`.

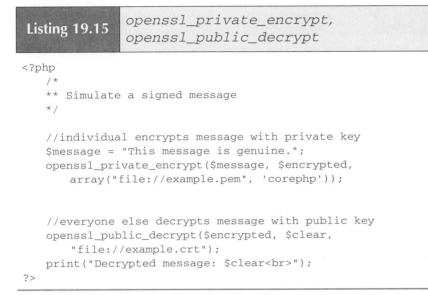

**Listing 19.15** *openssl_private_encrypt, openssl_public_decrypt*

```php
<?php
    /*
    ** Simulate a signed message
    */

    //individual encrypts message with private key
    $message = "This message is genuine.";
    openssl_private_encrypt($message, $encrypted,
        array("file://example.pem", 'corephp'));


    //everyone else decrypts message with public key
    openssl_public_decrypt($encrypted, $clear,
        "file://example.crt");
    print("Decrypted message: $clear<br>");
?>
```

### boolean openssl_public_encrypt(string data, string encrypted, resource key, integer padding)

The `openssl_public_encrypt` function encrypts a message with a public key. The optional `padding` argument defaults to OPENSSL_PKCS1_PADDING. You may also set it with one of the following constants: OPENSSL_SSLV23_PADDING, OPENSSL_PKCS1_OAEP_PADDING, OPENSSL_NO_PADDING.

### integer openssl_seal(string opened_data, string sealed_data, array envelope, array public)

The `openssl_seal` function (Listing 19.16) encrypts data using a randomly generated key. PHP encrypts the key with each of the given public keys and places them in the `envelope` argument. This allows the encryption of data and sending to multiple recipients.

**Listing 19.16** *openssl_open, openssl_seal*

```php
<?php
    //encrypt the data
    openssl_seal("some data", $sealed, $envelope,
        array('file://example.crt','file://example2.crt'));
```

---

**Listing 19.16**   *openssl_open, openssl_seal (cont.)*

```
//pretend that the owner of example.crt now decrypts
openssl_open($sealed, $opened, $envelope[0],
    array('file://example.pem', 'corephp'));

print($opened);
?>
```

---

### boolean openssl_sign(string data, string signature, resource private_key)

The `openssl_sign` function (Listing 19.17) generates a signature for the given data using the specified key, placing it in the `signature` argument.

---

**Listing 19.17**   *openssl_sign, openssl_verify*

```
<?php
    $data = "some data";

    //sign the data
    openssl_sign($data, $signature,
        array('file://example.pem', 'corephp'));

    //verify the signature
    if(1 == openssl_verify($data, $signature,
        'file://example.crt'))
    {
        print("Verified");
    }
    else
    {
        print("Not verified");
    }
?>
```

---

### integer openssl_verify(string data, string signature, resource public_key)

The `openssl_verify` function verifies the signature on signed data. It returns 1 if verified, 0 if not verified, and -1 if an error occurred.

### boolean openssl_x509_check_private_key(resource certificate, resource private_key)

The `openssl_x509_check_private_key` function checks if the given key belongs to the given certificate.

### boolean openssl_x509_checkpurpose(resource certificate, integer purpose, array ca, string untrusted)

The `openssl_x509_checkpurpose` function checks if the given certificate may be used for the given purpose. It returns -1 on error. Use one constant from Table 19.21 to specify the purpose. The `ca` argument should be an array of trusted certificate authorities. The optional `untrusted` argument may be the path to a file containing untrusted certificates.

**Table 19.21**   X.509 Purposes

| Constant | Description |
|---|---|
| X509_PURPOSE_ANY | All purposes |
| X509_PURPOSE_CRL_SIGN | Sign a certificate revocation list |
| X509_PURPOSE_NS_SSL_SERVER | Netscape SSL server |
| X509_PURPOSE_SMIME_ENCRYPT | Encrypt S/MIME email |
| X509_PURPOSE_SMIME_SIGN | Sign S/MIME email |
| X509_PURPOSE_SSL_CLIENT | SSL client |
| X509_PURPOSE_SSL_SERVER | SSL server |

### boolean openssl_x509_export(resource certificate, string output, boolean terse)

The `openssl_x509_export` function puts an X.509 certificate into the `output` argument. The optional `terse` argument controls whether the output includes extra, human-readable comments. It defaults to TRUE, meaning it does not include comments.

### boolean openssl_x509_export_to_file(resource certificate, string file, boolean terse)

The `openssl_x509_export_to_file` function puts an X.509 certificate into the specified file. The optional `terse` argument controls whether the output includes extra, human-readable comments. It defaults to TRUE, meaning it does not include comments.

### void openssl_x509_free(resource certificate)

Use this function to free memory associated with a certificate resource.

### array openssl_x509_parse(resource certificate, boolean short_names)

The `openssl_x509_parse` function returns an array describing the attributes of the given certificate. By default, PHP uses the short names for the array keys. Set the optional `short_names` argument to `FALSE` to use longer names.

### resource openssl_x509_read(string certificate)

The `openssl_x509_read` function creates a resource given the certificate as a string or a path to a file.

# 19.5  System V Messages

System V messages are one of three methods of inter-process communication provided by System V operating systems. They allow processes to communicate via formatted messages. Processes place messages of a fixed length in the queues of other processes.

A complete discussion of System V messages is beyond the scope of this text. There are plenty of resources for learning more about them. I recommend *Unix Network Programming* by W. Richard Stevens, published by Prentice Hall. The second edition was published in 1997 as two volumes.

Listings 19.18 and 19.19 implement a simple server that makes strings uppercase using System V messages. The server waits for clients to place messages in its queue. The server responds by placing the transformed text in client queues. The clients can also send a greeting or ask the server to shutdown.

| Listing 19.18 | *System V message server* |
| --- | --- |

```php
<?php
    //key for the server's queue
    define('SERVER_QUEUE', 1970);

    //message types
    define('MSG_SHUTDOWN', 1);
    define('MSG_TOUPPER', 2);
    define('MSG_HELLO', 3);
```

**Listing 19.18**   *System V message server (cont.)*

```
//create queue
$queue = msg_get_queue(SERVER_QUEUE);

//process messages
$keepListening = TRUE;
while($keepListening)
{
    //wait for a message
    msg_receive($queue, 0, $type, 1024, $message);

    switch($type)
    {
        case MSG_SHUTDOWN:
            $keepListening = FALSE;
            break;

        case MSG_HELLO:
            print($message . " says hello.\n");
            break;

        case MSG_TOUPPER:
            $clientQueue = msg_get_queue($message['caller']);
            $response = strtoupper($message['text']);
            msg_send($clientQueue, MSG_TOUPPER, $response);
            break;
    }
}

//remove the queue
msg_remove_queue($queue);
?>
```

**Listing 19.19**   *System V message client*

```
<?php
    //key for the server's queue
    define('SERVER_QUEUE', 1970);

    //message types
    define('MSG_SHUTDOWN', 1);
    define('MSG_TOUPPER', 2);
    define('MSG_HELLO', 3);
```

| Listing 19.19 | *System V message client (cont.)* |
|---|---|

```
//create queue
$qid = rand(1, 10000);
$queue = msg_get_queue($qid);
$serverQueue = msg_get_queue(SERVER_QUEUE);

//send a greeting
msg_send($serverQueue, MSG_HELLO, $qid);

//send a string to set to uppercase
msg_send($serverQueue, MSG_TOUPPER,
    array('caller'=>$qid,
        'text'=>'corephp'));

//wait for return from server
msg_receive($queue, 0, $type, 1024, $message);
print("$message\n");

//tell server to shutdown
msg_send($serverQueue, MSG_SHUTDOWN, NULL);

//remove the queue
msg_remove_queue($queue);
?>
```

### integer msg_get_queue(integer key, integer permission)

The `msg_get_queue` function creates or attaches to a message queue with the given key. The `permission` argument controls read and write privileges to the queue in the same way file permissions do. It defaults to 0666, which is read and write access for all users.

### boolean msg_receive(resource queue, integer desired_type, integer type, integer size, string message, boolean unserialize, integer flags, integer error)

The `msg_receive` function pulls the next message off the queue of the desired type. The queue argument must be a resource created by `msg_get_queue`. If you use 0 for the desired type, PHP returns the first message of any type. PHP puts the actual type of the message in the `type` argument. The `size` argument sets the maximum message size accepted. The `message` argument receives the message.

The optional `unserialize` argument controls whether the message is a serialized PHP variable needing to be unserialized. By default, this argument is set to TRUE. PHP uses the same serialization method used by the session functions.

The optional `flags` argument allows you to pass options to an underlying layer. Combine the constants in Table 19.22 with logical-OR operators.

If an error occurs, the `error` argument receives the error code.

**Table 19.22**    System V Message Receive Flags

| Constant | Description |
|---|---|
| MSG_EXCEPT | This flag causes `msg_receive` to look for a message whose type does not match the desired type. It has no effect when using 0 for the desired type. |
| MSG_IPC_NOWAIT | With this flag, `msg_receive` does not wait for messages. It sets `error` to `ENOMSG` and returns immediately if there are no messages. |
| MSG_NOERROR | With this flag, PHP truncates messages that are longer than the maximum size. |

### boolean msg_remove_queue(resource queue)
The `msg_remove_queue` function destroys the given message queue.

### boolean msg_send(resource queue, integer type, string message, boolean serialize, boolean block, integer error)
The `msg_send` function places a message of a specified type in the specified queue. The type must be greater than zero. By default, PHP serializes the message using the same method defined for sessions. You may set the `serialize` argument to `FALSE` to force PHP to send the message as a binary string.

If the `block` argument is set to `FALSE`, PHP will not wait in the event that the queue is full. Normally, PHP will wait indefinitely until space in the queue becomes available. If you turn off blocking and the queue is full, PHP sets `error` to `EAGAIN`.

### boolean msg_set_queue(resource queue, array data)
The `msg_set_queue` function sets parameters on the queue. The `queue` argument should be a resource returned by `msg_get_queue`. The data array should contain keys from the following list: `msg_perm.gid`, `msg_perm.mode`, `msg_perm.uid`, `msg_qbytes`. These correspond to the statistics returned by `msg_stat_queue` and described in Table 19.23.

Only the root user and the owner of the queue may change these values. Only the root user can change `msg_qbytes`.

**array msg_stat_queue(resource queue)**

The `msg_stat_queue` function returns an array describing the given queue and the last message pulled from the queue. Table 19.23 lists the statistics in the returned array.

**Table 19.23**   System V Message Statistics

| Statistic | Description |
| --- | --- |
| msg_ctime | The UNIX timestamp for the last change to the queue. |
| msg_lrpid | The process ID of the receiving process. |
| msg_lspid | The process ID of the sending process. |
| msg_perm.gid | The group ID of the queue owner. |
| msg_perm.mode | The file access mode of the queue. |
| msg_perm.uid | The user ID of the queue owner. |
| msg_qbytes | The number of bytes of space available in the queue. |
| msg_qnum | The number of messages in the queue. |
| msg_rtime | The UNIX timestamp for the last read from the queue. |
| msg_stime | The UNIX timestamp for the last write to the queue. |

# 19.6  System V Semaphores

PHP offers an extension for using System V semaphores. If your operating system supports this feature, you may add this extension to your installation of PHP. At the time of this writing, only the Solaris, Linux, and AIX operating systems were known to support semaphores.

Semaphores are a way to control a resource so that it is used by a single entity at once, inspired by the flags used to communicate between ships. The idea to use an integer counter to ensure single control of a resource was described first by Edsger Dijkstra in the early 1960s for use in operating systems.

A complete tutorial on semaphores is beyond the scope of this text. Semaphores are a standard topic for college computer science courses, and you will find adequate descriptions in books about operating systems. The whatis.com Web site `<http://www.whatis.com/>` references *Unix Network Programming* by W. Richard Stevens, published by Prentice Hall. The second edition was published in 1997 as two volumes.

### boolean sem_acquire(integer identifier)

The `sem_acquire` function (Listing 19.20) attempts to acquire a semaphore you've identified with the `sem_get` function. The function will block until the semaphore is acquired. Note that it is possible to wait forever while attempting to acquire a semaphore. One way is if a script acquires a semaphore to its limit and then tries to acquire it another time. In this case the semaphore can never decrement.

If you do not release a semaphore with `sem_release`, PHP will release it for you and display a warning.

| Listing 19.20 | *sem_acquire, sem_get, sem_release* |
| --- | --- |

```php
<?php
/*
** Semaphore example
**
** To see this in action, try opening two or more
** browsers and load this script at the same time.
** You should see that each script will execute the
** fake procedure when it alone has acquired the
** semaphore.  Pay attention to the output of the
** microtime function in each browser window.
*/

//Define integer for this semaphore
//This simply adds to readability
define("SEM_COREPHP", 1970);

//Get or create the semaphore
//This semaphore can be acquired only once
$sem = sem_get(SEM_COREPHP, 1);

//acquire semaphore
if(sem_acquire($sem))
{
    //perform some atomic function
    print("Faking procedure... " . microtime() .
        "<br>");
    sleep(3);
    print("Finishing fake procedure... " . microtime() .
        "<br>");
```

| Listing 19.20 | *sem_acquire, sem_get, sem_release (cont.)* |

```
        //release semaphore
        sem_release($sem);
    }
    else
    {
        //we failed to acquire the semaphore
        print("Failed to acquire semaphore!<br>\n");
    }
?>
```

### integer sem_get(integer key, integer maximum, integer permission)

Use sem_get to receive an identifier for a semaphore. If the semaphore does not exist, it will be created. The optional maximum and permission arguments are used only during creation. The maximum argument controls how many times a semaphore may be acquired. It defaults to 1. The permission argument controls read and write privileges to the semaphore in the same way file permissions do. It defaults to 0666, which is read and write access for all users. The key argument is used to identify the semaphore among processes in the system. The integer returned by sem_get may be unique each time it is called, even when the same key is specified.

### boolean sem_release(integer identifier)

Use sem_release to reverse the process of the sem_acquire function.

### boolean sem_remove(integer identifier)

Use sem_remove to remove a semaphore from memory.

# 19.7  System V Shared Memory

PHP offers an extension for using System V shared memory. It follows the same restrictions as the System V semaphore functions. That is, your operating system must support this functionality. Solaris, Linux, and AIX are known to work with shared memory.

Shared memory is virtual memory shared by separate processes. It helps solve the problem of communication between processes running on the same machine. An obvious method might be to write information to a file, but access to permanent storage is relatively slow. Shared memory allows the creation of system memory that may be accessed by multiple processes, which is much faster. Since exclusive use of this memory is essential, you must use some sort of locking. This is usually done with semaphores. If you use the shared memory functions, make sure you include support for System V semaphores as well.

A full discussion of the use of shared-memory functions is beyond the scope of this text. I found a short description of shared memory at whatis.com `<http://www.whatis.com/>`. You may also pursue college courses about operating systems or refer to *Unix Network Programming* by W. Richard Stevens to learn more about shared memory.

The shared memory extension was added to PHP by Christian Cartus.

### integer shm_attach(integer key, integer size, integer permissions)

The `shm_attach` function (Listing 19.21) returns an identifier to shared memory. The `key` argument is an integer that specifies the shared memory. The shared memory will be created if necessary, in which case the optional `size` and `permissions` arguments will be used if present.

The size of the memory segment defaults to a value defined when PHP is compiled. Minimum and maximum values for the size are dependent on the operating system, but reasonable values to expect are a 1-byte minimum and a 128K maximum. There are also limits on the number of shared memory segments. Normal limits are 100 total segments and six segments per process.

The permissions for a memory segment default to 0666, which is read and write permission to all users. This value operates like those used to set file permissions.

As with semaphores, calling `shm_attach` for the same key twice will return two different identifiers, yet they will both point to the same shared memory segment internally.

Keep in mind that shared memory does not expire automatically. You must free it using `shm_remove`.

| Listing 19.21 | *Using System V shared memory* |
| --- | --- |

```php
<?php
    /*
    ** Shared Memory example
    **
    ** This example builds on the semaphore example
    ** by using shared memory to communicate between
    ** multiple processes.  This example creates shared
    ** memory but does not release it.  Make sure you
    ** run the shm_remove example when you're done
    ** experimenting with this example.
    */
```

**Listing 19.21**    *Using System V shared memory (cont.)*

```
//Define integer for semaphore key
define("SEM_COREPHP", 1970);

//Define integer for shared memory key
define("SHM_COREPHP", 1970);

//Define integer for variable key
define("SHMVAR_MESSAGE", 1970);


//Get or create the semaphore
//This semaphore can only be acquired once
$sem = sem_get(SEM_COREPHP, 1);

//acquire semaphore
if(sem_acquire($sem))
{
    //attach to shared memory
    //make the memory 1K in size
    $mem = shm_attach(SHM_COREPHP, 1024);

    //attempt to get message variable, which
    //won't be there the first time
    if($old_message = shm_get_var($mem, SHMVAR_MESSAGE))
    {
        print("Previous value: $old_message<br>\n");
    }

    //create new message
    $new_message = getmypid() . " here at " . microtime();

    //set new value
    shm_put_var($mem, SHMVAR_MESSAGE, $new_message);

    //detach from shared memory
    shm_detach($mem);

    //release semaphore
    sem_release($sem);
}
else
{
    //we failed to acquire the semaphore
    print("Failed to acquire semaphore!<br>\n");
}
?>
```

## boolean shm_detach(integer identifier)

Use `shm_detach` to free the memory associated with the identifier for a shared-memory segment. This does not release the shared memory itself. Use `shm_remove` to do this.

## value shm_get_var(integer identifier, integer key)

The `shm_get_var` function returns a value stored in a variable with `shm_put_var`.

## boolean shm_put_var(integer identifier, integer key, value)

The `shm_put_var` function sets the value for a variable in a shared memory segment. If the variable does not exist, it will be created. The variable will last inside the shared memory until removed with `shm_remove_var` or when the shared memory segment itself is destroyed with `shm_remove`. The value argument will be serialized with the same argument used for the `serialize` function. That means you may use any PHP value or variable—with one exception: at the time of this writing, objects lose their methods when serialized.

## boolean shm_remove(integer identifier)

Use `shm_remove` (Listing 19.22) to free a shared memory segment. All variables in the segment will be destroyed, so it is not strictly necessary to remove them. If you do not remove shared memory segments with this function, they may exist perpetually.

---

**Listing 19.22**    *shm_remove*

```php
<?php
    /*
    ** Shared Memory example 2
    **
    ** This example removes shared memory created
    ** by the previous shared memory example.
    */

    //Define integer for semaphore key
    define("SEM_COREPHP", 1970);

    //Define integer for shared memory key
    define("SHM_COREPHP", 1970);

    //Define integer for variable key
    define("SHMVAR_MESSAGE", 1970);
```

**Listing 19.22**    *shm_remove (cont.)*

```
//Get or create the semaphore
//This semaphore can be acquired only once
$sem = sem_get(SEM_COREPHP, 1);

//acquire semaphore
if(sem_acquire($sem))
{
    //attach to shared memory
    //make the memory 1K in size
    $mem = shm_attach(SHM_COREPHP, 1024);

    //remove variable
    shm_remove_var($mem, SHMVAR_MESSAGE);

    //remove shared memory
    shm_remove($mem);

    //release semaphore
    sem_release($sem);
}
else
{
    //we failed to acquire the semaphore
    print("Failed to acquire semaphore!<br>\n");
}

?>
```

### boolean shm_remove_var(integer identifier, integer key)

The `shm_remove_var` function frees the memory associated with a variable within a shared memory segment.

# XML

**Topics in This Chapter**

- DOM XML
- Expat XML
- WDDX

# Chapter

The functions in this chapter manipulate XML documents. The extensible mark-up language, XML, has steadily grown in popularity since being introduced in 1996. XML is a first cousin to HTML in that it, too, is derived from SGML, a generalized mark-up language that is nearly 20 years old. Like HTML, XML documents surround textual data with tags. Unlike HTML, XML can be used to communicate any type of data. The best place to start learning about XML is its home page at the W3C `<http://www.w3.org/XML/>`. Among the resources there, you will find book recommendations.

PHP offers two methods for working with XML documents: DOM and event handling. In the former method, the XML document appears as a collection of objects. In the latter method, you read through an XML document and PHP executes various handlers you define. This chapter also discusses WDDX, an XML language for serializing data.

The examples in this chapter often refer to the XML document shown in Listing 20.1. Listing 20.2 shows its DTD. Listing 20.3 demonstrates an external unparsed entity. Listing 20.4 shows a simple XSL document.

| Listing 20.1 | *Example XML document* |

```
<?xml version='1.0'?>
<!DOCTYPE example SYSTEM "corephp.dtd" [
<!ENTITY externalEntity SYSTEM "corephp_entity.xml">
<!ENTITY capture SYSTEM
"http://www.php.net/gifs/php_logo.gif" NDATA gif>
<!NOTATION gif SYSTEM "/usr/local/bin/view_gif">
]>
<example output="capture"
    xmlns:xhtml="http://www.w3.org/1999/xhtml">
    <title>An Example XML Document</title>
    <code>
    This section contains some PHP code.
    <?phpphp
        print("Core PHP");
    ?>
    <xhtml:br />
    </code>
    &externalEntity;
    <table border="yes">
        <row><cell>A</cell><cell>D</cell></row>
        <row><cell>B</cell><cell>E</cell></row>
        <row><cell>C</cell><cell>F</cell></row>
    </table>
</example>
```

| Listing 20.2 | *Example DTD* |

```
<!ELEMENT example (title,code,table*)>
<!ATTLIST example output CDATA #IMPLIED>
<!ELEMENT title (#PCDATA)>
<!ELEMENT code (#PCDATA)>
<!ELEMENT table (row*)>
<!ATTLIST table border CDATA #REQUIRED>
<!ELEMENT row (cell*)>
<!ELEMENT cell (#PCDATA)>
```

| Listing 20.3 | *Example external entity* |

```
<?xml version="1.0" ?>
This is the external entity.
```

| Listing 20.4 | *Example XSL document* |

```
<xsl:stylesheet version="1.0"
    xmlns:xsl='http://www.w3.org/1999/XSL/Transform'>
    <xsl:template match="/">
        <h1><xsl:value-of select="//title"/></h1>
        <pre>
            <xsl:value-of select="//code"/>
        </pre>
        <xsl:value-of select="$myParam" />
    </xsl:template>
</xsl:stylesheet>
```

# 20.1 DOM XML

The Document Object Model (DOM) is an interface for allowing programs to read and update the elements of an XML document. Each element of the document appears as an object with methods and attributes a program can manipulate. One popular use of the DOM is JavaScript within browsers updating the contents of an HTML page. From PHP's perspective, the DOM allows a natural way of treating an XML document as an ordinary data structure. Compare this approach to that of the Expat XML functions discussed later in this chapter.

PHP wraps the GNOME XML library <http://www.xmlsoft.org/> in order to offer the functions described in this section. You can find the latest version of the specification at the W3C site: <http://www.w3.org/DOM/>. A detailed discussion of DOM is beyond the scope of this text, but you may find the specification is enough to get you started. You find a copy of Joe Marini's *Document Object Model: Processing Structured Documents*.

PHP creates several classes to mirror those described by the DOM specification. In order to maintain namespace integrity, the PHP classes have a Dom prefix. For example, the specification's node class is DomNode in PHP. The PHP classes implement both attributes and methods defined in the specification as methods. The names of the PHP methods follow conventions for PHP functions, which includes using underscores to separate words. Where the specification calls for an ownerDocument property of the node class, PHP implements an owner_document method on the DomNode class.

Several of the methods described below are not implemented at the time of writing. However, because they appear in the source code and the DOM specification, it's likely they will work soon.

### string DomAttribute::name()

The `name` method (Listing 20.5) returns the name of the attribute.

| Listing 20.5 | *DomAttribute::name, DomAttribute::value* |
|---|---|

```php
<?php
    //load the document
    $dom = domxml_open_file("corephp.xml");

    //grab the first table element
    list($table) = $dom->get_elements_by_tagname('table');

    //get the first attribute
    list($a) = $table->attributes();

    print("Attribute " . $a->name() . " is " .
        $a->value());
?>
```

### boolean DomAttribute::specified()

If the XML document specifies the value of the attribute, this method returns TRUE. If the attribute is implied, this method returns FALSE.

### string DomAttribute::value()

The `value` method returns the value of the attribute.

### object DomDocument::create_attribute(string name, string value)

The `create_attribute` method returns a `DomAttribute` object with the given name and value.

### object DomDocument::create_cdata_section(string cdata)

The `create_cdata_section` method returns a `DomCData` object.

### object DomDocument::create_comment(string comment)

The `create_comment` method returns a `DomComment` object.

### object DomDocument::create_element(string name)

The `create_element` method returns a `DomElement` object.

### object DomDocument::create_element_ns(string uri, string name, string prefix)

The `create_element_ns` method returns a `DomElement` object for the given namespace. The `prefix` argument is optional. If left out and the specified namespace does not exists, PHP generates a random prefix.

### object DomDocument::create_entity_reference(string content)

The `create_entity_reference` method returns a `DomEntityReference` object.

### DomDocument::create_processing_instruction(string target, string content)

The `create_processing_instruction` method returns a `DomProcessingInstruction` object.

### object DomDocument::create_text_node(string content)

The `create_text_node` method returns a `DomText` object.

### object DomDocument::doctype()

The `doctype` method returns a `DomDocumentType` object.

### object DomDocument::document_element()

The `document_element` method returns the `DomElement` object corresponding to the root of the document.

### integer DomDocument::dump_file(string file, integer compression, boolean format)

The `dump_file` method writes an XML document to a file and returns the number of bytes written. The optional `compression` argument sets the level of GZIP compression applied to the file. Use 0 for no compression. The optional `format` argument controls whether PHP preserves whitespace. By default, PHP strips unnecessary whitespace.

### string DomDocument::dump_mem(boolean format)

The `dump_mem` method (Listing 20.6) returns an XML document. By default, PHP removes all unnecessary whitespace. If you set the optional `format` argument to TRUE, PHP keeps formatting whitespace in the document.

---

**Listing 20.6**  *DomDocument::dump_mem*

```php
<?php
    //create new document
    $dom = domxml_new_doc("1.0");

    //start ordinary HTML document
    $root = $dom->append_child($dom->create_element("html"));
    $head = $root->append_child($dom->create_element("head"));
    $title = $head->append_child($dom->create_element("title"));
    $body = $root->append_child($dom->create_element("body"));

    //start body with some PHP code
    $body->append_child(
        $dom->create_processing_instruction(
            'php',
            'print(date("Y-m-d"));'));
    $body->append_child($dom->create_element("br"));

    $body->set_attribute('id', 'corephp');

    //set title text with current time
    $title->append_child($dom->create_text_node(time()));

    //dump the entire document
    print($dom->dump_mem(TRUE));
?>
```

---

### object DomDocument::get_element_by_id(string id)

The `get_element_by_id` method returns the `DomElement` object with the given `id` attribute.

### array DomDocument::get_elements_by_tagname(string tagname)

The `get_elements_by_tagname` method returns an array of `DomElement` objects with the given tag name.

### string DomDocument::html_dump_mem()

The `html_dump_mem` method returns the XML document in a form suitable for HTML browsers. This is almost identical to the output of the `dump_mem` method, with a few XML-specific tags left out.

## DomDocument::xinclude()

The `xinclude` method implements the `XInclude` tags in the document.
`XInclude` is described in the following document: `<http://www.w3.org/TR/xinclude/>`.

## array DomDocumentType::entities()

The `entities` method returns an array of entities.

## string DomDocumentType::name()

The `name` method returns the name of the document type.

## array DomDocumentType::notations()

The `notations` method returns an array of notations for the document type.

## string DomDocumentType::public_id()

The `public_id` method returns the public ID for the document type.

## string DomDocumentType::system_id()

The `system_id` method returns the system ID for the document type.

## string DomElement::get_attribute(string attribute)

The `get_attribute` method returns the value of the given attribute.

## object DomElement::get_attribute_node(string attribute)

The `get_attribute_node` method returns a `DomAttribute` object for the named attribute.

## array DomElement::get_elements_by_tagname(string tagname)

The `get_elements_by_tagname` method returns the elements with the given tag name inside the element. Compare this to `DomDocument::get_elements_by_tagname`, which returns elements for a `DomDocument` object.

## boolean DomElement::has_attribute(string name)

The `has_attribute` method tests for the presence of an attribute.

## boolean DomElement::remove_attribute(string name)

The `remove_attribute` method removes an attribute from an element.

### object DomElement::set_attribute(string name, string value)

The `set_attribute` method sets the value of the given attribute on the element. If the attribute doesn't exist, it's created. It returns the new attribute object.

### object DomElement::set_attribute_node(object attribute)

The `set_attribute_node` method adds the given `DomAttribute` object to the element.

### string DomElement::tagname()

The `tagname` method returns the tag name of the element.

### boolean DomNode::add_namespace(string uri, string prefix)

The `add_namespace` method adds the given namespace to the node.

### object DomNode::append_child(object node)

The `append_child` method appends a node to another as a child and returns a reference to the child. If the child node belonged to another document, PHP detaches and moves it. All the children of the appending node come along, of course. If you wish to copy a node, use the `DomNode::clone_node` method.

### object DomNode::append_sibling(object node)

The `append_sibling` method adds the given node to the document immediately after a node.

### array DomNode::attributes()

The `attributes` method returns an array of attributes of the given node.

### array DomNode::child_nodes()

The `child_nodes` method returns an array of child nodes belonging to the node.

### object DomNode::clone_node(boolean deep)

The `clone_node` method returns a copy of the node. The optional `deep` argument controls whether PHP should copy all children. It's `FALSE` by default.

### string DomNode::dump_node(object node, boolean format, integer level)

The `dump_node` method returns a partial XML document in the same manner as `DomDocument::dump_mem`. The `node` argument is the root of the returned tree. The `format` argument controls whether PHP formats the document with whitespace. The `level` argument is the so-called imbrication level, as defined by the GNOME XML library.

### object DomNode::first_child()

The `first_child` method returns the first child of the node, or NULL if no children exist.

### string DomNode::get_content()

The `get_content` method returns all text node children of the node concatenated into a single `string.boolean DomNode::has_attributes()` method. The `has_attributes` method returns TRUE if the node contains at least one attribute.

### boolean DomNode::has_child_nodes()

The `has_child_nodes` returns TRUE if the node contains at least one child.

### object DomNode::insert_before(object new_node, object existing_node)

The `insert_before` method (Listing 20.7) inserts a new node immediately before an existing node and returns the inserted node. If the `new_node` is part of the existing document, PHP simply moves it. If you set `existing_node` to NULL, PHP adds the node to the end of the list of children.

---

**Listing 20.7**    *DomNode::insert_before*

```php
<?php
    //load the document
    $dom = domxml_open_file("corephp.xml");

    //grab the first row element
    list($table) = $dom->get_elements_by_tagname('table');
    $child = $table->first_child();

    //make new row
    $row = $dom->create_element('row');
    $text = $dom->create_text_node('X');
    $cell = $dom->create_element('cell');
    $cell->append_child($text);
    $row->append_child($cell);
    $text = $dom->create_text_node('Y');
    $cell = $dom->create_element('cell');
    $cell->append_child($text);
    $row->append_child($cell);
```

| Listing 20.7 | `DomNode::insert_before` *(cont.)* |
|---|---|

```
    //insert the new row
    $table->insert_before($row, $child);

    //dump the document
    print($dom->dump_mem(TRUE));
?>
```

### boolean DomNode::is_blank_node()

The `is_blank_node` method returns TRUE if the node is empty.

### object DomNode::last_child()

The `last_child` method returns the last child of the node, or NULL if no children exist.

### object DomNode::next_sibling()

The `next_sibling` method returns the next node of the same level. You may use this method and `first_child` to iterate over every child of a given node.

### string DomNode::node_name()

The `node_name` method returns the name of a node for the following subclasses: `DomAttribute`, `DomDocumentType`, `DomElement`, `DomEntity`, `DomEntityReference`, `DomNotation`, `DomProcessingInstruction`. For `DomCDataSection`, `DomComment`, `DomDocument`, and `DomText` PHP returns #cdata-section, #comment, #document, and #text, respectively.

### integer DomNode::node_type()

The `node_type` method returns an integer matching one of the type constants in Table 20.1.

**Table 20.1**   Node Type Constants

| Constant | Description |
|---|---|
| XML_ATTRIBUTE_NODE | Attribute |
| XML_CDATA_SECTION_NODE | CData Section |
| XML_COMMENT_NODE | Comment |
| XML_DOCUMENT_FRAG_NODE | Document Fragment |

**Table 20.1**  Node Type Constants *(cont.)*

| Constant | Description |
| --- | --- |
| XML_DOCUMENT_NODE | Document |
| XML_DOCUMENT_TYPE_NODE | Document Type |
| XML_ELEMENT_NODE | Element |
| XML_ENTITY_NODE | Entity |
| XML_ENTITY_REF_NODE | Entity Reference |
| XML_NOTATION_NODE | Notation |
| XML_PI_NODE | Processing Instruction |
| XML_TEXT_NODE | Text |

### string DomNode::node_value()

The node_value method returns the value contained by the node for the following subclasses: DomAttribute, DomCDataSection, DomComment, DomProcessingInstruction, DomText. For other subclasses, it returns NULL.

### object DomNode::owner_document()

The owner_document method returns the document to which the node belongs.

### object DomNode::parent_node()

The parent_node method returns the parent of the node or NULL if the node has no parent.

### string DomNode::prefix()

The prefix method returns the prefix for the given node.

### DomNode::previous_sibling()

The previous_sibling method returns the node of the same level that appears immediately before the node in the document. It returns NULL if there is no previous node. You can use this method with last_child to iterate over all children.

### object DomNode::remove_child(object child)

The remove_child method removes a child from a node and returns it. It returns FALSE on failure.

### object DomNode::replace_child(object old_child, object new_child)

The `replace_child` method removes the child specified by the first argument and puts the object specified by the second argument in its place. It returns the replaced child. If the new child is part of the node's document, it is moved, not copied.

### object DomNode::replace_node(object node)

The `replace_node` method (Listing 20.8) replaces a node with a new node and returns the old node.

| Listing 20.8 | *DomNode::replace_node* |
| --- | --- |

```php
<?php
    //load the document
    $dom = domxml_open_file("corephp.xml");

    //grab the code element
    list($code) = $dom->get_elements_by_tagname('code');

    //loop over children
    for($c = $code->first_child(); $c !== NULL;
        $c = $c->next_sibling())
    {
        //if we find a block of PHP code, eval it
        //and replace it with a text node
        if(($c->node_type() == XML_PI_NODE) AND
            ($c->target() == 'php'))
        {
            //execute code and capture output
            ob_start();
            eval($c->data());
            $output = ob_get_contents();
            ob_end_clean();

            //replace pi node with text node
            $c->replace_node($dom->create_text_node($output));
        }
    }

    //dump the document
    print($dom->dump_mem(TRUE));
?>
```

### boolean DomNode::set_content(string content)

The `set_content` method adds content to the node. If the node has children, PHP adds the content to the end of the list of children.

### boolean DomNode::set_name(string name)

The `set_name` method sets the name of the node. The following subclasses allow for setting the name: `DomAttribute`, `DomDocumentType`, `DomElement`, `DomEntity`, `DomEntityReference`, `DomNotation`, `DomProcessingInstruction`.

### DomNode::set_namespace(string uri, string prefix)

The `set_namespace` method sets the namespace for the node. Optionally, you may set the prefix with the `prefix` argument. Otherwise, PHP generates a random prefix.

### DomNode::unlink_node()

The `unlink_node` method detaches a node from its document.

### string DomProcessingInstruction::data()

The `data` method returns the contents of the `DomProcessingInstruction` object. If the complete processing instruction appears as `<?phpphp phpinfo(); ?>` in the document, this method returns `phpinfo();`.

### string DomProcessingInstruction::target()

The `target` method returns the target of the `DomProcessingInstruction` object. If the complete processing instruction appears as `<?phpphp phpinfo(); ?>` in the document, this method returns `php`.

### object domxml_new_doc(string version)

The `domxml_new_doc` function returns a `DomDocument` object with the XML version set to the given `version` argument.

### object domxml_open_file(string file)

The `domxml_open_file` function loads an XML document from a file and returns a `DomDocument` object.

### object domxml_open_mem(string document)

The `domxml_open_mem` function loads an XML document from a string and returns a `DomDocument` object.

### string domxml_version()

The `domxml_version` function returns the version of the XML library.

### object domxml_xmltree(string document)

The `domxml_xmltree` function reads an entire XML document and returns the root node. Each node contains a `children` property, which is an array of objects. The objects also include the properties defined by the DOM specification.

You cannot use these objects with the method discussed in this section.

### object domxml_xslt_stylesheet(string document)

The `domxml_xslt_stylesheet` function returns a `DomXsltStyleSheet` object given the contents of an XSL document.

### string domxml_xslt_version()

The `domxml_xslt_version` function returns a string representing the version of the XSLT library compiled into PHP.

### object domxml_xslt_stylesheet_doc(object document)

The `domxml_xslt_stylesheet_doc` function returns a `DomXsltStyleSheet` object given a `DomDocument` object.

### object domxml_xslt_stylesheet_file(string file)

The `domxml_xslt_stylesheet_file` function returns a `DomXsltStyleSheet` object given a path to a file.

### object DomXsltStylesheet::process(object document, array parameters, boolean xpath_parameters, string profile_file)

The `process` method (Listing 20.9) applies a style sheet to a `DomDocument` object. The optional `parameters` argument should be an associative array matching parameters needed by the style sheet. The optional `xpath_parameters` argument specifies whether the parameters are plain strings or XPath expressions. Set the optional `profile_file` argument with a path, and PHP writes profiling information.

---

**Listing 20.9**  *DomXsltStyleSheet::process*

```php
<?php
    //load a document
    $dom = domxml_open_file("corephp.xml");

    //load a style sheet
    $xslt = domxml_xslt_stylesheet_file("corephp.xsl");

    //apply the stylesheet to the document
    $dom2 = $xslt->process($dom, array('myParam'=>'use this'));
```

**Listing 20.9** *DomXsltStyleSheet::process (cont.)*

```
    //dump the styled document
    print($dom2->dump_mem());

    print($xslt->result_dump_mem($dom2));
?>
```

### DomXsltStylesheet::result_dump_file(object document, string filename, integer compression)

The `result_dump_file` method dumps a `DomDocument` object returned by the `process` method into a file. The optional `compression` argument sets the level of GZIP compression applied to the file.

Unlike `DomDocument:dump_file`, this method does not force the output document into being a well-formed XML document.

### string DomXsltStylesheet::result_dump_mem(object document)

The `result_dump_mem` method returns a string containing a styled `DomDocument`. Unlike `DomDocument:dump_file`, this method does not force the output document into being a well-formed XML document.

### array XPathContext::xpath_eval(string xpath, object node)

The `xpath_eval` method (Listing 20.10) returns an array of `XPathObject` objects matching the `xpath` argument. Use the optional `node` argument for expressions that require an additional context.

`XPathObject` objects contain no methods. The `nodeset` property is an array of nodes objects.

**Listing 20.10** *XPathContext::xpath_eval*

```
<?php
    //load the document
    $dom = domxml_open_file("corephp.xml");

    //create xpath context
    $context = xpath_new_context($dom);

    //find title
    $xpath = $context->xpath_eval("//title");

    //print contents
    print($xpath->nodeset[0]->get_content());
?>
```

**boolean XPathContext::xpath_register_ns(string prefix, string uri)**

The `xpath_register_ns` method registers the given namespace.

**object xpath_new_context(object document)**

The `xpath_new_context` function returns an `XPathContext` object for the given `DomDocument` object.

**xptr_new_context**

You may use `xptr_new_context` as an alias to `xpath_new_context`.

# 20.2  Expat XML

The functions in this section wrap the Expat library developed by James Clark <http://www.jclark.com/xml/>. This library is part of the PHP distribution, and its purpose is parsing XML documents. A stream of data is fed to the parser. As complete parts of the data are recognized, events are triggered. These parts are the tags and the data they surround. You register the events with a handler, a function you write. You may specify FALSE for the name of any handler, and those events will be ignored.

Stig Bakken added the XML extension to PHP.

**string utf8_decode(string data)**

The `utf8_decode` function takes UTF-8 text and returns ISO-8859-1 text.

**string utf8_encode(string data)**

The `utf8_encode` function returns the `data` argument as UTF-8 text.

**string xml_error_string(integer error)**

The `xml_error_string` function returns the description for the given error code.

**integer xml_get_current_byte_index(resource parser)**

The `xml_get_current_byte_index` function returns the number of bytes parsed so far.

**integer xml_get_current_column_number(resource parser)**

The `xml_get_current_column_number` function returns the column number in the source file where the parser last read data. This function is useful for reporting where an error occurred.

## integer xml_get_current_line_number(resource parser)

The `xml_get_current_line_number` function returns the line number in the source file where the parser last read data. This function is useful for reporting where an error occurred.

## integer xml_get_error_code(resource parser)

The `xml_get_error_code` function returns the last error code generated on the given parser. Constants are defined for all the errors. They are listed in Table 20.2. If no error has occurred, `XML_ERROR_NONE` is returned. If given an invalid parser identifier, `FALSE` is returned.

**Table 20.2** XML Error Constants

| |
|---|
| XML_ERROR_ASYNC_ENTITY |
| XML_ERROR_ATTRIBUTE_EXTERNAL_ENTITY_REF |
| XML_ERROR_BAD_CHAR_REF |
| XML_ERROR_BINARY_ENTITY_REF |
| XML_ERROR_DUPLICATE_ATTRIBUTE |
| XML_ERROR_EXTERNAL_ENTITY_HANDLING |
| XML_ERROR_INCORRECT_ENCODING |
| XML_ERROR_INVALID_TOKEN |
| XML_ERROR_JUNK_AFTER_DOC_ELEMENT |
| XML_ERROR_MISPLACED_XML_PI |
| XML_ERROR_NONE |
| XML_ERROR_NO_ELEMENTS |
| XML_ERROR_NO_MEMORY |
| XML_ERROR_PARAM_ENTITY_REF |
| XML_ERROR_PARTIAL_CHAR |
| XML_ERROR_RECURSIVE_ENTITY_REF |
| XML_ERROR_SYNTAX |
| XML_ERROR_TAG_MISMATCH |
| XML_ERROR_UNCLOSED_CDATA_SECTION |
| XML_ERROR_UNCLOSED_TOKEN |
| XML_ERROR_UNDEFINED_ENTITY |
| XML_ERROR_UNKNOWN_ENCODING |

## boolean xml_parse(resource parser, string data, boolean final)

The `xml_parse` function scans over data and calls handlers you have registered. The size of the `data` argument is not limited. You could parse an entire file or a few bytes at a time. A typical use involves fetching data within a `while` loop.

The `final` argument is optional. It tells the parser that the data you are passing is the end of the file.

## boolean xml_parse_into_struct(resource parser, string data, array structure, array index)

The `xml_parse_info_struct` function (Listing 20.11) parses an entire document and creates an array to describe it. You must pass the `structure` argument as a reference. Elements numbered from zero will be added to it. Each element will contain an associative array indexed by `tag`, `type`, `level`, and `value`. The `index` argument is optional. You must pass it by reference as well. It will contain elements indexed by distinct tags found in the XML file. The value of each element will be a list of integers. These integers are indices into the `structure` array. It allows you to index the elements of the `structure` array that match a given tag.

If you set any handlers, they will be called when you use `xml_parse_into_struct`.

**Listing 20.11**  *xml_parse_into_struct*

```php
<?php
    //create parser
    if(!($parser = xml_parser_create()))
    {
        print("Could not create parser!<br>");
        exit();
    }

    //get entire file
    $data = file_get_contents("corephp.xml");

    //parse file into array
    xml_parse_into_struct($parser, $data, $structure, $index);

    //destroy parser
    xml_parser_free($parser);
```

**Listing 20.11** *xml_parse_into_struct (cont.)*

```
print("Structure:<br>" .
    "<table border=\"1\">" .
    "<tr>" .
    "<th>tag</th>" .
    "<th>type</th>" .
    "<th>level</th>" .
    "<th>value</th>" .
    "<tr>");

foreach($structure as $s)
{
    if(!isset($s["value"]))
    {
        $s["value"] = "";
    }

    print("<tr>" .
        "<td>{$s["tag"]}</td>" .
        "<td>{$s["type"]}</td>" .
        "<td>{$s["level"]}</td>" .
        "<td>{$s["value"]}</td>" .
        "<tr>");
}

print("</table>");

print("Element Reference:<br>");
foreach($index as $key=>$value)
{
    print("$key:");
    foreach($value as $i)
    {
        print(" $i");
    }
    print("<br>");
}
?>
```

### resource xml_parser_create(string encoding)

Calling xml_parser_create is the first step in parsing an XML document. An identifier to be used with most of the other functions is returned. The optional encoding argument allows you to specify the character set used by the parser. The three character sets accepted are ISO-8859-1, US-ASCII, and UTF-8. The default is ISO-8859-1.

### resource xml_parser_create_ns(string encoding, string separator)

The `xml_parser_create_ns` function creates a parser, as `xml_parser_create` does, with the addition of processing namespaces. The optional `separator` argument specifies a single character used to separate name parts.

### boolean xml_parser_free(resource parser)

The `xml_parser_free` function releases the memory being used by the parser.

### value xml_parser_get_option(resource parser, integer option)

The `xml_parser_get_option` function returns an option's current value. Table 20.3 lists the available options.

**Table 20.3**   XML Option Constants

| |
| --- |
| XML_OPTION_CASE_FOLDING |
| XML_OPTION_SKIP_TAGSTART |
| XML_OPTION_SKIP_WHITE |
| XML_OPTION_TARGET_ENCODING |

### xml_parser_set_option(resource parser, integer option, value data)

Use `xml_parser_set_option` to change the value of an option. Table 20.3 lists the available options.

### boolean xml_set_character_data_handler(resource parser, string function)

Character data is the text that appears between tags, and `xml_set_character_data_handler` sets the function that executes when it is encountered. Character data may span many lines and may cause several events. PHP will not concatenate the data for you.

The function specified in the `function` argument must take two arguments. The first is the parser identifier, an integer. The second is a string containing the character data.

You may also specify the handler function as a class method or an object method by supplying an array of two elements. The first element may be the name of a class or an instantiation. The second element must be the name of the method.

### boolean xml_set_default_handler(resource parser, string function)

The `xml_set_default_handler` function captures any text not handled by the other handlers. This includes the DTD declaration and the XML tag.

The function specified in the `function` argument must take two arguments. The first is the parser identifier, an integer. The second is a string containing the data.

You may also specify the handler function as a class method or an object method by supplying an array of two elements. The first element may be the name of a class or an instantiation. The second element must be the name of the method.

### boolean xml_set_element_handler(resource parser, string start, string end)

Use `xml_set_element_handler` (Listing 20.12) to assign the two functions that handle start tags and end tags.

The `start` argument must name a function you've created that takes three arguments. The first function is the parser identifier. The second is the name of the start tag found. The third is an array of the attributes for the start tag. The indices of this array are the attribute names. The elements are in the same order as they appeared in the XML.

The second function handles end tags. It takes two arguments, the first of which is the parser identifier. The other is the name of the tag.

You may also specify the handler functions as class methods or object methods by supplying an array of two elements. The first element may be the name of a class or an instantiation. The second element must be the name of the method.

| Listing 20.12 | `xml_set_element_handler` |
|---|---|

```php
<?php
    /*
    ** define functions
    */
    function cdataHandler($parser, $data)
    {
        print($data);
    }

    function startHandler($parser, $name, $attributes)
    {
```

**Listing 20.12**   *xml_set_element_handler (cont.)*

```
    switch($name)
    {
        case 'EXAMPLE':
            print("<hr>\n");
            break;
        case 'TITLE':
            print("<b>");
            break;
        case 'CODE':
            print("<pre>");
            break;
        default:
            //ignore other tags
    }
}

function endHandler($parser, $name)
{
    switch($name)
    {
        case 'EXAMPLE':
            print("<hr>\n");
            break;
        case 'TITLE';
            print("</b>");
            break;
        case 'CODE':
            print("</pre>");
            break;
        default:
            //ignore other tags
    }
}

function piHandler($parser, $target, $data)
{
    if($target == "php")
    {
        eval($data);
    }
    else
    {
        print(htmlentities($data));
    }
}
```

**Listing 20.12**   *xml_set_element_handler (cont.)*

```
function defaultHandler($parser, $data)
{
    global $defaultText;

    $defaultText .= $data;
}

function ndataHandler($parser, $name, $base, $systemID,
    $publicID, $notation)
{
    print("<!--\n");
    print("NDATA\n");
    print("Entity: $name\n");
    print("Base: $base\n");
    print("System ID: $systemID\n");
    print("Public ID: $publicID\n");
    print("Notation: $notation\n");
    print("-->\n");
}

function notationHandler($parser, $name, $base, $systemID,
    $publicID)
{
    print("<!--\n");
    print("Notation: $name\n");
    print("Base: $base\n");
    print("System ID: $systemID\n");
    print("Public ID: $publicID\n");
    print("-->\n");
}

function externalHandler($parser, $name, $base, $systemID,
    $publicID)
{
    //here you could create another parser
    print("<!--Loading $systemID-->\n");

    return(TRUE);
}


/*
** Initialize
*/
```

| Listing 20.12 | *xml_set_element_handler (cont.)* |
|---|---|

```
//create parser
if(!($parser = xml_parser_create()))
{
    print("Could not create parser!<br>\n");
    exit();
}

//register handlers
xml_set_character_data_handler($parser, "cdataHandler");
xml_set_element_handler($parser, "startHandler",
    "endHandler");
xml_set_processing_instruction_handler($parser, "piHandler");
xml_set_default_handler($parser, "defaultHandler");
xml_set_unparsed_entity_decl_handler($parser, "ndataHandler");
xml_set_notation_decl_handler($parser, "notationHandler");
xml_set_external_entity_ref_handler($parser,
    "externalHandler");


/*
** Parse file
*/
if(!($fp = fopen("corephp.xml", "r")))
{
    print("Couldn't open corephp.xml!<br>\n");
    xml_parser_free($parser);
    exit();
}

while($line = fread($fp, 1024))
{
    if(!xml_parse($parser, $line, feof($fp)))
    {
    //Error, so print full info
        print("ERROR: " .
        xml_error_string(xml_get_error_code($parser)) .
        " at line " .
        xml_get_current_line_number($parser) .
        ", column " .
        xml_get_current_column_number($parser) .
        ", byte " .
        xml_get_current_byte_index($parser) .
        "<BR>\n");
    }
}
```

| Listing 20.12 | *xml_set_element_handler (cont.)* |

```
//destroy parser
xml_parser_free($parser);

print("Text handled by the default handler:\n");
print("<pre>" . htmlentities($defaultText) . "</pre>\n");
?>
```

### boolean xml_set_end_namespace_decl_handler(resource parser, string function)

The xml_set_end_namespace_decl_handler function handles when PHP finds the end of a namespace declaration. The handler should receive one argument. It receives the prefix.

You may also specify the handler function as a class method or an object method by supplying an array of two elements. The first element may be the name of a class or an instantiation. The second element must be the name of the method.

### boolean xml_set_external_entity_ref_handler(resource parser, string function)

XML entities follow the form of HTML entities. They start with an ampersand and end with a semicolon. Between these two characters is the name of the entity. An external entity is defined in another file. This takes the form <!ENTITY externalEntity SYSTEM "entities.xml"> in your XML file. Each time the entity appears in the body of the XML file, the handler you specify in xml_set_external_entity_ref_handler is called.

The handler function must take five arguments. First is the parser identifier. Next is a string containing the names of the entities open for this parser. Then come the base, the system ID, and the public ID.

You may also specify the handler function as a class method or an object method by supplying an array of two elements. The first element may be the name of a class or an instantiation. The second element must be the name of the method.

### boolean xml_set_notation_decl_handler(resource parser, string function)

The handler registered with xml_set_notation_decl_handler receives notation declarations. These are formed like <!NOTATION jpg SYSTEM "/usr/local/bin/jview"> and are meant to suggest a program for handling a data type.

The handler must take five arguments, the first of which is the parser identifier. The second is the name of the notation entity. The rest are base, system ID, and public ID, in that order.

You may also specify the handler function as a class method or an object method by supplying an array of two elements. The first element may be the name of a class or an instantiation. The second element must be the name of the method.

### xml_set_object(resource parser, object container)

The xml_set_object function (Listing 20.13) associates an object with a parser. You must pass the parser identifier and a reference to an object. This is best done within the object using the this variable. After using this function, PHP will call methods of the object instead of the functions in the global scope when you name handlers.

| Listing 20.13 | *xml_set_object* |
| --- | --- |

```php
<?php
    class myParser
    {
        var $parser;

        function parse($filename)
        {
            //create parser
            if(!($this->parser = xml_parser_create()))
            {
                print("Could not create parser!<br>");
                exit();
            }

            //associate parser with this object
            xml_set_object($this->parser, $this);

            //register handlers
            xml_set_character_data_handler($this->parser,
                "cdataHandler");
            xml_set_element_handler($this->parser,
                "startHandler", "endHandler");
```

**Listing 20.13**   *xml_set_object (cont.)*

```
    /*
    ** Parse file
    */
    if(!($fp = fopen($filename, "r")))
    {
        print("Couldn't open example.xml!<br>");
        xml_parser_free($this->parser);
        return;
    }

    while($line = fread($fp, 1024))
    {
        xml_parse($this->parser, $line, feof($fp));
    }

    //destroy parser
    xml_parser_free($this->parser);
}


function cdataHandler($parser, $data)
{
    print($data);
}

function startHandler($parser, $name, $attributes)
{
    switch($name)
    {
        case 'EXAMPLE':
            print("<hr>");
            break;
        case 'TITLE':
            print("<b>");
            break;
        case 'CODE':
            print("<pre>");
            break;
        default:
            //ignore other tags
    }
}
```

| Listing 20.13 | *xml_set_object (cont.)* |
|---|---|

```
        function endHandler($parser, $name)
        {
            switch($name)
            {
                case 'EXAMPLE':
                    print("<hr>");
                    break;
                case 'TITLE';
                    print("</b>");
                    break;
                case 'CODE':
                    print("</pre>");
                    break;
                default:
                    //ignore other tags
            }
        }
    }

    $p = new myParser;
    $p->parse("corephp.xml");
?>
```

### boolean xml_set_processing_instruction_handler(resource parser, string function)

The `xml_set_processing_instruction_handler` function registers the function that handles tags of the following form: `<?phptarget data?>`. This may be familiar; it's how PHP code is embedded in files. The `target` keyword identifies the type of data inside the tag. Everything else is data.

The `function` argument must specify a function that takes three arguments. The first is the parser identifier. The second is the target. The third is the data.

You may also specify the handler function as a class method or an object method by supplying an array of two elements. The first element may be the name of a class or an instantiation. The second element must be the name of the method.

### xml_set_start_namespace_decl_handler(resource parser, string function)

The `xml_set_start_namespace_decl_handler` function handles the start of a namespace declaration. The handler should accept two arguments. The first receives the prefix and the second receives the URI.

You may also specify the handler function as a class method or an object method by supplying an array of two elements. The first element may be the name of a class or an instantiation. The second element must be the name of the method.

### boolean xml_set_unparsed_entity_decl_handler(resource parser, string function)

This function specifies a handler for external entities that contain an NDATA element. These take the form of `<!ENTITY php-pic SYSTEM "php.jpg" NDATA jpg>`, and they specify an external file.

You may also specify the handler function as a class method or an object method by supplying an array of two elements. The first element may be the name of a class or an instantiation. The second element must be the name of the method.

# 20.3 WDDX

The Web Distributed Data Exchange, or WDDX, is an XML language for describing data in a way that facilitates moving it from one programming environment to another. The intent is to relieve difficulty associated with sending data between applications that represent data differently. Traditionally this has been done by designing special interfaces for each case. For instance, you may decide that your PERL script will write out its three return data separated with tabs, using a regular expression to extract the text you later convert to integers. WDDX intends to unify the effort into a single interface. If you wish to learn more about WDDX, visit the home site at `<http://www.openwddx.org/>`.

Andrei Zmievski added WDDX support to PHP.

### wddx_add_vars(integer packet_identifier, string variable, ...)

The `wddx_add_vars` function is one of three functions for creating packets incrementally. After creating a packet with `wddx_packet_start`, you may add as many variables as you wish with `wddx_add_vars`. After the `packet_identifier` argument, you may pass strings with the names of variables in the local scope or arrays of strings. If necessary, PHP will explore multidimensional arrays for names of variables. The variables will be added to the packet until you use `wddx_packet_end` to create the actual packet as a string.

### value wddx_deserialize(string packet)

The wddx_deserialize function (Listing 20.14) returns a variable representing the data contained in a WDDX packet. If the packet contains a single value, it will be returned as an appropriate type. If the packet contains multiple values in a structure, an associative array will be returned.

---

**Listing 20.14**    *wddx_deserialize*

```php
<?php
    //simulate WDDX packet
    $packet = "<wddxPacket version='1.0'>" .
        "<data>" .
        "<string>Core PHP Programming</string>" .
        "</data>" .
        "</wddxPacket>";

    //pull data out of packet
    $data = wddx_deserialize($packet);

    //test the type of the variable
    if(is_array($data))
    {
        //loop over each value
        foreach($data as $key=>$value)
        {
            print("$key: $value<br>\n");
        }
    }
    else
    {
        //simply print the value
        print("$data<br>\n");
    }
?>
```

---

### string wddx_packet_end(integer packet_identifier)

The wddx_packet_end function returns a string for the packet created with wddx_packet_start and wddx_add_vars.

### integer wddx_packet_start(string comment)

The `wddx_packet_start` function (Listing 20.15) returns an identifier to a WDDX packet you can build as you go. The optional `comment` argument will be placed in the packet if supplied. Use the returned packet identifier with `wddx_add_vars` and `wddx_packet_end`.

| Listing 20.15 | *wddx_packet_start* |
|---|---|

```php
<?php
    //create test data
    $Name = "Leon Atkinson";
    $Email = "corephp@leonatkinson.com";
    $Residence = "Martinez";

    $Info = array("Email", "Residence");

    //start packet
    $wddx = wddx_packet_start("Core PHP Programming");

    //add some variables to the packet
    wddx_add_vars($wddx, "Name", $Info);

    //create packet
    $packet = wddx_packet_end($wddx);

    //print packet for demonstration purposes
    print($packet);
?>
```

### string wddx_serialize_value(value data, string comment)

The `wddx_serialize_value` function creates a WDDX packet containing a single value. The data will be encoded with no name. The optional comment field will be added to the packet as well.

### string wddx_serialize_vars(string variable, …)

Use `wddx_serialize_vars` (Listing 20.16) to create a packet containing many variables. You may specify any number of variable names in the local scope. Each argument may be a string or an array. PHP will recursively explore multi-dimensional arrays for more names of variables if necessary. A WDDX packet is returned.

**Listing 20.16** *wddx_serialize_vars*

```php
<?php
    //create test data
    $Name = "Leon Atkinson";
    $Email = "corephp@leonatkinson.com";
    $Residence = "Martinez";

    $Info = array("Email", "Residence");

    //print packet
    print(wddx_serialize_vars("Name", $Info));
?>
```

# ALGORITHMS

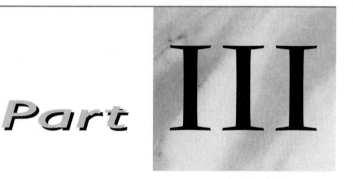

Part **III**

An algorithm is a recipe for solving a problem. This section discusses broad problems in computer science and how to solve them, all in the context of PHP. These problems are inherent in any programming endeavor, but in most cases PHP makes handling them easier. However, the particular circumstances of the Web offer the seasoned programmer a new set of challenges. This section brings these issues to your attention.

Chapter 21 examines sorting and searching, along with a related topic, random numbers. Although PHP has built-in functions for sorting data, this chapter explores the theory behind sorting. This gives you the knowledge to code custom sorting functions when the need arises.

Chapter 22 discusses parsing and string evaluation. Much of this chapter is about regular expressions, a powerful way to describe patterns that are compared to strings. These are useful for validating user input.

Chapter 23 describes integrating PHP with a database. MySQL is used in the examples because it's Open Source. Databases allow you to manipulate data in powerful ways and are necessary for many Web applications.

Chapter 24 is about network issues, such as sending HTTP headers. Because PHP scripts execute as Web pages, network issues appear frequently.

Chapter 25 explores generating graphics with PHP. It develops examples that create buttons and graphs dynamically.

# SORTING, SEARCHING, AND RANDOM NUMBERS

**Topics in This Chapter**

- Sorting
- Built-In Sorting Functions
- Sorting with a Comparison Function
- Searching
- Indexing
- Random Numbers
- Random Identifiers
- Choosing Banner Ads

# Chapter 21

Sorting and searching are two fundamental concepts of computer science. They are closely tied to almost every application: databases, compilers, even the World Wide Web. The more information you have online, the more important it becomes to know exactly where that information is.

Admittedly, sorting is not as serious a topic in the context of PHP as it is for C++. PHP offers some very powerful sorting functions, even one that allows you to define how to compare two elements. This chapter deals with some classic problems of computer science. You may be interested in learning about the concepts that become useful as you use more generalized languages like C or Ada. But further than that, these concepts will help you understand the internal workings of databases, Web servers, even PHP itself. You will be more capable of dealing with the inevitable problem unsolved by any built-in PHP function.

This chapter also discusses random numbers, which are useful for putting data out of order. The practical application of this usually takes the form of unique identifiers, for files or sessions.

## 21.1  Sorting

To sort means to put a set of like items into order. The rules of ordering can be simple, such as strings sorted by the order of the alphabet. They could be complex, such as sorting addresses first by country, then by state, then by city. The process of sorting can take several forms but always involves comparing two elements with a set of rules for ordering. The result of the comparison determines whether the two items are in order or out of order, therefore needing to be swapped.

There are three classes of sorts: exchange, insert, and select. In an exchange method, two elements are compared and possibly exchanged. This process continues until the list is in order. In an insert method, the elements are removed and placed in another list, one by one. Each time an element is moved, it is inserted into the correct position. When all elements are moved, the list is in order. A selection sort involves building a second list by scanning the first and repeatedly selecting the lowest value. Insertion and selection sorts are two sides of a coin. The former scans the new list; the latter scans the old list.

As I said earlier, a sorting algorithm is essentially comparison and possible movement of elements in a list. On average, moving an element takes the same amount of time, no matter which algorithm you use. Likewise, the comparison is independent of the actual sort. If we take these to be constants, then the most important question to ask about each algorithm is, How many times does the algorithm perform either of these costly actions?

Of course, the sort must be kept in context with the data. Some algorithms perform very well when the data are completely unordered but are slow when the data are already in order or in reverse order. Some sorts perform very poorly when there are many elements; others have such an overhead as to be inappropriate for smaller data sets. Like any technician, the programmer matches the tool to the job.

## 21.2  Built-In Sorting Functions

Usually, it will not be necessary to write your own sort functions. PHP offers several functions for sorting arrays. The most basic is `sort`. This function is described, along with the other sorting functions in Chapter 11. It's instructive to compare `sort` to `rsort`, `asort`, and `ksort`.

The `sort` function puts all the elements in the array in order from lowest to highest. If the array contains any strings, then this means ordering them by the ASCII codes of each character. If the array contains only numbers, then they are ordered by their values. The indices—the values used to reference the elements— are discarded and replaced with integers starting with zero. This is an important effect, which Listing 21.1 demonstrates; Figure 21.1 shows the output. Notice that although I use some numbers and a string to index the array, after I sort it, all the elements are numbered zero through four. Keep this in mind if you ever need to clean up the indices of an array.

| Listing 21.1 | *Sorting with* `sort` |
|---|---|

```php
<?php
    /*
    ** Fill fruit array with random values
    */
    $fruit[1] = "Apple";
    $fruit[13] = "apple";
    $fruit[64] = "Blueberry";
    $fruit[3] = "pear";
    $fruit["last"] = "Watermelon";

    //sort the array
    sort($fruit);

    //dump array to show new order
    print("<pre>");
    print_r($fruit);
    print("</pre>\n");
?>
```

```
Array
(
    [0] => Apple
    [1] => Blueberry
    [2] => Watermelon
    [3] => apple
    [4] => pear
)
```

**Figure 21.1**   Output of Listing 21.1.

Another point worth noting in Listing 21.1 is the order of the output: Apple, Blueberry, Watermelon, apple, pear. A dictionary might list apple just before or just after Apple, but the ASCII code for A is 65. The ASCII code for a is 97. Appendix B lists all the ASCII codes. Later in this chapter I'll explain how to code a case-insensitive sort.

The `rsort` function works exactly like `sort` except that it orders elements in the reverse order. Try modifying the code in Listing 21.1 by changing `sort` to `rsort`.

Two other two sort functions, `asort` and `arsort`, work in a slightly different way. They preserve the relationship between the index and the element. This is most useful when you have an associative array. If the array is indexed by numbers, you probably do not want to preserve their indices. On the other hand, what if you did? Listing 21.2 illustrates a possible scenario; output is shown in Figure 21.2.

---

**Listing 21.2**   *Using the asort function*

```php
<?php
    // Fill and array in order of preference
    $pasta = array(1=>"ravioli",
        "spaghetti",
        "vermicelli",
        "lasagna",
        "gnocchi",
        "rigatoni");

    // Sort the array, keeping indices
    asort($pasta);

    // Print array, now in alphabetical order
    foreach($pasta as $rank=>$name)
    {
        print("$name was ranked number $rank<br>\n");
    }
?>
```

---

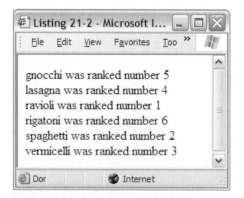

**Figure 21.2**   Output of Listing 21.2.

Listing 21.2 gets each element in the order in which the elements exist in memory. They retain their original indices, which are the numbers starting with zero used when the elements were added to the array. If I had used `arsort`, the order would have been the exact opposite. Listing 21.3 is perhaps a more typical use of these functions. It is important to keep the elements in the array returned by `getdate` associated with their indices. Listing 21.3 sorts the array in reverse order by the elements. It may not be particularly useful but illustrates the use of this function. The output is shown in Figure 21.3.

| Listing 21.3 | *Using the `arsort` function* |
|---|---|

```php
<?php
    //get an array from getdate
    $today = getdate();

    //Sort the array, keeping indices
    arsort($today);

    //Print array, now in descending order
    print("<pre>");
    print_r($today);
    print("</pre>\n");
?>
```

**Figure 21.3**  Output of Listing 21.3.

The last sorting function I want to discuss in this section is `ksort`. This function sorts an array on the values of the indices. I've modified the code in Listing 21.3 to use `ksort` instead of `arsort`. Notice that now all the elements are in the order of their indices, or keys.

The `ksort` function is perhaps most useful in situations where you have an associative array and you don't have complete control over the contents. In Listing 21.4 the script gets an array generated by the `getdate` function. If you run it with the `ksort` line commented out, you will see that the order is arbitrary. It's simply the order chosen when the function was coded. I could have typed a couple of lines for each element based on the list of elements found in the description of the `getdate` function in Chapter 14. A more readable solution is to sort on the keys and to print each element in a loop. As you might have guessed, the `krsort` function sorts an array by its indices in reverse.

---

**Listing 21.4**    *Using the `ksort` function*

```php
<?php
    // get an array from getdate
    $today = getdate();

    // Sort the array, keeping indices
    ksort($today);

    //Print array, now ordered by keys
    print("<pre>");
    print_r($today);
    print("</pre>\n");
?>
```

---

# 21.3  Sorting with a Comparison Function

The built-in sorting functions are appropriate in the overwhelming majority of situations. If your problem requires a sort that performs better than the one used in the built-in functions, you are faced with coding your own. If your problem is that you need to compare complex elements, such as objects or multidimensional arrays, the solution is to write a comparison function and plug it into the `usort` function.

The `usort` function allows you to sort an array using your own comparison function. Your comparison function must accept two values and return an integer. The two arguments are compared, and if a negative number is returned, then the values are considered to be in order. If zero is returned, they are considered to be equal. A positive number signifies that the numbers are out of order.

In Listing 21.5, I've created a multidimensional array with three elements for name, title, and hourly rate. Sometimes I want to be able list employees by name, but other times I might want to list them by title or how much they make per hour. To solve this problem, I've written three comparison functions. Output is shown in Figure 21.4.

| Listing 21.5 | *Using the usort function* |
|---|---|

```php
<?php
    class EmployeeTracker
    {
        static $title = array(
            "President"=>1,
            "Executive"=>2,
            "Manager"=>3,
            "Programmer"=>4
            );

        public $employees;

        public function __construct($data)
        {
            $this->employees = $data;
        }

        // byName
        // compare employees based on name
        function byName($left, $right)
        {
            return(strcmp($left[0], $right[0]));
        }

        // byTitle
        // compare employees based on title
        function byTitle($left, $right)
        {
            if($left[1] == $right[1])
            {
                return(0);
            }
            else
            {
                return(EmployeeTracker::$title[$left[1]] -
                    EmployeeTracker::$title[$right[1]]);
            }
        }
    }
```

| Listing 21.5 | *Using the* usort *function (cont.)* |

```php
    // bySalary
    // compare employees based on salary, then name
    function bySalary($left, $right)
    {
        if($left[2] == $right[2])
        {
            return(byName($left, $right));
        }
        else
        {
            return($right[2] - $left[2]);
        }
    }

    // printEmployees
    // send entire list of employees to browser
    function printEmployees()
    {
        foreach($this->employees as $value)
        {
            printf("%s (%s) %.2f/Hour <br>\n",
                $value[0],
                $value[1],
                $value[2]);
        }
    }
}

// Create some employees (Name, Title, Rate)
$e = new EmployeeTracker(array(
    array("Mckillop, Jeff", "Executive", 50),
    array("Porter, Carl", "Manager", 45),
    array("Marazzani, Rick", "Manager", 35),
    array("Dibetta, Bob", "Programmer", 65),
    array("Atkinson, Leon", "President", 100)));

print("<b>Unsorted</b><br>\n");
$e->printEmployees();

print("<B>Sorted by Name</B><br>\n");
usort($e->employees, array($e, "byName"));
$e->printEmployees();
```

**Listing 21.5**    *Using the* usort *function (cont.)*

```
    print("<b>Sorted by Title</b><br>\n");
    usort($e->employees, array($e, "byTitle"));
    $e->printEmployees();

    print("<b>Sorted by Rate</b><br>\n");
    usort($e->employees, array($e, "bySalary"));
    $e->printEmployees();
?>
```

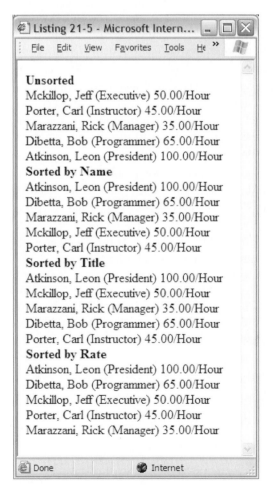

**Figure 21.4**    Output of Listing 21.5.

The `byName` function is a simple wrapper for `strcmp`. Names will be ordered by ASCII code. The `byTitle` function assigns an integer value to each title and then returns the comparison of these integers. The `bySalary` function compares the wage element, but if two employees make the same amount of money per hour, their names are compared.

# 21.4  Searching

Sorting organizes information into a form that aids in finding the exact piece being looked for. If you need to look up a phone number, it's easy to flip through the pages of a phone book until you find the approximate area where the number might be. With a bit of scanning you can find the number, because all the names are in order. For most of us, this process is automatic.

If you want to duplicate this process inside a PHP script, you have to think about each of the steps. The simplest way is to start at the beginning and look at every entry until you find the one you want. If you get to the end and haven't found it, it must not exist. I don't have to tell you this is probably the worst way to search, but sometimes this is all you have. If the data are unsorted, there is no better way.

You can dramatically improve your search time by doing a binary search. The requirement is that the data be sorted. Luckily, I've shown this to be relatively simple. The binary search involves repeatedly dividing the list into a half that won't contain the target value and a half that will.

To perform a binary search, start in the middle of the list. If the element in the middle precedes the element you are searching for, you can be sure it's in the half of the list that follows the middle element. You will now have half as many elements to search through. If you repeat these steps, you will zero in on your targeted value very quickly. To be precise, the worst case is that it will take log $n$, or the base-two logarithm of the number of elements in the data. If you had 128 numbers, it would take at most seven guesses. Listing 21.6 puts this idea into action.

| Listing 21.6 | *A binary search* |
| --- | --- |

```php
<?php
    // byName
    // compare employees based on name
    function byName($left, $right)
    {
        return(strcmp($left[0], $right[0]));
    }
```

**Listing 21.6**   *A binary search (cont.)*

```php
//Create some employees (Name, Title, Rate)
$employee = array(
    array("Mckillop, Jeff", "Executive", 50),
    array("Porter, Carl", "Instructor", 45),
    array("Marazzani, Rick", "Manager", 35),
    array("Dibetta, Bob", "Programmer", 65),
    array("Atkinson, Leon", "President", 100));

//Sort the list
usort($employee, "byName");

print("<pre>");
print_r($employee);
print("</pre>\n");

//Pick target
$Name = "Porter, Carl";
print("Searching for $Name<br>\n");

//Set range to search in
$lower_limit = 0;
$upper_limit = count($employee) - 1;

//Pick mid-point
$index = floor(($lower_limit + $upper_limit)/2);
while($lower_limit < $upper_limit)
{
    if(strcmp($employee[$index][0], $Name) < 0)
    {
        //Target in upper half
        $lower_limit = $index + 1;
    }
    elseif(strcmp($employee[$index][0], $Name) > 0)
    {
        //Target in lower half
        $upper_limit = $index - 1;
    }
    else
    {
        //Target found
        $lower_limit = $index;
        $upper_limit = $index;
    }
```

| Listing 21.6 | *A binary search (cont.)* |
|---|---|

```
        //Pick mid-point
        $index = floor(($lower_limit + $upper_limit)/2);
    }

    // Print results
    print("Position $index<br>\n");
    print("{$employee[$index][0]} {$employee[$index][1]}<br>\n");
?>
```

# 21.5 Indexing

By sorting the data, you spend time up front, betting it will pay off when you need to search. But even this searching costs something. A binary search may take several steps. When you need to do hundreds of searches, you may look for further improvement in performance. One way is to perform every possible search beforehand, creating an index. A lot of work is done at first, which allows searches to be performed fast.

Let's explore how we can transform the binary search in Listing 21.6 into a single lookup. We want an array that, given a name, returns its position in the original array, so we'll build a list of matches. Refer to the code in Listing 21.7. We won't bother sorting the list. It won't help, because we will be visiting every element of the array. As we visit each element, we create a new array. The index of this array is the name of the employee. Each element of the index will be an array of indices in the employee array. Once the index is created, finding an employee is a single statement. If the name is found in the array, we can retrieve the index values for the employee array.

| Listing 21.7 | *Building an index* |
|---|---|

```
<?php
    //Create some employees (Name, Title, Rate)
    $employee = array(
        array("Mckillop, Jeff", "Executive", 50),
        array("Porter, Carl", "Instructor", 45),
        array("Marazzani, Rick", "Manager", 35),
        array("Dibetta, Bob", "Programmer", 65),
        array("Atkinson, Leon", "President", 100));
```

**Listing 21.7** — *Building an index (cont.)*

```
//build index
$employeeIndex = array();
foreach($employee as $id=>$val)
{
    $employeeIndex[$val[0]] = $id;
}

//where's Carl?
$index = $employeeIndex["Porter, Carl"];
print("Position $index<br>\n");
print("{$employee[$index][0]} {$employee[$index][1]}<br>\n");
?>
```

This example is not very realistic because we're only making one search, and we're building the index with each request. The index needs to be built only once as long as the `employee` array doesn't change. You could save the array to a file, perhaps using PHP serialization functionality, and then load it when needed. I wrote similar code for the FreeTrade project that indexes keywords that appear in pages of a Web site.

Of course, databases present a larger solution to managing data. In most cases, it's best to rely on a database to store large amounts of data, because databases have specialized code for searching and sorting. Databases are discussed in Chapter 23.

# 21.6 Random Numbers

Closely tied to sorting and searching is the generation of random numbers. Often, random numbers are used to put lists out of order. They offer the opportunity to create surprise. They allow you to squeeze more information onto a single page by choosing content randomly for each request. You see this every day on the Web in the form of quotes of the day, banner ads, and session identifiers.

There are two important qualities of truly random numbers: Their distribution is uniform, and each successive value is independent of the previous value. To have a uniform distribution means that no value is generated more often than any other. The idea of independence is that given a sequence of numbers returned by the generator, you should be unable to guess the next. Of course, we can't write an algorithm that really generates independent values. We have to have some formula, which by its nature is predictable. Yet, we can get pretty close using what is called a pseudorandom number generator. These use simple mathematical expressions that return seemingly random numbers. You provide a starting input called a seed. The first call to the function uses this seed for input, and subsequent calls use the previous value. Keep in mind that a seed will begin the same sequence of output values any time it's used. One way to keep things seeming different is to use the number of seconds on the clock to seed the generators.

The standard C library offers the `rand` function for generating random numbers, and PHP wraps it in a function of the same name. You pass upper and lower limits, and integers are returned. You can seed the generator with the `srand` function, or just let the system seed it for you with the current time. Unfortunately, the standard generator on some operating systems can be inadequate. Fortunately, Pedro Melo added a new set of functions to PHP that use the Mersenne twister algorithm.

I won't attempt to describe the algorithm behind the Mersenne Twister algorithm because it's out of the scope of this text. You can visit the home page for more information <http://www.math.keio.ac.jp/~matumoto/emt.html>. You can read a careful description there to convince yourself of the validity of the algorithm if you wish.

Listing 21.8 is a very simple example that generates 100 random numbers between 1 and 100, using the `mt_rand` function. It then computes the average and the median. If the distribution of numbers is uniform, the average and median will be very close. The sample set is really small, though, so you will see lots of variance as you rerun the script. The output is shown in Figure 21.5.

| Listing 21.8 | *Getting random numbers* |
|---|---|

```php
<?php
    // Seed the generator
    mt_srand(doubleval(microtime()) * 100000000);

    // Generate numbers
    print("<h3>Sample Set</h3>\n");
    $size = 100;
    $total = 0;
    for($i=0; $i < $size; $i++)
    {
        $n = mt_rand(1, $size);
        $sample[$i] = $n;
        $total += $n;
        print("$n ");
    }
    print("<br>\n");

    print("Average: " . ($total/$size) . "<br>\n");

    sort($sample);
    print("Median: " . ($sample[intval($size/2)]) . "<br>\n");
?>
```

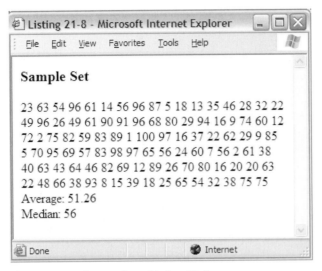

**Figure 21.5**   Output from Listing 21.8.

# 21.7  Random Identifiers

If you ever need to track users through a site, you will need to assign unique identifiers. You can store all the information you know about the user in a database and pass the identifier from page to page either through links or with cookies. You will have to generate these identifiers randomly; otherwise, it is too easy for anyone to masquerade as a legitimate user. Fortunately, random identifiers are easy to generate.

Listing 21.9 illustrates how this works. A pool of characters to use in the session identifier is defined. Characters are picked randomly from the list to build a session identifier of the specified length. That identifier is used inside a link so that it is passed to the next page. This method works for any browser, even Lynx. Chapter 23 discusses the integration of this technique with a database.

It's very important to have random numbers here. Suppose you simply used the seconds on the clock. For an entire second, every session identifier would be the same. And it's very likely many people will be accessing a Web site during a single second. In Listing 21.9, I've used the time on the microsecond clock to seed the random generator, but even this allows the window of opportunity for getting a duplicate session identifier. One way to avoid this situation is to use a lockable resource that holds a seed—for example, a file. Once you lock the file, you can read the seed and write back a new one, at which point you are assured that two concurrent processes never get the same seed.

| Listing 21.9 | *Generating a session identifier* |
|---|---|

```php
<?php
    // SessionID
    // generates a session id
    function getSessionID($length=16)
    {
        // Set pool of possible characters
        $Pool = "ABCDEFGHIJKLMNOPQRSTUVWXYZ";
        $Pool .= "abcdefghijklmnopqrstuvwxyz";
        $lastChar = strlen($Pool) - 1;
        $sid = "";

        for($i = 0; $i < $length; $i++)
        {
            $sid .= $Pool[mt_rand(0, $lastChar)];
        }

        return($sid);
    }

    // Seed the generator
    mt_srand(100000000 * (double)microtime());

    if(isset($_REQUEST['sid']))
    {
        print("Old Session ID was {$_REQUEST['sid']}<br>\n");
    }

    $sid = getSessionID();

    print("<a href=\"{$_SERVER['PHP_SELF']}?sid=$sid\">");
    print("Get Another Session ID");
    print("</a>\n");
?>
```

# 21.8  Choosing Banner Ads

Another use for random numbers is selecting banner ads. Suppose you've signed up three sponsors for your Web site. Each has a single banner you promise to display on an equal proportion of hits to your site. To accomplish this, generate a random number and match each number to a particular banner. In Listing 21.10, I've used a switch statement on a call to mt_rand. In a situation like this, you don't need to worry too much about using good seeds. You simply want a reasonable distribution of the three choices. Someone guessing which banner will display at midnight poses no security risk.

**Listing 21.10**   *Random banner ad*

```php
<?php
    //Seed the generator
    mt_srand(doubleval(microtime()) * 100000000);

    //choose banner
    switch(mt_rand(1,3))
    {
        case 1:
            $bannerURL = "http://www.leonatkinson.com/random/";
            $bannerImage = "leon_banner.png";
            break;
        case 2:
            $bannerURL = "http://www.php.net/";
            $bannerImage = "php_banner.png";
            break;
        default:
            $bannerURL = "http://www.phptr.com/";
            $bannerImage = "phptr_banner.png";
    }

    //display banner
    print("<a href=\"$bannerURL\">");
    print("<img src=\"$bannerImage\" ");
    print("width=\"400\" height=\"148\" border=\"0\">");
    print("</a>");
?>
```

# PARSING AND STRING EVALUATION

**Topics in This Chapter**

- Tokenizing
- Regular Expressions
- Defining Regular Expressions
- Using Regular Expressions in PHP Scripts

# Chapter 22

Parsing is the act of breaking a whole into components, usually a sentence into words. PHP must parse the code you write as a first step in turning a script into an HTML document. There will come a time when you are faced with extracting or verifying data collected in a string. This could be as simple as a tab-delimited list. It could be as complicated as the string a browser uses to identify itself to a Web server. You may choose to tokenize the string, breaking it into pieces. Or you may choose to apply a regular expression. This chapter examines PHP's functions for parsing and string evaluation.

## 22.1 Tokenizing

PHP allows for a simple model for tokenizing a string. Certain characters, of your choice, are considered separators. Strings of characters between separators are considered tokens. You may change the set of separators with each token you pull from a string, which is handy for irregular strings—that is, ones that aren't simply comma-separated lists.

Listing 22.1 accepts a sentence and breaks it into words using the `strtok` function, described in Chapter 12. As far as the script is concerned, a word is surrounded by a space, punctuation, or either end of the sentence. Single and double quotes are left as part of the word. Output is shown in Figure 22.1.

**Listing 22.1**    *Tokenizing a string*

```php
<?php
    /*
    ** If submitted a sentence, parse it
    */
    if(isset($_REQUEST['sentence']))
    {
        $total=0;

        print("<b>Submitted text:</b>");
        print("{$_REQUEST['sentence']}<br>\n<br>\n");

        //set characters that separate tokens
        $separators = " ,!.?";

        //get each token
        for($token = strtok($_REQUEST['sentence'], $separators);
            $token !== FALSE;
            $token = strtok($separators))
        {
            //skip empty tokens
            if($token != "")
            {
                // count each word
                if(!isset($word_count[strtolower($token)]))
                {
                    $word_count[strtolower($token)]=1;
                }
                else
                {
                    $word_count[strtolower($token)]++;
                }
                $total++;
            }
        }

        //first sort by word
        ksort($word_count);

        //next sort by frequency
        arsort($word_count);

        print("<b>$total Words Found</b>\n");
        print("<ul>\n");
        foreach($word_count as $key=>$value)
```

**Listing 22.1**    *Tokenizing a string (cont.)*

```
    {
        print("<li>$key ($value)</li>\n");
    }
    print("</ul>\n");
}

print("<form action=\"{$_SERVER['PHP_SELF']}\" " .
    "method=\"post\">\n");
print("<input name=\"sentence\" size=\"40\">\n");
print("<input type=\"submit\" value=\"Parse\">\n");
print("</form>\n");
?>
```

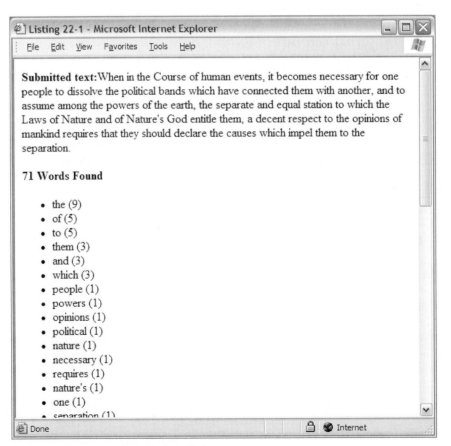

**Figure 22.1**    Output from Listing 22.1.

Note the use of the `for` loop in this example. Instead of incrementing an integer, it gets tokens, one by one. When `strtok` encounters the end of input, it returns FALSE. Your first inclination might be to test for FALSE in the `for` loop with the `!=` operator. Recall that an empty string is considered equivalent to FALSE. If two separators follow each other, `strtok` will return an empty string, as you'd expect. Since we don't want to stop tokenizing at the first repeated separator, we must check for a genuine FALSE with the `!==` operator.

The `strtok` function is useful only in the most simple and structured situations. An example might be reading a tab-delimited text file. The algorithm might be to read a line from a file, pulling each token from the line using the tab character, then continuing by getting the next line from the file.

# 22.2  Regular Expressions

Fortunately, PHP offers something more powerful than the `strtok` function: regular expressions. Written in a language of their own, regular expressions describe patterns that are compared to strings. The PHP source code includes an implementation of regular expressions that conforms to the POSIX 1003.2 standard. This standard allows for expressions of an older style but encourages a modern style that I will describe. All the regular expression functions are described in Chapter 12.

In 1999 Andrei Zmievski added support for regular expressions that follow the style of Perl. They offer two advantages over PHP native regular expressions. They make it easier to copy an expression from a Perl script, and they take less time to execute.

It is beyond the scope of this text to examine regular expressions in depth. It is a subject worthy of a book itself. I will explain the basics as well as demonstrate the various PHP functions that use regular expressions. An excellent resource for learning more about regular expressions is Chapter 2 of Ellie Quigley's *UNIX Shells by Example*. If you are interested in PERL-style regular expressions, check the official PERL documentation site first `<http://www.perldoc.com/perl5.8.0/pod/perlre.html>`. You will then need to read the documentation at the PHP site itself that lists the differences between Perl and the PHP implementation `<http://www.php.net/manual/pcre.pattern.syntax.php>`. There are several differences in the PHP implementation, but most PERL expressions execute unmodified in PHP.

# 22.3  Defining Regular Expressions

At the highest level, a regular expression is one or more branches separated by the vertical bar character ( | ). This character is considered to have the properties of a logical-OR. Any of the branches could match with an evaluated string. Table 22.1 provides a few examples.

**Table 22.1**    Branches in a Regular Expression

| Sample | Description |
| --- | --- |
| Apple | Matches the word apple. |
| apple\|ball | Matches either apple or ball. |
| begin\|end\|break | Matches either begin, end, or break. |

Each branch contains one or more atoms. Characters that modify the number of times the atom may be matched in succession may follow these atoms. An asterisk (*) means the atom can match any number of times. A plus sign (+) means the atom must match at least once. A question mark (?) signifies that the atom may match once or not at all.

Alternatively, the atom may be bound, which means it is followed by curly braces, { and }, that contain integers. If the curly braces contain a single number, then the atom must be matched exactly that number of times. If the curly braces contain a number followed by a comma, the atom must be matched that number of times or more. If the curly braces contain two numbers separated by a comma, the atom must match at least the first number of times, but not more than the second number. See Table 22.2 for some examples of repetition.

**Table 22.2**    Allowing Repetition of Patterns in Regular Expressions

| Sample | Description |
| --- | --- |
| a(b*) | Matches a, ab, abb, . . .—an a plus any number of b's. |
| a(b+) | Matches ab, abb, abbb, . . .—an a plus one or more b's. |
| a(b?) | Matches either a or ab—an a possibly followed by a b. |
| a(b{3}) | Matches only abbb. |
| a(b{2,}) | Matches abb, abbb, abbbb, . . .—an a followed by two or more b's. |
| a(b{2,4}) | Matches abb, abbb, abbbb—an a followed by two to four b's. |

An atom is a series of characters, some having special meaning, others simply standing for a character that must be matched. A period (.) matches any single character. A carat (^) matches the beginning of the string. A dollar sign ($) matches the end of the string. If you need to match one of the special characters (^ . [] $ () | * ? {} \), put a backslash in front of it. In fact, any character preceded by a backslash will be treated literally even if it has no special meaning. Any character with no special meaning will be considered just a character to be matched, backslash or not. You may also group atoms with parentheses so that they are treated as an atom.

Square brackets ([]) are used to specify a range of possible values. This may take the form of a list of legal characters. A range may be specified using the dash character (-). If the list or range is preceded by a carat (^), the meaning is taken to be any character not in the following list or range. Take note of this double meaning for the carat.

In addition to lists and ranges, square brackets may contain a character class. These class names are further surrounded by colons, so that to match any alphabetic character, you write [:alpha:]. The classes are alnum, alpha, blank, cntrl, digit, graph, lower, print, punct, space, upper, and xdigit. You may wish to look at the man page for ctype to get a description of these classes.

Finally, two additional square bracket codes specify the beginning and ending of a word. They are [:<:] and [:>:], respectively. A word in this sense is defined as any sequence of alphanumeric characters and the underscore characters. Table 22.3 shows examples of using square brackets.

**Table 22.3**   Square Brackets in Regular Expressions

| Sample | Description |
|---|---|
| a.c | Matches aac, abc, acc, . . .—any three-character string beginning with an a and ending with a c. |
| ^a.* | Matches any string starting with an a. |
| [a-c]*x$ | Matches x, ax, bx, abax, abcx—any string of letters from the first three letters of the alphabet followed by an x. |
| b[ao]y | Matches only bay or boy. |
| [^Zz]{5} | Matches any string, five characters long, that does not contain either an uppercase or lowercase z. |
| [[:digit:]] | Matches any digit, equivalent to writing [0-9]. |
| [[:<:]]a.* | Matches any word that starts with a. |

# 22.4 Using Regular Expressions in PHP Scripts

The basic function for executing regular expressions is `ereg`. This function evaluates a string against a regular expression, returning TRUE if the pattern described by the regular expression appears in the string. In this minimal form, you can check that a string conforms to a given pattern. For example, you can ensure that a U.S. postal ZIP code is in the proper form of five digits followed by a dash and four more digits. Listing 22.2 demonstrates this idea; Figure 22.2 shows the output.

| Listing 22.2 | *Checking a ZIP code* |
|---|---|

```php
<?php
    /*
    ** Check a ZIP code
    ** This script will test a zip code, which
    ** must be five digits, optionally followed by
    ** a dash and four digits.
    */

    /*
    ** if zip submitted evaluate it
    */
    if(isset($_REQUEST['zip']))
    {
        if(ereg("^([0-9]{5})(-[0-9]{4})?$", $_REQUEST['zip']))
        {
            print("{$_REQUEST['zip']} is a valid ZIP code.<br>\n");
        }
        else
        {
            print("{$_REQUEST['zip']} is <b>not</b> " .
                "a valid ZIP code.<br>\n");
        }
    }

    //start form
    print("<form action=\"{$_SERVER['PHP_SELF']}\">\n");
    print("<input type=\"text\" name=\"zip\">\n");
    print("<input type=\"submit\">\n");
    print("</form>\n");
?>
```

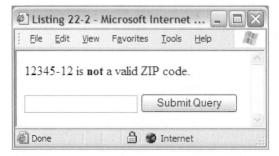

**Figure 22.2**   Output from Listing 22.2.

The script offers a form for inputting a ZIP code. It must have five digits and may be followed by a dash and four more digits. The functionality of the script hinges on the regular expression `^([0-9]{5})(-[0-9]{4})?$,` which is compared to user input. It's instructive to examine this expression in detail.

The expression starts with a carat. This causes the expression to match only from the beginning of the evaluated string. If this were left out, the ZIP code could be preceded by any number of characters, such as `abc12345-1234`, and still be a valid match. Likewise, the dollar sign at the end of the expression matches the end of the string. This stops matching of strings like `12345-1234abc`. The combination of using a carat and a dollar sign allows us to match only exact strings.

The first subexpression is `([0-9]{5})`. The square-bracketed range allows only characters from zero to nine. The curly braces specify that there must be exactly five of these characters.

The second subexpression is `(-[0-9]{4})?`. Like the first, it specifies exactly four digits. The dash is a literal character that must precede the digits. The question mark specifies that the entire subexpression may match once or not at all. This makes the four-digit extension optional.

You can easily expand this idea to check phone numbers or dates. Regular expressions provide a neat way of checking variables returned from forms. Consider the alternative of nesting `if` statements and searching strings with the `strpos` function.

You may also choose to have subexpression matches returned in an array. This is useful in situations where you need to break a string into components. The string a browser uses to identify itself is a good string for this method. Encoded in this string are the browser's name, version, and the type of computer it's running on. Pulling this information out into separate variables will allow you to customize your site based on the capabilities of the browser.

Listing 22.3 is a script for creating a set of variables that aid in cloaking a site for a particular browser. For the purpose of illustration, we will customize a link based on the browser being used. If the user visits the page with Netscape Navigator, we will provide a link to the download page for Microsoft Internet Explorer. Otherwise, we'll put a link to Netscape's download page. This is an example of customizing content, but the same method can be used to decide whether to use advanced features.

| Listing 22.3 | *Evaluating user agent* |
|---|---|

```php
<?php
    //evaluate user agent like
    //Mozilla/4.0 (compatible; MSIE 6.0; Windows NT 5.1; Q312461)
    ereg("^([[:alpha:]]+)/([[:digit:]\.]+)( .*)$",
        $_SERVER['HTTP_USER_AGENT'], $match);

    $browserName = $match[1];
    $browserVersion = $match[2];
    $browserDescription = $match[3];

    //look for clues that this is MSIE
    if(eregi("msie", $browserDescription))
    {
        //looking for something like:
        //(compatible; MSIE 6.0; Windows NT 5.1; Q312461)
        eregi("MSIE ([[:digit:]\.]+);",
            $browserDescription, $match);

        $browserName = "MSIE";
        $browserVersion = $match[1];
    }

    print("You are using $browserName " .
        "version $browserVersion!<br>\n" .
        "You might want to try ");

    if(eregi("mozilla", $browserName))
    {
        print("<a href=\"" .
            "http://www.microsoft.com/ie/download/default.asp\">");
        print("Internet Explorer");
        print("</a> ");
    }
    else
    {
        print("<a href=\"" .
            "http://www.netscape.com/computing/download/".
            "index.html" ."\">");
        print("Navigator");
        print("</a> ");
    }

    print("for comparison.<br>\n");
?>
```

In this script the main `ereg` function is not used in an `if` statement. It assumes the browser will identify itself minimally as a name, a slash, and the version. The `match` array gets set with the parts of the evaluated string that match with the parts of the regular expression. There are three subexpressions for name, version, and any extra description. Most browsers follow this form, including Navigator and Internet Explorer. Since Internet Explorer always reports that it is a Mozilla (Netscape) browser, extra steps must be taken to determine if a browser is really a Netscape browser or an imposter. This is done with a call to `eregi`.

If you are wondering why element zero is ignored, that's because the zero element holds the substring that matches the entire regular expression. In this situation it is not interesting. Usually, the zero element is useful when you are searching for a particular string in a larger context. For example, you may be scanning the body of a Web page for URLs. Listing 22.4 fetches the PHP home page and lists all the links on the page. The output is shown in Figure 22.3.

| **Listing 22.4** | *Scanning text for URLs* |
|---|---|

```php
<?php
    //set URL to fetch
    $URL = "http://www.php.net/";

    //open file
    $page = fopen($URL, "r");

    print("Links at $URL<br>\n");
    print("<ul>\n");

    while(!feof($page))
    {
        //get a line
        $line = fgets($page, 1024);

        //loop while there are still URLs present
        while(eregi("href=\"[^\"]*\"", $line, $match))
        {
            //print out URL
            print("<li>{$match[0]}</li>\n");

            //remove URL from line
            $replace = ereg_replace("\?", "\?", $match[0]);
            $line = ereg_replace($replace, "", $line);
        }
    }

    print("</ul>\n");

    fclose($page);
?>
```

**Figure 22.3**   Output from Listing 22.4.

The main loop of this script gets lines of text from the file stream and looks for `href` properties. If one is found in a line, it will be placed in the zero element of the `match` array. The script prints it out and then removes it from the line using the `ereg_replace` function. This function replaces text matched with a regular expression with a string. In this case the script replaces the `href` property with an empty string. The reason for finding the link and then removing it is that it is possible for two links to be on one line of HTML. The `eregi` function will match the first substring only. The solution is to find and remove each link until none remain.

Notice that when removing the link, a `replace` variable is prepared. Some links might contain a question mark, a valid character in a URL that separates a filename from form variables. Since this character has special meaning to regular expressions, the script places a backslash before it to let PHP know it's to be taken literally.

I frequently use `ereg_replace` to convert text for use in a new context. You can use `ereg_replace` to collapse multiple spaces into a single space. Listing 22.5 demonstrates this idea. The output is shown in Figure 22.4.

| Listing 22.5 | *Replacing multiple spaces* |
|---|---|

```php
<?php
    /*
    ** if text submitted show it
    */
    if(isset($_REQUEST['text']))
    {
        print("<b>Unfiltered</b><br>\n" .
            "<pre>{$_REQUEST['text']}</pre>" .
            "<br>\n");

        $_REQUEST['text'] = ereg_replace("[[:space:]]+",
            " ", $_REQUEST['text']);

        print("<b>Filtered</b><br>\n" .
            "<pre>{$_REQUEST['text']}</pre>" .
            "<br>\n");
    }
    else
    {
        $_REQUEST['text'] = "";
    }

    //start form
    print("<form action=\"{$_SERVER['PHP_SELF']}\">\n" .
        "<textarea name=\"text\" cols=\"40\" rows=\"10\">" .
        "{$_REQUEST['text']}</textarea><br>\n" .
        "<input type=\"submit\">\n" .
        "</form>\n");
?>
```

**Figure 22.4**   Output from Listing 22.5.

# DATABASE
# INTEGRATION

**Topics in This Chapter**

- Building HTML Tables from SQL Queries
- Tracking Visitors with Session Identifiers
- Storing Content in a Database
- Database Abstraction Layers

# Chapter

PHP has strong support for many databases. If native support for your favorite database doesn't exist, there's always ODBC, which is a standard for external database drivers. Support for new databases seems to show up regularly. The universal remark in this regard from the PHP developers has been "give us a machine to test on, and we'll add support."

MySQL is undoubtedly the most popular database used by PHP coders. Apart from being free, it suits Web development because of its blazing speed. In the examples for this chapter I'll assume you have a MySQL database. If you don't, you can either go to the MySQL Web site `<http://www.mysql.com/>` and investigate downloading and installing, or you can pursue changing the examples to work with another database.

Most relational databases use the Structured Query Language, or SQL. It is a fourth-generation language (4GL), which means it reads a bit more like English than PHP source code. A tutorial on SQL is beyond the scope of this book. If you're completely new to SQL, look for my other book, *Core MySQL*, also published by Prentice Hall Professional Technical Reference.

# 23.1 Building HTML Tables from SQL Queries

Perhaps the simplest task you can perform with a database and PHP is to extract data from a table and display it in an HTML table. The table could contain a catalog of items for sale, a list of projects, or a list of Internet name servers and their ping times. For illustration purposes, I'll use the first scenario. Imagine that a supermarket wants to list the items it has for sale on its Web site. As a proof of concept, you must create a page that lists some items from a database. We'll use the test database that's created when MySQL is installed. The PHP script for viewing the catalog of products will reside on the same machine as the database server.

The first step is to create the table. Listing 23.1 displays some SQL code for creating a simple, three-column table. The table is named catalog. It has a column called ID that is an integer with at most 11 digits. It cannot be null, and new rows will automatically be assigned consecutive values. The last line of the definition specifies ID as a primary key. This causes an index to be built on the column and disallows duplicate IDs. The other two columns are Name and Price.

| Listing 23.1 | *Creating catalog table* |
| --- | --- |

```
CREATE TABLE catalog
(
    ID INT(11) NOT NULL AUTO_INCREMENT,
    Name CHAR(32),
    Price DECIMAL(6,2),

    PRIMARY KEY (ID)
);
```

Name is a character string that may be up to 32 characters long. Price is a six-digit number with two decimal places, which is a good setup for money. Next, we will need to put some items in the table. Since we're only creating a demo, we'll fill in some items we might expect in a supermarket along with some dummy prices. To do this we'll use the INSERT statement. Listing 23.2 is an example of this procedure.

---

| Listing 23.2 | *Inserting data into catalog table* |
|---|---|

```
INSERT INTO catalog (Name, Price) VALUES
    ('Toothbrush', 1.79),
    ('Comb', 0.95),
    ('Toothpaste', 5.39),
    ('Dental Floss', 3.50),
    ('Shampoo', 2.50),
    ('Conditioner', 3.15),
    ('Deodorant', 1.50),
    ('Hair Gel', 6.25),
    ('Razor Blades', 2.99),
    ('Brush', 1.15);
```

Each SQL statement ends with a semicolon, much as in PHP. We're telling the MySQL server that we want to insert a number of rows into the catalog table, and we'll be supplying only the name and price. Since we're leaving out ID, MySQL creates one. This is due to our defining the column as AUTO_INCREMENT. The VALUES keyword lets the server know we are about to send the values we promised earlier in the command. Notice the use of single quotes to surround text, as is standard in SQL. MySQL allows inserting multiple rows in one statement by separating rows with commas. Most other database servers require a separate statement for each row.

Just to check that everything went well, Figure 23.1 shows the output you would get if you selected everything from the catalog table from within the MySQL client. I got this output by typing SELECT * FROM catalog; in the MySQL client.

```
+----+--------------+-------+
| ID | Name         | Price |
+----+--------------+-------+
|  1 | Toothbrush   |  1.79 |
|  2 | Comb         |  0.95 |
|  3 | Toothpaste   |  5.39 |
|  4 | Dental Floss |  3.50 |
|  5 | Shampoo      |  2.50 |
|  6 | Conditioner  |  3.15 |
|  7 | Deodorant    |  1.50 |
|  8 | Hair Gel     |  6.25 |
|  9 | Razor Blades |  2.99 |
| 10 | Brush        |  1.15 |
+----+--------------+-------+
10 rows in set (0.00 sec)
```

**Figure 23.1**   SELECT * FROM catalog.

The last step is to write a PHP script that gets the contents of the table and dresses it up in an HTML table. Listing 23.3 lists PHP code for extracting the name and price values, then displaying them in an HTML table. The output is shown in Figure 23.2. The first step in communicating with a database server is to connect to it. This is done with the `mysql_connect` function. It takes a hostname, a username, and a password. I usually create a user named `httpd` in my MySQL databases with no password. I also restrict this user to connections made from the local server. I name it after the UNIX user who will be executing the scripts—in other words, the Web server. If you are renting space from a hosting service, you may have a MySQL user and database assigned to you, in which case you'll need to modify the function arguments, of course.

---

**Listing 23.3**   *Creating HTML table from a query*

```php
<?php
    //connect to server, then test for failure
    if(!($dbLink = mysql_connect("localhost", "httpd", "")))
    {
        print("Failed to connect to database!<br>\n");
        print("Aborting!<br>\n");
        exit();
    }

    //select database, then test for failure
    if(!($dbResult = mysql_query("USE test", $dbLink)))
    {
        print("Can't use the test database!<br>\n");
        print("Aborting!<br>\n");
        exit();
    }

    // get everything from catalog table
    $Query = "SELECT Name, Price " .
        "FROM catalog " .
        "ORDER BY Name ";
    if(!($dbResult = mysql_query($Query, $dbLink)))
    {
        print("Couldn't execute query!<br>\n");
        print("MySQL reports: " . mysql_error() . "<br>\n");
        print("Query was: $Query<br>\n");
        exit();
    }
```

**Listing 23.3**  *Creating HTML table from a query (cont.)*

```
//start table
print("<table border=\"0\">\n");

//create header row
print("<tr>\n");
print("<td bgcolor=\"#cccccc\"><b>Item</b></td>\n");
print("<td bgcolor=\"#cccccc\"><b>Price</b></td>\n");
print("</tr>\n");

// get each row
while($dbRow = mysql_fetch_assoc($dbResult))
{
    print("<tr>\n");

    print("<td>{$dbRow['Name']}</td>\n");
    print("<td align=\"right\">{$dbRow['Price']}</td>\n");

    print("</tr>\n");
}

//end table
print("</table>\n");
?>
```

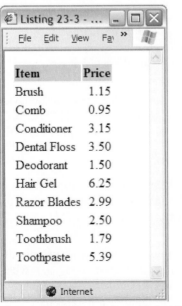

Figure 23.2    Output from Listing 23.3.

If the connection is successful, a MySQL link identifier will be returned. Notice that I'm testing for failure and performing the connection on one line. The function used to connect to the database is `mysql_connect`. If you've flipped through the descriptions of the MySQL functions in Chapter 17, you might remember another function called `mysql_pconnect`. These two functions operate identically inside a script, but `mysql_pconnect` returns persistent connections.

Most of the database functions that PHP offers incorporate the idea of a persistent connection—a connection that does not close when your script ends. If the same Web process runs another script later that connects to the same database server, the connection will be reused. This has the potential to save overhead. In practice, the savings are not dramatic, owing to the way Apache 1.3.x and earlier use child processes instead of threads. These processes serve a number of requests and then are replaced by new processes. When a process ends, it takes its persistent connection with it, of course.

The next step is to select a database. Here I've selected the database named `test`. Once we tell PHP which database to use, we get all rows from the `catalog` table. This is done with the `mysql_query` function. It executes a query on the given link and returns a result identifier. We will use this result identifier to fetch the results of the query.

Before we begin pulling data from the results, we must begin building an HTML table. This is done, as you might expect, by using an opening table tag. I've created a header row with a gray background and left the rest of the table behavior as default.

Now that the header row is printed, we can fetch each row from the result set. The fastest way to do this, executionwise, is to use `mysql_fetch_assoc`. This expresses each column in the result as an element of an associative array. The names of the columns are used for the keys of the array. You could also use `mysql_fetch_row` or `mysql_fetch_object`, which are equally efficient. You should avoid `mysql_result`, since this function does a costly lookup into a two-dimensional array.

When no more rows remain, `FALSE` will be returned. Capitalizing on this behavior, I put the fetch of the row inside a `while` loop. I create a row in the HTML table, printing object properties inside the table cells. When no rows remain, I close the table. I don't bother to close the connection to the database because PHP will do this automatically.

This is an extremely simple example, but it touches on all the major features of working with a database. Since each row is created in a loop, each is uniform. If the data change, there is no need to touch the code that turns them into HTML. You can just change the data in the database.

A good example of this technique in action is the Random Band Name Generator `<http://www.leonatkinson.com/random/index.php?SCREEN=band>`, which creates random band names from a table of words stored in a MySQL database to which anyone can add. Each refresh of the page fetches another ten names.

# 23.2 Tracking Visitors with Session Identifiers

As Web sites evolve into Web applications, the problem of maintaining state arises. The issue is that, from page to page, the application needs to remember who is visiting the page. The Web is stateless. Your browser makes a connection to a server, requests one or more files, and then closes the connection. Five minutes later, when you click to a connecting page, the routine happens all over again. While a log is kept, the server doesn't remember you. Any information you gave it about yourself three pages back may be saved somewhere, but it's not associated with you after that.

Imagine a wizardlike interface for ordering a pizza. The first screen asks you how many pizzas you want. Then you go through a page for each pizza, picking toppings and type of crust. Finally, a page asks for your name and number so that your order can be emailed to the nearest pizza parlor. One way to handle this problem is to pass all the information gathered up to that point with each form submission. As you go from page to page, those data grow and grow. You're telling the server a partial version of your order many times. It works, but it's definitely wasteful of network bandwidth.

Using a database and a session identifier, you can store information as it becomes available. A single identifier is used as a key to the information. Once your script has the identifier, it can remember what has gone on before.

How the script gets the identifier is another issue. You have two choices. One is to pass the identifier as a variable inside every link or form. In a form this is simple to do with a hidden variable. In a link you have to insert a question mark and a variable definition. If your session ID is stored in a variable called `session`, then you might write something like `print("<a href=\"page2.php?session=$session\">next</a>");` to send `session` to the next page. This technique works with all browsers, even Lynx.

An alternative is to use cookies. Like `GET` and `POST` form variables, cookies are turned into variables by PHP. So, you could create a cookie named `session`. The difference would be that since cookies may only be set in headers, you'll have to send them to the browser before sending any HTML code. Check out the `setcookie` function in Chapter 8 if you wish to pursue this strategy. A more complex strategy attempts to use cookies, but falls back on `GET` variables if necessary.

In fact, PHP can handle all these details for you. See the discussion of sessions in Chapter 7. What's missing from the standard functionality is database integration. You can use `session_set_save_handler` to keep the session data in a database. The big advantage is that PHP takes care of generating session identifiers and sending them to the browser. The big disadvantage is that PHP keeps the session data as a serialized array. If you need to manipulate the session data before storing it or before returning it to PHP, you must first use `unserialize`, change the array, then serialize the array again before passing it along.

Why would you need to manipulate the variables in the session? Perhaps you wish to disallow certain variables from sessions. More likely you'd like to keep certain variables as columns in the session table so you can run queries with them. For example, each user in a store may have an active order. If you add a column to the session table for the order ID, you can run queries that show which users have invoices underway or even which items they have in their baskets.

For the purposes of comparison, let's examine using PHP's session handling versus a system written in PHP. The first step is to create a table to hold the sessions. Listing 23.4 is SQL code for creating a simple session table in a MySQL database.

| **Listing 23.4** | *Creating session table* |
| --- | --- |

```
CREATE TABLE session
(
    ID VARCHAR(32) NOT NULL,
    LastAction DATETIME,
    Invoice INT(11),
    SessionData TEXT,

    PRIMARY KEY (ID)
);
```

The primary key of this table is PHP's session identifier, a 32-character string. Each time the user moves to a new page, the application updates the `LastAction` column. That way we can clear out any sessions that appear to be unused. The `Invoice` column holds a pointer to a row in an invoice table and the `SessionData` holds the serialized variables in the user's session.

Listing 23.5 uses PHP's session handler with routines for storing the session data in the table from Listing 23.4. The `mySession` class encapsulates the routines for storing the session data in the table. In addition, a block of code takes care of reading and writing the `Invoice` column. It's nice that PHP handles sending the session identifier between the server and client without any extra work. It's unfortunate that the session handler must execute its own queries separate from those that manipulate the `Invoice` column.

| Listing 23.5 | *PHP sessions saved in a MySQL database* |
| --- | --- |

```php
<?php
    class mySession
    {

        private $dbLink;

        public function open()
        {
            if(!($this->dbLink =
                mysql_connect("localhost", "httpd", "")))
            {
                return(FALSE);
            }

            //select database, then test for failure
            if(!($dbResult =
                mysql_query("USE test", $this->dbLink)))
            {
                return(FALSE);
            }

            return(TRUE);
        }

        public function close()
        {
            mysql_close($this->dbLink);
            return(TRUE);
        }

        public function read($id)
        {
            $Query = "SELECT SessionData " .
                "FROM session " .
                "WHERE ID = '" . addslashes($id) . "'";
            if(!($dbResult = mysql_query($Query, $this->dbLink)))
            {
                return(FALSE);
            }
            $dbRow = mysql_fetch_assoc($dbResult);

            //mark the session as being accessed
            $Query = "UPDATE session " .
                "SET " .
                "LastAction=NOW() " .
                "WHERE ID='".addslashes($id)."' ";
```

**Listing 23.5**    *PHP sessions saved in a MySQL database (cont.)*

```php
        if(!($dbResult = mysql_query($Query, $this->dbLink)))
        {
            return(FALSE);
        }

        return($dbRow['SessionData']);
    }

    public function write($id, $data)
    {
        //create the session if it doesn't exist
        $Query = "INSERT IGNORE " .
            "INTO session (ID) " .
            "VALUES ('".addslashes($id)."')";
        if(!($dbResult = mysql_query($Query, $this->dbLink)))
        {
            return(FALSE);
        }

        //update the session
        $Query = "UPDATE session " .
            "SET " .
            "SessionData='".addslashes($data)."', " .
            "LastAction=NOW() " .
            "WHERE ID='".addslashes($id)."' ";
        if(!($dbResult = mysql_query($Query, $this->dbLink)))
        {
            return(FALSE);
        }

        return(TRUE);
    }

    public function destroy($id)
    {
        $Query = "DELETE session " .
            "WHERE ID='".addslashes($id)."' ";
        if(!($dbResult = mysql_query($Query, $this->dbLink)))
        {
            return(FALSE);
        }

        return(TRUE);
    }
```

| Listing 23.5 | *PHP sessions saved in a MySQL database (cont.)* |
| --- | --- |

```php
    public function garbage($lifetime)
    {
        $Query = "DELETE session " .
            "WHERE (LastAction + $lifetime) < NOW() ";
        if(!($dbResult = mysql_query($Query, $this->dbLink)))
        {
            return(FALSE);
        }

        return(TRUE);
    }

}

$s = new mySession();

session_set_save_handler(
    array($s, 'open'),
    array($s, 'close'),
    array($s, 'read'),
    array($s, 'write'),
    array($s, 'destroy'),
    array($s, 'garbage')
    );

//start session
session_start();

//Increment counter with each page load
if(isset($_SESSION['Count']))
{
    $_SESSION['Count']++;
}
else
{
    //start with count of 1
    $_SESSION['Count'] = 1;
}

//connect to database
if(!($dbLink = mysql_connect("localhost", "httpd", "")))
{
    print("Couldn't connect to database!<br>\n");
}
```

| Listing 23.5 | *PHP sessions saved in a MySQL database (cont.)* |

```php
//select database, then test for failure
if(!($dbResult = mysql_query("USE test", $dbLink)))
{
    print("Couldn't use test database!<br>\n");
}

//if the user changes the invoice ID, update
//the column and the session
if(isset($_REQUEST['invoice']))
{
    //force invoice to be integer
    $_REQUEST['invoice'] = (integer)$_REQUEST['invoice'];

    if(!($dbLink = mysql_connect("localhost", "httpd", "")))
    {
        print("Couldn't connect to database!<br>\n");
    }

    //select database, then test for failure
    if(!($dbResult = mysql_query("USE test", $dbLink)))
    {
        print("Couldn't use test database!<br>\n");
    }

    $Query = "UPDATE session " .
        "SET Invoice={$_REQUEST['invoice']} " .
        "WHERE ID = '" . session_id() . "' ";
    if(!($dbResult = mysql_query($Query, $dbLink)))
    {
        print("Couldn't update invoice!<br>\n");
    }

    $Invoice = $_REQUEST['invoice'];
}
else
{
    //get the invoice
    $Query = "SELECT Invoice FROM session " .
        "WHERE ID = '" . session_id() . "' ";
    if(!($dbResult = mysql_query($Query, $dbLink)))
    {
        print("Couldn't get invoice!<br>\n");
    }
    $dbRow = mysql_fetch_assoc($dbResult);
    $Invoice = $dbRow['Invoice'];
}
?>
```

| Listing 23.5 | *PHP sessions saved in a MySQL database (cont.)* |
|---|---|

```
<html>
<head>
<title>Listing 23-5</title>
</head>
<body>
<?php
    print("You have viewed this page {$_SESSION['Count']}
        times!<br>\n");
    print("Current Invoice: $Invoice<br>\n");

    //show form for getting name
    print("<form " .
        "action=\"{$_SERVER['PHP_SELF']}\" " .
        "method=\"post\">" .
        "<input type=\"text\" name=\"invoice\" " .
            "value=\"\">\n" .
        "<input type=\"submit\" value=\"set order number\"><br>\n" .
        "</form>");

    //use a link to reload this page
    print("<a href=\"{$_SERVER['PHP_SELF']}\">reload</a><br>\n");
?>
</body>
</html>
```

Compare the technique in Listing 23.5 with the one in Listing 23.6. The first time you load Listing 23.6, it will create a session for you. Each click of the "reload" link causes the script to check the session. If the session identifier is not in the session table, then the script rejects the session identifier and creates a new one. You can try submitting a bad session identifier by erasing a character in the location box of your browser.

| Listing 23.6 | *Customer session handling* |
|---|---|

```
<html>
<head>
<title>Listing 23-6</title>
</head>
<body>
<?php
    //create a session identifier
    function SessionID($length=32)
    {
```

**Listing 23.6**    *Customer session handling (cont.)*

```
    // Set pool of possible characters
    $Pool = "ABCDEFGHIJKLMNOPQRSTUVWXYZ" .
        "abcdefghijklmnopqrstuvwxyz";
    $lastChar = strlen($Pool) - 1;

    $sid = "";
    for($i = 0; $i < $length; $i++)
    {
        $sid .= $Pool[mt_rand(0, $lastChar)];
    }

    return($sid);
}

//connect to database
if(!($dbLink = mysql_connect("localhost", "httpd", "")))
{
    print("Couldn't connect to database!<br>\n");
}

//select database, then test for failure
if(!($dbResult = mysql_query("USE test", $dbLink)))
{
    print("Couldn't use test database!<br>\n");
}

//clear out any old sessions
$Query = "DELETE FROM session " .
    "WHERE DATE_ADD(LastAction, INTERVAL 1800 SECOND) < " .
        "NOW()";
if(!($dbResult = mysql_query($Query, $dbLink)))
{
    //can't execute query
    print("Couldn't remove old sessions!<br>\n");
}

//check session
$mySession = NULL;
if(isset($_REQUEST['sid']))
{
    //we have a session, so check it
    $Query = "SELECT SessionData, Invoice " .
        "FROM session " .
        "WHERE ID='" . addslashes($_REQUEST['sid']) . "' ";
```

| Listing 23.6 | *Customer session handling (cont.)* |
|---|---|

```php
    if(!($dbResult = mysql_query($Query, $dbLink)))
    {
        //can't execute query
        print("Couldn't query session table!<br>\n");
        print("MySQL Reports: " . mysql_error() . "<br>\n");
    }

    //if we have a row, then the match succeeded
    if($dbRow = mysql_fetch_assoc($dbResult))
    {
        //get session data
        $mySession = unserialize($dbRow['SessionData']);
        $mySession['Invoice'] = $dbRow['Invoice'];
    }
    else
    {
        //session is bad
        print("Bad Session ID ({$_REQUEST['sid']})!<br>\n");
        unset($_REQUEST['sid']);
    }
}

//if session is empty, we need to create it
if(!isset($_REQUEST['sid']))
{
    //no session, so create one
    $_REQUEST['sid'] = SessionID();

    $mySession = array('Count'=>0);

    //insert session to database
    $Query = "INSERT INTO session " .
        "(ID, SessionData, LastAction) " .
        "VALUES (" .
        "'" . addslashes($_REQUEST['sid']) . "', " .
        "'" . addslashes(serialize($mySession)) . "', " .
        "NOW()) ";
    if(!($dbResult = mysql_query($Query, $dbLink)))
    {
        //can't execute query
        print("Couldn't insert into session table!<br>\n");
        print("MySQL Reports: " . mysql_error() . "<br>\n");
        exit();
    }
}
```

**Listing 23.6**    *Customer session handling (cont.)*

```php
//if the user changes the invoice ID, update
//the column and the session
if(isset($_REQUEST['invoice']))
{
    //force invoice to be integer
    $_REQUEST['invoice'] = (integer)$_REQUEST['invoice'];

    $Query = "UPDATE session " .
        "SET Invoice={$_REQUEST['invoice']} " .
        "WHERE ID = '" . addslashes($_REQUEST['sid']) . "' ";
    if(!($dbResult = mysql_query($Query, $dbLink)))
    {
        print("Couldn't update invoice!<br>\n");
    }

    $mySession['Invoice'] = $_REQUEST['invoice'];
}


//increment view count
$mySession['Count']++;

if(!isset($mySession['Invoice']))
{
    $mySession['Invoice'] = 'NULL';
}

print("You have viewed this page " .
    "{$mySession['Count']} times!<br>\n");
print("Current Invoice: {$mySession['Invoice']}<br>\n");

//show form for getting name
print("<form " .
    "action=\"{$_SERVER['PHP_SELF']}\" " .
    "method=\"post\">" .
    "<input type=\"hidden\" name=\"sid\" " .
        "value=\"{$_REQUEST['sid']}\">" .
    "<input type=\"text\" name=\"invoice\" " .
        "value=\"\">\n" .
    "<input type=\"submit\" value=\"set order number\">" .
        "<br>\n" .
    "</form>");
```

---

| Listing 23.6 | *Customer session handling (cont.)* |

```php
//use a link to reload this page
print("<a href=\"" .
    "{$_SERVER['PHP_SELF']}?sid={$_REQUEST['sid']}\">reload" .
    "</a><br>\n");


/*
** save the session
*/

//pull invoice out
$Invoice = $mySession['Invoice'];
unset($mySession['Invoice']);

$Query = "UPDATE session " .
    "SET LastAction = NOW(), " .
    "Invoice = $Invoice, " .
    "SessionData = '" . serialize($mySession) . "' " .
    "WHERE ID='" . addslashes($_REQUEST['sid']) . "' ";
if(!($dbResult = mysql_query($Query, $dbLink)))
{
    //can't execute query
    print("Couldn't update session table!<br>\n");
    print("MySQL Reports: " . mysql_error() . "<br>\n");
    exit();
}

?>
</body>
</html>
```

---

# 23.3  Storing Content in a Database

Information stored in a database is not limited to short strings, like the 32-character item name from Listing 23.3. You can create 64K blobs, which are enough to store a good-sized Web page. The advantage here is that pages exist in a very structured environment. You can identify them with a number, and relationships can be drawn between them using only these numbers. The disadvantage is that since the information is now in a database, you can't just load the file into your favorite editor. You have to balance the costs and benefits; most Web sites don't need every piece of content stored in a database.

A situation where it makes a lot of sense to put the content in a database is a Bulletin Board System, or BBS. The system stores messages, which are more than just Web pages. Each message has its own title, creation time, and author. This structure can be conveniently wrapped up into a database table. Furthermore, since each message can be given a unique identifier, we can associate messages in a parent-child tree. A user can create a new thread of discussion that spawns many other messages. Messages can be displayed in this hierarchical structure to facilitate browsing.

As with all database-related systems, the first step is to create a table. Listing 23.7 creates a table for storing messages. Each message has a title, the name of the person who posted the message, when the message was posted, a parent message, and the body of text. The parent ID might be NULL, in which case we understand the message to be the beginning of a thread. The body doesn't have to be plaintext. It can contain HTML. In this way it allows users to create their own Web pages using their browsers.

| Listing 23.7 | *Create message table* |
| --- | --- |

```
CREATE TABLE Message
(
    ID INT NOT NULL AUTO_INCREMENT,
    Title VARCHAR(64),
    Poster VARCHAR(64),
    Created DATETIME,
    Parent INT,
    Body BLOB,
    PRIMARY KEY(ID)
);
```

The script in Listing 23.8 has two modes: listing message titles and viewing a single message. If the messageID variable is empty, the script shows a list of every message in the system organized by thread. It accomplishes this with the showMessages function. You might want to turn back to Chapter 4, specifically the section on recursion. The showMessages function uses recursion to travel to every branch of the tree of messages. It starts by getting a list of all the messages that have no parent. These are the root-level messages, or beginnings of threads. After showing each root-level message, showMessages is called for the thread. This process continues until a message is found with no children. Unordered-list tags display the message titles. The indention aids the user in understanding the hierarchy.

**Listing 23.8**    *A simple BBS*

```html
<html>
<head>
<title>Listing 23-8</title>
</head>
<body>
<?php
    print("<h1>Leon's BBS</h1>\n");

    //connect to server, then test for failure
    if(!($dbLink = mysql_connect("localhost", "httpd", "")))
    {
        print("Failed to connect to database!<br>\n");
        print("Aborting!<br\n");
        exit();
    }

    //select database, then test for failure
    if(!($dbResult = mysql_query("USE test", $dbLink)))
    {
        print("Can't use the test database!<BR>\n");
        print("Aborting!<BR>\n");
        exit();
    }

    /*
    ** recursive function that spits out all
    ** descendent messages
    */
    function showMessages($parentID)
    {
        global $dbLink;

        $dateToUse = Date("U");

        print("<ul>\n");

        $Query = "SELECT ID, Title, Created " .
            "FROM bbsMessage " .
            "WHERE Parent=$parentID " .
            "ORDER BY Created ";

        if(!($dbResult = mysql_query($Query, $dbLink)))
        {
            //can't execute query
            print("Couldn't query bbsMessage table!<br>\n");
            print("MySQL Reports: " . mysql_error() . "<br>\n");
            exit();
        }
```

Listing 23.8    *A simple BBS (cont.)*

```php
    while($row = mysql_fetch_assoc($dbResult))
    {
        //show message title as a link to view the body
        print("<li>({$row['Created']}) " .
            "<a href=\"" .
            "{$_SERVER['PHP_SELF']}?messageID={$row['ID']}" .
            "\">" .
            "{$row['Title']}</a></li>\n");

        //show children of this message
        showMessages($row['ID']);
    }

    print("</ul>\n");
}


/*
** print out a form for adding a message with
** parent id given
*/
function postForm($parentID, $useTitle)
{
    print("<form action=\"{$_SERVER['PHP_SELF']}\" " .
        "method=\"post\">\n" .
        "<input type=\"hidden\" name=\"inputParent\" " .
        "value=\"$parentID\">\n" .

        "<input type=\"hidden\" name=\"ACTION\" " .
        "value=\"POST\">\n" .

        "<table border=\"1\" cellspacing=\"0\" " .
        "cellpadding=\"5\" width=\"400\">\n" .

        "<tr>\n" .

        "<td width=\"100\"><b>Title</b></td>\n" .

        "<td width=\"300\">" .
        "<input type=\"text\" name=\"inputTitle\" " .
        "size=\"35\" maxlength=\"64\" value=\"$useTitle\">" .
        "</td>\n" .

        "</tr>\n" .

        "<tr>\n" .
```

Listing 23.8 *A simple BBS (cont.)*

```
            "<td width=\"100\"><b>Poster</b></td>\n" .

            "<td width=\"300\">" .
            "<input type=\"text\" name=\"inputPoster\" " .
            "size=\"35\" maxlength=\"64\">" .
            "</td>\n" .

            "</tr>\n" .

            "<tr>\n" .

            "<td colspan=\"2\" width=\"400\">" .
            "<textarea name=\"inputBody\" " .
            "cols=\"45\" rows=\"5\"></textarea>" .
            "</td>\n" .

            "</tr>\n" .

            "<tr>\n" .

            "<td colspan=\"2\" width=\"400\" align=\"middle\">" .
            "<input type=\"submit\" value=\"Post\">" .
            "</td>\n" .

            "</tr>\n" .

            "</table>\n" .
            "</form>\n");
}

/*
** perform actions
*/
if(isset($_REQUEST['ACTION']))
{
    if($_REQUEST['ACTION'] == "POST")
    {
        $Query = "INSERT INTO bbsMessage " .
            "(Title, Poster, Created, Parent, Body)" .
            "VALUES(" .
            "'" . addslashes($_REQUEST['inputTitle']) . "', " .
            "'" . addslashes($_REQUEST['inputPoster']) . "', " .
            "NOW(), {$_REQUEST['inputParent']}, " .
            "'" . addslashes($_REQUEST['inputBody']) . "')";
```

| Listing 23.8 | *A simple BBS (cont.)* |
|---|---|

```php
            if(!($dbResult = mysql_query($Query, $dbLink)))
            {
                //can't execute query
                print("Couldn't insert into bbsMessage " .
                    "table!<br>\n");
                print("MySQL Reports: " . mysql_error() .
                    "<br>\n");
                exit();
            }
        }

    }


/*
** Show Message or show list of messages
*/
if(isset($_REQUEST['messageID']) AND
    ($_REQUEST['messageID'] > 0))
{
    $Query = "SELECT ID, Title, Poster, Created, " .
        "Parent, Body " .
        "FROM bbsMessage " .
        "WHERE ID={$_REQUEST['messageID']} ";

    if(!($dbResult = mysql_query($Query, $dbLink)))
    {
        //can't execute query
        print("Couldn't query bbsMessage table!<br>\n");
        print("MySQL Reports: " . mysql_error() . "<br>\n");
        exit();
    }

    if($row = mysql_fetch_assoc($dbResult))
    {
        print("<table border=\"1\" cellspacing=\"0\" " .
            "cellpadding=\"5\" width=\"400\">\n" .

            "<tr>" .
            "<td width=\"100\"><b>Title</b></td>" .
            "<td width=\"300\">{$row['Title']}</td>" .
            "</tr>\n" .

            "<tr>" .
            "<td width=\"100\"><b>Poster</b></td>" .
            "<td width=\"300\">{$row['Poster']}</td>" .
            "</tr>\n" .
```

| Listing 23.8 | *A simple BBS (cont.)* |

```
                "<tr>" .
                "<td width=\"100\"><b>Posted</b></td>" .
                "<td width=\"300\">{$row['Created']}</td>" .
                "</tr>\n" .

                "<tr>" .
                "<td colspan=\"2\" width=\"400\">" .
                "{$row['Body']}" .
                "</td>" .
                "</tr>\n" .

                "</table>\n");

            postForm($row['ID'], "RE: {$row['Title']}");

        }

        print("<a href=\"{$_SERVER['PHP_SELF']}\">" .
            "List of Messages</a><br>\n");

    }
    else
    {
        print("<h2>List of Messages</h2>\n");

        // get entire list
        showMessages(0);

        postForm(0, "");

    }
?>
</body>
</html>
```

For the efficiency-minded, this use of recursion is not optimal. Each thread will cause another call to showMessages, which causes another query to the database. There is a way to query the database once and traverse the tree of messages in memory, but I'll leave that as an exercise for you.

If a message title is clicked on, the page is reloaded with messageID set. This causes the script to switch over into the mode where a message is displayed. The fields of the message are displayed in a table. If the message contains any HTML, it will be rendered by the browser, because no attempt is made to filter it out. This restriction is best applied as part of the code that adds a new message.

Regardless of the two modes, a form is shown for adding a message. If a message is added while the list of messages is shown, the message will be added to the root level. If a message is added while the user is viewing a message, then it will be considered a reply. The new message will be made a child of the viewed message.

This BBS is simple. A more sophisticated solution might involve allowing only authenticated users to add messages or keeping messages private until approved by a moderator. You can use this same structure to build any application that manages user-submitted data, such as a guest book. If you are searching for a sophisticated BBS solution, I suggest checking out Brian Moon's Phorum project `<http://www.phorum.org/>`.

# 23.4  Database Abstraction Layers

Imagine creating a Web application that uses MySQL and later being asked to make it work with Oracle. All the PHP functions are different, so you'd have to change every one. In addition, as MySQL and Oracle each use slightly different SQL, you will probably have to change most of your queries. One way of coping with this problem is an abstraction layer. This separates your business logic—the rules of your application—from the code that interfaces with the database. A single function calls the right function based on the type of database you need to query.

Perhaps the most popular database abstraction layer is part of PEAR `<http://pear.php.net/>`. This library also contains code for session management.

Despite abstraction layers, incompatibilities between databases continue to offer challenges. MySQL uses a special qualifier for column definitions called `AUTO_INCREMENT`. It causes a column to be populated automatically with integers in ascending order. In Oracle this functionality can be approximated using a sequence and a trigger. The differences are difficult to reconcile systematically. In 1999 Scott Ambler proposed a solution in his white paper "The Design of a Robust Persistence Layer for Relational Databases" `<http://www.ambysoft.com/persistenceLayer.html>`. A careful analysis of the problem is explored as well as a detailed design, neither of which I can do justice to in the context of this chapter.

An abstraction layer trades some performance in favor of robustness. Certain unique, high-performance features of each database must be abandoned. The abstraction layer will provide the common set of functionality. But what you gain is independence from any particular database.

# NETWORKS

**Topics in This Chapter**

- HTTP Authentication
- Controlling the Browser's Cache
- Setting Document Type
- Email with Attachments
- HTML Email
- Verifying an Email Address

# Chapter 24

Most anything you write in PHP will be in the context of a network. It's a language intended primarily to produce HTML documents via the HTTP protocol. PHP allows you to code without worrying about the underlying protocols, but it also allows you to address the protocols directly when necessary. This chapter deals intimately with two important protocols: HTTP and SMTP. These are the protocols for transferring Web documents and mail. I've attempted to describe some common problems and provide solutions. This chapter may address a particular problem you face, such as protecting a Web page with basic HTTP authentication, but it also illustrates generally how to use HTTP headers and communicate with remote servers.

## 24.1 HTTP Authentication

If you have any experience with the Web, you're familiar with basic HTTP authentication. You request a page, and a small dialog window appears asking for username and password. As described in Chapter 9, PHP allows you to open URLs with the `fopen` function. You can even specify a username and password in the URL in the same way you do in Navigator's location box. Authentication is implemented using HTTP headers, and you can protect your PHP pages using the `header` function.

   To protect a page with basic HTTP authentication, you must send two headers. The WWW-Authenticate header tells the browser that a username and password are required. It also specifies a realm that groups pages. A username and password are good for an entire realm, so users don't need to authenticate themselves with each page request. The other header is the status, which should be HTTP/1.0 401 Unauthorized. Compare this to the usual header, HTTP/1.0 200 OK.

Listing 24.1 is an example of protecting a single page. The HTML to make a page is put into functions because it needs to be printed whether the authentication succeeds or fails. PHP creates the PHP_AUTH_USER and PHP_AUTH_PW elements of the _SERVER array automatically if the browser passes a username and password. The example requires *leon* for the username and *secret* for the password. A more complex scheme might match username and password against a list stored in a file or a database.

| Listing 24.1 | *Requiring authentication* |
| --- | --- |

```php
<?php
    /*
    ** Define a couple of functions for
    ** starting and ending an HTML document
    */
    function startPage()
    {
        print("<html>\n");
        print("<head>\n");
        print("<title>Listing 24-1</title>\n");
        print("</head>\n");
        print("<body>\n");
    }

    function endPage()
    {
        print("</body>\n");
        print("</html>\n");
    }

    /*
    ** test for username/password
    */
    if(($_SERVER['PHP_AUTH_USER'] == "leon") AND
        ($_SERVER['PHP_AUTH_PW'] == "secret"))
    {
        startPage();

        print("You have logged in successfully!<br>\n");

        endPage();
    }
```

| Listing 24.1 | *Requiring authentication (cont.)* |

```
    else
    {
        //Send headers to cause a browser to request
        //username and password from user
        header("WWW-Authenticate: " .
            "Basic realm=\"Leon's Protected Area\"");
        header("HTTP/1.0 401 Unauthorized");

        //Show failure text, which browsers usually
        //show only after several failed attempts
        print("This page is protected by HTTP " .
            "Authentication.<br>\nUse <b>leon</b> " .
            "for the username, and <b>secret</b> " .
            "for the password.<br>\n");
    }
?>
```

Now that you know how to protect a page, it may be instructive to work in the other direction, requesting a protected page. As I said earlier, the `fopen` function allows you to specify username and password as part of a URL, but you may have a more complicated situation in which you need to use `fsockopen`. An Authentication request header is necessary. The value of this header is a username and password separated by a colon. This string is base64 encoded in compliance with the HTTP specification.

Listing 24.2 requests the script in Listing 24.1. You may need to modify the URI to make it work on your Web server. The script assumes you have installed all the examples on your Web server in `/corephp/listings`. If you are wondering about the `\r\n` at the end of each line, recall that all lines sent to HTTP servers must end in a carriage return and a linefeed.

| Listing 24.2 | *Requesting a protected document* |

```
<html>
<head>
<title>Listing 24-2</title>
</head>
<body>
<pre>
<?php
    //open socket
    if(!($fp = fsockopen("localhost", 80)))
    {
        print("Couldn't open socket!<br>\n");
        exit;
    }
```

| Listing 24.2 | *Requesting a protected document (cont.)* |
|---|---|

```
//make request for document
fputs($fp, "HEAD /corephp/listings/24-1.php HTTP/1.0\r\n");

//send username and password
fputs($fp, "Authorization: Basic " .
    base64_encode("leon:secret") .
    "\r\n");

//end request
fputs($fp, "\r\n");

//dump response from server
fpassthru($fp);
?>
</pre>
</body>
</html>
```

# 24.2 Controlling the Browser's Cache

One hassle of writing dynamic Web pages is the behavior of caches. Browsers maintain their own cache, and by default they will check for a newer version of the page only once per session. Some ISPs provide their own cache as well. The intention is to avoid wasteful retransmission of pages. However, if the content on your page potentially changes with each request, it can be annoying if an old version appears. If you are developing an e-commerce site, it can be critical that each page is processed anew.

On the other hand, your page may be dynamically building a page that contains information that doesn't change very often. My experience has been that caches are smart enough to store URLs that appear to be ordinary HTML files, but not URLs that contain variables following a question mark. Your PHP may use variables in the URL, though. If the information on these pages changes infrequently, you want to let the cache know.

RFC 2616 describes the HTTP 1.1 protocol, which offers several headers for controlling the cache. Listing 24.3 shows the headers to send to prevent a page from being cached. The `Last-Modified` header reports the last time a document was changed, and setting it to the current time tells the browser this version of the page is fresh. The `Expires` header tells the browser when this version of the document will become stale and should be requested again. Again, we use the current time, hopefully causing the browser to keep the document out of the cache. Perhaps the most important header, Cache-Control tells the browser how to cache the page. In this situation, we are requesting the page not be cached. The fourth header is for the benefit of older browsers that understand only HTTP 1.0. Try reloading the script in Listing 24.3 rapidly. You should see the date update each time.

**Listing 24.3** *Sending headers to prevent caching*

```php
<?php
    header("Last-Modified: " . gmdate("D, d M Y H:i:s") . " GMT");
    header("Expires: " . gmdate("D, d M Y H:i:s") . " GMT");
    header("Cache-Control: no-store, no-cache, must-revalidate ");
    header("Cache-Control: post-check=0, pre-check=0", false);
    header("Pragma: no-cache");
?>
<html>
<head>
<title>Listing 24-3</title>
</head>
<body>
The time is <?php print(date("D, d M Y H:i:s")); ?><br>
</body>
</html>
```

Listing 24.4 causes a page to be cached for 24 hours. Like Listing 24.3, the Last-Modified, Expires, and Cache-Control headers are used to control cache behavior. The last modification time is sent as the actual modification of the file. The expiration time is sent as 24 hours from now. And the cache is instructed to let the document age for 86,400 seconds, the number of seconds in a day. To prove to yourself that the file is being returned by the cache, try reloading the page quickly. The dates on the page should remain the same.

**Listing 24.4** *Sending headers to encourage caching*

```php
<?php
    //report actual modification time of script
    $LastModified = filemtime(__FILE__) + date("Z");
    header("Last-Modified: " .
        gmdate("D, d M Y H:i:s", $LastModified) . " GMT");

    //set expiration time 24 hours (86400 seconds) from now
    $Expires = time() + 86400;
    header("Expires: " .
        gmdate("D, d M Y H:i:s", $Expires) . " GMT");
```

| Listing 24.4 | *Sending headers to encourage caching (cont.)* |

```
    //tell cache to let page age for 24 hours (86400 seconds)
    header("Cache-Control: max-age=86400");
?>
<html>
<head>
<title>Listing 24-4</title>
</head>
<body>
The time is <?php print(gmdate("D, d M Y H:i:s")); ?> GMT<br>
<br>
This document was last modified
<?php print(gmdate("D, d M Y H:i:s", $LastModified)); ?> GMT<br>
It expires
<?php print(gmdate("D, d M Y H:i:s", $Expires)); ?> GMT<br>
</body>
</html>
```

Notice that all the dates in these two examples use GMT, or Greenwich Mean Time. This is specified by the HTTP protocol. Forgetting to convert from your local time zone to GMT can be an annoying source of bugs.

# 24.3  Setting Document Type

By default, PHP sends an HTTP header specifying the document as being HTML. The `Content-Type` header specifies the MIME type `text/html`, and the browser interprets the code as HTML. Sometimes you will wish to create other types of documents with PHP. Chapter 25 discusses creating images, which may require an `image/png` content type. MIME types are administered by IANA, the Internet Assigned Numbers Authority. You can find a list of official media types at <http://www.isi.edu/in-notes/iana/assignments/media-types/>.

At times, you may wish to take advantage of how browsers react to different types of content. For example, `text/plain` displays in a fixed-width font with no interpretation of HTML. If you use `*/*` for the content type, the browser displays a dialog window for saving the file. Perhaps the most interesting use is for launching a helper application.

Listing 24.5 creates a tab-delimited text file that may launch Microsoft Excel. Take note that the computer must meet a few qualifications, however. First, it probably needs to be running Windows, and it must have Microsoft Excel installed. Newer versions of Excel associate the `application/vnd.ms-excel` content type with `.xls` files. My experience has been that these headers will cause an Excel OLE container inside either MSIE or Netscape Navigator on a Windows machine, but your experience may differ. Other browsers will likely ask the user if the file should be saved.

Notice the second header in Listing 24.5, `Content-Disposition`. This is not part of the HTTP 1.1 standard, but most browsers recognize it. It allows you to suggest a filename. If you add `attachment;` to the header, the browser may choose to open Excel in a separate window.

| Listing 24.5 | *Sending a tab-delimited Excel file* |
| --- | --- |

```php
<?php
    //set the document type
    header("Content-Type: application/vnd.ms-excel");
    header("Content-Disposition: filename=\"listing24-5.txt\"");

    //send some tab-delimited data
    print("Listing 24-5\r\n");

    for($i=1; $i < 100; $i++)
    {
        print("$i\t");
        print(($i * $i) . "\t");
        print(($i * $i * $i) . "\r\n");
    }
?>
```

Using `Content-Type` this way is almost black magic, since browsers don't follow a standard when encountering different MIME types. This technique has proven to be most successful for me when writing intranet applications where I had the luxury of serving a narrow set of browsers.

# 24.4 Email with Attachments

Sending plain email with PHP is easy. The `mail` function handles all the messy protocol details behind the scenes. But if you want to send attachments, you will need to dig into an RFC, specifically RFC 1341. This RFC describes MIME, Multipurpose Internet Mail Extensions. You can read it at the faqs.org site <http://www.faqs.org/rfcs/rfc1341.html>, but I'll show you a somewhat naïve implementation.

There are several example implementations to be found on the Web. Check out David Sklar's networking section <http://px.sklar.com/section.html?id=10>. Most of these put functionality into a class and attempt to incorporate every aspect of the standard. Listing 24.6 contains code that sends email with multiple attachments using two simple functions. Use this example as a basis for learning the process, and expand its functionality if necessary.

**Listing 24.6**  *Sending attachments*

```
<html>
<head>
<title>Listing 24-6</title>
</head>
<body>
<?php
    /*
    ** Function: makeAttachment
    ** Input: ARRAY attachment
    ** Output: STRING
    ** Description: Returns headers and data for one
    ** attachment.  It expects an array with elements
    ** type, name, and content.  Attachments are naively
    ** base64 encoded, even when unnecessary.
    */
    function makeAttachment($attachment)
    {
        //send content type
        $headers = "Content-Type: " . $attachment["type"];

        if(isset($attachment["name"]))
        {
            $headers .= "; name=\"{$attachment["name"]}\"";
        }

        $headers .= "\r\n" .
            "Content-Transfer-Encoding: base64\r\n" .
            "\r\n" .
            chunk_split(base64_encode($attachment["content"])) .
            "\r\n";

        return($headers);
    }
```

**Listing 24.6**    *Sending attachments (cont.)*

```php
/*
** Function: mailAttachment
** Input: STRING to, STRING from, STRING subject,
** ARRAY attachment
** Output: none
** Description: Sends attachments via email.  The attachment
** array is a 2D array.  Each element is an associative array
** containing elements type, name and content.
*/
function mailAttachment($to, $from, $subject, $attachment)
{
    //add from header
    $headers = "From: $from\r\n";

    //specify MIME version 1.0
    $headers .= "MIME-Version: 1.0\r\n";

    //multiple parts require special treatment
    if(count($attachment) > 1)
    {
        //multiple attachments require special handling
        $boundary = uniqid("COREPHP");

        $headers .= "Content-Type: multipart/mixed" .
            "; boundary = $boundary\r\n\r\n" .
            "This is a MIME encoded message.\r\n\r\n" .
            "--$boundary";

        foreach($attachment as $a)
        {
            $headers .= "\r\n" .
                makeAttachment($a) .
                "--$boundary";
        }

        $headers .= "--\r\n";
    }
    else
    {
        $headers .= makeAttachment($attachment[0]);
    }

    //send message
    mail($to, $subject, "", $headers);
}
```

| Listing 24.6 | *Sending attachments (cont.)* |
| --- | --- |

```
//add text explaining message
$attach[] = array("content"=>"This is Listing 24-6",
    "type"=>"text/plain");

//add script to list of attachments
$fp = fopen(__FILE__, "r");
$attach[] = array("name"=>basename(__FILE__),
    "content"=>fread($fp, filesize(__FILE__)),
    "type"=>"application/octet-stream");
fclose($fp);

//send mail to root
mailAttachment("root@localhost",
    "httpd@localhost",
    "Listing 24-6",
    $attach);

print("Mail sent!<br>\n");
?>
</body>
</html>
```

The `mailAttachment` function assembles the parts that make up a MIME message. These parts are sent in the fourth argument of the `mail` function, which is generally used for headers. In the case of a MIME message, this area is used for both headers and attachments. After the customary From headers are sent, a MIME-Version header is sent. Unless there's only one attachment, a boundary string must be created. This is used to divide attachments from one another. We want to avoid using a boundary value that might appear in the message itself, so we use the `uniqid` function.

Each attachment is surrounded by the boundaries that always start with two dashes. The attachment itself is prepared by the `makeAttachment` function. Each attachment requires `Content-Type` and `Content-Transfer-Encoding` headers. The type of content depends on the attachment itself. If an image file is being sent, it might be `image/jpg`. These are the same codes discussed above with regard to the HTTP protocol. For the sake of simplicity, this function always encodes attachments using base64, which can turn binary files into 7-bit ASCII. This prevents them from being corrupted as they travel through mail servers that accept only 7-bit ASCII. As you might imagine, text files don't require encoding, and complete implementations encode attachments based on content type.

It may be instructive to see the assembled message in full. Try sending yourself a message. On a UNIX operating system, you should be able to peek at the file itself inside `/var/spool/mail` before reading it, or perhaps inside `~/Mail/received` afterward.

# 24.5  HTML Email

An HTML email is a message presented in HTML instead of plain text. This allows control of colors and fonts for decoration, and it even allows the inclusion of images in a message. It's easy to send HTML email from your client, but it's not as easy from a PHP script. The key is to understand how to form MIME messages.

But first, you should decide whether the advantages of sending an HTML email fits your needs and whether you can do so ethically. The first reason to consider HTML email is the greater control over presentation you'll gain. Plaintext is fine when an email is a simple narrative, but if you want to present a table, you will have difficulty. Most GUI email clients use a variable-width font to display messages. As a result, it's impossible to align text in columns using tabs or spaces.

Consider an order summary sent to a customer. Information such as items purchased, prices, and other data need to be presented in an email. Although a table seems like a natural way to organize the information, it's only possible with HTML.

HTML offers the value of making a better presentation. It lets you control fonts, colors, and general layout with tables, an important feature to many people. Those in the advertising industry surely see the value in the increased control this type of email provides.

There can also be an issue of usability. Image tags work in most email clients, so you can even put graphics in your messages. Because you can put images inline, you can also take advantage of the client's need to retrieve those images when the message is opened. Although there is a standard that includes all necessary images in one large email (called MHTML), few clients support it. So, your images must be hosted on a Web server.

You can measure how many times your message was viewed by looking at your Web server logs. But you can go further than that. It's easy to put the URL to a PHP script in for the image source attribute. The script can return an image, but before it does, it can capture some information generated by the request—such as the name of the client, the IP address of the requester, or even some extra information you've put in the URL as GET variables.

By now, you're probably detecting the distinct smell of spam. These are the tricks of those annoying people who send out advertisements for anything from cable television descramblers to pornography sites. These tricks are also used by sites you've requested to notify you of sales or new products. There are a few issues to consider before you decide to send HTML emails. The most important one is privacy. With HTML emails, it's very easy to track who opened the email you sent, when they opened it, and maybe even more.

Imagine putting a bit of code like this into an HTML email:

```
<img src="http://www.spam.com/saveinfo.php?sentTo=you@yourhost.com"
width="1" height="1" border="0">
```

When the recipient opens the email, the email client fetches the image, but the email address is sent along with the request. Now the operator knows that out of the thousands of people he spammed, this particular person opened it. In most cases, this is rude. You can even gather information about someone without disclosing the practice. In fact, if you make it a tiny 1x1 image, they may not even have the clue of seeing an image in the email.

You should also consider people who have slow connections to the Internet or do not have the ability to view HTML email. If you send an HTML email to people with limited or no ability to view HTML email, they may end up just receiving your raw HTML code.

Sending an email with a lot of large images is a problem for people who use modems to connect to the Internet, regardless of which software they use. This is the same problem you face when creating a Web page, except people aren't used to waiting five minutes for their email to display. They may not be online when they open their email. As a result, the image may be displayed as broken or it may cause their computer to attempt to reconnect to the Internet. Either scenario can be annoying.

There are situations where it is appropriate to send an HTML email, and other times when it's definitely not. Sending unsolicited email, especially a duplicate message to a large group, is definitely not nice in most cases. Gathering information about people without their consent isn't good either. If someone gives you permission, HTML email can be a tool to improve the experience of reading a message.

Your message must use MIME headers in order to use HTML. Sending messages with attachments is similar to sending attachments. Instead of sending a `multipart/mixed` message, send a `multipart/alternative` message. This alerts the client that several versions of the same message are included, and the client should pick the best version. The simplest case is to include a plain text version and an HTML version. If the client understands HTML, that version should be presented instead of the plaintext version.

Listing 24.7 demonstrates a simple HTML email. I used base64 encoding instead of quoted-printable because Microsoft's email clients appear to have trouble with quoted-printable messages.

**Listing 24.7**   *HTML email*

```php
<?php
    //add From: header
    $headers = "From: webserver@localhost\r\n";

    //specify MIME version 1.0
    $headers .= "MIME-Version: 1.0\r\n";

    //unique boundary
    $boundary = uniqid("COREPHP");

    //tell e-mail client this e-mail contains
    //alternate versions
    $headers .= "Content-Type: multipart/alternative" .
        "; boundary = $boundary\r\n\r\n";

    //message to people with clients who don't
    //understand MIME
    $headers .= "This is a MIME encoded message.\r\n\r\n\r\n";

    //plain text version of message
    $headers .= "--$boundary\r\n" .
        "Content-Type: text/plain; charset=UTF-7\r\n" .
        "Content-Transfer-Encoding: base64\r\n\r\n";
    $headers .= chunk_split(base64_encode(
        "This is the plain text version!"));

    //HTML version of message
    $headers .= "--$boundary\r\n" .
        "Content-Type: text/html; charset=UTF-7\r\n" .
        "Content-Transfer-Encoding: base64\r\n\r\n";
    $headers .= chunk_split(base64_encode(
        "This the <b>HTML</b> version!"));

    //send message
    mail("root@localhost", "An HTML Message", "", $headers);

    print("HTML Email sent!");
?>
```

# 24.6 Verifying an Email Address

It doesn't take much experience with email to discover what happens when it is mis-addressed. The email is returned to you. This is called bounced email. Consider for a moment a Web site that allows users to fill out a form that includes an email address and sends a thank-you message. Certainly, many people will either mistakenly mistype their addresses or purposely give a bad address. You can check the form of the address, of course, but a well-formed address can fail to match to a real mail box. When this happens, the mail bounces back to the user who sent the mail. Unfortunately, this is probably the Web server itself.

Reading through the bounced email can be interesting. Those running an e-commerce site may be concerned about order confirmations that go undelivered. Yet, the volume of mail can be very large. Add to this that delivery failure is not immediate. To the process that sends the mail, it appears to be successful. It may be worthwhile to verify an email address before sending mail.

RFC 821 describes the SMTP protocol, which is used for exchanging email. You can read it at the faqs.org Web site <http://www.faqs.org/rfcs/rfc821.html>. It lives up to its name, Simple Mail Transfer Protocol, in that it's simple enough to use interactively from a telnet session. In order to verify an address, you can connect to the appropriate SMTP server and begin sending a message. If you specify a valid recipient, the server will return a 250 response code, at which point you can abort the process.

It sounds easy, but there's a catch. The domain name portion of an address, the part after the @, is not necessarily the same machine that receives email. Domains are associated with one or more mail exchangers—machines that accept STMP connections for delivery of local mail. The getmxrr function returns all DNS records for a given domain.

Now consider Listing 24.8. The verifyEmail function is based on a similar function written by Jon Stevens. As you can see, the function attempts to fetch a list of mail exchangers. If a domain doesn't have mail exchangers, the script guesses that the domain name itself accepts mail.

| Listing 24.8 | *Verifying an email address* |
| --- | --- |

```
<html>
<head>
<title>Listing 24-8</title>
</head>
<body>
<?php
    /*
    ** Function: verifyEmail
    ** Input: STRING address, REFERENCE error
    ** Output: BOOLEAN
    ** Description: Attempts to verify an email address by
    ** contacting a mail exchanger.  Registered mail
    ** exchangers are requested from the domain controller first,
    ** then the exact domain itself.  The error argument will
    ** contain relevant text if the address could not be
    ** verified.
    */

    function verifyEmail($address, &$error)
    {
        $mxhost = array();
        $mxweight = array();

        list($user, $domain) = split("@", $address, 2);

        //make sure the domain has a mail exchanger
        if(dns_check_record($domain, "MX"))
        {
            //get mail exchanger records
            if(!dns_get_mx($domain, $mxhost, $mxweight))
            {
                $error =
                    "Could not retrieve mail exchangers!<br>\n";
                return(FALSE);
            }
        }
        else
        {
            //if no mail exchanger, maybe the host itself
            //will accept mail
            $mxhost[] = $domain;
            $mxweight[] = 1;
        }
```

**Listing 24.8**    *Verifying an email address (cont.)*

```
//create sorted array of hosts
$weighted_host = array();
for($i = 0; $i < count($mxhost); $i++)
{
    $weighted_host[($mxweight[$i])] = $mxhost[$i];
}
ksort($weighted_host);

//loop over each host
foreach($weighted_host as $host)
{
    //connect to host on SMTP port
    if(!($fp = fsockopen($host, 25)))
    {
        //couldn't connect to this host, but
        //the next might work
        continue;
    }

    /*
    ** skip over "220" messages
    ** give up if no response for 10 seconds
    */
    stream_set_blocking($fp, FALSE);

    $stopTime = time() + 10;
    $gotResponse = FALSE;

    while(TRUE)
    {
        //try to get a line from mail server
        $line = fgets($fp, 1024);

        if(substr($line, 0, 3) == "220")
        {
            //reset timer
            $stopTime = time() + 10;
            $gotResponse = TRUE;
        }
        elseif(($line == "") AND ($gotResponse))
        {
            break;
        }
        elseif(time() > $stopTime)
        {
            break;
        }
    }
```

**Listing 24.8**    *Verifying an email address (cont.)*

```php
        if(!$gotResponse)
        {
            //this host was unresponsive, but
            //maybe the next will be better
            continue;
        }

        stream_set_blocking($fp, TRUE);

        //sign in
        fputs($fp, "HELO {$_SERVER['SERVER_NAME']}\r\n");
        fgets($fp, 1024);

        //set from
        fputs($fp, "MAIL FROM: " .
            "<httpd@{$_SERVER['SERVER_NAME']}>\r\n");
        fgets($fp, 1024);

        //try address
        fputs($fp, "RCPT TO: <$address>\r\n");
        $line = fgets($fp, 1024);

        //close connection
        fputs($fp, "QUIT\r\n");
        fclose($fp);

        if(substr($line, 0, 3) != "250")
        {
            //mail server doesn't recognize
            //this address, so it must be bad
            $error = $line;
            return(FALSE);
        }
        else
        {
            //address recognized
            return(TRUE);
        }
    }

    $error = "Unable to reach a mail exchanger!";
    return(FALSE);
}
```

| Listing 24.8 | *Verifying an email address (cont.)* |

```
    if(verifyEmail("leon@clearink.com", $error))
    {
        print("Verified!<br>\n");
    }
    else
    {
        print("Could not verify!<br>\n");
        print("Error: $error<br>\n");
    }
?>
</body>
</html>
```

SMTP servers precede each message with a numerical code, such as the 250 code mentioned above. When first connecting with a server, it may send any number of 220 messages. These contain comments, such as the AOL servers' reminders not to use them for spam. No special code marks the end of the comments; the server simply stops sending lines. Recall that by default the fgets function returns after encountering the maximum number of characters specified or an end-of-line marker. This will not work in the case of an indeterminate number of lines. The script will wait forever after the last comment. Socket blocking must be turned off to handle this situation.

When set_socket_blocking turns off blocking, fgets return immediately with whatever data is available in the buffer. The strategy is to loop continually, checking the buffer each time through the loop. There will likely be some lag time between establishing a connection and receiving the first message from the server. Then, as 220 messages appear, the script must begin watching for the data to stop flowing, which means the server is likely waiting for a command. To avoid the situation where a server is very unresponsive, a further check must be made against a clock. If 10 seconds pass, the server will be considered unavailable. Of course, this may reject addresses on slow servers.

# GENERATING GRAPHICS

**Topics in This Chapter**

- Dynamic Buttons
- Generating Graphs on the Fly
- Bar Graphs
- Pie Charts
- Stretching Single-Pixel Images

# Chapter

This chapter explores generating graphics using the GD extension functions described in Chapter 16. It is important to be aware of the issues involved with the creation of graphics on the fly. The first is that it is relatively costly in terms of CPU time. In most cases the flexibility of dynamic graphics is not worth what you pay in the load imposed on the server. Another issue is that making nice-looking graphics from PHP functions is not easy. Many techniques available in graphics editors are next to impossible. As you will see in the examples that follow, a lot of work goes into creating simple, flat charts. Last, while there is adequate support for text, functions you'd expect in a word processor do not exist. Text does not wrap at line ends. There is no concept of leading, spacing, or descenders. Regardless, generating graphics makes sense in some situations. This chapter contains some real examples that you can start using with very little modification.

## 25.1 Dynamic Buttons

Images wrapped in anchor tags are a common navigational device. Instead of plaintext, this method allows you to create buttons similar to those created in the operating system or even to create fanciful icons. In most cases it is best to leave these as graphics created in your favorite graphics editor, because the time between changes is relatively long. However, if you have a button that changes often, it may make sense to create it dynamically with PHP. The content of the button, the label, needs to be available as a string in PHP. It could be a statement setting the value of a variable. It could also be a value retrieved from a file or a database.

An illustration will make this idea clear. Many corporate Web sites have a section for press releases. Instead of just a list of text links, your client wants a graphic of a flaming newspaper for each press release, all under the title "Hot off the Press." Each burning newspaper has text over the top with the headline from the press release. With a small company that issues only one press release a month, you are better off creating these graphics by hand. With a company that issues a press release each week, it starts to make sense to automate the process. You can put the press releases into a database and generate a graphic on the fly as surfers view the list of press releases. One advantage of this approach is that if the CEO finds out you're putting flaming newspapers on the site, you can make a minor modification and the graphics become the company logo with the press-release title over it.

Seriously, you must consider the tradeoffs associated with dynamically created graphics. You don't want to save yourself 15 minutes a month if it makes every page download 30 seconds longer. If you've been working with the Web for any time at all, you know to reuse graphics throughout the site because the browser caches them. The first page may take longer to load, but each successive page is faster because the graphics are already loaded in the browser. Dynamic graphics can be cached, of course, but the browser uses the URL to cache files. The `GET-method` form variables are part of the URL, so `http://www.site.com/button.php?label=home&from=1` and `http://www.site.com/button.php?label=home&from=2` may create two identical graphics but are different as far as the browser cache is concerned.

These are only some of the issues involved with dynamic buttons. To demonstrate the process, I'll provide an example and describe the steps. Listing 25.1 is a script that creates a PNG image of a button with a text label. The button is rectangular and has some highlighting and shadowing. The label has a drop-shadow effect applied to it and is centered both vertically and horizontally. The output is shown in Figure 25.1.

| Listing 25.1 | *PNG button* |
| --- | --- |

```php
<?php
    /*
    ** PNG button
    ** Creates a graphical button based
    ** on form variables.
    */

    class Button
    {
        private $image;
```

| Listing 25.1 | *PNG button (cont.)* |
|---|---|

```php
public function __construct($width, $height, $label, $font)
{
    $this->image = imagecreate($width, $height);
    $colorBody = imagecolorallocate($this->image,
        0x99, 0x99, 0x99);
    $colorShadow = imagecolorallocate($this->image,
        0x33, 0x33, 0x33);
    $colorHighlight = imagecolorallocate($this->image,
        0xCC, 0xCC, 0xCC);

    //create body of button
    imagefilledrectangle($this->image,
        1, 1, $width-2, $height-2,
        $colorBody);

    //draw bottom shadow
    imageline($this->image,
        0, $height-1,
        $width-1, $height-1,
        $colorShadow);

    //draw right shadow
    imageline($this->image,
        $width-1, 1,
        $width-1, $height-1,
        $colorShadow);

    //draw top highlight
    imageline($this->image,
        0, 0,
        $width-1, 0,
        $colorHighlight);

    //draw left highlight
    imageline($this->image,
        0, 0,
        0, $height-2,
        $colorHighlight);

    //determine label size
    $labelHeight = imagefontheight($font);
    $labelWidth = imagefontwidth($font) * strlen($label);

    //determine label upper left corner
    $labelX = ($width - $labelWidth)/2;
    $labelY = ($height - $labelHeight)/2;
```

| Listing 25.1 | *PNG button (cont.)* |
|---|---|

```php
        //draw label shadow
        imagestring($this->image,
            $font,
            $labelX+1,
            $labelY+1,
            $label,
            $colorShadow);

        //draw label
        imagestring($this->image,
            $font,
            $labelX,
            $labelY,
            $label,
            $colorHighlight);
    }

    public function drawPNG()
    {
        header("Content-type: image/png");
        imagepng($this->image);
    }

    public function drawJPEG()
    {
        header("Content-type: image/jpeg");
        imagejpeg($this->image);
    }
}

//set parameters if not given
if(!isset($_REQUEST['width']))
{
    $_REQUEST['width'] = 100;
}

if(!isset($_REQUEST['height']))
{
    $_REQUEST['height'] = 30;
}

if(!isset($_REQUEST['label']))
{
    $_REQUEST['label'] = "CLICK";
}
```

| Listing 25.1 | *PNG button (cont.)* |

```
    if(!isset($_REQUEST['font']))
    {
        $_REQUEST['font'] = 5;
    }

    $b = new Button($_REQUEST['width'], $_REQUEST['height'],
        $_REQUEST['label'], $_REQUEST['font']);
    $b->drawPNG();
?>
```

**CLICK**

**Figure 25.1**   Output from Listing 25.1.

The first step the script takes is to make sure it has valid information for all the parameters. These include the size of the button and the text with which to label the button. I've chosen to use the built-in fonts, which are numbered one through five. Chapter 16 has descriptions of functions for loading different fonts, and I encourage you to modify my script to incorporate them.

The next step is to create an image. There are two ways to do this. You can create a blank image of a specific size, or you can load an existing image file. I've chosen the former because it allows the script to make buttons of any size. You can make much more stylish buttons using the latter method. This is another good exercise.

The button will be drawn with three colors: a body color, a highlight color, and a shadow color. I've chosen to go with three shades of gray. These colors must be allocated with the `imagecolorallocate` function. Using the body color, the script makes a rectangle that is one pixel smaller than the entire image. The border around this rectangle is created with four lines. The lines on the bottom and right sides are drawn in the shadow color, and the top and left sides are drawn with the highlight color. This creates an illusion of the button being three-dimensional.

To finish the button, the script draws the label. First, the text is drawn slightly off center in the shadow color. Then the text is drawn in the highlight color over it and exactly centered, making the text look as though it is floating over the button.

At this point the script has created the image and needs to send it to the browser. It is very important that the header be sent to let the browser know that this file is an image. Without it, you get a garbled bunch of strange characters.

This wraps up the script that creates a button, but to really make use of it, we have to use it in the context of a Web page. Listing 25.2 demonstrates the minimal steps. I've created an array of four button labels I want to create. I then loop through the array, each time creating an image tag. The source of the image is the previous script. I pass the script some parameters to set the size of the button and the label. I leave the font as the default, but I could have set that as well. The output is shown in Figure 25.2.

**Listing 25.2**    *Creating buttons dynamically*

```php
<?php
    //define button labels
    $label = array("HOME",
        "ABOUT US",
        "OUR PRODUCTS",
        "CONTACT US");

    //display all buttons
    foreach($label as $text)
    {
        //link back to this page
        print("<a href=\"$SERVER['PHP_SELF']}\">");

        //create dynamic image tag
        print("<img src=\"25-1.php");
        print("?label=" . htmlentities($text));
        print("&amp;width=145");
        print("&amp;height=25");
        print("\" border=\"0\"");
        print("width=\"145\" height=\"25\">");

        print("</a><br>\n");
    }
?>
```

**Figure 25.2**    Output from Listing 25.2.

# 25.2 Generating Graphs on the Fly

Perhaps a more likely use of dynamic graphics is in generating graphs. Since graphs rely on data, they lend themselves to formula-driven creation. If the data change often, using PHP to generate the graphs is a good idea. In the following examples, I've written the data into the script, but pulling data from a database is not difficult. Sending the data from a form is probably not a practical idea for large amounts of data. The GET method imposes a relatively small limit on the total size of a URL that varies between Web servers. You could use the POST method, however. The two examples I'll show are a bar graph and a pie chart. Each uses the same set of data, which is a fictitious survey of favorite meat.

# 25.3 Bar Graphs

Bar graphs are a good way to compare values to each other. Creating them is a relatively simple task because each data point is a rectangle. The height of the rectangle represents the value of the data point. To make the transition, a scaling factor is used. In Listing 25.3 the graph is 200 pixels tall and the scaling factor is two. This means that a data point with the value 75 will be 150 pixels tall. The output is shown in Figure 25.3.

| Listing 25.3 | *Creating a bar graph* |
| --- | --- |

```php
<?php
    /*
    ** Bar graph
    */

    //fill in graph parameters
    $GraphWidth = 400;
    $GraphHeight = 200;
    $GraphScale = 2;
    $GraphFont = 5;
    $GraphData = array(
        "Beef"=>"99",
        "Pork"=>"75",
        "Chicken"=>"15",
        "Lamb"=>"66",
        "Fish"=>"22");
```

| Listing 25.3 | *Creating a bar graph (cont.)* |
| --- | --- |

```php
//create image
$image = imagecreate($GraphWidth, $GraphHeight);
imageantialias($image, TRUE);

//allocate colors
$colorBody = imagecolorallocate($image, 0xFF, 0xFF, 0xFF);
$colorGrid = imagecolorallocate($image, 0xCC, 0xCC, 0xCC);
$colorBar = imagecolorallocate($image, 0xFF, 0xFF, 0x00);
$colorText = imagecolorallocate($image, 0x00, 0x00, 0x00);

//fill background
imagefill($image, 0, 0, $colorBody);

//draw vertical grid line
$GridLabelWidth = imagefontwidth($GraphFont)*3 + 1;
imageline($image,
    $GridLabelWidth, 0,
    $GridLabelWidth, $GraphHeight-1,
    $colorGrid);

//draw horizontal grid lines
$styleDashed = array_merge(array_fill(0, 4, $colorGrid),
    array_fill(0, 4, IMG_COLOR_TRANSPARENT));
imagesetstyle($image, $styleDashed);
for($index = 0;
    $index < $GraphHeight;
    $index += $GraphHeight/10)
{
    imageline($image,
        0, $index,
        $GraphWidth-1, $index,
        IMG_COLOR_STYLED);

    //draw label
    imagestring($image,
        $GraphFont,
        0,
        $index,
        round(($GraphHeight - $index)/$GraphScale),
        $colorText);
}

//add bottom line
imageline($image,
    0, $GraphHeight-1,
    $GraphWidth-1, $GraphHeight-1,
    $colorGrid);
```

**Listing 25.3** *Creating a bar graph (cont.)*

```
//draw each bar
$BarWidth = (($GraphWidth-$GridLabelWidth)/count($GraphData))
    - 10;
$column = 0;
foreach($GraphData as $label=>$value)
{
    //draw bar
    $BarTopX = $GridLabelWidth +
        (($column+1) * 10) + ($column * $BarWidth);
    $BarBottomX = $BarTopX + $BarWidth;
    $BarBottomY = $GraphHeight-1;
    $BarTopY = $BarBottomY - ($value * $GraphScale);

    imagefilledrectangle($image,
        $BarTopX, $BarTopY,
        $BarBottomX, $BarBottomY,
        $colorBar);

    //draw label
    $LabelX = $BarTopX +
        (($BarBottomX - $BarTopX)/2) -
        (imagefontheight($GraphFont)/2);
    $LabelY = $BarBottomY-10;

    imagestringup($image,
        $GraphFont,
        $LabelX,
        $LabelY,
        "$label: $value",
        $colorText);

    $column++;
}

//output image
header("Content-type: image/png");
imagepng($image);
?>
```

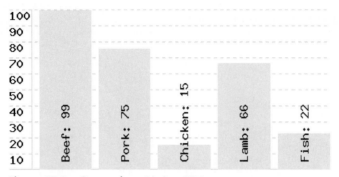

**Figure 25.3**   Output from Listing 25.3.

The business of creating the graph is similar to the process described earlier in which a button is created. A blank image is created, several colors are allocated, and functions are called for drawing shapes into the image. The script allows the width of the bars to adapt to the width of the graph. The width of the graph is divided by the number of bars drawn. A 10-pixel gutter is drawn between the bars. In the center of the bar the data point's label is written along with its value.

# 25.4  Pie Charts

Pie charts are a good way to see how a value represents a percentage of a whole. Each data point is a slice of a pie with a unique color. A legend associates the colors with each data point's label and value.

Since the pie chart is round, it represents a slightly more complex problem than the bar graph. PHP's image functions allow you to draw a pie slice, solid or outlined. Because each slice represents a portion of the whole, the script must calculate how many degrees to dedicate to the slice by dividing the value by the total of all slice values. Then it's a matter of calling `imagefilledarc`.

As with the bar graph, the data used in the chart come from an array hardcoded into the script in Listing 25.4. It is possible to keep the chart up to date by editing every time the data change, but it may be better to link it with a database. The output is shown in Figure 25.4.

**Listing 25.4** *Creating a pie chart*

```php
<?php
    //fill in chart parameters
    $ChartDiameter = 300;
    $ChartFont = 5;
    $ChartFontHeight = imagefontheight($ChartFont);
    $ChartData = array(
        "Beef"=>"99",
        "Pork"=>"75",
        "Chicken"=>"15",
        "Lamb"=>"66",
        "Fish"=>"22");

    //determine graphic size
    $ChartWidth = $ChartDiameter + 20;
    $ChartHeight = $ChartDiameter + 20 +
        (($ChartFontHeight + 2) * count($ChartData));

    //determine total of all values
    $ChartTotal = array_sum($ChartData);

    //set center of pie
    $ChartCenterX = $ChartDiameter/2 + 10;
    $ChartCenterY = $ChartDiameter/2 + 10;

    //create image
    $image = imagecreate($ChartWidth, $ChartHeight);
    imageantialias($image, TRUE);

    //create a round brush for drawing borders
    $dot = imagecreate(10, 10);
    $dotColorBlack = imagecolorallocate($dot, 0, 0, 0);
    $dotColorTransparent = imagecolorallocate($dot, 255, 0, 255);
    imagecolortransparent($dot, $dotColorTransparent);
    imagefill($dot, 0, 0, $dotColorTransparent);
    imagefilledellipse($dot, 4, 4, 5, 5, $dotColorBlack);
    imagesetbrush($image, $dot);


    //allocate colors
    $colorBody = imagecolorallocate($image, 0xFF, 0xFF, 0xFF);
    $colorBorder = imagecolorallocate($image, 0x00, 0x00, 0x00);
    $colorText = imagecolorallocate($image, 0x00, 0x00, 0x00);
    $colorSlice = array(

        imagecolorallocate($image, 0xFF, 0x00, 0x00),
        imagecolorallocate($image, 0x00, 0xFF, 0x00),
        imagecolorallocate($image, 0x00, 0x00, 0xFF),
        imagecolorallocate($image, 0xFF, 0xFF, 0x00),
```

| Listing 25.4 | *Creating a pie chart (cont.)* |
|---|---|

```
        imagecolorallocate($image, 0xFF, 0x00, 0xFF),
        imagecolorallocate($image, 0x00, 0xFF, 0xFF),
        imagecolorallocate($image, 0x99, 0x00, 0x00),
        imagecolorallocate($image, 0x00, 0x99, 0x00),
        imagecolorallocate($image, 0x00, 0x00, 0x99),
        imagecolorallocate($image, 0x99, 0x99, 0x00),
        imagecolorallocate($image, 0x99, 0x00, 0x99),
        imagecolorallocate($image, 0x00, 0x99, 0x99));

//fill background
imagefill($image, 0, 0, $colorBody);


/*
** draw each slice
*/
$Degrees = 0;
$slice=0;
foreach($ChartData as $label=>$value)
{
    $StartDegrees = round($Degrees);
    $Degrees += (($value/$ChartTotal)*360);
    $EndDegrees = round($Degrees);

    $CurrentColor = $colorSlice[$slice%(count($colorSlice))];

    //draw pie slice
    imagefilledarc(
        $image,
        $ChartCenterX, $ChartCenterY,
        $ChartDiameter,$ChartDiameter,
        $StartDegrees, $EndDegrees,
        $CurrentColor, IMG_ARC_PIE);


    //draw legend for this slice
    $LineY = $ChartDiameter + 20 +
        ($slice*($ChartFontHeight+2));

    imagerectangle($image,
        10,
        $LineY,
        10 + $ChartFontHeight,
        $LineY+$ChartFontHeight,
        $colorBorder);
```

**Listing 25.4** | *Creating a pie chart (cont.)*

```
    imagefilltoborder($image,
        12,
        $LineY + 2,
        $colorBorder,
        $CurrentColor);

    imagestring($image,
        $ChartFont,
        20 + $ChartFontHeight,
        $LineY,
        "$label: $value",
        $colorText);

    $slice++;
}


//draw border
imageellipse($image,
    $ChartCenterX, $ChartCenterY,
    $ChartDiameter,$ChartDiameter,
    IMG_COLOR_BRUSHED);

//output image
header("Content-type: image/png");
imagepng($image);
?>
```

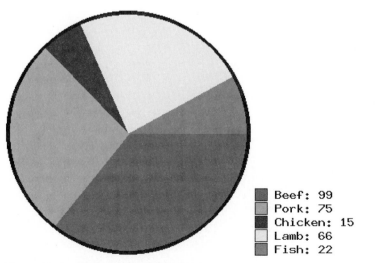

**Figure 25.4** Output from Listing 25.4.

# 25.5  Stretching Single-Pixel Images

The following technique takes advantage of the behavior of most browsers with the width and height properties of the image tag. It does not require the GD extension, because it doesn't actually manipulate an image. It relies on the browser to stretch an image to match the width and height specified in the IMG tag. This allows you to stretch a single-pixel image into a large bar.

Refer to Listing 25.5. An HTML table is used to line up graph labels with bars. The largest data element will fill 100 percent of the graph width, which is specified by the graphWidthMax variable. Each element is pulled from the data array and used to scale graphWidthMax. This produces a horizontally oriented bar graph, but the same method can make a vertical graph too. You may wish to add a second, clear image to the right of each bar to ensure the graph renders correctly on all browsers. See Figure 25.5.

| Listing 25.5 | *Bar graph using stretched images* |
| --- | --- |

```php
<?php
    //fill in graph parameters
    $graphWidthMax = 400;
    $graphData = array(
        "Beef"=>"99",
        "Pork"=>"75",
        "Chicken"=>"15",
        "Lamb"=>"66",
        "Fish"=>"22");
    $barHeight = 10;
    $barMax = max($graphData);

    print("<table border=\"0\">\n");

    foreach($graphData as $label=>$rating)
    {
        //calculate width
        $barWidth = intval($graphWidthMax * $rating/$barMax);

        print("<tr>\n");

        //label
        print("<th>$label</th>\n");
```

**Listing 25.5**     *Bar graph using stretched images (cont.)*

```
        //data
        print("<td>");
        print("<img src=\"reddot.png\" ");
        print("width=\"$barWidth\"  height=\"$barHeight\" ");
        print("border=\"0\">");
        print("</td>\n");

        print("</tr>\n");
    }

    print("</table>\n");
?>
```

**Figure 25.5**   Output from Listing 25.5.

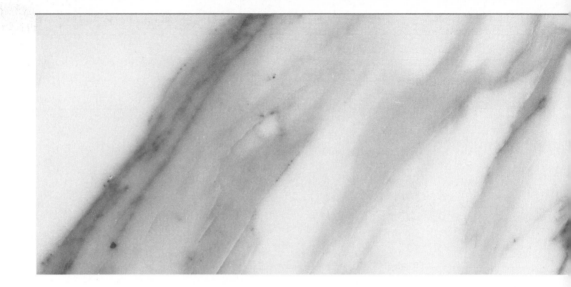

# SOFTWARE
# ENGINEERING

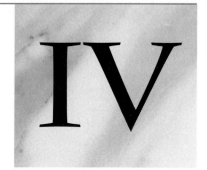

Part IV

S oftware engineering is more than just programming. Like a civil engineer carefully designs and builds a skyscraper, a software engineer carefully designs and implements software systems. Even small PHP scripts may benefit from software engineering concepts. This section explores the issues involved in using PHP in a Web site.

Chapter 26 is about integrating PHP and HTML. You can use PHP just in key places or in generating every page of a site. This chapter helps you decide.

Chapter 27 discusses system specification and design. It develops an approach for designing a system with PHP, including a phase of careful requirements analysis. A survey is made of existing methods for designing with PHP.

Chapter 28 touches on issues of efficiency and debugging. It provides information to help measure performance, and it describes remote debugging.

Chapter 29 discusses implementing design patterns in PHP.

# INTEGRATION WITH HTML

**Topics in This Chapter**

- Sprinkling PHP within an HTML Document
- Using PHP to Output All HTML
- Separating HTML from PHP
- Generating HTML with PHP

# Chapter 26

By this time, you have learned the basics of PHP. You have a reference for the functions, and you've been introduced to some fundamental problems of programming. But all the examples I've shown have been pieces, snippets for the sake of illustration. This chapter discusses how to integrate PHP into a Web site. It will help you decide whether to build a site completely with PHP, to sprinkle PHP throughout the site, or to simply create a few key PHP-driven pages. It also discusses issues involved in using PHP to generate HTML.

## 26.1 Sprinkling PHP within an HTML Document

The first and most obvious approach to using PHP is to build HTML files as you have always done, inserting PHP tags as if they were HTML tags. This could take the form of repeating HTML that you replace with a call to a PHP function. It could take the form of a large block of PHP code that generates database output. Or it could be a script that processes a form submission. These are all situations in which the impact of PHP on the site is low. This is a good first step for those new to programming. You are able to insert the smallest amount of PHP code as a test. As your experience and confidence grow, so will your reliance on PHP.

Aside from simple tasks, such as inserting today's data with `<?php print(date('Y/m/d')); ?>`, you can write your own function for wrapping a block of HTML. Listing 26.1 defines a class for printing HTML tables.

**Listing 26.1**    *Formatting function*

```php
<?php
    /*
    ** Simple class for creating HTML tables
    */
    class HTMLTable
    {
        static function start($header=FALSE)
        {
            print("<table border=\"1\">\n");

            if(is_array($header))
            {
                print("<tr>\n");

                foreach($header as $h)
                {
                    print("<th>" .
                        strtoupper($h) .
                        "</th>\n");
                }

                print("</tr>\n");
            }
        }

        static function end()
        {
            print("</table>\n\n");
        }

        static function printRow($label, $field)
        {
            print("<tr>\n");

            //label
            if($label !== "")
            {
                print("<th>" .
                    strtoupper($label) .
                    "</th>\n");
            }
```

**Listing 26.1**   *Formatting function (cont.)*

```php
            if(!is_array($field))
            {
                $field = array($field);
            }

            foreach($field as $key=>$value)
            {
                print("<td>");
                if($value === "")
                {
                    print(" ");
                }
                else
                {
                    print($value);
                }
                print("</td>\n");
            }

            print("</tr>\n");
        }

        static function printSet($set)
        {
            foreach($set as $field)
            {
                if(isset($field['label']))
                {
                    $label = $field['label'];
                    unset($field['label']);
                }
                else
                {
                    $label = "";
                }
                HTMLTable::printRow($label, $field);
            }
        }

    }
?>
<html>
<head>
<title>Listing 26-1</title>
</head>
```

| Listing 26.1 | *Formatting function (cont.)* |
|---|---|

```
<body>
<p>
This is an example of using a function to repeat
a commonly-used piece of HTML code.  It builds
out a table, like this one.
</p>
<?php
    //show table with labels on the left
    HTMLTable::start();
    HTMLTable::printRow('step 1', 'Start the table');
    HTMLTable::printRow('step 2', 'Print rows');
    HTMLTable::printRow('step 3', 'End the table');
    HTMLTable::end();
?>
<p>
The HTMLTable class allows you to draw all HTML
tables in the same way.  To change the look of
all tables, you need only edit the class.  Cascading
Style Sheets offer similar technology, but implementing
in PHP means we can make unlimited changes to the
data before building the HTML.  It also means we
can neatly indent the data without affecting the
placement on the final document.
</p>
<?php
    //show a table with labels on top
    HTMLTable::start(array('artist', 'song'));
    HTMLTable::printSet(array(
        array('Thelonious Monk', 'Bemsha Swing'),
        array('John Coltrane', 'Spiral'),
        array('Charlie Parker', 'Koko')
        ));
    HTMLTable::end();
?>
</body>
</html>
```

One benefit of this technique is that every table renders in exactly the same way. Less text to type for each table means less chance of leaving out part of the formula. This is nice to the programmer, who undoubtedly is eager to find a shortcut to typing long segments of identical HTML. A higher degree of quality is ensured. If a call to the function is mistyped, PHP displays an error. If no errors are displayed, the tables are most likely displayed identically and in the correct format.

If the format of the table needs changing, the code must be altered in only one place. Furthermore, PHP offers the opportunity to make changes to the data before displaying it. In Listing 26.1, the code switches labels to uppercase. Note how the class operates in two modes, labels on top or labels on the left.

Another similar use of PHP is to dress up what is essentially CGI output: a large block of PHP surrounded by HTML so that the output of the code simply appears in a larger page. This is a similar approach offered by SSI (Server-Side Includes). An SSI tag may call a CGI and insert the output in its place.

The approach is appropriate in situations in which your site is mostly static, but certain key areas must be dynamic. The advantage is low impact on the Web server. PHP is used only when absolutely needed. In Listing 26.2 the code generates information that doesn't change, but it's easy to imagine code that pulls stock quotes from a database. It eliminates the need to edit the HTML page each time the information changes, but parts that don't change often, like the layout of the page, are left as static HTML.

| Listing 26.2 | *Dressing up CGI output* |
| --- | --- |

```
<html>
<head>
<title>Listing 26-2</title>
</head>
<body>
<h1>Color Chart</h1>
<p>
The following chart displays the colors
safe for displaying in all browsers.  These
colors should not dither on any computer
with a color palette of at least 256
colors.
</p>
<p>
This chart will only display on browsers
that support table cell background colors.
</p>
<?php
    $color = array("00", "33", "66", "99", "CC", "FF");
    $nColors = count($color);

    for($Red = 0; $Red < $nColors; $Red++)
    {
        print("<table>\n");
```

| Listing 26.2 | *Dressing up CGI output (cont.)* |
|---|---|

```
        for($Green = 0; $Green < $nColors; $Green++)
        {
            print("<tr>\n");

            for($Blue = 0; $Blue < $nColors; $Blue++)
            {
                $CellColor = $color[$Red] .
                    $color[$Green] . $color[$Blue];

                print("<td bgcolor=\"#$CellColor\">");
                print("<tt>$CellColor</tt>");
                print("</td>\n");
            }

            print("</tr>\n");
        }

        print("</table>\n");
    }
?>
</body>
</html>
```

While Listing 26.2 is an example of dynamic output, you are often faced with the opposite situation. Your site may be completely static, but you need to accept catalog requests. PHP is a good solution for accepting form submissions. The first step is to create an HTML page that asks for name and address. Listing 26.3 demonstrates.

| Listing 26.3 | *Catalog request form* |
|---|---|

```
<html>
<head>
<title>Listing 26-3</title>
</head>
<body>
<p>
Please enter name and address to receive a free catalog.
</p>
<form action="26-4.php">
<table>
<tr>
    <td>Name</td>
    <td><input type="text" name="name"></td>
</tr>
```

**Listing 26.3** *Catalog request form (cont.)*

```
<tr>
    <td>Address</td>
    <td><input type="text" name="address"></td>
</tr>
<tr>
    <td>City</td>
    <td><input type="text" name="city"></td>
</tr>
<tr>
    <td>State</td>
    <td><input type="text" name="state"></td>
</tr>
<tr>
    <td>ZIP</td>
    <td><input type="text" name="zip"></td>
</tr>
<tr>
    <td><input type="reset"></td>
    <td><input type="submit"></td>
</tr>
</table>
</form>
</body>
</html>
```

The page in Listing 26.3 is a very simple submission form. Each of the input tags will be turned into the _REQUEST array when the submit button is clicked. This calls the script listed in Listing 26.4. The script opens a file named requests.txt for appending and writes each of the form fields into the file. Each field is separated by tab characters, which allows you to import the file into a spreadsheet easily.

**Listing 26.4** *Form submission*

```
<html>
<head>
<title>Listing 26-4</title>
</head>
<body>
<?
    /*
    ** process form input, append it to file
    */
```

| Listing 26.4 | Form submission (cont.) |
|---|---|

```php
$fp = fopen("/tmp/requests.txt", "a");
if($fp)
{
    //massage user input
    $_REQUEST['name'] = substr(0, 16, $_REQUEST['name']);
    $_REQUEST['address'] = substr(0, 32, $_REQUEST['address']);
    $_REQUEST['city'] = substr(0, 16, $_REQUEST['city']);
    $_REQUEST['state'] = substr(0, 2, $_REQUEST['state']);
    $_REQUEST['zip'] = substr(0, 10, $_REQUEST['zip']);

    //lock the file
    flock($fp, (LOCK_SH));

    //write request
    fputs($fp, $_REQUEST['name'] . "\t" .
        $_REQUEST['address'] . "\t" .
        $_REQUEST['city'] . "\t" .
        $_REQUEST['state'] . "\t" .
        $_REQUEST['zip'] . "\n");

    //release lock
    flock($fp, LOCK_UN);

    //close the file
    fclose($fp);
}

?>
<p>
Thank you for your catalog request!
</p>
<p>
<a href="26-3.html">Return to site</a>
</p>
</body>
</html>
```

# 26.2 Using PHP to Output All HTML

Any of the examples in the previous section is an excellent first step toward introducing PHP into a Web site. Their impact in terms of server load is relatively low. I like to think of sites using similar approaches as being PHP-enabled, as if they had a small injection of PHP that makes them extraordinary. The step beyond this is what I think of as PHP-powered: a site made completely of PHP. In this approach every byte of output comes from PHP. The `print` function sends HTML tags. Every page is a script inside a single pair of PHP tags.

You might have noticed that most of the examples in the book take this approach. I have found that while this requires extra time up front, the code is much more maintainable. Once information is put in the context of a PHP variable, it's easy to add something dynamic to it later. It also has the advantage of ultimately being more readable as the page becomes more complex. Compare the simple examples in Listing 26.5 to Listing 26.6. Both change the background color of the page depending on the time of day.

---

**Listing 26.5**   *Mixing PHP and HTML*

```
<html>
<head>
<title>Listing 26-5</title>
</head>
<?php
    $Hour = date("H");
    $Intensity = round(($Hour/24.0)*(0xFF));
    $PageColor = dechex($Intensity) .
        dechex($Intensity) .
        dechex($Intensity);
?>
<body bgcolor="#<?php print($PageColor); ?>">
<h1>Listing 26-5</h1>
</body>
</html>
```

---

**Listing 26.6**   *Converting script to be completely PHP*

```
<?php
    //start document
    print("<html>\n");
    print("<head>\n");
    print("<title>Listing 26-6</title>\n");
    print("</head>\n");

    $Hour = date("H");
    $Intensity = round(($Hour/24.0)*(0xFF));
    $PageColor = dechex($Intensity) .
        dechex($Intensity) .
        dechex($Intensity);
```

| Listing 26.6 | *Converting script to be completely PHP (cont.)* |
| --- | --- |

```
    //show body
    print("<body bgcolor=\"#$PageColor\">\n");
    print("<h1>Listing 26-6</h1>\n");
    print("</body>\n");
    print("</html>\n");
?>
```

My experience has been that having all the HTML inside the PHP script allows very quick changes. I don't have to search for the opening and closing tags buried inside the HTML as in Listing 26.5. It also allows me to break code up into separate lines in the source code that appear as a single line in the output. An example is the header text. I can enhance the readability but not sacrifice the presentation. This has become very handy when dealing with tables. Leaving any whitespace between a `td` tag and an image causes an extra pixel to appear. In an HTML file, the solution is to run the whole thing together on one line. Inside a PHP script I can have many `print` calls and send an endline only in the last. The result is a single line in the output, but very readable source code.

The usefulness of these techniques, like that of many others, increases with the size of the project. I've created 50-page Web applications using both approaches and can attest to the value of putting everything inside the PHP code.

# 26.3 Separating HTML from PHP

The last approach I want to discuss involves using the `include` and `require` functions. As you may recall from Chapter 7, these functions include a file in the PHP code. The file is considered to be a PHP file regardless of the extension on the name. If PHP code appears in the included file, it is surrounded by `<?php` and `?>` tags. You may want to turn back to the functional reference to refresh yourself on the differences between `include` and `require`, but they aren't particularly important to this discussion.

Certain chunks of HTML must appear on every well-formed page. Additionally, you may develop repeating elements such as a company logo. Rather than write them into every page, you may choose to put them into a file and dynamically include them. Listing 26.7 contains HTML you might include at the top of every page on a site. In Listing 26.8 are two lines to close a page. Listing 26.10 wraps the content in Listing 26.9 with the opening and closing code to form a complete page.

**Listing 26.7**  *Start of HTML page*

```
<html>
<head>
<title>PHP</title>
</head>
<body>
```

**Listing 26.8**  *End of HTML page*

```
</body>
</html>
```

**Listing 26.9**  *Page content*

```
<p>
This is the body of the page.
It's just a bit of HTML.
</p>
```

**Listing 26.10**  *Page-building script*

```
<?php
    // include code to open HTML page
    require("26-7");

    // include content
    require("26-9");

    // include code to close HTML page
    require("26-8");
?>
```

In this way, HTML and PHP are separated into modules. In this example, I have hardcoded the inclusion of a two-line HTML file, but I could just as easily have included the color tables from Listing 26.2. The HTML in Listing 26.7 can be reused from page to page, and if I need to add something to every page on the site, I need to edit only that one file. I might want to add the PHP function from Listing 26.1. It will then be available for use inside the code from Listing 26.9.

It may occur to you that this approach is exhibiting another pattern. Every page on the site will simply become three calls to `require`. The first and last calls will always be the same. In fact, every page on the site will vary simply by the name of the file included in the second `require` statement. This takes us beyond the issue of integrating HTML and PHP and into the structural design of a site. It is possible to create a site that has exactly one PHP script. This idea is developed in Chapter 27.

# 26.4  Generating HTML with PHP

An HTML `select` tag allows you to list several options that appear as a pull-down menu. I am often in the situation of creating the contents of the list on the fly. Sometimes the contents are pulled from a database, such as for choosing from among users in a Web application. Other times the contents are generated, such as choosing month, day, and year. There are two aspects to this problem. First, there is the fairly simple problem of creating all the values for the `option` tags. This is best accomplished in a loop. The second issue deals with preselecting one of the options.

Regardless of the source of the contents, database or otherwise, the technique is similar. To illustrate, I'll develop a function for generating three `select` fields for getting a date from the user: month, day, and year. To generate a list of the months, it is best to draw from an array to display their names. Days and years are numbers, so their values and displayed names are the same. Listing 26.11 demonstrates.

| Listing 26.11 | *Date selector* |
|---|---|

```php
<?php
    /*
    ** Get three selectors for month, day, year
    */
    function getDateSelectors($name, $date=NULL)
    {
        static $monthName = array(1=>"January",
        "February", "March", "April", "May",
        "June", "July", "August", "September",
        "October", "November", "December");

        if($date === NULL)
        {
            $date = time();
        }
```

**Listing 26.11**   *Date selector (cont.)*

```php
//make Month selector
$givenMonth = date("m", $date);
$fields = "<select name=\"{$name}[month]\">\n";
for($m = 1; $m <= 12; $m++)
{
    $fields .= "<option value=\"$m\"";
    if($m == $givenMonth)
    {
        $fields .= " selected";
    }
    $fields .= ">" . $monthName[$m] . "</option>\n";
}
$fields .= "</select>\n";

$fields .= "<select name=\"{$name}[day]\">\n";
$givenDay = date("d", $date);
for($d=1; $d <= 31; $d++)
{
    $fields .= "<option value=\"$d\"";
    if($d == $givenDay)
    {
        $fields .= " selected";
    }
    $fields .= ">$d</option>\n";
}
$fields .= "</select>\n";

$fields .= "<select name=\"{$name}[year]\">\n";
$givenYear = date("Y", $date);
$lastYear = date('Y')+5;
for($y = date('Y')-5; $y <= $lastYear; $y++)
{
    $fields .= "<option value=\"$y\"";
    if($y == $givenYear)
    {
        $fields .= " selected";
    }
    $fields .= ">$y</option>\n";
}
$fields .= "</select>\n";

return($fields);
}
```

**Listing 26.11** *Date selector (cont.)*

```
//start document
print("<html>\n" .
    "<head>\n" .
    "<title>Listing 26-11</title>\n" .
    "</head>\n");

//start body
print("<body>\n");


//choose default date
if(isset($_REQUEST['sample']))
{
    //construct time
    $UseDate = mktime(0, 0, 0,
        $_REQUEST['sample']['month'],
        $_REQUEST['sample']['day'],
        $_REQUEST['sample']['year']);
}
else
{
    //use default
    $UseDate = NULL;
}

//make simple form
print("<form action=\"{$_SERVER['PHP_SELF']}\">\n");
print(getDateSelectors("sample", $UseDate));
print("<input type=\"submit\">\n");
print("</form>\n");

//close HTML document
print("</body>\n" .
    "</html>\n");
?>
```

The options for each selector are generated in a `for` loop. Months range from 1 to 12, days from 1 to 31. For years, I've chosen to present an 11-year range around the current year. Notice that if you submit a date, it refreshes the page and sets the form with the date you chose. The key is the addition of the `if` statement. Each time through the loop, the current value is tested against the one to be selected.

Note how the three selectors pass their values as part of an array. PHP understands to create array elements from form fields named with square brackets. If you duplicate this technique, do not include quotes around the associative key. That is, use `{$name}[month]` instead of `{$name}['month']`. When parsing form fields, PHP does not expect string delimiters around the key.

# DESIGN

**Topics in This Chapter**

- Writing Requirements Specifications
- Writing Design Documents
- Change Management
- Modularization Using `include`
- FreeEnergy
- Templates
- Application Frameworks
- PEAR
- URLs Friendly to Search Engines

# Chapter 27

Building a Web site with PHP is not the same as building a static Web site. If you choose simply to sprinkle PHP code occasionally throughout the site, the effect may be minimal, of course. If you choose to use PHP to generate every page, you will find many opportunities for transforming patterns into functions. As I wrote in Chapter 26, elements such as opening and closing body tags can be put into a function or an included file. The consequence of this situation is that you no longer have just a Web site. You have a Web application.

When this happens, it becomes more important to draw upon formal development techniques. Certainly, structured design is useful when building static Web sites. The case is made plainly in *Web Site Engineering* by Thomas Powell. The addition of PHP makes careful design critical. PHP applications may not be mission-critical endeavors that include thousands of programmers, but there are some ideas from software engineering that can benefit small projects. I can't cover every topic of software engineering as it applies to Web applications in the context of a chapter. I recommend reading Powell's book as an excellent starting point. I also recommend Pete McBreen's *Software Craftsmanship*. His ideas frame the experience of PHP-powered development well.

After introducing the basics of software requirements and design, I will explore some specific design issues and solutions.

# 27.1  Writing Requirements Specifications

Before you can design a system, it is important to understand what it's supposed to do. Too often this comes in the form of a verbal request such as, "We need a home page with a guest book and a visitor counter," which is never further defined. This usually leads to the building of a prototype that is 25 percent of what the client wants. Changes are made to the prototype, and the site is now 50 percent of what the client wants now. During the time the changes were made, the client has moved the target.

The solution to this problem is to set a target and stick with it. This should start with a statement of the goals for the project. In my experience the most important question left unasked is about motivation. When a client asks for a large, animated scene to appear on his index page, often the motivation is a desire to seem familiar with leading-edge technology. Instead of blindly fulfilling the client's request, it is better to look for the best solution for the *Why?* A slick graphical design can say more about the client's attention to advances in technology.

Once you have asked Why? enough times, you should have a list of several goals for the project. These goals should suggest a set of requirements. If one of the system's goals is to generate more business, one requirement may be to raise visitor awareness of items in the client's catalog. This may evolve into a requirement that products appear throughout the site on a rotational basis. This could be implemented as banners or kickers strategically placed within the site. Don't, however, tie yourself down with design issues. This earliest stage of site development should concentrate solely on the goals of the system.

From a solid base of goals, you can begin to describe the system requirements. This usually takes the form of a requirements specification document, a formal description of the black-box behavior expected from the site. The goals will suggest a collection of functional requirements and constraints on the design. As I've said, having a goal of increasing sales suggests, among other things, that the site should raise customer awareness of catalog items. Another requirement could be that the site provides some free service to attract visitors. An example is a loan company offering a mortgage calculator. It is a good idea to informally explore possible solutions to requirements, but it's still important to keep design decisions out at this time.

The requirements specification is formal and structured, but it should be understandable by nonexperts in the implementation technology. The description of the system's behavior serves partially as a contract between the client and developer. Clear statements will eliminate misunderstandings that have a high cost later in development. That is not to say that the document shouldn't be precise. When possible, state requirements in measurable terms. Constraining page size to 30K is an objective standard and easily tested. Requiring the site to inspire confidence in the client company is not easily measurable, but sometimes it's all you have.

Table 27.1 lists six things toward which a requirements specification should aspire. It should only specify external behavior. Every requirement should be expressed as the answer to a *What?* question. It should specify constraints. These are best expressed as quantities: How many hits per day? Maximum page size? Maximum page depth? The requirements specification should allow you to change it later. While you should use natural language, don't write a long narrative. Number sections of the document and use diagrams where necessary. It should be a document that helps a future programmer learn about the system. Don't be surprised if that programmer is you six months later.

The requirements should pay attention to the entire life of the system. If the system needs to be able to recover from a catastrophic failure within an hour, write it into the specification. And the follow-up to this idea is that you should describe how the system deals with adversity—not just disaster, but also illegal user input. Some systems ignore user input that is not understood. How many times have you seen a "404 Document Not Found" error? It's nice when that page includes a link to the index page of the site.

**Table 27.1**  Properties of Requirements Specifications

Specifies only external system behavior

Specifies constraints on the implementation

Allows easy modification

Serves as a reference tool for system maintainers

Records forethought about the lifecycle of the system

Characterizes acceptable responses to undesired events

Keeping these guidelines in mind, refer to Table 27.2, which outlines the structure of a requirements specification. The overview should be a page or less that reviews the goals of the site. If the goals were detailed in another document, make this document available. It is important to preserve the thought that went into the project at each phase. The requirements build on the goals, and in turn the design builds on the requirements. But being able to refer to the original goals of the system will be helpful to the designer and even the implementer.

**Table 27.2**   Requirements Specification Document Structure

Overview of system goals

Operating and development environments

External interfaces and data flow

Functional requirements

Performance requirements

Exception handling

Implementation priorities

Foreseeable modifications

Design suggestions

The operating and development environments are sometimes overlooked in requirements specifications. This includes both the browser and the Web server. If you are developing an intranet application, you may be fortunate enough to optimize for a particular browser version. I've found that while a large company may impose a standard browser for the organization for which you've developed an application, another standard may apply to the users in another organization a thousand miles away. The most popular browsers operate closer to a standard than they did in the early days of the Web, so this is less of an issue than it was.

The Web server is perhaps more under your control and certainly less finicky about differences in source code. If you are using PHP, most likely you will be using Apache. It's a good idea to use identical versions of both Apache and PHP for your development and live environments.

For the most part, your list of external interfaces will include the Internet connection between the browser and the Web server, the local file system, and possibly a database connection. I find it helpful to create a diagram that shows the relationship between data elements, the simplest of which might be a box labeled Browser connected to a box labeled Server. The line would have arrows at each end to show that information travels in both directions. This diagram is a description of the context, not a design of the data structure. Whether you will be using a database may be obvious, but which database may not be. If the system will be storing data somehow, just show data flowing into a box that could be database or flat file. The goal is to describe how data moves around in the system.

The functional requirements will certainly be the largest part of the document. If you have drawn a data flow diagram, you may have a very good idea of how the system breaks up into modules. The more you can partition the functionality into distinct pieces, the easier it will be to group the functional requirements. I've written many requirements documents for Web applications that are essentially data warehouses. My approach has been to dedicate a section to each of the major data entities. A project management application might have a collection of project descriptions, a collection of users, and a collection of comments. Each of these would have a section in the functional requirements that lists first all the information it stores and then the ways the information can be manipulated.

The performance requirements are constraints on the functionality. You may wish to outline a minimum browser configuration for use of the site. Maximum page weights are a good idea. If the client is dictating that a certain technology be used, it should be noted in this section. It's good to know in advance that while you will be allowed to use PHP, you have to deal with Oracle and Internet Information Server on Windows XP.

The exception-handling section describes how the system deals with adversity. The two parts of this are disaster and invalid input. Discuss what should happen if the Web server suddenly bursts into flame. Decide whether backups will be made hourly, daily, or weekly. Also decide how the system handles users entering garbage. For example, define whether filling out a form with a missing city asks the user to hit the back button or automatically redisplays the form with everything filled out and the missing field marked with a red asterisk.

If the client has a preference for the order of implementation, outline it. My experience has been that, faced with a dire deadline before the project begins, the client will bargain for which functionality will appear in the first round. Other requirements may not be critical to the system, and the client is willing to wait. If there is a preference in this area, it is very important for the designer and implementers to know in advance.

Farther in the future are the foreseeable modifications. The client may not be ready to create a million-dollar e-commerce site just yet, but may expect to ask you to plug this functionality into the site a year from now. It may not make sense to use an expensive database to implement a 50-item catalog, but building a strong foundation for later expansion will likely be worthwhile.

The last part of the requirements specification is a collection of design hints. This represents the requirements writer's forethought about pitfalls for the designer. You might summarize a similar project. You might suggest a design approach.

# 27.2 Writing Design Documents

Once you have created a requirements specification document, you will have to decide whether to write a design document. Often it is not necessary, especially when a few people are working on a small project. You may wish to choose key elements of a complete design document and develop them to the point of usefulness.

The first part of design is concerned with the architecture of the system. The system should be broken into sections that encompass broad groups of functionality. A Web application for project management might break down into a module that handles project information, a module that handles users, and a module that handles timesheet entries. An informational Web site can be broken down by the secondary pages—that is, the pages one click away from the home page. The "About Us" section serves to inform visitors about the company itself, while a catalog area is a resource for learning about the items the company sells.

Depending on the type of site, you should choose some sort of diagram that shows the subsystems and how they relate to each other. These are called entity relationship diagrams. I almost always create a page-flow diagram. Each node in the graph is a page as experienced by the user. Lines representing links connect the page to other pages on the site. Another useful diagram is one that shows the relationships between database tables. Nodes represent tables, and you may wish to list the fields inside boxes that stand for the tables. Lines connect tables and show how fields match. It's also helpful to indicate whether the relationship between the tables is one to one or one to many.

The next phase of design is interface specification. This defines how subsystems communicate. It can be as simple as listing the URLs for each page. If the site has forms, all the fields should be enumerated. If you are tracking user sessions, you will want to specify how you will be doing this, with cookies or form variables. Define acceptable values for the session identifier. If the site will be communicating with files or a database, this phase will define names of files or login information for databases.

The largest part of a design document is a detailed description of how each module works. At this point it's acceptable to specify exactly the method for implementing the module. For example, you may specify that a list of catalog items be presented using the `ul` tag. On the other hand, if it doesn't matter, leave it out. The programmer will have the best idea for solving the problem.

I suggest pursuing a style guide, which may be part of the design document or may stand alone. This document specifies the style of the code in the project. You'll find an example in Appendix G, but don't bother flipping there now. The style guide deals with issues like how to name variables and where to place curly braces. Many of these issues are arbitrary. What's important is that a decision is made and followed. A large body of code formatted according to a standard is easier to read.

For the rest of this chapter I'd like to present some design ideas you may choose to adopt. PHP's dynamic nature allows for structural designs that can't be achieved in plain HTML. It is a shame to waste this functionality by using PHP as a faster alternative to CGI. I encourage you to consider using PHP as the engine that powers a completely dynamic Web site.

# 27.3  Change Management

Anyone who's worked with a team on a Web application knows the pain of dividing the tasks among team members. For small teams, it usually works to shout over cubicle walls. For larger teams, you may need a manager to coordinate the development process. However, Gantt charts don't seem to fit the shoot-from-the-hip mentality of the typical Web programmer. It feels natural to wander through the files of the project, changing them as you tackle a problem without worrying if someone else is editing them.

Sometimes changes are lost, but people cope by keeping backups. Alternatively, team members can warn each other not to touch some files for short period. If a file is destroyed, you may hunt through archives to find an older version. Developers can guard against losing newer changes by keeping local copies of every change they make, but it feels like a big hassle.

Web sites evolve through many iterations. The team works on a project, and it integrates the changes when it finishes. There are two typical methods for putting the changes into production. The brute force method involves replacing all application files. This ensures that you don't miss any files. Alternatively, you can copy just the new files and the files that changed.

Instead of trying to control the source code through ad hoc activities, consider using a source code control system. Popular among C programmers, source code control works well with most programming languages. The PHP development team uses source code control to coordinate the hundreds of people contributing to PHP, as do many open-source projects.

The overwhelming favorite source code control system among open-source developers is CVS (concurrent versions system). CVS is an open-source project itself. At its core is the functionality of the `diff` and `patch` utilities that are part of most operating systems. You can use `diff` to compare two files and find the differences. The `patch` utility can apply the differences to a third file to bring it up to date.

CVS keeps a repository for a project that includes every incremental change to every file. Users interact with the repository by running shell commands on the server. Remote users must use a remote shell, which is `rsh` by default. It's wise to avoid `rsh` and use `ssh` if you can, as `rsh` sends passwords and traffic through the net unencrypted. Some open-source projects provide a read-only account for grabbing a current development version without allowing changes.

After checking out files from a repository, a developer may make any number of changes to files without disturbing any other developer. Under normal use, CVS does not grant exclusive use of a file to one user. These are called unreserved copies. Developers work on files concurrently, and CVS takes care of tracking changes as they are checked in. CVS distributes changes on demand to developers. The changes integrate into source files even if the developer updates a file with changes that aren't checked in.

CVS does support reserved copies, but most users find them unnecessary. In most contexts, CVS can resolve differences between files without human intervention. When conflicts do occur, CVS alerts the developer and marks conflicting code plainly.

Although I present a brief tutorial here, find Karl Fogel's book, *Open Source Development with CVS* <http://cvsbook.red-bean.com/>. The chapters that deal with CVS specifically are free to download, but I recommend buying the book if you decide to use CVS. Beyond the mechanics of CVS itself, it documents how CVS fits into the development process. Also, keep an eye on the Subversion project <http://subversion.tigris.org/>, which aims to build a CVS replacement.

If you're running Linux or FreeBSD, CVS may be installed already. If not, use a package manager appropriate for your system, such as RPM or `apt-get`. If you're using Windows, you can run CVS clients with no problem, but CVS servers don't work well. You can set up a server that allows local CVS usage with which to experiment, but you need a UNIX operating system to use CVS seriously.

The CVS Web site <http://www.cvshome.org/> has links for downloading binaries for many operating systems. You can also download source code and compile it yourself, but I won't go over those steps. The compilation follows typical steps because it uses `autoconf`. See the installation instructions in the source code archive.

CVS requires just one binary that's typically installed as `/usr/local/bin/cvs`. This is the client application, but it also makes changes on the server through a remote shell. To start using a host as a CVS server, you only need to create a repository.

All CVS functionality goes through the `cvs` command-line utility. The `init` command to `cvs` creates a new repository. The `-d` option sets the path to the repository. CVS creates this directory and places several files inside it. Figure 27.1 is a capture from my shell as I created a new repository and listed the contents.

```
# cvs -d /home/cvshome init
# ls -R /home/cvshome
/home/cvshome:
CVSROOT

/home/cvshome/CVSROOT:
Emptydir          config,v          loginfo       rcsinfo
checkoutlist      cvswrappers       loginfo,v     rcsinfo,v
checkoutlist,v    cvswrappers,v     modules       taginfo
commitinfo        editinfo          modules,v     taginfo,v
commitinfo,v      editinfo,v        notify        verifymsg
config            history           notify,v      verifymsg,v

/home/cvshome/CVSROOT/Emptydir:
```

**Figure 27.1**   Creating a CVS repository.

I created this directory as the root user. This doesn't allow anyone else to use the repository. I created a group named `cvs` in `/etc/group` and used `chgrp` to allow users in this group to use the repository.

Traditionally, CVS uses a password server process on port 2401 for connections. Installation involves adding the server to `inetd`'s list of daemons. CVS manages a set of users and passwords separate from those in `/etc/passwd` with the `pserver` daemon. All commands through the password server execute as a single user.

Using `pserver` is good for public repositories, such as those for open-source projects. If you're using it for your internal team, don't bother with it. It's complicated and less secure than SSH.

CVS uses `rsh` by default. Set the `CVS_RSH` environment variable to switch it to SSH. For example, I added the lines in Figure 27.2 to my `.bash_profile` file.

```
#make sure cvs uses SSH
CVS_RSH=ssh
export CVS_RSH
```

**Figure 27.2**  Additions to bash profile.

To access the CVS server remotely, you must use special notation. CVS uses colons to separate information about the authentication method and the hostname of the server. For example, `:ext:leon@192.168.123.194:/home/cvshome` matches my repository.

In this mode, CVS will prompt you for your password each time you execute `cvs`. Some people find this annoying, so they generate an authorized key. This is a function of SSH, not CVS. You can read about this on the OpenSSH site `<http://www.openssh.org/>`.

Use the `import` command to create a project inside your repository. This command creates a directory in the repository and copies all the files in your current directory recursively. For example, I started a new project in a directory called `myproject`. Inside the directory is a single PHP script. To create a directory in the repository, I issued the commands in Figure 27.3. Note how I used backslashes to keep the lines from wrapping.

The `-d` option appears again, specifying the path to the repository. The `-m` option applies to the `import` command. It sets a comment to associate with the CVS action. This comment can be as long as you need, and if you leave out the `-m` option, CVS will launch an editor for you. The last three commands specify the project name, the vendor tag, and the release tag. These names are up to you. The project name will be the name used for the directory on the server, and it's how you refer to the project, so choose a short name. What you choose for the vendor tag and the release tag aren't important usually. I use the name of the company and `start` by default.

```
/tmp/myproject> cvs \
-d :ext:leon@192.168.123.194:/home/cvshome import \
-m 'starting my project' myproject mycompany start
leon@192.168.123.194's password:
N myproject/index.php

No conflicts created by this import

/tmp/development/myproject>
```

**Figure 27.3**    Importing a project into CVS.

CVS created a directory on the server, but it hasn't changed any of the files I imported. To work with the files in the repository, you must make a checkout.

The checkout command copies files from the server to your local machine. It also creates directories named CVS in every subdirectory of the project. These subdirectories keep track of the status of the files and where they came from. After making a checkout, you no longer need to specify the path to the repository. CVS will find it in the CVS directory.

Figure 27.4 shows how I made a checkout of my new project.

```
~> cvs -d :ext:leon@192.168.123.194:/home/cvshome \
checkout myproject
leon@192.168.123.194's password:
cvs server: Updating myproject
U myproject/index.php
~>
```

**Figure 27.4**    Checking out a project from CVS.

Once you checkout the project, you can start editing files. Other developers can make their own checkouts. When you finish working on a file, use a commit command to integrate your changes into the project. CVS examines all the files in the current directory and in any subdirectories. It then coordinates with the server to find changes and apply them to the server's copies of the files. Figure 27.5 shows the results of making a commit.

You and other developers can commit changes as often as you wish, and the server keeps the most current version at all times. Your own files do not receive updates unless you ask for them explicitly with the update command. CVS will check all files recursively. If the server has a newer version, it applies the changes to your files. Your changes are not lost. CVS does its best to merge your changes with those committed since you last updated your files.

```
~/myproject>cvs commit -m 'added navigation code'
leon@192.168.123.194's password:
Checking in index.php;
/home/cvshome/myproject/index.php,v   <--   index.php
new revision: 1.2; previous revision: 1.1
done
~/myproject>
```

**Figure 27.5**   Checking changes into CVS.

Updating your files often helps keep your work coordinated with other developers and avoids conflicts. Conflicts occur when two developers disagree on a particular part of the source code. For example, consider the following sequence of events. In the beginning state, a line in the source code states $a=3. Later, another developer changes the line to $a=5 and commits the file. This sets the official version of the line. If you issue an update before changing this line, you will receive the change with no conflicts, and you can change it yourself. However, if you change the line before issuing an update, you will encounter a conflict. CVS marks the conflicting sections of code and inserts both versions in the source code. To resolve the conflict, you must edit the file and choose one version or the other.

Regularly updating files helps avoid conflicts. It also alerts you to changes in files. As you issue an update, CVS notifies you of which files have changed since your last update. You can also configure CVS to email changes to a mailing list. If all developers subscribe to the mailing list, they can monitor activity on the project. This isn't a substitute for proper communication among team members, but it reduces the need to consult constantly with each other about who's editing which file.

When you're ready to make the project live, you have two options. If releases are infrequent, you may wish to make an export of the project and replace existing files on the production server. Use the `export` command to make a checkout that contains no CVS directories.

For a site that gets frequently updated, I prefer making an ordinary CVS checkout on the production server. When making a new version of the site live, you need to log in to the production server and issue an `update` command. This is faster and less hassle than replacing all existing files. It also avoids those errors associated with missing files or incorrect paths.

# 27.4   Modularization Using `include`

Despite its name, the `include` function is not equivalent to C's preprocessor command of the same name. In many ways it is like a function call. Given the name of a file, PHP attempts to parse the file as if it appeared in place of the call to `include`.

The difference from a function is that the code will be parsed only if the `include` statement is executed. You can take advantage of this by wrapping calls to `include` in `if` statements. The `require` function, however, will always include the specified file, even if it is inside an `if` block that is never executed. It has been discussed several times on the PHP mailing list that `require` is faster than `include` because PHP is able to inject the specified file into the script during an early pass across the code. However, this applies only to files specified by a static path. If the call to `require` contains a variable, it can't be executed until runtime. It may be helpful to adopt a rule of using `require` only when outside a compound statement and when specifying a static path.

Almost anything I write in PHP uses `include` extensively. The first reason is that it makes the code more readable. The other reason is that it breaks the site into modules. This allows multiple people to work on the site at once. It forces you to write code that is more easily reused within the existing site and on your next project. Most Web sites have to rely on repeating elements. Consistent navigation aids the user, but it is also a major problem when building and maintaining the site. Each page has to have a similar code block pasted into it. Making this a module and including it allows you to debug the code once, making changes quickly.

You can adopt a strategy that consists of placing functions into include modules. As each script requires a particular function, you can simply add an `include`. If your library of functions is small enough, you might place them all into one file. However, you likely will have pieces of code that are needed on just a handful of pages. In this case, you'll want this module to stand alone.

As your library of functions grows, you may discover some interdependencies. Imagine a module for establishing a connection to a database, plus a couple of other modules that rely on the database connection. Each of these two scripts will include the database connection module. But what happens when both are themselves included in a script? The database module is included twice. This may cause a second connection to be made to the database, and if any functions are defined, PHP will report the error of a duplicate function.

In C programmers avoid this situation by defining constants inside the included files. In PHP you can use the `include_once` statement. A function named `printBold` is defined in Listing 27.1. This function is needed in the script shown in Listing 27.2. I've purposely placed a bug in the form of a second `include`. The second time the module is included, it will return before redeclaring the function.

**Listing 27.1** *Preventing a double `include`*

```php
<?php
    function printBold($text)
    {
        print("<b>$text</b>");
    }
?>
```

| Listing 27.2 | *Attempting to include a module twice* |

```php
<?php
    //load printBold function
    include_once("27-1.php");

    //try loading printBold function again
    include_once("27-1.php");

    printBold("Successfully avoided a second include");
?>
```

# 27.5 FreeEnergy

I used the technique of including modules on several Web applications, and it led me to consider all the discrete elements of a Web page. Headers and footers are obvious, and so are other repeating navigational elements. Sometimes you can divide pages up into the content unique to the page, the stuff that comes before it, and the stuff that comes after it. This could be hard to maintain, however. Some of the HTML is in one file, some in another. If nothing else, you'll need to flip between two editor windows.

Consider for a moment a Web page as an object—that is, in an object-oriented way. On the surface, a Web page is a pair of `html` tags containing `head` tags and `body` tags. Regardless of the design or content of the page, these tags must exist, and inside them will be placed further tags. Inside the `body` tags a table can be placed for controlling the layout of the page. Inside the cells of the table are either links to other pages on the site or some content unique to the page.

FreeEnergy is a system that attempts to encapsulate major pieces of each page into files to be included on demand. Before I proceed, I want to state my motivations clearly. My first concern when developing a Web site is that it be correct and of the highest quality. Second is that it may be developed and maintained in minimal time. After these needs are addressed, I consider performance. Performance is considered last because of the relatively cheap cost of faster hardware. Moore's law suggests that eighteen months from now, CPU speed and memory capacity will have doubled for the same price. This doubling costs nothing but time. Also, experience has shown that a small minority of code contributes to a majority of the time spent processing. These small sections can be optimized later, leaving the rest of the code to be written as clearly as possible.

The FreeEnergy system uses more calls to `include` than you would find if you simply make a few includes at the top of your pages. Hits to the file system do take longer than function calls, of course. You could place everything you might need in one large file and include it on every page, but you will face digging through that large file when you need to change anything. A trade has been made between the performance of the application and the time it takes to develop and maintain it.

I called this system FreeEnergy because it seems to draw power from the environment that PHP provides. The `include` function in PHP is quite unique and central to FreeEnergy, especially the allowance for naming a script with a variable. The content unique to a page is called a screen. The screen name is passed to a single PHP script, which references the screen name in a large array that matches the screen to corresponding layout and navigation modules.

The FreeEnergy system breaks Web pages into five modules: action, layout, navigation, screen, and utility. Action modules perform some sort of write function to a database, a file, or possibly to the network. Only one action module executes during a request, and it is executed before the screen module. An action module may override the screen module named in the request. This is helpful in cases where an action module is attempting to process a form and the submitted data are incomplete or otherwise unsatisfactory. Action modules never send data directly to the screen. Instead, they add messages to a stack to be popped later by the layout module. It is possible that an action module will send header information, so it's important that no output be produced.

Layout modules contain just enough code to arrange the output of screen and navigation modules. They typically contain `table` tags for controlling the layout of a Web page. Inside the table cells, calls to `include` are placed. They may be invoking navigation modules or screen modules.

Navigation modules contain links and repeating elements. In the vernacular used by engineers I work with, these are "top nav," "bottom nav," and "side nav." Consider the popular site, Yahoo!. Its pages generally consist of the same navigation across the top and some at the bottom. Its top nav includes the logo and links to important areas of the site. If the Yahoo! site were coded in FreeEnergy, there would probably be a dynamic navigation module for generating breadcrumbs for the current section, such as `Home > Computers and Internet > Software > Internet > World Wide Web > Servers > Server Side Scripting > PHP`.

Screen modules contain the content unique to the particular page being displayed. They may be plain HTML, or they may be primarily PHP code, depending on context. A press release is static. Someone unfamiliar with PHP can prepare it. He needs only know that the screen module is an HTML fragment.

Any module may rely on a utility module in much the same way utility files are used in other contexts. Some utility modules are called with each page load. Others are collections of functions or objects related to a particular database table.

All modules are collected in a `modules` directory that further contains a subdirectory for each module type. To enhance security, it is placed outside of the Web server's document root. Within the document root is a single PHP script index.php. This script begins the process of calling successive modules and structuring their output with the standard HTML tags.

# 27.6 Templates

Another approach to modularizing PHP applications can be called templatizing. Loose coupling is a fundamental principle of good system design. Aside from avoiding confusing people who don't understand PHP, a separation offers the benefit of switching to a different presentation language, such as XML, without disturbing the business logic.

Using templates, interface designers insert simple tags into prototypical files (templates) composed mostly of HTML. They insert short bits of a simple templating language that a PHP script parses in order to replace markers with generated information.

As with most solutions, there's a tradeoff. The cost of a templating system is increased work for PHP with each page load. PHP includes an efficient parser written in C by the geniuses at Zend. Writing your own parser in PHP itself is bound to be less than optimal, or so the argument goes. Yet, a simple syntax can help keep parsing fast, and some caching tricks can avoid most of the heavy lifting.

I'm optimistic about the average person being able to learn to program in PHP. Templating pessimistically guesses that the average person won't learn PHP but can understand a simpler middle ground between PHP and HTML. I like to teach people to understand PHP, but I also understand there's usually a context for a good tool.

FastTemplate is perhaps the oldest of the templating systems. It was ported from the original Perl implementation. It uses `.tpl` files to hold templates. These templates contain HTML and markers inside curly braces. A PHP script loads a template, sets values for each of the markers, and parses the template to produce a final chunk of HTML ready to send to the browser.

**Listing 27.3** *Main template*

```
<html>
<head><title>{TITLE}</title>
</head>
<body>
<h1>{TITLE}</h1>
<table>
<tr>
<td valign="top">{SIDENAV}</td>
<td valign="top">{MAIN}</td>
</tr>
</table>
</body>
</html>
```

Listing 27.3 shows a simple template. Look for the markers in curly braces. This template uses three: TITLE, SIDENAV, and MAIN. These are chunks of content generated inside the main PHP script. The first is a simple variable assignment, and the second will contain another template file. The last is a standard name used by FastTemplate to stand for the main content of any screen. Listing 27.4, Listing 27.5, and Listing 27.6 are a few other templates used in this example.

| Listing 27.4 | *Side navigation* |
| --- | --- |

```
<a href="home.php">Home</a><br>
<a href="about.php">About Us</a><br>
<a href="contact.php">Contact Us</a><br>
```

| Listing 27.5 | *Table template* |
| --- | --- |

```
<table border="1">
<tr><th>n</th> <th>n^2</th> <th>n^3</th></tr>
{ROWS}
</table>
```

| Listing 27.6 | *Row template* |
| --- | --- |

```
<tr>
    <td>{NUMBER}</td> <td>{SQUARE}</td>  <td>{CUBE}</td>
</tr>
```

The side navigation is a simple set of links to other scripts, as you might expect. The table includes three columns for a number, its square, and its cube. A template stored in row.tpl further defines the rows of the table. The PHP script in Listing 27.7 calls this template for each row of the table.

**Listing 27.7**   *Script using templates*

```php
<?php
    //get FastTemplate class
    require_once("class.FastTemplate.php");

    //instantiate
    //use templates in current directory
    $tpl = new FastTemplate(".");

    //set list of templates used
    $tpl->define(
        array(
            "main"=>"27-3.tpl",
            "side"=>"27-4.tpl",
            "table"=>"27-5.tpl",
            "row"=>"27-6.tpl"
        )
    );

    //set the value of the TITLE variable
    $tpl->assign(array("TITLE"=>"FastTemplate Test"));

    //get side navigation
    $tpl->parse("SIDENAV", "side");

    //create rows for the table
    for($n=1; $n <= 10; $n++)
    {
        //set values
        $tpl->assign(
            array(
                "NUMBER"=>$n,
                "SQUARE"=>pow($n,2),
                "CUBE"=>pow($n,3)
            )
        );

        //parse row template and append it to ROWS
        $tpl->parse("ROWS",".row");
    }

    //parse table, main and put it in MAIN
    $tpl->parse("MAIN", array("table","main"));

    //send entire contents to the browser
    $tpl->FastPrint("MAIN");
?>
```

Most of the code in this example ought to be easy to follow. The template files need to be in a subdirectory, as shown in the instantiation. The `assign` method sets one or more variables to a fixed value, and the `parse` method parses a template. You must define marker values before parsing a template, of course.

This example produces a table of numbers generated in a loop. Each row of the table is appended to the `ROWS` variable by assigning variable values and parsing the template. Note that the call to `parse` uses a period before the name of the template, `row`. This tells FastTemplate to append instead of replace.

FastTemplate also uses another syntax for repeating blocks. You mark part of the HTML with HTML comments that must follow a strict form. There's no room for adding extra spacing or breaking the comment onto two lines. These are called dynamic blocks, and they are really embedded templates.

PHPLib is a large framework for building Web applications. It includes a class that uses templates very similar to those used by FastTemplate. You must download the entire package to get the template class, but it's usable by itself.

Like FastTemplate, PHPLib's template class uses curly braces for markers. It also supports repeating blocks using HTML comment syntax. Other than the differences in method names, this class works like FastTemplate.

Two other similar solutions are AvantTemplate and TemplatePower. These classes use the same approach to templating defined by FastTemplate: markers that stand for replaceable values. They also add support for including templates directly instead of using a marker.

Choosing between these templating systems is largely one of personal preference. You might prefer the syntax of one of them over others. TemplatePower claims to be faster than FastTemplate by six times. Naturally, if you use PHPLib, its included templating class is your best choice.

The consequence of the extra layer keeping HTML and PHP logic separate is a hit to performance. Every page load requires parsing templates and filling in values for markers. It can have a significant effect on the time it takes to assemble a page. Some data must be regenerated with each request, such as the contents of a shopping basket, but most information on a Web site is static. We can save a lot of work if we cache the parsed templates.

In computer terms, a cache is temporary, fast storage. Space in the cache is limited, and data placed there is volatile. Caches rely on the idea that a request for data now predicts another request for the same data in the near future. If an application behaves this way and the cache is sufficiently large, you will experience a performance increase by using a cache.

The `cachedFastTemplate` class adds caching to the original PHP FastTemplate implementation. Two new methods allow reading from and writing to text files stored in `/tmp`. The `write_cache` method stores fully parsed templates in a directory named after the Web server's host name. The `is_cached` method will load the contents from the directory if the template was cached previously.

The appeal of this class is that it's a drop-in replacement for the original class. You don't need to update your templates. Changes to your PHP scripts are minor, and they will continue to function even without modification. They just won't cache.

There are a few other templating systems that use caching, but Smarty is an industrial-strength solution. First, Smarty compiles templates into native PHP. The template file edited by interface designers is parsed only once. Calls to templates cause the PHP engine to run a `.php` file. This eliminates the overhead of running a parser written in PHP.

Compilation of scripts occurs behind the scenes, with no commands in your script. If a page request calls for a template that hasn't been compiled yet, Smarty compiles it. If the template file changes after this compilation, Smarty will recompile the next time your script uses the template.

Additionally, Smarty includes caching functionality, increasing the performance for static pages. For those pages with static content, Smarty will process the template into a plaintext file. As with other caching implementations, you can set an expiration time, after which the file will be regenerated.

Smarty's templating system includes more than just marker replacement. It also includes sophisticated control flow, such as if-else statements. This allows interface designers to make simple logical decisions without bothering programmers. The system also includes loops and a function for including other templates in place.

Templating systems are clearly a satisfying solution for some people; otherwise, they wouldn't be so popular. FastTemplate is simple, and I'm sure anyone comfortable with HTML can handle working around the markers. The complex solutions, such as Smarty, may be nearly as intimidating as PHP itself. This is not to suggest that Smarty has no value. Its approach certainly will be attractive to many programmers, and careful communication with novices can help keep them away from the more complex syntax.

Most of these templating systems use {name} as a marker for some value to be placed later by a PHP script. It's only slightly more complicated to write `<?php=$name?>`. The biggest disadvantage to using PHP tags is that they don't show up visually in browsers, which treat them as unrecognized tags.

# 27.7 Application Frameworks

Taking application development to the next logical level, application frameworks attempt to organize reusable components to a ready platform for application development. The bargain made with these tools is trading some flexibility and performance for a large library of ready-made components. This can lead to rapid development.

BinaryCloud `<http://www.binarycloud.com/>` is a complete application-hosting environment written in PHP, meant for building enterprise-level applications. Alex Black and his company, Turing Studio, lead the maintenance of BinaryCloud. BinaryCloud compiles its own source files into PHP scripts. It uses the Smarty template engine discussed earlier in the chapter. The source code is freely available under a GNU license.

Another approach to Web site design with PHP is the Midgard project `<http://www.midgard-project.org/>`. The maintainers are Jukka Zitting and Henri Bergius. Rather than code a solution in PHP alone, they have pursued integrating PHP into their own application server. Midgard is capable of organizing more than 800,000 pages of content using a Web-based interface. For this reason it is ideal for operating Magazine sites.

Midgard is an open-source project, of course. You can download an official release or grab a snapshot through CVS. Binary downloads are available as well.

Ariadne is a Web application framework from Muze, a development agency in the Netherlands. It's available under the GNU Public License. Auke van Slooten leads the project. The source code can be downloaded from the Muze site `<http://www.muze.nl/software/ariadne/>`.

Ariadne stores PHP source code as objects in a MySQL database. These objects interact with each other using a virtual file system. A rich user interface is presented to the user through Web pages, but advanced users may dig deeper, as well. Another major component controls access rights for users or groups.

Horde `<http://www.horde.org/>` is the application framework used for IMP, a popular email client written in PHP. Chuck Hagenbuch started the Horde Project. Currently, Eric Rostetter maintains the project, which is available under a GNU license. The framework evolved from the backend of the original IMP application, and its heritage shows in its ability to build quality Web applications for communicating with Internet servers.

# 27.8 PEAR

PEAR `<http://pear.php.net/>` is the PHP Extension and Application Repository. It's part of the PHP project, and you get a copy of the core PEAR library when you install PHP. In some ways, PEAR is a parallel to Perl's CPAN. It collects many general-purpose PHP scripts into a cohesive library. You can fetch components as you need them using part of PEAR itself. Stig Bakken, a longtime PHP contributor, leads the PEAR project.

A core set of PEAR classes comes along with PHP. Although some packages have a narrow purpose, PEAR as a whole is general purpose. Downloading a PEAR package is easy. The PHP distribution includes a shell script named `pear`. Running `pear` without any arguments lists available commands. To get a list of packages available for installation, run `pear remote-list`. To install a package, execute something like `pear install XML_Tree`. The script downloads and installs the package.

Using a PEAR class is easy too. PHP keeps the downloaded PEAR classes in `/usr/local/lib/php` by default. This path should be in your include path, which means you can include a PEAR class simply by naming it. For example, `require_once('XML/Tree.php')` gets the XML Tree class. Listing 27.8 demonstrates the use of `XML_Tree`, which allows the creation of an XML document without having the DOMXML extension available.

---

**Listing 27.8** *Using a PEAR class*

```php
<?php
    //load XML_Tree
    require_once('XML/Tree.php');

    //create a document
    $tree = new XML_Tree;
    $root =& $tree->addRoot('catalog');
    $section =& $root->addChild('section');
    $section->addChild('A');
    $section->addChild('B');
    $section->addChild('C');
    $section =& $root->addChild('section');
    $section->addChild('X');
    $section->addChild('Y');
    $section->addChild('Z');

    //dump XML document
    header('Content-Type: text/xml');
    $tree->dump();
?>
```

---

# 27.9 URLs Friendly to Search Engines

Search engines such as Google <http://www.google.com/> and All the Web <http://www.alltheweb.com/> attempt to explore the entire Web. They have become an essential resource for Internet users, and anyone who maintains a public site benefits from being listed. Search engines use robots, or spiders, to explore pages in a Web site, and they index PHP scripts the same way they index HTML files. When links appear in a page, they are followed. Consequently, the entire site becomes searchable.

Unfortunately, many robots do not follow links that appear to contain form variables. Links containing question marks may lead a robot into an endless loop, so they are programmed to avoid them. This presents a problem for sites that use form variables in links. Passing form variables in anchor tags is a natural way for PHP to communicate, but it can keep your pages out of the search engines. To overcome this problem, data must be passed in a format that resembles ordinary URLs.

First, consider how a Web server accepts a URI and matches it to a file. The URI is a virtual path, the part of the URL that comes after the hostname. It begins with a slash and may be followed by a directory, another slash, and so forth. One by one, the Web server matches directories in the URI to directories in the file system. A script is executed when it matches part of the URI, even when more path information follows. Ordinarily, this extra path information is thrown away, but you can capture it.

Look at Listing 27.9. This script works with Apache compiled for UNIX but may not work with other Web servers. It relies on the PATH_INFO environment variable, which may not be present in a different context. Each Web server creates a unique set of environment variables, although there is overlap.

**Listing 27.9**    *Using path info*

```php
<?php
   if(isset($_SERVER['PATH_INFO']))
   {
       //remove .html from the end
       $path = str_replace(".html",
           "", $_SERVER['PATH_INFO']);

       //remove leading slash
       $path = substr($path, 1);

       //iterate over parts
       $pathVar = array();
       $v = explode("/", $path);
       $c = count($v);
       for($i=0; $i<$c; $i += 2)
       {
           $pathVar[($v[$i])] = $v[$i+1];
       }
```

| Listing 27.9 | *Using path info (cont.)* |
|---|---|

```
    print("You are viewing message " .
        "{$pathVar['message']}<br>\n");
}

//pick a random ID
$nextID = rand(1, 1000);
print("<a href=\"{$_SERVER["SCRIPT_NAME"]}/message/
    $nextID.html\">" .
    "View Message $nextID</a><br>\n");
?>
```

You may be accessing the code in Listing 27.9 from the URL http://localhost/corephp/27-9.php/message/1234.html. In this case, you are connecting to a local server that contains a directory named corephp in its document root. A default installation of Apache might place this in /usr/local/apcache/htdocs. The name of the script is 27-9.php, and everything after the script name is then placed in the PATH_INFO variable. No file named 1234.html exists, but to the Web browser it appears to be an ordinary HTML document. It appears that way to a spider as well.

The code in Listing 27.9 doesn't really do much. It splits the path info into pairs used for variable name and value. The script pretends message is an identifier. It could be referencing a record in a relational database. I've added some code to use a random number to create a link to another imaginary record. Remember the BBS from Chapter 23? This method could be applied, and each message would appear to be a single HTML file.

I've introduced only the essential principles of this method. There are a few pitfalls, and there are a few enhancements to be pursued. Keep in mind that Web browsers do their best to fill in relative URLs, and using path information this way may foil their attempts to request images that appear in your scripts. Therefore, you must use absolute paths. You might also wish to name your PHP script so that it doesn't contain an extension. This is possible with Apache by setting the default document type, using the DefaultType configuration directive. You can also use Apache's mod_rewrite. I encourage you to read about these parts of Apache at its home site <http://www.apache.org/docs/>.

# EFFICIENCY AND DEBUGGING

## Topics in This Chapter

- Optimization
- Measuring Performance
- Optimize the Slowest Parts
- When to Store Content in a Database
- Debugging Strategies
- Simulating HTTP Connections
- Output Buffering
- Output Compression
- Avoiding `eval`
- Don't Load Extensions Dynamically
- Improving Performance of MySQL Queries
- Optimizing Disk-Based Sessions
- Don't Pass by Reference
- Avoid Concatenation of Large Strings
- Avoid Serving Large Files with PHP-Enabled Apache
- Understanding Persistent Database Connections
- Avoid Using `exec`, Backticks, and `system` If Possible
- Use `php.ini-recommended`
- Don't Use Regular Expressions Unless You Must
- Optimizing Loops
- IIS Configuration

# Chapter 28

This chapter touches upon some issues of efficiency and debugging, which are more art than science. Efficiency should not be your first concern when writing code. You must first write code that works, and hopefully your second concern is keeping the code maintainable.

You will pick up some tactical design issues as you gain more experience in programming. These begin to gel as idioms—repeated structures applied to similar problems. Individuals and organizations tend to develop their own idioms, and you will notice them in code found in magazine articles and code repositories. Once you accept an idiom as your own, you can consider it a solved problem. This consistency saves time when writing code and when reading it later.

In most projects, a tiny minority of code is responsible for most of the execution time. Consequently, it pays to measure first and optimize the slowest section. If performance increases to acceptable levels, stop optimizing.

When a bug appears in your script, the time you spent writing meaningful comments and indenting will pay off. Sometimes just reading over troublesome code reveals its flaws. Most of the time you must print incremental values of variables to understand the problem.

Among the many books on the subject, I can recommend two. The first is *Writing Solid Code* by Steve Maguire. It's oriented toward writing applications in C, but many of the concepts apply to writing PHP scripts. The other is *The Practice of Programming* by Brian Kernighan and Rob Pike; Chapter 7 will be of particular interest.

# 28.1  Optimization

One reason I like PHP is that it allows the freedom to quickly create Web applications without worrying about following all the rules of proper design. When it comes to rapid prototyping, PHP shines. With this power comes the responsibility to write clean code when it's time to write longer-lasting code. Sticking to a style guide helps you write understandable programs, but eventually you will write code that doesn't execute fast enough.

Optimization is the process of fine-tuning a program to increase speed or reduce memory usage. Memory usage is not as important as it once was, because memory is relatively inexpensive. However, shorter execution times are always desirable.

Before you write a program, commit yourself to writing clearly at the expense of performance. Follow coding conventions, such as using `mysql_fetch_row` instead of `mysql_result`. But keep in mind that programming time is expensive, especially when programmers must struggle to understand code. The simplest solution is usually best.

When you finish a program, consider whether its performance is adequate. If your project benefits from a formal requirements specification, refer to any performance constraints. It's not unusual to include maximum page load times for Web applications. Many factors affect the time between clicking a link and viewing a complete page. Be sure to eliminate factors you cannot control, such as the speed of the network.

If you determine that your program needs optimization, consider upgrading the hardware first. This may be the least expensive alternative. In 1965 Gordon Moore observed that computing power doubled every 18 months. It's called Moore's law. Despite the steep increase in power, the cost of computing power drops with time. For example, despite CPU clock speeds doubling, their cost remains relatively stable. Upgrading your server is likely less expensive than hiring programmers to optimize the code.

After upgrading hardware, consider upgrading the software supporting your program. Start with the operating system. Linux and BSD UNIX have the reputation of squeezing more performance out of older hardware, and they may outperform commercial operating systems, especially if you factor in server crashes.

If your program uses a database, consider the differences between relational databases. If you can do without the few advanced features not yet part of MySQL, it may offer a significant performance enhancement over other database servers. Check out the benchmarks provided on their Web site. Also, consider giving your database server more memory.

Two Zend products can help speed execution times of PHP programs. The first is the Zend Optimizer. This optimizes PHP code as it passes through the Zend Engine.

It can run PHP programs 40 percent to 100 percent faster than without it. Like PHP, the Zend Optimizer is free. The next product to consider is the Zend Cache. It provides even more performance over the optimizer by keeping compiled code in memory. Some users have experienced 300 percent improvements. Visit the Zend Web site <http://www.zend.com/> to purchase the Zend Cache.

# 28.2  Measuring Performance

Before you can begin optimizing, you must be able to measure performance. There are two easy methods: inserting HTML comments and using Apache's ApacheBench utility. PHP applications run on a Web server, but the overhead added by serving HTML documents over a network should be factored out of your measurements.

You need to isolate the server from other activity, perhaps by barring other users or even disconnecting it from the network. Running tests on a server that's providing a public site may give varying results, as traffic changes during the day. Run your tests on a dedicated server even if the hardware doesn't match the production server. Optimizations made on slower hardware should translate into relative gains when put into production.

The easiest method you can use is insertion of HTML comments into your script's output. This method adds to the overall weight of the page, but it doesn't disturb the display. I usually print the output of the `microtime` function. Insert lines like `print("<!--" . microtime() . "-->\n")` at the beginning, end, and at key points inside your script. To measure performance, request the page in a Web browser and view the source. This produces lines like those in Figure 28.1.

```
<!-- 0.57843700 1046300374 -->
<!-- 0.71726700 1046300374 -->
<!-- 0.10676900 1046300375 -->
```

**Figure 28.1**   Measuring performance with `microtime`.

The `microtime` function returns the number of seconds on the clock. The first figure is a fraction of seconds, and the other is the number of seconds since January 1, 1970. You can add the two numbers and put them in an array, but I prefer to minimize the effect on performance by doing the calculation outside of the script. In the example above, the first part of the script takes approximately 0.14 seconds, and the second part takes 0.39.

If you decide to calculate time differences, consider the method used in Listing 28.1. Entries to the clock array contain a one-word description followed by the output of `microtime`. The `explode` function breaks up the three values so the script can display a table of timing values. The first column of the table holds the number of seconds elapsed since the last entry.

---

**Listing 28.1**     *Calculating `microtime` differences*

```php
<?php
    //start clock
    $clock[] = 'Start ' . microtime();

    //fake some long calculation
    $value = 0;
    for($index = 0; $index < 10000; $index++)
    {
        $value += (cos(time()%pi()));
    }

    //end clock
    $clock[] = 'cos ' . microtime();


    //write to file
    $fp = fopen("/tmp/data.txt", "w");
    for($index = 0; $index < 10000; $index++)
    {
        fputs($fp, "Testing performance\n");
    }
    fclose($fp);

    //end clock
    $clock[] = 'fputs ' . microtime();

    //print clock
    $entry = explode(' ', $clock[0]);
    $lastVal = $entry[1] + $entry[2];
    print('<table border="1">');
    foreach($clock as $c)
    {
        $entry = explode(' ', $c);

        print('<tr>');

        print('<td>' . ($entry[1] + $entry[2] - $lastVal) .
            '</td>');
        print('<td>' . $entry[0] . '</td>');
        print('<td>' . ($entry[1] + $entry[2]) . '</td>');
```

| Listing 28.1 | *Calculating `microtime` differences (cont.)* |

```
    print('</tr>');

    $lastVal = $entry[1] + $entry[2];
}
print('</table>');
?>
```

Inserting HTML comments is my favorite method, because it takes no preparation. But its big weakness is a small sample size. I always try three or four page loads to eliminate any variances due to caching or periodic server tasks.

The Apache Web server includes a program that addresses this problem by measuring the number of requests your server can handle. It's called ApacheBench, but the executable is ab. ApacheBench makes a number of requests to a given URL and reports on how long it took. Figure 28.2 shows the results of running 1,000 requests for a simple HTML script. The line in bold is the part I typed into my shell.

I requested an HTML document to get an idea of the baseline performance of my server. Any PHP script ought to be slower than an HTML document. Comparing the figures gives me an idea of the room for improvement. If I found my server could serve a PHP script at 10 requests per second, I'd have a lot of room for improvement.

Keep in mind that I'm running ApacheBench on the server. This eliminates the effects of moving data over the network, but ApacheBench uses some CPU time. I could test from another machine to let the Web server use all the system resources.

By default, ApacheBench makes one connection at a time. If you use 100 for the -n option, it connects to the server 100 times sequentially. In reality, Web servers handle many requests at once. Use the -c option to set the concurrency level. For example, -n 1000 -c 10 makes one thousand connections with 10 requests active at all times. This usually reduces the number of requests the server can handle, but at low levels the server is waiting for hardware, such as the hard disk.

The ApacheBench program is a good way to measure overall change without inconsistencies, but it can't tell you which parts of a script are slower than others. It also includes the overhead involved with connecting to the server and negotiating for the document using HTTP. You can get around this limitation by altering your script. If you comment out parts and compare performance, you can gain an understanding of which parts are slowest. Alternatively, you may use ApacheBench together with `microtime` comments.

```
# /usr/local/apache/bin/ab -n 10000 http://localhost/50k.html
This is ApacheBench, Version 1.3d <$Revision: 1.65 $> apache-1.3
Copyright (c) 1996 Adam Twiss, Zeus Technology Ltd,
http://www.zeustech.net/
Copyright (c) 1998-2002 The Apache Software Foundation,
http://www.apache.org/

Benchmarking localhost (be patient)
Completed 1000 requests
Completed 2000 requests
Completed 3000 requests
Completed 4000 requests
Completed 5000 requests
Completed 6000 requests
Completed 7000 requests
Completed 8000 requests
Completed 9000 requests
Finished 10000 requests
Server Software:        Apache/1.3.26
Server Hostname:        localhost
Server Port:            80

Document Path:          /50k.html
Document Length:        51205 bytes

Concurrency Level:      1
Time taken for tests:   20.161 seconds
Complete requests:      10000
Failed requests:        0
Broken pipe errors:     0
Total transferred:      514950000 bytes
HTML transferred:       512050000 bytes
Requests per second:    496.01 [#/sec] (mean)
Time per request:       2.02 [ms] (mean)
Time per request:       2.02 [ms] (mean, across all concurrent
requests)
Transfer rate:          25541.89 [Kbytes/sec] received

Connnection Times (ms)
              min   mean[+/-sd] median    max
Connect:        0     0    0.0       0       2
Processing:     1     1    0.0       1       4
Waiting:        0     0    0.0       0       2
Total:          1     1    0.1       1       4

Percentage of the requests served within a certain time (ms)
  50%       1
  66%       1
  75%       1
  80%       1
  90%       1
  95%       1
  98%       1
  99%       1
 100%       4 (last request)
```

**Figure 28.2**   ApacheBench output.

Whichever method you use, be sure to test with a range of values. If your program uses input from the user, try both the easy cases and the difficult ones, but concentrate on the common cases. For example, when testing a program that analyzes text from a `textarea` tag, don't limit yourself to typing a few words into the form. Enter realistic data, including large values, but don't bother with values so large they fall out of normal usage. People rarely type a megabyte of text into a text area, so if performance drops off sharply when you do, it's probably not worth worrying about.

Remember to measure again after each change to your program, and stop when you achieve your goal. If a change reduces performance, return to an earlier version. Let your measurements justify your changes.

# 28.3 Optimize the Slowest Parts

Although there are other motivations, such as personal satisfaction, most people optimize a program to save money. Don't lose sight of this as you spend time increasing the performance of your programs. There's no sense in spending more time optimizing than the optimization itself saves. Optimizing an application used by many people is usually worth the time, especially if you benefit from licensing fees. It's hard to judge the value of an open-source application you optimize, but I find work on open-source projects satisfying as recreation.

To make the most of your time, try to optimize the slowest parts of your program where you stand to gain the most. Generally, you should try to improve algorithms by finding faster alternatives. Computer scientists use a special notation called big-O notation to describe the relative efficiency of an algorithm. An algorithm that must examine each input datum once is $O(n)$. An algorithm that must examine each element twice is still called $O(n)$, as linear factors are not interesting. A really slow algorithm might be $O(n^2)$, or O of n-squared. A really fast algorithm might be $O(n \log n)$, or n times the logarithm of n. This subject is far too complex to cover here. You can find detailed discussions of this topic on the Internet and in university courses. Understanding it may help you choose faster algorithms.

Permanent storage, such as a hard disk, is much slower than volatile storage, such as RAM. Operating systems compensate somewhat by caching disk blocks to system memory, but you can't keep your entire system in RAM. Parts of your program that use permanent storage are good candidates for optimization.

If you are using data stored in files, consider using a relational database instead. Database servers can do a better job of caching data than the operating system because they view the data with a finer granularity. Database servers may also cache open files, saving you the overhead in opening and closing files.

Alternatively, you can try caching data within your own program, but consider the lifecycle of a PHP script execution. At the end of the request, PHP frees all memory. If during your program you need to refer to the same file many times, you may increase performance by reading the file into a variable.

Consider optimizing your database queries too. MySQL includes the EXPLAIN statement, which returns information about how the join engine uses indexes. MySQL's online manual includes information about the process of optimizing queries.

Here are two tips for loops. If the number of iterations in a loop is low, you might get some performance gain from replacing the loop with a number of statements. For example, consider a for loop that sets 10 values in an array. You can replace the loop with 10 statements, which is a duplication of code but may execute slightly faster.

Also, don't recompute values inside a loop. If you use the size of an array in the loop, use a variable to store the size before you enter the loop instead of calling count each time through the loop. Likewise, look for parts of mathematical expressions that factor into constant values.

Function calls carry a high overhead. You can get a bump in performance if you eliminate a function. Compiled languages, such as C and Java, have the luxury of replacing function calls with inline code. You should avoid functions that you call only once. One technique for readable code is to use functions to hide details. This technique is expensive in PHP.

If all else fails, you have the option of moving part of your code into C, wrapping it in a PHP function. This technique is not for the novice, but many of PHP's functions began as optimizations. Consider the in_array function. You can test for the presence of the value in an array by looping through it, but the function written in C is much faster.

# 28.4  When to Store Content in a Database

When I speak of content, I mean static text, perhaps containing HTML. There is no rule saying that content should never be placed in a database or that it should always be put in a database. In the case of a bulletin board, it makes sense to put each message in a database. Messages are likely to be added continually. It is convenient to treat them as units, manipulating them by their creation dates or authors. At the other extreme, a copyright message that appears at the bottom of every page of a site is more suited to a text file that is retrieved with the require function.

Somewhere between these two extremes is a break-even point. The reason is that databases provide a tradeoff. They allow you to handle data in complex ways. They allow you to associate several pieces of information around a common identifier. However, you trade away some performance, as retrieving data is slower than if you opened a file and read the contents.

Many Web sites are nothing more than a handful of pages dressed up in a common graphic theme. A hundred files in a directory are easy to manage. You can name each one to describe its contents and refer to it in a URL, such as `http://www.example.com/index.php?screen=about_us`, and still get the benefit of systematically generating the layout and navigation. Your PHP script can use the value of the `screen` variable as the name of a local file, perhaps in a directory named `screens`. Developers can work on the page contents as they are accustomed, because they know the code is stored in a file named `about_us` in a directory named `screens`.

When the content grows to a thousand pages, keeping each in a separate file starts to become unmanageable. A relational database will help you better organize the content. With a site so large, it's likely that there will be many versions of the navigation. In a database it is easy to build a table that associates page content with navigation. You can also automate hyperlinks by creating one-way associations between pages. This would cause a link to automatically appear on a page.

The biggest problem with this approach is the lack of good tools for editing the site. Developers are used to fetching files into an editor via FTP. Asking these same people to start using a database shell is most likely out of the question. The cost of teaching SQL to anyone who might work on the site may eliminate any benefit gained when the content is put into the database. So, you are faced with creating your own tools to edit the content. The logical path is to create Web-based tools, since coding a desktop application is a major project in itself, especially if both Windows and Macintosh users are to be accommodated. As you might guess, Web-based site editors are less than ideal. However, with very large sites they become bearable, because the alternative of managing such a large static site is a greater evil, so to speak.

# 28.5  Debugging Strategies

There are times when code produces unexpected results. Examining the code reveals nothing. In this case the best thing to do is some in-line debugging. PHP scripts generate HTML to be interpreted by a browser, and HTML has a comment tag. Therefore, it is a simple matter to write PHP code that reports diagnostic information inside HTML comments. This allows you to put diagnostic information into an application without affecting its operation.

Often I create database queries dynamically, based on user input. A stray character or invalid user input can cause the query to return an error. Sometimes I print the query itself. I also print the results of the error functions, such as `mysql_error`. The same applies to code unrelated to databases. Printing diagnostic information, even if it is as simple as saying "got here," can help.

Chapter 9 describes many debugging-related functions. The `print_r` function can be particularly helpful.

You can go a long way toward finding bugs in your applications by turning on all errors, warnings, and notices. Warnings and notices may not halt your scripts, but they can indicate potential problems. Consider how PHP allows the use of a variable before initializing it. If you mistype the name of a variable, PHP creates a new variable with an empty value. PHP generates a notice if you use the value of a variable before initializing it.

It may be easiest to turn on notices inside `php.ini`, assuming the Web server is dedicated to development. A production server should not display error messages as a security precaution. You can always turn on full error reporting from within your script with the `error_reporting` function.

If you don't wish to disturb the HTML output of your scripts, you can write messages to a log file. The `error_log` and `syslog` functions are two solutions built into PHP. Of course, you can always open a text file in your code and write diagnostic information. If you use Apache, you can also use the `apache_note` function to pass debugging information up to the Apache process where it may be included in Apache's logs. Refer to the Apache documentation to learn how to create custom logs.

Finally, there are several tools available for debugging PHP scripts. Zend Studio, for example, includes a remote debugger that allows you to step over each line of your script.

# 28.6  Simulating HTTP Connections

When writing PHP scripts, it is not necessary to understand every detail of the HTTP protocol. I would be straying to include a treatise here, but you ought to have enough understanding so that you could simulate a connect by using telnet. You may know that Web servers listen on port 80 by default. HTTP is a text-based protocol, so it's not hard to telnet directly to a Web server and type a simple request. HTTP has several commands that should be familiar; GET and POST are used most often. HEAD is a command that returns just the headers for a request. Browsers use this command to test whether they really want to get an entire document.

It is especially helpful to simulate an HTTP connection when your script sends custom headers. Figure 28.3 is an example showing a request I made to an Apache server. The text in bold is what I typed. The remote server returned everything else.

```
# telnet www.example.com 80
Trying 192.168.178.111...
Connected to www.example.com.
Escape character is '^]'.
HEAD / HTTP/1.0

HTTP/1.1 200 OK
Date: Wed, 26 Feb 2003 23:19:07 GMT
Server: Apache/1.3.26 (Unix) AuthMySQL/2.20 PHP/4.1.2
mod_gzip/1.3.19.1a mod_ssl/2.8.9 OpenSSL/0.9.6g
X-Powered-By: PHP/4.1.2
Connection: close
Content-Type: text/html

Connection closed by foreign host.
[root@www tmp]#
```

**Figure 28.3**   Simulating an HTTP connection.

# 28.7  Output Buffering

Output buffering is an advanced feature added in PHP 4. Enabling output buffering makes PHP direct the output of applications to a memory buffer instead of sending it directly to the client browser. Once in the buffer, applications can manipulate the output. This manipulation may be compression, conversion from XML to HTML, or even changing embedded URLs. Afterwards, the application emits the processed results to the browser.

Even if you have no need to perform postprocessing on the output your applications emit, output buffering can improve the performance of PHP-based Web sites by decreasing the number of I/O calls to the Web server's infrastructure. Calling the I/O layer of the Web server is typically an expensive operation. Gathering the output into one big block and performing just one I/O operation can be much faster than performing an I/O call every time PHP emits a piece of output—that is, every time you call `print` or `echo`.

If your PHP scripts emit HTML pages larger than 10K, allocating and reallocating the buffer can consume more time than is saved from the reduced number of I/O calls. As in many other cases in computer science, you achieve the best performance by finding a good balance between no buffering at all and complete buffering.

Thankfully, PHP's output buffering layer allows users to strike this balance. Instead of telling PHP to buffer all output, you can enable *chunked* output buffering. Chunked output buffering limits the amount of buffered data to a designated value and flushes the buffer every time the buffer fills up. A good balanced value for chunked output buffering is 4K. It significantly reduces the number of I/O calls your script triggers without consuming significant amounts of memory or imposing noticeable allocation overhead. For instance, if the average size of a PHP-generated HTML page on your site is 50K, PHP will typically perform between 500 and 10,000 I/O calls. With a 4K buffer, it would perform between 12 and 13 I/O calls, resulting in a noticeable gain.

To enable a 4KB output buffer for your entire site, set the `output_buffering` directive to 4096. If you wish to enable output buffering on a per-script basis, use `ob_start`. For example, you might write `ob_start(null, 4096)` to use a 4K buffer.

# 28.8  Output Compression

Even considering the growing availability of personal broadband Internet access, many sites still address the market of dialup users. If you happen to be running one of them, you probably know that the size of your pages has direct influence on the amount of time your users have to wait before they can see your Web site. Regardless of your Web server's performance, delivery to the client remains at the mercy of the network. Reducing the size of your content reduces the impact of network performance on the overall request-to-response time.

Typically, giving up on certain elements in your Web site just to improve performance is not an option. That is, graphics designers go through their own process of optimizing the design with respect to application requirements. One practical solution is compression of your content. As you would hope, PHP comes to your aid if you need to make use of compression.

PHP's output compression support takes advantage of the fact that most of the popular browsers (including Internet Explorer, Netscape Navigator, and Mozilla) are capable of seamlessly decompressing compressed pages. Such browsers send a special entry in their HTTP request (`Accept-Encoding: deflate, gzip`), which hints to the server that they know how to handle compressed content. Most servers don't do anything with this information, but with PHP you can easily turn this into smaller pages and faster download times. Document sizes typically reduce by 2 to 10 times!

If enabled, output compression will detect the special entry in the browser's request and will seamlessly compress any output that is emitted by your application. To enable output compression (only for browsers that support it; the behavior for browsers that don't will not be affected), simply turn on the `zlib.output_compression` directive in `php.ini`.

If you wish to enable output compression for a specific page only, you can do so with `ob_start`. For example, `ob_start("ob_gzhandler", 4096)` activates compression and buffers the output. Note that PHP implements output compression on top of the output buffering mechanism. Unlike regular chunked output buffering, which simply sends out the contents of the output buffer each time it fills up, when output compression is enabled the contents of the buffer go through a special compression filter each time it has to be flushed. The size of the buffer directly affects the efficiency of the compression. If you use a smaller buffer size, compression ratios will be worse. Using larger buffers will usually result in better compression ratios, but typically comes with a price of higher allocation overhead. As with regular output buffering, 4096 bytes is a good, balanced chunk size. Unless you have a good reason to change it, you should stick to the defaults.

Because compressing information is a CPU-intensive task, it only makes sense if

- your pages are large,
- a large percentage of your users accesses your Web site over slow connections, and
- your Web server has CPU cycles to spare.

If some of these factors are not true in your case, enabling output compression may actually decrease the overall performance. In case you're interested in output compression without having to pay the CPU overhead price, consider the Zend Performance Suite. Zend Performance Suite combines output compression with content caching, which means you get all the benefits of output compression without having to wait for the data to compress each time.

# 28.9 Avoiding `eval`

Before we get into the gory details, the best way to remember this tip is to remember the catchy phrase *eval( ) is evil*. You should do your best to avoid it: `eval` suffers from slow performance because in order to execute the code, it must invoke the runtime compiler component in the Zend Engine, which is an expensive operation. In many situations, you can replace a call to `eval` with equivalent code that does not make use of `eval`.

The most common case where `eval` can be replaced with faster code is when you use it for accessing variables or functions dynamically. Consider Listing 28.2.

| Listing 28.2 | *Unnecessary use of `eval`* |
|---|---|

```php
<?php
    function assign($varname, $value)
    {
        eval("global \$$varname; \$$varname = \$value;");
    }

    for($i=0; $i<100; $i++)
    {
        assign("foo", 5);
        print($foo);
    }
?>
```

In this example, `assign` can be used to assign values into variables when you have the variable name handy and not the variable itself. In our case, the `eval` string will expand to `global $foo; $foo = $value;` which assigns 5 to the global `foo` variable, and when we print it, we get 5, as expected. You can achieve the same functionality without using `eval` by using an indirect reference. See Listing 28.3.

| Listing 28.3 | *Removing unnecessary use of `eval`* |
|---|---|

```php
<?php
    function assign($varname, $value)
    {
        global $$varname;
        $$varname = $value;
    }

    for($i=0; $i<100; $i++)
    {
        assign("foo", 5);
        print($foo);
    }
?>
```

Prefixing variable `varname` with an extra `$` tells PHP to fetch the variable whose name is the value of `var`. This feature is called an *indirect reference*. In our case, the value of variable is `foo`, so PHP globalizes `foo` and assigns the value to it. Since it doesn't have to invoke the runtime compiler, this new version will yield approximately twice as many requests per second as the `eval` version!

Another way to eliminate repeated calls to eval involves creating a function dynamically. Let's assume that we have a few lines of code in a variable named code, possibly fetched from a database, passed from a different part of the program or constructed locally. Listing 28.4 shows a naïve implementation.

---

**Listing 28.4** *Call to dynamic code with eval*

```php
<?php
    //create some example code
    $code = "sqrt(pow(543, 12));";

    for($i=0; $i<100; $i++)
    {
        eval($code);
    }
?>
```

---

As mentioned before, this is exceptionally slow. PHP invokes the Zend Engine runtime compiler for each iteration. The technique in Listing 28.5 offers a better solution.

---

**Listing 28.5** *Using a dynamic function to eliminate eval*

```php
<?php
    //create some example code
    $code = "sqrt(pow(543, 12));";

    //create a function to wrap
    //the loaded code
    $func = create_function('', $code);

    for($i=0; $i<100; $i++)
    {
        $func();
    }
?>
```

---

The create_function function creates a new function from the code passed to it, as discussed in Chapter 11. While the results of Listing 28.4 and Listing 28.5 are identical, Listing 28.5 is several times faster. The reason is simple: Listing 28.4 invokes the runtime compiler 100 times, each time we eval the code. Using create_function, the script invokes the runtime compiler only once and declares an *anonymous function*, which it calls 100 times. This saves 99 invocations of the runtime compiler, which results in a huge performance boost.

# 28.10  Don't Load Extensions Dynamically

The dl function allows applications to *dynamically load* extensions into PHP, thereby adding functionality to the PHP engine. It is the runtime equivalent of exten-sion=/path/to/extension.so in php.ini. However, using dl has many drawbacks over using php.ini. We strongly encourage you not use it.

Dynamically loading a library for each script execution is much slower than doing it once on server startup. You're actually getting hurt twice, because if you load it using the extension directive in php.ini, it gets loaded once for all of the Web server processes instead of being loaded for each process separately.

Due to the nature of memory management under UNIX, loading an extension once on server startup is much more efficient than loading it later, separately for each server process. An extension loaded on server startup, by the Apache parent process, is shared among all the child processes. However, when we load an extension in runtime into specific Web server processes, each copy we load ends up consuming its own chunk of memory, which is not shared with any other process, thereby consuming much more memory.

What if I'm a Windows user and don't care too much about Apache or UNIX?, you may ask. In that case, the motivation for not using dl is even simpler—dl is not supported by the thread-safe version of PHP. Because virtually all of the PHP builds for Windows are built in thread-safe mode, dl is typically not an option if you're a Windows user.

# 28.11  Improving Performance of MySQL Queries

The mysql_query function is perhaps the most popular function in PHP. If you're a MySQL user, you use it routinely to issue queries to the MySQL server and receive result sets. What you may not know is that when a query returns large result sets or queries large databases, mysql_query can be very inefficient.

In order to understand the reason for the inefficiency, you must understand how `mysql_query` works. When you issue a SELECT statement using `mysql_query`, PHP sends it to the MySQL server. The MySQL server parses it, creates an execution plan, and starts to iterate over the table rows, looking for valid results. Every time it finds a valid result, the server sends it back over the network to the client. On the client side, PHP appends each row to a buffer, until the server sends a message that acknowledges that no rows remain. When this happens, `mysql_query` returns control to the PHP application and allows it to iterate over the result buffer.

The performance problem arises when we deal with large result sets or when we're querying very big databases. In such cases, the time that passes from receiving the first result row and receiving the last one can be quite long. Even though our client is idle and is virtually doing nothing, we cannot use this time to begin processing the results. We have to wait until the server sends the very last row, and only after we get control back can we process the results. If we could start processing the result rows as soon as they start arriving instead of having to wait for the last row, performance would improve significantly. As usual, PHP doesn't disappoint us.

In addition to `mysql_query`, PHP offers an additional version of the function, named `mysql_unbuffered_query`. The API for the two functions is identical, but `mysql_unbuffered_query` does not buffer the result rows before returning control to the PHP application. Instead, it returns control to PHP as soon as it issues the query successfully. Each time we fetch a row, the MySQL module attempts to read the next row from the server and returns control to the application as soon as it fetches the row. That way, we can process the rows as they arrive instead of having to wait for the entire result set to become available.

If unbuffered queries are so good, why does PHP even let you use regular, buffered queries? Unfortunately, there's a good reason for that—unbuffered queries are not always a good idea. If the server sends the rows faster than the client reads them, the server will keep the relevant tables locked for more time than necessary. SQL statements needing to write to the table must wait until the read operation finishes. Since this may result in a huge performance degradation for pages that make changes to the database, using unbuffered queries is recommended only if the amount of processing your pages perform on each row is sufficiently small or if updates are infrequent.

# 28.12 Optimizing Disk-Based Sessions

Many Web applications use *HTTP sessions* to retain information about specific users for the duration of their visit. The default and most common storage for the session information is disk files, located in /tmp. With heavily loaded Web sites that serve large number of users, accessing the session store on the disk may become extremely inefficient, since most file systems (including Linux's ext2 and Windows' NTFS) don't handle a large number of files in the same directory very efficiently. As the number of files in the /tmp directory grows due to a large number of active sessions, the time it takes to open each session file becomes longer.

A good first step would be moving the session storage directory from /tmp into a dedicated directory in the file system. You can do that by setting the session.save_path directive in php.ini. Using a different directory removes the overhead of non-PHP sessions-related files if any reside in /tmp. However, this is indeed just a first step and not necessarily a very big one. Given enough active sessions, the number of other files in /tmp may be negligible.

As if out of habit, PHP comes to the rescue and allows you to easily distribute the session files to multiple directories without any hassle. PHP has built-in support to treat the first *n* letters in the session key as hashing directories. For those of you not familiar with this methodology, let's illustrate. Consider we have a session with the key 3fdb6cd5748e5ef2ecc415530a3f167e. Assuming we've set session.save_path to /tmp/php_sessions, PHP stores this session in a file named /tmp/php_sessions/ sess_3fdb6cd5748e5ef2ecc415530a3f167e. However, if we change php.ini to session.save_path = 2;/tmp/php_sessions, PHP stores the session information in /tmp/php_sessions/3/f/sess_3fdb6cd5748e5ef2ecc415530a3f167e. Note the extra directories separating php_sessions and the session file itself. Similarly, if we set the session.save_path to 4;/tmp/php_sessions, PHP stores the session file in /tmp/php_sessions/3/f/d/b/sess_3fdb6cd5748e5ef2ecc415530a3f167e. The optional semicolon-separated number in session.save_path is named the *session save path depth*.

Thanks to the exponential nature of this algorithm, the number of files per directory is reduced by a power of 36 that equals the session save path depth, 36 being the number of characters used for session identifiers. This means that there usually isn't a need to go beyond a depth of 2 or 3.

Garbage collection may be improved too. Garbage collection is the process of removing old session files after a certain expiration timeout. By default, PHP takes care of garbage collection automatically. However, due to architectural constraints, PHP's built-in garbage collection takes place inside the context of a request. This means that at least one request will end up being blocked for the duration of the cleanup, which can sometimes take more than a few seconds. Moreover, PHP's automated cleanup supports only the default depth setting of 0. As soon as we move to use a different depth, automated garbage collection will no longer work, and session files will begin to pile up.

The best solution for the garbage collection issue is to move it out of PHP and into a cron job. For instance, if you would like to remove sessions after 24 hours and perform collection every hour, you could add the following line to the system's crontab:

```
0 * * * * nobody find /tmp/php_sessions -name sess_\* -ctime +1 |
xargs rm -f
```

Using this mechanism works regardless of any `session.save_path` depth you may be using and prevents any requests from getting stuck for long periods of time due to garbage collection. Of course, you may want to tune the frequency of garbage collection by using different cron settings or change the expiration limit for session file by using different find settings.

# 28.13  Don't Pass by Reference (or, Don't Trust Your Instincts)

Telling people not to trust their instincts may be startling, but in the context of PHP it can be good advice. One of the most common examples of a popular bad hunch is the urge to pass variables by reference for performance reasons. Admittedly, it sounds very convincing. Instead of passing a copy of the variable, a script passes the variable itself. That's bound to be faster, isn't it? Well, no. In order to understand why, we need to understand a bit more about how the Zend Engine handles values.

The Zend Engine implements a *reference-counted, copy-on-write* value system. This means that multiple variables may point to the same value without consuming multiple blocks of memory. Consider Listing 28.6.

| Listing 28.6 | *Zend Engine reference counting* |
|---|---|

```php
<?php
    //create an array
    $apple = array(1=>'a', 2=>'b', 3=>'c');

    //make a copy, ZE keeps one version only
    $ball = $apple;
?>
```

In this example we assign `apple` to `ball`, but PHP copies no data. Instead, it updates `ball` to point to the same location in memory `apple` does, a location that contains the array that we originally assigned to `apple`. For bookkeeping purposes, PHP notifies the array and updates it with a *reference count* of 2. The Zend Engine takes responsibility to ensure that the reference count of each value in the system reflects the number of symbols referencing it. So much for the *reference-counted* part. Let's enhance our example with the code in Listing 28.7.

| Listing 28.7 | *Zend Engine splitting references on write* |
| --- | --- |

```php
<?php
    //create an array
    $apple = array(1=>'a', 2=>'b', 3=>'c');

    //make a copy, ZE keeps one version only
    $ball = $apple;

    //apple changes, ZE makes separate versions
    //for apple and ball
    $apple[1] = 'd';

    //element 1 of ball remains a
    print($ball[1]);
?>
```

Of course, we don't expect that modifying `apple[1]` will change `ball[1]` and hope that the contents of `ball[1]` will remain `a`. If you try running it, you'll find out that indeed it does not get affected by the assignment to `apple[1]`. But how could this be if we just said that `a` and `ball` point to the very same location in memory?

This is where the *copy-on-write* part kicks in. As soon as the Zend Engine detects a write operation to a value that is referenced by more than one symbol, it replicates the value, creating an identical value that sits in a different place in memory, disconnected from any other symbols. Only then does it allow the write operation to continue. This just-in-time duplication greatly improves performance without any functional side effects thanks to avoiding unnecessary data copies.

How does all of this relate to passing-by-reference being a bad idea? A good start would be understanding *why it doesn't help,* and the reason is that thanks to the engine's reference-counting mechanism, there's no need to explicitly pass any variables by reference. The engine will automatically avoid unnecessary duplication if at all possible.

Okay, so it's not a good idea. It still doesn't mean it will do any harm—or does it? In reality, it turns out that it does. Let's go back to our `apple` and `ball` arrays and add a function that displays their contents. See Listing 28.8.

| Listing 28.8 | *Unnecessary pass by reference* |
|---|---|

```php
<?php
    //function to print the count of an array
    //passed by reference
    function printArray(&$arr)
    {
        print(count($arr));
    }

    //create an array
    $apple = array(1=>'a', 2=>'b', 3=>'c');

    //make a copy, ZE keeps one version only
    $ball = $apple;

    //print array
    printArray($apple);
?>
```

Seemingly, there's nothing wrong with this code. It produces the expected results. However, this implementation is roughly 30 percent slower than it would have been if you declared `printArray` to receive its argument by value instead of by reference. When the engine comes to pass `apple` to `printArray`, it detects that it needs to pass it by reference. It then detects that the value in question has a reference count of 2. Since we're passing `apple` by reference, and any changes that `printArray` might make must not be reflected in `ball`, the Zend Engine must make separate copies for `apple` and `ball`. If you pass a variable into a function by value, the Zend Engine simply can increment the reference count.

Never use pass-by-reference for performance reasons. Use it only when it makes sense from a functional point of view—let the engine take care of passing arguments!

# 28.14  Avoid Concatenation of Large Strings

A very common practice in PHP is to needlessly concatenate large chunks of data before printing them. Compare Listing 28.9 to Listing 28.10. The concatenation of `subject` and `contents` has to happen before the script calls `print`, and if the size of `contents` is very big, it can consume a lot of time. Listing 28.10 calls `print` multiple times; PHP never needs to concatenate `subject` and `contents` in memory, which saves valuable time. Note that since calling `print` itself has some overhead, it may not always be advisable to separate concatenations into multiple print statements. In certain cases it may also make the code less readable. For that reason, it's best if you follow this practice only when displaying large strings.

---

**Listing 28.9**    *Concatenation of large strings*

```php
<?php
    $subject = "some subject";
    $contents = "...a very large block of text...";
    print("Subject:  $subject\n\n$contents");
?>
```

---

**Listing 28.10**    *Avoiding concatenation of large strings*

```php
<?php
    $subject = "some subject";
    $contents = "...a very large block of text...";
    print("Subject:  $subject\n\n");
    print($contents);
?>
```

---

# 28.15  Avoid Serving Large Files with PHP-Enabled Apache

This isn't a coding tip, but rather a server setup tip. If your Web site serves large files for downloading, it may be a good idea to set up a special Web server for serving them instead of serving them through the PHP-enabled Apache Web server. There are several reasons for doing so.

Large downloads can take a significant amount of time. The number of concurrent processes that Apache uses is typically limited by a relatively small number. Every Apache process that serves a download file remains unavailable for the duration of the download. This reduces the number of concurrent users that your Web site can handle.

Apache processes consume relatively large amounts of memory for each process, especially if Apache is PHP-enabled. Even if increasing the maximum number of concurrent Apache processes is an option for you, you will be wasting a large amount of memory needlessly.

To set up a download server, consider using the throttling Web server thttpd <http://www.acme.com/software/thttpd/>. It is extremely lightweight and imposes almost no overhead on the server, which makes it one of the most suitable Web servers for serving large amount of static content such as download files.

# 28.16  Understanding Persistent Database Connections

Persistent database connections are one of the least understood features in PHP. Many people don't understand the meaning of persistent links, misconfigure their setup, get beaten by connection problems, and dump persistent connections altogether. Since in many situations, using persistent connections yields significant performance gains, it is important to understand how to properly set them up so that they get a fair trial.

The first important thing to understand about persistent connections is what they are *not*. Persistent connections are *not* the same as connection pooling, functionality offered by ODBC, JDBC, and certain database drivers. Connection pooling, the process of juggling a pool of connections to server threads, is not suitable for PHP because the typical PHP environment is not multithreaded. In Apache 1.x (and also in version 2.0, when using the prefork MPM), concurrency is implemented by having several *processes*. Since database connections cannot be shared among different processes, there's no way to implement connection pooling. That is, if we open a connection in process, it cannot be used by any other process.

As opposed to pooled connections, persistent connections are connections that are simply not closed at the end of the request, as are ordinary connections. Future requests that are handled by the same process can then reuse the opened connection, thus avoiding the overhead of establishing a new database connection in each request. The fundamental difference between pooled and persistent connections is therefore that persistent connections keep one connection open per Web server instance, whereas with pooled connections, a relatively small number of opened connections is shared between all server instances.

Given this knowledge, we can now make more informed decisions about whether it makes sense for us to use persistent connections, and if so, how to set them up. Here are a couple of guidelines to follow.

When using persistent connections, given a long enough uptime, there will be one connection open for each running Apache process. This means that your database server must be able to handle at least as many active connections as your Apache server's MaxClients setting. Having a few extra free connections in excess of MaxClients is best so that you will still be able to connect to the database server for administration purposes.

Persistent connections make sense only if your database server handles a large number of open connections efficiently. Certain database servers suffer from a significant performance hit when working with a large number of open connections, even if they are mostly idle. Other servers may have licensing restrictions on the number of simultaneous connections that can be made to them in any given time. With such servers, persistent connections are not recommended. One example of a server that does handle a large number of simultaneous connections very efficiently is MySQL, so using persistent connections in conjunction with it is highly recommended.

# 28.17 Avoid Using `exec`, Backticks, and `system` If Possible

A common mistake that many PHP programmers make is overusing external processes for tasks that can be performed using PHP's built-in native functions. For instance, `exec("/bin/ls -a $dirname", $files)`, which uses the external `/bin/ls` program, can be replaced by code in Listing 28.11.

| Listing 28.11 | *Avoiding executing an external process* |
| --- | --- |

```php
<?php
    $dir = opendir($dirname);
    while($entry = readdir($dir))
    {
        $files[] = $entry;
    }
?>
```

Even though it's a few more lines of code, Listing 28.11 is *much* faster and is also much less prone to security hazards. The `exec` version requires you to make sure that `dirname` contains no malicious switches or code that may end up doing something other than you expect.

Whenever you find yourself using `exec`, `system`, or backticks, check whether there's a way to implement the same functionality using native PHP code. If it can be done with reasonable effort, always prefer the native PHP approach to external program invocation.

# 28.18 Use `php.ini-recommended`

The PHP distribution includes a file named `php.ini-recommended` alongside the standard `php.ini-dist` file. Unlike `php.ini-dist`, which comes preconfigured for PHP's default settings, `php.ini-recommended` has a list of nonstandard settings, which improve PHP's security and performance. Each nonstandard setting is thoroughly documented in the body of `php.ini-recommended`, which describes the consequences of enabling it as well as the category of improvement to which this setting is related, such as performance or security. When installing PHP for the first time, or when you want to tune your PHP server for performance, try to use `php.ini-recommended`.

# 28.19 Don't Use Regular Expressions Unless You Must

PHP features a very large library of string functions, some of which are extremely powerful. However, in many situations two or more functions can be used to perform the same task, but with great differences in performance.

Perhaps the most commonly overused functions are `ereg_replace` and `preg_replace`. These regular-expression-based pattern-replacing functions are often used even when the replacement pattern is completely static and there's no need for compiling a complex regular expression. For instance,

```
$str = ereg_replace("sheep", "lamb", "Mary had a little sheep");
```

can be up to 10 times slower than the equivalent

```
$str = str_replace("Mary had a little sheep", "sheep", "lamb");
```

Use regular expressions only when you absolutely have to!

If you do have to use a regular expression, try to use the Perl-compatible functions, such as `preg_match` and `preg_replace` instead of the older regular expression functions, such as `ereg` and `ereg_replace`. Besides being more powerful, the Perl-compatible functions are typically quicker than the old, POSIX regular expressions.

# 28.20  Optimizing Loops

A very common performance mistake in PHP is creating loops that iterate over an array without caching the number of elements in the array. For example, consider Listing 28.12. The first loop can be optimized to perform about 50 percent faster by caching the value of count($arr) in a variable instead of calling count over and over again. You can even get the count inside the for loop's initialization step. Wherever possible, see if you can take static code, which is invariant of the loop's iterator, out of the loop.

| Listing 28.12 | *Count array elements once* |
| --- | --- |

```php
<?php
    //setup sample array
    $arr = array("Cosmo" , "Elaine", "George", "Jerry");

    //loop over elements, recounting each time
    for ($i=0; $i < count($arr); $i++)
    {
        print $arr[$i];
    }

    //loop over elements, make count first
    $n = count($arr);
    for ($i=0; $i < $n; $i++)
    {
        print $arr[$i];
    }

    //put count into init step
    for ($i=0, $n = count($arr); $i < $n; $i++)
    {
        print $arr[$i];
    }
?>
```

# 28.21  IIS Configuration

If you have a performance-sensitive PHP server deployed on Microsoft IIS under Windows, you should be aware of the different setup options that IIS allows. The different settings allow you to trade reliability and security for performance.

Inside the your PHP application's properties window in Internet Services Manager, select the Home Directory tab. In that tab, you will see an Application Protection pull-down menu, which determines the isolation level of the application. By default, IIS sets it to Medium, which means that PHP pages will be running in a separate process of IIS. In practice, it means that if PHP experiences a crash, perhaps due to memory corruption or stack overflow, the only the PHP-dedicated IIS process is affected. Other applications are served by other processes and are not effected.

While this setting helps make your server more robust, it comes at the price of a big performance hit. The other applicable Application Protection setting, *Low*, would make IIS run PHP in the main `inetinfo.exe` process. Requests will not have to be relayed to external processes, and performance will be dramatically increased. However, the price may come in the form of reduced stability—any PHP crash will bring the entire Web server down with it. Unfortunately, because not all of PHP's modules and the third-party libraries they use are entirely thread-safe, such crashes cannot be avoided.

For a performance-sensitive Web site, we recommend that you first try using PHP with the Low Application Protection setting. Only if you experience trouble should you switch to the Medium setting.

# DESIGN PATTERNS

**Topics in This Chapter**

- Patterns Defined
- Singleton
- Factory
- Observer
- Strategy

# Chapter 29

Popular among fans of Java and C++, design patterns are not a topic often discussed among PHP programmers. Yet, they are an important part of computer science. Furthermore, they apply to all programming languages.

Design patterns have their root in the work of Christopher Alexander in the context of designing buildings and cities. However, his work applies to any design activity, and it soon inspired computer scientists. The first popular book about software design patterns was *Design Patterns: Elements of Reusable Object-Oriented Software* by Erich Gamma, Richard Helm, Ralph Johnson, and John Vlissides. People commonly refer to them as the Gang of Four, or GoF.

# 29.1  Patterns Defined

Intuitively, we recognize patterns in our programming with almost every line of code. Given an array, you have a favorite idiom for looping over it. Since the `foreach` statement appeared in PHP, it's been my favorite.

From a larger perspective, we encounter the familiar problem of where to place functionality in PHP scripts. Most projects require dividing functionality into several modules. A flat, informational site benefits well from a simple scheme using headers and footers applied with `include` or `require`. Both examples have problems to be solved and memorized solutions. The conditions define a problem that has a known solution. Furthermore, after solving the problem a number of times, you gain an appreciation for the side effects, good and bad, of the solution.

The formal definition of design patterns includes four parts: a name, a description of the problem, a solution, and a set of consequences. The name gives us a convenient way to refer to the pattern. The problem description defines a particular set of conditions to which the pattern applies. The solution describes a best general strategy for resolving the problem. Finally, the pattern explains any consequences of applying the pattern.

Pattern solutions are not particularly fancy. They don't require the use of obscure features. They represent careful refinement over time, based on experience. They tend to optimize for reusability rather than efficiency. Naturally, a solution optimized for speed takes advantage of a particular situation and therefore is not well suited to the general case. For example, if you need the sum of three numbers, you can easily write them in a line of code. You would not use a general solution for the sum of 10,000 numbers, such as looping over an array.

Although patterns have their roots in building architecture, in the context of computer science they are closely linked to object-oriented design. Object-oriented programming aims to produce generalized software modules called objects. Design patterns seek to produce generalized solutions to common problems. This avoids the reinvention of the proverbial wheel.

Prior to PHP 5, PHP programmers found it difficult to implement design patterns efficiently in PHP. Thanks to PHP 5's revamped object model, design patterns are now easy to implement and are becoming a key ingredient in development of object-oriented PHP applications.

There are several advantages to using design patterns in your code. You don't need to think through the solution as long as you recognize that the problem matches the one solved by the pattern. You don't need to analyze the consequences of applying the pattern. You don't need to spend time optimizing the implementation.

Instead of having to come up with a solution, you only have to recognize what kind of problem you are facing. If the problem has an applicable design pattern, then you may be able to skip much of the design overhead and go directly to the implementation phase.

The consequences of using a certain design pattern are written in the pattern description. Instead of having to analyze the possible implications of using a certain algorithm—or worse, figure out why the algorithm you chose is not right for you after you implement it—you can refer to the pattern description. Implementing a solution from a design pattern gives you a fairly good idea about the complexity, limitations, and overhead of the solution.

The solutions supplied in design patterns tend to be efficient, especially in terms of reducing development and maintenance times. Simply put, you put other people's brains to work on your problem for free, which is a bargain.

If you've written large applications, it's quite possible that you would recognize similarities between some of the algorithms you used and the algorithms described in certain design patterns. That is no coincidence—design patterns are there to solve real-world problems that you are likely to encounter regularly. It's quite possible that after performing a thorough investigation of a certain problem, the solution you came up with is similar to that in the design pattern. If you were aware of design patterns back then, it would have saved you at least some of the design time.

While this chapter is not meant to provide thorough coverage of design patterns, it acquaints you with some of the most popular ones and includes PHP implementation examples. If you're interested in further enhancing your knowledge of design patterns, definitely find a copy of the GoF book mentioned earlier. Craig Larman's *Applying UML and Patterns: An Introduction to Object-Oriented Analysis and Design and the Unified Process* is another well-recommended resource.

# 29.2 Singleton

Singleton is a design pattern that is useful when you want to create an object that should be accessible for different, distinct parts of your application. Especially if this object is supposed to contain large chunks of information, instantiating it over and over again may prove to be extremely inefficient. Instead, if you had a way of sharing the same instance between all of the different parts of the application, it would be ideal. Of course, global variables come to mind, but they require you to manage initialization. That is, you must make sure that nobody erases this variable by mistake, that nobody instantiates another instance of this class, and so forth. Relying on the application code to properly use the infrastructure is definitely not object-oriented. In object-oriented design, you would instantiate your own class to expose an API allowing you to take care of these things in the class itself instead of having to rely on every piece of application code to maintain system integrity.

Figure 29.1 shows the structure of a Singleton implementation in PHP.

Analyzing this class, you can spot three key features: a private, static property holding the single instance; a public, static method that returns the single instance; and a private constructor.

A private, static property holds a single instantiation of the class. As previously mentioned in the description of static class properties, static variables are similar to global variables. In this case, however, we take advantage of our ability to make this property private, thereby preventing application code from reading it or changing it.

A public, static method returns the only instantiation of the class. This single access point allows us to initialize the variable exactly once, before the application code accesses it. Thanks to its being static, we don't need to instantiate an object before we can call this method.

```
class Singleton
{
    static private $instance = NULL;

    private function __construct()
    {
        ... perform initialization as necessary ...
    }

    static public function getInstance()
    {
        if (self::$instance == NULL)
        {
            self::$instance = new Singleton();
        }

        return self::$instance;
    }

    ... class logic goes here ...
}
```

**Figure 29.1**    Singleton pattern.

The constructor is private. A Singleton class is one of the few situations in which it makes sense to use a private constructor. The private constructor prevents users from instantiating the class directly. They must use the `getInstance` method. Trying to instantiate the class using `$obj = new Singleton` will result in a fatal error, since the global scope may not call the private constructor.

One real-world example with which you can use the Singleton class is a configuration class, which wraps around your application's configuration settings. Listing 29.1 is a simple example. Thanks to the Singleton pattern, there's never more than one copy of the configuration file in memory. Any changes made to the configuration automatically persist.

**Listing 29.1**    *Configuration Singleton*

```
<?php
    /*
    ** Configuration file singleton
    */
    class Configuration
```

| Listing 29.1 | *Configuration Singleton (cont.)* |
| --- | --- |

```
{
    static private $instance = NULL;
    private $ini_settings;
    private $updated = FALSE;
    const INI_FILENAME = "/tmp/corephp.ini";

    private function __construct()
    {
        if(file_exists(self::INI_FILENAME))
        {
            $this->ini_settings =
                parse_ini_file(self::INI_FILENAME);
        }
    }

    private function __destruct()
    {
        //if configuration hasn't changed, no need
        //to update it on disk
        if(!$this->updated)
        {
            return;
        }

        //overwrite INI file with the
        //version in memory
        $fp = fopen(self::INI_FILENAME, "w");
        if(!$fp)
        {
            return;
        }

        foreach ($this->ini_settings as $key => $value)
        {
            fputs($fp, "$key = \"$value\"\n");
        }

        fclose($fp);
    }

    public function getInstance()
    {
        if(self::$instance == NULL)
        {
            self::$instance = new Configuration();
        }
```

| Listing 29.1 | *Configuration Singleton (cont.)* |

```
            return self::$instance;
        }

    public function get($name)
    {
        if(isset($this->ini_settings[$name]))
        {
            return $this->ini_settings[$name];
        }
        else
        {
            return(NULL);
        }
    }

    public function set($name, $value)
    {
        //update only if different from what
        //we already have
        if(!isset($this->ini_settings[$name]) OR
            ($this->ini_settings[$name] != $value))
        {
            $this->ini_settings[$name] = $value;
            $this->updated = TRUE;
        }
    }
}

//Test the class
$config = Configuration::getInstance();
$config->set("username", "leon");
$config->set("password", "secret");
print($config->get("username"));
?>
```

# 29.3 Factory

Factory is a design pattern aimed at decoupling the instantiation of your objects from the application code that uses them. For example, you may want to use different kinds of objects depending on the situation. If you have two rendering classes, HtmlRenderer and WmlRenderer, and want your application to transparently use the right one depending on what kind of client is connected, you can easily do that using the Factory design pattern.

There are many different variants of the Factory design pattern. In Figure 29.2 we pick a simple one, which simply uses a global function.

```php
<?php
    //define abstract factory class
    class Renderer
    {
        private $document;

        abstract function render()
        {
        }

        function setDocument($document)
        {
            $this->document = $document;
        }
    }

    class HtmlRenderer extends Renderer
    {
        function render()
        {
            ... HTML rendering ...
        }
    }

    class WmlRenderer extends Renderer
    {
        function render()
        {
            ... WML rendering ...
        }
    }

    //Create the right kind of Renderer
    function RendererFactory()
    {
        $accept = strtolower($_SERVER["HTTP_ACCEPT"]);
        if(strpos($accept, "vnd.wap.wml") > 0)
        {
            return new WmlRenderer();
        }
        else
        {
            return new HtmlRenderer();
        }
    }

    //Application code
    $renderer = RendererFactory();
    $renderer->setDocument(…content…);
    $renderer->render();
?>
```

**Figure 29.2** Factory pattern.

The Factory method receives no arguments, but in many situations you may wish to pass information to the Factory that will help it determine what kind of object should be instantiated. Nothing in the Factory pattern prevents you from passing arguments to the constructor.

A popular case for using factory methods is implementing an unserializer—a piece of code that takes a two-dimensional, serialized stream and turns it into objects. How do we write general-purpose code that will be able to instantiate any type of object that may appear in the stream? What if you want to specify different arguments to the constructor, depending on the type of object you're instantiating? Listing 29.2 contains an implementation.

| Listing 29.2 | *Registered classes with the Factory pattern* |
| --- | --- |

```php
<?php
    class Factory
    {
        private $registeredClasses = array();
        static private $instance = NULL;

        private function __construct() {}

        static function getInstance()
        {
            if(self::$instance == NULL)
            {
                self::$instance = new Factory();
            }
            return self::$instance;
        }

        function registerClass($id, $creator_func)
        {
            $this->registeredClasses[$id] = $creator_func;
        }

        function createObject($id, $args)
        {
            if(!isset($this->registeredClasses[$id]))
            {
                return(NULL);
            }
            return($this->registeredClasses[$id]($args));
        }
    }
```

| Listing 29.2 | *Registered classes with the Factory pattern (cont.)* |
|---|---|

```php
class MyClass
{
    private $created;
    public function __construct()
    {
        $created = time();
    }

    public function getCreated()
    {
        return($this->created);
    }
}

function MyClassCreator()
{
    return(new MyClass());
}

$factory = Factory::getInstance();
$factory->registerClass(1234, "MyClassCreator");
$instance = $factory->createObject(1234, array());
?>
```

Those of you who are familiar with the bits and bytes of PHP's syntax know that there's a simpler way of doing it. Listing 29.2 demonstrates a more object-oriented way to solve the problem, as it is done in other languages. It also allows for flexibility should you wish to implement additional logic in the creator (possibly sending some information to the constructor). In practice, it's accurate to say that PHP has built-in support for factory methods, utilized by simply writing `$object = new $classname`.

# 29.4  Observer

Observer is one of the most useful design patterns for developing large-scale object-oriented applications. It allows you, with the use of messages, to interconnect objects without their having to know anything about each other. At the heart of the Observer pattern are two main actors: observers and subjects. Observer objects find subject objects interesting and need to know when the subject changes. Typically, multiple observers monitor a single subject.

Listing 29.3 contains a simple implementation of the Observer pattern.

| Listing 29.3 | *Observer pattern* |
|---|---|

```php
<?php
    interface Message
    {
        static function getType();
    };

    interface Observer
    {
        function notifyMsg(Message $msg);
    };

    class Subject
    {
        private $observers = array();

        function registerObserver(Observer $observer, $msgType)
        {
            $this->observers[$msgType][] = $observer;
        }

        private function notifyMsg(Message $msg)
        {
            @$observers = $this->observers[$msg->getType()];
            if(!$observers)
            {
                return;
            }

            foreach($observers as $observer)
            {
                $observer->notifyMsg($msg);
            }
        }

        function someMethod()
        {
            //fake some task
            sleep(1);

            //notify observers
            $this->notifyMsg(new HelloMessage("Zeev"));
        }
    }
```

---

**Listing 29.3**   *Observer pattern (cont.)*

```php
class HelloMessage implements Message
{
    private $name;

    function __construct($name)
    {
        $this->name = $name;
    }

    function getMsg()
    {
        return "Hello, $this->name!";
    }

    static function getType()
    {
        return "HELLO_TYPE";
    }
}


class MyObserver implements Observer
{
    function notifyMsg(Message $msg)
    {
        if ($msg instanceof HelloMessage)
        {
            print $msg->getMsg();
        }
    }
}

$subject = new Subject();
$observer = new MyObserver();
$subject->registerObserver($observer,
    HelloMessage::getType());
$subject->someMethod();
?>
```

---

The beauty in the Observer pattern is that it allows subject objects to activate Observer objects without the subjects having any knowledge about the objects that observe them other than that they support the notification interface. The Observer pattern enables developers to connect dependent objects in different parts of the application, dynamically and as necessary, without having to provide specialized APIs for each type of dependency. It also allows different Observer objects to select what kind of information interests them without having to change any code in the subject object.

One thing to worry about when implementing Observer is cyclic notification paths. An object may both observe other objects and be observed by other objects—that is, be both a Subject and an Observer. If two objects observe each other and deliver messages that trigger another message in their observing object, an endless loop occurs. In order to avoid it, it's best if you avoid delivering notification messages in your notification handler. If it's not possible, try to create a simple, one-sided flow of information, which will prevent cyclic dependencies.

# 29.5  Strategy

The Strategy pattern applies when you have a general problem to be solved by two or more algorithms. The choice of solutions represents a decision the user makes. For example, a graphics program allows for saving an image in many different formats, each with unique code for writing a file. The input to each of these routines is identical.

This pattern can also solve the problem of presenting a Web application in various languages or styles. Very simple schemes can get by with an array of translated words or colors for a theme, but complex customization may require code to produce dynamic results. I encountered this situation when trying to allow for international versions of an e-commerce site.

Aside from differences in language, people of the world format numbers differently. The `number_format` function goes a long way to solve this problem, of course. It doesn't address figures of money. Americans use $ to the left of numbers to represent dollars. Europeans may expect EUR, the symbol for a Euro. It's possible prices for Japanese customers should have yen to the right of the figure, depending on the situation.

To implement the strategy pattern, you must define a shared interface for all algorithms. You may then proceed with various implementations of this interface. In PHP we can implement this by defining a general class and extending it with subclasses. We can take advantage of polymorphism to promote a consistent interface to the functionality.

Listing 29.4 contains the base class, `localization`. It defines two methods, `formatMoney` and `translate`. The first method returns a formatted version of a money figure. The second method attempts to translate an English phrase into a local representation. The base class defines default functionality. Subclasses can choose to use the defaults or override them.

| Listing 29.4 | *Strategy pattern* |
|---|---|

```php
<?php
    //Strategy superclass
    class Localization
    {
        function formatMoney($sum)
        {
            number_format($sum);
        }

        function translate($phrase)
        {
            return($phrase);
        }
    }
?>
```

Listing 29.5 contains an English subclass of localization. This class takes special care to place negative signs to the left of dollar signs. It doesn't override the translate method, since input phrases are assumed to be in English.

| Listing 29.5 | *English subclass* |
|---|---|

```php
<?php
    //get Localization
    include_once('29-4.php');

    class English extends Localization
    {
        function formatMoney($sum)
        {
            $text = "";

            //negative signs precede dollar signs
            if($sum < 0)
            {
                $text .= "-";
                $sum = aba($sum);
            }

            $text .= "$" . number_format($sum, 2, '.', ',');

            return($text);
        }
    }
?>
```

Listing 29.6 contains a German subclass of `localization`. This class uses periods to separate thousands and commas to separate decimals. It also includes a crude `translate` method that handles only yes and no. In a realistic context, the method would use some sort of database or external interface to acquire translations.

| Listing 29.6 | *German subclass* |
| --- | --- |

```php
<?php
    include_once('29-4.php');

    class German extends Localization
    {
        public function formatMoney($sum)
        {
            $text = "EUR " . number_format($sum, 2, ',', '.');

            return($text);
        }

        public function translate($phrase)
        {
            if($phrase == 'yes')
            {
                return('ja');
            }

            if($phrase == 'no')
            {
                return('nein');
            }

            return($phrase);
        }
    }
?>
```

Finally, Listing 29.7 is an example of using the `localization` subclasses. A script can choose between available subclasses based on a user's stated preference or some other clue, such as HTTP headers or domain name. This implementation depends on classes kept in files of the same name. After initialization, all use of the localization object remains the same for any language.

| Listing 29.7 | *Using localization* |
|---|---|

```php
<?php
    print("Trying English<br>\n");
    include_once('29-5.php');
    $local = new English;
    print($local->formatMoney(12345678) . "<br>\n");
    print($local->translate('yes') . "<br>\n");

    print("Trying German<br>\n");
    include_once('29-6.php');
    $local = new German;
    print($local->formatMoney(12345678) . "<br>\n");
    print($local->translate('yes') . "<br>\n");
?>
```

One advantage of this pattern is the elimination of big conditionals. Imagine a single script containing all the functionality for formatting numbers in every language. It would require a `switch` statement or an `if-else` tree. It also requires parsing more code than you would possibly need for any particular page load.

Also consider how this pattern sets up a nice interface that allows later extension. You can start with just one localization module, but native speakers of other languages can contribute new modules easily. This applies to more than just localization. It can apply to any context that allows for multiple algorithms for a given problem.

Keep in mind that Strategy is meant for alternate functionality, not just alternate data. That is, if the only difference between strategies can be expressed as values, the pattern may not apply to the particular problem. In practice, the example given earlier would contain much more functionality differences between languages, differences which might overwhelm this chapter.

You will find the Strategy pattern applied in PEAR_Error, the error-handling class included in PEAR. Sterling Hughes wrote PEAR's error framework so that it uses a reasonable set of default behaviors, while allowing for overloading for alternate functionality depending on context.

# ESCAPE
# SEQUENCES

# Appendix A

The following codes may be included in strings and have special meaning when printed to the browser or to a file. It is important to note that they do not have special meaning when passed to other functions, such as those communicating with a database or evaluating a regular expression.

| Code | Description |
|------|-------------|
| \" | Double Quotes |
| \\ | Backslash Character |
| \n | New Line |
| \r | Carriage Return |
| \t | Horizontal Tab |
| \x00 - \xFF | Hex Characters |

# ASCII Codes

# Appendix

The following table lists the first 128 characters of the ASCII code. PHP allows for ASCII codes ranging from 0 to 255, but above code 127 the representation differs across operating systems.

| Decimal | Hex | Character | Description |
|---------|-----|-----------|-------------|
| 0 | 00 | | Null |
| 1 | 01 | | Start of Heading |
| 2 | 02 | | Start of Text |
| 3 | 03 | | End of Text |
| 4 | 04 | | End of Transmission |
| 5 | 05 | | Enquiry |
| 6 | 06 | | Acknowledge |
| 7 | 07 | | Bell |
| 8 | 08 | | Backspace |
| 9 | 09 | | Character Tabulation |
| 10 | 0A | | Line Feed |

| Decimal | Hex | Character | Description |
| --- | --- | --- | --- |
| 11 | 0B | | Line Tabulation |
| 12 | 0C | | Form Feed |
| 13 | 0D | | Carriage Return |
| 14 | 0E | | Shift Out |
| 15 | 0F | | Shift In |
| 16 | 10 | | Datalink Escape |
| 17 | 11 | | Device Control One |
| 18 | 12 | | Device Control Two |
| 19 | 13 | | Device Control Three |
| 20 | 14 | | Device Control Four |
| 21 | 15 | | Negative Acknowledge |
| 22 | 16 | | Synchronous Idle |
| 23 | 17 | | End Of Transmission Block |
| 24 | 18 | | Cancel |
| 25 | 19 | | End of Medium |
| 26 | 1A | | Substitute |
| 27 | 1B | | Escape |
| 28 | 1C | | File Separator |
| 29 | 1D | | Group Separator |
| 30 | 1E | | Record Separator |
| 31 | 1F | | Unit Separator |
| 32 | 20 | | Space |
| 33 | 21 | ! | Exclamation Mark |
| 34 | 22 | " | Quotation Mark |
| 35 | 23 | # | Number Sign |
| 36 | 24 | $ | Dollar Sign |

| Decimal | Hex | Character | Description |
| --- | --- | --- | --- |
| 37 | 25 | % | Percent Sign |
| 38 | 26 | & | Ampersand |
| 39 | 27 | ' | Apostrophe |
| 40 | 28 | ( | Left Parenthesis |
| 41 | 29 | ) | Right Parenthesis |
| 42 | 2A | * | Asterisk |
| 43 | 2B | + | Plus Sign |
| 44 | 2C | , | Comma |
| 45 | 2D | – | Hyphen-Minus |
| 46 | 2E | . | Period |
| 47 | 2F | / | Forward Slash |
| 48 | 30 | 0 | Zero |
| 49 | 31 | 1 | One |
| 50 | 32 | 2 | Two |
| 51 | 33 | 3 | Three |
| 52 | 34 | 4 | Four |
| 53 | 35 | 5 | Five |
| 54 | 36 | 6 | Six |
| 55 | 37 | 7 | Seven |
| 56 | 38 | 8 | Eight |
| 57 | 39 | 9 | Nine |
| 58 | 3A | : | Colon |
| 59 | 3B | ; | Semicolon |
| 60 | 3C | < | Less-Than Sign |
| 61 | 3D | = | Equals Sign |
| 62 | 3E | > | Greater-Than Sign |

| Decimal | Hex | Character | Description |
|---------|-----|-----------|-------------|
| 63 | 3F | ? | Question Mark |
| 64 | 40 | @ | At Symbol |
| 65 | 41 | A | Uppercase A |
| 66 | 42 | B | Uppercase B |
| 67 | 43 | C | Uppercase C |
| 68 | 44 | D | Uppercase D |
| 69 | 45 | E | Uppercase E |
| 70 | 46 | F | Uppercase F |
| 71 | 47 | G | Uppercase G |
| 72 | 48 | H | Uppercase H |
| 73 | 49 | I | Uppercase I |
| 74 | 4A | J | Uppercase J |
| 75 | 4B | K | Uppercase K |
| 76 | 4C | L | Uppercase L |
| 77 | 4D | M | Uppercase M |
| 78 | 4E | N | Uppercase N |
| 79 | 4F | O | Uppercase O |
| 80 | 50 | P | Uppercase P |
| 81 | 51 | Q | Uppercase Q |
| 82 | 52 | R | Uppercase R |
| 83 | 53 | S | Uppercase S |
| 84 | 54 | T | Uppercase T |
| 85 | 55 | U | Uppercase U |
| 86 | 56 | V | Uppercase V |
| 87 | 57 | W | Uppercase W |
| 88 | 58 | X | Uppercase X |

| Decimal | Hex | Character | Description |
|---------|-----|-----------|-------------|
| 89 | 59 | Y | Uppercase Y |
| 90 | 5A | Z | Uppercase Z |
| 91 | 5B | [ | Left Square Bracket |
| 92 | 5C | \ | Backslash |
| 93 | 5D | ] | Right Square Bracket |
| 94 | 5E | ^ | Carat |
| 95 | 5F | _ | Underscore |
| 96 | 60 | ` | Accent |
| 97 | 61 | a | Lowercase A |
| 98 | 62 | b | Lowercase B |
| 99 | 63 | c | Lowercase C |
| 100 | 64 | d | Lowercase D |
| 101 | 65 | e | Lowercase E |
| 102 | 66 | f | Lowercase F |
| 103 | 67 | g | Lowercase G |
| 104 | 68 | h | Lowercase H |
| 105 | 69 | i | Lowercase I |
| 106 | 6A | j | Lowercase J |
| 107 | 6B | k | Lowercase K |
| 108 | 6C | l | Lowercase L |
| 109 | 6D | m | Lowercase M |
| 110 | 6E | n | Lowercase N |
| 111 | 6F | o | Lowercase O |
| 112 | 70 | p | Lowercase P |
| 113 | 71 | q | Lowercase Q |
| 114 | 72 | r | Lowercase R |

| Decimal | Hex | Character | Description |
|---------|-----|-----------|-------------|
| 115 | 73 | s | Lowercase S |
| 116 | 74 | t | Lowercase T |
| 117 | 75 | u | Lowercase U |
| 118 | 76 | v | Lowercase V |
| 119 | 77 | w | Lowercase W |
| 120 | 78 | x | Lowercase X |
| 121 | 79 | y | Lowercase Y |
| 122 | 7A | z | Lowercase Z |
| 123 | 7B | { | Left Curly Bracket |
| 124 | 7C | \| | Vertical Line |
| 125 | 7D | } | Right Curly Bracket |
| 126 | 7E | ~ | Tilde |
| 127 | 7F |  | Delete |

If you are interested in how characters are rendered in a particular browser, the script in Listing B.1 will print each character in a table.

**Listing B.1**    *ASCII characters*

```
<html>
<head>
<title>ASCII Characters</title>
</head>
<body>
<table border="1" cellspacing="0" cellpadding="5">
<?
    for($index=32; $index <= 255; $index++)
    {
        print("<tr>");
        print("<td>$index</td>");
        print("<td>".chr($index)."</td>");
        print("</tr>\n");
    }
?>
</table>
</body>
</html>
```

# OPERATORS

# Appendix

| Precedence | Operator | Operation It Performs | Associativity |
|---|---|---|---|
| 1 | !<br>~<br>++<br>--<br>@<br>(int)<br>(float)<br>(string)<br>(bool)<br>(array)<br>(object) | logical not<br>bitwise not<br>increment<br>decrement<br>silence operator<br>integer cast<br>floating-point cast<br>string cast<br>boolean cast<br>array cast<br>object cast | Right |
| 2 | *<br>/<br>% | multiply<br>divide<br>modulo | Left |
| 3 | +<br>−<br>. | add<br>subtract<br>concatenate | Left |
| 4 | <<<br>>> | bitwise shift left<br>bitwise shift right | Left |

| Precedence | Operator | Operation It Performs | Associativity |
|---|---|---|---|
| 5 | <br><=<br>><br>>= | is smaller<br>is smaller or equal<br>is greater<br>is greater or equal | Nonassociative |
| 6 | ==<br>!=<br>===<br>!== | is equal<br>is not equal<br>is identical<br>is not identical | Nonassociative |
| 7 | && | logical and | Left |
| 8 | \|\| | logical or | Left |
| 9 | ? : | question mark operator | Left |
| 10 | =<br>=&<br>+=<br>-=<br>*=<br>/=<br>%=<br>^=<br>&=<br>\|=<br>.= | assign<br>assign by reference<br>assign add<br>assign subtract<br>assign multiply<br>assign divide<br>assign modulo<br>assign bitwise xor<br>assign bitwise and<br>assign bitwise or<br>assign concatenate | Right |
| 11 | AND | logical and | Left |
| 12 | XOR | logical xor | Left |
| 13 | OR | logical or | Left |

# PHP Tags

# Appendix D

There are several ways to mark an area of PHP script in a Web page, displayed below. The results of the script, if any, will take the place in the final output. If a line break follows the closing tag, it will be removed. This helps you write more readable code.

```
<?
?>
```

This is the classic method for marking PHP code. Many of the examples found on the Internet use this method, probably because it's been available the longest. PHP 2 used this method, except that the second question mark was omitted.

This method is called *short tags,* and support for it may be turned on or off. One way is to use the `short_tags` function described in Chapter 15. A directive in the `php.ini` file controls enabling short tags for all scripts. You can also configure PHP to enable short tags before you compile it.

```
<?=
?>
```

Unlike other methods, these tags are shorthand for a call to the `echo` function. This is probably best illustrated with an example.

```
<? $name="Leon"; ?>
Hi, my name is <?= $name ?>.
<?php
?>
```

This method was added to make PHP scripts compatible with XML, which gets confused by the short tags described above.

```
<script language="php">
</script>
```

Some text editors, Microsoft's Frontpage in particular, do not understand tags that start with `<?`, so support for this longer tagging method was added.

```
<%
%>
<%=
%>
```

These methods emulate ASP-style tags. They are otherwise identical to the form using question marks.

Finally, you can run a script from the command line, like `php test.php`. By default, the PHP compilation process creates a command-line interface version of PHP. Windows users can find the CLI version of PHP in its own subdirectory of the PHP distribution.

# PHP COMPILE-TIME CONFIGURATION

# Appendix E

The following are commands accepted by the `configure` script. Typing `./configure --help` in your shell will get you more information about what each does.

```
--disable-all
--disable-cgi
--disable-cli
--disable-ctype
--disable-inline-optimization
--disable-ipv6
--disable-libtool-lock
--disable-mbregex
--disable-path-info-check
--disable-posix
--disable-rpath
--disable-session
--disable-short-tags
--disable-tokenizer
--disable-xml
--enable-all
--enable-bcmath
--enable-calendar
--enable-dba
--enable-dbase
--enable-dbx
--enable-debug
--enable-dio
--enable-discard-path
```

```
--enable-dmalloc
--enable-embed[=TYPE]
--enable-exif
--enable-fast-install[=PKGS]
--enable-fastcgi
--enable-filepro
--enable-force-cgi-redirect
--enable-ftp
--enable-gd-native-ttf
--enable-libgcc
--enable-magic-quotes
--enable-maintainer-zts
--enable-mbstring
--enable-memory-limit
--enable-pcntl
--enable-roxen-zts
--enable-safe-mode
--enable-shared[=PKGS]
--enable-shmop
--enable-sigchild
--enable-sockets
--enable-static[=PKGS]
--enable-sysvmsg
--enable-sysvsem
--enable-sysvshm
--enable-ucd-snmp-hack
--enable-versioning
--enable-wddx
--enable-xslt
--enable-yp
--with-adabas[=DIR]
--with-aolserver=DIR
--with-apache-hooks-static[=DIR]
--with-apache-hooks[=FILE]
--with-apache[=DIR]
--with-apxs2handler[=FILE]
--with-apxs2[=FILE]
--with-apxs[=FILE]
--with-birdstep[=DIR]
--with-bz2[=DIR]
--with-caudium=DIR
--with-cdb[=DIR]
--with-config-file-path=PATH
--with-config-file-scan-dir=PATH
--with-cpdflib[=DIR]
--with-crack[=DIR]
--with-curlwrappers
--with-curl[=DIR]
--with-custom-odbc[=DIR]
```

```
--with-cyrus[=dir]
--with-db
--with-db2[=DIR]
--with-db3[=DIR]
--with-db4[=DIR]
--with-dbmaker[=DIR]
--with-dbm[=DIR]
--with-dom-exslt[=DIR]
--with-dom-xslt[=DIR]
--with-dom[=DIR]
--with-empress-bcs[=DIR]
--with-empress[=DIR]
--with-esoob[=DIR]
--with-exec-dir[=DIR]
--with-expat-dir=DIR
--with-expat-dir=DIR
--with-expat-dir=DIR
--with-fam
--with-fbsql[=DIR]
--with-fdftk[=DIR]
--with-flatfile
--with-freetype-dir[=DIR]
--with-gdbm[=DIR]
--with-gd[=DIR]
--with-gettext[=DIR]
--with-gmp
--with-gnu-ld
--with-hwapi[=DIR]
--with-hyperwave
--with-ibm-db2[=DIR]
--with-iconv-dir=DIR
--with-iconv-dir=DIR
--with-iconv[=DIR]
--with-imap-ssl=<DIR>
--with-imap[=DIR]
--with-informix[=DIR]
--with-ingres[=DIR]
--with-inifile
--with-interbase[=DIR]
--with-iodbc[=DIR]
--with-ircg
--with-ircg-config=PATH
--with-isapi=DIR
--with-jpeg-dir[=DIR]
--with-jpeg-dir[=DIR]
--with-jpeg-dir[=DIR]
--with-kerberos[=DIR]
--with-layout=TYPE
--with-ldap[=DIR]
```

```
--with-libedit[=DIR]
--with-mcal[=DIR]
--with-mcrypt[=DIR]
--with-mcve[=DIR]
--with-mhash[=DIR]
--with-milter=DIR
--with-mime-magic[=FILE]
--with-ming[=DIR]
--with-mm[=DIR]
--with-mnogosearch[=DIR]
--with-mod_charset
--with-mod_charset
--with-msession[=DIR]
--with-msql[=DIR]
--with-mssql[=DIR]
--with-mysql-sock[=DIR]
--with-mysqli[=DIR]
--with-mysql[=DIR]
--with-ncurses[=DIR]
--with-ndbm[=DIR]
--with-nsapi=DIR
--with-oci8[=DIR]
--with-openlink[=DIR]
--with-openssl[=DIR]
--with-oracle[=DIR]
--with-ovrimos[=DIR]
--with-pdflib[=DIR]
--with-pear=DIR
--with-pfpro[=DIR]
--with-pgsql[=DIR]
--with-phttpd=DIR
--with-pi3web=DIR
--with-pic
--with-png-dir[=DIR]
--with-png-dir[=DIR]
--with-pspell[=DIR]
--with-qtdom
--with-readline[=DIR]
--with-recode[=DIR]
--with-regex=TYPE
--with-roxen=DIR
--with-sablot-js=DIR
--with-sapdb[=DIR]
--with-servlet[=DIR]
--with-snmp[=DIR]
--with-solid[=DIR]
--with-swf[=DIR]
--with-sybase-ct[=DIR]
--with-sybase[=DIR]
```

```
--with-t1lib[=DIR]
--with-thttpd=SRCDIR
--with-tiff-dir[=DIR]
--with-tiff-dir[=DIR]
--with-tsrm-pthreads
--with-tsrm-pth[=pth-config]
--with-tsrm-st
--with-ttf[=DIR]
--with-tux=MODULEDIR
--with-unixODBC[=DIR]
--with-webjames=SRCDIR
--with-xmlrpc[=DIR]
--with-xpm-dir[=DIR]
--with-xslt-sablot=DIR
--with-yaz[=DIR]
--with-zip[=DIR]
--with-zlib-dir=<DIR>
--with-zlib-dir[=DIR]
--with-zlib-dir[=DIR]
--with-zlib-dir[=DIR]
--with-zlib-dir[=DIR]
--with-zlib[=DIR]
--without-pcre-regex
--without-pear
```

# INTERNET
# RESOURCES

# Appendix F

The first place to look for information about PHP on the Internet is PHP's home site
`<http://www.php.net/>`. Many of the sites listed in this appendix appear on pages
of that site. You can download the latest source code and executables there. You can
read the latest news. You will also find information about the various mailing lists,
which can be a great source of support. To subscribe to the general mailing list, send
mail to `php-general-subscribe@lists.php.net`. You will get an email to confirm
your subscription. Be prepared to get hundreds of messages a day. I suggest sending
the messages into their own folder using a filter. If you'd prefer to just browse the
messages, try the archives at the AIMS group mailing list archives
`<http://marc.theaimsgroup.com/?l=php-general>`.

Another great resource is Nathan Wallace's FAQTS.com site
`<http://php.faqts.com/>`, a collection of frequently asked questions, including a
large section about PHP.

The links below are just a sample of what's available. The PHP home site and the
portals below list many more.

# F.1  Portals

| | |
|---|---|
| `<http://www.zend.com/>` | Zend |
| `<http://www.phpbuilder.com/>` | PHP Builder |
| `<http://www.weberdev.com/` | WeberDev |
| `<http://devshed.com/Server_Side/PHP/>` | DevShed's PHP Resources |
| `<http://www.phpwizard.net/>` | PHP Wizard |
| `<http://www.php-center.de/>` | PHP Center (in German) |
| `<http://www.phpindex.com/>` | PHP Index (in French) |

# F.2   Software

| | |
|---|---|
| `<http://px.sklar.com/>` | PX: PHP Code Exchange |
| `<http://phplib.sourceforge.net/>` | PHP Base Library |
| `<http://www.phpclasses.org/>` | PHP Classes Repository |
| `<http://www.hotscripts.com/PHP/Scripts_and_Programs/>` | HotScripts' PHP Section |
| `<http://sourceforge.net/projects/php4ue/>` | UltraEdit word files for PHP |
| `<http://dcl.sourceforge.net/>` | Double Choco Latte, a bug tracking system |
| `<http://www.phorum.org/>` | Phorum, threaded discussions |
| `<http://horde.org/imp/>` | Web to mail interface |
| `<http://www.phpmyadmin.net/>` | MySQL Web interface |

# PHP
# STYLE GUIDE

# Appendix G

This is a sample style guide based on the one used by the FreeTrade project <http://share.whichever.com/freetrade/>. You may wish to compare it to the style guide used by the PEAR project <http://pear.php.net/>.

## G.1 Comments

Every file should start with a comment block describing its purpose, version, author, and a copyright message. It should be a block comment in the style below.

```
/*
** File: test
** Description:  This is a test program
** Version: 1.0
** Created: 1/1/2004
** Author: Leon Atkinson
** Email: leon@leonatkinson.com
**
** Copyright (c) 2000 Your Group.  All rights reserved.
*/
```

Every function should have a block comment specifying name, input/output, and what the function does.

```
/*
** Function: doAdd
** Input:   INTEGER a,  INTEGER b
** Output: INTEGER
** Description:  Adds two integers
*/
function doAdd($a, $b)
{
    return(a+b);
}
```

Ideally, every `while`, `if`, `for`, and similar block of code should be preceded by a comment explaining what happens in the block. Sometimes this is unnecessary.

```
// get input from user char by char
while(getInput($inputChar))
{
    storeChar($inputChar);
}
```

Explain sections of code that aren't obvious.

```
//TAB is ASCII 9
define(TAB, 9);

//change tabs to spaces in userName
for($index=0; $index < count($userName); $index++)
{
    $userName[$index] = ereg_replace(TAB, " ", $userName[$index]);
}
```

# G.2 Function Declarations

As previously stated, functions should have a comment block explaining what they do and their input/output. The function block should align starting at one tab from the left margin, unless the function is part of a class definition. Opening and closing braces should also be one tab from the left margin. The body of the function should be indented two tabs.

```
<?php
    /*
    ** doAdd
    ** Adds two integers
    ** Input:  $a, $b
    ** Output: sum of $a and $b
```

```
    */
    function doAdd($a, $b)
    {
        return(a+b);
    }
?>
```

# G.3  Compound Statements

Flow-control primitives should be compound statements, even if they contain only one instruction. Like functions, compound statements should have opening braces that start at column zero relative to scope. Code within the braces forms a new scope and should be indented.

```
// tell the user if a is equal to ten
if($a==10)
{
    printf("a is ten.\n");
}
else
{
    printf("a is not ten.\n");
}
```

# G.4  Naming

The names of variables, constants, and functions should begin with a lowercase letter. In names that consist of more than one word, the words are written together and each word starts with an uppercase letter. Use short names for variables used in a small scope, such as just inside a `for` loop. Use longer names for variables used in larger scopes. Function names should begin with a lowercase letter and use capitals for subsequent words.

```
/*
** Function getAddressFromEnvironment
** Input: $Prefix - prefix used to generate address form
** Return: array suitable for addressFields
*/
function getAddressFromEnvironment($Prefix)
{
    global $AddressInfo;
```

```
    //get list of all address fields
    //from the AddressInfo array
    reset($AddressInfo);
    while(list($field, $info) = each($AddressInfo))
    {
        $ReturnValue[$field] = trim($GLOBALS[($Prefix .
            $info[ADDR_VAR])]);
    }

    return($ReturnValue);
}
```

Function names should suggest an action or verb. Use names like `updateAddress` or `makeStateSelector`. Variable names should suggest a property or noun, such as `userName` or `Width`. Use pronounceable names, such as `User`, not `usr`. Use descriptive names for variables used globally; use short names for variables used locally.

Be consistent and use parallelism. If you are abbreviating number as `num`, always use that abbreviation. Don't switch to using `no` or `nmbr`.

Values that are treated as constants—that is, are not changed by the program—should be declared in the beginning of the scope in which they are used. In PHP this is done with the `define` function. Each of these constants should be paired with a comment that explains its use. They should be named exclusively with uppercase letters, with underscores to separate words. You should use constants in place of any arbitrary values to improve readability.

```
// maximum length of a name to accept
define("MAX_NAME_LENGTH",  32);
print("Maximum name length is " . MAX_NAME_LENGTH);
```

Constants that belong to a specific module should use a consistent prefix.

```
//text with which to label the field
define("ADDR_LABEL", 0);

//name of the form field (sans prefix of course)
define("ADDR_VAR", 1);

//error message to display for missing fields
define("ADDR_ERROR", 2);
```

Variables are to be declared with the smallest possible scope. This means using function parameters when appropriate. Lines should not exceed 78 characters. Break long lines at common separators, and align the fragments in an indented block.

```
if(($size <0) OR
    ($size > max_size) OR
    (isSizeInvalid($size)))
{
    print("Invalid size");
}
```

# G.5  Expressions

Write conditional expressions so that they read naturally aloud. Sometimes eliminating a not operator (!) will make an expression more understandable. Use parentheses liberally to resolve ambiguity. Using parentheses can force an order of evaluation. This saves the time a reader may spend remembering precedence of operators.

Keep each line simple. The trinary operator (x ? 1 : 2) usually indicates too much code on one line. if..elseif..else is usually more readable. Don't sacrifice clarity for cleverness.

# Index

http://www.phptr.com/

Prentice Hall PTR   InformIT   InformIT Online Books   Financial Times Prentice Hall   ft.com   PTG Interactive   Reuters

TOMORROW'S SOLUTIONS FOR TODAY'S PROFESSIONALS

Prentice Hall **Professional Technical Reference**

| Browse | Book Series | What's New | User Groups | Alliances | Special Sales | Contact Us |

Search | Help | Home

*Quick Search*

## PTR Favorites

Find a Bookstore

Book Series

Special Interests

Newsletters

Press Room

International

Best Sellers

Solutions Beyond the Book

 Shopping Bag

*Keep Up to Date with*

# PH PTR Online

We strive to stay on the cutting edge of what's happening in professional computer science and engineering. Here's a bit of what you'll find when you stop by **www.phptr.com**:

**(!) What's new at PHPTR?** We don't just publish books for the professional community, we're a part of it. Check out our convention schedule, keep up with your favorite authors, and get the latest reviews and press releases on topics of interest to you.

**(@) Special interest areas** offering our latest books, book series, features of the month, related links, and other useful information to help you get the job done.

**User Groups** Prentice Hall Professional Technical Reference's User Group Program helps volunteer, not-for-profit user groups provide their members with training and information about cutting-edge technology.

**Companion Websites** Our Companion Websites provide valuable solutions beyond the book. Here you can download the source code, get updates and corrections, chat with other users and the author about the book, or discover links to other websites on this topic.

**Need to find a bookstore?** Chances are, there's a bookseller near you that carries a broad selection of PTR titles. Locate a Magnet bookstore near you at www.phptr.com.

**Subscribe today! Join PHPTR's monthly email newsletter!** Want to be kept up-to-date on your area of interest? Choose a targeted category on our website, and we'll keep you informed of the latest PHPTR products, author events, reviews and conferences in your interest area.

Visit our mailroom to subscribe today! **http://www.phptr.com/mail_lists**